AF797235

THE OXFORD HANDBOOK OF

PROSECUTORS AND PROSECUTION

THE OXFORD HANDBOOK OF

PROSECUTORS AND PROSECUTION

Edited by

RONALD F. WRIGHT, KAY L. LEVINE,

and

RUSSELL M. GOLD

OXFORD
UNIVERSITY PRESS

OXFORD
UNIVERSITY PRESS

Oxford University Press is a department of the University of Oxford. It furthers the University's objective of excellence in research, scholarship, and education by publishing worldwide. Oxford is a registered trade mark of Oxford University Press in the UK and certain other countries.

Published in the United States of America by Oxford University Press
198 Madison Avenue, New York, NY 10016, United States of America.

© Oxford University Press 2021

All rights reserved. No part of this publication may be reproduced, stored in a retrieval system, or transmitted, in any form or by any means, without the prior permission in writing of Oxford University Press, or as expressly permitted by law, by license, or under terms agreed with the appropriate reproduction rights organization. Inquiries concerning reproduction outside the scope of the above should be sent to the Rights Department, Oxford University Press, at the address above.

You must not circulate this work in any other form
and you must impose this same condition on any acquirer.

Library of Congress Cataloging-in-Publication Data
Names: Wright, Ronald F., 1959– editor. | Levine, Kay L., editor. | Gold, Russell M., editor.
Title: The Oxford handbook of prosecutors and prosecution / edited by
Ronald F. Wright, Kay L. Levine, Russell M. Gold.
Description: [New York] : Oxford University Press, [2021]
Identifiers: LCCN 2020044243 (print) | LCCN 2020044244 (ebook) |
ISBN 9780190905422 (hardback) | ISBN 9780190905446 (epub) | ISBN 9780190905453 (ebook)
Subjects: LCSH: Prosecution. | Public prosecutors. | Prosecution
(International law)
Classification: LCC K5425 .O94 2021 (print) | LCC K5425 (ebook) |
DDC 345/.05042—dc23
LC record available at https://lccn.loc.gov/2020044243
LC ebook record available at https://lccn.loc.gov/2020044244

3 5 7 9 8 6 4

Printed by Sheridan Books, Inc., United States of America.

Table of Contents

Preface: Prosecutors' Changing Roles at the Hub of Criminal Justice ix
Hon. Stephanos Bibas

List of Contributors xix
Introduction: Understanding Prosecutors in All Their Contexts xxiii
Ronald F. Wright, Kay L. Levine, and Russell M. Gold

PART I PHASES OF CRIMINAL PROCEEDINGS

1. Public Prosecutors in Criminal Investigations: A Comparative Law Study 3
Stefano Ruggeri

2. Selecting Charges 35
Matt Barno and Mona Lynch

3. Testing Charges 59
Roger A. Fairfax, Jr.

4. Prosecutors and Plea Bargaining 75
Brian D. Johnson and Raquel Hernandez

5. Disclosure, Security, Technology: Challenges in Pre-trial Access to Evidence 101
Darryl K. Brown

6. Prosecutors and Trials 117
Alexander Heinze

7. Prosecutors and Sentencing 153
Nora V. Demleitner

8. Prosecutors Post-Conviction 171
Brandon L. Garrett

9. Accountability Courts and Diversion Programs 183
SALMON SHOMADE

PART II WORKING ENVIRONMENTS AND RELATIONSHIPS

10. Hiring and Learning Strategies in Prosecution Services 207
RASMUS H. WANDALL

11. The Necessity of Performance Measures for Prosecutors 227
LAUREN-BROOKE EISEN AND MIRIAM ARONI KRINSKY

12. Specialized Units and Vertical Prosecution Approaches 259
CASSIA SPOHN

13. Courtroom Workgroups: "A Prosecutor, a Defense Attorney, and a Judge Walk into a Bar..." 273
MILTON HEUMANN, RICK KAVIN, AND ANU CHUGH

14. Law Enforcement Organization Relationships with Prosecutors 291
DANIEL C. RICHMAN

15. Bar Authorities and Prosecutors 309
BRUCE A. GREEN

16. Prosecutors and Their Legislatures, Legislatures and Their Prosecutors 327
RUSSELL M. GOLD

17. The Relationship Between Prosecutors and Defenders 351
ELLEN YAROSHEFSKY

18. Victims and Prosecutors 373
AMANDA KONRADI AND TIRZA JO OCHRACH-KONRADI

19. Prosecutors and Voters 399
CARISSA BYRNE HESSICK

20. Community Prosecution and Building Trust Across a Racial Divide 413
RONALD F. WRIGHT

PART III PROSECUTION IN SPECIALIZED CONTEXTS

21. Prosecutors and the Immigration Enforcement System in the United States 431
JENNIFER CHACÓN

22. Prosecuting Race and Adolescence 447
KRISTIN HENNING

23. Corporate Criminal Law Unbounded 475
MIRIAM H. BAER

24. Law Enforcement Agent Defendants and Prosecutors 497
STEPHEN RUSHIN

25. Prosecuting Misdemeanors 513
JENNY ROBERTS

26. Prosecutors and National Security 539
KENT ROACH

27. Shrinking the Accountability Deficit in Capital Charging 559
SHEROD THAXTON

Index 585

Preface

PROSECUTORS' CHANGING ROLES AT THE HUB OF CRIMINAL JUSTICE

HON. STEPHANOS BIBAS

The Long Arm of the Law

Criminal justice has always been a topic of vital social concern. Our newspapers, crime dramas, and true-crime stories have long reflected our fascination with criminal justice and punishment. It is central to what citizens expect of their government.

In times past, smaller, more homogeneous societies agreed more on right and wrong. They relied mainly on families, churches, community pressure, and shame to suppress and remedy disorder. Zoning, curfews, and other non-criminal laws hid vice and made it less prevalent. Troublemakers were sometimes shunted off to the military, the frontier, or even asylums. So criminal justice was a backstop (Bibas 2012, 2).

But times have changed. This essential task has grown increasingly important in the United States in modern times, as crime—and especially perceptions of crime—has grown. As other norms, customs, and laws have weakened, the backstop became more important and less of a last resort. Its scope expanded beyond classic mala in se (inherently wrongful acts, like murder) to mala prohibita (acts that are wrong only because they are outlawed, like regulatory offenses). And media spread sensational crime stories even when crime rates are flat or falling, increasing people's fear of crime even and spurring calls for even more criminal enforcement. Because of this expansion, American criminal justice has reached an unprecedented scale, prosecuting several million felonies and 10 to 13 million misdemeanors each year (Natapoff 2018, 13, 40–41). Those millions of prosecutions largely revolve around a central actor with tremendous power and discretion: the prosecutor.

The Prosecutor as the Central Actor in Criminal Justice

The growth in criminal law has gone hand-in-hand with the growth of an American criminal justice bureaucracy. That bureaucracy has developed around the prosecutor. The prosecutor's role has grown and adapted, tracking the transformation of American criminal justice from a public morality play to a hidden plea-bargaining assembly line. The lynchpins of this new machinery of criminal justice are prosecutors. They have morphed from courtroom advocates seeking convictions to policymakers who secure pleas and set the course of our criminal-justice system.

From Victims to Public Prosecutors

In the colonial era, there were hardly any lawyers. Victims prosecuted their own crimes without lawyers and defendants defended themselves without lawyers. Even judges lacked formal legal training, and juries decided both guilt and punishment. Convicted defendants were not sent to prison. There was, in short, no bureaucracy of criminal justice (Bibas 2012, 3–5).

All of that changed in the nineteenth century. Because victims varied in their means, abilities, and articulateness, states created professional prosecutors to represent them, as well as the public's interest in justice. The professionalization is now so complete that victims are marginalized, reduced mostly to potential witnesses and suppliers of victim-impact information for sentencing. The victims' rights movement has done only a bit to push back at the margins. Chapter 18 discusses victims' continuing role, but prosecutors now control whom to charge.

From Reactive to Proactive

At first, prosecutors were entirely reactive: they prosecuted cases brought to them. Newly created professional police forces changed all that. The police brought prosecutors cases—many of which would not have been prosecuted before. And prosecutors began working with police and overseeing some of their investigations. Prosecutors thus had to screen out cases that they viewed as weak or low priority. And they negotiated away (or down) cases based on their perceived importance (Bibas 2012, 15–18). Chapter 18 discusses prosecutors' roles in police investigations.

From Adversary to Bargainer

So victims lost their influence, and soon juries did too. As George Fisher shows in his magisterial history *Plea Bargaining's Triumph*, American prosecutors were busy and not personally invested in each case's outcome, so they developed plea bargaining to lighten their crushing dockets and ensure victories (Fisher 2003, 13, 40–48). And many crimes have broad sentencing ranges and trigger several charges, so prosecutors have many tools to encourage bargains. Plea bargaining resolves 95 percent of criminal convictions today.

That cut juries out of the picture, sidestepped or coopted judges, and put defense lawyers in a reactive position. Prosecutors and defense lawyers built on their professional knowledge and relationships as repeat players to develop a plea-bargaining market. Both sides had a sense of how similar cases had been charged and sentenced recently, so they could peg charges and sentences to the going rate for particular crimes (Bibas 2012, 19).

Pre-trial proceedings today are thus largely about working together toward a negotiated outcome, seeking compromise instead of trial. Sometimes this helps everyone, as when a defendant cooperates against other wrongdoers in exchange for a lighter sentence.

As a rule, prosecutors set sentences. Judge Gerard Lynch, in his famous article "Our Administrative System of Criminal Justice," explains how defense lawyers can negotiate pleas with prosecutors by advocating to supervisory prosecutors as they would to judges (Lynch 1998). Prosecutors thus start to look a bit like inquisitorial judges in the continental European tradition.

In short, prosecutors are the hub of the courtroom working group, framing the terms of debate with judges and defense counsel. Chapter 13 of this volume surveys how courtroom workgroups function today, and Chapters 14 and 17 explore law enforcement and defense counsel's roles in these workgroups.

From Litigator to Office Manager

To handle all these cases, pleas, and investigations, prosecutors needed to organize their resources and manage their personnel. Prosecutors' central identity was and still is that of courtroom litigators. But litigating in court, especially before a jury, now takes up much less of a prosecutor's day. Prosecutors work not in isolation but often as part of much larger offices, usually broken down into units that specialize by crime or by stage of a case. Larger offices have supervisors and often internal policies, procedural and sometimes substantive, to guide their line prosecutors' discretion. Chapters 10 through 12 address some of the organizational challenges prosecutors face in structuring and running their offices.

Prosecutors are at the center of a web of government bureaucracy—a professional network that includes judges, public defenders, police, probation officers, parole officers, prison officials, legislatures, and sentencing commissions. That professional network is not only local, but also reaches across the country to other localities and levels of government. Head prosecutors may also deal with public and private diversion programs, juvenile justice groups, and others, as Chapters 8 and 9 discuss.

From Lawyer to Policymaker

Prosecutors have also become powerful political actors. Both the public and politicians support their work, so they have the ear of legislatures. That gives them the power to block reforms that stifle plea bargaining, like completely indeterminate sentences. Prosecutors also developed new tools to undercut statutory sentences, like probation (Fisher 2003, 64–90). And as Bill Stuntz has shown, they persuaded legislatures to seem tough on crime by creating new crimes and new penalties, only to trade them away quietly as plea-bargaining chips (Stuntz 2001). Chapters 2 and 16 of this volume explore prosecutors' relationships with legislatures, ranging from their role in reform to their impact on state budgets.

Prosecutors also took on other roles beyond seeking convictions. They advocated for changes in the law. They helped promote public safety. And they became public educators, speaking out on topics like drug abstinence and abuse. Chapters 8 (reentry), 9 (diversion), and 20 (community groups), among others, reflect on some of these broader roles. In short, prosecutors today have tremendous power over the criminal justice system.

Prosecutorial Discretion: The Lynchpin of U.S. Criminal Justice

Prosecutors' substantial power is not fettered by much legal regulation. In continental Europe, prosecutors have long operated under the principle of legality, requiring them to charge and pursue every crime of which they have enough proof. True, that principle was not rigidly followed and may have loosened in recent years, particularly as prosecutors have had to process more cases. Even so, the principle of legality still constrains how European prosecutors do their jobs and think about their roles.

Nothing like the European principle of legality has ever taken root in America. As John Langbein observed, victims in England long had the discretion to bring or dismiss their own cases. Prosecutors inherited that discretion, which fueled the rise of plea bargaining (Langbein 1979). And it let prosecutors do triage. Triage has many advantages: it lightens workloads, focuses effort on the strongest proof of the most serious crimes, and averts prosecution of technical or otherwise less blameworthy violations. But it also risks being arbitrary, discriminatory, opaque, and unaccountable.

As legislatures kept expanding criminal codes and punishment in response to the societal pressures mentioned above, prosecutors' triage became especially important. There are far more crimes and cases than prosecutors can bring. The surfeit of cases is not a bug but a feature: it keeps us from living in a police state, letting prosecutors use judgment and common sense to ignore trivial wrongs and to narrow overbroad laws in practice. But triage also means speeding up cases to the point of cutting corners, thereby sacrificing the role of the jury and defendants' and victims' day in court.

Now more than ever, prosecutors use their judgment to run the show. They make delicate judgments of how blameworthy and how dangerous a particular wrongdoer is. They weigh priorities and factor in costs. And they decide whether mandatory minimum sentences, sentence enhancements, or collateral consequences (like deportation) ought to apply. Prosecutorial discretion is a theme that runs throughout this volume, especially Chapters 2 (selecting charges), 4 (plea bargaining), and 7 (sentencing).

American prosecutors have historically proceeded case by case, ex post. That case-by-case discretion is in tension with our historical expectation in a democracy that officials will make reasoned decisions, justifying their exercises of public power through public policy. Unlike ordinary bureaucrats, prosecutors need not and usually do not explain their actions.

Prosecutors' decisions thus risk being arbitrary. True, their habits of disposition sometimes solidify into de facto rules or at least rules of thumb, guiding their own future dispositions ex ante. Yet these de facto rules are seldom codified, rarely publicized, and never made binding. This hidden discretion thus creates a gap—an "acoustic separation"—between the conduct rules on the books and the decision rules in practice (Dan-Cohen 1984). Some defendants and defense counsel will learn and play by the rules in practice. Others will remain the dark. But in the end, the discretion lies wholly with the prosecutor, who can change or break the de facto rules at will. Prosecutors' discretion is thus the true lynchpin of our criminal justice system.

The Fragmentation of Prosecutions

It is hard to measure how well this lynchpin succeeds because prosecution takes no one form. American prosecution is hardly a single entity, let alone a rational and unified bureaucracy. Instead, it reflects the varied levels of government, fragmentation within each office, difficulty of measuring success, and varied political and policy expectations.

Levels of Government

America's federalist system of government is mirrored in its systems of prosecution. American criminal justice is fragmented across the federal, state, county, municipal, and even sublocal systems of government. Most police are organized at the city level, most prosecutors at the county level, and most prisons at the state level. That creates what is sometimes called a "correctional free lunch," encouraging county prosecutors to send prisoners to state prisons without worrying about the impact on the state budget. More generally, the incentives at each level do not match up. Jurisdictional divisions make it hard to coordinate actions, or even to measure, predict, and hold actors accountable for their performance (Bierschbach and Bibas 2017).

Fragmentation within Each Prosecuting Agency

The span of large prosecuting offices fragments decision-making and incentives even more. State and national offices are headed by an attorney general, who is sometimes elected but sometimes appointed. County offices are usually headed by an elected district attorney. "The elected," as he or she is sometimes dubbed, may set some high-level policies, but often does not offer much concrete guidance, oversight, or direction.

Particularly when the elected does not set much policy or insist on uniformity from the top, there may be much variation even within a single office. Much depends on the office's culture, its supervisors, and its structure, as Chapter 12 discussess.

Below the single elected and what is often a thin layer of supervisors, line prosecutors compose most of the office. But if there is little guidance from the top and little office policy, formal training, or oversight, line prosecutors may be on their own. That risks creating idiosyncratic variation. It also makes it hard to measure success and hold offices as a whole accountable. Few incentives are directly tied to line prosecutors' performance; most are paid fixed salaries. Line prosecutors' risk aversion and their own desires to reduce their workloads may encourage them to get rid of cases more quickly and cheaply than the elected or the public might prefer. Chapter 10 explores how hiring and training prosecutors influence prosecution.

Office structure also shapes line prosecutors' roles and expertise in another way. Larger offices are often divided up either horizontally or vertically. That means that line prosecutors belong to units that specialize either in a particular stage of cases (like charging, plea negotiation, trial, or sentencing) or in particular kinds of cases (like petty offenses, sex crimes, or homicides). So some line prosecutors develop expertise in how to prosecute sex crimes, for instance. But many remain generalists, rotating through a range of units or cases.

This bewildering array of jurisdictions, offices, office structures, and individual variation creates a methodological headache. It makes it extremely hard to study American prosecution in the aggregate.

Metrics of Success

Another challenge in studying prosecution is the difficulty in framing what makes one a good prosecutor or prosecutor's office. What should prosecutors maximize? That is one of the subjects of Chapter 11. Economists often start by modeling prosecutors as maximizing sentences. But that is a poor proxy for justice or public safety: many scholars have critiqued mass incarceration. And there is widespread agreement that legislatures overcriminalize and trust prosecutors to tailor the punishment to the crime.

A second approximation might be to expect prosecutors to maximize convictions. That is at least descriptively more realistic, as prosecutors may claim victory yet be sensitive to how much punishment fits each crime and defendant. And it is tempting to focus on such outputs because they are easy to measure. Prosecutors are known to brag about their conviction rates. That quantitative approach is often absorbed in law school (Bibas 2012, 33). The notches-on-the-belt mindset is alluring.

But this common focus on the quantity of convictions can obscure their quality. The quantity-based mindset tempts one to focus on punishment over crime prevention and deterrence. And it slights qualitative measures that matter greatly to non-lawyers. These include procedural justice (the sense that one has been treated fairly and respectfully and had one's day in court), healing, vindication, and reintegration.

Perhaps prosecution's obsessive focus on quantity is inevitable. It is far easier for big-city prosecutors to hurry each case along than to take the time to let victims and defendants have their say and be heard. Limited funding is a big constraint. So is poor information technology. And it can be hard to agree upon, let alone to measure and improve, qualitative performance. While big businesses put a lot of effort into soliciting customer feedback and improving customer satisfaction, prosecutors' offices do not. Chapter 11 delves into how prosecutors can and should use performance measures to gauge and improve their performance.

Democracy vs. Civil Service; Populism vs. Expertise

Another large divide is between technocratic and populist approaches to criminal justice. In continental Europe, prosecutors are often apolitical civil servants who enter into and stay on a career track. Their role is built on a bureaucratic vision of rationality and neutrality. Prosecutors are neither elected nor accountable to voters, so they can resist majority preferences. And the centralization of many European governments leaves less room for local variation.

American prosecutors, by contrast, are both much more local and in theory much more subject to democratic control. But those democratic checks do not work as they did even a century ago. Grand and petit juries were designed to ensure popular participation and accountability. But today, both kinds of juries are rare.

And electoral checks work better in theory than in practice. Most district attorneys are elected and prosecute in the name of The People. Yet most district attorney races are not competitive; incumbents enjoy huge advantages (Wright 2009). Prosecutors' decisions are hidden and opaque, making them less accountable. So there is a danger of agency costs: prosecutors' self-interests can color serving the interests of the public. And our populist system lacks the formal training and defined role expectations that accompany European civil-service systems. In other words, American prosecutors have both more discretion and less guidance or oversight.

The fragmentation of prosecutions across levels of government and within each office exacerbates the problem, impeding oversight and accountability. That can warp prosecutors' incentives and perspectives. Prosecutors may want to do justice, but in practice that may mean following their gut sense of justice and succumbing to bureaucratic pressure to maximize volume and move cases along. Electoral checks may not be enough to offset those incentives. Because of the problems just discussed, the electorate often cannot do much to weigh in and trade off one priority against another in any reflective, meaningful way. And the frustration that voters feel risks costing the system legitimacy—especially when a minority community feels ignored and mistreated by those in power. Chapter 19 addresses the role of voters generally, and Chapter 21 focuses more specifically on the role of under-represented groups like racial minorities and immigrants.

Prospects for Reform

The range of prosecution systems is enormous; each has strengths and weaknesses. Different observers will disagree about the merits of each. Academics and foreign observers often blame populism as a weakness of American criminal justice. But that democratic input can also be a strength, or at least an avenue of change. Much depends on one's political theory and the value one puts on democratic legitimacy.

Philosophers wedded to a single theory of punishment may decry how far actual prosecution deviates from their chosen ideal. They may thus reject populist systems with all their fragmentation and inconsistencies in favor of apolitical, insulated civil services like those in continental Europe, pursuing a unified vision of crime control or rehabilitation. But those who emphasize democracy and consent of the governed may welcome prosecutors' responsiveness to democratic pressure and look for ways to improve it. And voters are often more pluralistic than experts, expecting prosecutors to balance the competing purposes of punishment.

America's decentralized layers of government also create myriad laboratories of democracy. And now that the reflexive tough-on-crime ratchet is breaking down, criminal-justice policy no longer divides along neat partisan lines but is politically contested. The cost of criminal justice is another pressure spurring policymakers to try new approaches, especially at state and local levels where policing, prosecution, and imprisonment take up large shares of budgets (as Chapter 16 notes). These costs and political contests generate a wider range of approaches in the more democratic systems of prosecution.

Many American policy entrepreneurs and public-interest groups have thus stepped in to advocate and support new ways to prosecute. The Vera Institute has long worked on issues like bail reform, and the Laura and John Arnold Foundation has recently joined them. George Soros and others have begun to support reform-minded district attorneys, leading to the election of ex-defense lawyers promising less-punitive approaches in cities as large as Philadelphia. The Innocence Project and others have worked with prosecutors' offices to support the creation of conviction-integrity units to catch and remedy wrongful convictions. And America's decentralized, federalist system of government fosters such democratic experimentalism, especially at lower levels of government.

As one can see, there is not one clear answer to the many issues raised by prosecution. But there is an enormous range of fascinating questions, each of which calls for further research and study. This is a timely and important volume to reflect on where we stand and to spur more research, debate, and experimentation.

References

Bibas, Stephanos. 2012. *The Machinery of Criminal Justice*. New York: Oxford University Press.
Bierschbach, Richard A., and Stephanos Bibas. 2017. "Rationing Criminal Justice." *Michigan Law Review* 116(2): 187–246.
Dan-Cohen, Meir. 1984. "Decision Rules and Conduct Rules: On Acoustic Separation in Criminal Law." *Harvard Law Review* 97(3): 625–677.
Fisher, George. 2003. *Plea Bargaining's Triumph*. Stanford: Stanford University Press.
Langbein, John H. 1979. "Understanding the Short History of Plea Bargaining." *Law and Society Review* 13(2): 261–272.
Lynch, Gerard F. 1998. "Our Administrative System of Criminal Justice." *Fordham Law Review* 66(6): 2117–2151.
Natapoff, Alexandra. 2018. *Punishment Without Crime*. New York: Basic Books.
Stuntz, William J. 2001. "The Pathological Politics of Criminal Law." *Michigan Law Review* 100(3): 505–600.
Wright, Ronald F. 2009. "How Prosecutor Elections Fail Us." *Ohio State Journal of Criminal Law* 6(2): 581–610.

List of Contributors

Miriam H. Baer is a Professor of Law at Brooklyn Law School, and Senior Fellow, Carol and Lawrence Zicklin Center for Business Ethics Research at the Wharton School.

Matt Barno is a Ph.D. student at the University of California, Irvine.

Stephanos Bibas is a federal judge serving on the United States Court of Appeals for the Third Circuit.

Darryl K. Brown is the O. M. Vicars Professor of Law and Barron F. Black Research Professor of Law at the University of Virginia School of Law.

Jennifer Chacón is a Professor of Law at the UCLA School of Law.

Anu Chugh has been a Lloyd C. Gardner Fellow at Rutgers University, School of Arts and Sciences.

Nora V. Demleitner is the Roy L. Steinheimer, Jr., Professor of Law at Washington and Lee University School of Law.

Lauren-Brooke Eisen is the Director of the Justice Program at the Brennan Center for Justice.

Roger A. Fairfax, Jr., is the Patricia Roberts Harris Research Professor of Law and Founding Director of the Criminal Law and Policy Initiative at George Washington University Law School.

Brandon L. Garrett is the L. Neil Williams, Jr., Professor of Law at Duke University School of Law.

Russell M. Gold is an Associate Professor of Law at the University of Alabama School of Law.

Bruce A. Green is the Louis Stein Chair of Law and Director of the Louis Stein Center for Law and Ethics at Fordham University School of Law.

Alexander Heinze is Assistant Professor of Law at the Georg-August-University of Göttingen, Institute for Criminal Law and Justice, Department of Foreign and International Criminal Law.

Kristin Henning is the Agnes N. Williams Research Professor, Director of the Juvenile Justice Clinic, and Associate Dean for Clinics and Experiential Learning at the Georgetown University Law Center.

Raquel Hernandez is a Ph.D. student in Criminology at the University of Maryland.

Carissa Byrne Hessick is the Anne Shea Ransdell and William "Buck" Ransdell, Jr., Distinguished Professor of Law and Director of the Prosecutors and Politics Project at the University of North Carolina School of Law.

Milton Heumann is the Distinguished Professor of Political Science at Rutgers University.

Brian D. Johnson is Professor of Criminology at the University of Maryland.

Rick Kavin is a Graduate Student in the Political Science Department at Rutgers University.

Amanda Konradi is an Associate Professor of Sociology at Loyola University Maryland.

Miriam Aroni Krinsky is the Executive Director of Fair and Just Prosecution.

Kay L. Levine is a Professor of Law at the Emory University School of Law.

Mona Lynch is Professor of Criminology, Law and Society at University of California, Irvine.

Tirza Jo Ochrach-Konradi is a graduate of Scripps College, in Claremont, California.

Daniel C. Richman is the Paul J. Kellner Professor of Law at Columbia University Law School.

Kent Roach is a Professor and the Prichard Wilson Chair in Law and Public Policy on the Faculty of Law at the University of Toronto.

Jenny Roberts is a Professor of Law and the Co-Director of the Criminal Justice Clinic at the Washington College of Law, American University.

Stefano Ruggeri is Professor of Italian, European, and Comparative Criminal Justice at Messina University (Italy), Law Department.

Stephen Rushin is an Associate Professor of Law at Loyola University Chicago School of Law.

Salmon Shomade is an Associate Professor of Political Science at Oxford College of Emory University.

Cassia Spohn is the Foundation Professor and Director of Graduate Programs in the School of Criminology and Criminal Justice at Arizona State University.

Sherod Thaxton is Professor of Law at the UCLA School of Law. He also holds courtesy appointments in the Department of African American Studies and the Department of Sociology.

Rasmus H. Wandall is a Research Fellow, Faculty of Law, University of Lund, and Attorney-at-Law with Jon Palle Buhl Law Firm, Copenhagen.

Ronald F. Wright is the Needham Y. Gulley Professor of Criminal Law at Wake Forest University School of Law.

Ellen Yaroshefsky is the Howard Lichtenstein Distinguished Professor of Legal Ethics, Associate Dean for Research and Faculty Development, and Executive Director of the Monroe H. Freedman Institute for the Study of Legal Ethics at Hofstra University, Maurice A. Deane School of Law.

Introduction

Understanding Prosecutors in All Their Contexts

RONALD F. WRIGHT, KAY L. LEVINE, AND RUSSELL M. GOLD

We inhabit a world where antisocial behavior, destructive personal interactions, nuisances, and petty law violations occur every day, in homes and on public thoroughfares, in rural areas, suburbs, and inner cities, in corporations and in families. Sometimes there are good reasons for circumventing the law, such as stealing bread to feed one's starving family. Sometimes there aren't. And while law-breakers are portrayed in the entertainment industry as social deviants, street corner gangsters, or sophisticated financial syndicates, they are also ordinary citizens. For many people, the law violation reflects a momentary lapse in judgment, or a way to deal with stressful life circumstances during a particular period, rather than a commitment to a dangerous or depraved lifestyle. In short, humans engage in a range of behaviors that cause physical or financial harm to others, offend moral sensibilities, and disrupt the peace, and they do so for understandable and unjustifiable (and sometimes incomprehensible) reasons.

Criminal law offers one especially powerful response to wrongful acts. Treating an action as a crime can trigger interventions by the police, courts, corrections officers, and community surveillance officers. Moreover, the crime label can lead to consequences for the actor both inside the criminal justice system (such as pre-trial detention, post-conviction incarceration, fines, and even the death penalty) and outside, in realms as diverse as employment, food and housing assistance, immigration, firearms ownership, child custody, and voting.

Who decides whether to engage the machinery of criminal justice (Bibas 2015), or to use alternative social responses, or to look the other way? This is not the decision of any single person, but many of the key choices belong to the criminal prosecutor. The prosecutor's office is the gatekeeper to the justice system, preventing some people from becoming enmeshed in the system entirely, diverting others out of the system at some mid-way point, and funneling still others through to the end. It is a position that carries enormous power, and this power, if left unchecked (or under-checked), can dramatically influence the percentage of the population that is under surveillance or caged in the name of public safety. What is more, an unsupervised gatekeeper could disproportionately deploy system resources against vulnerable populations.

The prosecutor's role in choosing society's response to wrongful acts has grown stronger over the years. The law gives prosecutors greater influence today than they had in the past over the sentences that criminal defendants face (Bjerk 2005; Frase 2013) and the collateral consequences that shape their lives. While prosecutors have long attracted the attention of scholars in many social science disciplines (Wright and Levine 2017), we believe that the time has arrived for "prosecution studies" to be understood as a distinct sub-discipline. This book captures the state-of-the-art scholarship for entry-level scholars, experienced researchers, and engaged professionals.

Deductive and Inductive Approaches to Prosecution Scholarship

Keeping competing interests in sight, and in balance, is generally regarded as the primary challenge of the prosecutor's job, although scholars disagree on what a balanced prosecution portfolio looks like. The answer to this question is grounded in the interplay between theory and practice, between deductive and inductive styles of inquiry (Garland 2001, vii–xii).

A few general theories of prosecution have emerged lately in the sociolegal literature as a counterpoint to the prosecutorial tendency to declare simply that their job is to "do the right thing," a prescription that carries great moral weight but offers little actual guidance. Jeff Bellin, for example, posits that prosecutors ought to think of themselves as servants of the law (Bellin 2020; see also Fish 2017). Bellin invokes the description of the prosecutor's job commonly encountered in civil law countries such as Germany to argue that prosecutors should make their charging and case resolution choices in support of a rational, functional legal system. Such a system provides a relatively clear set of instructions that prosecutors ought to follow; hence, prosecutors should subordinate the wishes of the public and the victim regarding enforcement or non-enforcement, and they should reject vague objectives such as "public safety" or "substantive justice."

Bruce Green and Rebecca Roiphe characterize the prosecutor as a fiduciary of the public trust (Green and Roiphe 2020). Like Bellin, they hope to develop a theory of the prosecutor's role that offers more concrete guidance than the traditional "do justice" command, but they emphasize the fiduciary duties of care and loyalty, rather than a duty to the formal law itself. For example, these duties exclude choices based on personal or private advantage, obligate prosecutors to make choices based on the common good, and call for prosecutors to reveal more about their internal office processes. But the public interests that prosecutors vindicate are sufficiently abstract, according to Green and Roiphe, to allow prosecutors to make just choices in individual cases, setting aside the case-specific views of local actors in order to further or mitigate other systemic effects of their work.

David Sklansky, by contrast, emphasizes that prosecutors can never count on a well-defined set of objectives or a pre-ordered script. Instead, they serve a mediating function in criminal justice (Sklansky 2016), which means the job requires flexibility more than servitude. Sklansky tells us that members of the public hold incompatible goals for the legal system, alternating between (or sometimes combining) desires for rules and discretion, for police and for courts, for law and politics. Prosecutors have the necessary ideological, institutional, and operational tools to satisfy the public despite some of their incompatible goals. The contours of what satisfaction looks like may change on a case-by-case basis, but the prosecutor pulls the strings.

While each of these theories of prosecution provides valuable insights—both descriptive and normative—about the work of prosecutors today, we believe that they fail to account for the full range of prosecutor activities. In particular, these theories concentrate on the role of the prosecutor in the criminal courts and neglect the prosecutor's relationships with other governmental actors, non-profits, or the community more generally. Theories of prosecution need to account for the prosecutor's work upstream and downstream from the criminal courts in order to fully capture the job. A comprehensive theory therefore should account for the prosecutor's efforts to balance criminal enforcement with other social responses to dangerous actions, and should look beyond the propriety of the prosecutors' decisions after their cases have entered the criminal court realm.

Another limitation of some of these theories—both Bellin's and Green and Roiphe's in particular—is their tendency to view the job in a uniform way. They assume that all prosecutors everywhere should do the job in the same way, regardless of the particulars of the socio-legal landscape in which they practice. In particular, they do not leave appropriate room for the public to shape the work of local prosecutors—guidance that differs from place to place—while acknowledging that prosecutors must remain within the outer bounds that the law sets (Gold 2011; Levine 2020; Murray 2020; Wright 2017).[1] Moreover, the "servant of the law" and "fiduciary" accounts of prosecution describe well the functions of the office in some countries, but they do not fit so comfortably with the expansive job description of prosecutors in the United States. In short, it is possible to draw theoretical insights from routine practice, but it is unlikely that a single theory could draw together the many aspects of the prosecutor's role, as performed in many different places.

In this volume we offer the reader an inductive, evidence-based approach to assessing what prosecutors actually do in their working lives. In other words, however one sets the proper equilibrium between public safety and justice, we believe that abstract ideals do not guide prosecutors in the field as they maintain their own sense of balance. Instead, choices that prosecutors make every day define the equilibrium, fortify it, or threaten it. For example, the prosecutor needs to devise systems to distinguish reliable from unreliable accusations, and to hold accusers accountable for errors and biases that lead them to short-circuit their investigations. The prosecutor also must decide how to correct for case-sorting decisions that could reinforce racial and socioeconomic disparities.

Whatever their implicit theories of the job, prosecutors must operationalize them within the communities that the local office serves, accounting for the entities and forces operating in the same sociopolitical landscape. With all of these groups, the prosecutor needs to ensure that communication is a two-way street, to reconcile public safety objectives with fiscal responsibility, public accountability, and ethical practice. For example, modern prosecutors are often involved in crafting or redirecting criminal justice policy at the macro level: they may lobby state legislatures regarding the drafting of new legislation, or they may seek to educate judges about the need to take certain categories of crime more seriously.

Modern prosecutors also take an interest in improving the long-term safety, wellness, and fair treatment of communities, looking beyond the cases generated by local police to a deeper set of priorities. Toward that end, they might help non-profits to secure funding for training programs or other social services, to keep would-be offenders out of the justice system or to facilitate the re-entry of defendants after their carceral sentences have ended. In short, the chief prosecutors who neglect these outward-facing roles to focus exclusively on managing an internal caseload lose the opportunity to craft a more structurally sound, fiscally responsible justice system, in conjunction with (instead of at odds with) community players.

In focusing on how prosecution is operationalized, rather than on how it is theorized, this collection of essays asks the reader to consider prosecution functions from a variety of law and social science disciplines and from a variety of jurisdictions. While the emphasis is on the United States, many of the chapters offer evidence of practices and trends from other nations, to put the practices we see in the United States into comparative perspective. Moreover, the United States itself offers a rich variety of approaches to most criminal justice system questions, as there are at least fifty-one distinct justice systems operating at any given time—and considerably more when one accounts for the degree of local variation within each state. Acquiring knowledge about just the federal prosecution approach in the United States is therefore unwise, if the scholar or policymaker wants to understand how most prosecutions are operating across the fifty states.

Themes

Turning now to the larger themes of the book: the chapters in Part I and Part III examine the prosecutor as a case manager and courtroom actor but offer views of the prosecutor at various stages of a case, and in various kinds of cases. Meanwhile, the chapters in Part II zoom out to examine the prosecutor's relationships with other actors and institutions in the sociolegal landscape, encompassing their work outside the judicial process.

The Shape of Discretion

When the prosecutor acts in the case manager capacity, two main features of the job take center stage: discretion and triage. A vast body of literature has established that prosecutors in both the United States and in foreign systems possess significant discretion. They wield almost unchecked power to make decisions about who gets prosecuted, for what crimes, and with what results. As Lynch and Barno discuss in Chapter 1, and Johnson and Hernandez discuss in Chapter 4, discretion is at its apex when prosecutors are making filing decisions and plea offers, two areas in which the U.S. Supreme Court has failed to impose meaningful restraints on prosecutorial choices. Lynch and Barno further demonstrate that once legislatures—particularly the U.S. Congress—reined in judicial sentencing discretion, they transferred that discretionary power to prosecutors in what is known as a "hydraulic displacement of discretion." This point emerges as well in Demleitner's essay (Chapter 7) discussing a prosecutor's role in post-conviction sentencing and in Hessick's essay (Chapter 19) documenting the inability of elections to hold prosecutors accountable for their choices in most instances.

But discretion also arises because of the prosecutor's need to triage cases: there are too many cases on the calendar but not enough time to handle all of them with in-depth care, and a greater-still number of cases that prosecutors could bring because of the breadth of criminal law but choose not to. Prosecutors thus need to identify which cases merit the use of their resources and which they can resolve through alternate mechanisms. The move toward summary trials in some countries has further aggrandized prosecutors' power, as Heinze explains in his comparative look at trial practices in Chapter 6; the development of accountability courts and diversion programs has done the same elsewhere, as ably shown by Shomade in Chapter 9.

The chapters in Part III, by highlighting the prosecution of distinct defendant populations and case types, lay bare the complexity of the decision to file criminal charges. These chapters show the fallacy of a "one-size-fits-all" approach to understanding this crucial intercept point from the prosecution perspective. For example, in Chapter 21, Chacón explains how some modern state prosecutors exercise their charging discretion to mitigate the federal immigration effects of a criminal conviction, while Henning (Chapter 22) and Roberts (Chapter 25) argue that prosecutors ought to engage in more creative tinkering or outright declination to benefit the population of juvenile or misdemeanor defendants. Thaxton (Chapter 27) calls for more outside review of charging decisions in death penalty cases to minimize both the sheer number of capital cases and the degree of racial disparity, while Baer (Chapter 23) urges prosecutors and academics to tame their enthusiasm for unprincipled enforcement of corporate criminal laws. Rushin (Chapter 24) turns a critical eye toward the prosecutors who must decide whether to file charges against police officers; he offers keen insight into the institutional barriers that prevent objective consideration of the evidence in these cases. Lastly, in Chapter 26 Roach brings the charging decision into the national security arena, where international cooperation, independence, and the need for secrecy render the decision to file (or not) politically fraught and always subject to second-guessing.

Outside of the charging and bargaining arenas, the use of discretion can be found in many of the prosecutor's other pre-trial choices as well. For instance, chapters by Fairfax (Chapter 3), Brown (Chapter 5), and Garrett (Chapter 8) demonstrate that prosecutors consider whether to present exculpatory evidence at pre-trial probable cause hearings, whether to undertake their pre-trial disclosure obligations generously or narrowly, and whether to cooperate with defense investigators who assert a post-conviction claim of innocence. Moreover, these discretionary choices at various phases of a case are interrelated, as prosecutors often decide at the time of filing what a case will be "worth" at the time of plea bargaining, and may craft pre-trial strategies (such as disclosure and motions) to increase their leverage in negotiations.

Sometimes these decisions are heavily shaped by office policies, but in other instances the individual prosecutor has autonomy to craft a unique approach. In the absence of statutory or constitutional rules constraining the available choices, this level of autonomy becomes the handmaiden of discretion. When discretion and autonomy are at their highest levels, the prosecutor's willingness and ability to balance responsibilities as an advocate with responsibilities as a minister of justice become particularly important. Ruggieri's exploration of the porous boundary between prosecutors and judges in continental systems in Chapter 1 provides a novel perspective on this problem, as the prosecutor's duties shift in relation to the judge's duties at different stages of a criminal investigation. Brown's entry (Chapter 5) likewise explores the salience of autonomy when prosecutors are charged with fulfilling their disclosure obligations. Roach's essay (Chapter 26) offers a contrasting view of the value of independence, as he describes the need for cooperation across nations when prosecutors make decisions about terrorism and national security prosecutions. Finally, Chacón's chapter (Chapter 21) explores the degree to which state prosecutors exercise their autonomy in a federalist system – choosing to reject the tight coil imposed by federal immigration laws in favor of softer approaches to enforcement of state criminal codes.

Independence within Relationships

As the chapters in Part II show, the prosecutor's network of connections to victims, the state bar, politicians, and law enforcement make the job of prosecution both more textured and more challenging than the courtroom-centric view allows us to see. Moreover, competing obligations to courtroom workgroups, the state legislature, and the larger community complicate the prosecutor's ability to focus exclusively on cases to the detriment of larger concerns.

To begin, the prosecutor must interact with a variety of individuals in order to do the job well, but those individuals often have agendas that differ from the prosecutor's own priorities. The prosecutor must therefore approach these individuals in the spirit of cooperation but always retain a sense of skepticism about when and where their respective values and objectives diverge. Relatedly, in professional relationships prosecutors are not and cannot be partners in the true sense of the word. They serve multiple constituencies at the same time, which renders their sense of loyalty to any single constituency somewhat diffuse.

The theme of connection-but-not-subservience emerges starkly in Richman's chapter about law enforcement relationships (Chapter 14) and Wright's chapter about community groups (Chapter 20). Both authors note that prosecutors risk doing both too much and too little to satisfy the desires of these often outspoken groups, and that they must communicate carefully around expectations and boundaries in order not to offend or alienate. Spohn's essay (Chapter 12) describing prosecutorial approaches in specialized units and Konradi and Konradi's chapter about victims (Chapter 18) likewise highlight prosecutorial ambivalence about being beholden to those who are relative outsiders to the justice system. Prosecutors need to maintain a sense of detachment in order to preserve their professional judgment while continuing to show respect for victims and keep them as reliable witnesses.

Aside from remaining alert to the sometimes shifting equilibrium, the prosecutor cannot develop an attorney-client fiduciary relationship with either the police or the victim, as that might heighten adversariness with the prosecutor's courtroom workgroup. The workgroup signals to the prosecutor that she should prioritize efficiency and the maintenance of professional relationships with other criminal justice actors (like the defense bar and the judiciary). What is more, the prosecutor must serve the rule of law and justice even if (especially if) those ideals conflict with the victim's or law enforcement's immediate desires. Heumann, Kavin, and Chugh illustrate this strain in their chapter about courtroom workgroups (Chapter 13); Yaroshefsky does the same in her essay documenting the connective tissue between prosecutors and defenders (Chapter 17). She portrays the relationship between these two sets of attorneys as far from unidimensional; instead, it bounces between collegiality and advocacy depending on office, context, and personality.

Tensions exist with the state capitol as well. As explained by Gold in his chapter about prosecutors and their legislatures (Chapter 16), the prosecutor relies on the menu of crimes provided by the legislature in the criminal code but does not approach the criminal code merely as its servant. Prosecutors' authority to exercise discretion (to keep certain offenders out of the justice system, and to mitigate the effects of the justice system for others) keeps them from being a tool of full enforcement. At the same time they have a role in shaping what future laws will be, through lobbying efforts, media blasts, and congressional testimony.

In these various contexts, the prosecutor must navigate a web of interlocking relationships so as not to be out-maneuvered or to generate a sense of betrayal that might limit future pathways to success. Prosecutors must also stay apprised of their professional obligations as members of the state bar, as Green instructs in his chapter on bar authorities (Chapter 15), while simultaneously remaining alert to attempts by the bar to limit their authority in individual cases. All in all, the terrain is fraught with difficulty for the prosecutor who fails to attend to institutional incentives and or who ignores competing narratives about prosecutorial power and restraint in the public square.

Beyond placing these relationships in the spotlight, the chapters in this volume consider the connections between the roles we ask prosecutors to play and the professional environment in which prosecutors develop their skills. Metrics that a community establishes for what makes a "good prosecutor" emerge from and reinforce the case-centric view of prosecution, and prosecutors tend to be hired and promoted in accordance with those metrics. In other words, the metrics and the behavior of prosecutors can be regarded as mutually constitutive. That is not to say they are written in stone, however. Wandall points out in his chapter about hiring and training standards (Chapter 10), and Eisen and Krinsky emphasize in their piece about performance measures (Chapter 11), that a new set of metrics could and should capture the full range of tasks that comprise the modern prosecutor's portfolio. A new, more diverse set of metrics would allow us to better assess the true performance of each person who holds the office and would send a signal to those interested in the profession about what skills really matter.

Disparities by Race, Gender, and Socioeconomic Status

As in any writing about the criminal justice system, concerns about racial, gender, and socio-economic disparities emerge frequently throughout this book. We regard these patterns as too pervasive and too important to confine to any single chapter. No honest account of criminal justice can ignore the impact of race, gender, and class on the outcomes of the system (Alexander 2010; Ulmer, Kurlychek, and Kramer 2007).

We asked all of our authors to consider the race, gender, and class dimensions of the prosecutorial policies they were discussing writ large. Explicitly thoughtful connections between prosecution and race, gender, and class can be found throughout the book, but we highlight a few here: Lynch and Barno's chapter about charging (Chapter 2), Johnson and Hernandez's chapter on plea bargaining (Chapter 4), Eisen and Krinsky's chapter about performance metrics (Chapter 11), Konradi and Konradi's chapter about victims (Chapter 18), Wright's chapter about community groups (Chapter 20), Henning's chapter about the juvenile justice system (Chapter 22), and Thaxton's chapter about the death penalty (Chapter 27).

The Spread of Reform Ideas

Finally, the authors in this volume ably demonstrate that discontent with the status quo provides flat ground for new ideas to travel, spread, and sometimes swirl into a storm of innovation. These chapters provide us with abundant evidence from non-U.S. jurisdictions about various ways that prosecutors might engage in dialogue across professional and geographic boundaries. For instance, when we consider Ruggieri's take on the prosecutorial role in investigations, Heinze's chapter on trials, and Wandall's entry on hiring and training standards, we can learn from techniques and procedures that other nations have embraced to evaluate more critically those that dominate in the United States. These authors have opened up new channels of thought for prosecutors everywhere to reimagine their professional identities and ways of the doing the job.

The banquet of ideas that this volume brings to the table could be especially welcome for newly elected reformer or "progressive" prosecutors in various jurisdictions across the United States. In areas such as charge declinations, pre-trial release and post-conviction integrity units, dozens of newly elected office leaders are signaling that conventional ways of performing the prosecution function are too expensive, racially compromised, and bereft of compassion (Bazelon 2019; Davis 2019; Levin 2020; Levine 2020). We also hope that this volume can set the research agenda for students, scholars recently arriving to this field, and others formulating their interests and agendas in the field of prosecution. And finally, for experienced scholars of prosecutors and prosecutions, we anticipate that the range of subjects addressed here can prompt a rethinking of the topics that merit attention going forward.

Chapter-by-Chapter Summaries

Chapter 1 focuses on prosecutors' role in investigations. The author demonstrates that the extent of prosecutor control over police investigations varies significantly from country to country and varies depending on the nature of the investigative tools used. Prosecutors' investigative power has increased in many places as the distinction between investigation and prosecution has softened.

Chapter 2 documents prosecutors' vast charging discretion and the negligible limitations that the U.S. Supreme Court has placed on that discretion for prosecutors in both state and federal courts. It discusses four factors that have emerged in the literature as significant shapers of charging discretion: case factors, demographic factors, socio-structural factors, and local factors. Lastly, the chapter considers the role of mandatory minimum sentencing provisions in shaping charging decisions that have, in turn, accounted for nearly all of the racial disparities in American criminal sentencing and contributed to mass incarceration.

Chapter 3 guides the reader through the various processes by which prosecutors' charging decisions can be tested in a criminal case: judicial probable cause hearings to validate arrests, preliminary hearings, grand juries, plea hearings, trials, post-trial motions (such as motions for judgment of acquittal or a new trial), appeals for sufficiency of evidence, or actual innocence claims on collateral review. The author further explains how and why grand juries could be used more effectively to check prosecutors' charging power.

Chapter 4 explains the extraordinary importance of plea bargains in modern American criminal law practice. It recounts the historical evolution and rise of plea bargaining, and then articulates the various normative positions that various scholars have taken concerning the wisdom and morality of the practice. The author concludes with policy prescriptions, including more judicial regulation of plea bargaining, formal limits on the size of plea discounts, complete discovery during bargaining, and greater financial support for public defender offices.

Chapter 5 analyzes prosecutors' disclosure obligations—often referred to as discovery—and the ways in which disclosure regimes vary across jurisdictions. Although most of the common law world requires broad disclosure, many U.S. states allow discretion to prosecutors to determine what they wish to disclose—such as by determining whether a particular piece of evidence is material—and when. Such narrow disclosure rules implicitly treat prosecutors as the actors best positioned to assess the risks of potential disclosure, the author contends.

Chapter 6 offers the reader a comparative look at the prosecutor's conduct while in trial. It emphasizes the multiplicity of roles played by the prosecutor during this process: executive officer, judicial branch official, impartial minister of justice, forceful advocate for victims, officer of the court, and leader of law enforcement. It also discusses the rarity of full trials, both in the United States and around the world, the decline of juries, and the prosecutor's role in jury selection before trial.

Chapter 7 explores prosecutors' power over sentencing, beginning with the charging power and continuing through prosecutors' involvement in potential parole or clemency decisions. The author shows that as federal judges' discretion declined in the United States in the latter part of the twentieth century, prosecutors' power to influence the post-conviction sentence increased. That same pattern emerged in other common law countries and in continental Europe, as discretion and prosecutors' ability to bargain increased across jurisdictions.

Chapter 8 contrasts the traditional way in which American prosecutors have operated post-conviction (by maintaining their adversarial posture and defending their convictions) with a recent trend (using a less adversarial approach and cooperating with defense investigations into claims of innocence). Some prosecutors' offices have formed conviction integrity units and have even assumed an affirmative responsibility to investigate closed cases after conviction. The author suggests that this model ought to be described as investigative or remedial, rather than conventionally adversarial.

Chapter 9 describes prosecutors' role in the creation, operation, and perpetuation of accountability courts (such as drug courts) and diversion programs. After detailing the history of accountability courts in the United States and abroad, the author explains the non-adversarial approach that prosecutors take in such programs. Rather than arguing for a conviction, prosecutors in these courts work with a team including a defense lawyer, a judge, a probation officer, and other non-court actors such as drug treatment centers, to help the defendant restructure his life so as to avoid future law-breaking.

Chapter 10 considers the various approaches to hiring and training prosecutors that exist around the globe. It particularly contrasts the decentralized approach that characterizes hiring and training in state jurisdictions across America with the tightly organized bureaucratic models of many continental nations. The author emphasizes the impact on consistency and robust professional development that the bureaucratic model produces, two values that seem largely absent in the American landscape.

Chapter 11 takes the reader on a tour through the landscape of prosecutorial performance measures that currently exist (most of which focus on conviction and sentencing statistics). It then invites the reader to consider alternative measures that capture the full range of the prosecutor's roles, particularly in an office that is committed to reforms that reduce a jurisdiction's carceral footprint and level of racial injustice.

Chapter 12 introduces two important aspects of the prosecutor's office architecture: the use of specialized units and vertical prosecution models. Specialized units help prosecutors develop expertise in certain kinds of cases, particularly those with sensitive victim issues; vertical prosecution models allow one prosecutor to handle a case from filing through sentencings. These two features often co-exist. The authors explore existing research documenting the influence of vertical specialized units (for sexual assault, domestic violence, and gang homicides) on case management decisions and outcomes.

Chapter 13 offers the reader a close-up view of courtroom workgroups, the particular combination of courtroom personnel (most specifically, judges and defense attorneys) with whom prosecutors interact on a daily basis. Using original interview data, the authors challenge the conventional wisdom that the workgroup itself is the primary driver of courtroom and case outcomes. They assert instead that the workgroup is merely one factor among many that influence case-processing decisions.

Chapter 14 takes up the issue of how prosecutors form relationships with law enforcement officers and teams, and the degree to which those relationships influence both the prosecutor's work and the work of law enforcement. The author contends that dialogue and friction between prosecutors and law enforcement agents sometimes inhibits, and sometimes promotes, productive deliberation about public safety, the rule of law, and community values.

Chapter 15 addresses the role of bar authorities in regulating prosecutorial behavior and explores the influence that prosecutors can wield in the development of professional ethics standards. For the most part, the author asserts, prosecutors regard the imposition of ethical standards by these organizations as unwelcome; this leads prosecutors to resist them or to actively seek changes in standards they feel are too constraining.

Chapter 16 illuminates the complex, but often symbiotic, relationship between prosecutors and legislative authorities. While legislatures formally possess the authority to draft criminal prohibitions, prosecutors influence those laws in two significant ways. First, prosecutors have the power to enforce or to ignore criminal statutes in service of local priorities; second, prosecutors can shape the content of statutes through their lobbying efforts. In this setting both prosecutors and legislators prefer broadly worded criminal prohibitions, as they allow legislators to demonstrate a firm commitment to public safety while knowing that prosecutors will limit the laws' reach through their enforcement discretion.

Chapter 17 examines the multidimensional set of connections between prosecutors and defense attorneys. Drawing on original interviews, the author illuminates the interrelated factors that affect such relationships in the United States and abroad, particularly the power imbalance that heavily favors prosecutors, the social architecture of the prosecutor's office, the reward structures, and the lawyer's individual characteristics. The chapter also considers structural changes in the legal system that have the capacity to shift the nature of these relationships, such as open disclosure rules and the election of reform-minded prosecutors.

Chapter 18 focuses on the interaction between prosecutors and victims in criminal cases. Starting from the basic premise that victims long ago relinquished formal power to public prosecutors, the authors consider the various ways in which the relationship with the victim can significantly influence the trajectory of the criminal case throughout the prosecution. The chapter also brings attention to the capacity of victim legal clinics to shape prosecutorial choices.

Chapter 19 draws on existing literature to inquire whether prosecutors are, or can be, meaningfully held accountable by the electorate for the choices they make. The author compares the United States, in which most chief state prosecutors are elected by local communities, to other countries, in which such elections are rare. The author emphasizes that the issue of electoral responsiveness is one aspect of the tension between prosecutorial accountability and the desire for prosecutorial independence, particularly in highly charged cases.

Chapter 20 considers prosecutors' relationships with the communities they serve, specifically through the lens of community prosecution strategies. In adopting these approaches, prosecutors try to build or to fortify a sense of trust, at least in part by allowing the community to shape office priorities. But where the communities have experienced a history of racial injustice, the author argues, the twin goals of enhancing public safety and increasing the legitimacy of the criminal justice system can be difficult to achieve.

Chapter 21 tracks the interaction between criminal prosecutors in the state courts and immigration enforcement officials at the national level in the United States. Because the immigration consequences of criminal convictions have expanded and intensified over the past generation, the charging decisions of prosecutors now create remarkably diverse immigration effects. Some state prosecutors try to supplement the immigration enforcement efforts of the federal government, while others apply the criminal law of the state in ways that mitigate the immigration effects of a criminal conviction.

Chapter 22 addresses the performance of prosecutors as gatekeepers of juvenile court jurisdiction, and their failure at times to apply principles of adolescent development equitably across race and class lines. Drawing on recent findings in developmental psychology and the cognitive science of bias, the chapter offers a framework to improve prosecutorial decision-making, enhance public safety and help all youth achieve a healthy and productive transition to adulthood.

Chapter 23 criticizes the tendency of contemporary corporate crime scholarship to enhance and legitimate the government's power to prosecute corporate defendants. If the prospect of unbounded enforcement and lawmaking powers are troubling when it comes to most criminal defendants, the same concerns ought to apply to corporate offenders, the author argues. This chapter considers the normative implications of an "unbound" corporate criminal law, and proposes legislative reforms that would impose needed restraints on the prosecutors who currently implement corporate criminal law.

Chapter 24 considers the unique challenges that prosecutors face when they investigate and charge police officers suspected of criminal misconduct. Prosecutors rarely pursue criminal charges against police officers and secure convictions even less often. The chapter explores some of the possible reasons for the lack of success in these cases, including potential conflicts of interest and institutional barriers. It also reviews some of the most compelling scholarly recommendations to improve the investigation and prosecution of criminal conduct by police officers.

Chapter 25 discusses the role of prosecutors in the misdemeanor system. It argues that prosecutors under-utilize their discretion to decline and dismiss low-level cases. Informed prosecutorial decision-making in this arena is critical for several reasons: the enormous volume of arrests, structural and institutional realities that weaken the role of other lower court actors, racial disparities in the impact of misdemeanor charges, and the need to mitigate the myriad disproportionate effects of the ever-growing number of collateral consequences that flow from a minor criminal record.

Chapter 26 examines the distinct operational and ethical challenges that prosecutors face in national security and terrorism cases. The operational challenges include demands for specialization, the availability of special investigative powers, and the complexity of international co-operation. The ethical challenges require prosecutors to balance legitimate claims of secrecy against equally compelling demands for disclosure, and to maintain prosecutorial independence while recognizing the effects of national security cases on the whole of society.

Chapter 27 explores the prosecutor's role in death penalty cases. The author argues that limiting the most aggressive prosecutorial decisions in potentially capital cases might reduce the prevalence of error and the expense of these cases. The chapter proposes reforms to prosecutor decision-making, including advisory opinions from a reviewing authority to assess the appropriateness of a prosecutor's decision to seek the death penalty, and cost-shifting mechanisms to discourage prosecutorial overreaching in capital charging.

Note

1. Green and Roiphe allow prosecutors, as fiduciaries, only a limited authority to account for public sentiment and preferences on a policy level. They should consider the preferences of their states as a whole (or the country as a whole, for federal prosecutors) rather than their particular localities (Green and Roiphe 2020, 819, 841–842).

References

Alexander, Michelle. 2010. *The New Jim Crow: Mass Incarceration in the Age of Colorblindness.* New York: The New Press.

Bazelon, Emily. 2019. *Charged: The New Movement to Transform American Prosecution and End Mass Incarceration.* Random House.

Bellin, Jeffrey. 2020. "Theories of Prosecution." *California Law Review* 108(4): 1203–1253.

Bibas, Stephanos. 2015. *The Machinery of Criminal Justice.* Oxford and New York: Oxford University Press.

Bjerk, David. 2005. "Making the Crime Fit the Penalty: The Role of Prosecutorial Discretion Under Mandatory Minimum Sentencing." *Journal of Law and Economics* 48(2): 591–625.

Davis, Angela J. 2019. "Reimagining Prosecution: A Growing Progressive Movement." *UCLA Criminal Justice Law Review* 3(1): 1–27.

Fish, Eric S. 2017. "Prosecutorial Constitutionalism." *Southern California Law Review* 90(2): 237–306.

Frase, Richard S. 2013. *Just Sentencing: Principles and Procedures for a Workable System. Just Sentencing.* Oxford, New York: Oxford University Press.

Garland, David. 2001. *The Culture of Control: Crime and Social Order in Contemporary Society.* Chicago: University of Chicago Press.

Gold, Russell M. 2011. "Promoting Democracy in Prosecution." *Washington Law Review* 86(1): 69–124.

Green, Bruce A., and Rebecca Roiphe. 2020. "A Fiduciary Theory of Prosecution." *American University Law Review* 69(3): 805–862.

Levin, Benjamin. Forthcoming 2021. "Imagining the Progressive Prosecutor." *Minnesota Law Review* 105: __.

Levine, Kay L. 2020. "Should Consistency Be Part of the Reform Prosecutor's Playbook?" *Hastings Journal of Crime and Punishment* 1(2): 169–193.

Murray, W. Kerrel. Forthcoming 2021. "Populist Prosecutorial Nullification." *N.Y.U. Law Review* 96: __.

Sklansky, David A. 2016. "The Nature and Function of the Prosecutorial Power." *Journal of Criminal Law & Criminology* 106(3): 473–520.

Ulmer, Jeffery T., Megan C. Kurlychek, and John H. Kramer. 2007. "Prosecutorial Discretion and the Imposition of Mandatory Minimum Sentences." *Journal of Research in Crime and Delinquency* 44(4): 427–458.

Wright, Ronald F. 2017. "Reinventing American Prosecution Systems." *Crime and Justice: A Review of Research* 46: 395–439.

Wright, Ronald F., and Kay L. Levine. 2017. "Place Matters in Prosecution Research." *Ohio State Journal of Criminal Law* 14(2): 675–703.

PART I

PHASES OF CRIMINAL PROCEEDINGS

CHAPTER 1

PUBLIC PROSECUTORS IN CRIMINAL INVESTIGATIONS

A Comparative Law Study

STEFANO RUGGERI

1.1 Introduction

There is little doubt that public prosecutors constitute one of the most significant and, at the same time, most controversial figures of modern criminal justice (Ruggieri 2008, 998). In the current era, the start of criminal proceedings needs prosecutorial action, for models of criminal proceedings initiated *ex officio* by judicial authorities have almost disappeared.[1] Though the historical evolution of public prosecutors followed different paths in national jurisdictions, some common lines could be drawn. The ways in which these peculiar bodies act and the aims they pursue in criminal proceedings reflect the constant tension between the victim's eagerness for justice and the need of dominant forces to maintain their power to enforce penalties.

This tension emerged long before the foundation of modern states, particularly in civil law countries, when the development of absolute monarchies entailed the concentration of the power to impose sentences and to control judges as well (Orlandi 2008, 943f.). It is largely recognized that most European public prosecutorial offices, such as the German *Staatsanwaltschaft* or the Spanish *Fiscalía*, have one single common origin, which traces back to the French absolutism of the fourteenth century (Orlandi 2008, 943). It should not be overlooked, however, that the concentration of political powers in royal absolutism did not melt them, and that even the power to impart justice, although being formally brought together with other powers in the king's hands, already held autonomous relevance (Satta 1962, 800). The original function of the first prosecutorial officers to protect the king's interests should therefore be understood in this sense.

Doubtless, the French *procureur publique* or the English Attorney General have had enormous influence on the developments that have taken place in a number of criminal justice systems worldwide. Yet, beyond these common lines, it would probably be meaningless to identify similarities with, or divergences from, ancient models, which emerged to satisfy the specific needs of a certain society in a historical period. In Italy, for instance, a king's prosecutor (*procuratore del Re*) still survived under the 1930 code of criminal procedure, with remarkable powers to terminate criminal proceedings, while his legal action was hierarchically subordinated to the oversight of the Executive. But although Italian criminal justice is still largely inspired by the French judiciary system of *parquet* comprising both judges and prosecutors, the hierarchical subordination of public prosecutorial offices to the Ministry of Justice was abolished after the fall of the fascist regime.[2] A close examination of individual jurisdictions, moreover, reveals that significant changes have often characterized the functions or organizational structure of public prosecutorial offices within the same country over the years, which makes it almost impossible to draw the lines of the public prosecutor in France or Spain, as if it were an immortal being.

Comparative law research, if conducted with a functional and dynamic method, may instead seem to be of great usefulness. This perspective suggests looking at the ways national models satisfy the state's need to initiate and bring forward its legal action in criminal trials, although this need has always emerged differently in various countries, depending on the social tensions and criminal law policy of a specific historical period. But what counts as "prosecution" in criminal matters? Does prosecution only mean instituting a criminal trial by bringing individuals to court to face an accusation? What is the nature of the prosecutor's legal action in the pre-trial inquiries, which aim at verifying whether and with what procedure defendants have to be brought to court?

Legal scholarship has long dealt with such questions.[3] Piero Calamandrei, one of the most influential scholars of civil procedural law of the twentieth century, emphasized the high relativism of legal theories on civil law action (Calamadrei 1943, 115), comparing its multiple forms with the legendary story of the thousand and one nights (Di Chiara 2003, 242). A look at the difficult problems concerned with criminal prosecution, however, reveals that criminal law action remains polyhedral in modern times, its features varying according to a number of factors, such as the type of prosecutorial services, the stages or instances of the proceedings, the existence of special rules applying to certain (serious) crimes, and so on. This confirms that the role of public prosecutorial offices cannot be studied in abstract terms but necessitates a dynamic approach, which looks at the solutions enacted in a specific legal context. It is only the analysis of the forms in which these special bodies *act* in criminal proceedings that can tell us what they *are* in a specific jurisdiction.

This approach, however, complicates things even more than what one would expect in civil justice. Thus, what is the meaning of a legal action instituted by a body, such as the public prosecutorial office, which aspires to a certain degree of impartiality but acts as a party in the proceedings? What would the legal system be without prosecutorial action? The fact that most criminal justice systems today make large use of public prosecution, or have even maintained monopolistic forms of public legal actions, should not necessarily be viewed in negative terms (Marzaduri 1996, 5), or as an attack on civil liberties, as it was partially seen in the nineteenth century (Carrara 1875, 5ff.). Private prosecution entails a number of risks, particularly if it rests in the hands of the victim: a criminal trial might be initiated for revenge in the absence of sufficient evidence, or vice versa a criminal investigation might be discontinued in a case in which a criminal process would be necessary. Similar reasons led the Italian Constitutional Court to allow for criminal prosecution being instituted by private parties or bodies other than public prosecutors, on condition that such legal actions can never block the initiative of the competent public prosecutors (Constitutional Court, judgments 61/1967, 84/1979, 474/1993).

In sum, the way public prosecution materializes in criminal matters, despite being a universal problem, is definitively a problem of positive law, which reflects the forms in which judicial proceedings are instituted (Satta 1959, 822) and is therefore open to multiple answers. The purpose of this study is to analyze, by way of comparative law, the public prosecutor's role in criminal investigations, which for the aforementioned reasons is tantamount to asking how criminal law actions are carried out in the pre-trial inquiries. At first glance, examining criminal prosecution in the investigative stage may seem to be misleading, as its aim is precisely to ascertain whether or not prosecution is to be instituted. But we shall see that the paradox is only apparent, as prosecutorial actions can clearly be identified during the pre-trial inquiry, a very delicate phase in which a number of relevant intrusive measures can be enforced that severely interfere with fundamental rights on the basis of a criminal charge. The analysis of pre-trial investigations, therefore, provides a privileged viewpoint to grasp the complexity and intrusiveness of criminal prosecution. Criminal prosecution is best understood as something more than a request for judgment on a specific charge;[4] it extends to the decision whether or not to institute a criminal trial.

1.2 Public Prosecution, Charging Decisions, and Pre-trial Inquiries: The Need for a Broad Understanding of Criminal Law Action

The problem of the public prosecutor's theoretical role in criminal investigations turns out to be the problem of how public prosecution is actually carried out in criminal investigations. A comparative law approach to this complex topic, however, immediately reveals the difficulty of identifying a public prosecution in the pre-trial inquiry, which largely depends on the features of the investigative phase, as well as the dynamics between the prosecutorial and other public (judicial and police) authorities in each criminal justice system. For instance, in Brazil, which opted for a model of police inquiry (Lopes Jr. and Glockner 2014), public prosecution may seem to be confined to a secondary role. A similar conclusion appears to apply to those countries (such as France, Portugal, and Spain)[5] which still assign a dominant role to the investigating judge or magistrate during a criminal inquiry. Remarkably, even in countries such as Italy, where the court proceedings are preceded by a pre-trial inquiry generally[6] headed by the public prosecutor and the investigating magistrate has been replaced by a judge guarantor, there does not seem to be room for public prosecution in a strict sense during the investigative phase.

To put it in other words, public prosecution and public investigation do not appear to live together under the same roof in several jurisdictions. The simple and rather tautological reason is that the pre-trial inquiries generally aim to gather all the necessary evidence to enable the competent body (a prosecutor or a judge) to decide whether or not a criminal law action must be initiated by bringing one or more individuals to court.[7]

On close examination, neither this solution nor the placement of the decision on whether to institute the court proceedings constitute decisive arguments to conclude that the prosecutorial legal action during the pre-trial inquiry falls outside the scope of public prosecution. This remains true even in countries, such as Italy and Germany, rooted in the principle of mandatory public prosecution (Marzaduri 1996, 2). Positive law rarely deals with criminal prosecution in abstract terms but usually regulates the ways in which criminal law actions can be instituted and carried out, and as a result, the forms that criminal proceedings can hold depending on who initiates them and how they are conducted. Indeed, public prosecution—similar to what is stressed in relation to civil law action (Satta 1948, 78)—is neither a power nor a right but is simply legal action. In this light, *persecutio criminalis*, legally understood, is definitively also a fact (Satta 1948, 78), or even better, a complex factual phenomenon, namely the powerful movement that leads to the institution and completion of the overall criminal process. But since this process does not only consist of a trial, a prosecutorial legal action can already be observed at the time of the criminal inquiry. From this it follows that prosecution can be identified with the overall criminal proceedings (Cordero 1987, 39), whose features depend on a number of relevant factors and questions, such as whether positive law assigns prosecutorial competences to individuals or public bodies, which procedures and forms govern the exercise of these competences in specific cases, and so on.

Yet even this approach, though reducing the criminal law action to its essential terms, does not enable us to entirely grasp the complexity of public prosecution within the pre-trial inquiry from a comparative law perspective. If the institution of a criminal trial necessitates the filing of one or more charges, does the possibility of filing a charge also represent a sufficient condition for identifying a criminal-law action in the pre-trial inquiry? This possibility may seem to be denied by those countries, which opt for a model of pre-trial inquiry in which the decision on whether to file formal charges is placed at the end rather than at the beginning of the investigations. Italian law, for instance, does not provide for the filing of a preliminary charge in a strict sense during the pre-trial inquiry.[8] However, the institution of a prosecutorial investigation presupposes that the competent public prosecutor registered a *notitia criminis* under a specific legal classification. This is precisely the "fact" of which suspects must be informed before being questioned (Art. 65 CCP), which is tantamount to saying that they must be charged with an alleged offense prior to questioning.

It is true that both the police and the competent prosecutor can conduct their inquiries against unknown persons. This is perhaps one of the main differences between the investigative phase and the court proceedings, which in all jurisdictions must always be directed against specific individuals (or legal persons, in the countries that provide for this possibility). But this difference is not a good argument to rule out the existence of a prosecutorial legal action in the investigative phase. On close examination, the filing of one or more charges defines the necessary content of every criminal law action from the beginning of a criminal proceeding, and therefore during the pre-trial inquiry as well. As has been observed, positive law can assign the competence to charge to bodies other than public prosecutorial services and independent from them, as was the case for England and Wales, which traditionally assigned to the police the decision on whether to charge. It is interesting to note, however, that the 2003 Criminal Justice Act shifted to the Crown Prosecution Service (CPS) the general power to charge suspects unless in trivial cases, for reasons mainly concerned with the lack of legal knowledge by the police, which negatively affected the accuracy of the charges filed and the outcome of the process instituted (Darbyshire 2008, 86f.). Remarkably, such reasons largely coincided with those that in some countries, such as Italy, led to the concentration of the charging decision in the hands of the public prosecutorial offices.

The awareness of the need to connect the decision to charge with the decision to prosecute, therefore, suggests viewing criminal prosecution as a flow starting when a criminal investigation is commenced on the basis of a suspicion that one or more specific individuals committed one or more specific offenses. It is not necessary that these individuals are brought to court with a formal accusation, and that a judge or tribunal is therefore requested to adjudicate the case.

The broad reach of criminal prosecution probably marks the main difference from civil law actions. The Italian code of civil procedure, enacted a decade after the 1930 code of criminal procedure, focused on the institution of legal action (*Dell'esercizio dell'azione*) rather than on legal action itself. That a civil-law action consists of a request for adjudication, and therefore legal action is taken by commencing a court proceeding, does not mean that criminal-law actions must follow the same patterns. Thus, a criminal process has incomparable costs for individual freedoms, which explains why almost all criminal justice systems, regardless of their structure and inspiration, require the trial to be preceded by criminal investigations. And since the institution and carrying out of a criminal inquiry lie with public bodies, this reveals the public nature that widely characterizes criminal prosecution worldwide, which is not contradicted by the choice of some countries to permit private criminal law actions.[9]

Yet, if suspicion of the alleged crime—the so-called *fumus delicti*—may not suffice to justify a criminal investigation, it does not automatically support the delicate decision to charge. Thus, the institution of a criminal inquiry always presupposes that a generic suspicion of guilt, no matter whether taken autonomously by the investigative authorities or received by private parties or public bodies, is converted into a specific hypothesis regarding one or more facts having criminal law relevance. National arrangements significantly differ from each other as to the competent body to formulate this hypothesis, as well as the procedures governing its formalization, the tools of oversight (if any), and so on. But the definition of such a criminal law hypothesis is a necessary condition for commencing a criminal inquiry everywhere and is altogether the result of a complex assessment, which also involves relevant legal aspects. The choice of a specific legal classification instead of another, in particular, inevitably conditions the direction of the pre-trial inquiry, the possibility of using special investigative means, and the outcome of the investigation, that is, the decision on whether or not to institute prosecution. Besides, the discretion of the investigative authorities would be unlimited without a clear factual hypothesis, which therefore serves the fundamental goal of defining the lawful area of investigation (Nobili 1998, 39ff.).

But can any criminal law hypothesis be deemed to be a "charge"? Is it enough to justify the commencement of a public prosecution, in the broad sense underlined hitherto? The answer appears to be negative, even in all those jurisdictions that opt for a centralized model of prosecutorial investigation.[10] Since the filing of charges presupposes that sufficient evidence has been gathered to direct the criminal investigations against one or more persons, a public prosecutorial decision can only be observed from this moment on, which radically modifies the structure of criminal investigations, and therefore, of the overall criminal trial. In the past, one could have argued, by way of a comparative law survey, that no specific procedural act was necessary to charge someone with a criminal offense.[11] Yet today any model of criminal trial shaped by human rights law would make this conclusion somewhat outdated. The establishment of a formal charge, indeed, constitutes an essential safeguard for the suspect, who must be given legal certainty as to whether or not he was charged with a criminal offense, and, in the affirmative case, the specific contents of the charges preferred again him, as well as the rights which he enjoys from this moment on, starting with the right to detailed information. Developments in various countries, both in Europe and Latin America, clearly confirm this conclusion.[12] The need to fulfill the forms of procedural law, however, must not lead to rigid formalism. The analysis of case law from the European Court of Human Rights in Strasbourg, in particular, appears to be extremely relevant for the purposes of the present discussion, for it highlights a clear preference for a non-formalistic approach to the right to information about the "accusation," which must also be properly granted in the pre-trial inquiry.[13]

EU law seems to confirm the unitary structure of prosecution in these terms as well. Of course, unitary structure does not mean forced uniformity. On the contrary, public prosecution offers several different types of notice to the accused. Remarkably, even though the right to know the charge is a guarantee of such importance that it must be granted to both suspects and accused, the forms and intensity of this guarantee vary depending on the phases of criminal proceedings, and even within the pre-trial inquiry, according to the stages of the investigations (Art. 6 Directive 2012/13/EU). Yet, as noted, public prosecution always necessitates a charge that has already been filed, or is about to be.[14]

1.3 Prosecutorial Action and the Relational Networks in the Pre-trial Inquiry

1.3.1 Criminal Law Actions and the Complex Dynamics of Pre-trial Investigations

The subjective direction that is inherent in every charging decision, which establishes a clear link between the alleged offenses and the person against whom the charge is filed, marks the emergence of a set of legal relationships that characterize the subsequent course of a criminal investigation. Ancient legal scholarship, relying on civil law notions, used to look at the criminal process as a network of legal relationships (*rapporto giuridico processuale*). This approach, however, revealed a sort of contractual view of criminal proceedings, whose main terms projected the relationship between the state, as the holder of *jus puniendi*, and the perpetrator, as the person subject to the obligation to undergo punishment. This explained the dominant role of public prosecutors as representatives of *jus persequendi*, which, being the necessary way of satisfying the state's right to punishment, held a fundamental position despite its autonomous relevance from substantive criminal law. The quite natural implication of this approach was that the defendant—*vis-à-vis* the state's prosecutorial representative—occupied a somewhat passive role, namely as the holder of the obligation to undergo a criminal trial rather than the holder of procedural rights. The 1930 Italian code of criminal procedure departed from this approach, albeit in a rather contradictory way. Although it was already clear that the criminal law action could no longer be identified with *res in iudicium deducta* (Cordero 1987, 6), the drafters of the Rocco code still assigned primary importance to criminal prosecution and its public nature, thus pointing out the state's monopoly in the institution of criminal trials.

While criminal law scholarship largely maintained this contractual view of the criminal process for a long time,[15] civil procedural law doctrine abandoned such a static understanding of legal actions, particularly in countries, such as Italy, in which statutory law provided good arguments for grasping the dynamic structure of civil law actions (Satta 1948, 74f.). Yet precisely the dynamic features of criminal law actions allow us to clearly see the potential of the relational networks which are involved in the decision to institute proceedings. Due to the structure and aims of criminal inquiries, they can gain a subjective direction even before the institution of the court proceedings. It has been noted that during a criminal inquiry a number of relevant investigative measures (wiretaps, technical surveillance, home search, etc.) can be adopted to ascertain whether or not charges are to be filed, or to identify the individuals against whom these charges are to be addressed; in the latter case, in particular, such measures can severely affect the fundamental rights of third persons. But the institution of a criminal law action by way of filing charges radically changes the networks of legal relationships in a criminal investigation. As has been observed, any criminal law action contains all the elements of the future process and, to a great extent, determines the way in which criminal law will materialize in a specific case. Therefore, most depends on the way the charging decision is taken and who is empowered to prosecute.

Here, however, some important differences separate the prosecutorial initiative aimed at the institution of the court proceedings from the criminal law action which initiates an investigation against a person for an alleged offense. Comparative law shows various ways that court proceedings can be instituted, for some criminal justice systems empower individuals or bodies other than the public prosecutorial offices to do so. On the other hand, pre-trial inquiries—even if activated following the initiative of a private party, such as the victim—are always conducted by public authorities, their main purpose being to ascertain whether and how a criminal trial is to be instituted later. This does not mean that the investigative action of public bodies always materializes without any contact with the defense, or without involving private parties in the activities. Indeed, a modern, fair trial-oriented view of criminal investigations reveals a number of different arrangements, through which private parties can actively take part in pre-trial inquiries, either by way of being involved in the legal action conducted by the investigative bodies or by carrying out their own investigations, if allowed.

1.3.2 The Relationships among Public Bodies: The Interaction between Public Prosecutors and the Police, and the Role of the Judicial Authority in the Pre-trial Inquiry

These brief remarks set the foundation for understanding the complex networks that follow the institution of a prosecutorial action, starting with the relationships that arise from the charging decision and which develop among public authorities during investigation. Doubtless, the decision-making process underlying the exercise of the charging powers is one of the most delicate moments of criminal proceedings. Every model of fair criminal justice seeks mechanisms to justify "putting the person to the trouble of mounting a defense," as well as to "protect the innocent by removing or lessening the possibility of miscarriages of justice" (Campbell, Ashworth, and Redmayne 2018, 193).

Such mechanisms vary considerably. Some jurisdictions opt for oversight of the charging decisions by an independent body, which therefore highlights a first, important relationship between the person or body which is competent to file a criminal charge and the authority empowered to control it. Other countries even entrust the charging decision to a judicial authority. An emblematic example of this model is provided by Spanish criminal justice, which even today assigns such strong powers to the *juez de instrucción* that the judge has to decide whether or not a criminal judicial inquiry is to be opened, and furthermore the judge takes charge of the overall pre-trial investigations. The provision for judicial power at the start of a criminal inquiry, moreover, should not be seen solely as a guarantee for the person being investigated but also for other private parties, since Spanish law makes it possible for individuals to request the initiation of the investigation, or to challenge the decision not to do so. This approach is also in line with the general features of Spanish legal system, in which the institution of a criminal prosecution is considered to be a fundamental right in Spain, being an expression of the general right to effective judicial protection enshrined by constitutional law (Gimeno Sendra 2015, 251ff.). Compared to the enhanced prosecutorial powers of private parties in the institution of the court proceedings,[16] their proactive role in the charging decisions in the investigative phase should, however, not be overestimated, for the exercise of prosecutorial powers entails grave implications for the person against whom a criminal process is addressed. Despite the vague formulation of Article 118 of the Spanish Law of Criminal Procedure (LECrim) and the existence of a number of provisions enabling not only public authorities (the police and the public prosecutors) but also private parties, and even other individuals (witnesses, co-defendants) to charge the suspect with a criminal offense (Gimeno Sendra 2015, 416ff.), both legal scholarship and case law tend to maintain a restrictive notion of *imputación* by stressing the need that formal charges be filed by the judiciary (Armengot Vilaplana 2013, 202ff.).

Furthermore, other European countries enhance the public prosecutor's competence to the extent that they rule out any possibility of external supervision of the charging decisions. Italian law, for instance, does not foresee any control by the competent judge, who is not empowered to check the timing and form chosen by the competent prosecutor for the registration of *notitia criminis* with a specific legal classification. Neither can the judge supervise the public prosecutor's decision to direct the investigation against one or more individuals for specific offenses. The main reason for this approach lies in constitutional law, which enshrines the general obligation of public prosecutors to institute a criminal law action. Indeed, public prosecutors fulfill their constitutional law obligation not only by bringing defendants to court but also beforehand by initiating a criminal investigation, and directing it against the alleged offender once sufficient evidence requires them to do so.

The drafters of the 1988 Italian code of criminal procedure, moreover, strengthened the public prosecutor's power during the investigation by enacting a centralized model of prosecutorial inquiry. This model ruled out the possibility of autonomous police investigations after the competent prosecutor assuming the leadership of the investigative phase, i.e., at a stage possibly prior to the filing of charges against one or more suspects. But we saw that this model was almost immediately repealed mainly for practical reasons, with the result that during the prosecutorial inquiry the police today can either carry out investigations under the direction and according the guidelines set by the competent prosecutor, or continue to investigate autonomously. Although in specific areas, such as that of the criminal proceedings falling under the jurisdiction of the justices of the peace, the investigative powers of the police have been enhanced, the charging decisions still lie with public prosecutorial offices.[17] This centralization of the charging competences in the hands of public prosecutors, moreover, strengthens prosecutorial discretion in the registration of *notitia criminis*. Since the early years of the new code, the practical need to avoid unnecessary proceedings has led prosecutors to deal with borderline situations in a distinctive form. Thus, *notitiae criminis* that are considered to be inconsistent are treated as "pseudo-offenses" (*pseudo notizie di reato*), being recorded in a specialized register. This registration usually gives rise to a preparatory enquiry (*pre-inchiesta*) with the aim of ascertaining whether criminal investigations must be initiated (Aprati 2010, 45ff.), a practice whose lawfulness, despite being confirmed by the Supreme Court (Court of Cassation, Joint Sections, 22 November 2000, p.m. in c. ignoti), is still doubtful.

Similar arrangements can also be observed in other European countries. In France, since the principle of mandatory prosecution does not govern criminal justice, "it is for the prosecutor to determine what action should be taken in cases referred to her," that is, to decide which charges to be preferred and whether or not an inquiry of *juge d'instruction* is to be instituted (Beale 2015, 42). A high degree of discretion, furthermore, characterizes the prosecutorial legal action in Germany. Notwithstanding the fact that the principle of legality places on state prosecutors the general duty to investigate every complaint, a selection of complaints takes place de facto, "particularly when the reported offence is not a serious crime" (Huber 2008, 297). Significantly, the police generally make such selections. Although state prosecutorial offices lead the pre-trial investigative procedure (*Ermittlungsverfahren*) and can give directives to the police, in practice the police here also carry out their own investigations with considerable autonomy. Moreover, German law has empowered police officers having the status of "auxiliary officers supporting the state prosecution" (*Hilfsbeamte der Staatsanwaltschaft*) with wider investigative powers (Huber 2008, 297ff.). Nonetheless, state prosecutors still maintain full responsibility for the decisions as to whether or not a court proceeding is to be instituted, and we shall see that German prosecutors have greater decision-making powers than those of prosecutorial bodies in other European jurisdictions (below, § 1.5).

The relationships that arise from the charging decision between public prosecutorial services and law enforcement authorities vary in accordance with the general features of every criminal justice system, and in some cases have significantly changed over the years within the same country. In England and Wales, for instance, the introduction of a Crown Prosecution Service (CPS) in 1986 shifted the considerable historic charging powers of the police over to this new body. The enactment of important structural and functional reforms in the 2003 Criminal Justice Act—the establishment of a duty prosecutor in large police stations and the definition of statutory charging criteria—strengthened the CPS's prosecutorial powers. Meanwhile, a pilot program launched some years ago returned considerable charging responsibilities to the police by restricting the CPS's competence to more serious offenses (Campbell, Ashworth, and Redmayne 2018, 197f.). Yet it is worth observing that, unlike in continental Europe, public prosecutors in England and Wales have no power to direct the inquiries that the police conduct (Darbyshire 2008, 86f.). Furthermore, even in those jurisdictions traditionally characterized by a functional subordination of law enforcement authorities to public prosecutors, the police have gained more and more autonomy in conducting their own investigations. This result, as we observed while dealing with Italian criminal justice, is unconnected to charging powers.

In Latin America, Brazil provides a model of pre-trial inquiry characterized by a consistent imbalance of the investigative powers in favor of law enforcement authorities. It is true that significant developments have recently taken place in the charging decision, in order to enact a formal statute on *indiciamento*. Yet the police still maintain exclusive powers in deciding whether or not to charge, and in defining the specific charge to be filed. Regardless of the types of proceedings and the power of public prosecutorial offices or private parties in the institution of the court proceedings, the charging decisions in the pre-trial inquiry still lie in the hands of the police. Without a doubt, the legislative reform of 2013 strengthened the responsibility of police officers, which are required to have technical knowledge while analyzing the information available and selecting the correct charge to file. In this framework, the obligation for the police to give reasons for their charging decisions is also of utmost importance, ruling out any form of unjustified or automatic charges filed by the police. In spite of these positive developments, Brazilian law does not specify whether and at what stage of the pre-trial inquiry, exactly, the police should file *indiciamento*, which, determining a significant change in the status of the suspect, also entails the granting of a number of important safeguards.[18] Notwithstanding the dominant role of the police in the Brazilian pre-trial inquiries, the relationships between law enforcement authorities and other public authorities, particularly with the public prosecutor, are moving towards new schemes. Thus, while it is unquestionable that public prosecutors can request the institution of a police inquiry, as well as specific investigative measures, it is doubtful whether they can also order or carry out autonomous investigations. Though case law tends to provide a positive answer, Brazilian criminal justice today still provides a model of pre-trial inquiry without functional subordination of the police to public prosecutorial services (Lopes Jr. 2018, 122).

Even more complex relationships characterize the various phases of the investigation. Here also, a number of different solutions emerge from a comparative analysis of domestic jurisdictions. In those criminal justice systems that still rely on an investigative judge or magistrate, this authority holds the dominant role in the pre-trial inquiry. As noted, Spain provides a clear example of this model, for the *juez de instrucción* is not only competent to commence a criminal investigation and to file formal charges, but furthermore generally leads all the investigative activities aimed at the ascertainment of facts and the identification of the alleged perpetrators (Gascón Inchausti and Villamarín López 2008, 606). Judicial authority is further enhanced in cases of investigative measures affecting fundamental rights, and Spanish constitutional case law has specified the essential qualitative conditions that a *juez de instrucción* must satisfy by ordering such measures, such as the requirement of a reasoned decision, respect for the proportionality principle, and so on (Gascón Inchausti and Villamarín López 2008, 576f.).

The requirement of judicial oversight in cases of investigations interfering with fundamental rights is also of utmost importance in countries with a different model of pre-trial inquiry. We saw, for instance, that in Brazil the huge dimension of national territory led the drafters of the current code not to import the system, widely used in Europe at that time, of a judicial pre-trial inquiry, led by an investigative judge. Therefore, the model of a police inquiry was maintained to ensure prompt investigative intervention in all of Brazil. Despite the dominant role of law enforcement authorities in the pre-trial inquiry, however, Brazilian criminal justice has a judge guarantor (*juiz de garantias*), who is empowered to authorize and supervise any measures restricting fundamental rights (Lopes Jr. 2018, 119ff.). Yet recent legislative reforms have changed the functions of the judicial authority in Brazil, by strengthening the powers of the judiciary during the pre-trial inquiry. In particular, Law 11.690/2008 enabled judges to collect—at their own initiative—urgent evidence during the police inquiry. This power—although being subject to compliance with the principles of necessity, adequacy, and proportionality of the measure adopted—can give rise to abuses, allowing judges to follow their own investigative goals. This can distort the balance between the police and the individuals charged with a criminal offense, while shifting from the model of a judge responsible for procedural safeguards to a model of active judicial intervention in the investigations, typical of the mixed systems of criminal justice, characterized by an investigating judge or magistrate (Lopes Jr. 2018, 123). Following this approach, Brazilian Law 12.403/2011 also empowered judges to order pre-trial detention *ex officio* (Art. 311 CCP). There is no doubt that this power also jeopardizes the impartiality of judicial authority (Giacomolli 2014, 376f.), and therefore creates a risk that no independent body will be available to hear from a suspect subject to coercive measures. Moreover, the 2011 reform maintained the code's rules, which enabled both the police and the complainant (*querelante*), alongside the public prosecutor, to request the adoption of pre-trial detention. This autonomous power of the police can give rise to human rights concerns.[19]

A proactive power, such as that granted by Brazilian law to the police, is generally unknown in European countries, for even in those jurisdictions in which the law enforcement authorities have gained more and more investigative powers, the authority to request remand detention and further restrictions on freedom generally lies with public prosecutors. In Italy, the police directly depend on, and must generally follow the directives of, public prosecutors. Although law enforcement authorities, as noted, have increasing autonomy in their investigations even during the public prosecutor's inquiry, they are not entitled to file requests to the competent judge for the pre-trial inquiry. Unlike the investigative magistrate under the Rocco code, this judge lacks any proactive power and is not authorized to gather evidence for the purposes of the trial decision-making at the judge's own initiative. Indeed, even if the judicial procedure of *incidente probatorio* has progressively been strengthened over the years, mainly with a view to protecting minor victims and other vulnerable individuals (Art. 392 et seqq. CCP), the judge for the pre-trial inquiry can take information at the request of either the public prosecutor or the defendant.

1.3.3 The Interaction between Investigative Authorities and Private Parties

Notwithstanding the dominant role of the investigative authorities in pre-trial inquiries, the interaction between the competent body for charging and other public authorities does not exhaust the complex relational networks produced by the filing of a criminal law action, for these also encompass the relationships between the prosecutorial authority and private parties. In several jurisdictions, the investigative authorities cannot autonomously start a criminal investigation until they receive a notice of a crime. Even today, the reports or complainants lodged by the victim or the damaged party play an essential role in the activation of criminal inquiries in almost all criminal justice systems.[20] In the current era, furthermore, models of prosecutorial or police inquiry can no longer be maintained in absolute terms. It is noteworthy that even in those jurisdictions, such as Germany and Italy, in which public prosecutors are called upon to conduct their inquiries in the broadest and most objective way, namely by collecting information both against and in favor of the defendant, this approach does not exclude the involvement of private parties.

Doubtless, international human rights law—in the European scenario, together with EU law—has enhanced a participatory approach to criminal investigations. The focus on fair trial rights by international human rights charters has progressively led international jurisprudence and later EU lawmakers to acknowledge a number of fundamental safeguards—starting with the right to be informed about the accusation, the right to have the necessary time and facilities to prepare one's own defense, and so on—triggered by the filing of criminal charges, and therefore, applicable in the investigative phases as well. These safeguards are so important that in several countries, such as Germany and Italy, constitutional law protects them through specific provisions. These acknowledgments set the foundations for a variety of interactions between the investigative action conducted by public bodies and private parties. Several arrangements not only emerge from a comparative examination of domestic criminal justice systems but also often have been developed within the same jurisdiction.

A widespread method of involving the defense counsel of private parties in pre-trial inquiries is to allow their participation in specific investigative measures. In Italian criminal justice under the 1930 code, constitutional case law attenuated the unilateral features of the prosecutorial inquiry (*istruzione sommaria*) by permitting various forms of participation by the defense. The 1988 code further enhanced this approach, to the extent that legal scholarship invoked the category of "imperfect *contradictoire*" to define the defense's participation in the prosecutorial and police investigations even if no judge is involved (Cordero 2012, 891). Despite the clear attempt to strengthen participatory rights in the pre-trial inquiry, it is doubtful that the individuals concerned can have a fair opportunity to become actively involved in evidence-gathering procedures prior to trial, particularly if such investigations are ordered or headed by the same body (public prosecutor) that formulated the charge. Clearly, the absence of an impartial body and the dominant role of the investigative authorities cannot satisfy the requirement of fair evidence-gathering, based the principle of equality of arms, a requirement that holds constitutional relevance in Italy. As long as the investigative authorities lead their investigations, the involvement of the defense will inevitably remain at a secondary level. Thus, during questioning of suspects by the police, the defense lawyer is generally only allowed a somewhat passive role. Lawyers are instead permitted a more active role in the prosecutorial interrogation, being able to make specific requests and observations to the competent authority, which, however, leads the suspect's examination.

It is questionable, moreover, whether suspects or the aggrieved parties can conduct their own investigations by means of their defense lawyers in parallel to the inquiries carried out by the investigative authorities. Comparative law does not reveal any uniform solutions in this regard, and several jurisdictions still lack a formal statute on defense investigations, which of course negatively affects the admissibility of the information collected. Most jurisdictions historically favored a rather paternalistic approach, particularly in those countries in which public prosecutors are required to conduct their inquiries impartially during the pre-trial phase. Here, indeed, private parties can often ask the prosecutor to carry out investigations on their behalf, or can forward the results of their own informal investigations to the prosecutor, so that a public body will present it at trial. It is worth observing that such approaches are still alive in countries, such as Italy, which has since 2000 used a detailed set of procedural rules governing the investigations of defense lawyers and the usability at trial of the evidence gathered by them (Arts. 391-*bis* et seqq. CCP). Allowing for the defense to conduct such formal investigations during the pre-trial inquiries carried out by the investigative bodies, to the extent that defense lawyers gain a similar status to that of public officers, is probably not a proper solution to compensate private parties for the imbalance in favor of the authorities in charge of the criminal inquiry. The question arises whether a forced equality of arms turns out to weaken that participatory approach to evidence-gathering, which necessitates the effective interaction between different parties rather than separate investigative channels (Nobili 2001, 6ff.).

1.4 Prosecutorial Investigations, Interference with Fundamental Rights, and Fair Trial Safeguards

The enhancement of prosecutorial powers during investigation can also be observed from another viewpoint. In recent years, we have witnessed the increasing worldwide use of intrusive measures of investigation, mainly of unprecedented investigative tools that could interfere with fundamental rights because of their hidden nature or their reliance on new technological means, or for both reasons. Comparative law shows that recourse to undercover investigations, technical surveillance, online search, and so on, is more and more frequent, which measures cannot easily be traced back to the traditional tools of investigation. Doubtless, the traditional approach to coercive investigations is unable to respond to the complexity of such developments, mainly because these measures do not restrict fundamental rights by way of using coercion in a strict sense.

Legislation has slowly responded to these developments, but not without difficulties and contradictions. For instance, installing malware in tablets or smartphones can be used for very different investigative purposes: cyber investigations have a polyhedral nature, as is shown by the diverse regulations enacted by European jurisdictions on remote search through spyware (Spain),[21] cyber-interception of communications through malware (Italy),[22] and so on. The increasing amount of data that can be stored in mobile tools and their widespread use magnify the risks for the person against whom the investigation is conducted, and even more so for third parties. Indeed, unlike what happens with traditional forms of seizure or interception of telecommunications, the investigative use of spyware carries consequences that are not foreseeable, and the degree of intrusiveness of these new tools of investigation is further enhanced if spyware is used to seize data that are not stored in a specific device but in an intangible space, such as the cloud.

In various countries, legislative reforms have defined the limits of lawful use of such measures of investigation. Yet most of these reforms could solve only a part of the problems that arise in the practice, and it is precisely the atypical nature of several technological means of investigation that poses today enormous challenges for lawyers and case law, while enhancing the powers of investigative bodies. To a great extent, the enactment of specific legislative regulations on new measures of investigation in various jurisdictions has strengthened the investigative reach of public prosecutors. It might be surprising that the enhancement of the public prosecutors' power to order new investigative means has been accompanied by the progressive reduction of exclusive investigative authority of prosecutorial offices. In Italy, we saw that, while the 1988 code invoked a centralized model of prosecutorial inquiry, subsequent legislation progressively increased the investigative competences of law enforcement authorities. Today they can autonomously conduct a number of relevant coercive measures, also through new technological means. Similar developments have taken place in other countries as well. The reduction of exclusively prosecutorial authority to perform criminal investigations, however, should not be seen solely in light of the constant overload of domestic criminal justice systems, but is also the natural result of the high specialization of new investigative tools, which require specific knowledge that prosecutors or state attorneys inevitably lack.

Another relevant aspect of such developments is the increase of prosecutorial power to decide whether coercive measures of investigation—depending on the arrangements of domestic law—are to be performed or continued or validated, if carried out autonomously by law enforcement authorities. The prosecutorial decision-making powers have also been enhanced in those countries in which the authorization or the oversight of restrictions on fundamental rights in the pre-trial phase traditionally fall under the authority of the judiciary. In Germany, a physical examination or a genome analysis needs judicial authorization, but to avoid dispersal of evidence, state prosecutors and the investigative authorities in general can order them too. Similar conclusions apply to Italian criminal justice, for here the exceptional investigative powers of the police to carry out measures, such as searches or the sampling of biological materials to establish the suspect's identity, need subsequent validation by the public prosecutor. Moreover, in Italy the investigative authorities are not required to perform solely the measures regulated by the law, for the general obligation to carry out all the necessary means of investigation to enable the prosecutor to decide whether to institute a criminal trial also empowers them to conduct investigations without any legal basis. This expansive approach holds implications of utmost practical relevance for new technological measures with enormous potential for intrusiveness, such as online searches.[23]

Beyond the arrangements made by domestic law, moreover, the increase of the public prosecutor's power to order and perform intrusive measures of investigation in Europe carries important implications from the viewpoint of ECHR law as well. It has been observed that the European Court of Human Rights has long developed an autonomous understanding of the notion of "criminal charge," while assessing the compliance by domestic countries with fundamental safeguards, such as the reasonable length of criminal proceedings and the right to be informed of the accusation. This approach, which is largely independent from national law, looks at the impact of a criminal inquiry on the fundamental rights of the individuals concerned, which requires national authorities to provide them with information on the charges that "substantially affects" their position.[24] The most difficult problem posed by new intrusive investigations is that their success mostly depends on the possibility of carrying them out in a hidden form. This feature of such investigative measures highlights a tension between the need to preserve the efficiency of a criminal inquiry and the individual right to information that arises in the context of an investigative activity.

Against this background, the question arises whether a proper alternative could be to enhance the decision-making powers of the judicial authority, e.g., by means of establishing a fast-track judicial procedure aimed at the oversight of intrusive investigations in urgent cases, falling within the authority of a judge guarantor (if any) or another judicial body. The main advantage of such a solution is that the fundamental control of proportionality would be entrusted to a body other than the one in charge of the investigation, which should circumscribe the use of new intrusive inquires to strictly necessary cases, thus reducing the risk of arbitrariness. This result, however, presupposes that such judicial authority can carry out its tasks fairly: thus, the independence of the judicial body may not be enough but must also be coupled with the independence of judicial oversight. This obvious condition is unfortunately often undermined by legislation. In Italy, for instance, the public prosecutor's power to order the interception of telecommunications in urgent cases, as well as the interception of communications by means of spyware between present persons, is limited by the obligation to request validation from the judge, who must do so within forty-eight hours. Nonetheless, the initial or subsequent control by the judge in the pre-trial inquiry is largely jeopardized by the serious possibility that the public prosecutor could withhold from the judicial authority relevant information supporting the request for such intrusive means. From this it follows that the judge inevitably sees with the public prosecutor's eyes.

While the powers of investigative authorities, and of public prosecutorial services in particular, increase progressively, private parties in contrast hold no law enforcement powers. In several countries, the lack of in-depth reflection on the link among the equality of arms, the principle of *contradictoire*, and the guarantee of judicial oversight has led the lawmakers to ignore proper alternatives, such as that of strengthening the *jus postulandi* of private parties. In Italy, except in the case of access to private places or areas not open to the public that can be requested by a lawyer, defense lawyers are not empowered to apply for intrusive investigative measures, which can still be ordered solely upon request of the competent prosecutor. The main concern that prevented the legislature from reforming this set-up was the fear that the granting of *jus postulandi* to private parties could re-introduce the old prosecutorial inquiry in a new version, transferred to the defense and also prone to misuse (Marzaduri 2000, 770). But this concern was certainly excessive, taking into account that under the current code, the judicial authority is always required to give reasons when measures interfering with fundamental rights are needed.

1.5 Prosecutorial Decision-Making and Discretionary Adjudication

Alongside the increase of the investigative powers of public prosecutorial services, a comparative examination of criminal investigations also highlights the enhancement (or the maintenance) of other relevant prosecutorial decision-making powers. This phenomenon can be observed from different viewpoints. As noted, the adjudication powers of public prosecutors have been strengthened in direct proportion to the expansion of their power to authorize or order intrusive measures of investigation. Remarkably, in countries such as Italy, where the law enforcement authorities are empowered (more or less exceptionally) to carry out several coercive investigations, the police must request validation from the prosecutor. We saw, moreover, that even when a judge is authorized to order highly intrusive measures, such as wiretaps or restrictions on liberty, the possibility of effectively independent decision-making is often undermined by the prosecutor's power not to disclose relevant information either to the defense or to the judge.

It is doubtful that such enhancement of the public prosecutor's power, however, is in line with ECHR law. A problematic case concerns the coercive sampling of biological materials under Italian law. By going beyond the investigative powers assigned to the police, Law 85/2009, through which Italy adhered to the Prüm Convention and set up a national DNA database, empowered public prosecutors to order compulsory biological sampling in urgent cases without requesting judicial intervention during the pre-trial inquiry (Art. 359-*bis* CCP). It is true that the sampling must be carried out without endangering human health or physical integrity and while respecting the dignity of the person concerned. Nevertheless, Italian legislation does not clarify the precise category of cases that would allow for prosecutorial initiative, and the general reference to the threshold of a maximum of three years of detention does not ensure proportionality between the coercion used during the investigation and the expected sentence.

Beyond these new grants of authority, public prosecutorial offices still hold general powers of investigation during the preliminary inquiry, which often entail the use of coercion and can be used without a specific showing of urgency and without requiring the intervention of the judge. Germany provides a number of relevant examples of this approach. In Italy, the maintenance of consistent investigative powers in the hands of public prosecutors is mainly justified by the fact that under Italian judicial organization, public prosecutors are representatives of the judiciary as well and can therefore exercise specific powers of the judicial authority during the pre-trial inquiry, such as the ordering of searches, inspections, and so on. Such an arrangement is inconsistent with the European Convention, a fact that is apparent from the judgment in *Brazzi v. Italy* (2018), in which the European Court, although dealing with a transnational case, examined the problem concerned with the public prosecutor's power to order (or validate) home searches during the investigative phase.[25] Thus, beyond the problems concerned with this specific case, Italian law has structural deficiencies for not providing for any judicial protection of the fundamental requirements of lawfulness and necessity of such intrusive measures during the prosecutorial inquiry. Nor can the affected person challenge the prosecutorial order before a judge or a court, since Italian law provides for judicial review solely in cases of seizure. Therefore, the absence of independent oversight, as highlighted in the *Brazzi* case, increases the risk of abuse and arbitrary interference with fundamental rights.

In addition to these decision-making powers regarding some interim decisions, the comparative analysis of the investigative phases reveals that public prosecutors still retain further relevant decision-making authority on whether to institute prosecution or to terminate the proceedings. At first glance, it might be argued that such prosecutorial adjudication powers reflect the quasi-judicial power of public prosecutors, and should therefore be limited to those jurisdictions that treat them as representatives of the judiciary. As has been observed, France provides an emblematic example of this approach, since public prosecutors in France have wide decision-making powers, which encompass the decision to request supplementary investigations, or to establish whether or not a criminal law action is to be instituted by starting a judicial inquiry (Vogler 2008, 202f.). Focusing exclusively on these jurisdictions, however, could mean oversimplifying a complex development, which materializes with diverse features in countries characterized by different judicial organization and criminal justice systems. In Italy, the 1930 code empowered public prosecutors to decide autonomously whether to terminate the proceedings, a power abolished by Royal Legislative Decree No. 288/1944.

It is interesting to note that Germany, whose criminal justice is also strongly based upon the principle of legality, walked a somewhat different road by reinforcing the prosecutorial adjudication powers in various ways. The examination of German law displays a complex picture. In general terms, the code of criminal procedure, after acknowledging the general duty to institute public prosecution, leaves considerable discretion to state prosecutors on whether to discontinue the proceedings in misdemeanors (*Vergehen*), if the alleged offender's guilt was considered to be of a minor nature and there was no public interest in the prosecution (§ 153[1] CCP). It is true that termination of the proceedings needs the approval of the court.[26] But this approval has never been deemed to be a judicial decision and does not therefore require the suspect's examination, nor can it be challenged through a so-called "*Klageerzwingungsverfahren*" (Meyer-Goßner and Schmitt 2019, § 153, Rn. 10 et seqq.); and as a result, the prosecutorial decision to dispense with prosecution only terminates the proceedings on a provisional basis (Kühne 2010, Rn. 606).

Alongside this traditional form of discontinuance of the proceedings based on opportunity reasons, the German legislature subsequently enacted a number of provisions that allow state prosecutors to dispense with prosecution without any judicial approval (offenses committed abroad, criminal offenses under the code of crimes against international law, etc.). In other situations, the state prosecutor not only needs the approval of the competent court but also the consent of the defendant, in order to decide not to go forward with public charges. The most significant provision following this scheme is perhaps § 153a CCP, which enables the prosecutor in some categories of cases to establish the conditions and instructions to be imposed on the accused so as to eliminate the public interest in criminal prosecution. Some examples of these conditions include performing a specified service to make reparations, paying a sum of money to a non-profit-making institution or to the Treasury, or performing some other service of a non-profit-making nature. A condition that holds particular relevance for both theoretical and practical reasons consists of the defendant making a serious attempt to reach a mediated agreement with the aggrieved person (the so-called "perpetrator-victim mediation" or *Täter-Opfer-Ausgleich*) with a view to reparation for his offense (§ 153a[5] CCP). This provision further strengthens the discretionary powers of state prosecutors, who are called upon to define the conditions that best fit the challenges of the specific case, and which are expected to achieve the consent of both the judicial authority and the defendant.

Interestingly, such mechanisms bring German experience closer to the solutions enacted by other countries, which have introduced alternative forms of termination of the proceedings. France, in particular, has in recent decades given public prosecutors a number of different alternatives to prosecution too, such as terminating the case on condition, reparation, or mediation, as well as a specific procedure of "penal composition" (Vogler 2008, 203). In Italy, recent reforms have assigned public prosecutors new powers, enabling them to apply for discontinuance of the proceedings in case of low severity of the alleged offense; a procedure that, significantly, involves both the suspect and the victim (Art. 411[1-*bis*] CCP). This legislation reveals not only an increasing attention towards new mechanisms aimed at preventing the risks of a criminal trial but also a participatory approach that more and more characterizes the criminal process.

1.6 The Public Prosecutor's Role in Transnational Criminal Justice

1.6.1 Prosecutorial Powers in EIO Investigations

The investigative powers of public prosecutors are further strengthened in the field of transnational criminal justice. Judicial cooperation in the EU area in recent years provides significant examples of this phenomenon, such as a new, wide-ranging instrument of transnational evidence-gathering, known as the European investigation order (hereafter, EIO). The relevant legal instrument, Directive 2014/41/EU (hereafter, DirEIO), aimed at in-depth legal assistance among EU countries. Though the results were not fully in line with such expectations, this legal instrument still brought about important changes. In particular, the EIO legislation combined the logic of mutual recognition of judicial orders with a system in which transborder investigations can proceed by means of coercive measures or measures affecting fundamental rights—unlike what happened in the traditional forms of intergovernmental judicial cooperation in criminal matters.

This legislative framework contributed to the enhancement of the investigative powers of public prosecutorial services within EU countries. Regardless of the structure of the criminal justice system of each member state, the EIO Directive clearly favored a quasi-judicial view of public prosecutors by equating them with a judge, a court, or an investigating magistrate. Each of those actors may issue or validate a European investigation order, if the legislation of the issuing state gives that actor the power to order the gathering of evidence (Art. 2[c][i-ii] DirEIO). Interestingly, EU institutions construed this tool of evidence-gathering in a way that enables the defense to play a proactive role in transnational inquiries, thus acknowledging the right of private parties to request the issuing of an EIO. Nevertheless, this innovative solution is probably not enough to erase the imbalance on the defense's account and to compensate private parties for the dominant role of public prosecutors and investigative magistrates. Thus, only suspects and defendants were given such *jus postulandi*, while other private parties have no means of requesting the activation of the European procedure. Most significantly, suspects and defendants must address their request for a European investigation order to the issuing authority, which may be one of the aforementioned actors. As a consequence, there is nothing to ensure that the merits of the defense's request are assessed by an independent body.

The risk of further imbalance on the defense's account is increased by the rules on the execution of the sought investigation. The 2010 proposal for Directive had already provided for the possibility of authorities of the trial country assisting with the investigation they seek. Neither the nature of these authorities nor their relationship with the issuing authority was in any way specified, nor did the draft proposal clarify the exact terms of their assistance. EU institutions made it clear that the supporting authorities in the trial country are in principle bound by *lex loci* and have no law enforcement powers in the country executing the EIO. The Directive, however, provides for one significant exception: the foreign authorities can exercise law enforcement powers on national territory, provided that it is not prohibited by *lex loci* and the competent bodies in the executing state agree with this arrangement (Art. 9[5] DirEIO). This mechanism introduces an unprecedented system of almost extraterritorial inquiries within the mutual recognition model, which goes beyond the distinctions of earlier models of international assistance, while raising many human rights concerns. In particular, there is still no specification of the role and position of these "authorities," which could lead administrative authorities, regardless of their functional relationship with the competent authorities for the criminal proceedings, to take investigative actions that interfere with the fundamental rights of the target.

National implementation has made heavy use of these margins of maneuver, thus furthering the role of public prosecutors in transnational cases. Italy provides an emblematic example of these developments. Apparently, the Italian Implementing Law (Legislative Decree 108/2017) limited itself to establishing the general requirement that the European investigation order meet the same conditions that the requested investigation would have to satisfy in a similar national case (Art. 27[1]). From this somewhat vague formulation it seems to follow that public prosecutors and judges can order European orders within the limits of their respective powers in national cases. On closer examination, Italian treated prosecutors differently for EIO requests than for domestic cases. A clear example regards a highly intrusive form of evidence-gathering, namely interception of telecommunications: while in domestic proceedings, as noted, the prosecutorial competence is limited to urgent cases, public prosecutors are generally competent to order wiretapping in transnational cases (Art. 43).

The same pattern holds true for cyber-interception of communications through spyware. Domestic regulation in Italy empowers prosecutors to order this intrusive measure in urgent cases regarding the proceedings for a number of serious crimes (criminal organization, drug trafficking, etc.), on condition that the judicial authority validates the prosecutorial order within strict time-limits. By contrast, the failure of Legislative Decree 108/2017 to enact either a validation procedure or a means of challenging prosecutorial orders[27] in transnational cases deprives the addressee of an independent assessment of their lawfulness and necessity.

Other European jurisdictions have walked a different road, which appears to offer a higher level of protection of the individuals concerned. For instance, the Spanish Implementing Law (Law 3/2018, which amended Law 23/2014) bars public prosecutors from requesting foreign authorities to enforce transnational investigative measures affecting fundamental rights (Art. 187[1] of amended Law 23/2014). Neither can they execute a similar measure in Spain, if requested by a foreign authority (187[2][a] of amended Law 23/2014). In these cases, the authority shifts to the judge or court in charge of the proceedings, which are explicitly required to consider the rights of the suspected person or the accused (Art. 189[1][a] of amended Law 23/2014).

1.6.2 The New Investigative Powers of the EPPO in Transborder Cases

In 2017, EU institutions launched another important model of transnational evidence-gathering, which is destined to further strengthen the investigative powers of public prosecutorial bodies. Regulation 2017/1939/EU (hereafter, RegEPPO) introduced an unprecedented European Public Prosecutor's Office (hereafter, EPPO) with the main aim of investigating and prosecuting crimes affecting the EU financial interests. For the purposes of the present discussion, I shall focus on the new rules governing the EPPO's investigative powers in transborder cases (Bachmaier Winter 2018, 117ff.).

The procedural framework for cross-border investigations by the EPPO appears in Regulation 2017/1939/EU. Because of the wide-ranging powers of the EPPO, these rules will not only apply to offenses involving fraud to the Union's financial interests, but also to offenses that may have a domestic dimension, such as participation in a criminal organization as defined by Framework Decision 2008/841/JHA, if the focus of the criminal activity of this criminal organization is to commit any of the PIF offenses (crimes that affect the financial interests of the EU), as well as the commission of further offenses that are "inextricably linked" to PIF offenses (Art. 22[2-3]). In such cases, the transnational character of the EPPO's investigation will not necessarily reflect the cross-border nature of the offenses under investigation, but will reflect the procedural requirements for collecting specific pieces of evidence in other EU countries.

Whichever the reasons for conducting transborder inquiries are, the EPPO Regulation enacted an unprecedented model that can be traced back neither to traditional legal assistance procedures nor to the most recent forms of mutual recognition-based investigative cooperation within the EU area. If relevant information is sought in another member state, it will not be collected by means of requests or orders forwarded to foreign authorities, or in the context of joint transborder inquiries conducted by cooperating bodies belonging to different countries. Instead, these investigations are carried out as a joint venture among European Delegated Prosecutors of the countries concerned, who are called upon to "act in close cooperation by assisting and regularly consulting each other in cross-border cases" (Art. 31[1]). Investigative cooperation will materialize by means of a system of assignment, which enables the handling European Delegated Prosecutor to require a European Delegated Prosecutor from another member state to carry out the requested measure in its territory, without any need for recognition and consequently without any possibility of refusal (Bachmaier Winter 2018, 122).

The broad investigative powers conferred on the European Public Prosecutor's Office pose delicate problems in relation to the use of intrusive measures, which are magnified in transborder cases. This specific authority has undergone significant developments from 2013 legislative proposal (hereafter, PRegEPPO) to the text approved in 2017, and a comparative overview of the proposal and the final text raises several human rights concerns. The Commission's proposal contained a wider list of investigative measures that ought to be made available to European Delegated Prosecutors, than that enacted into the 2017 Regulation. Although most of these measures had a clear impact on a number of fundamental rights, the 2013 proposal did not specify any thresholds of punishment, thus allowing the use of intrusive investigations even in cases punishable with low sentences. As a sort of compensation for this result, the Commission required respect for the principles of proportionality and necessity by requiring the applicant to use the least intrusive means. The proposal also required judicial authorization in relation to a number of particularly intrusive investigative measures (e.g., search of computer systems, freezing of instrumentalities or proceeds of crime, wiretaps, real-time surveillance of telecommunications, etc.). Remarkably, the proposal also provided for judicial authorization of such intrusive measures irrespective of the provisions of domestic law, while in relation to different measures, this requirement was conditioned on the normal operation of *lex loci* (Art. 26[5] PRegEPPO). This strong focus on judicial authorization reflected the general approach of the 2013 proposal, which aimed at strengthening the EPPO's accountability "with a strict regime of judicial control whereby the European Public Prosecutor's Office can only use coercive investigation powers subject to prior judicial authorisation" (Recital 11 PRegEPPO).

A close examination of the rules enacted by the 2017 Regulation, particularly of those regarding the use of coercive measures of investigation, reveals a clear tendency to soften the need for harmonized standards of human rights protection and the adoption of much more flexible solutions than those proposed in 2013. It is true that, regardless of the transnational or national nature of the inquiry conducted by a European Delegated Prosecutor, the Regulation provides for a much shorter list of investigative measures that must be made available to the competent Prosecutor, compared to that established by the Commission's proposal; and the adoption of these measures also requires a minimum threshold of at least four years of imprisonment (Art. 30[1] RegEPPO). Moreover, the EPPO Regulation introduced a detailed set of rules aims at ensuring consistency of the EPPO's investigative action by enhancing the requirement of judicial authorization of specific investigative means, as well as the assessment of the principle of proportionality and the rule of law. In this regard, however, the new rules raise serious human rights concerns. There are no clear indications as to whether the EPPO's authority is to order or to request those investigative measures that must be made available to the prosecutor, since all of them make judicial authorization necessary only if required by national law (Art. 30[2-3] RegEPPO). EU institutions specifically focus on judicial authorization in cases of cross-border investigations, but only if provided for by either the domestic law of the country in which the handling European Delegated Prosecutor operates or the home jurisdiction of the assisting European Delegated Prosecutor (Art. 31[3] RegEPPO).

Interestingly, the original intention to link the EPPO's accountability with a strict regime of prior judicial control of coercive investigations was also not reproduced in the final text. The requirement of judicial authorization, if needed to satisfy binding constitutional safeguards of the country where the sought evidence is to be taken, is so important that the Regulation envisages the possibility of authorization being refused, with the result that the handling European Delegated Prosecutor must withdraw the assignment.

Doubtless, this series of events could frustrate the aims of the EPPO's investigation and the full implementation of the mutual recognition principle. It is doubtful, however, that to avoid this risk—and to ensure consistency with the validation procedure laid down by Article 2(d) of the EIO Directive—the requirement of judicial authorization should be interpreted to mean formal oversight without any assessment of the principles of necessity and proportionality (Bachmaier Winter 2018, 128f.). Indeed, respect for these essential requirements characterizes the overall investigative action of the new EPPO both in national and transborborder cases. The handling European Prosecutor is required not only to justify the use of a specific measure in relation to the requested evidence, but also to ensure that its use entails the minimum impact on fundamental rights. The problem is how to ensure the achievement of such an ambitious result.

Since judicial control may not be required, the entire responisibility for establishing whether a specific measure is truly necessary and whether there is no less intrusive measure available which could achieve the same objective lies solely with the European Public Prosecutor. The negative consequences that can derive from the possible absence of independent oversight increase in transborder inquiries. Here, where the assisting European Prosecutor believes that the requested measure does not exist under *lex loci* or is only available under specific conditions, or an alternative less intrusive means would be available, assistance will not be denied at all, but the assisting European Prosecutor must inform a supervising European Prosecutor and consult with the handling European Delegated Prosecutor (Art. 31[5] RegEPPO). The Regulation clearly favours the achievement of a consensual solution of the problem, without, however, giving any clear indication as to how this result can be obtained. Worse still, there is no trace of any involvement of the individuals concerned and their defense lawyers, even in cases that under domestic law would allow participation in such a delicate decision. An even more worrisome situation arises, moreover, where a bilateral arrangement is not achieved within seven working days. In this situation, the matter will be referred to the Permanent Chamber of the EPPO, which "shall to the extent necessary hear the European Delegated Prosecutors concerned by the case and then decide without undue delay, in accordance with applicable national law as well as this Regulation, whether and by when the assigned measure needed, or a substitute measure, shall be undertaken by the assisting European Delegated Prosecutor" (Art. 31[7-8] RegEPPO). Therefore, it may well happen that the either the handling and the assisting European Prosecutors or the Permanent Chamber will decide—without any independent oversight—to authorize the enforcement of an investigative measure, even if *lex loci* does not provide for it or even forbids it, or submits it to stricter conditions that do not occur in the specific case, or another measure would achieve the same result with less intrusive means. It is truly not understandable how this can be tolerated in a legal regime aimed at the protection of freedom, security, and justice. It also difficult to understand how in these cases such a measure can be adopted "in accordance with applicable national law." At any rate, this provision magnifies the decision-making powers of the Permanent Chamber, namely of a body that is neither independent from the investigation at stake nor is necessarily familiar with the laws of the country in which the requested measure is to be enforced (Bachmaier Winter 2018, 126f.).

Another problematic issue involves the interaction of procedural rules from different jurisdictions. Following the approach adopted by several international law instruments, such as the EU Convention on Mutual Legal Assistance, as well as the EIO Directive, the EPPO Regulation requires the assigned investigative measures to be carried out pursuant to *lex loci*, yet "formalities and procedures expressly indicated by the handling European Delegated Prosecutor shall be complied with unless such formalities and procedures are contrary to the fundamental principles of law of the member state of the assisting European Delegated Prosecutor" (Art. 32). This formulation, favoring a combination of procedural laws, does not establish any criteria for applying different national procedures in a consistent way, nor does it ensure the individuals concerned any certainty as to the applicable choice of law. Unlike what happens under the EIO procedure, which enables a judicial body to act as an issuing authority, the establishment of formalities and procedures is here in the hands of the handling Delegated Prosecutor. Furthermore, there is nothing to ensure that the requested procedures do not negatively affect the defense rights of the addressee of the investigation and are also necessary for the validity of the requested evidence, as instead required by Framework Decision 2003/577/JHA on orders freezing property or evidence (Art. 5[1]). Nor does the EPPO Regulation provide any mechanisms to ensure consistency among European Delegated Prosecutors in the selection of the procedures applicable to intrusive investigations in similar cases, notwithstanding that consistency of prosecutorial policy falls within the general tasks of the College (Art. 9[2]).

Even more worryingly, there is no trace of any involvement of the defense in the enforcement of a transnational investigation assigned to another EDP, or of any independent oversight of the procedure of execution. The EPPO Regulation devoted scant and contradictory attention to defense rights and the right to legal assistance in the EPPO's investigation (Bachmaier Winter 2018, 132ff.). To be sure, EU institutions extended the usual rules on admissibility and free assessment of evidence to the information gathered by the defendant, while requiring respect for the safeguards granted by the EU legislation to defendants and suspects. Nevertheless, there is no general acknowledgment of the exercise of investigative powers by defense lawyers, beyond the reference to the domestic law arrangements regarding the possibility of presenting evidence, requesting the appointment of experts or expert examination and hearing of witnesses, and so on (Art. 41[3]). The main problem probably lies in the fact that, notwithstanding the harmonization of a number of defense rights and particularly of the right to legal assistance and legal aid, there is still no coherent supranational statute on defense investigations. EU institutions, while establishing a set of procedural rules on the investigations of the European Public Prosecutor's Office, missed an important opportunity to address the investigative powers of defense lawyers in this specific area. Even more worryingly, unlike from what we saw in relation to the EIO Directive, the drafters of the EPPO Regulation also failed to recognize a *jus postulandi* for the defense. As a result, when specific investigations must be made available to European Delegated Prosecutors, defense lawyers can only request them to the extent allowed by domestic law. Remarkably, the Regulation sponsored a mechanism that is quite outdated in the field of domestic criminal inquiries, acknowledging the possibility of the individuals concerned to ask "the EPPO to obtain such measures on behalf of the defense" (Art. 41[3]). The establishment of a European Public Prosecutor's Office with such broad investigative powers should call for in-depth reflection on the need to introduce a Eurodefensor, an institution proposed more than ten years ago which would be particularly useful in transborder cases (Nestler 2006, 415ff.).

1.7 Conclusions

The analysis of this problematic area, based on a comparative approach, reveals the considerable enhancement of the role of public prosecutors in criminal investigations at various levels and in countries with different traditions and different criminal justice systems. The strengthening of the prosecutor's charging authority, while softening the traditional distinction between investigation and prosecution, shows a clear and increasing prosecutorial influence in the pre-trial inquiry. In several jurisdictions, this result is also strictly linked with the growth of the investigative powers of public prosecutors aimed at the enforcement of a number of coercive measures and further intrusive means of investigation, including some that rely on new technological methods. While all forms of interference with fundamental rights require a suspicion of the alleged offense, the existence of *fumus delicti* specifically regarding the person investigated provides the basis for the decision to file a criminal charge, a decision of such complexity that is more and more entrusted to a judge or a public prosecutor, regardless of their position in the domestic judicial organization. The enhancement of the criminal law action of public prosecutors in the investigative phase, therefore, in turn increases the discretion of the prosecutorial decision-making in filing charges, a phenomenon which is increasingly evident in transnational cases.

It is not an easy task to critically assess such developments. Much depends—and will depend more and more in the near future—on whether and how domestic law can ensure a fair balance between the legal action of public prosecutorial offices and the rights of the individuals involved in criminal inquiries. But it is apparent that a true equal treatment in the delicate phase of criminal investigation, characterized by the dominant role of the investigative bodies, requires that the enhancement of the prosecutorial powers be accompanied, in a sort of direct proportion, by the strengthening of the tasks of independent authorities, such as the judges guarantors, with a view to compensating for the imbalance that the defendant still experiences in criminal justice.

NOTES

1. In Italy, until the 1930 code of criminal procedure (the so-called "Rocco code") was in force, there were still a few forms of judicial prosecution, namely the proceedings instituted by a district court judge (*pretore*) or by the investigating magistrate after rejecting the public prosecutor's request for discontinuance of the inquiry. It is, however, doubtful that the ancient principle *ne procedat judex ex officio* is always incompatible with the qualitative requirements of a fair trial (Cordero 1987, 60). The main problem regards the impartiality of the judge who is called upon to adjudicate the case, if the same person files the charges against the defendant and then adjudicates those same charges. A similar concern was expressed, under the 1988 code, in relation to the complaint that the aggrieved person can lodge before the justice of the peace. If the competent prosecutor neither files charges nor rejects the complaint, the question arises whether the justice of the peace must summon the parties to a court hearing or reject the victim's complaint by forwarding it to the public prosecutorial office. Italian courts have largely advocated the second solution, which was also shared by constitutional case law (dec. 381/2005). In the course of this study, however, we shall see that while the public prosecutor's competences do not necessarily entail a monopoly of criminal prosecution, the concerns regarding the need for impartiality also arise from the maintenance, and in some cases even the growth, of the decision-making competences of the public prosecutors (Marzaduri 2018, 1234f.).
2. Royal Legislative Decree 511/1946 amended Article 69 of the Courts Act, i.e., Royal Decree 12/1941. See Caprioli (1994, 35).
3. From the viewpoint of Italian criminal justice, see Marzaduri (1996, 8ff., 17ff.).
4. On the theoretical relationship between legal action and request for judgment see Satta (1964, 816ff.).
5. As to Spain, however, it is interesting to note that recent proposals of reform were oriented towards the enhancement of the role of public prosecutorial services. See Bujosa Vadell (2015, 15).
6. A significant exception can be observed in the field of the proceedings falling under the competence of the justices of the peace, since here the pre-trial inquiries are normally carried out by the police, while the public prosecutor's investigations only aim at filling eventual gaps of the police inquiries. The decision on whether or not to institute the court proceedings, however, entirely lie with the public prosecutor (Legislative Decree 274/2000).
7. Departing from the approach followed by the previous codification, the current Italian code of criminal procedure, enacted in 1988, placed the charging decision at the end of a long pre-trial inquiry, in which the investigative authorities—namely the competent public prosecutor and the police—are required to carry out their inquiries as exhaustively as possible, collecting all the relevant information not only against but also in favor of the suspects (Arts. 326, 358 CCP).
8. Remarkably, the concept of "preliminary charge" was already enacted into a draft, elaborated at the beginning of the 1960s by Professor Francesco Carnelutti in his function as President of a Ministerial Commission for the reform of the code of criminal procedure, the so-called "Bozza Carnelutti" (Carnelutti 1963, 19f., 61).
9. Under Italian procedural law, where a victim lodges a criminal law complaint before the justice of the peace (see note 1 above), there does not seem to be any room for prosecutorial investigations. It must, however, be taken into account that the public prosecutor is

called upon to decide whether or not to bring the case before the justice of the peace on the basis of the information contained in the complaint of the aggrieved person, whom Italian law requires not only to identify the possible charge in clear and detailed terms but also to provide it with all the necessary evidence aimed at supporting it at trial (Marzaduri 2018, 1231).

10. In Italy, although the police are required to start their investigations autonomously after receiving or obtaining *notitia criminis*, they must inform promptly the competent public prosecutorial office, and a public prosecutor will be charged with the case and register the alleged offense (Art. 335 CCP). From this moment on, the public prosecutor assumes the leadership of the pre-trial inquiry. It is true that the police can continue their autonomous inquiries even afterwards (Art. 348 CCP), but only on condition that the competent prosecutor decides to initiate a pre-trial criminal investigation.
11. The 1930 Italian code did not provide for a list of procedural acts through which public prosecutors could institute criminal proceedings (Conso 1950, 360).
12. Along with the developments that took place in Italian criminal justice after the entry into force of the 1988 code, which required a public prosecutor to formally register *notitia criminis* and enacted an exhaustive list of procedural acts through which public prosecutors could institute criminal proceedings, it is worth noting that Brazil recently carried out an important reform (Law 12.830/2013), which aimed at solving the problems arising from the lack of a formal charge in the police inquiry.
13. The European Convention stands out among other human rights charters for acknowledging the right of every person "charged" with a criminal offense to be informed of the "accusation" preferred against them. This reference may seem to provide this guarantee with a more restrictive scope than that of the other fair trial guarantees laid down in Article 6(3) ECHR, and it is worth noting that some commentators interpreted the right to information as relating to the act through which the court proceedings are instituted with a formal accusation (Trechsel 2005, 198ff.). This approach is debatable for several reasons. First, focusing on specific procedural acts aimed at charging the defendant with an offense not only restricts the scope of the guarantee but also deprives it of much of its dynamic force. Thus, linking the right to information to the beginning of the court proceedings would mean accepting that the Convention left individuals largely unprotected in the pre-trial inquiry, notwithstanding that most intrusive measures are usually carried out in this phase. Second, this negative result would not remain limited to the right to information. As is well-known, the fair trial rights are strictly connected with each other: without information on the charge, suspects would not be able to properly prepare their de, make themselves heard, and so on. Furthermore, it is worth observing that the European Court has never followed such a restrictive interpretation of Article 6(3)(a) ECHR, while promoting a flexible approach that largely departs from the domestic understanding of "charge," which imposes on the competent authority precise obligations aimed at enabling the effective exercise of fair trial rights (*Drassich v. Italy* 2007). This approach makes the right to information of the accusation as an extremely dynamic safeguard, which cannot be rigidly confined to specific procedural stages (Kühne 2009, Rn. 496).
14. A significant exception relates to the "persons other than suspects or accused persons who, in the course of questioning by the police or by another law enforcement authority, become suspects or accused persons" (Art. 2[3] Directive 2013/48/EU). This extension entails serious human rights risks from a human rights perspective, as "there is no precise

moment where it can be undoubtedly stated that a witness becomes a suspect," and national countries regulate this delicate change of status in very different ways. In this sense see Bachmaier Winter (2015, 114).

15. To be sure, some Italian scholars departed from this criminal law-oriented approach by promoting an autonomous concept of criminal prosecution in light of the needs of procedural law. See, in particular, Giovanni Leone, who conceived even of discontinuance of proceedings as a form of prosecution (1959, 859f.).
16. The role of private parties reaches its peak in cases of libel or slander, since here in Spain the institution of criminal proceedings lies exclusively in the hands of the victim, any initiative of the public prosecutorial office being ruled out.
17. Again, some peculiarities characterize the criminal proceedings before the justices of the peace, which are of the utmost importance from the perspective of this study. Since the police are generally competent to investigate autonomously, registration of *notitia criminis* is here not the first procedural act of the pre-trial inquiry but usually follows the completion of the investigative phase, when the police are required to forward a final report to the competent public prosecutor. Moreover, according to the original text of Legislative Decree 274/2000, the police were also actively involved in the institution of the judicial proceedings, being empowered to summon the defendant to court on the basis of the charges preferred by the prosecutorial office. This arrangement, however, did not appear to be fully in line with the constitutional law principle of mandatory prosecution, and it was repealed by Law 155/2005 (Marzaduri 2018, 1224ff.).
18. On this topic and the problems concerned with this legislative reform see Lopes Jr. (2018, 169ff.).
19. Furthermore, it is not clear what role the victim can exactly play in the initiation of the remand proceedings. On close examination, the legal formulation is misleading in that it generally refers to the complainant. However, Article 311 CCP surely cannot be interpreted as also empowering the complainant to request pre-trial detention in cases of private criminal action, which is allowed where the minimum sentence is less than four years of imprisonment, i.e., the threshold laid down by Law 12.403/2011 as the minimum sentence to order remand detention. The only case in which the complainant can request the defendant's remand detention is therefore that of private legal action subsidiary to the public prosecution (Lopes Jr. 2018, 631ff.). Here also, however, the victim plays a rather ambiguous role in remand proceedings, since the code does not provide for any form of hearing of the aggrieved party either before or after the measure has been enforced.
20. This was the case for Italy under the Rocco code, while the 1988 codification for the first time enabled the investigative authorities either to receive notices of crime or to seek them at their own initiative (Art. 330). This innovation has been of the utmost importance, empowering public prosecutors and the police to initiate criminal investigations without the need for an external input either by a public body or private parties.
21. On the problems concerned with remote computer searches in Spain, see Bachmaier Winter (2017, 205ff.).
22. On interception through malware in Italian law, see among others Giostra and Orlandi (eds.) (2018).
23. New rules on cyber-interception of communications by means of malware have recently been enacted into the Italian code through various legislative reforms. See Legislative Decree 216/2017, followed by Law-Decree 161/2019, converted into Law 7/2020, and finally Law-Decree 28/2020, converted into Law 70/2020. It is worth noting, however, that these

reforms have not eradicated the wide possibilities of online searches through such devices, which are today still allowed in all cases other than those regulated by the new rules on cyber-interception. In this sense see already Parlato (2018, 295).

24. Compare *Corigliano v. Italy* (1982), with *Brozicek v. Italy* (1989).
25. *Brazzi v. Italy* (2018).
26. The approval of the court is instead not required in the case of a misdemeanor which is not subject to an increased minimum penalty and where the consequences ensuing from the offense are minimal (§ 153[1] CCP).
27. A similar challenge was instead provided for in relation to European orders of seizure of assets (Art. 28 of Legislative Decree 108/2017).

References

Aprati, Roberta. 2010. *La notizia di reato nella dinamica del procedimento penale*. Naples: Jovene.

Armengot Vilaplana, Alicia. 2013. *El imputado en el proceso penal*. Pamplona: Aranzadi.

Bachmaier Winter, Lorena. 2015. "The EU Directive on the Right to Access to a Lawyer: A Critical Assessment." In *Human Rights in European Criminal Law: New Developments in European Legislation and Case Law after the Lisbon Treaty*. Edited by Stefano Ruggeri, 111–131. Heidelberg: Springer.

Bachmaier Winter, Lorena. 2017. "Remote Computer Searches under Spanish Law: The Proportionality Principle and the Protection of Privacy." *Zeitschrift für die Gesamte Strafrechtswissenschaft* 129: 205–231.

Bachmaier Winter, Lorena. 2018. "Cross-Border Investigations under the EPPO Proceedings and the Quest for Balance." In *The European Public Prosecutor's Office: The Challenges Ahead*. Edited by Lorena Bachmaier Winter, 117–139. Cham: Springer.

Beale, Sara Sun. 2015. "Prosecutorial Discretion in Three Systems: Balancing Conflicting Goals and Providing Mechanisms for Control." In *Discretionary Criminal Justice in a Comparative Context*. Edited by Michele Caianiello and Jacqueline S. Hodgson, 27–58. Durham: Carolina Academic Press.

Brazzi v. Italy. 2018. Appl. No. 57278/11, Eur. Ct. Hum. Rts.

Brozicek v. Italy. 1989. Appl. No. 10964/84, Eur. Ct. Hum. Rts.

Bujosa Vadell, Lorenzo Mateo. 2015. "Discretionary Justice at the Initiation of a Criminal Investigation." In *Discretionary Criminal Justice in a Comparative Context*. Edited by Michele Caianiello and Jacqueline S. Hodgson, 13–26. Durham: Carolina Academic Press.

Calamandrei, Piero. 1943. *Istituzioni di diritto processuale civile secondo il nuovo codice*. Padua: Cedam.

Campbell, Liz, Andrew Ashworth, and Mike Redmayne. 2018. *The Criminal Process*. 5th ed. Oxford: Oxford University Press.

Caprioli, Francesco. 1994. *L'archiviazione*. Naples: Jovene

Carnelutti, Francesco. 1963. *Verso la riforma del processo penale*. Naples: Morano.

Carrara, Francesco. 1875. "Azione penale." In *Rivista penale*, 5–20.

Conso, Giovanni. 1950. "Il provvedimento di archiviazione." In *Rivista italiana di diritto penale*, 320–361.

Cordero, Franco. 1987. *Procedura penale*. 9th ed. Milan: Giuffrè.

Cordero, Franco. 2012. *Procedura penale*. 9th ed. Milan: Giuffrè.

Corigliano v. Italy. 1982. Appl. No. 8304/78, Eur. Ct. Hum. Rts.

Darbyshire, Penny. 2008. "Criminal Procedure in England and Wales." In *Criminal Procedure in Europe*. Edited by Richard Vogler and Barbara Huber, 39–169. Berlin: Duncker & Humblot.

Di Chiara, Giuseppe. 2003. "Diritto processuale penale." In *Una introduzione al sistema penale: per una lettura costituzionalmente orientata*. Edited by Giovanni Fiandaca and Giuseppe Di Chiara. Naples: Jovene.

Drassich v. Italy. 2007. Appl. No. 25575/04, Eur. Ct. Hum. Rts.

Gascón Inchausti, Fernando, and María Luisa Villamarín López. 2008. "Criminal Procedure in Spain." In *Criminal Procedure in Europe*. Edited by Richard Vogler and Barbara Huber, 541–653. Berlin: Duncker & Humblot.

Giacomolli, Nereu José. 2014. *O devido processo penal: abordagem conforme a Cconstituição federal e o Pacto de São José da Costa Rica*. São Paulo: Atlas S.A.

Gimeno Sendra, Vicente. 2015. *Derecho procesal penal*. 2nd ed. Pamplona: Civitas-Thomson Reuters.

Giostra, Glauco, and Renzo Orlandi, eds. 2018. *Nuove norme in tema di intercettazioni: tutela della riservatezza, garanzie difensive e nuove tecnologie informatiche*. Turin: Giappichelli.

Huber, Barbara. 2008. "Criminal Procedure in Germany." In *Criminal Procedure in Europe*. Edited by Richard Vogler and Barbara Huber, 269–371. Berlin: Duncker & Humblot.

Kühne, Hans-Heiner, Herbert Miehsler, and Theo Vogler. 2009. "Article 6." In *Internationaler Kommentar zur Europäischen Menschenrechtskonvention*. Edited by Katharina Pabel and Stefanie Schmahl, 2013. Cologne: Carl Heymanns.

Kühne, Hans-Heiner. 2010. *Strafprozessrecht: Eine systematische Darstellung des Deutschen und Europäischen Strafverfahrensrechts*. 8th ed. Heidelberg: C. F. Müller.

Leone, Giovanni. 1959. "Azione penale." In *Enciclopedia del diritto*. Vol. IV, 851–861. Milan: Giuffrè.

Lopes Jr., Aury. 2018. *Direito Processual Penal*. 15th ed. São Paulo: Saraiva

Lopes Jr., Aury, and Ricardo Jakobsen Glockner. 2014. *Investigação preliminar no processo penal*. 6th ed. São Paulo: Saraiva.

Marzaduri, Enrico. 1996. "Azione. IV) Diritto processuale penale." In *Enciclopedia giuridica*. Vol. IV, 1–23. Rome: Treccani.

Marzaduri, Enrico. 2000. "Commento all'art. 1 legge costituzionale 2/1999." *La legislazione penale*, 762–804.

Marzaduri, Enrico. 2018. "Procedimento penale davanti al giudice di pace." In *Compendio di procedura penale*. Founded by Giovanni Conso and Vittorio Grevi. Edited by Marta Bargis, 1207–1257. 9th ed. Milan: Wolters Kluwer-Cedam.

Meyer-Goßner, Lutz, and Bertram Schmitt. 2019. *Strafprozessordnung*. 69th ed. Munich: C. H. Beck.

Nestler, Cornelius. 2006. "European Defence in Trans-national Criminal Proceedings." In *Ein Gesamtkonzept für die Europäische Strafrechtspflege: A Programme for European Criminal Justice*. Edited by Bernd Schünemann, 415–428. Cologne: Carl Heymanns.

Nobili, Massimo. 1998. *Scenari e trasformazioni del processo penale*. Padua: Cedam.

Nobili, Massimo. 2001. "Giusto processo e indagini difensive: verso una nuova procedura penale?" In *Diritto penale e processo*, 5–14.

Orlandi, Renzo. 2008. "Pubblico ministero (ufficio del)." In *Enciclopedia del diritto*. Annali vol. II-2, 943–955. Milan: Giuffrè.

Parlato, Lucia. 2018. "Problemi insoluti: le perquisizioni *On-line*." In *Nuove norme in tema di intercettazioni: tutela della riservatezza, garanzie difensive e nuove tecnologie informatiche*. Edited by Glauco Giostra and Renzo Orlandi, 289–324. Turin: Giappichelli.

Ruggieri, Francesca. 2008. "Pubblico ministero (diritto processuale penale)." In *Enciclopedia del diritto*. Annali vol. II-1, 998–1015. Milan: Giuffrè.

Satta, Salvatore. 1948. *Diritto processuale civile*. Padua: Cedam.

Satta, Salvatore. 1959. "Azione in generale. b) L'azione nel diritto positivo." In *Enciclopedia del diritto*. Vol. IV, 822–825. Milan: Giuffrè.

Satta, Salvatore. 1962. "Corte di cassazione (diritto processuale civile)." In *Enciclopedia del diritto*. Vol. X, 797–829. Milan: Giuffrè.

Satta, Salvatore. 1964. "Domanda giudiziale. e) Diritto processuale civile." In *Enciclopedia del diritto*. Vol. XIII, 816–826. Milan: Giuffrè.

Trechsel, Stefan. 2005. *Human Rights in Criminal Proceedings*. Oxford: Oxford University Press.

Vogler, Richard. 2008 "Criminal Procedure in France." In *Criminal Procedure in Europe*. Edited by Richard Vogler and Barbara Huber, 171–268. Berlin: Duncker & Humblot.

CHAPTER 2

SELECTING CHARGES

MATT BARNO AND MONA LYNCH

2.1 Introduction

The selection of criminal charges has been described as "the most important prosecutorial power and the strongest example of the influence and reach of prosecutorial discretion" (Davis 2007, 22). Through their initial charging decisions, prosecutors not only determine who will be subject to the state's penal power but also define the terms under which defendants will strategize and negotiate to mitigate their potential punishment (Vorenberg 1981). For this reason, initial charging decisions have a lasting impact on the entire criminal process, from the initiation of formal proceedings to the imposition of the final sentence upon conviction. Although criminal charging has been a frequent subject of legal writing, the empirical body of research examining how these decisions are made in practice is both sparser and more fragmentary than the legal commentary (Wright, Levine, and Miller 2014). Empirical researchers face significant obstacles in examining this critical stage of the criminal process, both because prosecutorial charging decisions are generally made outside of public view, and because the key processes attending the charging process, like grand jury indictment proceedings, are by rule and tradition shrouded in secrecy (Richman 1999).

This chapter provides an overview of the discretionary aspects of the criminal charging process, including the legal parameters within which prosecutors exercise their charging discretion and how that discretion is exercised in practice. We begin by reviewing the legal standards governing prosecutorial charging decisions. We address both constitutional limits on the power to *initiate* criminal charges, as well as limits on the *severity* of charges, which have primarily been tested in the context of plea negotiations. We then turn to the socio-legal theory and empirical research on prosecutorial charging discretion. Within that framework, we describe how formal legal structures governing criminal sentencing interact with prosecutors' power and incentives in the charging stage of the criminal process. We then review both the empirical literature documenting variations in charging practices and the key theoretical explanations for those variations. We conclude with several suggestions for future lines of research.

2.2 Legal Standards Surrounding Prosecutorial Charging Discretion

Depending on the jurisdiction and the seriousness of the alleged offense, prosecutors initiate formal charges against a defendant either through a grand jury indictment or the filing of an information directly with the court (Chemerinsky and Levenson 2017). In the federal system and in roughly one-third of the states, a grand jury indictment is required to initiate felony charges. In the remaining states, prosecutors can initiate felony charges through the filing of an information, so long as probable cause is established in a preliminary hearing before a judicial magistrate.[1] Neither a grand jury indictment nor a preliminary hearing is required in misdemeanor cases—prosecutors can generally initiate misdemeanor charges directly through the filing of an information or complaint. Professional conduct codes in all U.S. jurisdictions require that a prosecutor's decision to bring criminal charges be supported by probable cause (Davis 2007; Model Rules of Professional Conduct 2016). Beyond this minimal requirement, however, there are virtually no legal standards governing a prosecutor's charging decisions. Prosecutors exercise nearly unlimited discretion to determine both who will be charged and what those charges will be, and over the last four decades, the U.S. Supreme Court has consistently foreclosed legal opportunities to rein in these discretionary charging powers (Applegate 1982; Barkow 2006; Davis 2007).

Oyler v. Boles (1962), was the first Supreme Court case of the modern era to address a constitutional challenge to prosecutorial charging discretion (Applegate 1982; Vorenberg 1981). The petitioners in *Oyler* were convicted under West Virginia's habitual criminal statute, which mandated a life sentence for any defendant convicted of a third offense punishable by imprisonment. The petitioners argued that because charges under the habitual criminal statute were only brought against a small minority of eligible defendants, district attorneys in West Virginia were engaged in selective prosecution in violation of the Due Process and Equal Protection Clauses. The Court ultimately held that as long as charging decisions are not based on impermissible factors such as race or religion, prosecutors have unreviewable discretion over whether to bring charges against a particular defendant. Where suspect categories are not involved, the principle of separation of powers bars judges from evaluating the discretionary enforcement decisions of executive officers, and thus prosecutors are generally free to make charging decisions in the absence of any meaningful judicial oversight.[2]

Even when charging decisions appear to be based on unconstitutional factors like a defendant's race, the Supreme Court's landmark decision in *United States v. Armstrong*

(1996), has made it exceedingly difficult to succeed on a claim of discriminatory prosecution (Davis 2007). The defendants in *Armstrong* sought to have their federal crack cocaine charges dismissed on grounds that the U.S. Attorney was selectively charging Black individuals in violation of the Equal Protection Clause. In support of their claim, the defendants produced preliminary evidence indicating that virtually all defendants charged with crack offenses in the district's federal court were Black, while virtually all White crack defendants were prosecuted in state court where sentences were much lighter. The *Armstrong* defendants initially succeeded on a discovery motion requiring the U.S. Attorney to produce records of the racial identity of all defendants charged with crack cocaine offenses in the district, as well as the criteria used to determine which cases to prosecute in federal court. The U.S. Attorney appealed the ruling on the discovery motion, and the dispute ultimately reached the Supreme Court.

In an 8-1 decision, the Court ruled that the evidence produced by the *Armstrong* defendants did not meet the threshold required to grant the discovery motion. Statistics demonstrating aggregate differences in charges levied against Black and White crack defendants were not sufficient to demonstrate unconstitutional racial bias in the U.S. Attorney's charging decisions. Rather, the defendants had to identify *specific* individuals who were "similarly situated" to the defendants in all relevant respects other than race—such as age, criminal history, frequency and location of drug use—but who had not been charged by the U.S. Attorney. Because the *Armstrong* defendants had not produced evidence identifying specific similarly situated White individuals who were not charged in federal court, the Court determined that the defendants were not entitled to pursue their selective prosecution claim further through the discovery motion. Legal scholar Angela J. Davis (2007, 103) has argued that the Court's holding in *Armstrong* makes it "practically impossible to challenge prosecutorial decisions that produce unwarranted racial disparities." Not only must a defendant identify similarly situated individuals of another race that the prosecutor declined to charge, but the defendant must do so without the benefit of discovery concerning the prosecutor's past charging decisions and the criteria used to make those decisions.

The Supreme Court has also explicitly condoned the practice of using criminal charges with strikingly harsh sentences as a weapon to compel defendants to plead guilty and to sacrifice their constitutional right to a jury trial. In *Bordenkircher v. Hayes* (1978), a defendant challenged a prosecutor's use of a threatened additional charge as leverage in plea negotiations, arguing that it violated his constitutional right to due process. Hayes was initially charged in Kentucky with forging a check worth $88.30, a crime that carried a sentence of two to ten years in prison. The prosecutor in Hayes' case offered to recommend a sentence of five years if Hayes pled guilty to the forgery charge. If Hayes decided not to plead guilty and proceeded to trial, the prosecutor threatened to seek an additional charge under Kentucky's Habitual Criminal Act, which would require Hayes to serve life in prison for the forgery as a result of his two prior felony convictions. When Hayes refused to plead, the prosecutor made good on the threat to seek the additional charge, and Hayes was ultimately convicted at trial and sentenced to life in prison.

The Supreme Court determined that the prosecutor's use of a threatened charge in the course of plea negotiations did not violate Hayes' constitutional right to due process. The Court began by acknowledging that "the guilty plea and the often concomitant plea bargain are important components of this country's criminal justice system" (361). In order to maintain "relatively equal bargaining power" between prosecution and defense (362), the Court argued that a prosecutor's use of threatened additional charges was "an inevitable—and permissible—attribute" of the negotiation process (364). The Court, however, neglected to recognize the subjective realities of such threats. In a system where prosecutors are provided with a plethora of opportunities for crafting extraordinarily harsh charging threats, the pressure on defendants to plead guilty becomes nearly insurmountable.

As a result of the Supreme Court's charging jurisprudence, prosecutors operate in an environment devoid of any significant legal checks on their discretion. Courts generally will not inquire into the criteria used to make charging decisions, leaving prosecutors free to determine who is formally brought into the criminal justice system in the absence of any meaningful oversight. Although the Constitution forbids prosecutors from using race or other suspect categorizations as a basis for bringing criminal charges, the Court has established a remarkably high evidentiary burden not only for proving discrimination in the context of prosecutorial charging decisions but even for obtaining discovery of the evidence required to make such a proof. The absence of legal oversight has bred what Radley Balko (2013) has described as a "culture of infallibility" and an "ethos of impunity" among prosecutors throughout the United States. Prosecutors are free to wield their virtually limitless charging discretion to ensure that they obtain their desired outcomes as easily as possible, and defendants are generally left without legal recourse to contest this immense power over the charging process.

Moreover, the power of charging discretion has been amplified over the last four decades, as the criminal law has expanded dramatically both in terms of the number of criminal statutes on the books and the length of sentences attached to a criminal conviction (Davis 2007; Pfaff 2017). Bill Stuntz argued that this expansion was motivated by a desire on the part of legislators not necessarily to expand the scope of criminal justice enforcement, but to enhance prosecutors' bargaining power in negotiating plea deals with defendants. Expansive criminal codes with overlapping crime definitions allow prosecutors to stack multiple charges against defendants for the same conduct, and the exceptionally punitive sentences available upon conviction amplify the risks that defendants face if they decline the prosecutor's plea offers and proceed to trial (Stuntz 2001, 537–538). A range of scholars and advocates have noted that these dynamics dominate the contemporary administration of criminal punishment, with nearly all criminal convictions coming via guilty pleas rather than convictions at trial (e.g., Davis 2007; HRW 2013; Lynch 2016; Pfaff 2017).

2.3 Prosecutorial Charging Discretion in Context: The "Hydraulic Displacement" Thesis

Several scholars have noted that the unbridled discretion exercised by prosecutors over charging decisions stands in stark contrast to recent movements throughout the criminal justice system to curb discretionary decision-making (Davis 2007; Johnson 2014; Vorenberg 1981). Over the last forty years, judges in particular have seen their discretionary power over the criminal justice process shrink considerably (Stemen and Rengifo 2012; Stith and Cabranes 1998). Prior to the 1980s, U.S. jurisdictions generally operated under indeterminate sentencing regimes in which individual judges had sole discretion to determine the initial sentences received by defendants upon conviction (Frankel 1973).[3] Indeterminate sentencing systems came under heavy criticism in the late 1970s and early 1980s, as both conservative and liberal figures took aim at the seemingly limitless power that idiosyncratic judges exercised over criminal punishment (Johnson 2014). Determinate sentencing regimes, in which sentences for particular crimes are fixed a priori and judges are given few if any opportunities to deviate from these fixed sentences, were viewed as the proper solution to the problem of unrestricted judicial discretion. One consequence of the shift to determinate sentencing was the further empowerment of prosecutors, who could now significantly control sentencing outcomes through their initial charging decisions (Barkow 2008).

Most of the research documenting the transition from indeterminate to determinate sentencing in the U.S. has focused on the federal criminal justice system (Stith and Cabranes 1998).[4] In 1984, Congress passed the Sentencing Reform Act, which created the U.S. Sentencing Commission and authorized the Commission to promulgate mandatory guidelines that federal judges would be obligated to follow, with very few exceptions, when sentencing convicted defendants (Lynch 2016). The first guidelines were implemented in 1987, thereby inaugurating the era of determinate sentencing in federal court. For nearly two decades, federal judges treated the Commission's guidelines as mandatory and generally sentenced defendants within its specified ranges. The Supreme Court's decision in *United States v. Booker* (2005) declared aspects of the guidelines system to be unconstitutional and mandated that the guidelines be treated as merely advisory. However, despite the relaxation of sentencing restrictions implied by *Booker*, federal judges are still required to calculate the guideline range prior to issuing a sentence, and ultimately many judges continue to sentence within the guideline ranges (Starr and Rehavi 2013). Moreover, since the late 1980s, Congress has continued to further constrain judicial discretion through the enactment of mandatory minimum statutes, which prohibit judges from administering a sentence below a specified floor if a defendant is convicted of a specified offense (Lynch 2016).

Numerous scholars have observed that the contraction of judicial discretion in the federal system simply magnified the consequences attached to federal prosecutors' initial charging decisions (Alschuler 1978; Bibas 2003; Lynch 2016; Nagel and Schulhofer 1992; Stith 2007; Stith and Cabranes 1998). Miethe (1987, 155–156) referred to this "zero-sum" process as the "hydraulic displacement of discretion," whereby discretion is never entirely eliminated from the criminal justice system, only displaced or transferred to different actors or institutions. Starr and Rehavi (2013, 13) are careful to note that restraints on judicial discretion did not necessarily *expand* prosecutorial discretion, which was "already almost boundless." Rather, constraints on judicial discretion increase prosecutorial "*power*" by amplifying the impact of prosecutors' charging decisions on defendants' final sentences. In a determinate sentencing regime, judges have no opportunity to counter-balance the effects of negotiated charges. In effect, the prosecutor determines the final sentence in the context of plea negotiations with a defendant, and the judge is only given the opportunity to rubber stamp the agreement made by the prosecutor. Furthermore, criminal code expansion in the latter half of the twentieth century substantially enhanced prosecutors' leverage in plea negotiations, providing them with a "menu" of punitive charges that could be strategically deployed to compel defendants to plead guilty (Stuntz 2006, 818).

The result is that prosecutors have become "the most powerful officials in the criminal justice system" (Davis 2013, 823; Pfaff 2017, 133). Behind closed doors and without significant oversight, prosecutors make virtually all of the key decisions that drive outcomes for criminal defendants. Through their initial charging decisions, prosecutors establish the terms under which defendants and the prosecution will negotiate over a plea agreement. The breadth of criminal charges available to prosecutors and the extreme penalties attached to certain charges (such as those carrying mandatory minimum sentences) afford prosecutors astounding leverage in these plea negotiations. Because defendants' ability to hold prosecutors to their burden of proving guilt beyond a reasonable doubt is essentially "obliterated by the sheer punitive force of the array of legal hammers in the prosecutor's toolbox," the overwhelming majority of criminal defendants plead guilty rather than proceeding to trial (Lynch 2016, 109). When the guilty plea is entered, judges in determinate sentencing regimes are then constrained by statutory mandates that dictate sentence terms and ranges. In the most restrictive of systems, prosecutors' charging discretion allows them to control the entire administration of the criminal law, from start to finish.

2.4 Empirical Research on Prosecutorial Charging Discretion

Early empirical research on prosecutorial charging decisions often approached the issue of discretion as a problem in need of management and control (Wright and Miller 2002).

Typically these studies focused on the case screening process, whereby prosecutors determined which suspects to formally charge and which cases to decline. The frequent critique was that "selective prosecution" in the screening process reflected arbitrariness and unjustified disparities in discretionary charging decisions (Davis 1969; Frase 1980, 280; Vorenberg 1981). The critique was often coupled with recommendations for how to cabin prosecutorial discretion, for example through internal office policies subject to judicial review (Abrams 1971) or case screening conferences involving input from defense attorneys (Vorenberg 1981). This initial wave of scholarship fit comfortably within the mold of "gap studies"—early sociolegal scholarship illustrating the ways in which formal law underdetermines actual legal practice, producing a gap between the law-on-the-books and law-in-action (Gould and Barclay 2012). Neither substantive nor procedural criminal law offered much guidance about case screening, and thus prosecutors were left to make their own decisions about which suspects to formally charge.

The initial spark of empirical inquiry into prosecutorial charging discretion was followed by a period of relative stagnation. To be sure, legal scholars continued to write extensively about the dangers of unfettered charging discretion, and they increasingly began to emphasize the notion that these discretionary charging decisions were infected with racial bias (Barkow 2008; Burke 2005; Davis 1998; Gershman 1991; McAdams 1997). For the most part, however, this legal scholarship has relied on anecdote, personal experience, and descriptions in appellate court opinions to understand how prosecutorial charging discretion operates in practice (Wright, Levine, and Miller 2014). Systematic empirical analysis of prosecutorial charging decisions is much rarer, primarily due to issues with data access. Charging decisions generally take place behind closed doors, outside of public view. These decisions are not subject to external oversight or scrutiny, and virtually no data are collected to track prosecutors' reasons for pursuing charges against some suspects and not others. Accordingly, scholars have often described the charging process as a "black box" whose opacity renders empirical research exceedingly difficult (Miller and Wright 2008).

Nevertheless, despite these data challenges, some researchers have been able to crack open the "black box," and the empirical research they have produced over the last three decades has expanded on the early "gap studies" in at least two meaningful respects. First, these studies examine not only discretionary decisions about which suspects to formally charge, but also decisions about the *content* of charges that will be filed. Given the wide array of charging options now available to prosecutors, understanding how and why prosecutors choose particular charges over others is key to understanding how outcomes are produced in the criminal justice system. Second, these studies go beyond simply acknowledging the gap between the formal law and actual charging practices by exploring the factors that define and structure this gap. The focus in these studies is not simply on recognizing the existence of broad prosecutorial charging discretion, but on understanding the features that shape the exercise of this discretion. The remainder of this section reviews empirical research on four key sets of factors influencing prosecutorial charging discretion: (1) case factors, (2) demographic factors, (3) social-structural factors, and (4) local factors.

2.4.1 Case Factors

Classic empirical studies of prosecutorial charging discretion typically focused on how evidence strength and offense seriousness influenced the decision to file charges against an arrestee (Miller 1970). An early study by Albonetti (1987), for example, examined how charging decisions were influenced by the degree of uncertainty in the prosecutor's ability to obtain a conviction at trial. Using case processing data from the U.S. Attorney's office in Washington, D.C., Albonetti found that prosecutors were significantly more likely to bring charges in cases where there was physical evidence or multiple forms of corroborating evidence. Conversely, prosecutors were significantly less likely to bring charges when exculpatory evidence was present or when only one witness was available. In a follow-up study of charge reductions at initial case filing in Jacksonville, Florida, Albonetti (1992) found that state prosecutors were significantly less likely to reduce a felony arrest charge to a misdemeanor in cases involving the use of a weapon, physical force, or threat of physical force. These studies provide empirical support to the common-sense notion that leniency in charging decisions is inversely related to both the strength of the case against the arrestee and the perceived seriousness of the alleged conduct.

More recent studies on domestic violence and sexual assault cases have continued to provide empirical support for these conclusions. With regard to evidence strength, Spohn, Beichner, and Davis-Frenzel (2001) qualitatively coded a sample of sexual battery cases presented to prosecutors in Miami, Florida, concluding that prosecutorial charging decisions were largely shaped by the victim's willingness to cooperate with the government and discrepancies in victim and witness statements about the incident. Kingsnorth et al. (2001, 2002) and Davis et al. (2003) similarly found that victim cooperation significantly influenced the decision to bring charges against domestic violence arrestees in Sacramento, California, and Milwaukee, Wisconsin, respectively. As to offense severity, Henning and Feder (2005) analyzed a sample of all domestic violence arrestees over a twelve-month period in Shelby County, Tennessee, finding that prosecutors were significantly more likely to bring charges in felony rather than misdemeanor cases and in cases where the victim was injured.

2.4.2 Demographic Factors

Many empirical studies have analyzed the extent to which prosecutorial charging decisions are influenced by the race, ethnicity, and gender of both defendants and victims. These studies have collectively produced mixed results, most likely due to variation in the types of cases studied.

With regard to charges filed in domestic violence and sexual assault cases, Kingsnorth and his colleagues conducted several studies concluding that neither race, ethnicity, nor gender influenced prosecutors' decisions to bring charges against an arrestee (Kingsnorth et al. 1998, 2001; Kingsnorth, MacIntosh, and Sutherland 2002). These findings were corroborated by Spohn, Beichner, and Davis Frenzel (2001), who similarly found null effects for demographic factors associated with both suspects and victims. Two studies that did find significant racial effects on prosecutorial charging decisions reached opposite conclusions concerning the direction of influence. Wooldredge and Thistlethwaite (2004) found that prosecutors were less likely to bring charges against Black suspects, while Henning and Feder (2005) found that prosecutors were more likely to bring charges against minority (non-White) suspects. Lastly, Spohn and Holleran (2001) found that while prosecutors in *stranger* sexual assault cases were significantly more likely to bring charges when the victim was White, there were no significant effects regarding the race or ethnicity of either the victim or the suspect in cases involving acquaintances or partners. As will be discussed further in section 2.4.3 below, these mixed findings may be a result of the powerful role that ideological factors, including myths about appropriate and sympathetic victims, play in shaping prosecutorial charging discretion in domestic violence and sexual assault cases. Prior research suggests that in such cases, prosecutors often make charging decisions based on their perceptions of how sympathetic the victim will appear to jurors, and these perceptions may not map directly onto racial or ethnic categories.

Studies of death penalty charging decisions have generally produced more consistent findings concerning victim and suspect demographics. David Baldus is often regarded as a pioneer in this field, given the prominent role that his research played in the most noteworthy constitutional challenge to the death penalty since the brief post-*Furman*[5] moratorium in the early 1970s. In *McCleskey v. Kemp* (1987), McCleskey relied upon research conducted by Baldus and his colleagues[6] to argue that the death penalty in Georgia was applied in a racially discriminatory manner in violation of the Equal Protection Clause. The "Baldus study," as it became known in the course of litigation, demonstrated that prosecutors were significantly more likely to seek the death penalty in cases where a Black defendant kills a White victim. This effect was primarily driven by "race-of-victim discrimination"—prosecutors were significantly more likely to bring capital charges in cases involving White victims rather than Black victims, and they were especially likely to seek the death penalty in Black-on-White homicides. The Supreme Court ultimately rejected McCleskey's constitutional challenge, holding that statistical evidence of the sort presented in the Baldus study is never sufficient in and of itself to prove racial discrimination in violation of the Equal Protection Clause. Nevertheless, subsequent studies by Baldus and others have continued to document race-of-victim disparities in death penalty charging decisions across numerous jurisdictions (Baldus and Woodworth 2003a; Free 2001; Paternoster et al. 2003; U.S. GAO 1990). Summarizing this research, Baldus and Woodworth (2003b, 1426) wrote, "The literature is clear that when race-of-victim disparities exist, the most common source is prosecutorial charging decisions."

Shermer and Johnson (2010) recently examined demographic variations in charge-reductions after initial case filing in the federal system. Overall, the researchers conservatively estimated that prosecutors reduced the severity of charges in about 12 percent of all cases as a plea negotiation strategy. However, those reductions varied significantly by gender. Women were more likely to receive reductions than men, and specifically young White women and Latinas were more likely to receive charge reductions compared to older White men.

Sometimes explicitly, but more often implicitly, studies on suspect and victim demographics adopt a "focal concerns" perspective on how race, ethnicity, and gender influence prosecutorial charging decisions (Spohn, Beichner, and Davis-Frenzel 2001, 208). The focal concerns perspective posits that disparities in the criminal justice system stem from stereotypical assumptions about race and gender, which serve as conceptual shortcuts for criminal justice practitioners tasked with making difficult decisions about defendants' culpability and the danger posed to the community (Steffensmeier, Ulmer, and Kramer 1998). According to this perspective, aggregate-level racial and gender disparities simply reflect the sum of atomized decisions shaped by these individual biases. Initially developed in the context of assessing judicial sentencing disparities, the focal concerns perspective has also been used to analyze prosecutorial charging decisions in sexual assault (Spohn, Beichner, and Davis-Frenzel 2001) and homicide cases (Pyrooz, Wolfe, and Spohn 2011), and it seems to undergird much of the largely atheoretical work of Baldus and his colleagues (see Baldus and Woodworth 2003b). More sociologically oriented scholars have critiqued the focal concerns perspective for over-emphasizing the role that individual cognitions play in producing broadly observed racial inequalities (Lynch 2013). Rather than seeing these inequalities as the product of biased assumptions at the individual level, sociologists highlight the role that institutional structures, organizational contexts, and socially constructed categories and schema play in structuring individual decision-making. The following subsection reviews research examining the influence of these social-structural factors in the context of prosecutorial charging discretion.

2.4.3 Social-Structural Factors

There is a robust line of research documenting the ways in which socially constructed categories about appropriate and sympathetic victims influence charging decisions in sexual assault cases. Frohmann (1991, 213) was among the first to critique static, binary conceptions of case factors, arguing that factors such as victim credibility are neither objective features of cases nor the result of individual biased assumptions, but rather "constructed and maintained through interaction." Prosecutors' perceptions of victim credibility are the product of the dynamic interplay between the victim, the prosecutor, and the prosecutor's understanding of how sexual assault is conceived of within the wider social body. Prosecutors develop "typifications of rape-relevant behavior" that are tied to the socially developed categories and schema used to make sense of sexual assault within the community of potential jurors (Frohmann 1991, 217). Assessments of victim credibility are then filtered through these typifications, and victim behavior that does not conform to these typifications is consequently viewed as suspect. Hence, charging decisions in sexual assault cases remain "orient[ed] to a 'downstream' concern with convictability... [and] constantly 'in dialogue with' anticipated defense arguments and anticipated judge and juror responses to case testimony" (Frohmann 1991, 224).

In a qualitative study of charging practices in a metropolitan city on the west coast, Frohmann (1991, 219) describes how prosecutors in sexual assault cases based their charging decisions on "common-sense assumptions about normal heterosexual relations that the prosecutors assume judges and juries use to assess the believability of the victim." For example, Frohmann (1991) documented how prosecutors deployed widely shared myths about the manner in which true victims report instances of sexual assault to evaluate and discredit victim witness statements. Victims who did not report early enough, who made contact with the alleged perpetrator after the incident, and whose demeanor did not adequately reflect distress were all considerably more likely to be seen by prosecutors as lacking credibility. In a follow-up study at the same research site, Frohmann (1997) emphasized the importance of local geographical knowledge in shaping sexual assault charging decisions. Prosecutors used their understanding of local micro-cultures to ascribe a set of moral values and behavioral norms to parties based on the neighborhoods they inhabited. Given the racial segregation in Frohman's research site, this reliance on local place-based knowledge was a key driver of racial disparities in prosecutorial charging decisions. Together, Frohmann's studies illustrate the significance of both broadly shared and locally situated categories and schema in determining how prosecutors exercise charging discretion.

Subsequent studies by Spohn and her colleagues have continued to highlight the impact of social knowledge structures on prosecutorial charging discretion in sexual assault cases. In an analysis of sexual offense charging practices in Detroit, Spears and Spohn (1997) found that the *only* significant predictors of prosecutors' charging decisions were variables associated with the victim's conformity to gendered behavioral norms. Prosecutors were significantly less likely to bring charges if the victim engaged in "risky" behavior prior to the alleged incident[7] or if the victim was viewed as morally suspect as a result of prior sexual behavior or substance abuse. When these variables were controlled for, case factors such as the strength of the evidence or the number of witnesses available were no longer significant predictors of charging decisions. Spohn, Beichner, and Davis-Frenzel (2001) examined charging decisions in Miami and similarly concluded that prosecutors were less likely to bring charges if the victim engaged in risky behavior prior to the incident or if there were questions about the victim's moral character, although the effects of evidentiary factors remained significant in their model. Finally, in a study of charging practices in Kansas City and Philadelphia, Spohn and Holleran (2001) found that the effect of a victim's "moral character" and pre-incident behavior varied depending on the type of sexual offense alleged. In cases involving acquaintances and partners, where gender norms exert a particularly strong influence on how sexual behavior is interpreted, Spohn and Holleran found that judgments about victims' moral character and pre-incident behavior significantly influenced charging decisions. However, in cases involving strangers, where gender norms exert less of an influence on how sexual behavior is interpreted, these factors did not significantly impact prosecutorial charging decisions.

With regard to race and ethnicity, scholars have increasingly applied institutional theories of racism to study the factors that structure prosecutorial charging discretion. Institutional theories of racism posit that racially disparate outcomes in the criminal justice system are not simply the result of biased actors discriminating against non-White defendants in individual cases. Rather, these racially disparate outcomes stem from an amalgam of situational, contextual, and structural forces that operate at the group level, even if shaped in part by individual-level factors (Haney López 2000; Lynch 2013). These group-level factors facilitate and recursively institutionalize biased action by reinforcing racial ideologies and naturalizing racially harmful responses as appropriate interventions. Consequently, racial bias is both systemic and systematized (or patterned), and not merely the outcome of sporadic, individualized action of single actors.

Ian Haney López's (2000) theory of institutional racism offers a particularly useful model for understanding how racial disadvantage is produced in the criminal justice system. For Haney López, institutional racism occurs when organizational actors engage in behavior that reinforces racial-status hierarchies—either by harming a disadvantaged group or benefitting an advantaged group—while relying upon "racial institutions." Haney López (2000, 1808) defines racial institutions as "any understanding of race that has come to be so widely shared within a community that it operates as an unexamined cognitive resource for understanding one's self, others, and the-way-the-world-is."

Haney López examined historical racially discriminatory grand jury selection procedures in Los Angeles County to illustrate how the deployment of racial institutions contributed to both the initial under-representation of Mexican-Americans in grand jury pools and the persistence of this underrepresentation over time. As racially biased ways of thinking and acting became normalized and routinized, racial institutions became further entrenched in the common sense understanding of Los Angeles County courts, and the organizational inertia impeding reform efforts grew stronger. In a study of crack cocaine enforcement in Cleveland, Lynch (2011) uses this framework to explain how the county prosecutor's office overcharged Black crack users from the city with felony drug possession when arrested just with paraphernalia (crack pipes). No other paraphernalia cases from anywhere in the county were charged as felonies, and crack pipe cases from outside the city were treated as misdemeanors. Moreover, even when presented with evidence of the harmful, racially disparate effect of this charging practice, the prosecutor's office declined to change it.

From the perspective of institutional theories of racism, prosecutorial charging decisions are particularly likely to reflect institutional biases that contribute to racial stratification. Institutional theories of racism emphasize that biased action is most likely to occur in circumstances "where institutional actors have the most decision-making authority and the least oversight" (Lynch 2013, 115). Because prosecutors exercise sole discretion over both the decision to file charges and what the content of those charges will be (within the bounds of what the evidence supports), the criteria used to make these decisions remain hidden from any significant judicial or public scrutiny. Consequently, prosecutors are not motivated to question the attitudes and worldviews that shape their charging decisions and contribute to racially disparate outcomes, nor are they necessarily cognizant of such biases. Furthermore, prosecutors are under significant role demands to produce convictions that demonstrate their contribution to public safety (Lynch 2011). Hence, they are particularly unlikely to empathize with the targets of their charging policies, as doing so would undermine the notion that prosecuting these targets makes the community safer.

These insights are reflected in Van Cleeve's (2016) ethnographic account of prosecutorial practices in Cook County (Chicago), Illinois. Van Cleeve recounts how prosecutors in "Crook County" deployed the cultural category of "mopes" to insulate themselves from claims that they were engaged in racially biased charging practices. To these prosecutors, "a mope represents someone who is uneducated, incompetent, degenerate, and lazy" (61). Prosecutors viewed their role as one of "sorting and managing [mopes]" in a manner "akin to the historic 'white man's burden' to socialize a racialized underclass that is 'half-devil and half-child'" (61). However, the racialized aspects of the "mope" category remained under the surface—ostensibly the "mope" label was a moral rather than a racial signifier. In Van Cleve's analysis, by justifying their charging decisions through this allegedly "colorblind logic," prosecutors were able to "ignore the ubiquity of race and racism" throughout the Cook County courts (60). In the absence of any meaningful oversight over their boundless charging discretion, prosecutors were never forced to account for the racially disparate outcomes that stemmed from their purportedly race-neutral focus on "mopes."

2.4.4 Local Factors

A long line of scholarship in the law and society tradition highlights the varying ways in which broad-level legal policy is translated into actual legal practice across diverse local settings (Abel 2010). Consistent with this tradition, classic law and society studies examined how local court communities developed collective norms regarding triable cases, the appropriate terms of plea-bargaining, and the "going rates" for prototypical cases (Church 1985; Dixon 1995; Einsenstein, Flemming, and Nardulli 1988; Heumann 1978). This also extends to what kinds of cases are charged and how charging options are used strategically by prosecutors in the plea negotiation process.

For instance, Schulhofer and Nagel (1989, 1996; Nagel and Schulhofer 1992) conducted several early studies on how charging and bargaining practices around the newly instituted federal sentencing guidelines varied across federal districts. These studies illustrate how local demands, conditions, and norms uniquely structured the performance of legal compliance with the federal sentencing guidelines in disparate districts. While these performances were conditioned and constrained by the structure and mandates of the guidelines, they nonetheless varied considerably across the districts under study. The deployment of these differing strategies was determined by the degree of supervision over local charging and bargaining practices, as well as the motivations of individual U.S. Attorneys in the different locales.

Lynch and Omori (2014) uncovered similar findings in research exploring district court responses to the Supreme Court's decision in *United States v. Booker* (2005), which rendered the federal sentencing guidelines merely advisory rather than mandatory. In a quantitative study of federal court sentencing outcomes, Lynch and Omori (2014) found that responses to *Booker* were significantly influenced by previous charging practices in each local district. Districts that had relied heavily on mandatory minimum charges pre-*Booker* were less likely to experience sentencing decreases post-*Booker* relative to districts that charged mandatory minimum offenses more sparingly. Hence, local legacies of past practice—the "law-before" (Verma 2015)—structured how these districts responded and adapted to the legal changes embodied in the *Booker* decision.

Moreover, Lynch and Omori (2014) also found that districts where prosecutors charged higher rates of mandatory minimum-eligible charges were the primary drivers of system-wide racial disparities in sentencing. This finding highlights not only the importance of prosecutorial charging decisions in shaping racially disparate outcomes, a topic discussed in greater detail below, but also the inherently local nature of criminal justice administration in the United States. Because prosecutors at the local jurisdictional-level (i.e., counties and federal districts) are granted such wide discretion over charging decisions, system-wide racial disparities ultimately reflect a myriad of discrete discretionary decisions, each of which are conditioned by both broad-level racial institutions and legal structures common across multiple jurisdictions, as well as unique local "idiocultures"—"'system[s] of knowledge, beliefs, behaviors, and customs' . . . that make up the local worlds in which these [prosecutors] work" (Lynch 2016, 110).

These quantitative findings were further confirmed by Lynch's (2016, 2018) ethnographic study of drug charging practices in four federal districts throughout the United States. Locales significantly differed in the severity and typology of drug cases brought to federal court and in the charging strategies deployed by local prosecutors, including the use of charges that triggered mandatory minimums. These charging decisions were hugely consequential for variations in eventual sentencing outcomes. Legal scholars Ronald Wright and Marc Miller have similarly emphasized the role of local "social norms" in shaping charging practices across prosecutorial offices (Miller and Wright 2008; Wright, Levine, and Miller 2014). In an analysis of charging practices in North Carolina, for example, Wright (2012, 212) found that despite a "common legal framework," prosecutor offices across the state pursued a "unique mix of criminal charges" calibrated to local interests and conditions.

The findings from this research have important implications for reform efforts designed to reduce racial and ethnic inequality in prosecutorial charging decisions. Any one-size-fits-all, top-down approach to addressing charging inequalities is unlikely to succeed in the face of these local variations in charging practices. The conditions that structure inequality in local jurisdictions differ from one another—sometimes dramatically—and thus the strategies for addressing inequality must be specifically tailored to account for varied local conditions if they are to be successful.

2.5 Role of Prosecutorial Charging Trends in Influencing Carceral Expansion and Racial Inequality

Recently, an intriguing line of scholarship has approached prosecutorial charging decisions not as an outcome to be explained, but as an independent variable driving contemporary trends in punishment. The early takeaway from this research is that prosecutorial charging decisions are a major contributor to the carceral trends that define mass incarceration. Pfaff (2017), for example, argues that prosecutors were the primary culprit behind the fivefold increase in the U.S. incarceration rate over the last four decades. While other academics commonly cite the War on Drugs, changes to criminal statutes, and longer sentences as explanations for the incarceration boom, Pfaff contends that these explanations do not account for nearly as much of the expansion as they are given credit for. Only 16 percent of those in state prisons are serving sentences for drug violations, and Pfaff argues that perhaps only 5 percent to 6 percent of those inmates are both low-level and non-violent (35–36). Pfaff also cites evidence indicating that while the incarceration rate increased dramatically over the last forty years, actual time served by inmates changed very little over that time (55–56).

Pfaff (2017) ultimately concludes that the incarceration boom was largely driven by an increase in felony charges filed, and since both crime and arrests were in decline, the increase in charges appears to have been driven by more aggressive prosecution. In a sample of state court data from 1994–2008, Pfaff found that increases in charges filed per felony arrest accounted for virtually all of the increase in prison admissions over that time (69–73). Pfaff offers several possible explanations for why prosecutors increased their felony filings during this time, including the fact that tougher sentencing laws made it easier for prosecutors to efficiently obtain guilty pleas from defendants. In the end, Pfaff argues that significant reductions in the incarceration rate will require changes in the incentives that motivate prosecutors to bring more charges. One of the solutions that Pfaff proposes is to "cut statutory maximums" in order to diminish some of the leverage that prosecutors have over defendants in the plea bargaining process (155), a suggestion also endorsed by one of the co-authors in prior work (Lynch 2016, 137–138).

Prosecutorial charging decisions have also been identified as one the principal sources of racial and ethnic inequality in the criminal justice system. In an analysis of factors influencing sentencing disparities between Black and White defendants in federal court, Starr and Rehavi (2013) found that prosecutorial charging decisions—in particular the decision to bring mandatory minimum charges—accounted for nearly all of the unexplained sentencing disparities between Black and White defendants. After controlling for arrest offense, Black defendants were considerably more likely to face charges subject to a mandatory minimum than were similarly situated White defendants. Starr and Rehavi contrast their findings with those of previous studies on federal sentencing disparities, which focused narrowly on the differences between the recommended guideline sentence and the final sentence issued by the judge. As Starr and Rehavi point out, the recommended guideline sentence is itself "the end product of charging, plea-bargaining, and sentencing fact-finding," each of which are shaped by the discretionary decisions of prosecutors (6). Hence, controlling for the recommended guideline sentence filters out the potential influence that prosecutorial charging discretion may have on final sentencing disparities. Starr and Rehavi overcome this problem by using defendants' arrest offense as a proxy for underlying criminal behavior, thereby allowing the authors to assess disparities in prosecutors' recommended sentences relative to underlying criminal behavior, in addition to disparities between recommended sentences and final sentences received. Ultimately, Starr and Rehavi conclude that the former set of disparities has a much stronger influence on overall racial inequality than the latter.

In a recent study of federal district courts, Lynch and Omori (2018) found that prosecutors' drug charging decisions were strongly predictive of Black-White disparities in conviction rates across a broad range of crimes. Lynch and Omori focused on federal crack cocaine charges, arguing that these charges offer "a useful window into how criminal law is differentially deployed as a racialized social control mechanism" (781). Given the history of racialized crack enforcement and the highly discretionary nature of federal drug crime prosecutions, contemporary crack charging practices in federal district court are particularly likely to reflect entrenched structures of institutionalized racism impacting a broad range of prosecutorial practices. Consistent with this view, Lynch and Omori found that, after controlling for relative crack use in the district, prosecutors' frequency in bringing crack cases predicted Black-White disparities in conviction rates not only for drug offenses, but for all offenses prosecuted within a given district. Thus, prosecutorial charging practices can be viewed as both a driver of racial inequality in the criminal justice system and a reflection of deeply seated racial institutions that facilitate the reproduction of racial inequality over time.

In recent qualitative work, Lynch has also drawn attention to the ways in which charging practices in different jurisdictions contribute to localized configurations of racial and ethnic inequality. Lynch (2016, 2018) examined charging and plea bargaining practices in federal drug cases in four districts throughout the United States: a northeastern district, a southeastern district, a southwestern district, and a rural district.[8] Lynch found that while the end-product of the process was substantially the same in each district—defendants were compelled to plead guilty by the prosecutors' threats of more severe punishments, often brought about through charging elements—the actual mechanisms deployed by prosecutors to achieve this goal were "shaped by localized norms and imperatives" (2016, 109). Both the circumstances that led to the filing of federal drug charges and the types of charges used to secure guilty pleas varied across locale, resulting in differing patterns of racial and ethnic inequality in each district.

In the liberal northeastern district, for example, federal prosecutors typically worked with local law enforcement to identify suspects, often those with prior drug convictions, who were viewed as a problem in poor Black communities. Prosecutors would then bring these suspects into federal court on drug charges for small street-level sales, where they could use the full punitive might of the federal criminal code to compel defendants to plead guilty and accept a lengthy term of imprisonment. The practice of using federal drug charges as a pretext for prosecuting allegedly dangerous Black suspects was so common in the northeastern district that it even had a nickname, named after the practice's primary proponent in the U.S. Attorney's office (Lynch 2018, 17). On the other hand, federal drug prosecutions in the southeast were typically driven by confidential informants (Lynch 2018, 21). Prosecutors used federal drug charges to bring defendants into court, where they would then use the threat of additional or more serious charges to induce defendants into cooperating with the government and disclosing the identity of others involved in drug transactions. As a result of this snow-ball method of case production, federal drug prosecutions in the southeast district tended to stay confined within the same neighborhoods and social networks, typically in the district's poorer Black communities (Lynch 2018, 23). Defendants were charged after being fingered by someone who knew them, and they secured reduced sentences by divulging the identities of other suspects they knew. In the abstract, the outcomes of these charging practices were ultimately very similar—federal drug prosecutions remained concentrated among young Black men in disadvantaged communities within each district. But the mechanisms that produced these outcomes were uniquely conditioned by local factors, resulting in differing patterns of charge dispersion in each locale.

2.6 Conclusion

Given the significance of prosecutorial charging decisions, the charge selection process remains notably under-researched. Nevertheless, the foregoing review of literature on prosecutorial charging discretion reveals several emerging strands of promising research that are worth highlighting. First, scholars have increasingly begun to focus on the local factors that structure prosecutorial charging discretion. While it is true that charging discretion is likely impacted by broadly influential demographic and social-structural factors, it is also important to recognize that the impact of these factors on prosecutorial charging decisions is mediated by the local environment. The discretion that prosecutors exercise over charge-selection is situated locally among county-level district attorneys and federal district-level U.S. Attorneys. Hence, local norms, conditions, and resources are likely to shape how factors such as a defendant's race impact prosecutorial charging decisions, and future empirical research must remain attentive to these local influences (Lynch 2016; Wright, Levine, and Miller 2014).

Second, by focusing on the content of charges selected in addition to the case screening process, scholars are further elucidating how prosecutorial charging discretion contributes to racial inequality in the criminal justice system. Starr and Rehavi's (2013) findings regarding the impact of mandatory minimum charging practices on racial disparities in federal court sentencing followed on the heels of a report from the

U.S. Sentencing Commission placing the blame for these disparities squarely on judges and the expansion of judicial discretion implied by the *Booker* decision (USSC 2012). The Commission's findings were distorted by a disregard for how discretionary decisions at earlier stages in the process impacted the sentences received by defendants upon conviction. By focusing on the relationship between initial charges filed and the facts alleged at arrest, Starr and Rehavi (2013) were able to uncover how prosecutorial charging decisions influenced racial disparities at sentencing. Ultimately, Starr and Rehavi found that virtually all of the Black-White disparities in sentencing could be explained by prosecutors' decisions to disproportionately charge Black arrestees with crimes involving mandatory minimum sentences, relative to similarly situated White arrestees. In other words, prosecutors were charging Black suspects more harshly than similarly situated White suspects, a finding that could only be revealed through an analysis of charge content.

Most of the recent research on prosecutorial charging discretion has focused on the federal system, where empirical data on charging practices are somewhat easier to obtain. However, the vast majority of criminal prosecutions take place in state court at the county level (Pfaff 2017). The dynamics of state court proceedings differ from federal court in important ways, and thus it would be valuable to explore the extent to which insights from prior federal court research could be extended into the state court context as well. However, the difficulty in penetrating the "black box" of prosecutorial charging practices at any level is likely to persist as long as these charging practices are permitted to take place in the absence of meaningful public oversight. While some individual prosecutors' offices have been open to empirical researchers, those willing to be transparent likely differ in fundamentally important ways from the majority that are not so willing (Wright and Levine 2017). At present, the prospects for future empirical research on prosecutorial charging discretion are dependent in some sense on the legal doctrine governing transparency in charging decisions, which to date has served as a formidable obstacle for researchers as well as for advocates who seek to challenge problematic practices.

In conclusion, as a matter of public policy, we echo recent calls for legislating more transparency on prosecutorial "performance measures" (Wright 2017, 424), including data related to charging decisions. There is reason to think that inroads can be made in this regard. For instance, in 2018, Florida enacted a bi-partisan criminal justice data transparency bill that provides the public significant access to system data (CSG Justice Center 2018). Nonprofits have also been effective in partnering with state and local jurisdictions on transparency efforts. Most notably, Measures for Justice, incorporated in 2011 as a non-profit to undertake a national effort to obtain county-level criminal justice data for all stages of the criminal process, has already earned cooperation in a number of states, with full data for multiple years now available for six states.[9] Beyond the goal of transparency and access to administrative data, we also urge expanded cooperation with qualitative researchers who study prosecutorial practices, including charging practices. The ability to talk to and learn from line prosecutors can significantly enhance the quality and accuracy of empirical work on the key decision-making stage of charging.

Notes

1. In a few states, prosecutors can initiate felony charges solely through the filing of an information without a probable cause hearing, and the Supreme Court has upheld such procedures as consistent with constitutional due process. See *Lem Woon v. Oregon* (1913); *Ocampo v. United States* (1914).
2. See also *Wayte v. United States* (1985).
3. Judicial discretion in indeterminate sentencing regimes was often counter-balanced by broad parole board discretion. Once a defendant was incarcerated, parole boards generally had the ability to shorten or lengthen the defendant's sentence without restriction (Dershowitz 1976). The decline of indeterminate sentencing was often coupled with the abolition of parole boards entirely.
4. By the late 1990s, most states had also transitioned to sentencing regimes that constrained judicial decision-making, partly as a result of funding incentives provided by the federal government (Turner, Greenwood, Chen, and Fain 1999). Research documenting these state-level transitions, however, is relatively sparse.
5. *Furman v. Georgia* (1972).
6. This research is summarized in Baldus, Woodworth, and Pulaski (1990).
7. The researchers defined risky behavior as including walking alone at night, being in a bar alone, using alcohol or drugs, hitchhiking, or inviting the alleged perpetrator to one's residence (Spears and Spohn 1997, 510–511).
8. Pseudonyms were used to preserve the anonymity of research participants.
9. See https://measuresforjustice.org/.

References

Abel, Richard L. 2010. "Law and Society: Project and Practice." *Annual Review of Law and Social Science* 6: 1–23.

Abrams, Norman. 1971. "Internal Policy: Guiding the Exercise of Prosecutorial Discretion." *UCLA Law Review* 19(1): 1–58.

Albonetti, Celesta A. 1987. "Prosecutorial Discretion: The Effects of Uncertainty." *Law & Society Review* 21(2): 291–314.

Albonetti, Celesta A. 1992. "Charge Reduction: An Analysis of Prosecutorial Discretion in Burglary and Robbery Cases." *Journal of Quantitative Criminology* 8(3): 317–333.

Alschuler, Albert W. 1978. "Sentencing Reform and Prosecutorial Power: A Critique of Recent Proposals for 'Fixed' and 'Presumptive' Sentencing." *University of Pennsylvania Law Review* 126(3): 550–577.

Applegate, Amy Grossman. 1982. "Prosecutorial Discretion and Discrimination in the Decision to Charge." *Temple Law Quarterly* 55(1): 35–88.

Baldus, David C., and George Woodworth. 2003a. "Race Discrimination in the Administration of the Death Penalty: An Overview of the Empirical Evidence with Special Emphasis on the Post-1990 Research." *Criminal Law Bulletin* 39(2): 194–226.

Baldus, David C., and George Woodworth. 2003b. "Race Discrimination and the Legitimacy of Capital Punishment: Reflections on the Interaction of Fact and Perception." *DePaul Law Review* 53(4): 1411–1496.

Baldus, David C., George Woodworth, and Charles A. Pulaski. 1990. *Equal Justice and the Death Penalty: A Legal and Empirical Analysis*. Boston: Northeastern University Press.

Balko, Radley. 2013. "The Untouchables: America's Misbehaving Prosecutors, and the System That Protects Them." *Huffington Post*, August 1, 2013. https://www.huffingtonpost.com/2013/08/01/prosecutorial-misconduct-new-orleans-louisiana_n_3529891.html.

Barkow, Rachel E. 2006. "Separation of Powers and the Criminal Law." *Stanford Law Review* 58(4): 989–1054.

Barkow, Rachel E. 2008. "Institutional Design and the Policing of Prosecutors: Lessons from Administrative Law." *Stanford Law Review* 61(4): 869–921.

Bibas, Stephanos. 2003. "The Feeney Amendment and the Continuing Rise of Prosecutorial Power to Plea Bargain." *Journal of Criminal Law and Criminology* 94(2): 295–308.

Bordenkircher v. Hayes. 1978. 434 U.S. 357.

Burke, Alafair S. 2005. "Improving Prosecutorial Decision Making: Some Lessons of Cognitive Science." *William and Mary Law Review* 47(5): 1587–1634.

Chemerinsky, Erwin, and Laurie L. Levenson. 2017. *Criminal Procedure*. New York: Wolters Kluwer Law & Business.

Church, Thomas W., Jr. 1985. "Examining Local Legal Culture." *Law & Social Inquiry* 10(3): 449–510.

Council of State Governments Justice Center [CSG Justice Center]. 2018. "Landmark Florida Legislation Sets New Standard for Data Collection and Transparency."

Davis, Angela J. 1998. "Prosecution and Race: The Power and Privilege of Discretion." *Fordham Law Review* 67(1): 13–68.

Davis, Angela J. 2007. *Arbitrary Justice: The Power of the American Prosecutor*. Oxford: Oxford University Press.

Davis, Angela J. 2013. "In Search of Racial Justice: The Role of the Prosecutor." *N.Y.U. Journal of Legislation and Public Policy* 16(4): 821–852.

Davis, Kenneth Culp. 1969. *Discretionary Justice: A Preliminary Inquiry*. Baton Rouge: Louisiana State University Press.

Davis, Robert C., Barbara E. Smith, and Bruce Taylor. 2003. "Increasing the Proportion of Domestic Violence Arrests That Are Prosecuted: A Natural Experiment in Milwaukee." *Criminology and Public Policy* 2(2): 263–282.

Dershowitz, Alan M. 1976. "Background Paper." In *Fair and Certain Punishment: Report of the Twentieth Century Fund Task Force on Criminal Sentencing*. New York: McGraw-Hill.

Dixon, Jo. 1995. "The Organizational Context of Criminal Sentencing." *American Journal of Sociology* 100(5): 1157–1198.

Eisenstein, James, Roy B. Flemming, and Peter F. Nardulli. 1988. *The Contours of Justice: Communities and Their Courts*. Boston: Little, Brown, and Company.

Frankel, Marvin E. 1973. *Criminal Sentences: Law without Order*. New York: Hill and Wang.

Frase, Richard S. 1980. "The Decision to File Federal Criminal Charges: A Quantitative Study of Prosecutorial Discretion." *The University of Chicago Law Review* 47(2): 246–330.

Free, Marvin D. 2001 "Racial Bias and the American Criminal Justice System: Race and Presentencing Revisited." *Critical Criminology* 10(3): 195–223.

Frohmann, Lisa. 1991. "Discrediting Victims' Allegations of Sexual Assault: Prosecutorial Accounts of Case Rejections." *Social Problems* 38(2): 213–226.

Frohmann, Lisa. 1997. "Convictability and Discordant Locales: Reproducing Race, Class, and Gender Ideologies in Prosecutorial Decisionmaking." *Law & Society Review* 31(3): 531–556.

Furman v. Georgia. 1972. 408 U.S. 238.

Gershman, Bennett L. 1991. "The New Prosecutors." *University of Pittsburgh Law Review* 53(2): 393–458.

Gould, Jon B., and Scott Barclay. 2012. "Mind the Gap: The Place of Gap Studies in Sociolegal Scholarship." *Annual Review of Law and Social Science* 8: 323–335.
Haney López, Ian F. 2000. "Institutional Racism: Judicial Conduct and a New Theory of Racial Discrimination." *Yale Law Journal* 109(8): 1717–1884.
Henning, Kris, and Lynette Feder. 2005. "Criminal Prosecution of Domestic Violence Offenses: An Investigation of Factors Predictive of Court Outcomes." *Criminal Justice and Behavior* 32(6): 612–642.
Heumann, Milton. 1978. *Plea Bargaining: The Experiences of Prosecutors, Judges, and Defense Attorneys*. Chicago: University of Chicago Press.
Human Rights Watch [HRW]. 2013. *An Offer You Can't Refuse: How US Federal Prosecutors Force Drug Defendants to Plead Guilty*. New York: Human Rights Watch.
Johnson, Brian D. 2014. *The Missing Link: Examining Prosecutorial Decision-Making across Federal District Courts*. Ipswich, MA: National Institute of Justice.
Kingsnorth, Rodney, John Lopez, Jennifer Wentworth, and Debra Cummings. 1998. "Adult Sexual Assault: The Role of Racial/Ethnic Composition in Prosecution and Sentencing." *Journal of Criminal Justice* 26(5): 359–371.
Kingsnorth, Rodney F., Randall C. MacIntosh, Terceira Berdahl, Carrie Blades, and Steve Rossi. 2001. "Domestic Violence: The Role of Interracial/Ethnic Dyads in Criminal Court Processing." *Journal of Contemporary Criminal Justice* 17(2): 123–141.
Kingsnorth, Rodney F., Randall C. MacIntosh, and Sandra Sutherland. 2002. "Criminal Charge or Probation Violation? Prosecutorial Discretion and Implications for Research in Criminal Court Processing." *Criminology* 40(3): 553–578.
Lem Woon v. Oregon. 1913. 229 U.S. 586.
Lynch, Mona. 2011. "Crack Pipes and Policing: A Case Study of Institutional Racism and Remedial Action in Cleveland." *Law & Policy* 33(2): 179–214.
Lynch, Mona. 2013. "Institutionalizing Bias: The Death Penalty, Federal Drug Prosecutions, and Mechanisms of Disparate Punishment." *American Journal of Criminal Justice* 41(1): 91–132.
Lynch, Mona. 2016. *Hard Bargains: The Coercive Power of Drug Laws in Federal Court*. New York: Russell Sage Foundation.
Lynch, Mona. 2018. "Prosecutorial Discretion, Drug Case Selection, and Inequality in Federal Court." *Justice Quarterly* 35(7): 1309–1336.
Lynch, Mona, and Marisa Omori. 2014. "Legal Change and Sentencing Norms in the Wake of *Booker*: The Impact of Time and Place on Drug Trafficking Cases in Federal Court." *Law & Society Review* 48(2): 411–445.
Lynch, Mona, and Marisa Omori. 2018. "Crack as Proxy: Aggressive Federal Drug Prosecutions and the Production of Black–White Racial Inequality." *Law & Society Review* 52(3): 773–809.
McAdams, Richard H. 1997. "Race and Selective Prosecution: Discovering the Pitfalls of *Armstrong*." *Chicago-Kent Law Review* 73(2): 605–668.
McCleskey v. Kemp. 1987. 481 U.S. 279.
Miethe, Terance D. 1987. "Charging and Plea Bargaining Practices under Determinate Sentencing: An Investigation of the Hydraulic Displacement of Discretion." *Journal of Criminal Law and Criminology* 78(1): 155–176.
Miller, Frank William. 1970. *Prosecution: The Decision to Charge a Suspect with a Crime*. Boston: Little, Brown, and Company.
Miller, Marc L., and Ronald F. Wright. 2008. "The Black Box." *Iowa Law Review* 94(1): 125–196.
Model Rule of Professional Conduct 3.8. 2016. In *ABA Model Rules of Professional Conduct*. American Bar Association.

Nagel, Ilene H., and Stephen J. Schulhofer. 1992. "A Tale of Three Cities: An Empirical Study of Charging and Bargaining Practices under the Federal Sentencing Guidelines." *Southern California Law Review* 66(1): 501–566.

Ocampo v. United States. 1914. 234 U.S. 91.

Oyler v. Boles. 1962. 368 U.S. 448.

Paternoster, Raymond, Robert Brame, Sarah Bacon, Andrew Ditchfield, Karen Beckman, and Nadine Frederique. 2003. *An Empirical Analysis of Maryland's Death Sentencing System with Respect to the Influence of Race and Legal Jurisdiction: Final Report*. College Park: University of Maryland.

Pfaff, John. 2017. *Locked In: The True Causes of Mass Incarceration—and How to Achieve Real Reform*. New York: Basic Books.

Pyrooz, David C., Scott E. Wolfe, and Cassia Spohn. 2011. "Gang-Related Homicide Charging Decisions: The Implementation of a Specialized Prosecution Unit in Los Angeles." *Criminal Justice Policy Review* 22(1): 3–26.

Richman, Daniel C. 1999. "Grand Jury Secrecy: Plugging the Leaks in An Empty Bucket." *American Criminal Law Review* 36(3): 339–356.

Schulhofer, Stephen J., and Ilene H. Nagel. 1989. "Negotiated Pleas under the Federal Sentencing Guidelines: The First Fifteen Months." *American Criminal Law Review* 27(2): 231–288.

Schulhofer, Stephen J., and Ilene H. Nagel. 1996. "Plea Negotiations under the Federal Sentencing Guidelines: Guideline Circumvention and Its Dynamics in the Post-*Mistretta* Period." *Northwestern University Law Review* 91(4): 1284–1316.

Shermer, Lauren O'Neill, and Brian D. Johnson. 2010. "Criminal Prosecutions: Examining Prosecutorial Discretion and Charge Reductions in US Federal District Courts." *Justice Quarterly* 27(3): 394–430.

Spears, Jeffrey W., and Cassia C. Spohn. 1997. "The Effect of Evidence Factors and Victim Characteristics on Prosecutors' Charging Decisions in Sexual Assault Cases." *Justice Quarterly* 14(3): 501–524.

Spohn, Cassia, Dawn Beichner, and Erika Davis-Frenzel. 2001. "Prosecutorial Justifications for Sexual Assault Case Rejection: Guarding the 'Gateway to Justice.'" *Social Problems* 48(2): 206–235.

Spohn, Cassia, and David Holleran. 2001. "Prosecuting Sexual Assault: A Comparison of Charging Decisions in Sexual Assault Cases Involving Strangers, Acquaintances, and Intimate Partners." *Justice Quarterly* 18(3): 651–688.

Starr, Sonja B., and M. Marit Rehavi. 2013. "Mandatory Sentencing and Racial Disparity: Assessing the Role of Prosecutors and the Effects of *Booker*." *Yale Law Journal* 123(1): 2–80.

Steffensmeier, Darrell, Jeffery Ulmer, and John Kramer. 1998. "The Interaction of Race, Gender, and Age in Criminal Sentencing: The Punishment Cost of Being Young, Black, and Male." *Criminology* 36(4): 763–798.

Stemen, Don, and Andres F. Rengifo. 2012. "Charting the Evolution of Structure and Determinacy in State Sentencing and Corrections Policies 1970–2010." *Justice Research and Policy* 14(2): 1–46.

Stith, Kate. 2007. "The Arc of the Pendulum: Judges, Prosecutors, and the Exercise of Discretion." *Yale Law Journal* 117(7): 1420–1497.

Stith, Kate, and Jose A. Cabranes. 1998. *Fear of Judging: Sentencing Guidelines in the Federal Courts*. Chicago: University of Chicago Press.

Stuntz, William J. "The Pathological Politics of Criminal Law." 2001. *Michigan Law Review* 100(3): 505–600.
Stuntz, William J. "The Political Constitution of Criminal Justice." 2006. *Harvard Law Review* 119(3): 780–851.
Turner, Susan, Peter W. Greenwood, Elsa Chen, and Terry Fain. 1999. "The Impact of Truth-in-Sentencing and Three Strikes Legislation: Prison Populations, State Budgets, and Crime Rates." *Stanford Law and Policy Review* 11(1): 75–92.
U.S. General Accounting Office [U.S. GAO]. 1990. "Death Penalty Sentencing: Research Indicates Pattern of Racial Disparities." Washington, D.C.: U.S. General Accounting Office.
U.S. Sentencing Commission [USSC]. 2012. *Report on the Continuing Impact of* United States v. Booker *on Federal Sentencing*. Washington, D.C.: U.S. Sentencing Commission.
United States v. Armstrong. 1996. 517 U.S. 456.
United States v. Booker. 2005. 543 U.S. 220.
Van Cleve, Nicole Gonzalez. 2016. *Crook County: Racism and Injustice in America's Largest Criminal Court*. Stanford: Stanford University Press.
Verma, Anjuli. 2015. "The Law-Before: Legacies and Gaps in Penal Reform." *Law & Society Review* 49(4): 847–882.
Vorenberg, James. 1981. "Decent Restraint of Prosecutorial Power." *Harvard Law Review* 94(7): 1521–1573.
Wayte v. United States. 1985. 470 U.S. 598.
Wooldredge, John, and Amy Thistlethwaite. 2004. "Bilevel Disparities in Court Dispositions for Intimate Assault." *Criminology* 42(2): 417–456.
Wright, Ronald F. 2012. "Persistent Localism in the Prosecutor Services of North Carolina." *Crime and Justice* 41(1): 211–264.
Wright, Ronald F. 2017. "Reinventing American Prosecution Systems." *Crime and Justice* 46(1): 395–439.
Wright, Ronald F., and Kay L. Levine. 2017. "Place Matters in Prosecution Research." *Ohio State Journal of Criminal Law* 14(2): 675–704.
Wright, Ronald F., Kay L. Levine, and Marc L. Miller. 2014. "The Many Faces of Prosecution." *Stanford Journal of Criminal Law and Policy* 1: 27–47.
Wright, Ronald, and Marc Miller. 2002. "The Screening/Bargaining Tradeoff." *Stanford Law Review* 55(1): 29–118.

CHAPTER 3

TESTING CHARGES

ROGER A. FAIRFAX, JR.

3.1 Introduction

ALTHOUGH there are a number of significant actors in the criminal justice system, none is more consequential than the prosecutor. The prosecutor is the linchpin of the apparatus designed to administer and enforce the criminal law. The most salient feature of the prosecutor's role is the exercise of discretion; that is, the decision whether and what to charge. While this discretion is often described as plenary and virtually boundless, there are mechanisms designed to test the soundness of charges that are brought forward by the prosecutor. These various checks, described below, all serve to screen out meritless and unfounded charges, but they operate in different ways and at different stages of criminal proceedings. Most involve a judge's scrutiny of the charges being advanced by the prosecutor, but the grand jury—despite its shortcomings—features an important *popular* check on prosecutorial discretion and mechanism for testing charges.

3.2 Screening Role of the Prosecutor

The prosecutor plays an outsize role in American criminal justice. With myriad and overlapping criminal prohibitions in state and federal codes, the prosecutor is entrusted with determining which statutes are enforced, which crimes are prosecuted, and—often—which sentences are handed down (*United States v. Batchelder* 1979).

Typically, chief prosecutors in the United States are selected through popular election, although a handful of jurisdictions have chief prosecutors appointed by elected officials (Barkow 2019, 154; Davis 2007, 10–11; Wright 2009, 589). Regardless of how they assume authority, these chief prosecutors set the enforcement priorities for the office and they supervise lower-level colleagues—often referred to as assistant or "line" prosecutors—who handle the day-to-day responsibilities of the prosecuting agency. In the United States, line prosecutors are civil servant lawyers aligned with the Executive Branch of government, unlike in some countries in the continental tradition, such as Italy, in which the prosecutors are affiliated with the judiciary (Caianiello 2015; Luna and Wade 2015), or in most of Australia where minor offenses are prosecuted by specially-trained, non-attorney police officers (Marcus and Waye 2010, 347). Often, prosecutor offices in the United States are divided into units, supervised by more experienced line prosecutors, and organized around certain types of offenses (Wright and Levine 2018, 1671).

The prosecutor plays a multi-faceted role, working closely with law enforcement, advising them and—sometimes—directing them in their investigative activities (Bibas 2001, 1100; Fairfax 2017b, 227). The prosecutor also acts as a screen for charges that law enforcement or citizens seek to have prosecuted. This function of "papering" a case gives the prosecutor significant power to determine what types of crimes are prosecuted in a jurisdiction. The prosecutor also engages closely with defense counsel, often seeking to reach agreement on a pre-trial resolution of criminal charges through a plea bargain. Indeed, the vast majority of criminal convictions in the United States derive from guilty pleas (*Lafler v. Cooper* 2012; Fairfax 2016, 1397–1398). For those cases that do go to trial, the prosecutor is an advocate, litigating preliminary issues that will shape the evidence at trial, presenting that evidence to the fact-finder at trial, and defending convictions in post-trial motions or on appeal after trial. Prosecutors also have other duties, arguably unrelated to these core charging and litigation functions. These include "[f]orensics, correction, clemency" and other policy roles as part of what one commentator as described as prosecutors' "tangential policy portfolio" (Barkow 2019, 145–146).

3.3 Prosecutorial Discretion over Charges

Prosecutors have virtually unfettered discretion to bring criminal charges. For any episode of alleged criminal conduct, there are often dozens of statutes that reasonably could apply. The prosecutor must determine which, among the many criminal prohibitions that could apply, the state will allege in a given case against a given defendant (Fairfax 2011). These decisions involve more than an analysis of whether the elements of a given offense may be satisfied by a potential defendant's conduct. Factors such as enforcement priorities, enforcement resources, and the characteristics of the defendant, including criminal history and the likelihood of recidivism, are but a few that may come into play. This discretion over charge selection extends to determining how a case will be resolved through tools such as charge bargaining, offers of pre-trial diversion or deferred prosecution, or sentence bargaining.

In the context of minor or lower-level offenses, the line prosecutor to whom the case has been assigned often makes charging decisions alone and without any meaningful supervision. However, with more serious or complex offenses, the prosecutorial decision is often made in a more collaborative manner, with supervisory or more senior prosecutors conferring or weighing in on the decision to charge, sometimes after a "prosecution memorandum" has been submitted to the group for review (United States Department of Justice, Justice Manual 2020, 9-110.210, 9-110.400, 9-110.815). Despite this practice of consulting senior prosecutors in the United States, there are no rights of appeal created for a defendant desiring a reconsideration of the line prosecutor's decision, as may be found in other systems (United States Department of Justice, Justice Manual 2018, 9-27.130, 9-27.140, 9-27.150; Johnson 2012). That said, the chief (or other high-ranking) prosecutor may observe the occasional practice of informally "sitting down" with defense counsel to give a fair hearing on the merits of prosecution or charges in a given case.

Although this charging discretion is often described as "plenary," there are sometimes guidelines prosecutors can consult to help guide that discretion. A prosecuting agency could adopt guidelines to help channel or cabin a prosecutor's discretion. For example, a set of guidelines referred to as the Principles of Federal Prosecution provide guidance to federal prosecutors in the exercise of their prosecutorial discretion (United States Department of Justice, Justice Manual 2018, 9-27.000). These guidelines do not create any rights for the defendant, but violations theoretically could constitute the basis for internal discipline by the U.S. Department of Justice.

In addition, the American Bar Association promulgated standards that provide guidance to prosecutors in the exercise of their discretion (American Bar Association Criminal Justice Standards 2015). The Criminal Justice Standards complement the ethical rules that guide prosecutorial discretion as a matter of professional responsibility (American Bar Association, Model Code of Professional Responsibility 1969, Disciplinary Rule 7-103; American Bar Association, Model Rules of Professional Conduct 1983, 3.8). Failure to adhere to the ethical rules of the state in which the prosecutor practices or is licensed can lead to professional discipline and even disbarment. Nevertheless, the prosecutor's exercise of discretion in a given case is rarely scrutinized and almost never challenged (Davis 2007).

3.4 Testing Charges

Given prosecutors' expansive authority to bring charges and the resulting consequences to the accused, it is essential that there be checks on those charging decisions. The reasons for this are manifold. A prosecutor's decision to charge an offense could be informed by bias or prejudice against a particular defendant. Public passion or sentiment could unduly influence a prosecutor to bring meritless charges against an unpopular defendant. Dubious criminal charges in a high-profile case might be brought to bring down a political enemy, or to advance the prosecutor's own career interests. A weak case might have been permitted to proceed to trial because the prosecutor withheld exculpatory evidence at the preliminary stages. Even where there is little doubt about the factual guilt of the accused, a case might be improperly built upon evidence obtained in violation of the defendant's constitutional rights.

Therefore, the ability to vet or "test" the charges lodged by the prosecutor is crucial to protecting the rights of the defendant, due process, and the integrity of the criminal justice system writ large. Nevertheless, the Supreme Court has explained that there is no independent constitutional right to judicial review of the decision to prosecute or bring charges (*Albright v. Oliver* 1994; *Gerstein v. Pugh* 1975). However, there are a variety of checks on the prosecutorial decision to charge that derive from specific federal or state constitutional commands—such as the Fourth Amendment prohibition on seizures in the absence of probable cause, the Fifth Amendment's Grand Jury Clause, and the Due Process Clauses of the Fifth and Fourteenth Amendments—or statutes, rules, or ethical provisions. These mechanisms for "testing charges" may be grouped into several categories, from initial charges during the very earliest engagement in the criminal process to the time after jeopardy has attached and even after a guilty verdict has been rendered.

In some legal systems outside the United States, victims of alleged crimes (and sometimes other people) can obtain administrative review within the prosecutorial service when a prosecutor *declines* to bring charges (Johnson 2012). In this chapter, however, we primarily direct our attention to review of prosecutor decisions to file charges.

3.5 Initial Charges

3.5.1 Arrests Pursuant to Warrant

Many times, the earliest test of charges in a criminal case comes about in connection with the arrest of the alleged offender. In situations in which there is an arrest warrant, the prosecutor often will have obtained a criminal complaint, which means that he or she has demonstrated to a neutral magistrate that there is probable cause to believe that an offense has been committed and that the alleged offender committed it. The criminal complaint is the first and earliest charging document and gives law enforcement the right to obtain an arrest warrant or, if it is preferable, a summons to bring in the defendant to answer charges.

When the prosecutor is directly engaged in the process of procuring a warrant (Gold 2014, 1646), the prosecutor typically establishes the probable cause necessary to obtain the underlying criminal complaint by presenting evidence—often in unchallenged hearsay form—through a sworn testimonial affidavit by one of the lead law enforcement officers on the case. Although the evidentiary standards are much more relaxed than those governing an eventual trial, the process does represent at least an early assessment of the credibility of the law enforcement officer, who is often one of the government's central witnesses at trial. If the neutral magistrate is persuaded that probable cause is established by the evidence and testimony presented by the prosecutor, then the criminal complaint will issue. However, if the evidence and testimony do not persuade the magistrate that probable cause exists, then the criminal complaint will not be approved and the arrest warrant will be denied.

3.5.2 Probable Cause Hearing Following a Warrantless Arrest

In the case of a warrantless arrest, the prosecutor will have to work with law enforcement to establish probable cause for the underlying charge, certainly if the alleged offender remains in custody, and sometimes even if he or she is not detained. A defendant who is detained pursuant to a warrantless arrest typically is entitled to a probable cause hearing before a judicial officer within forty-eight hours of that arrest (*County of Riverside v. McLaughlin* 1991). Such hearing does not need to be adversarial; no cross-examination of government witnesses or defense presentation of evidence need be permitted. However, the hearing does require that the prosecutor present enough evidence to convince the judicial officer that probable cause exists to justify continued detention.

3.5.3 Preliminary Hearing

There is sometimes a mechanism for the judicial evaluation of charges at the bail and pre-trial detention stage. However, this assessment is usually combined with the other early stage evaluations of charges and does not represent a significant distinct opportunity for the testing of charges. By contrast, the preliminary hearing is typically the most robust and formal mechanism for the testing of initial charges. The preliminary hearing is often an adversarial hearing, at which the government must present witnesses and evidence sufficient to establish probable cause. The defense counsel may cross-examine government witnesses and often has the ability to present evidence. The presiding judge may discharge the defendant and dismiss the case if she is not satisfied that the government has presented evidence establishing probable cause (Fairfax 2017a, 36–37).

Preliminary hearings can create very real strategic advantages for the defense:

> With its requirement that [the] government offer testimony and evidence sufficient to establish probable cause, there can be significant advantages to the defendant who receives a preliminary hearing. The hearing forces the government to tip its hand as to the theory of the case very early in the proceedings. Good defense attorneys will use the [preliminary] hearing as an opportunity for fact discovery they otherwise would not have had at this stage of the case. Also, because the proceedings are on the record, the [preliminary] hearing "locks in" the testimony of the testifying case agent or other important fact witnesses for the government. Thus, the early testimony can serve as the basis for impeachment if the witness's testimony at trial strays from that given at the [preliminary] hearing in the beginning stages of the case.
>
> (Fairfax 2017a, 36)

To be sure, despite the opportunity for defense discovery and the locking in of government witness testimony, there are significant limitations to the effectiveness of preliminary hearings for testing charges. First, hearsay evidence is generally permissible, so prosecutors will often use an experienced law enforcement officer rather than a lay witness to testify in a summary fashion as to the essential facts related to the elements of the crime. Second, a savvy prosecutor will attempt to limit the efficacy of the defense "fishing expedition" at the preliminary hearing by keeping the direct examination very narrow, thus limiting the scope of cross-examination. Finally, and just as importantly, defense counsel generally cannot object to the evidence presented at this hearing on the grounds that it was illegally seized (Fairfax 2017a, 36–37).

In some jurisdictions, these limitations may result in a high incidence of defense counsel's waiver of the preliminary hearing. Nevertheless, the preliminary hearing, which is generally sought after by defendants, represents enough of a burden and check on prosecutors and their charging discretion that they often seek to obviate the need for the hearing. This can typically be done by obtaining a grand jury indictment prior to the deadline for holding a preliminary hearing. As a result, prosecutors will often have an incentive to move expeditiously toward obtaining a grand jury indictment, which generally cuts off the entitlement to a preliminary hearing (*Kaley v. United States* 2014).

Whether a case of a formal complaint and arrest warrant, or where there has been a showing of probable cause after a warrantless arrest, an independent judicial officer reviews the charges and determines whether probable cause exists. This judicial scrutiny of the prosecutor's proposed charges represents an early mechanism for testing charges.

3.6 Formal Charges

3.6.1 The Grand Jury

Although earlier charging stages could just as easily be termed "formal," the grand jury stage—for those jurisdictions requiring grand jury indictment—is the point at which the charges likely to drive the trial are crystallized. The grand jury is a lay body, typically numbering between twelve and twenty-three persons, called upon to determine whether there is sufficient evidence supporting allegations against an accused. In many jurisdictions, the government is powerless to force a defendant to stand trial unless a grand jury first returns an indictment. The grand jury also has significant authority to compel sworn testimony and the production of tangible evidence. As such, the grand jury is a powerful tool used by law enforcement to investigate crime (Fairfax 2010).

The grand jury has a proud and robust history, having evolved from its fourteenth-century origins as a primarily accusatory body:

> The grand jury began to earn its reputation as a protection for the accused over the next few centuries, as grand-jury indictment became a prerequisite for criminal prosecution and after high-profile instances of English grand juries refusing attempts to prosecute religious rivals of the monarchy. In the eighteenth century, American colonial grand juries followed suit, using their power to frustrate the Crown's prosecutions as a form of resistance to, and protest of, monarchical rule. . . . The level of respect accorded to the grand jury by the Founding generation led to the inclusion of the right to grand-jury indictment in the Bill of Rights.
>
> (Fairfax 2017d, 6–7)

Grand jury indictment is mandated by the Fifth Amendment to the U.S. Constitution for the prosecution of serious crimes in federal court. However, the U.S. Supreme Court held in the late nineteenth century that the Fifth Amendment's right to grand jury indictment is not incorporated through the Fourteenth Amendment to apply to the states (*Hurtado v. California* 1884). Indeed, the right to grand jury indictment stands virtually alone as a core criminal procedural right in the Bill of Rights that does not constrain the states (*Timbs v. Indiana* 2019; *Ramos v. Louisiana* 2020). To date, however, about half of the states require grand jury indictment for serious state crimes, and most give the prosecutor the option of a grand jury indictment in criminal cases.

However, after England, from which the American grand jury tradition derives, abolished the grand jury between World Wars I and II, there were legislative efforts in the United States to eliminate the federal grand jury. Critics of the grand jury often cited as unnecessary and unjustified the expense of the grand jury's scrutiny of criminal charges when there are professional prosecutors and other mechanisms to ensure proper review (Fairfax 2008, 428–430). Although these grand jury abolition efforts were unsuccessful, they signaled the diminished respect accorded the grand jury in many quarters (Leipold 1995; Fairfax 2010).

Although there is a great deal of dispute regarding the modern efficacy and relevance of the grand jury (Fairfax 2010), one undeniable function played by the institution is the testing of charges proposed by the prosecutor (Fairfax 2008; Kuckes 2006). The grand jury determines whether there is probable cause to support the charges presented by the prosecutor. If the grand jurors vote to approve proposed charges, then an indictment issues. If, however, the grand jurors do not concur in the charges, the prosecution may not go forward. In this way, the grand jury operates as a check on the prosecutor's ability to bring a criminal case to trial.

There are features of the grand jury's testing of charges that set it apart from the earlier instances. First, the earlier mechanisms for testing prosecutorial charges are employed before the case has fully taken shape. Probable cause hearings and preliminary hearings take place in the earliest stages of the case and often focus on just one of the charges that may eventually be brought against the defendant. Indeed, this singular charge may not even be part of the core charges that drive the disposition of the case in the end. However, by the grand jury stage, the prosecutor typically has made a determination of the full scope of the allegations underpinning the case against the defendant, and the full panoply of charges that will be pursued.

The grand jury also can be distinguished from probable cause hearings and preliminary hearings in that it represents a *popular* check on prosecutorial charging decisions. As Justice Harlan explained in his dissent in *Hurtado v. California*, "[O]ne of the peculiar benefits of the grand jury system, as it exists in this country, is that it is composed, as a general rule, of private persons who do not hold office at the will of the government, or at the will of the voters" (*Hurtado v. California* 1884, 554). Lay grand jurors necessarily bring a different perspective to the task of evaluating proposed charges than do judicial officers, and the grand jury represents an additional protection of individual liberty—particularly for those defendants who might be deemed unpopular—given its ability to protect against unfounded charges against the "weak and helpless—proscribed, perhaps, because of their race, or pursued by an unreasoning public clamor" (*Hurtado v. California* 1884, 554–555; *Powell v. Alabama* 1932; *Norris v. Alabama* 1935; Carter 2007).

The grand jury's feature of lay participation also presents a number of concrete enhancements to the process of testing charges and certain advantages to prosecutors. Although not learned in the law, lay grand jurors offer a common-sense view more representative of community norms (Fairfax 2008, 2016). As such, the grand jury can perform as a sounding board of sorts for the prosecutor, who can audition theories of the prosecution before a cross-section of the community (Fairfax 2008). This provides the prosecutor ready feedback on the reasonableness or viability of criminal charges before proceeding to trial, when jeopardy attaches. The grand jury process also assists the prosecutor in sharpening the presentation of evidence and weeding out witness testimony that proves damaging or ineffective.

Beyond facilitating the testing of the efficacy of evidence and prosecution theories of proof, the grand jury, as a representative of the community, can also play a role in influencing the prosecutor's exercise of discretion. Even for charges for which the prosecutor has sufficient evidence (admissible proof beyond a reasonable doubt), the grand jury can provide feedback on the wisdom of bringing a particular criminal charge. Indeed, the grand jury has the power, if not the right, to decline to approve an indictment on grounds beyond the sufficiency of the evidence, including the equities associated with bringing a criminal charge that the prosecutor is able to prove (Fairfax 2008).

These features of the grand jury function notwithstanding, there are well-established criticisms of its ability to effectively test charges. The grand jury has long been cast as a mere tool of the prosecution—a rubber stamp that does not represent a significant check on prosecutorial charging decisions (Leipold 1995). The primary arguments for this critique are that the prosecutor acts as both advocate for the government and sole legal advisor to the grand jury, runs the grand jury sessions in secret without defense or third-party scrutiny of the proceedings, and controls the scope of evidentiary presentation to the grand jury and is not bound by evidentiary or constitutional limits on what the grand jurors can consider, or constitutional mandates to disclose exculpatory evidence. To be sure, despite the fact that many states have modeled their grand jury procedures after the federal system (Md. Cts. & Jud. Proc. Code § 8-507; Mass. R. Crim. P. 5; Minn. Statutes § 628.41; Texas Code of Crim. Proc. Art. 20.02[a]), some states have adopted alternate approaches that bolster the grand jury's ability to serve as a meaningful check on the prosecutor (NY Crim. Pro. Law §§ 190.50, 190.52). Nevertheless, many of the aforementioned critiques are fair observations, and are the subject of longstanding reform efforts (National Association of Criminal Defense Lawyers 2000; Fairfax 2010, 346–350; Fairfax 2017c, 403).

However, many consider the single most powerful criticism of the efficacy of the grand jury in testing charges the fact that grand juries return an indictment in nearly every case in which prosecutors ask them to. For example, a recent U.S. Department of Justice study of federal grand juries showed that grand juries refused indictments in only eleven of the over 160,000 federal criminal cases prosecuted in a certain year (Bureau of Justice Statistics 2013, 12; Casselman 2014). The high rate of approval of prosecutors' proposed charges has received even greater scrutiny in the wake of many high-profile grand jury decisions not to indict police officers accused of the unjustified killings of unarmed African Americans (Fairfax 2017c, 403). In 2014, a Missouri grand jury declined to indict Darren Wilson, a police officer who shot and killed an unarmed African American teenager, Michael Brown, who was weeks from starting college. That same year, a Staten Island, New York grand jury declined to indict Daniel Pantaleo, a police officer who administered a prohibited chokehold that killed an unarmed 43-year-old father, Eric Garner, who was suspected of selling loose cigarettes (Fairfax 2017c, 399–400). These two cases galvanized a national and international movement, Black Lives Matter, and highlighted the seeming inability of the grand jury to provide accountability for law enforcement officers accused of killing unarmed African Americans (Fairfax 2017b, 214–216, 219–220). Unfortunately, this pattern would repeat itself in subsequent cases in which grand juries failed to indict officers who killed 12-year-old Tamir Rice and 26-year-old Breonna Taylor in highly publicized incidents (Fairfax 2017b, 217-218; Berman 2020; Dewan 2020).

That disconnect aside, the grand jury's overwhelming tendency to approve charges is certainly a damning critique. However, the statistics may not tell the entire story, as there are reasonable explanations for the high rate of indictment. First, it must be remembered that the probable-cause standard employed by grand juries is a relatively modest threshold to meet compared to the proof-beyond-a-reasonable-doubt standard required at trial. Furthermore, the prosecutor in the grand jury is unencumbered by evidentiary rules, fully free to use hearsay evidence and other evidence that would be inadmissible at trial. In addition, prosecutors have the ability to poll the grand jury informally to obtain an indication of how the grand jurors perceive the strengths and weaknesses of the case before requesting that the grand jurors vote on the indictment. If there are issues that would jeopardize obtaining a probable-cause finding, the prosecutor could present additional evidence to fill any gaps, or could simply choose not to request a vote. Either way, the statistics would not reflect a declination by the grand jury (Fairfax 2017d, 12).

That said, there are ways in which the grand jury process could be enhanced to make it a more robust check on the charging decisions of prosecutors. Among these are extending to the defendant the right to testify before the grand jury, requiring the prosecutor to present exculpatory evidence to the grand jury, disclosing to the defendant the legal instructions given to the grand jurors, and making a neutral legal advisor available to the grand jury (Fairfax 2017d, 18). Indeed, some states already have embraced a number of these proposed reforms. For example, New York state procedure gives the defendant the right to testify in the grand jury proceeding, and permits an attorney for a testifying witness to be present in the grand jury during the testimony (NY Crim. Pro. Law §§ 190.50, 190.52).

3.6.2 Post-arraignment

Following formal arraignment on criminal charges, pre-trial opportunities for testing of charges are generally very limited. A criminal defendant has a limited ability to move to dismiss the charges in a criminal case, although such opportunity is typically confined to issues unrelated to the factual merits of the charges. For example, a motion to dismiss may be allowed because of procedural irregularities associated with the initiation of criminal proceedings, the failure of the charging document to allege conduct falling within the terms of the criminal statute, or a meritorious challenge to the constitutionality of the statute under which the defendant is being charged. Likewise, a court may grant a pre-trial motion to dismiss because of prosecutorial misconduct, or matters relating to discovery violations on the part of the government, or a violation of a defendant's constitutional or statutory speedy trial rights.

However, there is a context in which a post-arraignment, pre-trial assessment of the merits would be proper—when a motion to suppress evidence is dispositive. When a defendant's successful motion to suppress evidence results in the exclusion of key evidence in a case—such as the firearm in a felon-in-possession of a firearm case, or the narcotics in a narcotics possession case—it often leads to the court dismissing the charges.

Finally, when a court considers a guilty plea—whether before or after arraignment on formal charges, it will determine whether there exists a factual basis for the guilty plea (Fairfax 2016). To be sure, this factual determination is largely pro forma, as the defendant presumably has admitted the conduct underlying the charged offense, and there is typically a stipulated statement of facts to which the defendant and the government have agreed. However, the court is tasked with satisfying itself that, were the case to proceed to trial, the government would be able to produce sufficient admissible evidence to establish every element of the crime beyond a reasonable doubt. Therefore, the court's review of the factual basis for the plea does represent another mechanism for testing a prosecutor's charges.

3.6.3 Trial

Although the vast majority of convictions in the United States come by way of the guilty plea process described above, the bench trial or jury trial—and its concomitant higher evidentiary burden of proof beyond a reasonable doubt—operates as the most powerful check on the prosecutor's charging decision. The proof beyond a reasonable doubt standard, which is similar to burdens of proof employed in the criminal adjudication systems of other countries around the world, is a constitutional fixture in the United States (OSCE 2017; Secli 2019; Zongzhi 2014). As the United States Supreme Court has made clear, "[l]est there remain any doubt about the constitutional stature of the reasonable-doubt standard, we explicitly hold that the Due Process Clause protects the accused against conviction except upon proof beyond a reasonable doubt of every fact necessary to constitute the crime with which he is charged" (*In re Winship*, 1970). The Court in *Winship* went on to explain the role that the standard plays in testing charges:

> The reasonable-doubt standard plays a vital role in the American scheme of criminal procedure. It is a prime instrument for reducing the risk of convictions resting on factual error. The standard provides concrete substance for the presumption of innocence—that bedrock "axiomatic and elementary" principle whose "enforcement lies at the foundation of the administration of our criminal law."

At trial, the fact-finder obviously has the opportunity to consider the evidence presented, make credibility determinations, and render judgment on the allegations brought forward by the prosecutor. Applying the aforementioned reasonable doubt standard, the fact-finder serves as a check on the prosecutor's charging decision. In the case of a jury trial, this is a *popular* check. The United States Supreme Court, in the case guaranteeing jury trial in all state cases involving serious crimes, illuminates the crucial role of jury trial in testing charges brought against an accused by the government:

> The right to jury trial is granted to criminal defendants in order to prevent oppression by the Government. Those who wrote our constitutions knew from history and experience that it was necessary to protect against unfounded criminal charges brought to eliminate enemies and against judges too responsive to the voice of higher authority. The framers of the constitutions strove to create an independent judiciary but insisted upon further protection against arbitrary action. Providing an accused with the right to be tried by a jury of his peers gave him an inestimable safeguard against the corrupt or overzealous prosecutor and against the compliant, biased, or eccentric judge.
>
> (*Duncan v. Louisiana* 1968)

Over the past two decades, the U.S. Supreme Court has further bolstered the importance of the right to trial by jury, holding the Sixth Amendment requires that factual determinations traditionally associated with the sentencing decision must be made by a jury rather than a judge in certain circumstances (*Apprendi v. New Jersey* 2000; *Blakeley v. Washington* 2004; *United States v. Booker* 2005).

However, even where the trial is without a jury, a judge is duty bound to apply the same proof beyond a reasonable doubt standard. The judge also has a role to play in the jury trial context, considering motions for judgment of acquittal. Such motions, which can be made by a defendant after the government's case-in-chief, the defendant's case, or after the verdict, require the judge to determine whether, after viewing the evidence in the light most favorable to the government, no reasonable jury could find proof beyond a reasonable doubt (Federal Rule of Criminal Procedure 2018, 29). Thus, the judge presiding over a jury trial has tremendous power to test the prosecutor's charges, including even overturning a jury's verdict of guilty if she feels the evidence did not support it.

3.6.4 Post-trial, Appeal, and Collateral Review

Aside from the consideration of a post-verdict motion for judgment of acquittal, there are other post-trial mechanisms for testing charges in a criminal case. A judge entertaining a motion for a new trial may determine that the evidence does not support a conviction. The standard of review for a motion for a new trial is different from that for a motion for judgment of acquittal, in that the former permits the judge to make her own assessment of the weight of the evidence and the credibility of the witnesses (Federal Rule of Criminal Procedure 2018, 33). By contrast, the standard for a motion for judgment of acquittal, as discussed above, is whether, after viewing the evidence in the light most favorable to the government, no reasonable person could find proof beyond a reasonable doubt. This "light most favorable" standard is the same used on appeal when a defendant challenges a guilty verdict on the grounds of sufficiency of the evidence (*Jackson v. Virginia* 1979). Finally, post-conviction actual innocence claims face procedural hurdles but may enjoy collateral review under prevailing law (Litman 2018, 423–436).

3.7 Conclusion

Scrutiny of the prosecutor's charges is an important feature of due process. There are a number of opportunities for the testing of criminal charges, either at trial or during post-trial proceedings, appeal, or collateral review. In addition, there might be the ability to utilize civil remedies to challenge improper prosecutorial decisions to charge, although such avenues have been severely limited by the courts (*Bivens v. Six Unknown Named Agents* 1971; 42 U.S.C. § 1983; *Albright v. Oliver* 1994; *Connick v. Thompson* 2011). However, given the "economic, reputational, and personal harm" and other burdens that are visited upon an accused when he or she is charged with a criminal offense (Kaley 2014), it is essential to have mechanisms for testing a prosecutor's charges earlier in the criminal process, prior to trial. Of these, the most robust are the preliminary hearing and the grand jury, with the latter having the most potential, if properly utilized, to insert a popular check on prosecutorial charging decisions and to play its "historical role of protecting individuals from unjust persecution" (*Gerstein v. Pugh* 1975, 117).

References

42 U.S.C. § 1983.

Albright v. Oliver. 1994. 510 U.S. 266.

American Bar Association. 1969. *Model Code of Professional Responsibility*.

American Bar Association. 1983. *Model Rules of Professional Conduct*. https://www.americanbar.org/groups/professional_responsibility/publications/model_rules_of_professional_conduct/

American Bar Association. 1993. *Standards on Criminal Justice: Prosecution Function*. https://www.americanbar.org/groups/criminal_justice/standards/ProsecutionFunctionFourthEdition/

Apprendi v. New Jersey. 2000. 530 U.S. 466.

Barkow, Rachel E. 2019. *Prisoners of Politics: Breaking the Cycle of Mass Incarceration*. Cambridge, MA: Harvard University Press.

Berman, Mark. 2020. "Breonna Taylor's Case Shines Spotlight on Grand Juries, Which Usually Operate Out of Public Eye," *Washington Post*, October 2, 2020.

Bibas, Stephanos. 2001. "Judicial Fact-Finding and Sentence Enhancements in a World of Guilty Pleas." *Yale Law Journal* 110(7): 1097–1185.

Bivens v. Six Unknown Named Agents. 1971. 403 U.S. 388.

Blakeley v. Washington. 2004. 542 U.S. 296.

Bureau of Justice Statistics. 2013. *U.S. Department of Justice, Federal Justice Statistics 2010—Statistical Tables*.

Caianiello, Michele. 2015. "The Italian Public Prosecutor: An Inquisitorial Figure in Adversarial Proceedings?" In *The Prosecutor in Transnational Perspective*. Edited by Erik Luna and Marianne Wade, 250–267. Oxford: Oxford University Press.

County of Riverside v. McLaughlin. 1991. 500 U.S. 44.

Carter, Dan T. 2007. *Scottsboro: A Tragedy of the American South*. Baton Rouge: Louisiana State University Press.

Casselman, Ben. 2014. "It's Incredibly Rare for a Grand Jury to Do What Ferguson's Did." *Five Thirty Eight*, November 24, 2014.

Connick v. Thompson. 2011. 563 U.S. 51.

Davis, Angela J. 2007. *Arbitrary Justice: The Power of the American Prosecutor*. Oxford: Oxford University Press.

Dewan, Shaila et. al. 2020. "In the Breonna Taylor Case, a Battle of Blame Over the Grand Jury." *New York Times*, October 2, 2020.

Duncan v. Louisiana. 1968. 391 U.S. 145.

Fairfax, Roger A., Jr. 2008. "Grand Jury Discretion and Constitutional Design." *Cornell Law Review* 93(4): 703–763.

Fairfax, Roger A., Jr. 2010. "Grand Jury 2.0: Toward a Functional Makeover of the Ancient Bulwark of Liberty." *William and Mary Bill of Rights Journal* 19(2): 339–368.

Fairfax, Roger A., Jr. 2011. "Prosecutorial Nullification." *Boston College Law Review* 52(4): 1243–1281.

Fairfax, Roger A., Jr. 2016. "Thinking outside the Jury Box: Deploying the Grand Jury in the Guilty Plea Process." *William and Mary Law Review* 57(4): 1395–1413.

Fairfax, Roger A., Jr. 2017a. *Adjudicatory Criminal Procedure: Cases, Statutes and Materials*. St. Paul: West Academic.

Fairfax, Roger A., Jr. 2017b. "The Grand Jury and Police Violence against Black Men." In *Policing the Black Man: Arrest, Prosecution, and Imprisonment*. Edited by Angela J. Davis, 209–233. New York: Penguin Random House.

Fairfax, Roger A., Jr. 2017c. "The Grand Jury's Role in the Prosecution of Unjustified Police Killings—Challenges and Solutions." *Harvard Civil Rights-Civil Liberties Law Review* 52(2): 397–419.

Fairfax, Roger A., Jr. 2017d. "Grand Jury." In *Academy for Justice: Reforming Criminal Justice*. Edited by Erik Luna, vol. 3, 5–20. Phoenix: Academy for Justice.

Federal Rules of Criminal Procedure 29, 33. 2018.

Gerstein v. Pugh. 1975. 420 U.S. 103.

Gold, Russell M. 2014. "Beyond the Judicial Fourth Amendment: The Prosecutor's Role." *U.C. Davis Law Review* 47(5): 1591–1666.

Hurtado v. California. 1884. 110 U.S. 516.

In re Winship. 1970. 397 U.S. 358.

Jackson v. Virginia. 1979. 443 U.S. 307.

Johnson, David T. 2012. "Japan's Prosecution System." *Crime and Justice* 41(1): 35–74.

Kaley v. United States. 2014. 571 U.S. 320.

Kuckes, Niki. 2006. "The Democratic Prosecutor: Explaining the Constitutional Function of the Federal Grand Jury." *Georgetown Law Journal* 94(5): 1265–1318.

Lafler v. Cooper. 2012. 566 U.S. 166.

Leipold, Andrew D. 1995. "Why Grand Juries Do Not (and Cannot) Protect the Accused." *Cornell Law Review* 80(2): 260–324.

Litman, Leah M. 2018. "Legal Innocence and Federal Habeas." *Virginia Law Review* 104(3): 417–495.

Luna, Erik, and Marianne Wade, eds. 2015. *The Prosecutor in Transnational Perspective*. Oxford: Oxford University Press.

Marcus, Paul, and Vicki Waye. 2010. "Australia and the United States: Two Common Criminal Justice Systems Uncommonly at Odds, Part 2." *Tulane Journal of International and Comparative Law* 18(2): 335–401.

Md. Cts. & Jud. Proc. Code § 8-507.

Mass. R. Crim. P. 5.

Minn. Statutes § 628.41.

Mo. Rev. Statutes. 2018. 540.021.

National Association of Criminal Defense Lawyers. 2000. *Federal Grand Jury Bill of Rights*.

NY Crim. Pro. Law §§ 190.50, 190.52

Norris v. Alabama. 1935. 294 U.S. 587.

Organization for Security and Cooperation in Europe (OSCE). 2017. *Doubt in Favour of the Defendant, Guilty beyond a Reasonable Doubt: Comparative Study*. Helsinki: Organization for Security and Cooperation in Europe.

Powell v. Alabama. 1932. 287 U.S. 45.

Ramos v. Louisiana. 2020. 590 U.S. ___, 140 S. Ct. 1390.

Seclì, Chiara. 2019. "Reaching the 'Beyond Reasonable Doubt' Standard in International Criminal Law Cases: A Comparison with Italian Doctrine and Jurisprudence." *Faculty of Law, Stockholm University Research Paper No. 67*.

Texas Code of Crim. Proc. Art. 20.02(a).

Timbs v. Indiana. 2019. 586 U.S. __, 139 S. Ct. 682.

United States Department of Justice, Justice Manual. 2018.

United States v. Batchelder. 1979. 442 U.S. 114.
United States v. Booker. 2005. 543 U.S. 220.
Wright, Ronald F. 2009. "How Prosecutor Elections Fail Us." *Ohio State Journal of Criminal Law* 6(2): 581–610.
Wright, Ronald L., and Kay L. Levine. 2018. "Career Motivations of State Prosecutors." *George Washington Law Review* 86(6): 1667–1710.
Zongzhi, Long. 2014. "'Beyond Reasonable Doubt' in the Chinese Legal Context." *Peking University Law Journal* 1(2): 339–371.

CHAPTER 4

PROSECUTORS AND PLEA BARGAINING

BRIAN D. JOHNSON AND RAQUEL HERNANDEZ

4.1 Introduction

As Supreme Court Justice Anthony Kennedy opined, plea bargaining "is not some adjunct to the criminal justice system; it is the criminal justice system" (*Missouri v. Frye* 2012). More than 95 percent of criminal convictions in American courts result from a guilty plea. In large urban courts (Reaves 2013) and in the federal justice system (Johnson 2019a) it exceeds 97 percent, and for misdemeanor offenses it is even higher (Kutateladze and Lawson 2018). This equates roughly to a guilty plea every two seconds during normal working hours (Colquitt 2001), and many county courts have not experienced a single trial in years (Wright et al. 2018). Without a doubt, criminal punishment in America today is the product of negotiated justice.

Although diverse explanations exist for the ubiquity of plea bargaining (Smith 2005), court actors tend to view it as an organizational necessity that ensures efficient case processing and high conviction rates. Popular views suggest plea bargaining prevents untenable backlogs that would grind the system to a halt, though empirical evidence is at best equivocal (Johnson 2019a; Smith 2005; Wooldredge 1989). Many argue that guilty pleas are essential to the allocation of appropriate punishment, mitigation of harsh sentences, and effective diversion of offenders, especially in "dead-bang" cases with clearly established factual guilt. Historically, the United States Supreme Court has taken a minimalist approach in regulating plea-bargaining in America, and its use has increasingly spread to other international contexts (Brook et al. 2016; Combs 2002; Turner 2009).

Despite its national omnipresence and growing international popularity, plea bargaining remains highly controversial. Critics maintain that proportionality and transparency in plea bargaining are sacrificed on the altar of organizational efficiency. Legal scholars emphasize its potential to result in coercion, contribute to false guilty pleas and wrongful convictions, and exacerbate social inequalities (Alschuler 1979, 1981; Bibas 2004; McCoy 2005). They note that plea agreements require defendants to forfeit constitutional due process rights and often lead to convictions that differ substantially from actual offense behavior (Johnson 2019). Research also provides strong evidence of a "trial penalty" in punishment, in which defendants convicted at trial receive substantially harsher sentences (Johnson 2019a). Some commentators maintain plea bargaining played a critical role in mass incarceration in America (Pfaff 2017), and legal scholars, social scientists, and policy pundits agree that significant reforms are needed.

This chapter examines the rise of plea bargaining in America, paying special attention to the growing power of criminal prosecutors.[1] It includes a normative discussion of ongoing philosophical debates and a review of the current state of empirical research, along with a summary of fruitful directions for future work. It identifies promising policy interventions to help constrain undue prosecutorial discretion, balance negotiating leverage in plea bargaining, and enhance fairness and accountability in one of the most consequential and least scrutinized outcomes in the justice system—the negotiated guilty plea.

4.2 The Historical Rise of Plea Bargaining

Jury trials have long been at the heart of the American system of justice (Vidmar and Hans 2007). In colonial America, virtually every criminal case was decided by jury, ensuring democratic representation and public legitimacy (Hans et al. 1986). Guilty pleas began their ascent in the mid-nineteenth century as part of the bureaucratization of justice in urban jurisdictions (Walker 1998). According to Smith (2005), four factors were primarily responsible for the rise of plea bargaining: (1) increased caseloads, (2) the juridification of law resulting in longer and more complex trials, (3) the advent of public prosecutors, which routinized guilty pleas, and (4) historical factors such as public elections of court officials and the introduction of suspended sentences.

The rise of plea bargaining is often viewed as the direct result of growing caseloads, though historians and legal scholars continue to disagree (Alschuler 1983; Feeley 1979; McCoy 2005; Meeker and Pontell 1985; Nardull 1979; Wooldredge 1989). In all likelihood, caseload pressure is important but not the sole explanation for plea bargaining. Both Langbein (1992) and Feeley (1997) note that early trials were summary affairs and suggest their increased complexity popularized plea bargaining. Friedman and Percival (1981) point to advances in policing that improved evidence quality, and other scholars highlight public elections that incentivized conviction rates (Ellis 2012; Ramsey 2002). More recent work emphasizes contemporary sentencing enhancements, which some have likened to discretionary "hammers" (Lynch 2016) that are selectively wielded to "bludgeon defendants into effectively coerced plea bargains" (Rakoff 2014, 4).

One underappreciated explanation for the rise in plea bargaining is the failure of the Supreme Court to effectively regulate it. Early court cases identified key legal challenges. In 1958, a federal appeals judge opined that "Justice and liberty are not the subjects of bargaining and barter" (*Sheldon v. United States* 1958). Shortly after, another court declared that "a plea of guilty induced by a promise of lenient treatment is an involuntary plea and hence void" (*Scott v. United States* 1965). By the 1970s, however, the future of plea bargaining was decided when the high court ruled it was "an essential component of the administration of justice" that "is to be encouraged" (*Santobello v. New York* 1970). With the endorsement of the Supreme Court, plea bargaining has become all but immune from appellate review, and over time prosecutors began to hold all of the cards at the negotiation table (Alschuler 1979).

To some extent, the overwhelming dominance of plea bargaining is understandable. Offering putative benefits to all involved, plea bargains result in significant punishment discounts for defendants and defense attorneys (Johnson 2003), clear crowded court dockets for judges (Alschuler 1976), and guarantee conviction for prosecutors while conserving resources and providing a mechanism for settling cases with thorny legal concerns (McCoy 2005). Over time, court actors have come to support the practice (Heumann 1978). Recent sentencing reforms, which are discussed in more detail in the next section, have shifted significant power from judges to prosecutors, allowing them to threaten excessive trial sentences and further contributing to the contemporary dominance of plea bargaining (Johnson 2019a).

4.3 The Rising Power of Prosecutors in Plea Negotiations

The capacious power of the prosecutor remains a focal point of legal scholars, criminal justice researchers, and policymakers alike (Alschuler 1968; Bibas 2004; Johnson et al. 2016; Pfaff 2017). In part, this reflects their expansive control over a wide range of punishment decisions (Bibas 2001; Johnson et al. 2016; Tonry 2012). Prosecutors accept and decline cases, select initial charges, alter or dismiss charges, and administer pre-trial diversion programs. Perhaps most importantly, prosecutors control myriad sentencing enhancements and concessions that can be threatened or selectively applied in the pursuit of a guilty plea. According to some, prosecutors have replaced judges and juries as the "central adjudicator(s) of facts" in the American courts (Lynch 2003, 1404).

Expansion of prosecutorial power in plea bargaining reflects both the impact of modern sentencing reforms and the lack of formal legal oversight in their decisions. First, modern policy reforms have increased the discretionary domain of prosecutors. Sentencing policy in the late twentieth century focused narrowly on judges, placing greater power in the hands of prosecutors (Miethe 1987; Tonry 2012). Mandatory minimums, truth in sentencing, parole abolition, and other sentencing reforms expanded charging options, increased punishment severity, disabled back-end correctional breaks, and elevated the importance of pre-sentence plea negotiations (Bibas 2001; Frase 2000; Miethe 1987). During the "tough on crime" era, punishment ceilings became so high that rational defendants, regardless of their guilt, could find it hard to refuse a plea deal (McCoy 2005). Second, prosecutorial plea decisions have remained largely immune from civic, legal, and academic scrutiny because plea negotiations are not typically part of the public record and not subjected to appellate review (Bibas 2001; Covey 2013). These plea deals are routinely "rubber stamped" by judges to produce de facto sentences (Alschuler 1976), allowing prosecutors to mobilize plea agreements to determine punishment in most criminal cases (Bibas 2001).

The growing leverage of prosecutors in guilty plea negotiations has sparked renewed debates over the merits and demerits of plea bargaining. This discourse reflects underlying value judgments about the relative priority of different purposes of punishment, from utilitarian goals related to moving cases to retributive notions of just deserts. Before evaluating the current state of empirical research, or identifying promising policy reforms, it is useful to review philosophical arguments on the pros and cons of plea bargaining.

4.4 Normative Perspectives on Plea Bargaining

Proponents of plea bargaining maintain that it streamlines case processing, eases conviction in cases with clear guilt, and endows prosecutors with requisite discretion to tailor appropriate punishments (Church 1979; Easterbrook 1992; Feeley 1979; Rosett and Cressey 1976; Ross 2006; Wilkinson 2014). They argue it encourages witness cooperation, maintains workgroup relations, helps settle cases with difficult legal issues, and spares vulnerable victims from testifying at trial (Bibas 2001; Eisenstein et al. 1988; Nardulli et al. 1988). Critics counter that plea bargaining entails systematic coercion that threatens transparency and fairness in punishment, while divesting defendants of their constitutionally guaranteed due process rights (Alschuler 1976, 1981; Covey 2008; McCoy 2005; Stuntz 2011; Wright 2005). They contend it contributes to false guilty pleas and wrongful convictions (Covey 2008; Gross et al. 2005; Langbein 1978; Rakoff 2014; Redlich et al. 2014; Wright 2005), and denounce it as "disaster" (Schulhofer 1992) or "torture" (Langbein 1978), while labeling it a "contrived, synthetic, and perfunctory substitute for real justice" (Blumberg 1974, 29).

Detractors of plea bargaining note that Supreme Court decisions have done little to curtail it. The *Brady* decision required guilty pleas to be both voluntary and knowing

(*Brady v. United States* 1970), meaning defendants must freely enter into them with full awareness of their consequences. However, in *Alford* the Court ruled that a defendant need not explicitly admit guilt for a court to accept a guilty plea (*North Carolina v. Alford* 1970, 38). Subsequent decisions have upheld the prosecutor's right to threaten more severe punishments for trial defendants, including life imprisonment (*Bordenkircher v. Hayes* 1978). Although recent cases ensure assistance of counsel, and require plea offers and their consequences be conveyed to defendants (*Padilla v. Kentucky* 2010; *Lafler v. Cooper* 2012, 170–172; *Missouri v. Frye* 2012), they do little to regulate prosecutorial power or to protect the constitutional rights of defendants. For instance, guilty pleas may be considered informed even when prosecutors fail to disclose exculpatory evidence (*United States v. Ruiz* 2002). The result is that prosecutors have immense leverage to unilaterally determine plea offers with limited defendant recourse or legal challenge.

Critics therefore question whether negotiated guilty plea decisions are truly voluntary (Covey 2008; Langbein 1978; Tata and Gormley 2016), especially when steep plea discounts are paired with the threat of lengthy sentences at trial (Dervan 2015; McCoy 2005; Zottoli et al. 2016). Prosecutors can often threaten uncooperative defendants with excessive trial sentences (Johnson 2019a; Kim 2015; Lynch 2016). The result is that innocent defendants may be persuaded to plead guilty (McCoy 2005), in part because they are seldom well versed in complicated legal argot, may lack social and financial resources, and often rely on public defenders who are incentivized to accept plea deals (Alschuler 2013; Bibas 2004; Sudnow 1965). False guilty pleas are especially likely to occur in cases that involve probation, death sentences, or defendants held in pre-trial detention (Blume and Helm 2014; Feeley 1979; Heaton et al. 2017; Stevenson and Mayson 2017). When plea discounts are large enough, empirical work suggests that innocents will in fact plead guilty (Blume and Helm 2014; Dervan 2015; Turner 2017).

Plea bargaining has also been heavily criticized for its covert nature (Sudnow 1965). According to Turner (2017, 75), it contributes to "incomplete investigations, inadequate disclosure, limited adversarial testing, perfunctory judicial oversight, and sizeable plea discounts," in addition to leading "defendants to plead guilty to crimes different from the ones they committed." Guilty pleas can sidestep discovery because legal statutes typically require full disclosure only at trial. This is exacerbated in offices that use "exploding plea offers" with strict time limits (Zottoli et al. 2016) and in jurisdictions with heavy caseloads and overburdened public defenders (Brown 2005). Plea offers often involve informal negotiations without clearly stated legal rationales or formal appeal mechanisms. Judges retain the authority to reject plea and sentence agreements, but in practice this seldom happens (Nagel and Schulhofer 1992). Judges have little incentive to fully investigate or challenge plea agreements, and many scholars suggest they are routinely "rubber stamped" (Alschuler 1976). Critics therefore emphasize the lack of accountability and legitimacy in plea bargaining, which is consistent with survey research that demonstrates low levels of public support for it (Herzog 2004).

The clandestine nature of plea bargaining also contributes to defendants being convicted of crimes that differ substantially from their actual offense behavior (Johnson and Larroulet 2019; Stemen and Escobar 2019; Sudnow 1965), which can undermine "ordinal proportionality in sentencing" (Roberts and Bradford 2015, 188) and limit the deterrent effects of punishment (Johnson 2019). Importantly, the choice to plead guilty is largely unrelated to retributive notions of desert and culpability (Alschuler 1981). ABA Standards for Guilty Pleas state that guilty pleas should not "be considered by the court as a mitigating factor," yet research evidence demonstrates consistent plea discounts in sentencing (Johnson 2003, 2019a; King et al. 2005). Critics assert that plea bargains are principally unrelated to the major purposes of punishment, which include fair, consistent, and proportional sentences, as well as community protection and crime control (Frase 2005). They also note that, although plea bargains appear to support greater leniency in sentencing, this is only in reference to severe sentences at trial (Alschuler 2013).

Another major critique is that defendants' due process rights are forfeited. Defendants who plead guilty "waive most procedural protections associated with trial" (Turner 2017, 76), including self-incrimination, the right to confront witnesses, appeal the sentence, and challenge ineffective counsel[2] (King and O'Neill 2005). In federal court, plea deals commonly require defendants to also waive their right to detention hearings, to challenge guidelines calculation errors, to file certain motions, and to request mitigating departures (Hofer 2011). For the most part, these standard protocols are in place not because they satisfy the purposes of punishment but because they grease the wheels of organizational efficiency and prevent convictions from being overturned. Moreover, some scholars maintain that the complexity of plea agreements further contributes to uninformed plea deals and diminished public legitimacy (Podgor 2011).

A final normative concern with plea bargaining is that it exacerbates inequalities in the criminal justice system. The nature of plea bargaining makes it a prime target for implicit biases tied to defendant race, ethnicity, and other characteristics (Smith and Levinson 2012). Implicit associations and widespread societal stereotypes are likely to shape prosecutorial assessments of culpability and harm. At the same time, lower status defendants are generally less trusting of the justice system (Hurwitz and Peffley 2005), have less bargaining power to procure favorable settlements (Savitsky 2012), and are more likely to risk harsher sentences at trial (Johnson 2019a). According to one leading critic, plea offers reflect "defense attorney charm" as well as the "race, wealth or bail status of the defendant" (Alschuler 1976, 1125; Bibas 2004).

It is worth noting that academic critiques of plea bargaining are in sharp contrast to strong normative support among court actors. Negotiated pleas reward defendants who admit guilt, maximize limited court resources, and allow prosecutors to individualize punishment. However, they may also coerce defendants into false guilty pleas, limit due process rights, obscure transparency, and contribute to inequalities in punishment. Although a number of empirical studies investigate false guilty pleas and charging disparities, relatively little empirical work focuses explicitly on negotiated guilty pleas in contemporary courts.

4.5 Empirical Research on Plea Bargaining

4.5.1 Wave I

Current assessments of punishment research lament the limited attention to plea bargaining (Johnson et al. 2016; Ulmer 2012). However, a wealth of scholarship dates back to the 1960s and 1970s when plea bargaining research was in its heyday (Alschuler 1968, 1976; Casper 1972; Mather 1973; Newman 1966). The first wave of plea bargaining research, Wave I, began in the 1960s and lasted up to 1980. Landes (1971) is often credited with developing the first formal model of plea bargaining, arguing that the decision to plead guilty depended on "the probability of conviction by trial, the severity of the crime, the availability and productivity of the prosecutor's and defendant's resources, trial versus settlement costs, and attitudes toward risk" (Landes 1971, 61). Other studies added to this discussion, focusing on defendant perspectives (Heumann 1978), judicial anecdotes (Alschuler 1976), and procedural aspects of plea-bargaining, including prosecutorial leverage to induce guilty pleas (Alschuler 1968). Related work examined "going rates" for pleas among typical offenders (Sudnow 1965) or local variations in plea practices across court communities (Eisenstein and Jacob 1977). Seminal work by Nardulli et al. (1988), for instance, distinguished between two models of the guilty plea process: the concessions model, which entailed adversarial bargaining over negotiated outcomes, and the consensus model, based on mutually agreed upon plea discounts. Their analysis of nine felony courts demonstrated that although both types of negotiation exist, the consensus model clearly predominated in most courts.

Although much was learned from this early work, research faltered as academic focus shifted to judicial discretion during the 1980s (Blumstein et al. 1983). Extensive data collections on guilty pleas were discontinued and empirical work on plea bargaining was largely replaced by research on sentencing outcomes (Blumstein et al. 1983; Johnson et al. 2016; Ulmer 2012). The next three decades witnessed a paucity of empirical plea scholarship as policy reforms targeted judicial discretion and further elevated the importance of plea bargaining in criminal court.

4.5.2 Wave II

Studies from about 1980 to the early twenty-first century represent a second wave of research, Wave II, which was primarily restricted to small samples, often focused on specific crimes, like intimate partner violence (e.g., Kingsnorth et al., 1999) or sexual assaults (e.g., LaFree 1980; Spohn et al. 2001), and limited to single charging decisions, like filing (e.g., Albonetti 1987) or case dismissal (Spohn et al. 1987). Most of this work focused on prosecutorial discretion and unwarranted disparity and found that charging decisions primarily reflect offense seriousness, evidence strength, and perceived harm and culpability of defendants. Relatively few studies in Wave II, however, concentrated explicitly on plea bargaining (but see, e.g., Albonetti 1990; Maynard 1982; Miethe 1987).

Evidence for inequalities in the second wave of plea research was inconsistent, suggesting male and minority defendants were often but not always disadvantaged (Kutateladze et al. 2012; Wooldredge and Griffin 2005; Wu 2016). For example, Spohn et al. (1987) reported that decisions to reject or dismiss charges were influenced by race and gender, with Hispanic males most likely to be prosecuted. Albonetti (1986) found that information related to the certainty of conviction influenced charging, with cases involving female and released defendants less likely to be prosecuted. Likewise, Farnworth and Teske (1995) observed that female defendants with no prior records were the most likely to receive charge reductions. Studies during this time also illustrated the importance of victim characteristics, finding that defendants were often treated less favorably in cases with White or female victims (Spears and Spohn 1997; Stolzenberg et al. 2004; Williams and Holcomb 2001). According to Frohmann (1997, 531), these patterns reflected race, class, and gender constructs that shape prosecutorial assessments of "case convictability" based on assessments of the "moral character of persons and of places."

Not all studies during this time revealed inequalities though. Several reports showed little or no evidence of race or gender disparity (Bishop and Frazier 1984; Holmes et al. 1987; Kingsnorth et al. 1998; Nardulli et al. 1988), and select studies found males or minority defendants received more favorable prosecution outcomes (Holmes et al. 1987). For example, Kingsnorth et al. (1998) found no evidence that the racial dyads of offenders and victims influenced the prosecution of sexual assaults, and Wooldredge and Thistlewaite (2004) concluded that African American offenders were less likely to be fully prosecuted for intimate assault. Only a small number of studies examined decisions explicitly related to plea bargaining such as charge or sentence reductions. Miethe (1987) reviewed the impact of sentencing guidelines in Minnesota and found they had minimal impact on preexisting patterns of plea bargaining. Albonetti (1992) analyzed a sample of burglary and robbery cases and found no evidence that charging reductions were related to defendant race or gender.

One important finding to emerge from the second wave of plea research is that defendants who plead guilty receive substantial sentencing discounts (Johnson 2019a). Economic approaches to plea bargaining emphasize that plea negotiations take place "in the shadow of the trial," meaning the threat of harsher trial sentences impacts defendant decision-making (Bibas 2004). Wright and Miller (2003, 1415) suggest that given the primacy of plea bargaining today, trials take "place in the shadow of guilty pleas." Research by Smith (1986) showed that average plea discounts were approximately equal to trial sentences discounted by the probability of acquittal (see also Abrams 2011). However, empirical studies overwhelmingly demonstrate a large "trial tax" at sentencing, indicative of large sentencing differentials for defendants convicted by plea versus trial (Bushway and Redlich 2012; Johnson 2003, 2019a; King et al. 2005; Wright 2005). Similar work shows that certain defendants are less likely to benefit from plea bargains. In general, male, Black, and Latino defendants are significantly less likely to accept plea deals and are disproportionately impacted by trial penalties (Albonetti 1990; Frenzel and Ball 2008; Johnson 2003).

4.5.3 Wave III

Although several important findings emerged from the second wave of plea research, in many ways it was quite limited. In contrast, recent work from the early twenty-first century represents a revival in academic scholarship on plea bargaining that is characterized by significant advances (Johnson et al. 2016). Key characteristics of the latest wave of research, Wave III, include new large-scale data collection efforts, collaborative research-practitioner partnerships, and innovative research questions and methodologies that address key limitations of prior work (e.g., Bushway et al. 2014; Frederick and Stemen 2012; Johnson 2019b; Johnson and Larroulet 2019; Kutateladze 2018; Kutateladze et al. 2016; Metcalfe and Chiricos, 2018; Redlich et al. 2014; Spohn and Tellis 2013; Stemen and Escobar 2019).

First, scholars have begun assembling new datasets that allow for more nuanced and holistic investigations of plea bargaining. Frederick and Stemen (2012), for example, collected detailed data on prosecutors using multiple research methods, including interviews, focus groups, and quantitative analyses. They examined multiple case outcomes in two counties, including plea offers and sentence recommendations. Their findings are complex but confirm that offense severity, evidence strength, and victim characteristics are all key considerations in plea bargaining, and they suggest prosecutors are especially concerned with "doing justice," maintaining public safety, and treating defendants fairly. They also found that a variety of organizational and contextual constraints influenced plea decisions. Similarly, Kutateladze et al. (2014) obtained unprecedented access to plea bargaining data by entering into a collaborative relationship with the District Attorney's Office of New York that provided detailed information on multiple stages of prosecution and sentencing. Among their many conclusions, they found disparities varied across decision-making stages and offense types, but that Black and Latino defendants were most likely to be detained, to receive custodial plea offers, and to be incarcerated. Their work suggests that plea bargaining plays an important role in imprisonment. These unique data collections have spurred a wealth of subsequent studies using novel approaches to study plea bargaining as well (e.g., Johnson and Larroulet 2019; Kutateladze 2018; Kutateladze et al. 2016).

Additional large data collection efforts include qualitative studies of federal prosecutors (Lynch 2016) and studies that link data across criminal justice agencies (Johnson 2019b; Rehavi and Starr 2014; Shermer and Johnson 2010; Spohn and Tellis 2013). Spohn and Tellis (2013), for instance, conducted in-depth analyses of police-prosecutor interactions in sexual assault cases. Shermer and Johnson (2010) linked federal data on prosecution to sentencing data to investigate the impact of charge bargaining on punishment. They found that defendants who had their charges reduced during plea bargaining received sentence lengths that were 19 percent shorter, and newer studies find even larger effect sizes (Johnson 2019b). Related work suggests mandatory minimums are especially important in plea bargaining (Rehavi and Starr 2014; Ulmer et al. 2007). Rehavi and Starr (2014), for example, concluded that racial disparities in federal court are mainly attributable to mandatory minimums being disproportionately applied to Black defendants.

Other emerging data collection efforts are also underway that will invigorate future plea-bargaining research. The non-profit organization Measures for Justice, for example, has collected case processing data from each county in multiple states that can support more comprehensive analyses of guilty pleas and punishment, and other researchers are in the process of collecting detailed multijurisdictional data on plea bargaining and prosecution as part of the broader Safety and Justice Challenge supported by the MacArthur Foundation. New large-scale data compilations that include detailed information on plea bargaining are one of the defining characteristics of the burgeoning Wave III of research on guilty pleas.

A second defining characteristic is new methods of data collection and analysis. Bushway et al. (2014), for example, collected online survey data from a large sample of prosecutors, defense attorneys, and judges to experimentally study the factors that impact plea bargaining. Manipulating hypothetical vignettes in a robbery case, they found that court actors expected plea deals to reduce sentences by four years, on average. They also found that criminal history and evidence strength had strong effects on perceived likelihood of conviction and that the "shadow of the trial" model was mostly supported for prosecutors and defense attorneys but not for judges. Similar work has furthered the study of key variables like case evidence. Redlich et al. (2016) conducted over 1,500 online interviews using hypothetical legal scenarios. They found that criminal history significantly influenced the likelihood of a plea discount and that defense attorneys placed stronger weight on case evidence. Similarly, Kutateladze et al. (2015) investigated the importance of evidence by coding details from case files for misdemeanor marijuana defendants to show that specific types of evidence, such as recordings, eyewitness identifications, or recovered currency, resulted in less favorable plea bargains. Other innovative methods have been developed to investigate the impact of plea bargaining on downstream punishments (Piehl and Bushway 2007; Rehavi and Starr 2014; Wright and Engen 2006), as well as the cumulative effects of disparity across multiple stages of plea bargaining (Johnson and Larroulet 2019; Kurlychek and Johnson 2019; Kutateladze 2018).

An emergent body of scholarship, driven by psychology and law scholars, has also begun to empirically document false guilty pleas and wrongful convictions in plea bargaining (Blume and Helm 2014; Dervan 2015; Dervan and Edkins 2013; Redlich et al. 2014; Redlich et al. 2016). This work finds evidence that innocent defendants will plead guilty, especially when plea-trial sentencing differentials are large, probation or death sentences are possible, and defendants are detained pre-trial (Blume and Helm 2014; Bordens 1984; Gross et al. 2005; Turner 2017; Wright 2005). For example,

Dervan and Edkins (2013, 17) analyzed vignette scenarios that indicated more than half of respondents falsely admitted guilt, leading them to conclude that even though it is challenging to accurately numerate false guilty pleas, "it is clear that plea bargaining has an innocence problem." Qualitative interviews with convicted defendants provide additional evidence. Zottoli et al. (2016) asked about guilty plea experiences and found that about 20 percent of adults and 25 percent of juveniles claimed to be innocent and only reported pleading guilty to obtain the plea discount. Additional work suggests that the innocence problem is greatest in cases with weak evidence because conviction at trial is least certain and prosecutors are motivated to offer larger discounts. Bushway et al. (2014), for example, demonstrate that larger plea reductions occur in cases with weaker evidence. Moreover, the National Registry of Exonerations found that 18 percent of exonerations were the result of false guilty pleas, and some scholars believe many more escape detection (Turner 2017). Given its centrality to core issues of justice, additional empirical research is clearly needed on this important and understudied issue.

Wave III research also boasts avant-garde approaches to understanding race and gender disparities in plea bargaining. Work by Sutton (2013), for example, analyzed sequential case outcomes for a large sample of male felons. Accounting for the cumulative impacts of race and ethnicity, Sutton concluded that Black and Latino defendants were 26 percent more likely to go to prison. Applying multilevel models to data from fifty jurisdictions, Wooldredge et al. (2015) found the effects of race and ethnicity operated indirectly through pre-trial detention, attorney type, prior record, and bond amounts. Kutateladze et al. (2014) also discovered evidence of cumulative disadvantage in New York City. Black and Latino defendants received less favorable outcomes across stages of case processing in misdemeanor marijuana cases. Using analogous data to study plea bargaining, Kutateladze (2018) found that approximately one-third of cases received a charge reduction, mostly at arraignment. Further, Black and Latino defendants were less likely than White defendants to have charges reduced during plea bargaining, while Asian Americans were more likely. Similarly, Metcalfe and Chiricos (2018) analyzed data from a Florida public defender's office and found that Black male defendants were least likely to plead guilty and received the least return for their guilty pleas. Finally, Johnson and Larroulet (2019) examined the average "distance traveled" during plea bargaining and found that it varied systematically across defendants, with negotiated guilty pleas reducing punishment less for male and minority defendants.

Modern studies of plea bargaining have also begun to examine variations across contexts. Franklin (2010) found that the odds of case dismissal were higher in counties with greater poverty and lower in more conservative counties. He suggested low-income communities may be devalued while conservatism elevates punitive attitudes. Stemen and Escobar (2019) gathered unique data from Wisconsin that included prosecutor backgrounds and found that few prosecutor characteristics influenced plea outcomes, but factors related to defense counsel were important in plea bargaining. Relatedly, Johnson (2019b) recently showed that charge reductions vary across federal courts. He reported that the likelihood of a charge reduction is related to court characteristics such as the size, caseload, departure rate, and historical charging norms of the jurisdiction.

Qualitative research reveals comparable jurisdictional variations in plea bargaining. Levine and Wright (2012, 1120) conducted interviews in three prosecutor offices, focusing on the importance of office structure and hierarchy and concluded that attitudes "toward autonomy (or conversely, the team) produce ripple effects" in relationships "with other lawyers and police" that shape the value one "places on achieving consistency across cases." More recently, Lynch (2016) collected data from court observations and in-depth interviews in three federal districts and identified unique organizational mechanisms and norms that prosecutors use to induce guilty pleas in drug cases. In addition to advances in data and methodology, then, Wave III research on plea bargaining has also begun to answer interesting new questions about social inequalities both within and across court contexts.

4.6 New Directions in Plea Bargaining Research

In general, significant improvements have characterized recent empirical work on guilty pleas, including innovations in data and methods, transdisciplinary and collaborative research efforts, and advances in measurement and analysis (Johnson et al. 2016; Spohn 2018). Nevertheless, many unanswered questions remain. Below we discuss remaining limitations and shortcomings that need to be addressed in future plea-bargaining research. These can be grouped broadly into three areas: (1) the operationalization and measurement of key variables, (2) advances in data and methods, and (3) expanding beyond traditional research questions.

First, pervasive measurement issues continue to plague plea bargaining research. For example, most studies are limited to binary measures that capture only whether or not a guilty plea or charge reduction occurs. Few studies carefully investigate the processes that generate guilty pleas or their impact on downstream punishment outcomes. Prosecutors design plea offers from an extensive array of charging and punishment options available within the "depth and distance" of the criminal code (Wright and Engen 2006). Narrowly focusing on single charging outcomes misses the nuance of charging concessions, sentencing enhancements, and the complexity of plea bargaining. It also risks faulty conclusions regarding fairness and equality. Certain types of pleas, like those that reduce felony charges to misdemeanors or invoke mandatory minimums, are especially consequential because they redefine the parameters of punishment. Some recent studies attempt to capture the relative value of a plea (Johnson and Larroulet 2019; Metcalfe and Chiricos 2018; Piehl and Bushway 2007) or account for the timing or type of guilty plea (Brook et al. 2016; LaFree 1985; Johnson 2003; Testa and Johnson 2020), but future studies can develop better ways of capturing the intricate nature of plea bargains.

Future work also needs to expand ways to capture key independent variables, including defendant race and ethnicity and evidentiary quality. Recent work demonstrates important variation within racial groups related to skin tone and appearance that could be extended to guilty pleas (Johnson and King 2017; King and Johnson 2016). Much has also been written about sentencing outcomes of immigrant defendants (Light et al. 2014) but little attention has been devoted to their prosecution, which is especially important in federal courts. At the same time, research shows that the quality of evidence has strong impacts on prosecution (e.g., Albonetti 1987), but data limitations often restrict the ability to capture it in statistical models (Kutateladze et al. 2015). Even when evidentiary measures are available, it can be difficult to quantify overall case strength. Creative research has utilized experimental methods and case vignettes to study evidence (Bushway et al. 2014; Dervan and Edkins 2013), but more research of this ilk is needed.

Second, better data and methods are paramount to sharpening our understanding of the social processes that shape plea bargains. Detailed information collected on the various negotiation stages of plea bargaining is a requisite. Even when researchers are privy to information on initial and final charges, discursive processes at the heart of plea bargaining such as multiple offers are rarely captured. Similarly, plea deals that involve fact stipulations, sentencing agreements, or other concessions beyond number and type of charges need to be collected. Scholars should also work to better contextualize the plea decision by examining it in relation to other key outcomes, including arrest, pre-trial detention, and sentencing options. The ability to track defendants through the justice system has increased remarkably with advances in online case automation, machine learning, and data-linking algorithms (Johnson 2019b; Rehavi and Starr 2014; Shermer and Johnson 2010; Stemen and Escobar 2019). Data collections spearheaded by non-profit and independent organizations, like Measures for Justice and the Vera Institute of Justice, are providing data across stages of the justice system that will support more holistic approaches to evidence-based research grounded in best practices in plea bargaining.

Achievements in data have created concomitant opportunities for new research methods to be applied to the study of guilty pleas. One emergent issue involves cumulative disadvantages that accrue across consecutive stages in case processing (Kurlychek and Johnson 2019; Kutateladze et al. 2014; Stolzenberg et al. 2013; Sutton 2013). Although studies are increasingly examining plea decisions in relation to other outcomes, few studies have developed comprehensive approaches for capturing cumulative disadvantages. Promising strategies include path analytic models designed to investigate the direct and mediating effects of independent variables (Brennan 2006; Hagan 1974), as well as latent class analysis, which may be valuable in identifying common "packages" of plea concessions. This approach has been used to study sentencing and probation (Kimchi 2019; Yan 2015) but has yet to be applied to plea bargaining. Datasets that include information on prosecutor characteristics support multilevel analysis of plea bargaining as well (Stemen and Escobar 2019), which could be extended to include the court context (Johnson 2006). One of the most propitious avenues for future research, though, is the expansion of mixed methods that combine qualitative and quantitative approaches to the study of guilty pleas (Frederick and Stemen 2012; Spohn and Tellis 2013). Targeted in-depth case studies of plea bargaining, popularized in earlier waves of research (Eisenstein and Jacob 1977; Nardulli et al. 1988), must be replicated in modern court contexts. Qualitative and ethnographic research remains critical to understanding plea bargaining practices across contexts even with the advent of "big data" (Lynch 2016).

Finally, it is essential that future work identifies new research questions that advance plea bargaining scholarship. Criminological research needs to move beyond traditional investigations of legal and extralegal factors and devote greater attention to understanding the legal parameters of criminal law and how it shapes plea decisions (Bushway and Forst 2013; Wright and Engen 2006). Explanations are necessary for determining how and why defendant characteristics, like race and gender, impact guilty plea processes (Alschuler 1968, 1978; Mather 1973). Additional theoretical and empirical development is needed to understand who pleads guilty and why. Little is known about differences in willingness to accept plea offers, how perceived legitimacy impacts these decisions, or how implicit biases on the part of court actors potentially shape plea outcomes. Few scholars have interviewed actual defendants to inquire about these issues (e.g., Zottoli et al. 2016), which is a promising avenue for future work. Lastly, research on false guilty pleas and wrongful convictions must be expanded, building upon the footing established in psychology and law (e.g., Dervan and Edkins 2013; Henderson and Levett 2018; Redlich et al. 2014). Overall, plea bargaining scholarship has progressed notably in the twenty-first century, but additional research is vital to furthering the empirical groundwork for evidence-based policy reforms.

4.7 Policy Reforms in Plea Bargaining

Legal scholars identify a host of serious moral and philosophical issues in plea bargaining, and empirical research raises a number of important corollary concerns. Among the most pressing are the lack of balance in negotiating leverage, which allows prosecutors to threaten long trial sentences to coerce guilty pleas; the limited transparency, accountability, and oversight in plea bargaining, which contributes to low levels of perceived legitimacy; and the hidden nature of the plea process, which raises the specter of inequality and leads to fundamental questions about fairness and impartiality in punishment. Although no antidote exists to cure the full array of concerns in plea bargaining, concrete policy reforms can begin to remedy some problematic aspects of the guilty plea process in American courts.

Traditionally, scholars have argued for the total abolition (Alschuler 1981; Langbein 1978; Schulhofer 1992) or continued maintenance (Easterbrook 1992; Scott and Stuntz 1992) of plea bargaining as an American institution, though recent approaches emphasize the need for a balanced evidence-based approach to identifying effective policy reforms (Johnson et al. 2016; Scott and Stuntz 2004; Wright 2005). This echoes the sentiments of scholars like Albert Alschuler (1983, 706–707) who recognized the "time for a crusade to prohibit plea bargaining has passed" and the focus must now shift to "[i]mproving the plea-bargaining process." Promising policy reforms include regulating plea bargaining with greater judicial involvement, ensuring core constitutional rights of defendants, improving financial support for public defenders' offices, placing formal limits on the size of plea discounts, and introducing new structural innovations like charging guidelines to constrain undue prosecutorial discretion.

First, rules in jurisdictions that prohibit judicial participation in plea negotiations should be relaxed, new policies ensuring more complete pre-trial discovery enacted, and greater constitutional protections guaranteed to defendants who plea bargain. According to Sklansky (2018, 460), what is required is "judicial supervision over prosecutorial decisions" including "what kinds of plea bargains to offer or to accept." Potential approaches might include expedited bench trial proceedings (Schulhofer 1984), guilty plea juries that validate the voluntariness of plea agreements (Appleman 2010), petit juries that accept plea agreements (Bibas 2012), or special "half-blown" trials that offer a compromise between guilty pleas and trials (*Lafler v. Cooper* 2012, Scalia, J., dissenting).

Judges should also be involved earlier in the plea negotiation process, asking questions and making suggestions during charge manipulations to guarantee a principled plea process (Alschuler 1976; King and Wright 2016; Rakoff 2014; Turner 2006, 2017). Further, defendants in plea negotiations should have the right to appeal, be guaranteed effective counsel (Turner 2017), and provided with full discovery (Turner and Redlich 2016). As in trial cases, prosecutors should be required to disclose any and all exculpatory evidence during plea negotiations. Currently, only a few states require it, even though pre-plea discovery "is the first step toward ensuring that parties are negotiating fair, well-informed, and factually based plea bargains and that innocent defendants are not coerced into pleading guilty" (Turner 2017, 97).

Second, negotiated plea offers and plea alterations should include written explanations as part of the public record that are subject to formal review (Bibas 2009; Miller and Wright 2008). A few jurisdictions have implemented requirements for written pleas, but they are the exception rather than the rule. Written records of plea-bargaining reasons offer several advantages: they provide a formal account of reduced or enhanced charges; protect defendants from uninformed pleas; guard prosecutors against unjustified disputes; provide judges with improved information when accepting plea deals; enhance the legitimacy of the process, and create tangible records to support empirical research (Johnson et al. 2016; Mallard 2014; Turner 2017). Recording requirements could also be useful in identifying disingenuous charge manipulations, overcharging practices, unwarranted disparities in prosecution, or problematic jurisdictions that use pressure tactics, like exploding offers, to coerce guilty pleas. To address the latter issue, a few states have established minimum time periods to pass before a plea can be accepted, but these types of procedural safeguards are still relatively rare (Turner 2017).

Lastly, recommendations that restore the balance of negotiating power include constraints on prosecutorial power that limit severe plea-trial disparities, steps that restrict the ability of plea agreements to unilaterally determine sentences, and structural provisions for better managing prosecutorial discretion. Limiting the magnitude of plea discounts would directly reduce coercion in plea bargaining. Plea discounts in England, for instance, cannot exceed one-third of the nominal sentence at trial (Ashworth and Roberts 2013; Roberts and Bradford 2015). Covey (2008) proposes an alternative policy involving punishment ceilings in which trial sentences cannot exceed plea outcomes by more than a modest amount. In addition, policies should be implemented to restrict the availability of discretionary "charging hammers" like mandatory minimums and habitual offender laws that can be used to threaten excessive trial sentences. Ideally, these types of sentencing enhancements would be presumptive rather than mandatory and shifted from prosecutor to judge, or at minimum, judicial vetoes would be available in the interests of justice (Tonry 2014). As Alschuler (2013, 707) counseled, effective policy reforms need to "cheer... measures that would reduce the bargaining leverage of prosecutors while booing... measures that would enhance it."

A more ambitious and comprehensive reform effort involves implementing plea guidelines to structure a broader range of charging decisions. Many prosecutor offices have internal charging policies such as screening requirements to limit plea bargaining (Wright and Miller 2002), and some international jurisdictions have developed formal charging guidelines (Tak 2001), but no U.S. jurisdiction employs legally binding plea-bargaining guidelines. Similar to sentencing guidelines for judges (Frankel 1973), presumptive charging guidelines could establish clear benchmarks in plea deals that set structural limits on what prosecutors can charge, amend, and threaten at trial (Pfaff 2017). Charging guidelines would help balance the playing field for prosecutors, defendants, and defense counsel, making it one of the many promising policy avenues for improving fairness and transparency in plea bargaining in American courts.

Although these proposals represent distinctive approaches to diverse aspects of plea bargaining, they hold the most promise to enhance consistency and impartiality if enacted conjointly. In many cases, reform efforts in one domain will require policy changes in another. For example, charging and plea-bargaining guidelines will only be effective if accompanied by judicial oversight to prevent prosecutorial circumvention (Pfaff 2017). Similarly, caps on plea discounts will require enforcement mechanisms, whereas written plea reasons will be most impactful if combined with new appellate rights for defendants. All of these pursuits should be united with redoubled efforts to ensure adequately funded defense counsel. With recent improvements in large plea-bargaining datasets, empirical research will need to play an ever-increasing role in achieving these goals. Research findings are essential to provide legitimacy and empiricism to ongoing policy debates too long directed by politicism and zealotry. In the end, to truly improve fairness, transparency, and effectiveness in plea bargaining, more balanced, evidence-based approaches will be required to improve our empirical knowledge base; this is more important today than ever before as the fate of criminal defendants is increasingly determined by bargained justice.

Notes

1. Parts of this chapter are modified from related arguments provided in Johnson (2019a).
2. In 2014, the Department of Justice issued a memorandum for all federal prosecutors stating that they should no longer seek waivers of the right to challenge ineffective counsel in federal plea agreements.

References

Abrams, David S. 2011. "Is Pleading Really a Bargain?" *Journal of Empirical Legal Studies* 8(1): 200–221.

Albonetti, Celesta A. 1986. "Criminality, Prosecutorial Screening, and Uncertainty: Toward a Theory of Discretionary Decision Making in Felony Case Processings." *Criminology* 24(4): 623–644.

Albonetti, Celesta A. 1987. "Prosecutorial Discretion: The Effects of Uncertainty." *Law and Society Review* 21(2): 291–314.

Albonetti, Celesta A. 1990. "Race and the Probability of Pleading Guilty." *Journal of Quantitative Criminology* 6(3): 315–334.

Albonetti, Celesta A. 1992. "Charge Reduction: An Analysis of Prosecutorial Discretion in Burglary and Robbery Cases." *Journal of Quantitative Criminology* 8(3): 317–333.

Alschuler, Albert W. 1968. "The Prosecutor's Role in Plea Bargaining." *The University of Chicago Law Review* 36(1): 50–112.

Alschuler, Albert W. 1976. "The Trial Judge's Role in Plea Bargaining, Part I." *Columbia Law Review* 76(7): 1059–1154.

Alschuler, Albert W. 1978. "Sentencing Reform and Prosecutorial Power: A Critique of Recent Proposals for 'Fixed' and 'Presumptive' Sentencing." *University of Pennsylvania Law Review* 126(3): 550–577.

Alschuler, Albert W. 1979. "Plea Bargaining and Its History." *Law and Society Review* 13(2): 211–245.

Alschuler, Albert W. 1981. "The Changing Plea Bargaining Debate." *California Law Review* 69(3): 652–730.

Alschuler, Albert W. 1983. "Implementing the Criminal Defendant's Right to Trial: Alternatives to the Plea Bargaining System." *The University of Chicago Law Review* 50(3): 931–1050.

Alschuler, Albert W. 2013. "*Lafler* and *Frye*: Two Small Band-Aids for a Festering Wound." *Duquesne Law Review* 51(3): 673–687.

American Bar Association (ABA). 1999. *ABA Standards for Criminal Justice Pleas of Guilty. 3d ed.* Washington, D.C.: American Bar Association.

Appleman, Laura I. 2010. "The Plea Jury." *Indiana Law Journal* 85(3): 732–776.

Ashworth, Andrew, and Julien V. Roberts. 2013. "The Origins and Nature of Sentencing Guidelines in England and Wales." In *Sentencing Guidelines: Exploring the English Model.* Edited by Andrew Ashworth and Julien V. Roberts. Introduction. Oxford: Oxford University Press.

Bibas, Stephanos. 2001. "Judicial Fact-Finding and Sentence Enhancements in a World of Guilty Pleas." *The Yale Law Journal* 110(7): 1097–1185.

Bibas, Stephanos. 2004. "Plea Bargaining Outside the Shadow of Trial." *Harvard Law Review* 117(8): 2463–2547.

Bibas, Stephanos. 2009. "Prosecutorial Regulation versus Prosecutorial Accountability." *University of Pennsylvania Law Review* 157(4): 959–1016.

Bibas, Stephanos. 2012. "Incompetent Plea Bargaining and Extrajudicial Reforms." *Harvard Law Review* 126(1): 150–175.

Bishop, Donna M., and Charles E. Frazier. 1984. "The Effects of Gender on Charge Reduction." *The Sociological Quarterly* 25(3): 385–396.

Blumberg, Abraham S., ed. 1974. *Current Perspectives on Criminal Behavior: Original Essays on Criminology*. New York: Alfred A. Knopf.

Blume, John H., and Rebecca K Helm. 2014. "The Unexonerated: Factually Innocent Defendants Who Plead Guilty." *Cornell Law Review* 100(1): 157–192.

Blumstein, Alfred, Jacqueline Cohen, Susan E. Martin, and Michael Tonry, eds. 1983. *Research on Sentencing: The Search for Reform*, vol. 1. Washington, D.C.: National Academy Press.

Bordenkircher v. Hayes. 1978. 434 U.S. 357.

Bordens, Kenneth S. 1984. "The Effects of Likelihood of Conviction, Threatened Punishment, and Assumed Role on Mock Plea Bargaining Decisions." *Basic and Applied Social Psychology* 5(1): 59–74.

Brady v. United States. 1970. 397 U.S. 742.

Brennan, Pauline K. 2006. "Sentencing Female Misdemeanants: An Examination of the Direct and Indirect Effects of Race/Ethnicity." *Justice Quarterly* 23(1): 60–95.

Brook, Carol A., Bruno Fiannaca, David Harvey, and Paul Marcus. 2016. "A Comparative Look at Plea Bargaining in Australia, Canada, England, New Zealand and the United States." *William and Mary Law Review* 57(4): 1147–1224.

Brown, Darryl K. 2005. "The Decline of Defense Counsel and the Rise of Accuracy in Criminal Adjudication." *California Law Review* 93(6): 1585–1590.

Bushway, Shawn D., and Allison D. Redlich. 2012. "Is Plea Bargaining in the 'Shadow of the Trial' a Mirage?" *Journal of Quantitative Criminology* 28(3): 437–454.

Bushway, Shawn D., Allison D. Redlich, and Robert J. Norris. 2014. "An Explicit Test of Plea Bargaining in the 'Shadow of the Trial.'" *Criminology* 52(4): 723–754.

Bushway, Shawn D., and Brian Forst. 2013. "Studying Discretion in the Processes that Generate Criminal Justice Sanctions." *Justice Quarterly* 30(2): 199–222.

Casper, Jonathan D. 1972. *American Criminal Justice: The Defendant's Perspective*. Englewood Cliffs: Prentice Hall.

Church, Thomas W. 1979. "In Defense of 'Bargain Justice.'" *Law and Society Review* 13(2): 509–525.

Colquitt, Joseph A. 2001. "Ad Hoc Plea Bargaining." *Tulane Law Review* 75(2): 695–776.

Combs, Nancy Amoury. 2002. "Copping a Plea to Genocide: The Plea Bargaining of International Crimes." *University of Pennsylvania Law Review* 151(1): 66–69.

Covey, Russell D. 2008. "Fixed Justice: Reforming Plea Bargaining with Plea-Based Ceiling." *Tulane Law Review* 82: 1237–1290.

Covey, Russell D. 2013. "Plea-Bargaining Law after *Lafler* and *Frye*." *Duquesne University Law Review* 51(3): 595–523.

Dervan, Lucian E. 2015. "The Injustice of the Plea-Bargain System." *Wall Street Journal*, December 3.

Dervan, Lucian E., and Vanessa A. Edkins. 2013. "The Innocent Defendant's Dilemma: An Innovative Empirical Study of Plea Bargaining's Innocence Problem." *Journal of Criminal Law and Criminology* 103(1): 1–48.

Easterbrook, Frank H. 1992. "Plea Bargaining as Compromise." *Yale Law Journal* 101(8): 1969–1978.

Eisenstein, James, and Herbert Jacob. 1977. *Felony Justice: An Organizational Analysis of Criminal Courts*. Boston: Little, Brown, and Company.

Eisenstein, James, Roy B. Flemming, and Peter F. Nardulli. 1988. *The Contours of Justice: Communities and Their Courts*. Boston: Little, Brown, and Company.

Ellis, Michael J. 2012. "The Origins of the Elected Prosecutor." *Yale Law Journal* 121(6): 1528–1569.

Farnworth, Margaret, and Raymond H. C. Teske, Jr. 1995. "Gender Differences in Felony Court Processing: Three Hypotheses of Disparity." *Women and Criminal Justice* 6(2): 23–44.

Feeley, Malcolm M. 1979 [1992]. *The Process Is the Punishment: Handling Cases in a Lower Criminal Court*. New York: Russell Sage Foundation.

Feeley, Malcolm M. 1997. "Legal Complexity and the Transformation of the Criminal Process: The Origins of Plea Bargaining." *Israel Law Review* 31(1): 183–222.

Frankel, Marvin E. 1973. *Criminal Sentences: Law without Order*. New York: Hill and Wang.

Franklin, Travis W. 2010. "Community Influence on Prosecutorial Dismissals: A Multilevel Analysis of Case- and County-Level Factors." *Journal of Criminal Justice* 38(4): 693–701.

Frase, Richard S. 2000. "Is Guided Discretion Sufficient-Overview of State Sentencing Guidelines?" *Saint Louis University Law Journal* 44(2): 425–450.

Frase, Richard S. 2005. "Punishment Purposes." *Stanford Law Review* 58(1): 67–83.

Frederick, Bruce, and Don Stemen. 2012. *The Anatomy of Discretion: An Analysis of Prosecutorial Decision Making Technical Report*. Technical Report, Vera Institute of Justice, New York.

Frenzel, Erika Davis, and Jeremy D. Ball. 2008. "Effects of Individual Characteristics on Plea Negotiations under Sentencing Guidelines." *Journal of Ethnicity in Criminal Justice* 5(4): 59–82.

Friedman, Lawrence M., and Robert V. Percival. 1981. *The Roots of Justice: Crime and Punishment in Alameda County, California, 1870—1910*. Chapel Hill: University of North Carolina Press.

Frohmann, Lisa. 1997. "Convictability and Discordant Locales: Reproducing Race, Class, and Gender Ideologies in Prosecutorial Decisionmaking." *Law and Society Review* 31(3): 531–556.

Gross, Samuel R., Kristen Jacoby, Daniel J. Matheson, and Nicholas Montgomery. 2005. "Exonerations in the United States 1989 Through 2003." *Journal of Criminal Law and Criminology* 95(2): 523–560.

Hagan, John. 1974. "Parameters of Criminal Prosecution: An Application of Path Analysis to a Problem of Criminal Justice." *Journal of Criminal Law and Criminology* 65(4): 536–544.

Hans, Valerie P., Neil Vidmar, and Hans Zeisel. 1986. *Judging the Jury*. New York: Plenum Press.

Heaton, Paul, Sandra Mayson, and Megan Stevenson. 2017. "The Downstream Consequences of Misdemeanor Pretrial Detention." *Stanford Law Review* 69(3): 711–794.

Herzog, Sergio. 2004. "Plea Bargaining Practices: Less Covert, More Public Support?" *Crime and Delinquency* 50(4): 590–614.

Henderson, Kelsey S., and Lora M. Levett. 2018. "Investigating Predictors of True and False Guilty Pleas." *Law and Human Behavior* 42(5): 427–441.

Heumann, Milton. 1978. *Plea Bargaining: The Experience of Prosecutors, Judges and Defense Attorneys*. Chicago: University of Chicago Press.

Hofer, Paul J. 2011. "Has *Booker* Restored Balance? A Look at Data on Plea Bargaining and Sentencing." *Federal Sentencing Reporter* 23(5): 326–332.

Holmes, M. D., H. C. Daudistel, and R. A. Farrell. 1987. "Determinants of Charge Reductions and Final Dispositions in Cases of Burglary and Robbery." *Journal of Research on Crime and Delinquency* 24(3): 233–254.
Hurwitz, Jon, and Mark Peffley. 2005. "Explaining the Great Racial Divide: Perceptions of Fairness in the US Criminal Justice System." *Journal of Politics* 67(3): 762–783.
Johnson, Brian D. 2003. "Racial and Ethnic Disparities in Sentencing Departures Across Modes of Conviction." *Criminology* 41(2): 449–490.
Johnson, Brian D. 2006. "The Multilevel Context of Criminal Sentencing: Integrating Judge- and County-Level Influences." *Criminology* 44(2): 259–298.
Johnson, Brian D. 2019a. "Trials and Tribulations: The Trial Tax and the Punishment Process." *Crime & Justice: A Review of Research* 48(2): 313–363.
Johnson, Brian D. 2019b. "In Search of the Missing Link: Examining Contextual Variation in Federal Charge Bargains across U.S. District Courts." *Justice Quarterly* 35(7): 1133–1165.
Johnson, Brian D., and Ryan D. King. 2017. "Facial Profiling: Race, Physical Appearance, and Punishment." *Criminology* 55(3): 520–547.
Johnson, Brian D., Ryan D. King, and Cassia Spohn. 2016. "Sociolegal Approaches to the Study of Guilty Pleas and Prosecution." *Annual Review of Law and Social Science* 12: 479–495.
Johnson, Brian D., and Pilar Larroulet. 2019. "The 'Distance Traveled': Investigating the Downstream Consequences of Charge Reductions for Disparities in Incarceration." *Justice Quarterly* 36(7): 1229–1257.
Johnson, Thea. 2019. "Fictional Pleas." *Indiana Law Journal* 94(3): 855–900.
Kim, Andrew Chongseh. 2015. "Underestimating the Trial Penalty: An Empirical Analysis of the Federal Trial Penalty and Critique of the Abrams Study." *Mississippi Law Journal* 84(5): 1195–1256.
Kimchi, Anat. 2019. "Investigating the Assignment of Probation Conditions: Heterogeneity and the Role of Race and Ethnicity." *Journal of Quantitative Criminology* 35(4): 715–745.
King, Nancy J., and Michael O'Neill. 2005. "Appeal Waivers and the Future of Sentencing Policy." *Duke Law Journal* 55(2): 209–262.
King, Nancy J., and Ronald F. Wright. 2016. "The Invisible Revolution in Plea Bargaining: Managerial Judging and Judicial Participation in Negotiations." *Texas Law Review* 95(2): 325–398.
King, Nancy J., David A. Soule, Sara Steen, and Robert R. Weidner. 2005. "Panel One: Prosecutorial Discretion and Its Challenges." *Columbia Law Review* 105(4): 959–1009.
King, Ryan D., and Brian D. Johnson. 2016. "A Punishing Look: Skin Tone and Afrocentric Features in the Halls of Justice." *American Journal of Sociology* 122(1): 90–124.
Kingsnorth, Rodney, John Lopez, Jennifer Wentworth, and Debra Cummings. 1998. "Adult Sexual Assault: The Role of Racial/Ethnic Composition in Prosecution and Sentencing." *Journal of Criminal Justice* 26(5): 359–371.
Kingsnorth, Rodney, Randall C. Macintosh, and Jennifer Wentworth. 1999. "Sexual Assault: The Role of Prior Relationship and Victim Characteristics in Case Processing." *Justice Quarterly* 16(2): 275–302.
Kurlychek, Megan C., and Brian D. Johnson. 2019. "Cumulative Disadvantage in the American Criminal Justice System." *Annual Review of Criminology* 2: 291–319.
Kutateladze, Besiki Luka. 2018. "Tracing Charge Trajectories: A Study of the Influence of Race in Charge Changes at Case Screening, Arraignment, and Disposition." *Criminology* 56(1): 123–153.

Kutateladze, Besiki Luka, Nancy R. Andiloro, and Brian D. Johnson. 2016. "Opening Pandora's Box: How Does Defendant Race Influence Plea Bargaining?" *Justice Quarterly* 33(3): 398–426.

Kutateladze, Besiki L., Nancy R. Andiloro, Brian D. Johnson, and Cassia C. Spohn. 2014. "Cumulative Disadvantage: Examining Racial and Ethnic Disparity in Prosecution and Sentencing." *Criminology* 52(3): 514–551.

Kutateladze, Besiki L., and Victoria Z. Lawson. 2018. "Is a Plea Really a Bargain? An Analysis of Plea and Trial Dispositions in New York City." *Crime and Delinquency* 64(7): 856–887.

Kutateladze, Besiki L., Victoria Z. Lawson, and Nancy R. Andiloro. 2015. "Does Evidence Really Matter? An Exploratory Analysis of the Role of Evidence in Plea Bargaining in Felony Drug Cases." *Law and Human Behavior* 39(5): 431–442.

Kutateladze, Besiki, Vanessa Lynn, and Edward Liang. 2012. "Do Race and Ethnicity Matter in Prosecution? A Review of Empirical Studies." New York: Vera Institute of Justice.

Landes, William M. 1971. "An Economic Analysis of the Courts." *Journal of Law and Economics* 14(1): 61–108.

Lafler v. Cooper. 2012. 566 U.S. 156, 170–172.

LaFree, Gary D. 1980. "The Effect of Sexual Stratification by Race on Official Reactions to Rape." *American Sociological Review* 45(5): 842–854.

LaFree, Gary D. 1985. "Adversarial and Nonadversarial Justice: A Comparison of Guilty Pleas and Trials." *Criminology* 23(2): 289–312.

Langbein, John H. 1978. "Torture and Plea Bargaining." *University of Chicago Law Review* 46(1): 3–22.

Langbein, John H. 1992. "On the Myth of Written Constitutions: The Disappearance of Criminal Jury Trial." *Harvard Journal of Law and Public Policy* 15(1): 119–128.

Levine, Kay L., and Ronald F. Wright. 2012. "Prosecution in 3-D." *Journal of Criminal Law and Criminology* 102(4): 1119–1181.

Light, Michael, Michael Massoglia, and Ryan D. King. 2014. "Citizenship and Punishment: The Salience of National Membership in U.S. Criminal Courts." *American Sociological Review* 79(5): 825–847.

Lynch, Gerard E. 2003. "Screening versus Plea Bargaining: Exactly What Are We Trading Off?" *Stanford Law Review* 55(4): 1399–1408.

Lynch, Mona. 2016. *Hard Bargains: The Coercive Power of Drug Laws in Federal Court*. New York: Russell Sage Foundation.

Mallard, John. 2014. "Putting Plea Bargaining on the Record." *University of Pennsylvania Law Review* 162: 683–718.

Mather, Lynn M. 1973. "Some Determinants of the Method of Case Disposition: Decision-Making by Public Defenders in Los Angeles." *Law and Society Review* 8(2): 187–216.

Maynard, Douglas W. 1982. "Defendant Attributes in Plea Bargaining: Notes on the Modeling of Sentencing Decisions." *Social Problems* 29(4): 347–360.

McCoy, Candace. 2005. "Plea Bargaining as Coercion: The Trial Penalty and Plea Bargaining Reform." *Criminal Law Quarterly* 50(1): 67–107.

Measures for Justice. 2019. Data accessed: December 2018.

Meeker, James W., and Henry N. Pontell. 1985. "Court Caseloads, Plea Bargains, and Criminal Sanctions: The Effects of Section 17 PC in California." *Criminology* 23(1): 119–143.

Metcalfe, Christi, and Ted Chiricos. 2018. "Race, Plea, and Charge Reduction: An Assessment of Racial Disparities in the Plea Process." *Justice Quarterly* 35(2): 223–253.

Miethe, Terance D. 1987. “Charging and Plea Bargaining Practices under Determinate Sentencing: An Investigation of the Hydraulic Displacement of Discretion.” *Journal of Criminal Law and Criminology* 78(1): 155–176.

Miller, Marc L., and Ronald F. Wright. 2008. “The Black Box.” *Iowa Law Review* 94(1): 125–196.

Missouri v. Frye. 2012. 566 U.S. 134.

Nagel, Irene, and Stephen J. Schulhofer. 1992. “A Tale of Three Cities: An Empirical Study of Charging and Bargaining Practices under the Federal Sentencing Guidelines.” *Southern California Law Review* 66: 501–566.

Nardulli, Peter F. 1979. “The Caseload Controversy and the Study of Criminal Courts.” *Journal of Criminal Law and Criminology* 70(1): 89–101.

Nardulli, Peter F., James Eisenstein, and Roy B. Flemming. 1988. *The Tenor of Justice: Criminal Courts and the Guilty Plea Process*. Urbana: University of Illinois Press.

Newman, Donald J. 1966. *Conviction: The Determination of Guilt or Innocence without Trial*. Boston: Little, Brown, and Company.

North Carolina v. Alford. 1970. 400 U.S. 25.

Padilla v. Kentucky. 2010. 559 U.S. 356.

Pfaff, John. 2017. *Locked In: The True Causes of Mass Incarceration and How to Achieve Real Reform*. New York: Basic Books.

Piehl, Anne M., and Shawn D. Bushway. 2007. “Measuring and Explaining Charge Bargaining.” *Journal of Quantitative Criminology* 23(2): 105–125.

Podgor, Ellen S. 2011. “Pleading Blindly.” *Mississippi Law Journal* 80(4): 1633–1647.

Rakoff, Jed S. 2014. “Why Innocent People Plead Guilty.” *New York Review of Books*, November 20.

Ramsey, Carolyn B. 2002. “The Discretionary Power of ‘Public’ Prosecutors in Historical Perspective.” *American Criminal Law Review* 39(4): 1309–1393.

Reaves, Brian A. 2013. *Felony Defendants in Large Urban Counties, 2009-Statistical Tables*. Washington, D.C.: U.S. Department of Justice.

Redlich, Allison D., James R. Acker, Robert J. Norris, and Catherine L. Bonventre, eds. 2014. *Wrongful Conviction: Stepping Back, Moving Forward*. Durham: Carolina Academic Press.

Redlich, Allison D., Shawn D. Bushway, and Robert J. Norris. 2016. “Plea Decision-Making by Attorneys and Judges.” *Journal of Experimental Criminology* 12(4): 537–561.

Rehavi, Marit M., and Sonja B. Starr. 2014. “Racial Disparity in Federal Criminal Sentences.” *Journal of Political Economy* 122(6): 1320–1354.

Roberts, Julian V., and Ben Bradford. 2015. “Sentence Reductions for a Guilty Plea in England and Wales: Exploring New Empirical Trends.” *Journal of Empirical Legal Studies* 12(2): 187–210.

Rosett, Arthur I., and Donald R. Cressey. 1976. *Justice by Consent: Plea Bargains in the American Courthouse*. Philadelphia: Lippincott.

Ross, Jacqueline E. 2006. “The Entrenched Position of Plea Bargaining in United States Legal Practice.” *American Journal of Comparative Law* 54: 717–732.

Santobello v. New York. 1970. 404 U.S. 257, 260.

Savitsky, Douglas. 2012. “Is Plea Bargaining a Rational Choice? Plea Bargaining as an Engine of Racial Stratification and Overcrowding in the United States Prison System.” *Rationality and Society* 24(2): 131–167.

Schulhofer, Stephen J. 1984. “Is Plea Bargaining Inevitable?” *Harvard Law Review* 97(5): 1037–1107.

Schulhofer, Stephen J. 1992. "Plea Bargaining as Disaster." *Yale Law Journal* 101(8): 1979–2009.

Scott, Robert E., and William J. Stuntz. 1992. "A Reply: Imperfect Bargains, Imperfect Trials, and Innocent Defendants." *Yale Law Journal* 101(8): 2011–2015.

Scott v. United States. 1965. 349 F.2d 641 (6th Cir.).

Sheldon v. United States. 1958. 242 F.2d 101 (5th Cir.).

Shermer, Lauren O., and Brian D. Johnson. 2010. "Criminal Prosecutions: Examining Prosecutorial Discretion and Charge Reductions in US Federal District Courts." *Justice Quarterly* 27(3): 394–430.

Sklansky, David A. 2018. "The Problems with Prosecutors." *Annual Review of Criminology* 1:451–469.

Smith, Bruce P. 2005. "Plea Bargaining and the Eclipse of the Jury." *Annual Review of Law and Social Science* 1: 131–149.

Smith, Douglas A. 1986. "The Plea Bargaining Controversy." *The Journal of Criminal Law and Criminology* 77(3): 949–968.

Smith, Robert J., and Justin D. Levinson. 2012. "The Impact of Implicit Racial Bias on the Exercise of Prosecutorial Discretion." *Seattle University Law Review* 35(3): 795–826.

Spears, Jeffery, and Cassia Spohn. 1997. "The Effect of Evidence Factors and Victim Characteristics on Prosecutors' Charging Decisions in Sexual Assault Cases." *Justice Quarterly* 14(3): 501–524.

Spohn, Cassia. 2018. "Reflections on the Exercise of Prosecutorial Discretion 50 Years After Publication of the Challenge of Crime in a Free Society." *Criminology and Public Policy* 17(2): 321–340.

Spohn, Cassia, Dawn Beichner, and Erika Davis-Frenzel. 2001. "Prosecutorial Justifications for Sexual Assault Case Rejection: Guarding the 'Gateway to Justice.'" *Social Problems* 48(2): 206–235.

Spohn, Cassia, John Gruhl, and Susan Welch. 1987. "The Impact of the Ethnicity and Gender of Defendants on the Decision to Reject or Dismiss Felony Charges." *Criminology* 35(1): 175–190.

Spohn, Cassia, and Katherine Tellis. 2013. *Policing and Prosecuting Sexual Assault: Inside the Criminal Justice System*. Boulder: Lynne Rienner Publishers, Inc.

Stemen, Don, and Gipsy Escobar. 2019. "Whither the Prosecutor? Prosecutor and County Effects on Guilty Plea Outcomes in Wisconsin." *Justice Quarterly* 35(7): 1166–1194.

Stevenson, Megan, and Sandra G. Mayson. 2017. "Bail Reform: New Directions for Pretrial Detention and Release." In *Academy for Justice, A Report on Scholarship and Criminal Justice Reform*. Edited by Erik Luna, vol. 3, 21–47. Phoenix: Academy for Justice.

Stolzenberg, Lisa, Stewart J. D'Alessio, and David Eitle. 2004. "A Multilevel Test of Racial Threat Theory." *Criminology* 42(3): 673–698.

Stolzenberg, Lisa, Stewart J. D'Alessio, and David Eitle. 2013. "Race and Cumulative Discrimination in the Prosecution of Criminal Defendants." *Race and Justice* 3(4): 275–299.

Stuntz, William J. 2004. "Plea Bargaining and Criminal Law's Disappearing Shadow." *Harvard Law Review* 117(8): 2548–2569.

Stuntz, William J. 2011. *The Collapse of American Criminal Justice*. Cambridge, MA: Harvard University Press.

Sudnow, David. 1965. "Normal Crimes: Sociological Features of the Penal Code in a Public Defender Office." *Social Problems* 12(3): 255–276.

Sutton, John R. 2013. "Structural Bias in the Sentencing of Felony Defendants." *Social Science Research* 42(5): 1207–1221.

Tak, Peter J. 2001. "Sentencing and Punishment in the Netherlands." In *Sentencing and Sanctions in Western Countries*. Edited by Michael Tonry and Richard S. Frase, 151–187. New York: Oxford University Press.

Tata, Cyrus, and Jay M. Gormley. 2016. *Sentencing and Plea Bargaining: Guilty Pleas versus Trial Verdicts*. Oxford: Oxford Handbooks Online.

Testa, Alex, and Brian D. Johnson. 2020. "Paying the Trial Tax: Race, Guilty Pleas, and Disparity in Prosecution." *Criminal Justice Policy Review* 31(4): 500–531.

Tonry, Michael. 2012. *Prosecutors and Politics: A Comparative Perspective*. Chicago: University of Chicago Press.

Tonry, Michael. 2014. "Remodeling American Sentencing: A Ten-Step Blueprint for Moving Past Mass Incarceration." *Criminology and Public Policy* 13(4): 503–533.

Turner, Jenia I. 2006. "Judicial Participation in Plea Negotiations: A Comparative View." *American Journal of Comparative Law* 54(1): 199–267.

Turner, Jenia I. 2009. *Plea Bargaining across Borders: Criminal Procedure*. New York: Wolters Kluwer Law and Business.

Turner, Jenia I. 2017. "Plea Bargaining." In *Reforming Criminal Justice: A Report of the Academy for Justice on Bridging the Gap between Scholarship and Reform*. Edited by Erik Luna, vol. 3, 73–100. Phoenix: Academy for Justice.

Turner, Jenia I., and Allison D. Redlich. 2016. "Two Models of Pre-plea Discovery in Criminal Cases: An Empirical Comparison." *Washington and Lee Law Review* 73(1): 285–408.

Ulmer, Jeffery T. 2012. "Recent Developments and New Directions in Sentencing Research." *Justice Quarterly* 29(1): 1–40.

Ulmer, Jeffery T., Megan C. Kurlychek, and John H. Kramer. 2007. "Prosecutorial Discretion and the Imposition of Mandatory Minimum Sentences." *Justice Quarterly* 44(4): 427–458.

United States v. Ruiz, 2002, 536 U.S. 622.

Vidmar, Neil, and Valerie Hans. 2007. *American Juries: The Verdict*. New York: Prometheus Books.

Walker, S. (1998). *Popular Justice: A History of American Criminal Justice*. 2nd ed. New York: Oxford University Press.

Wilkinson, J. Harvie, III. 2014. "In Defense of American Criminal Justice." *Vanderbilt Law Review* 67(4): 1099–1172.

Williams, Marian R., and Jefferson E. Holcomb. 2001. "Racial Disparity and Death Sentences in Ohio." *Journal of Criminal Justice* 29(3): 207–218.

Wooldredge, John D. 1989. "An Aggregate-Level Examination of the Caseload Pressure Hypothesis." *Journal of Quantitative Criminology* 5(3): 259–283.

Wooldredge, John, James Frank, Natalie Goulette, and Lawrence Travis. 2015. "Is the Impact of Cumulative Disadvantage on Sentencing Greater for Black Defendants?" *Criminology and Public Policy* 14(2): 187–223.

Wooldredge, John, and Timothy Griffin. 2005. "Displaced Discretion under Ohio Sentencing Guidelines." *Journal of Criminal Justice* 33(4): 301–316.

Wooldredge, John, and Amy Thistlewaite. 2004. "Bilevel Disparities in Court Dispositions for Intimate Assault." *Criminology* 42(2): 417–456.

Wright, Ronald F. 2005. "Trial Distortion and the End of Innocence in Federal Criminal Justice." *University of Pennsylvania Law Review* 154(1): 79–156.

Wright, Ronald F., Kami Chavis, and Gregory S. Parks. 2018. "The Jury Sunshine Project: Jury Selection Data as a Political Issue." *University of Illinois Law Review* 2018(4): 1407–1442.

Wright, Ronald F., and Rodney L. Engen. 2006. "The Charging and Sentencing Effects of Depth and Distance in a Criminal Code." *North Carolina Law Review* 84(6): 1935–1982.

Wright, Ronald F., and Marc Miller. 2002. "The Screening/Bargaining Tradeoff." *Stanford Law Review* 55(1): 29–118.

Wright, Ronald F., and Marc Miller. 2003. "Honesty and Opacity in Charge Bargains." *Stanford Law Review* 55(4): 1409–1415.

Wu, Jawjeong. 2016. "Racial/Ethnic Discrimination and Prosecution: A Meta-Analysis." *Criminal Justice and Behavior* 43(4): 437–458.

Yan, Shi. 2017. "Search for the Hidden Punishments: An Alternative Approach to Studying Alternative Sanctions." *Journal of Quantitative Criminology* 33(1): 21–44.

Zottoli, Tina M., Tarika Daftary-Kapur, Georgia M. Winters, and Conor Hogan. 2016. "Plea Discounts, Time Pressures, and False-Guilty Pleas in Youth and Adults Who Pleaded Guilty to Felonies in New York City." *Psychology, Public Policy, and Law* 22(3): 250–259.

CHAPTER 5

DISCLOSURE, SECURITY, TECHNOLOGY

Challenges in Pre-trial Access to Evidence

DARRYL K. BROWN

5.1 Introduction

THE rules that govern defense access to the prosecution's information about a criminal case—including the prosecution's intended trial evidence—vary widely across jurisdictions; they have changed substantially over time as well. Despite that variety, those rules have straightforward functions and negotiate a durable set of interests. On the one hand, those rules must accommodate public interests in *non*-disclosure—that is, individual (and corporate) interests in privacy for certain information, and the government's need to maintain secrecy in service of several interests, most notably to ensure the safety of evidentiary sources and the viability of ongoing investigations that rely on undercover actors or surreptitious surveillance. On the other hand, the same rules mandate disclosure of information before trial as a critical component in a system of fair and accurate adjudication. Beyond this central tension, rules accommodate other interests as well, especially managing and allocating the costs of gathering and sharing relevant information.

In theory, criminal judgments should be rendered by judges or jurors who have access at trial to all significant relevant evidence. In that process, all relevant evidence is disclosed at the trial; the question is how much information should be available to both parties (and perhaps the court) before trial. A primary justification for pre-trial disclosure is that it improves the accuracy of the trial process: allowing one party to withhold evidence until the trial leaves the opponent unprepared to respond to the evidence by, for example, identifying reasons to deem the source unreliable or presenting conflicting evidence from other sources. Leaving parties unprepared in this way undermines the quality of information on which fact-finders make decisions.

Two things are wrong with this picture. First, this view, which has been widely accepted in common law jurisdictions, for only (roughly speaking) the last half-century or so, still has not overcome traditional arguments against pre-trial disclosure in a significant number of U.S. criminal justice systems. Second, most criminal judgments are the products of guilty pleas, not trials. The plea bargaining process effectively shifts the fact-finding from the court to the parties. For party negotiations to be effective, both parties need access to most or all relevant information about the case. Yet disclosure rules in many jurisdictions are still designed for the pre-*trial* stage rather than the pre-*plea* stage. And without clear, mandatory disclosure obligations, disclosure is unlikely to happen. Numerous reports and court decisions across jurisdictions document prosecutors' failure to disclose important evidence even when they are required to do so (Armstrong and Possley 1999; Ridolfi and Possley 2010; Grissom, Murphy, and Dehn 2012; Shalom and Thomas 2012). At bottom, that is because disclosure duties conflict with adversarial interests: prosecutors, like defendants, would rather not share information that undermines their case and strengthens their opponent's, nor information that makes their favorable evidence vulnerable to an opponent's tampering. Prosecutors have additional reasons for wanting to avoid pre-trial or pre-plea disclosure: disclosure can be time-consuming and costly, and keeping defendants in the dark about weaknesses in the government's case can work to its advantage in plea negotiations.

Broadly speaking, criminal disclosure rules everywhere are organized around the same sets of sometimes-conflicting aims, values, and challenges. Nonetheless, one finds jurisdictions taking notably different approaches. I suggest in this chapter that pre-trial disclosure schemes can be divided, at a moderate level of generality, into three basic models. The differences do not arise primarily from what must be disclosed and what can be withheld. There is wide agreement, for example, that the government is justified in not disclosing before trial certain kinds of evidence in specific circumstances; all recognize the need to withhold information if disclosure poses a significant risk of endangering witnesses or hindering ongoing law enforcement operations. Likewise, there is little dissent from the principle that at some point the prosecution must disclose any "material" information known to government agents that is exculpatory in nature—i.e., that undermines the prosecution's case for defendant's guilt. Instead, the considerable differences in disclosure rules are best understood as differences about *who* gets to decide whether to withhold some information from the defense until trial, and *when* certain disclosures are made. Those choices are informed by different assessments of the competence and trustworthiness of the key players—prosecutors, judges, and the defense attorneys.

The greatest variety among disclosure regimes is found among U.S. jurisdictions, where rules in some states grant that authority over pre-trial disclosure to prosecutors by mandating only very limited obligations of pre-trial disclosure. But in other state court systems, as well as in the justice systems of other common law countries and European civil law systems, disclosure obligations are generally much broader, and judicial officials have the final call on whether circumstances justify withholding some information from the defense until trial. Those differences are significant; the timing of disclosure matters greatly to whether disclosure sufficiently well serves the core interest in accurate decision-making, and whether disclosure contributes to an adjudication regime that is accepted as sufficiently fair. The same goes for the choice of decision-maker—the prosecution or court when choices are a matter of case-by-case discretion, or the legislature when disclosure or confidentiality is defined as a fixed duty or privilege.

To explain these divergent policies on access to information before trial, the chapter puts less emphasis on the merits of competing policy arguments and more on how the institutional structure and professional norms of prosecution agencies, the defense bar, and the judiciary affect disclosure rules. Decisions about how to balance disclosure against, say, the need for confidential investigative tactics or the protection of at-risk witnesses differ a good deal according to these players' institutional power and their professional cultures. Jurisdictions tend to adopt broader disclosure policies when policymaking courts have the capacity to defy prosecutors' preferences (*R. v. Stinchcombe* 1991), or when political events such as high-profile wrongful-conviction scandals lead legislatures (and sometimes prosecutors) to see the virtues of broad pre-trial disclosure (Grissom 2013; Turner and Redlich 2016, 304–305).

In addition, the chapter highlights two changes in circumstances that affect disclosure policy debates and to which all disclosure schemes must adapt. The first is long standing: government policies, often coupled with new technologies, have steadily expanded law enforcement agencies' investigative and information-gathering capacities. Wiretap and video surveillance are familiar technology examples, as well as digitally based means of collecting and scouring all sorts of information. And scientific advances led to new modes of forensic analysis and expert diagnosis. Evidence based on scientific and technical expertise proved compatible with the movement toward early disclosure; opposing parties need time to prepare to challenge or counter specialized evidence. But over the same period, law enforcement also has steadily increased its use of low-tech tactics like undercover agents or private informants. Investigative tactics that rely on operational secrecy conflict with early disclosure policies, so even jurisdictions committed to expansive disclosure must accommodate the interests in preserving the secrecy on which some investigative techniques depend. How policymakers accomplish this leads to differences in the structure of disclosure schemes. Some jurisdictions put decisions about sensitive information in the hands of judges, who make those calls case-by-case. Others give that power to prosecutors by mandating comparatively little disclosure and leaving judges little or no power to require more. Rules also vary depending on whether policymakers trust the defense bar with access to sensitive information such as witness identities. Greater trust leads to broader disclosure. The structure of disclosure rules in many U.S. jurisdictions reflects the same choice favored in other areas of U.S. criminal procedure, from charging to sentencing decisions—policymakers trust prosecutors more than judges.

The second development is more recent, and it is one disclosure regimes have barely begun to accommodate: the rapidly expanding volume and availability of digital evidence. Some of the same interests in secrecy and privacy arise here as well, but just as often the key challenges are how to address the *security* of some digital evidence and how to provide meaningful *access* to it given the technical challenges (and sometimes high cost) of searching for the relevant needles in large digital haystacks. This trend seems likely to push judges into a more active managerial role, at least in those jurisdictions where they have traditionally been the most passive (Turner 2019). It is likely as well to trigger revisions of policies that allocate the costs of discovering information that is expensive to locate, as well as those dictating how much the prosecution or other government agencies must assist the defense in those tasks. To the extent such government discovery duties expand, it will represent a modest shift of the common law model of pre-trial practice toward the continental civil law model, in which defendants request that prosecutors or courts pursue a particular witness or source of evidence.

A point about terminology: in the United States, the standard term for all this is "discovery," whereas in England and other common law jurisdictions "disclosure" is standard. I will mostly use the latter, because the English have the better label here. U.S. criminal discovery rules (unlike their civil litigation counterparts) largely provide only that one party must *disclose* something it knows to its opponent; they provide few tools to *discover* information previously unknown to either party (Gold, Hessick, and Hessick 2017, 1646–1648). No more than a half-dozen states allow defendants to take witness depositions outside exceptional circumstances (Brown 2017, 156). Otherwise, authority for discovering relevant evidence is largely found elsewhere, primarily in the law defining the state's investigative powers.

5.2 Variations in Approaches to the Prosecution Disclosure

Information regulated by pre-trial disclosure rules is typically divided into three broad types, according to which party has initial possession and whether that party is likely to introduce that information as evidence at trial. The first is evidence in the government's possession that prosecutors expect to offer at trial to prove the defendant's guilt. The second is evidence in the government's possession that prosecutors do *not* plan to introduce, either because it undermines the case for guilt, prosecutors find it to be irrelevant or duplicative, or its value is simply unknown. (In English law this is denoted "unused evidence.") This includes potentially exculpatory evidence, a portion of which is known in U.S. law as *Brady* material. Finally, there is evidence that the defense possesses that it plans to present at trial. (With minor exceptions, U.S. disclosure rules generally do not address a fourth category: information the defense possesses but does not plan to offer at trial.)[1]

Notice that the first and third categories of information will be disclosed eventually, at trial; the only policy question is whether parties should have to disclose it to their opponents before trial—and if so when and how. But the second category might never be disclosed to the defense or the court because prosecutors have no adversarial incentive to do so (and sometimes an incentive *not* to do so). For this kind of information, disclosure duties are intended to solve a deficiency in the adversarial system (what in other contexts we might call a market failure), because prosecutors have no partisan incentive to provide the fact-finder with relevant evidence. All major common law jurisdictions now require prosecutors to share at least certain kinds of relevant, "unused" information with the defense before trial—in particular, exculpatory evidence that undermines the prosecution's evidence or affirmatively raises doubt about the defendant's guilt (*Brady v. Maryland* 1963; *R. v. Stinchcombe* 1991; *Dallison v. Caffrey* 1965). This legal duty is usually limited, however, to information that, in the prosecution's assessment, meets some standard of relevancy or materiality (*Smith v. Cain* 2012; *R. v. Keane* 1994). In the United States and elsewhere, professional responsibility rules and minister-of-justice norms generally require prosecutors to disclose all exculpatory evidence, regardless of its materiality.[2] The requirement to disclose relevant exculpatory evidence also exists in civil law jurisdictions, under domestic law and European treaty obligations (Caianiello 2019, 574–580). But in common law jurisdictions these disclosure duties are relatively recent developments; they were adopted only in the second half of the twentieth century. Before then, the common law tradition required both parties to disclose little if nothing in any of these categories of evidence. But in addition to prosecution disclosure duties, all systems now require also that the defense provide advance notice of certain types of evidence and case theories. Nearly everywhere defendants must disclose information about specific defenses such as alibi or insanity, including who they will call as trial witnesses on those topics. Additionally, both parties now must share some information in advance about expert witnesses and scientific analysis they will rely on at trial.

But there remains a significant split among jurisdictions regarding whether pre-trial disclosure is required for the first class of information—incriminating evidence the prosecution will offer at trial. A sizable minority of the state justice systems in the United States join nearly all common law jurisdictions outside the United States in mandating disclosure well before trial of the government's witnesses and other evidentiary sources, often with key details such as the prior witness statements or the expected content of trial testimony. In these states, prosecution disclosure is ordinarily due either upon "unsealing of the indictment" (N.J. Ct. R. 3:13-3[b]), "as soon as practicable after" that (Idaho Crim. R. 16), or a specific number of days after a defendant's request (Fla. R. Crim. P. 3.220[b]). But a number of U.S. states as well as the federal courts continue to allow prosecutors to withhold most of this information until the trial is underway (Fed. R. Crim. P. 16 and 26.2).

Few defend any longer the absence of pre-trial disclosure as serving the truth-finding enterprise by preventing intimidation of opposing witnesses or preparing false evidence based on advance knowledge of the opponent's case. Procedural rules now address those risks in other ways. The absence of disclosure was widely criticized as trial by "surprise" or "ambush" (Brennan 1963, 288–290; Williams 1959, 554; *R. v. Ward* 1993, 51). That risk is acute in the common law model of the concentrated trial that cannot be adjourned until a later time when one party presents evidence the other side did not anticipate and needs time to investigate its credibility or prepare counter evidence (Langbein 2012, 530). Instead, pre-trial disclosure is now regarded, in criminal as well as civil litigation, as maximizing the odds of accurate judgments by facilitating parties' preparation for trial. Additionally, advance notice of the government's evidence is widely viewed as a presumptive requirement of fair criminal trial process. Outside the United States, this shift has led to legal obligations on the prosecution to disclose much of its evidence to the defense in advance of trial. As a prerequisite of basic fairness, English courts have long recognized a common law duty on the prosecution to disclose to the defense before trial—and now, before guilty pleas—the evidence on which it will rely to prove guilt (*R. v. Brown*, 1606; *R. v. Ward* 1993, 51; Williams 1963). In the Crown Courts, the prosecution's disclosure "bundle" generally includes witness identities and key statements, notice of expert witnesses and scientific reports (Ashworth and Redmayne 2010, 259; Corker and Parkinson 2009, 61–72). Prosecution disclosure duties are similarly broad in Canada (Public Prosecution Service 2014, prin. 2.5.2; *R. v. Stinchcombe* 1991, 339 and 343; *R. v. Stinchcombe* 1995, 755; Canada Criminal Code, § 603), Australia (Commonwealth DPP 2017), and New Zealand (N.Z. Law Comm'n 2005, 18–20).

Among the fifty-one U.S. criminal justice systems, there is no such consensus and practices vary greatly. There is no "American model" of pre-trial disclosure law. Although the federal Constitution requires the prosecution to disclose exculpatory evidence to the defense by the time of trial, "there is no general constitutional right to discovery in a criminal case" (*Weatherford v. Bursey* 1977, 559; *Wardius v. Oregon* 1973, 474). Instead, one can describe disclosure practices in the states (where most prosecutions occur) and the federal system as following one of three or four basic approaches (Brown 2017).

About six states have adopted broad disclosure duties for the prosecution that are comparable to those in Commonwealth jurisdictions (Fla. R. Crim. P. 3.220; N.J. Ct. R. 3:13-3; N.C. Gen. Stat. § 15A-903). But a larger minority are at the other extreme. Perhaps fifteen state justice systems follow the model of the Federal Rules of Criminal Procedure, which define the most limited set of prosecution disclosure obligations in the common law world. Under these rules, prosecutors are required to disclose before trial little more than the identity of expert witnesses, the substance of expert analysis, physical items of evidence, and most prior statements of the defendant (Fed. R. Crim. P. 16; S.C.R. Crim. P. 5). Neither party is required to disclose the identities of their non-expert witnesses prior to trial, and disclosure of a witness's prior relevant statements need not be disclosed until the witness testifies at trial (Fed. R. Crim. P. 26.2). Another group of seven states largely follow this approach but modestly expand prosecution disclosure, notably by requiring advance notice of witnesses' identities. The remaining state justice systems—roughly half of U.S. jurisdictions—have adopted variations on a third approach that add a few more disclosure obligations. The particulars vary, but most grant the defense advance access not only to the names of prosecution witnesses but also to information such as their prior statements and criminal records (Cal. Penal Code §§ 1054.1–1054.9; Tex. Code Crim. P. arts. 39.14, 39.15).

There is a useful contrast in the approach of European civil law justice systems to these same issues. The key difference is conceptual: information about the case is not described as belonging to the *parties*. Instead, all relevant information is compiled in a single file or dossier that is generally understood as a *judicial* file. In practice, prosecutors are usually responsible for contributing most of its content. Depending on the jurisdiction, judicial officials may play an active role in the dossier's contents as well. And the defense can (or must) do the same, either by providing information (or objects) directly or requesting that state officials take statements from certain prospective witnesses. Failure to do so would be understood as improperly concealing evidence from the *court* as well as the prosecution. On this model, rules do not regulate what parties must *disclose* to each other; they regulate *access to the file*, which is presumptively available to both parties as well as the court. An important part of the context is that this process is not solely in preparation for a single, concentrated trial; the pre-trial and trial stages are part of a single, ongoing, judicially supervised adjudication (Caianiello 2019, 571–574).

5.3 Competing Interests in Pre-trial Litigation

In light of the consensus on prosecutorial obligations to disclose exculpatory information to the defense, the differences in pre-trial disclosure regimes largely have to do with the evidence that each party plans to offer at trial, particularly the names of witnesses and information about those witnesses. What accounts for these differences? There are two dimensions to the answer. The first looks to the strategies available for balancing the competing interests at stake in disclosure. Policies reflect very different views about how to manage disclosure in service of the same ends. The second points to the institutional forces and arrangements that help explain why policymakers in different places are convinced of the superiority of different strategies.

As noted earlier, disclosure rules balance conflicting interests. On the one hand, full disclosure before trial serves the interest in accurate fact-finding by enabling parties to prepare to confront and rebut opponents' evidence. With advance notice, they can identify a witness's bias or questionable competence, investigate the reliability of scientific or other expert analysis, and gather contradictory evidence. Facilitating thorough preparation underlies the ubiquitous requirement to give pre-trial notice of alibi (and alibi-rebuttal) evidence, expert testimony, or an insanity defense. But this interest in preparation and eliminating surprise conflicts with other interests that also improve fact-finding, and which would be better served by *not* disclosing evidence until trial. Foremost, these include (1) protecting witnesses from physical harm, intimidation, bribery, and the like; (2) protecting the integrity of other forms of evidence from destruction or contamination; and (3) safeguarding law enforcement investigative tactics that would be undermined by disclosure, such as the identity of undercover operatives and the existence of wiretaps or other surveillance. Those countervailing risks are not significant in many cases. Most witnesses don't face realistic risks for testifying; many cases don't involve secretive evidence-gathering tactics. Thus, the fact is that providing both parties with advance access to evidence is the best policy for assuring that all relevant evidence is presented and carefully scrutinized at trial *most of the time*. That is clearly true for expert evidence, for example, where preparation is essential and countervailing risks are especially low. Yet in certain circumstances, *not disclosing* information until trial best serves the aim of getting all relevant information before the fact-finder. That is the justification for withholding identity or contact information about witnesses who are deemed to face serious safety risks. (Keeping informers or surveillance operations confidential more often safeguards evidence production for a future case rather than the current one.)

Broad and narrow models of disclosure address these competing demands with different strategies. Holding aside considerable variations in details of various statutes, at bottom broad-disclosure schemes start with the default position that everything should be disclosed before trial and then provide for ways to make exceptions in particular circumstances, when the government has specific reasons for not disclosing specific evidence. Narrow or minimal disclosure schemes, by contrast, start with the opposite default rule: mandate disclosure only for specific kinds of evidence that never raise real risks of any kind, such as lab test results, expert analysis, and defendants' prior statements to police. Parties may withhold the rest until trial, although they are free to voluntarily disclose some or all evidence earlier (Douglass 2000, 2140–2141). Recognizing some of the costs of not disclosing most evidence before trial, jurisdictions provide a few modest mechanisms to compensate. Judges may have authority to order pre-trial disclosure upon a showing of substantial need (Ariz. R. Crim. P. 15[g]) or at least to encourage parties to cooperate in voluntary disclosure (McConkie 2017). And the defense should receive a mid-trial adjournment to review disclosures that occur only once the trial has begun, for prior statements of prosecution witnesses in particular (18 U.S.C. § 3500). (Broad-disclosure regimes employ that approach only to address inadvertent or improper failures to disclose earlier [Caianiello 2019, 567–570].) As one would expect, justifications for limited-disclosure schemes, such as those in U.S. federal courts, stress the concerns about risks from early disclosure to witnesses and investigative operations and downplay the costs of less thorough party preparation for accurate trial adjudication (*United States v. Ruiz* 2002, 631–632; Doucette 2016). Conversely, broad-disclosure jurisdictions—which describes most of the common law world but only a sizable minority of U.S. state criminal justice systems—rest on a primary commitment to eliminating evidentiary surprise and inadequate preparation that undermines adversarial testing of evidence, and so accommodate needs for non-disclosure through case-by-case exceptions. The same is true, broadly speaking, for European criminal justice systems in which presumptive early access to the dossier may be restricted to protect ongoing law enforcement activities and informant identities (Caianiello 2019, 565).

One could describe the basic difference between narrow and broad disclosure models to accommodating competing interests as a difference in *when* to disclose—at trial or before—that turns on how much weight policymakers give to one set of interests versus another. But there is another factor that drives the distinction in these policies as well. They reflect different choices about *who* controls disclosure, that is, who decides whether and when to disclose evidence prior to trial. This leads to what can be termed a structural difference between disclosure policies, meaning differences in how rules allocate authority among various players—parties, trial judges, and policymakers who draft the rules.

Of course, policymakers—legislatures or courts—make the first-order decisions about what kinds of evidence must be disclosed before trial and when. When they adopt expansive disclosure laws, policymakers, judges, and the parties are left with less authority. But since occasional exceptions from broad disclosure duties will be needed, such policies include second-order choices about who controls those decisions. In broad-disclosure regimes, that power almost always goes to judges; they rather than prosecutors decide whether particular circumstances justify withholding an item of evidence to protect, say, informers' identities, witness safety, or privileged information. Operational details usually take one of two forms: either prosecutors must get judicial permission to withhold information, or prosecutors can give notice that they have withheld something, and the defense can seek judicial review of that non-disclosure (Cal. Penal Code § 1054.7; *R. v. Stinchcombe* 1991; *R. v. Ward* 1993; Va. S. Ct. R. 3A:11). In addition, as just noted, rules allocate power to judges rather than parties in a different way, by authorizing them to order more disclosure than general rules dictate, based on some finding such as a substantial need for disclosure (Ariz. R. Crim. P. 15[g]).

The alternative, of course, is to give more authority to the parties than to judges, which primarily means more discretion to prosecutors. This is typically the structure of narrow-disclosure schemes, in which by definition policymakers have dictated few disclosure duties themselves. In theory such rules could put the discretion mostly in judges' hands, but in practice narrow disclosure mandates mean the parties mostly control what they will share with opponents before trial. Again the U.S. federal criminal procedure rules, and state rules based on them, are the clearest examples. Federal prosecutors, not judges, decide whether withholding the identities of government witnesses until trial is necessary to ensure their safety or integrity, or whether withholding evidence arising from wiretaps or other surveillance techniques should be withheld to protect continuing use of those techniques.

These choices about who controls disclosure decisions turn, at least implicitly and sometimes explicitly, on presumptions about the trustworthiness and competence of the various players. In most of the common law world (and also the civil law world; Caianiello 2019, 568–569), judges predominantly control whether parties may withhold information based on risks to witnesses or ongoing law enforcement efforts. This model considers judges fully competent to assess risks to witnesses or the needs of law enforcement in specific circumstances. But minimal disclosure regimes such as the U.S. federal rules, on the other hand, do not share that view. Instead, they take prosecutors to be the more competent actor for these judgments. By not mandating disclosure under general rules nor empowering judges to order disclosure in appropriate circumstances, they give prosecutors control over whether to disclose a great deal of important evidence before trial. This view emphasizes prosecutors' more intimate knowledge of the facts in the cases that they initiate, which makes them better positioned to assess witness risks or law enforcement's operational needs. Judges are comparatively less well positioned to make those calls, and judicial oversight would add administrative burdens and perhaps delays (*United States v. Ruiz* 2002, 631–632).

On the other hand, prosecutors are not as well positioned as judges to balance competing considerations objectively. That lesser objectivity (compared to judges) matters because withholding evidence until trial provides a tempting tactical advantage—minimizing the opponent's time to prepare confrontation and rebuttal strategies (Douglass 2000, 2140–2141). And that temptation can affect what should be a judgment solely about the competing interests of witness safety versus the public *value* of a better-prepared adversary. Prosecutors' unique role as ministers of justice is insufficient to offset this risk, as least in the judgment of policymakers in most Commonwealth criminal justice systems where broad disclosure duties now predominate. Prosecutors in the United Kingdom and other common law countries are not elected and enjoy civil service status, which should reinforce ministerial norms. Yet they are granted less authority over disclosure than U.S. prosecutors in minimal-disclosure jurisdictions, despite the U.S. practice of electing prosecutors contributing to a weaker minister-of-justice norm—an assessment I have defended at length elsewhere (Brown 2016, 44–50). Minimal-disclosure policies, then, trust prosecutors with a great deal of authority over pre-trial disclosure because they are especially convinced of the value of their unique case-specific knowledge about the risks that justify non-disclosure, which seems coupled with a relatively weaker commitment to the value of pre-trial disclosure for fair and accurate adjudication.

Finally, disclosure systems also reflect different degrees of trust in defense lawyers. A broad disclosure system seems less risky if defense attorneys collectively are assumed to be trustworthy professionals who would not betray professional obligations and public interests (e.g., witness safety) by compromising law enforcement confidentiality or facilitating a client's potential to intimidate witnesses. Where faith in defense lawyers' professionalism is sufficiently strong, disclosure of sensitive information can be broader by granting pre-trial access solely to defense *counsel* but not defendants themselves; lawyers must not share such information with their clients (Ariz. R. Crim. P. 39[b]; Cal. Penal Code § 1054.2; Ga. Code § 17-16-8). This form of limited access to the evidence dossier is a common feature in European criminal procedure (Caianiello 2019, 569). Thus, narrow-disclosure systems that lack this feature reflect a relatively low confidence in the trustworthiness of defense attorneys as well as in the competence of judges.

In sum, differences in disclosure policies reflect divergent judgments about the efficacy of various ways to manage the conflicting interests at stake in pre-trial disclosure, and divergent judgments follow from competing assumptions about the competence of judges, prosecutors, and defense lawyers to take responsibility in that process. But what leads policymakers in one jurisdiction to adopt one strategy, based on one set of assumptions, while those elsewhere, convinced of different premises, opt for another? An important part of the explanation, I submit, is the institutional power of various players in the policymaking process. Roughly speaking, the more influence that prosecution agencies have over disclosure policies, the more likely jurisdictions are to stick with narrow disclosure regimes that give prosecutors more control over pre-trial disclosures (Stuntz 2001). Conversely, where policymakers—whether courts or legislatures—have the institutional capacity to set disclosure policies by exercising independent judgment without undue deference from any single stakeholder, the result is usually some form of broad disclosure policy that shifts more power to the rule-makers themselves or to judges, and that reflects somewhat greater trust in defense lawyers. The Supreme Court of Canada's landmark decision in *R. v. Stinchcombe* (1991) is one example. Another is the Florida Supreme Court's record of procedural rule-making (for which it has more authority than many state courts), which has played a large role in Florida's especially broad pre-trial disclosure (and *discovery*) rules (Dimmig 1997, 52–55). Where legislatures make the policy, broad-disclosure reforms are often the result of political moments triggered by wrongful-conviction scandals that either diminish prosecutors' influence in debates or prompt prosecution agencies to support broader disclosure mandates. Reforms in Illinois, North Carolina, and Texas roughly fit that description (Grissom 2013; Turner and Redlich 2016, 304–305).

5.4 The Changing Nature of Evidence and Disclosure Reform

The twentieth-century expansion of government criminal investigation strategies—undercover agents, wiretaps, video surveillance, and much more—generated a large share of the justifications for restrictions on pre-trial disclosure. (The remaining rationales stem from victims' interests and risks to witnesses.) This final section looks briefly at the most recent important development in the nature of information subject to pre-trial disclosure—the rapid growth of digital evidence or electronically stored information (ESI). It considers how disclosure rules have begun to address this challenge, and how rules and practices are likely to change in the near future to deal with the exponentially increasing volume of this kind of evidence, which can be immensely valuable, but which also poses significant practical challenges.

The availability and volume of digital evidence in criminal investigation and litigation now comes from almost innumerable sources. For present purposes, we can note a few increasingly common sources such as cell phone data (which can include user location data as well as communication data); information from email and social media accounts, device hard drives, or web browser histories; and video recordings (often with audio) from surveillance cameras and police officers' vehicle-mounted and body-worn cameras. More than nine out of ten U.S. adults own cell phones, and U.S. police investigators make more than a million requests for cell-phone call records each year; an estimated

350 million surveillance cameras operate worldwide; 47 percent of U.S. law enforcement agencies—and sixty-two of the largest sixty-nine—have body-worn cameras. Sixty-nine percent have dashboard cameras (Anderson 2015; Hyland 2018; Starr 2014). And this leaves aside the trove of data from innumerable other devices in the rapidly expanding "internet of things," or networked, intelligent objects that store or generate digital data with some means of connectivity to communicate with other devices. By 2020, the number of such devices worldwide is expected to reach 50 billion (Danova 2013; Ferguson 2016, 812).

As Jenia Turner has considered in detail, ESI from these sources pose several challenges for pre-trial disclosure practices (Turner 2019). Simply storing data in a form that can be feasibly retrieved and examined can be costly, given the necessity of ensuring data security and sharing data between government agencies and private parties. Disputes can arise over the volume and format of data that law enforcement makes accessible to the defense, such as whether the government must provide data in a searchable format, or whether data files must include metadata—i.e., data that provides information about other "primary" data. Law enforcement often obtain data from third parties that lacks metadata, although that information can be critical to authenticate or understand primary data (Turner 2019). It can also have independent value, as confirmed by value that national security agencies' find in collecting solely metadata from phones and other devices (Szoldra 2016). These issues can trigger delay and raise the government's litigation costs. And even if the government has sufficient resources to handle data, individual defendants and their attorneys often do not (Turner 2019).

Further, overcoming these problems leaves others: prosecutors may share large volumes of data, including video from security cams or police cams, burdening defense teams with the laborious task—perhaps shortly before trial—of searching for the small, relevant needle in a large haystack of data (Anello and Albert 2017; Findling 2018). That problem—or tactic—is a familiar one in civil litigation with paper documents as well as digital data (Tidmarsh 2015, 868–869). Evolving solutions to this problem will likely take one of two basic forms. One is that the government will be required to identify for the defense the key data—in particular, exculpatory evidence—within large files and databases. Another is that the defense would have access to the rapidly evolving—often proprietary—technology to identify specific data within large collections. This option is technically feasible now for identifying many kinds of critical information in audio and video data. Instead of people watching hours of video in search of relevant moments and attempting to cross-reference and synchronize separate video sources of the same events, new tools can now search video files for particular faces, figures, vehicles, objects, behaviors (such as movement speed or direction), or sounds such as gun shots. They can also integrate multiple video files to provide a more comprehensive account from sources that individually provide only partial accounts, even if the video lacks key metadata that was stripped when it was uploaded to social media.

Even if it lives up to its promise, a key question will be whether this technology will be available to defendants, and even some prosecution offices (Liang et al. 2016; Briefcam.com). And the analysis of audio and video has proven a comparatively easier technical hurdle. Other domains are more challenging. Automating searches for syntactical meaning (as opposed to key words) in text is much more difficult; no comparable advance for that task is likely in the near term (Pickens 2018). And the reliability of conclusions drawn from analysis of other kinds of digital data, particularly user-generated event data, are still subjects of debate and are vulnerable to poor methodologies or analytical execution (Center for Statistics). Inferences about a cell phone's precise location, for example, are still not possible from data about ordinary phone calls such as the tower through which a call was routed (Grimm 2018; Starr 2014). And much of the software and methodologies developed for finding specific information in large data files, or drawing conclusions from data, is likely to be proprietary, which poses another barrier to disclosure and thus to independent assessment, or adversarial testing, of the reliability of those means of analysis (Wexler 2018).

How these developments will change disclosure rules in the future is unclear. So far only a few U.S. jurisdictions have taken steps—many relatively partial and modest—to address some of these challenges (Idaho Crim. R. 16[b][9]; N.J. Ct. R. 3:13-3 and 4:18). Turner seems correct to predict that the rapid growth of digital evidence is likely to require more resources for the criminal process—to securely transfer and store large volumes of data, to make analytical tools and experts available to both parties, and to probe the reliability of findings and inferences in the resulting analyses. And as it already has in civil litigation, that is likely to push criminal courts into the role of "managerial judging" (Turner 2019).

Yet in the longer run, it seems doubtful whether in the United States federal or state judges will have sufficient power under the federal Rules Enabling Act (28 U.S.C. § 2071) or its state equivalents, or through courts' inherent supervisory authority, to take on a much greater role in confronting the challenges digital evidence presents without further rule reforms. Dan McConkie has described how some federal district courts have dictated significant expansions of prosecutorial disclosure obligations through their local rule-making powers (McConkie 2017, 78–92). Yet those advances have notable limits. None require pre-trial disclosure of trial witness names, for example, much less names of persons with relevant knowledge whom the prosecution does not intend to call at trial. And because local rules cannot conflict with federal rules and statutes, trial judges cannot compel pre-trial disclosure of prosecution witnesses' prior statements (McConkie 2017, 114–115). Proposed Federal Rule of Criminal Procedure 16.1 is the first attempt of federal rule-makers to address disclosure of electronic information, but it would require merely that parties "confer, and try to agree on a timetable and procedures for pre-trial disclosure"; it pointedly does not expand judges' discretionary authority over disclosure of such materials. The era of ever-expanding digital evidence is likely to put pressure on this weak-judicial-power model of disclosure rules. One might expect that model, which, as noted, continues to prevail only in a minority of U.S. jurisdictions, gradually to further retreat in the face of this challenge and of the broader, long-term trend in the common law world to expand pre-trial disclosure and to shift final authority over disclosure from the parties to the judiciary.

Notes

1. For analogous disclosure duties on defendants in English and Welsh courts, see Criminal Justice Act 2003 §§ 32–40.
2. That issue is addressed in more detail in Bruce A. Green, "Bar Authorities and Prosecutors," Chapter 15 of this volume.

References

18 U.S.C. § 3500.

28 U.S.C. § 2071.

725 Ill. Comp. Stat. 5/114-13.

Ariz. R. Crim. P. 15 and 39(b)(11).

Armstrong, Ken, and Maurice Possley. 1999. "Trial and Error." *Chicago Tribune*, January 11–14, 1999.

Anderson, Monica. 2015. *The Demographics of Device Ownership*. Pew Research Center (October 29, 2015).

Anello, Robert J., and Richard F. Albert. 2017. "Coming Changes to Federal Criminal Discovery Rule?" *New York Law Journal* 257(63): 1–4.

Ashworth, Andrew, and Mike Redmayne. 2010. *The Criminal Process*, 4th ed. New York: Oxford University Press.

Brady v. Maryland. 1963. 373 U.S. 83.

Brennan, William J. 1963. "The Criminal Prosecution: Sporting Event or Quest for Truth?" *Washington University Law Quarterly* 1963(3): 279–295.

Briefcam. 2019. "About Briefcam."

Brown, Darryl K. 2016. *Free Market Criminal Justice*. New York: Oxford University Press.

Brown, Darryl K. 2017. "Discovery in State Criminal Justice." In *Reforming Criminal Justice: Pretrial and Trial Processes*. Edited by Erik Luna, vol. 3, 147–169. Phoenix: Academy for Justice.

Caianiello, Michele. 2019. "Access to and Limits on Evidence Dossiers in Civil Law Systems." In *The Oxford Handbook of Criminal Process*. Edited by Darryl Brown, Jenia I. Turner, and Bettina Weisser, 563–585. New York: Oxford University Press.

Cal. Const. art. I, § 28(b)(1).

Cal. Penal Code §§ 1054.1–1054.9.

Canada Criminal Code 1985. R.S.C. c. C-46, § 603.

Center for Human Rights Science and Center for Statistics and Applications in Forensic Evidence at Carnegie Mellon University.

Center for Statistics and Applications in Forensic Evidence, *Analyzing User-Generated Event Data (Digital)*.

Criminal Justice Act 2003 (England and Wales).

Colo. R. Crim. P. 16.

Commonwealth DPP. 2017. *Statement on Disclosure in Prosecutions Conducted by the Commonwealth* (Australia).

Commonwealth DPP. 2016. *CDPP Summary of State and Territory Disclosure Regimes* (Australia).

Corker, David, and Stephen Parkinson. 2009. *Disclosure in Criminal Proceedings*. New York: Oxford University Press.

Dallison v. Caffrey. 1965. 1 Q.B. 348 (England and Wales).

Danova, Tony. 2013. "Morgan Stanley: 75 Billion Devices Will Be Connected to the Internet of Things by 2020." *Business Insider*, October 2, 2013.

Dimmig, Howard. 1997. "Deposition Reform: Is the Cure Worse than the Problem?" *Florida Bar Journal* 71:52–55.

Doucette, Michael R. 2016. "Virginia Prosecutors' Response to Two Models of Pre-Plea Discovery in Criminal Cases: An Empirical Comparison." *Washington & Lee Law Review Online* 73: 415.

Douglass, John G. 2000. "Balancing Hearsay and Criminal Discovery." *Fordham Law Review* 68(6): 2097–2198.

Fed. R. Crim. P. 16.

Fed. R. Crim. P. 26.2.

Ferguson, Andrew Guthrie. 2016. "The Internet of Things and the Fourth Amendment of Effects." *California Law Review* 104(4): 805–880.

Findling, Drew. 2018. "Unable to Bear the Weight of the 'Document Dump': A Heavy Burden on Individuals and an Increasing Threat to Due Process." *The Champion*, (September/October), 5–8.

Fla. R. Crim. P. 3.220.

Ga. Code §§ 17-16-1 to -10.

Ga. Code Ann. § 17-16-8.

Gold, Russell, Carissa Byrne Hessick, and F. Andrew Hessick. 2017. "Civilizing Criminal Settlements." *Boston University Law Review* 97(5): 1607–1660.

Grimm, Paul. 2018. "Admissibility of Historical Cell Phone Location Evidence." *Litigation Journal* 44(4): 53–56.

Grissom, Brandi. 2013. "Perry Signs Michael Morton Act." *The Texas Tribune*, May 16.

Grissom, Brandi, Ryan Murphy, and Justin Dehn. 2012. "Errors in Judgment: The Consequences of Prosecutorial Mistakes." *The Texas Tribune*, July 5–10.

Hyland, Shelley S. 2018. *Body-Worn Cameras in Law Enforcement Agencies, 2016*. NJS 251775. Washington, D.C.: Bureau of Justice Statistics.

Idaho Crim. R. 16.

Ill. Sup. Ct. R. 412–415.

Langbein, John H. 2012. "The Disappearance of Civil Trial in the United States." *Yale Law Journal* 122(3): 522–573.

Leadership Conference on Civil and Human Rights. 2017. *Body-Worn Camera Scorecard*.

Liang, Junwei, et al. 2016. *Report: Video Synchronization and Sound Search for Human Rights Documentation and Conflict Monitoring*. Carnegie Mellon University Center for Human Rights.

McConkie, Daniel S., Jr. 2017. "The Local Rules Revolution in Criminal Discovery." *Cardozo Law Review* 39(1): 59–126.

N.J. Ct. R. 3:13-3, 3:13-4, 4:18.

N.C. Gen. Stat. §§ 15A-902 to 15A-910.

New Zealand Law Comm'n. 2005. *Criminal Pre-trial Processes: Justice through Efficiency*. Wellington, N.Z.: New Zealand Law Commission.

Ohio R. Crim. P. 12.1 and 16.

Pickens, Jeremy. 2018. "Deep Learning and E-Discovery—Fact or Fiction?" *BloombergLaw.com*, November 29, 2018.
Public Prosecution Service of Canada. 2014. *Public Prosecution Service of Canada Deskbook.* prin. 2.5.2.
R. v. Brown. 1994. 1 W.L.R. 1599.
R. v. Keane. 1994. 99 Cr. App. R. 1, 1994. 1 W.L.R. 746 (England & Wales).
R. v. Ward. 1993. 96 Cr. App. 1.
R. v. Stinchcombe. 1995. 1 S.C.R. 754 (Can.).
R. v. Stinchcombe. 1991. 3 S.C.R. 326(Can.).
Ridolfi, Kathleen M., and Maurice Possley. 2010. "Preventable Error: A Report on Prosecutorial Misconduct in California, 1997–2009." Veritas Initiative.
S.C. R. Crim. P. 5.
Shalom, Alexander, and George C. Thomas, III. 2012. *Trial and Error: A Comprehensive Study of Prosecutor Conduct in New Jersey*. ACLU of New Jersey.
Smith v. Cain. 2012. 565 U.S. 73.
Starr, Douglas. 2014. "What Your Cell Phone Can't Tell the Police." *New Yorker*, June 26.
Stuntz, William J. 2001. "The Pathological Politics of Criminal Law." *Michigan Law Review* 100(3): 505–600.
Szoldra, Paul. 2016. "Leaked NSA Document Says Metadata Collection Is One of Agency's 'Most Useful Tools.'" *Business Insider*, December 7.
Tex. Code Crim. P. art. 39.14, 39.15.
Tidmarsh, Jay. 2015. "The Litigation Budget." *Vanderbilt Law Review* 68(3): 855–918.
Turner, Jenia I., and Allison D. Redlich. 2016. *Washington & Lee Law Review* 73(1): 285–410.
Turner, Jenia I. 2019. "Managing Digital Discovery in Criminal Cases." *Journal of Criminal Law & Criminology* 109(2): 237–312.
United States v. Nobles. 1975. 422 U.S. 225.
United States v. Ruiz. 2002. 536 U.S. 622.
Utah R. Crim. P. 16.
Va. S. Ct. R. 3A:11.
Wardius v. Oregon. 1973. 412 U.S. 470.
Weatherford v. Bursey. 1977. 429 U.S. 545.
Wexler, Rebecca. 2018. "Life, Liberty and Trade Secrets." *Stanford Law Review* 70(5): 1343–1430.
Williams, Glanville. 1959. "Advance Notice of the Defence." *Criminal Law Review* (Eng.) 1959: 548.
Williams, Glanville. 1963. *The Proof of Guilt: A Study of the English Criminal Trial*. 3rd ed. San Antonio: Stevens & Sons Ltd.

CHAPTER 6

PROSECUTORS AND TRIALS

ALEXANDER HEINZE

6.1 Introduction

Ippolit Kyrillovich is a literary figure who has not been blessed with wide-spread popularity. In fact, Kyrillovich is hardly known even to the average reader of classical literature—even though he is a figure in Fyodor Dostoevsky's *The Brothers Karamazov*, one of Dostoevsky's most influential novels (Ruckaberle 2006). In the novel, Kyrillovich is "the prosecutor, actually the deputy prosecutor, but referred to as the prosecutor by everyone in the town" (Dostoevsky 1994). Nevertheless, Kyrillovich has a critical role in the book (Mayer 2007). As a prosecutor, he is committed to proving the guilt of Dimitri Karamazov, who is wrongfully accused of murdering his father and eventually convicted and sentenced to twenty years penal servitude in Siberia. In his closing speech, the prosecutor is less concerned with the accused himself but shows a (more consequentialist) goal of maintaining law and order, which Dostoevsky describes like this: "It is as well to remember that what gave his speech its strength was its sincerity: he did in all sincerity believe in the guilt of the accused; his address was not that of a hired hack going through the motions; in calling for 'retribution' he really was imbued with a desire to 'save society'" (Dostoevsky 1994).

Considering that the trial against Dimitri Karamazov was "basically fair" (Posner 2009) and yet, Karamazov was innocent, Kyrillovich personifies the prosecutor's dual role as a seeker of both procedural and substantive justice. Role duality is the very foundation of this chapter, which conducts an overview of the prosecutor's roles at trial. The main feature of the prosecutor's role at trial is that it could not be further away from singularity. The prosecutor belongs both to the executive and judicial branch, is both impartial minister of justice and forceful advocate of the victim, is both officer of the court with judicial functions and leader of law enforcement, is both centralized and decentralized, and is both elected and appointed.

A second feature of the prosecutor's role is a systemic one. The prosecutor's role at trial crucially depends on contextual factors: on the role of trial within the proceedings; on the nature of the proceedings; and eventually on the nature of the state itself. For instance, a preliminary reservation against using Kyrillovich as an example of the prosecutor's role duality could be that it does not apply to the American setting, since the novel plays in nineteenth-century Russia and Russia's criminal procedure model is (and was) "distinctly continental European" (Pakes 2019). However, compared to Dostoevsky's "Crime and Punishment," *The Brothers Karamazov* "depicts adversary procedure" (Posner 2009). It is thus much closer to American criminal procedure than it appears. Whether procedures follow an adversarial or inquisitorial model has a crucial influence on the prosecutor's role. Descriptions of procedural modelling are therefore inevitable in this chapter—as is scrutiny of the popular adversarial-inquisitorial dichotomy.

6.2 The Trial Phase

The first contextualization of the prosecutor's role at trial is the nature of the trial phase itself.

6.2.1 General Remarks and Definition

The lexical definition of the term "trial" is rather vague. It denotes "[t]he examination and determination of a cause by a judicial tribunal; determination of the guilt or innocence of an accused person by a court" or "[t]he action of testing or putting to the proof the fitness, truth, strength, or another quality of anything" (Onions 1973; Simpson and Weiner 1989/2002). For Ingraham, "trials"—more concretely—"are usually a review of facts collected by someone else (for example, by police, prosecutors, investigators, investigation judges or other officials, and defense lawyers) and presented to the decision-maker in open court or through a written record" (Ingraham 1987). It is rare that case law weighs in on the definition of "trial." In the Australian case *Dietrich v. The Queen* (1992), Justice Deane indicated that trial must take place before a magistrate, judge, or jury. Kirchengast interprets Deane's understanding of a criminal trial as being "separate from the various other pre- and post-trial processes that constitute the means by which defendants are held to account for their wrongdoing" (Kirchengast 2010). Vasiliev—albeit with a view to the International Criminal Trial—describes the trial phase as "the culmination of a host of preceding activities of the Prosecutor in investigating a case and preparing it for prosecution" (Vasiliev 2012). Vasiliev thus addresses an important restriction to the view of the trial as a separate phase: especially from a prosecutor's perspective, both the structure and the course of a trial depend on the phases preceding the trial phase, namely the pre-trial phase, investigation, arrest, etc. (Vasiliev 2012; Heinze 2020a). It is therefore necessary to locate the trial phase within the context of the criminal proceedings in general.

6.2.2 Normative Framework

Comparing the role of prosecutors at trial in various legal systems requires a certain abstraction, to the benefit of clarity and to the detriment of detail. It is the price that must be paid upon using comparative law's advantages, which include the improvement of an understanding of law and context by explaining reasons for differences and similarities or even the creation of a general jurisprudence (of prosecutorial conduct in our case). Comparing the details of the role of the prosecutor at trial is micro-comparison (de Cruz 2007). It requires broad comparative categories or models. In criminal procedure, those models are countless. Just to mention a few: adversarial vs. inquisitorial (both can have several different meanings) vs. accusatorial; crime control model vs. due process model vs. arms length model vs. liberal bureaucratic model vs. social disciplinary model vs. police model vs. victim participation model. Not to mention the normative models. I have described and compared those models elsewhere and argued that Damaška's concepts of coordinate vs. hierarchical officialdom and a reactive vs. an activist state (Damaška 1986) seem superior to all these models (Heinze 2014). Yet, space restrictions do not allow me to justify my selection, making a comparative analysis of the role of the prosecutor at trial on the basis of the coordinate vs. hierarchical officialdom and a reactive vs. an activist state dichotomy futile. Thus, I will use none of the models mentioned and simply refer to the civil law and common law traditions. In a way, this is a simplification to the detriment of accuracy, but it circumvents an abstract debate about procedural modelling.

6.2.3 Stages at Trial

For the purpose of this chapter, the trial will be divided into four main parts: an opening stage, presentation of evidence, a closing stage, and judgment/sentence (Vasiliev 2012). This general structure of course varies in different jurisdictions—as does the prosecutorial role within the stages. At times, it will therefore be necessary either to provide some context about the broader procedural picture in jurisdictions selected or to exceptionally add a part to the four mentioned above. It should also be noted that full trials have become a rarity these days, which I have addressed elsewhere (Ambos and Heinze 2017). In the United States, for instance, only a small percentage of cases go to trial (Cole, Smith, and DeJong 2018).

The tasks of the prosecutor at trial are—inter alia—to decide what evidence to bring to court (except in France and Germany), which witnesses to call, what questions to ask them, which documents to introduce into evidence, how to conduct cross-examination

(Heller 2015); to present the prosecution case, either orally or in writing; and often to make a sentencing recommendation (Wade 2006). In exceptional circumstances, some jurisdictions allow the prosecutor to alter the charge during trial (Netherlands: Blom and Smit 2006; Sweden: Zila 2006). In most civil law jurisdictions, the questioning of witnesses is primarily done by the court, and only subsequently by both prosecutor and defense. It is not the parties who present their evidence, it is the court who summons and examines the witnesses and experts (Bohlander 2012). In Germany, for instance, the role of the prosecutor at trial "is more akin to checking on the court's conduct of the trial, to object to questions by the court or other parties they consider inadmissible... and to fill in the gaps left after the court has finished its questioning, etc." (Bohlander 2012).

In this section, I will describe the role of the prosecutor in various stages of the trial. The objects of the comparative analysis will be (1) selected prosecutorial measures in (2) selected legal systems. The legal systems analyzed have been chosen to represent either the common law tradition (the United States, England and Wales) or civil law tradition (Germany and France). When no legal system is mentioned explicitly, I am referring to the United States or making general observations. To a comparative lawyer, this might seem unsatisfactory. Alas, it is. Yet, both time and space constraints will always curtail a comparative lawyer's ideal research.

6.2.3.1 *Jury Selection*

Since most legal systems relying on a civil law tradition do not conduct trials in front of a jury (although they may include lay participation), the first stage analyzed with regard to the involvement of the prosecutor is already an exceptional one. Even in systems that do use a jury trial, this trial has become a rarity (Burns 2009). In fact, legal systems relying on the common law tradition are tending to move away from the excesses of adversarial forms of adjudication, as well as from lay participation in fact-finding, as demonstrated through increased bench trials and fewer jury trials. In the United States, until 1976, only 3.4 percent of state criminal trials were jury trials. Between 1976 and 2002, jury trials fell to 1.3 percent (Burns 2009; Damaška 1997; Doran and Jackson 1997; Galanter 2004).

In those cases that are still argued in front of a jury, there are several ways for the prosecutor to influence the composition of the jury panel. The process of selecting the actual jurors from the pool of potential jurors by questioning them is called the *voir dire*—literally, "to speak the truth," also known as "jury selection" (Kadish et al. 2012; Grosso and O'Brian 2019). It is viewed as the first stage of a trial. The process of jury selection differs among the U.S. jurisdictions (Hall 2014) and the complexity varies with the seriousness of the crime (Grosso and O'Brian 2019). Lawyers for the prosecution and the defense are permitted to challenge prospective jurors either for cause or peremptorily, and eventually remove them from the jury panel (Scheb and Scheb 2013). In some jurisdictions, it is the trial judge who conducts the *voir dire* examination; he or she may invite the lawyers to suggest questions to ask the prospective jurors. In other jurisdictions, lawyers for each side conduct the *voir dire* (Scheb and Scheb 2013). A prosecutor's challenge for cause is a way to remove a juror demonstrating that he or she is biased (Samaha 2018). If the judge agrees, the juror is released. The numbers of jurors who may be removed this way is unlimited (Hall 2014).

Reasons for removal are—inter alia—"having a close relationship with counsel, being significantly involved in the case as a witness or in some other capacity, or having formed a definite opinion about the case" (Scheb and Scheb 2013). In addition to challenges for cause, the prosecutor may remove a juror using a peremptory challenge. Peremptory challenges are limited and do not have to be justified (Hall 2014). In the federal courts, both the prosecution and the defense have twenty peremptory challenges in capital offenses and three in misdemeanors. In felony cases, the prosecution has six, the defense ten (Samaha 2018). States have similar rules (Hall 2014). However, the prosecutor may not eliminate a juror because of race or gender (see below §6.3.3.1). To be able to use challenges effectively during the *voir dire* process, it is crucial to see how the prosecutors phrase the questions (Grosso and O'Brian 2019). Frederick defines four goals that should be achieved during *voir dire*: "eliciting information from jurors, developing rapport with jurors, educating jurors on key concepts, and persuading jurors to view the case from their perspective" (Frederick 2018). Nevertheless, in a recent empirical study, Grosso and O'Brian demonstrated that the effectiveness of the *voir dire* procedure to gain information about the bias of jurors is often overstated (Grosso and O'Brian 2019).

In England and Wales, a defendant's right to a jury trial was seriously weakened in the 1970s, and this trend has continued (Doran and Jackson 1997). Only Crown Court cases involve a jury (and a professional judge), while cases in the Magistrates' Court are tried by magistrates or by a judge sitting alone (Campbell, Ashworth, and Redmayne 2019; Darbyshire 2020). To provide a little context: all prosecutions start in the Magistrates' Court (Partington 2019). Whether they finish there depends on how the case is classified. If the charge is serious (for example, rape or murder), the case will go to the Crown Court on indictment (trial on indictment only). Most charges – for the least serious offenses – are dealt with summarily and tried only in the Magistrates' Court (summary trials) (Slapper and Kelly 2017; Spencer 1977/1995). Triable-either-way offenses (an intermediate category of offenses) may be tried either in a Magistrates' or Crown Court (Smartt 2006).

The jury will be sworn in, commonly referred to as being "empaneled" (Sharpley 2019). As is in the U.S. system, both the prosecution and the defense may challenge a potential juror on the ground that he or she may be biased for or against the accused. The party who alleges that a juror is biased bears the burden of proving bias. The prosecutor says "challenge" prior to the juror taking his or her oath and explains the reasons for the challenge to the judge (Hungerford-Welch 2019). In deviation from the U.S. system, the prosecution must provide prima facie evidence in support of the challenge before being (exceptionally) allowed to question the juror (*R. v. Chandler* 1964). A peculiarity of the jury selection process in England and Wales is the so-called "prosecution stand by," where in exceptional cases the prosecution (not the defense) may challenge a juror without giving reasons. To exercise this right, "prosecuting counsel says 'stand by' just before the juror takes his oath. It is then explained to the juror that he cannot sit on this jury, but will go back to the jury panel and may be called on to try another case" (Hungerford-Welch 2019).

6.2.3.2 *Opening Stage*

Once the jury has been empaneled and after the respective instructions, the trial begins with opening statements. Addressing the jury, the prosecutor makes the first opening statement, since he/she bears the burden of proof at trial (see below §6.2.3.3), outlining what he/she intends to prove (Ferdico, Fradella, and Totten 2009; Hall 2014). Thus, it is not argumentative; "inessential comment, irrelevant comment, is burdensome and can be extremely dangerous" (Du Cann 1993). Opening statements are often waived in bench trials, since the facts surrounding the charge cannot be presented (Hall 2014). Yet, the opening statement has a considerable influence on the determination of the outcome of the case (Ferdico, Fradella, and Totten 2009; Hall 2014; Lempert 1991).

In England and Wales, in all three trial options the prosecutor can make an opening speech. He/she usually speaks first, unless the preliminary issue of the sanity of the defendant is raised (Du Cann 1993). At the Crown Court, the prosecutor explains what the case is about and what evidence he/she intends to call—similar to the U.S. system. The opening speech will usually contain the following elements:

1. the legal elements of the offense(s) in the indictment;
2. an outline of the evidence the prosecutor intends to call (indicating the witnesses to be called and how these witnesses fit into the overall story); and
3. an explanation of the operation of the burden and standard of proof in a criminal case (Sharpley 2019).

At the Magistrates' Court, too, the purpose of the opening speech is to set the scene. It starts with the prosecuting solicitor:

> telling the magistrates the factual details about the charge which the defendant faces. He will then explain to the magistrates the relevant substantive law and will tell them what the prosecution will need to prove in order to secure a conviction. The prosecuting solicitor should remind the magistrates that the prosecution have the burden of proving beyond a reasonable doubt that the defendant is guilty, and that the defendant is entitled to an acquittal unless the magistrates are sure that he is guilty.... The prosecuting solicitor will outline what the prosecution case consists of, tell the court which witnesses he intends to call to give evidence for the prosecution, and summarise briefly the evidence that is to be given by these witnesses. He may also refer the magistrates to any points of law which he anticipates may arise during the trial (Sharpley 2019).

The Criminal Procedure Rules 2020 – "a concise, simple, consolidated statement of statutory and common law procedural rules" (Darbyshire 2020) – have concretised the prosecutor's opening speech in comparison to their predecessors from 2015: While the latter (merely) referred to the summarization of the prosecution case, "identifying the relevant law and facts" (former 24.3.[3][a] of the Criminal Procedure Rules 2015), the new Rule reads: "the prosecutor may summarise the prosecution case, concisely identifying the relevant law, outlining the facts and indicating the matters likely to be in dispute" (24.3.[3][a] of the Criminal Procedure Rules 2020). Criminal Practice Direction VI, para. 24B.1, emphasises that "[i]t will not usually be necessary, or helpful, to present a detailed account of all the prosecution evidence due to be introduced." In summary trials, opening speeches of the prosecutor are usually rather brief and sometimes waived (Hungerford-Welch 2019).

Everything that has been said so far does not apply to most trials within the civil law tradition. To take Germany as an example: if the court confirms the indictment, the trial phase is opened (*Eröffnungsbeschluss*), provided it seems likely that the accused will be sentenced (s. 203 of the German Code of Criminal Procedure [*Strafprozessordnung*—StPO]). After admission of the indictment, the trial court will prepare the hearing and set a date (s. 213 StPO). The court also formally opens the hearing, introduces the panel and establishes the identity of the defendant, counsel, prosecutor, and other parties (Bohlander 2012). The prosecutor takes a seat in front of the windows of the courtroom, which is not an official rule and yet the case in most courtrooms in Germany (Reinhard 2002). The unofficial reasons for this vary somewhat between practicality and myth: the prosecutor needs to be seated opposite the defendant, who should sit by the door; the defendant needs to be seated so the light of the windows can fall on him—since the prosecutor is supposed to sit opposite the defendant, he/she consequently needs to have the windows at his/her back; the prosecutor should sit in the light. In fact, the seating order of a courtroom is very illuminating in understanding the role of a prosecutor during trial. To compare the (usual) seating order in Crown Court trials with the order in Germany (for the average trial, i.e., regardless of a special circumstance), consider Figures 6.1 and 6.2.

In the two figures, the different understanding of the prosecutor's role becomes very visible. In the U.K. setting, the prosecutor is—at least with regard to the seating order—on equal footing with the defense, facing both bench and witness stand. In the German setting, the prosecutor is situated right next to the bench (at the window front), opposite the defendant. The witness faces the judge.

After the judge introduces the participants (and asks the witnesses, after they receive an initial caution, to leave the courtroom again), the prosecutor may ask the defendant questions about his/her identity, including first name, last name, date and place of birth, family status, affiliation, place of residence, and nationality. This does not fall into the category of an evidentiary questioning. In case the judge limits the introduction of the defendant to a minimum, i.e., to merely his/her identity, the prosecutor rarely asks follow up questions. Usually, however, this is the place in a trial when the defendant's past is elaborated upon, together with his/her personal and financial living conditions. The defendant has a right to remain silent about disclosing his/her identity in a narrow sense (Heghmanns 2017).

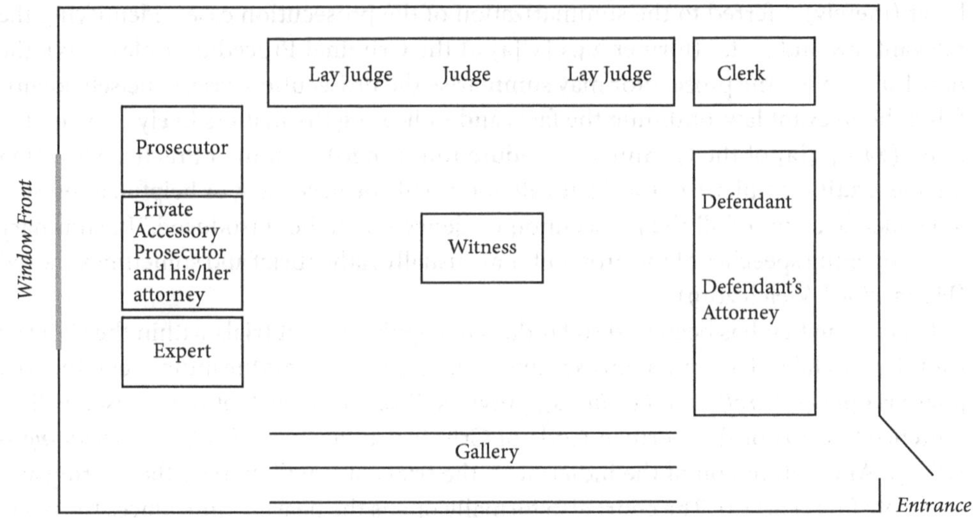

FIGURE 6.1 Seating Order in German Criminal Courts (generalized and simplified).

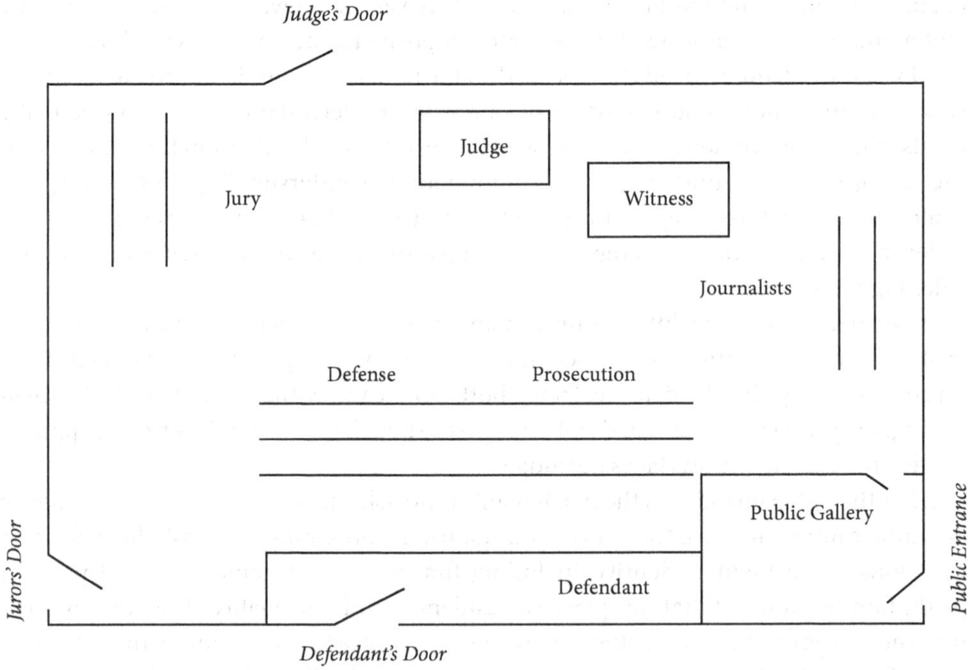

FIGURE 6.2 Seating Order in Crown Court (generalized and simplified from Heffer 2005).

If the defendant is absent, the prosecutor may apply for issuance of a penal order (s. 408a[1] StPO). I will come back to this central instrument of prosecutorial decision-making a little later. The prosecutor may make the application orally at the main hearing;

the essential content of the application for issuance of a penal order shall be included in the record made at the hearing (s. 408a[1] cl. 2 StPO). An arguable worst-case scenario for the defendant presents itself when he/she is absent, has no excuse for it, and the conditions of a penal order are not met: in this case, the prosecutor may apply for an order to bring the defendant before the court, or to issue an arrest warrant (s. 230[2] StPO). The prosecutor should refrain from issuing such an arrest order if the expected sentence would be rather low anyway (based on the proportionality principle) or if the accused lives far away from the trial location. In these circumstances, a penal order would be more appropriate. Finally, in the opening stage the prosecutor reads out the indictment, while omitting the essential results of the investigations (Bohlander 2012).

6.2.3.3 *Presentation of Evidence*

The presentation of evidence sits at the heart of the trial and is designed very differently across legal systems. A disclaimer at the outset: I do not discuss here the presentation of evidence and evidentiary rules (rules about the submission and admission of evidence and—depending on the legal system—its exclusion, probative value, or relevance, Heinze 2020a). It would go beyond the scope of this chapter to analyze in detail all of the prosecutor's opportunities, evidentiary objections, motions for exclusion, and objections to preserve issues for appeal.

In the United States, after the opening statement, the prosecutor introduces the government's proof in its case-in-chief. Here again, the prosecutor presents first due to its burden of persuasion and since he/she has brought charges. The prosecutor's case-in-chief begins with the direct examination of his/her first witness, "a person expected to give evidence favorable to the government's position. The examination of the witness is designed to produce evidence that will prove the prosecution's case against the defendant" (Ferdico, Fradella, and Totten 2009). The prosecutor's witnesses may also include experts (Scheb and Scheb 2013)—in criminal trials of the civil law traditions, expert witnesses are called by the judge/bench. Many evidentiary questions in U.S. criminal trials can be resolved prior to trial through a motion *in limine* (Hall 2014)—a similar platform is arguably present in the new Plea and Trial Preparation Hearing (PTPH) in England and Wales that shall be addressed in a moment.

Evidentiary questions occurring at trial are dealt with through objections: "Any time an attorney believes that a question, statement, or action of the opposing lawyer is improper, he or she may object. The court will then rule on the objection, and the trial will continue" (Hall 2014). While the prosecution needs to prove every element in the case, the defense frequently "stipulates" (agrees not to contest) some facts, particularly those that might prejudice the defendant's case—"detailed photographs and descriptions of a brutally murdered victim, for example" (Samaha 2018). The prosecutor may decline a stipulation (*People v. McClellan*, 1969). If the prosecutor decides not to call a material witness, he/she can ask the court to "inform the jury that a key witness is unavailable and not to draw negative inferences from his failure to testify" (Samaha 2018). In case a prosecutor is certain that a witness will invoke his/her constitutional privilege against self-incrimination, he/she may decide not to call this witness.

The "jury is not entitled to draw any inferences from the decision of a witness to exercise his constitutional privilege whether those inferences be favorable to the prosecution or the defense" (*Bowles v. United States* 1970).

Following cross-examination by the defense (as required by the Sixth Amendment confrontation clause), the prosecutor is entitled to clarify questions raised in cross-examination. This second round of questioning is called redirect examination. It is usually "strictly limited to matters raised on cross-examination. On rare occasions, a judge may permit re-cross-examination" (Ferdico, Fradella, and Totten 2009).

The prosecution may present rebuttal evidence to disprove the evidence of the defense, if the judge does not grant a motion for judgment of acquittal at the close of the defendant's evidence. Rebuttal proof is "limited to new material brought out in the defendant's presentation of evidence. Law enforcement officers may again be called as witnesses at this stage of the prosecution to correct errors or misleading impressions left after the defendant's presentation of evidence" (Ferdico, Fradella, and Totten 2009). The defense is then permitted to rebut the prosecution's rebuttal evidence (Hall 2014). If the prosecution aims at questioning the credibility of a defense witness, "the very starting point in 'exposing falsehood and bringing out the truth' through cross-examination must necessarily be to ask the witness who he is and where he lives. The witness's name and address open countless avenues of in-court examination and out-of-doors investigation" (Samaha 2018). The permissible scope of cross-examination varies in different jurisdictions (*Smith v. Illinois* 1968).

In England and Wales, the role of the prosecutor during the presentation of evidence again depends on the form of the trial. In the Magistrates' Court, the prosecution is asked to give evidence and each witness will be questioned on direct examination ("in-chief") by the prosecuting solicitor. After cross-examination by the defense, the prosecutor may then choose to re-examine the witness to ask brief clarifying questions. As a matter of custom, the first prosecution witness is the victim of the alleged crime (Sharpley 2019). If a witness simply duplicates the evidence of another witness, the prosecutor may "tender" that witness, i.e., "call him, establish his identity and relevance to the case, and then invite the defense to cross-examine. This is often done with police witnesses, where the evidence of one officer largely repeats that of another" (Hungerford-Welch 2019).

In case of a dispute about the admissibility of a piece of evidence, the magistrates will usually hold a hearing ("*voir dire*") to solve the dispute (Sharpley 2019). A similar hearing to solve evidentiary questions exists in the Crown Court: the PTPH, formerly known as Plea and Case Management Hearing (PCMH) or—prior to the PCMH—the Plea and Directions Hearing (PDH). PTPHs often concern issues such as pre-trial disclosure of evidence or unused material or the sudden unavailability of a witness (Darbyshire 2020). The Criminal Practice Directions provide that such hearings should only take place if there is some compelling reason.

In addition, under section 29(1) of the Criminal Procedure and Investigations Act 1996 (CPIA 1996), where it appears to a Crown Court judge that an indictment reveals a case of such complexity, or a case whose trial is likely to be of such length, that substantial benefits are likely to accrue from a preparatory hearing, a preparatory hearing may be held (Ward and Akhtar 2011). It can basically be held at any time before a jury is sworn in, on the application of any of the parties, or by the court on its own motion. As Sprack points out, the preparatory hearing "is in fact a stage of the trial itself, which may be used in order to settle various issues without requiring the jury to attend" (Sprack 2015). In cases of jury tampering (s. 44 of the Criminal Justice Act 2003 [CJA 2003]), terrorism charges (CPIA 1996, s. 29), or a trial of sample counts by jury and others by a judge alone (according to s. 17 of the Domestic Violence, Crime, and Victims Act 2004), such hearings are mandatory. A prosecutor who wants the court to order a trial without a jury must explain that the conditions in Rule 3.22 of the Criminal Procedure Rules 2020 are met.

At the Crown Court there are certain witnesses the prosecutor is required to call, such as witnesses whose statements were served on the defense when the case was transferred to the Crown Court (*R. v. Balmforth* 1992), albeit with a few exceptions:

1. the defense consent to the written statement of the witness being read to the court (under s. 9 of the Criminal Justice Act 1967);
2. the prosecution take the view that the witness is no longer credible (*R. v. Oliva* 1965); or
3. the witness would so fundamentally contradict the prosecution case that it would be better for that witness to be called by the defense (*R. v. Nugent* 1977; Hungerford-Welch 2019).

The summary trial largely follows the above-mentioned order, albeit in a somewhat telescoped manner.

In criminal trials relying on the civil law tradition, the role of the prosecutor at the stage of presenting evidence differs from the common law context, even though the picture is less coherent than it might appear prima facie. In fact, the term "presenting evidence" is already somewhat ill-suited, since there are no parties in the strict sense who "present evidence." It is the judge who takes the evidence or inquires into it and not the parties who present it. In fact, as already indicated, the prosecutor is not even a "party" *stricto sensu*. The different roles of judges in criminal trials—and the evidence-taking stage in particular—of the common law tradition, compared to those within the civil law tradition, is taken up by Pizzi, who compares the (alleged) common law–continental law antagonism with the difference between the American and European versions of football: while a professional American football game "requires many officials and many whistles on the field," there is only one referee (and two assistants) in a soccer game. Those contrasts have strong parallels when one compares American and European criminal trials (Pizzi 1999).

Thus, in Germany for instance, it is the judge who opens the phase of "taking evidence" (*Beweisaufnahme*). S. 238(1) StPO reads: "The presiding judge shall conduct the hearing, examine the defendant and take the evidence." He/she proceeds to examine witnesses, experts, and documents, usually followed by the trial participants; the prosecutor starts, followed by the defense counsel (s. 240 StPO). France deviates from this system: here, the responsibility for calling witnesses lies in the hands of prosecution and defense (Vogler 1996). Yet in France, in theory, the prosecutor does not directly question the witness but must ask questions through the presiding judge. In practice, however, the presiding judge will often allow the prosecutor to directly question the witness after the judge has finished his or her examination (Herrmann 1996). The same holds true in Germany, unless the accused is under 18 years of age: in this situation, the examination of witnesses "shall be conducted solely by the presiding judge" and the prosecutor "may request the presiding judge to ask the witnesses further questions. The presiding judge may permit these persons to put questions to witnesses directly if, according to his duty-bound discretion, no detriment to the well-being of the witness is to be expected" (s. 241a[1] and [2] StPO). Italy resembles the common law model (Perrodet 2002), and so does Sweden (Zila 2006).

In Germany, the judge asks the defendant after each piece of evidence whether he or she wishes to make comments and it is the judge who closes the phase of evidence-taking (Bohlander 2012). Under the rather strict regime of s. 244 StPO, the trial participants may make evidentiary motions (*Beweisantrag*), i.e., ask the judge to take certain pieces of evidence. While in earlier drafts of the law the judge could deny these motions with due discretion, he or she can now only deny it under certain enumerated conditions, the so-called *numerus clausus* (Arnoldi 2018). An evidentiary motion usually has the following structure:

1. application/motion (*Antrag*);
2. evidentiary claim (*Beweisbehauptung*);
3. form of evidence (*Beweismittel*);
4. connectivity between (2) and (3) (*Verknüpfung*);
5. recommendation on the selection of the form of evidence (*Vorschlag zur Beweismittelauswahl*).

Since it is the judge who interviews the witness, there is also no space for cross-examination—at least in practice. In theory, s. 239 StPO provides for a mild cross-examination, requiring a joint application by both prosecution and defense. In practice, this never happens. The rule is an "artifact" (Bohlander 2012), a relic from the beginnings of the German Code(s) of Criminal Procedure (Gaede 2016) that were both influenced and informed *inter alia* by an English trial model (Dezza 2017; Geppert 1979; Mittermaier 1845; von Feuerbach 1821). Cross-examination is (at least practically) also unknown in the Netherlands (Blom and Smit 2006).

These general and rather simplified observations of the evidence stage in selected legal systems do of course not do justice to the manifold peculiarities in this stage. Thus, two points of special interest shall be made with regard to the role of the prosecutor: the dossier and altering/supplementing the charges at trial. Witness preparation/familiarization might serve as a third point. Especially in common law legal systems, the guiding of witnesses at trial is essential for the success of the case (Du Cann 1993). Nevertheless, the topic will be neglected due to the fact that strictly speaking it only belongs to the trial phase in a broader sense and would be better understood in a pre-trial context.

6.2.3.3.1 THE DOSSIER

In legal systems relying on the civil law tradition, the written dossier is the backbone of the entire process and one of its main case-management tools, from the first stage of the proceeding in which the police intervene, to the phase of appeals against the verdict (Langer 2005). I have provided a detailed analysis of the dossier elsewhere (Heinze 2014). A judicial or prosecutorial official normally compiles the dossier, which includes information derived from the questioning of relevant witnesses, including defense witnesses, as well as the accused (McClelland 2002). In general terms, a case file distinguishes itself from a record of proceedings through two main components: a knowledge component and a weight component (Heinze 2020b). The knowledge component allows the judge at every stage of the proceedings to be fully informed about the entire background of the case. The dossier is also vital for the prosecutor: he or she can know, at every stage, what the case is about and the existing elements of proof (Heinze 2014).

Yet, whatever material is placed in the record or case file, as long as there is an additional decision about its admission (and thus its probative value and relevance), the document lacks a weight component. Evidence in a case file *stricto sensu* has a certain probative value and relevance. It is perceived credible evidence, regardless of how it was collected. In France and Belgium, "evidence" tends to mean a piece of information that receives attention by the dossier, whereas in English Law, nothing really counts as "evidence" until it has been heard orally at trial (de Smet 2009). The statements in the dossier have been accurately recorded in earlier inquiries, and their credibility may have been vouched for by other officials who heard the witnesses first-hand. Because these officials are supposed to be independent and impartial, statements accredited by them are entitled to much greater weight than out-of-court statements related by parties in the course of a contested trial (Doran, Jackson, and Seigel 1995). The idea of the prosecutor's impartiality leads to the belief that all the evidence he or she has gathered is credible regardless of how it was collected (Panzavolta 2004). The dossier provides knowledge, structure, and weight to the prosecutor and the evidence within a trial (Heinze 2014). Its inspection is equivalent to disclosure in common law systems (Turner 2016).

6.2.3.3.2 ALTERING/SUPPLEMENTING THE CHARGES AT TRIAL

It goes without saying that charging is normally the domain of the prosecutor. Yet, from a civil law perspective, with the termination of the investigation and the pertinent instrument of accusation, the authority shifts from the prosecutor to the judge(s). They have the power to amend the charges in their legal dimension in line with the principle *iura novit curia* ("the court knows the law"). From a common law (especially U.S.) perspective, any judicial amendment of the charges—in both their factual and legal contents—appears unacceptable, since their determination belongs to the exclusive domain of the prosecution and thus can only be amended by this institution itself. Exceptionally, the trial court may convict (only!) for a less serious—"lesser included"—offense (Ambos 2016).

Altering charges by judges needs to be distinguished from supplementary charges added at the trial. In Germany, the prosecutor may add new charges in respect of further criminal offenses committed by the defendant, and the court may, in an order, include them in the proceedings if it has jurisdiction and the defendant consents thereto (s. 266[1] StPO). It goes without saying that the defendant must have the opportunity to effectively defend himself against these charges.

6.2.3.4 *Closing Stage and Judgment*

After the presentation of evidence, both the prosecutor—who starts first—and the defense present their closing arguments or summations, arguing both facts and law. The prosecutor may present a short rebuttal (Ferdico, Fradella, and Totten 2009; Hall 2014). The prosecutor is entitled to sum up his/her case "graphically and forcefully. Indeed, where the circumstances of the case are grave, the prosecutor should not be expected to present the state's evidence in a manner appropriate to a lecture hall" (Henderson 1981). Both prosecutor and defence can comment on the jury instructions, given that the judge indicated prior to closing arguments how he or she intends to instruct the jury. Issues unrelated to the case or evidence that was not presented cannot be part of the summation. With regard to tactics at closing arguments, Lempert displays three possible avenues:

> The story model suggests several promising tactics. One is to assimilate the other side's evidence, or as much as can be accommodated, into one's own story or to reinterpret the other side's evidence to make it irrelevant. A second tactic is to point out gaps in the story the opponent attempts to tell. A third is to point to apparent facts which the opponent's story cannot accommodate. These are not mutually exclusive options, and the same closing statement may make an attempt at each of them (Lempert 1991).

Prosecutors cannot waive their right to make a closing argument and reserve their remarks for rebuttal; neither can they raise matters anew in rebuttal (Samaha 2018). The amount of time allotted for closing arguments is defined by statute or rule and/or left to the discretion of the trial judge (*State v. Dunkerton* 1929; Ferdico, Fradella, and Totten 2009; Hall 2014).

A similar picture appears in the Crown Court criminal trial in England and Wales: After the defense case has been concluded, both prosecutor—who starts first—and defense counsel will deliver a closing speech to the jury. At the Magistrates' Court, in summary trials, the prosecutor may make a closing speech ("may make final representations in support of the prosecution case") where "the defendant is represented by a legal representative, or whether represented or not, the defendant has introduced evidence other than his or her own" (Rule 24.3.[3][h] of the Criminal Procedure Rules 2020).

In Germany, representing a civil law legal system, the judge invites the prosecution, defense and other parties to make closing statements; the prosecution speaks first (along with other prosecuting participants) (Bohlander 2012). A similar procedure is visible in France (Vogler 1996). In Germany, the closing arguments of the prosecutor *aiming at a conviction* are usually structured as follows:

1. description of the facts (*Schilderung des Sachverhalts*);
2. evaluation of the evidence (*Beweiswürdigung*);
3. legal analysis (*rechtliche Würdigung*);
4. sentencing recommendation and application for a conviction (*Strafzumessung und Antrag auf Verurteilung*);
5. costs (*Kosten*).

If the prosecutor *aims at an acquittal*, he/she would start with the description of the original charge and would ask for an acquittal at step (4).

In the United States, on completion of the trial, if the judge or jury finds insufficient evidence to convict, the defendant is acquitted, that is, found not guilty of the crime. If the jury or the judge finds that the state has met its burden of proof, the defendant is found guilty and the matter moves to sentencing (McCord, McCord, and Bailey 2012). Rule 32 of the Federal Rules of Criminal Procedure and similar state court rules require judges to impose the sentence without unnecessary delay. This protects the defendant from a prolonged period of uncertainty about the future. Thus, sentencing usually occurs within a few weeks of conviction (Ferdico, Fradella, and Totten 2009). In a Crown Court trial in England and Wales, after deliberations, the jury delivers its verdict (Ward and Akhtar 2011). If the defendant pleads guilty, which happened in 66 percent of the cases in 2019 (UK Ministry of Justice 2019), or is convicted by the jury, he or she will be sentenced. In Germany, the trial concludes with the pronouncement of the judgment (*Urteil*, s. 260[1] StPO). The judges, who are triers of both fact and law, must give *explicit reasons* for their decision on guilt or innocence (s. 268[2] StPO).

Since the judgment lies in the hands of the decision-maker (single judge, bench, jury) and the role of the prosecutor at sentencing is covered by Nora V. Demleitner in Chapter 7 of this volume, at first glance it does not seem fruitful to analyze the role of the prosecutor with a view to judgment and sentencing any further. This conclusion, however, would only be sound if the prosecutor's role at this stage is observed in isolation, disconnected from the broader context of a trial. Yet, as mentioned at the outset, a role of any trial participant always depends on the broader context and character of the proceedings. There are in fact scenarios where the prosecutor's impact on a judgment and on sentencing—prior to these stages—cannot be overstated.

6.2.4 Prosecutors as Judges

6.2.4.1 *General Remarks*

Just as the identity of a person "grows out of a distinction between one's true inner self and an outer world of social rules and norms" (Fukuyama 2018), the role of the prosecutor—its procedural identity—must not only be viewed in the context of the procedural stage but also in juxtaposition to the main actor of the trial: the decision-maker or judge respectively. The prosecutorial role at trial is therefore defined through its differentiation from the judicial role. The reason for this is that the "power balance" (Vasiliev 2012) shifts once a case reaches the trial phase. In most legal systems, it is the judge who is now in control and this control may have considerable impact on the prosecutors' decision-making. The rise of judicial management is a world-wide phenomenon, especially at International Criminal Tribunals (Ambos 2016; Heinze 2017). In most legal systems, especially those leaning towards a civil law tradition, the control over the proceedings is transferred to the judiciary at trial (Vasiliev 2012).

However, the power balance experienced a readjustment once the handling of cases became unmanageable even for a well-equipped judiciary. Nowadays it is generally acknowledged that justice works slowly, as there are "simply too many offences, too many offenders, and too few resources to deal with them all" (Goldstein 1997). Similarly, the number of cases in U.S. lower criminal courts have increased substantially, "overwhelming prosecutors, defenders, and judges due to policies like over-policing" (Howell 2014). As a consequence, people increasingly lose confidence in the criminal justice system and its operators. One response has been the introduction of measures and methods to lower trial costs and expedite criminal trials (Jehle 2006). A common theme of these expedited trials is the leading role of public prosecutors in such proceedings (Ligeti 2019). As Gilliéron notes, "prosecutors in both the US and Europe have gradually slipped into the role of decision-makers" (Gilliéron 2014). In fact, prosecutors in some instances may act as the sole adjudicator of the criminal case (Gilliéron 2014).

The overburdening of our criminal justice systems has led to the introduction of "consensual" forms in criminal procedure, where agreements are reached which obviate the need for a criminal trial (Damaška 2001; Frase and Weigend 1995). In this respect, the principle of procedural economy has taken center stage (Thaman 2007). These measures include not only the charging process but also "penal orders" (see below §6.2.4.2 and Heinze and Fyfe 2019) and "plea bargaining" (Turner and Weigend 2019; Ambos and Heinze 2017), and they require the agreement of the accused.

6.2.4.2 *The Penal Order*

The discretion afforded to U.S. prosecutors throughout the criminal justice process has already been discussed in this Volume, as has the influence of the opportunity principle within U.S. criminal procedure and how it provides numerous opportunities for prosecutorial decision-making. The increasing need for curtailed criminal proceedings, however, has expanded the decision-making role of prosecutors to jurisdictions governed by the legality principle. Three ways of curtailing proceedings through a dominating role of the prosecutor deserve special attention: charging, plea bargaining, and the so-called "penal order." Since charging and plea bargaining are dealt with elsewhere in this volume, I will focus on the penal order—a procedural tool that is alien to common law systems.

There is a manifest similarity between what is known in the United States as the guilty plea and in Germany as the penal order (Ambos and Heinze 2017; Langbein 1974). According to a general and prefatory definition, a penal order can be seen as a "written proposal by the state to a defendant stipulating the crime committed and the penalty to be levied if the defendant does not object" (Felstiner 1979). In countries like Germany, France, and Italy the penal order may be used in cases sanctioned by fines, which practically applies to misdemeanors (such as traffic or shoplifting offenses) in most cases (Bouloc and Matsopoulou 2018; Corso 2000; Jehle 2013; Roxin and Schünemann 2017). Furthermore, the penal order may also be used in cases of imprisonment of up to six months in Italy (Jehle 2013), up to one year in Germany (Roxin and Schünemann 2017), up to five years in Luxembourg (Spielmann and Spielmann 2000), up to six years in the Netherlands (Vriend 2016), and up to ten years in Poland (Waltoś and Hofmański 2018).

In Germany, the prosecutor may submit an application for a penal order at any time, even after the beginning of trial (§ 408a StPO). Generally speaking, this penal order will inform the defendant that he or she will receive a specified sentence for a specified crime unless he or she objects within two weeks (Alschuler 1983), in which case the matter will proceed to a normal trial before the appropriate court by a single professional judge (ss. 407, 409 StPO). The judge must issue the penal order if he or she has no substantial objections (ss. 408 [3], 408a [2] StPO). In practice, this means that judges grant virtually all applications for a penal order as a matter of course—one reason for the recent call for the penal order's abolition in Germany (Bommer et al. 2019; Deiters 2018). The requirement of the defendant's consent entails the possibility of bargaining between the defense and the prosecution over the specific fine to be imposed (Dubber 1997).

Penal orders reflect even more prosecutorial power in France, where the *juge de police* delivers a judgment without giving any reasons, without a hearing, and even without the presence of a defense lawyer (Pradel 2000). Nearly the same procedural rules apply in Italy, where a penal order (*decreto penale*), regarded as a conviction, is issued upon request of the prosecutor, in the absence of the accused and without a trial (Corso 2000).

Needless to say, a penal order may not always be the appropriate answer to a crime. In France, *inter alia*, the public prosecutor may choose ordinary proceedings instead of a penal order for three reasons. First, if the facts present certain difficulties which can only be resolved in a hearing. Second, if a fine is not regarded as sufficient punishment in a particular case (Pradel 2000). Third, if a case is referred to the *juge de police* by the public prosecutor's department, and he or she refuses to deal with the case by penal order, instead taking the view that a more severe sentence should be imposed.

Further, once the decision for a penal order is made, the accused is by no means bound to that decision, but instead can apply for a review of the order (*opposition*). If he or she does so in France, the case will be publicly heard by the *juge de police* in an ordinary proceeding (Pradel 2000). The accused can also oppose the penal order in Germany, Italy (*opposizione*), and Luxembourg (Ambos and Heinze 2017). He or she then risks, of course, a costly trial, potentially resulting in a more severe penalty in court (Frase and Weigend 1995).

In 2019, the German prosecution services applied for a penal order in 595,954 cases, and in 147,923 cases these orders were opposed (Statistisches Bundesamt 2019). That is roughly 25 percent—a rather high number that indicates that the risks of going to trial are not so considerable in Germany to conclude that defendants are regularly pressured into plea bargaining (Kemme and Dunkel 2020). In Germany, a penal order might also be inappropriate whenever a full trial seems necessary for a full discovery of the facts or to further special or general prevention (No. 175[3] cl. 1 of the Guidelines for Criminal and Summary Proceedings [*Richtlinien für das Strafverfahren und das Bußgeldverfahren* (RiStBV)]). Both requirements reflect the role of the prosecutor who both aims at obtaining the truth and—a more consequentialist role—special and general prevention (about general prevention, Heinze 2018).

6.3 The Role of the Prosecutor at Trial: Ethical Framework

The distinctive roles played by prosecutors at trial are largely shaped by the aims of the particular criminal justice system (Weigend 2012). As individual actors within an institution, they are responsible for conscientiously performing certain straightforward tasks, yet they also wield discretionary authority to make decisions about individual cases and broader institutional policies. When a prosecutor faces a situation in which he or she has discretionary power, decision-making involves the goal or a set of goals, purposes, or objectives to be achieved (or maximized or minimized) (Gottfredson and Gottfredson 1988). Goals may be limited to the specific case or accused offender at hand, or they may take into account the larger impact of the singular case on the prosecutor's office and the entire criminal justice system. In this section, I explore the scope of prosecutorial decision-making and the role of fairness within the context of a criminal justice system's broad objectives and parameters.

6.3.1 Justice and Fairness Objectives at Trial

While the particular features of what constitutes justice vary between, and sometimes within, criminal justice systems, it always relates to fairness. A judicial or administrative body is tasked with serving the public, and in serving the public, a government body's most important higher-order goal is to treat every member of the public fairly. Here, procedural fairness, distributive fairness, and substantive fairness are of great

Table 6.1 Procedural Stages in the United States, England and Wales, and Germany

USA		Investigation	Arrest + Book.	Charge	Initial Appearance	Prelim./Grand Jury	Indictment/Information	Arraignment	Trial	Sentencing
		Police		Prosecution				Courts		
Eng/Wales	*Summ.*	**Investigation**	**Arrest**	**Charge**	**Initial Appearance**	**[Def. dealt with in Mag. or by single justice on the papers]**		**Summ. Trial**		**Sentencing**
	Indict. only				**First Hearing**	**Prelim.**	**Plea and Trial Preparation Hearing**	**Trial on Indictment**		**Sentencing [CC]**
	Either way					**Comm. Hearing**		**Jury Trial**		**Sentencing**
		Police		CPS Pros.	Mag.	Crown/Mag.	Crown Court	Mag./ Crown Court		
GER		**Investigation Phase**			**Intermediate Phase**			**Trial + Sentence**		
		(Arrest)	**Charge**		**Decision to confirm the charges**	**Decision to start the trial**				
State Prosecutor (Police)		Invest, judge for certain measures			Court			Court		

importance but cannot be subject to a deeper analysis in this chapter. I have done so elsewhere with Shannon Fyfe (Heinze and Fyfe 2018).

In an inquisitorial/policy-implementing system (for a categorization of procedural models see infra and Heinze 2014) such as Germany's, the criminal justice system seeks the truth, and all parties to the legal proceedings share this aim. This is especially true for the German Prosecution Service, where the employees view themselves as the "most objective civil servants in the world" (Boyne 2014). While both Article 20 (3) of the German Basic Law (Grundgesetz, GG)—in conjunction with Article 2 (1) GG—and Article 6 of the European Convention on Human Rights (ECHR) (Esser 2002; Geppert 1992; Roxin and Schünemann 2017; Schmitt 2020), ensure the right to a fair trial and other protections for the accused, a primary aim of the German criminal justice system is to seek the truth, or to seek the substantively fair result (in Germany, truth in the context of criminal procedure is only a "subgoal" of the goal "peace under the law," see Heinze 2018; Heinze and Fyfe 2019). As I explore in the next section, the German system is also aimed, to some extent, at distributive fairness.

The U.S. criminal justice system, on the other hand, purports to be aimed at procedural fairness. The Fourteenth Amendment of the U.S. Constitution states that no state shall "deprive any person of life, liberty, or property, without due process of law; nor deny to any person within its jurisdiction the equal protection of the laws" (U.S. Const. amend. XIV). The Fourth, Fifth, Sixth, and Eighth Amendments also provide protections for accused individuals. In this adversarial system, the prosecutor's role involves making the strongest case possible against a defendant, subject to the limitations imposed by due process and the supervision of the judge. Rule 3.8 of the American Bar Association (ABA) Model Rules of Professional Responsibility outlines these limitations, which include making reasonable efforts to ensure that the accused has the benefit of his or her own counsel, avoiding actions that will unfairly prejudice the public against the accused, promptly disclosing evidence to the defense when appropriate, and investigating or discontinuing a case where there is evidence of a defendant's innocence (Model R. Prof. Conduct 3.8 [ABA 2018]). Yet it remains the case that in an adversarial system like the United States, the judge is responsible for protecting the accused's due process rights, or procedural fairness, and the prosecutor is responsible for obtaining a substantively fair result within the parameters set by the judge (albeit through the adversarial process rather than a pure truth-seeking process). The same applies to the Crown Prosecution Service (CPS) in England and Wales (Darbyshire 2020), which searches for an "*approximation* of 'the truth,'" understanding "truth *as* proof" (Slapper and Kelly 2017), which appears to fall within the concept of "procedural truth" rather than "substantive truth." Cicchini (2018) argues that the truth-as-proof model is now also applied by prosecutors in the United States.

6.3.2 Prosecutorial Ethics at Trial

The normative foundations of prosecutorial ethics consist of two main concepts: a prosecutor's general duty to seek justice (Howell 2014; Zacharias 1991); and the moral theories that inform the corresponding, specific ethical obligations of the prosecutor. In both adversarial/conflict-solving and inquisitorial/policy-implementing procedural models, regardless of other specific duties and areas of discretion, the prosecutor is expected to seek justice (Heinze 2014; Kubicek 2006; Peters 1985). As noted earlier, while the particular features of what constitutes justice vary between, and sometimes within, criminal justice systems, it always has something to do with fairness.

The prosecutor's specific obligations for guaranteeing fair trials can be thought of in terms of deontological norms and consequentialist norms (on the question whether virtue theory can and should inform prosecutorial ethics, see Heinze and Fyfe 2018). Consequentialism identifies right actions based solely on the outcomes they produce, evaluated independently of how the end-states were achieved. The right action, for consequentialists, is the action that maximizes the good. The promotion of "the good," however, requires a conception of what is good and therefore worthy of promotion. In a criminal trial, we might conceive of goodness in terms of the substantive results of the trial. A criminal trial might be considered "good," or fair, if the person who committed a crime is convicted of said crime through the criminal trial process. A prosecutor who attempts to reach the correct substantive outcome in every case, and considers this to be the standard of what constitutes a fair trial, adopts a purely consequentialist view of her ethical obligations.

Deontology, conversely, "takes right action to be the primary evaluative notion; it recognizes various actions as obligatory, prohibited, or permitted on the basis of their intrinsic natures and independently of the value they produce" (Brink 2006). Deontological constraints identify what actions are impermissible because they violate duties not to harm people in various ways (McNaughton and Rawling 2006). Beyond the actions which are specifically required by duty, deontology allows for significant freedom of choice in our actions (Kant 1785). In a criminal trial, deontological constraints on a prosecutor will align more with considerations of procedural fairness. A prosecutor who is focused on deontological norms will be concerned with the reasons that support the choices that are made, respect for defendants' rights, and the way trials are conducted, independent of the end-states the trials produce.

This includes the degree of conviction on the part of the prosecutor as to the guilt of the accused, which also is a matter of prosecutorial ethics. Here again, a balance is struck between the prosecutor as an advocate striving for victory and a prosecutor as an officer of the court (Vasiliev 2012). As an officer of the court, the prosecutor is expected to prove guilt beyond reasonable doubt (Cicchini 2018; Duff et al. 2006). This heavy burden of proof is—at least in conflict-solving settings—seen as a concession to the equality of arms principle (Jackson and Summers 2012; about the equality of arms principle see Heinze 2014).

This is not the place to address the countless conundrums that surround the burden of proof. It goes deep into the meandering rivers of norm theory and democracy. I will therefore only provide a brief sketch of those topics within the burden of proof realm, that are relevant for this chapter and have sparked some controversy amongst judges and legal scholars. First, since this chapter has a comparative orientation, the term "burden of proof" creates rather diverse associations. In adversarial/conflict-solving settings, there is a "burden of production" and a "burden of persuasion" (Kokott 1998). The prosecutor (and the defense) has the burden to produce evidence (Jackson and Summers 2012; Darbyshire 2020)—a feature that does not apply in many civil law legal systems, where judges are not only entitled but also *required* to produce (or ask for the production of) evidence (Kokott 1998). Furthermore, the prosecutor also bears the risk of non-persuasion of the trier of fact, that is, he/she must prove the elements of the offense (Jackson and Summers 2012). This risk has developed within the jury system, which means that in Germany, for instance, there is no major difference between the burden of production (*subjektive Beweislast/Beweisführungslast*) and the burden of persuasion (*objektive Beweislast*) (Kokott 1998).

Second, while common law systems designate the standard of proof as proof beyond a reasonable doubt, civil law systems tend to refer to the "*in dubio pro reo*" principle (Fletcher 1968). In other words, the presumption of innocence provides the basis for the burden of proof that rests on the prosecutor (Volk and Engländer 2018; Dubber and Hörnle 2014). This leads to a third topic of controversy: Is the prosecutor obliged to treat the defendant as factually innocent during trial? The answer—again—depends on the role of the prosecutor and the ensuing ethical boundaries. For some, the presumption of innocence only applies to the fact-finder (Laudan 2006). The Louisiana Supreme Court clarified in 1979 that the presumption of innocence was "a guide to the jury. If it were absolute and operative at every stage of a prosecution, the defendant could never be jailed until conviction" (*State v. Green* 1973, 186). To view partisan prosecutors as objective and respecting the presumption of innocence is said to be "wishful thinking" and therefore rejected (Laudan 2006). As Bharara, former U.S. Attorney for the Southern District of New York, opines: "The presumption of innocence would be a dangerous standard for an investigator" (Bharara 2019). Others maintain that due to the role of prosecutors as officers of the court, the presumption of innocence applies throughout the proceedings (Ashworth 2006) and prosecutors must treat the accused as factually innocent during trial (Duff et al. 2007; Laufer 1995; Lippke 2014 with further references).

Deontological constraints are well suited to play the primary role in shaping prosecutorial ethics and promoting fair trials. Danner has argued that prosecutorial decisions will be both actually legitimate and perceived as such if they are taken in a principled, reasoned, and impartial manner (Danner 2003). The duty to treat every individual as an end in herself and thus apply the same rules impartially, without bias or concern about outcomes, lends itself to ensuring procedural fairness. A prosecutor is constrained by "rules which apply in an all-or-nothing, categorical manner without reference to the particular context or consequences of the prohibited or required behaviour" (Nicolson 2005). Deontological constraints do not permit individual rights to be violated, even if a rights violation could be "offset by benefits that arise elsewhere" in the justice system (Markovits 2010). Thus, deontological constraints are crucial to the foundations of prosecutorial ethics and procedural fairness.

Concerns about the substantive outcomes of criminal trials, the overall performance or record of a prosecutor, or the social and political impacts of criminal trials likely involve more consequentialist considerations (Mégret 2012). A prosecutor with an impeccable record of respect for defendants' rights, faced with the prospect of removal due to his or her failure to convict several accused persons, must consider whether he or she should treat a few defendants as a means to the end of staying employed. Another prosecutor, tasked with determining which members of a large criminal enterprise should be indicted and which should receive plea deals, will necessarily take the results of his or her decisions into account—and will likely be unable to achieve a fair result in distributional terms. Consequentialist considerations within prosecutorial decision-making became a matter of intense legal and political debate at the International Criminal Court (ICC) in the context of the Afghanistan situation and the authorisation of investigations against U.S. troops (ICC, *Situation Afghanistan*, Pre-Trial Chamber II, Decision Pursuant to Article 15 of the Rome Statute on the Authorisation of an Investigation into the Situation in the Islamic Republic of Afghanistan, ICC-02/17-33, 12 April 2019; Appeals Chamber, Judgment on the appeal against the decision on the authorisation of an investigation into the situation in the Islamic Republic of Afghanistan, ICC-02/17-138, 5 March 2020; Ambos and Heinze 2019).

Consequentialist considerations will be inappropriate at many points in a criminal trial, because they will constitute an impermissible failure of procedural fairness. These sorts of considerations should be impermissible during a criminal trial phase when they are incompatible with deontological constraints. In other instances, such as during the sentencing phase, it may be appropriate to consider a defendant's particular circumstances before determining the best method and duration of punishment.

In practically all domestic criminal justice systems, justice is distributed selectively according to certain, often policy-based criteria (Damaška 2008; Jehle 2006; Wade 2006), so consequentialist considerations may also be appropriate prior to the trial. It is impossible for a prosecutor to treat every *potential* defendant equally, even if it is possible to treat every *actual* defendant equally (Armenian 2016). A prosecutor's conduct should always be limited by deontological constraints prohibiting bias and the use of individuals as means rather than respecting them as ends. But it is appropriate, and perhaps even obligatory in some instances, for a prosecutor to consider the potential consequences of the decisions he or she makes regarding which situations to investigate and which individuals to prosecute.

6.3.3 Prosecutorial Misconduct at Trial

A prosecutor's failure to abide by legal or ethical obligations is considered prosecutorial misconduct. These professional obligations are intended to locate a prosecutor between extremes, thereby compelling him/her to seek justice and ensure that "guilt shall not escape nor innocence suffer" (*Berger v. United States* 1935, 88). In more concrete terms, in the United States for instance, the ABA Model Rules of Professional

Conduct serve as models for the ethics rules of most states. They were adopted by the ABA House of Delegates in 1983. Prior to the adoption of the Model Rules, the ABA model was the 1969 Model Code of Professional Responsibility. Preceding the Model Code were the 1908 Canons of Professional Ethics (last amended in 1963) (Heinze 2014).

A prosecutor is required to refrain from improper methods calculated to produce a wrongful conviction, while also using "every legitimate means to bring about a just one" (Heinze 2014). Specific types of prosecutorial misconduct include improper efforts to influence other parties to a trial, improper statements regarding evidence that has not been presented, failures to disclose evidence, and making abusive, insulting, inflammatory, or prejudicial statements (Alschuler 1972; Soubise and Woolley 2018).

6.3.3.1 *Prosecutorial Misconduct at Jury Selection*

Jury selection cannot be based on race or gender. Yet, in 2005 the U.S. public learned that it was standard practice in Alameda County, California, to remove Jews and women of color from juries in capital trials (Murphy 2005). A former Alameda prosecutor, John R. Quatman, said that a trial judge advised him during jury selection that "no Jew would vote to send a defendant to the gas chamber" (*In re Freeman* 2006). Prosecutors drawing racial lines in selecting juries establish "state-sponsored group stereotypes rooted in, and reflective of, historical prejudice" (*J.E.B. v. Alabama ex rel. T.B.* 1994, 128; *Miller-El v. Dretke* 2005, 238; Samaha 2018). The U.S. Supreme Court explained that "the very integrity of the courts is jeopardized when a prosecutor's discrimination 'invites cynicism respecting the jury's neutrality'" (*Miller-El v. Dretke* 2005 238, citing *Powers v. Ohio* 1991, 412). Discrimination undermines "public confidence in adjudication" (*Miller-El v. Dretke* 2005, 238, citing *Georgia v. McCollum* 1992, 49; *Edmonson v. Leesville Concrete Co.* 1991, 628). As a result, the U.S. Supreme Court has "consistently and repeatedly . . . reaffirmed that racial discrimination by the State in jury selection offends the Equal Protection Clause" (*Miller-El v. Dretke* 2005, 238, citing *Norris v. Alabama* 1935, 596).

In *Swain v. Alabama* (1965), the U.S. Supreme Court required the defendant to prove "a pattern of racial discrimination in which the State is significantly involved" for which the state is responsible. The Court remarked:

> [W]hen the prosecutor in a county, in case after case, whatever the circumstances, whatever the crime, and whoever the defendant or the victim may be, is responsible for the removal of Negroes who have been selected as qualified jurors by the jury commissioners and who have survived challenges for cause, with the result that no Negroes ever serve on petit juries, the Fourteenth Amendment claim takes on added significance. Cf. Yick Wo v. Hopkins, 118 U. S. 356. In these circumstances, giving even the widest leeway to the operation of irrational but trial-related suspicions and antagonisms, it would appear that the purpose of the peremptory challenge are being perverted (223–224).

Due to considerable criticism of the Supreme Court's ruling in *Swain v. Alabama*, especially with regard to the burden of proof (Samaha 2018), the Court returned to the problem in *Batson v. Kentucky* (1986). It held that:

> Once the defendant makes a *prima facie* showing, the burden shifts to the State to come forward with a neutral explanation for challenging black jurors. The prosecutor may not rebut a *prima facie* showing by stating that he challenged the jurors on the assumption that they would be partial to the defendant because of their shared race or by affirming his good faith in individual selections (96–98).

In 1991, the U.S. Supreme Court broadened the rule and held: "Under the Equal Protection Clause, a criminal defendant may object to race-based exclusions of jurors through peremptory challenges whether or not the defendant and the excluded jurors share the same race" (*Powers v. Ohio* 1991, 404).

In the late 1980s and early 1990s, incoherent court rulings addressed the issue of gender-based peremptory challenges (Scheb and Scheb 2013). In *J.E.B. v. Alabama ex rel. T.B.* (1994) the U.S. Supreme Court clarified that:

> Failing to provide jurors the same protection against gender discrimination as race discrimination could frustrate the purpose of *Batson* itself. Because gender and race are overlapping categories, gender can be used as a pretext for racial discrimination. Allowing parties to remove racial minorities from the jury not because of their race, but because of their gender, contravenes well-established equal protection principles and could insulate effectively racial discrimination from judicial scrutiny.

6.3.3.2 *Prosecutorial Misconduct at the Opening Stage and the Presentation of Evidence*

At the opening statement/speech, the prosecutor "has a duty to avoid raising the emotional temperature" (Du Cann 1993). Du Cann in his seminal work "The Art of the Advocate" emphasizes: "In criminal trials in particular there is much anguish and suffering which can give rise to strong reactions in the most detached and unbiased jury. He must never exploit this."

With regard to the presentation of evidence, as already mentioned, this chapter is not the place to analyze evidentiary rules in detail. Thus, only a few points shall be mentioned *exempli gratia*. In cross-examination, the prosecutor may attack the witness's credibility in the following ways:

1. showing the witness's inability to have viewed or heard the matters the witness has testified to, or inability to recall the event testified to;
2. demonstrating that the witness has made prior conflicting statements on an important point;

3. showing the witness has been convicted of a crime;
4. establishing that the witness bears a bad reputation for truthfulness in the community;
5. showing bias, prejudice, or motive to misrepresent the facts, or that the witness has a definite interest in the result of the trial (Scheb and Scheb 2013).

It would be a violation of due process if a state prosecutor sought to "impeach a defendant's exculpatory story, told for the first time at trial, by cross-examining the defendant about his failure to have told the story after receiving *Miranda* warnings . . . at the time of his arrest" (*Doyle v. Ohio* 1976). While in direct examination, the prosecutor is prohibited from asking leading questions (i.e., "questions which are so framed that the witness will understand from them the answer he is expected to give" [Du Cann 1993]), leading questions are allowed in cross-examination (Scheb and Scheb 2013). Whether to allow or deny leading questions is a decision that is conceptually based on the normative framework of a trial. As soon as this normative framework is either ambiguous or not clarified, disputes about procedural law will eventually be solved by judicial trial management. The ICC is an illustrative example: The legality of leading questions has been both rejected (*Prosecutor v. Gbagbo et al.*, Trial Chamber I, Transcript, 4 February 2016, ICC-02/11-01/15-T-14-ENG, p. 2, lines 5–9) and accepted (by the same Chamber: *Prosecutor v. Gbagbo et al.*, Decision adopting amended and supplemented directions on the conduct of the proceedings, 4 May 2016, ICC-02/11-01/15-498, para. 16).

Comments to the jury by a prosecutor in a state criminal trial "upon a defendant's failure to testify as to the matters which he can reasonably be expected to deny or explain because of facts within his knowledge or by the court that the defendant's silence under those circumstances evidences guilt" violate the Self-Incrimination Clause of the Fifth Amendment (*Griffin v. California* 1965). Moreover, the prosecutor is generally asked to refrain from linking the "poverty" of the defendant to the likelihood of committing a crime (*State v. Mathis* 1966; *State v. Stewart* 1978). However, in certain situations evidence of a defendant's financial situation may be admissible (Henderson 1981 with further references). Note also that the elaboration of the financial situation of the defendant is common in many legal systems relying on the civil law tradition (for the example of Germany, see above 6.2.3.2).

6.3.3.3 *Prosecutorial Misconduct at the Closing Stage*

A prosecutor in his closing statement must confine his argument to the facts and evidence presented at trial and the reasonable inferences that can be drawn therefrom. He/she must refrain from making an argument that is "undignified and intemperate, containing improper insinuations and assertions calculated to mislead the jury" (*Berger v. United States* 1935, 85). He/she can only comment on the defendant's credibility as long as the comments are based on evidence before the court and "in light of the considerable evidence supporting the conviction, the comment was not unduly prejudicial" (*United States v. Gallagher* 1978, 1041). Rule 3.4.(e) of the ABA Model Rules of Professional Conduct reiterates the case law. The prosecutor shall not "in trial, allude to any matter that the lawyer does not reasonably believe is relevant or that will not be supported by admissible evidence, assert personal knowledge of facts in issue except when testifying as a witness, or state a personal opinion as to the justness of a cause, the credibility of a witness, the culpability of a civil litigant or the guilt or innocence of an accused." The rule mirrors the fairness aspect of prosecutorial conduct mentioned above. Last but not least, a prosecutor should refrain from calling the defendant "any name that might inflame the jury and subsequently mandate a reversal," which includes "butcher boy," "leg breaker," "punk," and "comparing the accused to various forms of the animal species" (Henderson 1981). This also applies to attacks on defense attorneys. In *Fortune v. State* (2019), the South Carolina Supreme Court overturned a conviction after the prosecutor in his closing argument said: "My job is to show the truth. On the other hand, the defense attorneys' jobs are to manipulate the truth. Their job is to shroud the truth. Their job is [to] confuse jurors. Their job is to do whatever they have to—without regard for the truth—to get a not guilty verdict." The Supreme Court found the remark "inexcusable" and its compact overview of the case law on improper prosecutorial conduct at the closing stage is a recommended read.

6.3.3.4 *Intermediate Conclusion*

Each of these forms of misconduct is unprofessional, and this is one reason why prosecutors may face legal, professional, or social sanctions for engaging in these behaviors. But the most damning impact of prosecutorial misconduct is on individual cases, where defendants might be wrongfully convicted or wrongfully acquitted on the basis of biased or improper statements. The corresponding concern is the impact of unfairly influenced individual cases on the overall actual and perceived legitimacy of legal institutions, and on the profession of lawyers in general (Heinze 2020a).

Not all instances of unprofessionalism on the part of a prosecutor rise to the level of prosecutorial misconduct, and not every instance of prosecutorial misconduct rises to the level of appellate courts sanctioning prosecutors or overturning convictions. In the "ardor of advocacy, and in the excitement of trial, even the most experienced counsel are occasionally carried away" by the temptation to make abusive, insulting, inflammatory or prejudicial statements during the trial (Alschuler 1972, citing *Dunlop v. United States* 1897, 498). But arguably in any legal system, regardless of the prosecutor's specific role, rhetoric should not be necessary to obtain the most rational verdicts in criminal cases (Alschuler 1972). A view of the adversarial system as one in which a certain kind of rhetorical strategy with rhetorical flourish is desirable, if not necessary to obtain rational verdicts, looks like it will do little to discourage certain kinds of prosecutorial misconduct (or at least unprofessionalism). There is something to the thought that "if a judgment of criminal conviction should not rest upon emotionalism, we should encourage the prosecutor not to argue in emotional terms. If the basis for a criminal conviction should be a detailed sifting of the evidence, we should encourage the prosecutor to present arguments that will promote a careful sifting of the evidence" (Alschuler 1972).

6.4 Conclusion

Upon identifying the multiple roles of the prosecutor at trial, prosecutorial work is influenced by two role-related factors: role duality and role ambiguity (drawing on Heinze and Fyfe 2019). As to the former, the prosecutor is expected to fulfill dual roles, and these are often in conflict. To exemplify this with regard to the United States and Germany: first, the prosecutor is the seeker of both procedural and substantive justice. In the United States, the criminal justice system is aimed at ensuring procedural justice, yet the prosecutor is also expected to seek substantive justice within the framework of procedural due process constraints. In Germany, the prosecutor is tasked with seeking the truth, or a substantively fair result.

Second, the prosecutor is part of the executive branch or the judiciary. In Germany, the prosecution service is a judicial organ of the executive branch. In the United States, at the federal level, prosecutors also belong to the executive branch. They are part of the Department of Justice. At the state level, however, district attorneys have a unique position compared to other jurisdictions: even though they belong to the executive branch, they are completely independent, and usually only responsible to their voters (and their ethical obligations) (Gilliéron 2014).

Third, the prosecutor is led by the principle of mandatory prosecution and/or opportunity. While a U.S. prosecutor enjoys considerable discretion as to whether to prosecute, the German prosecutor is subject to the principle of legality. However, this domination is increasingly weakened by the opportunity principle in the face of an overloaded criminal justice system. This also has an impact on the prosecutor's role as a policy-implementer or conflict-solver. While in Germany the prosecutor is tasked with implementing the policy of the executive branch, the same might be true in the U.S. system, considering that prosecutors are part of the executive branch.

Fourth, the prosecutor is an impartial minister of justice and a forceful advocate of the victim. In conflict-solving procedures, the proceedings are characterized by partisan interests. In a pure conflict-solving (criminal) procedure, this conflict takes place between the representative of the victim and the alleged perpetrator. Strictly speaking, in a pure conflict-solving role, the prosecutor functions as the representative of the victim and mainly advocates for his or her interests.

Fifth, prosecutors are officers of the court with judicial functions and leaders of law enforcement. To cope with the caseloads, both the German and the U.S. system provide public prosecutors with an almost judicial role within abbreviated criminal proceedings. At the same time, German law assigns the prosecution service auxiliary police officers with special powers and a closer relationship with the prosecution. In the United States, however, the police are not accountable to the prosecutor.

Sixth, the prosecution service is centralized and decentralized. Both Germany and the United States are federal states and thus have a system of public prosecution that is decentralized. Within each state, each district has its own prosecutor's office with its own organization.

Seventh, the prosecutor is an elected and appointed official. In Germany, upon the proposal of the Minister of Justice and with the consent of the legislative chamber, the federal prosecutor general and federal prosecutors are appointed by the President of Germany. State prosecutors are appointed by the State Minister of Justice. Most state court chief prosecutors in the United States, by contrast, are elected. The U.S. Attorneys in the federal system are appointed by the President of the United States with the advice and consent of the Senate. In both instances, prosecutors are part of the executive branch, which consists of elected officials who are accountable to the public. The difference between the two jurisdictions is the nature of the accountability mechanism: while in the U.S. citizens directly elect the chief of the local prosecutor office (often called a "district attorney"), in Germany citizens vote for the party that nominates the government official who eventually appoints the prosecutors.

It goes without saying that these examples of role duality do not always unfold as cogently as necessary in order to perfectly assign prosecutorial roles to the conflict-solving or policy-implementing ideals. In fact, quite the opposite: more often than not, prosecutorial roles at trial that seem clear cut prima facie are, upon closer consideration, blurred. I borrow from Sklansky and refer to this departure from clear role duality as "role ambiguity." This ambiguity is not an accident, but rather seems to be a tool for permitting a prosecutor to select and characterize his or her own roles. In other words, to increase prosecutorial discretion and—eventually—power, the roles of the prosecutor are left largely undefined. According to Sklansky, this has had the effect of, *inter alia*, allowing the criminal justice system "to soften the edges of its purported commitments and to redirect its resources quickly and informally" (Sklansky 2016, 2018). At the same time, role ambiguity reduces transparency and accountability, and increases the opportunity for illegal prosecutorial acts of the prosecutor (Sklansky 2018).

References

Alschuler, Albert W. 1972. "Courtroom Misconduct by Prosecutors and Trial Judges." *Texas Law Review* 50(4): 629–735.

Alschuler, Albert W. 1983. "Implementing the Criminal Defendant's Right to Trial." *University of Chicago Law Review* 50(3): 931–1050.

Ambos, Kai. 2016. *Treatise on International Criminal Law*, Vol. 3: *International Criminal Procedure*. Oxford: Oxford University Press.

Ambos, Kai, and Alexander Heinze. 2017. "Abbreviated Procedures in Comparative Criminal Procedure." In *Abbreviated Criminal Procedures for Core International Crimes*. Edited by Morten Bergsmo, 27–100. Brussels: Torkel Opsahl Academic EPublisher.

Ambos, Kai, and Alexander Heinze. 2019. "Written Amicus Curiae Observations." In *Proceedings Relating to the Appeals Filed Against the 'Decision Pursuant to Article 15 of the Rome Statute on the Authorisation of an Investigation into the Situation in the Islamic Republic of Afghanistan' Issued on 12 April 2019 (ICC-02/17-33) and Pursuant to 'Decision on the participation of amici curiae, the Office of Public Counsel for the Defence and the cross-border victims' Issued on 14 October 2019 (ICC-02/17-97)*. November 14, 2019, ICC-02/17-108.

Armenian, Andre Vartan. 2016. "Selectivity in International Criminal Law: An Assessment of the 'Progressive Narrative.'" *International Criminal Law Review* 16(4): 642–672.

Arnoldi, Olaf. 2018. "Präsente Beweismittel in der Praxis." *Neue Zeitschrift für Strafrecht*: 305–312.

Ashworth, Andrew. 2006. "Four Threats to the Presumption of Innocence." *International Journal of Evidence & Proof* 10(4): 241–279.

Batson v. Kentucky. 1986. 476 U.S. 79.

Berger v. United States. 1935. 295 U.S. 78.

Bharara, Preet. 2019. *Doing Justice: A Prosecutor's Thoughts on Crime, Punishment, and the Rule of Law*. New York: Alfred A. Knopf.

Blom, Martine, and Paul Smit. 2006. "The Prosecution Service Function within the Dutch Criminal Justice System." In *Coping with Overloaded Criminal Justice Systems*. Edited by Jörg-Martin Jehle and Marianne Wade, 237–284. Heidelberg: Springer.

Bohlander, Michael. 2012. *Principles of German Criminal Procedure*. Oxford and Portland: Hart Publishing.

Bommer, Felix, et al. 2019. "Alternativentwurf Abgekürzte Strafverfahren im Rechtsstaat (AE-ASR)." *Goltdammer's Archiv für Strafrecht* 166: 1–128.

Bouloc, Bernard, and Haritini Matsopoulou. 2018. *Droit Pénal Général et Procédure Pénale*. 21st ed. Paris: Sirey.

Bowles v. United States. 1970. 439 F.2d 536 (D.C. Cir.).

Boyne, Shawn M. 2014. *The German Prosecution Service: Guardians of the Law?* Berlin and Heidelberg: Springer.

Brink, David O. 2006. "Some Forms and Limits of Consequentialism." In *The Oxford Handbook of Ethical Theory*. Edited by David Copp, 380–423. Oxford: Oxford University Press.

Burns, Robert P. 2009. *The Death of the American Trial*. Chicago and London: University of Chicago Press.

Campbell, Liz, Andrew Ashworth, and Mike Redmayne. 2019. *The Criminal Process*. 5th ed. Oxford: Oxford University Press.

Cicchini, Michael. 2018. "Spin Doctors: Prosecutor Sophistry and the Burden of Proof." *University of Cincinnati Law Review* 87(2): 489–521.

Cole, George F., Christopher E. Smith, and Christina DeJong. 2018. *Criminal Justice in America*. 9th ed. Boston: Cengage.

Corso, Piermaria. 2000. "Italy." In *Criminal Procedure Systems in the European Community*. Edited by Christine van den Wyngaert, 223–260. 2nd ed. London: Butterworths.

Damaška, Mirjan R. 1986. *The Faces of Justice and State Authority: A Comparative Approach to the Legal Process*. New Haven and London: Yale University Press.

Damaška, Mirjan R. 1997. *Evidence Law Adrift*. New Haven and London: Yale University Press.

Damaška, Mirjan R. 2001. "Models of Criminal Procedure." *Zbornik Pravnog Fakulleta u Zagrebu* 51: 477–516.

Damaška, Mirjan R. 2008. "What Is the Point of International Criminal Law?" *Chicago-Kent Law Review* 83(1): 329–365.

Danner, Allison M. 2003. "Enhancing the Legitimacy and Accountability of Prosecutorial Discretion at the International Criminal Court." *The American Journal of International Law* 97(3): 510–552.

Darbyshire, Penny. 2020. *Darbyshire on the English Legal System*. 13th ed. London: Sweet & Maxwell.

de Cruz, Peter. 2007. *Comparative Law in a Changing World*. 3rd ed. London and New York: Routledge-Cavendish.

Deiters, Mark. 2018. "Abgekürzte Strafverfahren." *Zeitschrift für die gesamte Strafrechtswissenschaft* 130: 491–512.

de Smet, Simon. 2009. "A Structural Analysis of the Role of the Pre-Trial Chamber in the Fact-Finding Process of the ICC." In *The Emerging Practice of the International Criminal Court*. Edited by Carsten Stahn and Göran Sluiter, 405–440. Leiden and Boston: Martinus Nijhoff Publishers.

Dezza, Ettore. 2017. *Geschichte des Strafprozessrechts in der Frühen Neuzeit*. Cham: Springer.

Dietrich v. The Queen. 1991. 177 CLR 292 (Austl.).

Doran, Sean, and John Jackson. 1997. "The Case for Jury Waiver." *Criminal Law Review* 1997: 155–172.

Doran, Sean, John D. Jackson, and Michael D. Seigel. 1995. "Rethinking Adversariness in Nonjury Criminal Trials." *American Journal of Criminal Law* 23(1): 1–69.

Dostoevsky, Fyodor. 1994 [1880]. *The Karamazov Brothers*. Translated by Ignat Avsey. New York: Oxford University Press.

Doyle v. Ohio. 1976. 426 U.S. 610.

Dubber, Markus D. 1997. "American Plea Bargains, German Lay Judges, and the Crisis of Criminal Procedure." *Stanford Law Review* 49(3): 547–572.

Dubber, Markus D., and Tatjana Hörnle, eds. 2014. *The Oxford Handbook of Criminal Law*. Oxford: Oxford University Press.

Du Cann, Richard. 1993. *The Art of the Advocate*. London: Penguin.

Duff, Antony, et al. 2006. "Introduction: Judgment and Calling to Account." In *The Trial on Trial*, vol. 2. Edited by Antony Duff et al., 1–13. Oxford and Portland: Hart.

Duff, Antony, et al. 2007. *The Trial on Trial*, vol. 2. Edited by Antony Duff et al. Oxford and Portland: Hart.

Dunlop v. United States. 1897. 165 U.S. 486.

Edmonson v. Leesville Concrete Co. 1991. 500 U.S. 614.

Esser, Robert. 2002. *Auf dem Weg zu einem europäischen Strafverfahrensrecht*. Berlin: De Gruyter.

Felstiner, William L. F. 1979. "Plea Contracts in West Germany." *Law and Society Review* 13(2): 309–325.

Ferdico, John N., Henry F. Fradella, and Christopher D. Totten. 2009. *Criminal Procedure for the Criminal Justice Professional*. 10th ed. Belmont: Wadsworth.

Fletcher, George P. 1968. "Two Kinds of Legal Rules: A Comparative Study of Burden-of-Persuasion Practices in Criminal Cases." *Yale Law Journal* 77(5): 880–935.

Fortune v. State. 2019. 428 S.C. 545.

Frase, Richard S., and Thomas Weigend. 1995. "German Criminal Justice as a Guide to American Law Reform: Similar Problems, Better Solutions?" *Boston College International and Comparative Law Review* 18(2): 317–360.

Frederick, Jeffrey T. 2018. *Mastering Voir Dire and Jury Selection*. 4th ed. Chicago: American Bar Association.

Fukuyama, Francis. 2018. *Identity*. London: Profile Books.

Gaede, Karsten. 2016. "§ 239 StPO". In *Münchener Kommentar zur Strafprozessordnung*, Band 2: *§§ 151–332 StPO*. Edited by Hartmut Schneider. Munich: C. H. Beck.

Galanter, Marc. 2004. "The Vanishing Trial: An Examination of Trials and Related Matters in Federal and State Courts." *Journal of Empirical Legal Studies* 1(3): 459–570.

Georgia v. McCollum. 1992. 505 U.S. 42.

Geppert, Klaus. 1979. *Der Grundsatz der Unmittelbarkeit im deutschen Strafverfahren*. Berlin and New York: Walter de Gruyter.

Geppert, Klaus. 1992. "Zum 'fair-trial-Prinzip' nach Art. 6 Abs. 1 Satz 1 der europäischen Menschenrechtskonvention.'" *Juristische Ausbildung*: 597–604.

Gilliéron, Gwladys. 2014. *Public Prosecutors in the United States and Europe*. Berlin: Springer.

Goldstein, Abraham S. 1997. "Converging Criminal Justice Systems: Guilty Pleas and the Public Interest." *Israel Law Review* 31: 169–182.

Gottfredson, Michael R., and Don M. Gottfredson. 1988. *Decision Making in Criminal Justice: Toward the Rational Exercise of Discretion*. Berlin: Springer Science & Business Media.

Griffin v. California. 1965. 380 U.S. 609.

Grosso, Catherine M., and Barbara O'Brian. 2019. "Lawyers and Jurors: Interrogating Voir Dire Strategies by Analyzing Conversations." *Journal of Empirical Legal Studies* 16(3): 515-541.

Hall, Daniel E. 2014. *Criminal Law and Procedure*. 7th ed. Belmont: Cangage.

Heffer, Chris. 2005. *The Language of Jury Trial*. New York: Palgrave MacMillan.

Heghmanns, Michael. 2017. *Das Arbeitsgebiet des Staatsanwalts*. 5th ed. Münster: Aschendorff.

Heinze, Alexander. 2014. *International Criminal Procedure and Disclosure*. Berlin: Duncker & Humblot.

Heinze, Alexander. 2017. "The Kosovo Specialist Chambers' Rules of Procedure and Evidence." *Journal of International Criminal Justice* 15: 985–1009.

Heinze, Alexander. 2018. "Bridge over Troubled Water—A Semantic Approach to Purposes and Goals in International Criminal Justice." *International Criminal Law Review* 18(6): 929–957.

Heinze, Alexander. 2020a. "Private International Criminal Investigations and Integrity." In *Integrity in International Justice*. Edited by Morten Bergsmo and Viviane Dittrich, 615–738. Brussels: Torkel Opsahl Academic EPublisher.

Heinze, Alexander. 2020b. "Falsa Demonstratio Non Nocet: The Record of the Proceedings at the ICC is a Case File–Now More Than Ever." In *Opinio Juris*, 25 June 2020, http://opinio-juris.org/2020/06/25/falsa-demonstratio-non-nocet-the-record-of-the-proceedings-at-the-icc-is-a-case-file-now-more-than-ever/.

Heinze, Alexander, and Shannon Fyfe. 2018. "Prosecutorial Ethics and Preliminary Examinations at the ICC." In *Quality Control in Preliminary Examination*, vol. 2. Edited by Morten Bergsmo and Carsten Stahn, 1–75. Brussels: Torkel Opsahl Academic EPublisher.

Heinze, Alexander, and Shannon Fyfe. 2019. " The Role of the Prosecutor." In *Core Concepts in Criminal Law and Criminal Justice*, vol. 1. Edited by Kai Ambos, Antony Duff, Julian Roberts, and Thomas Weigend, 343–388. Cambridge: Cambridge University Press.

Heller, Kevin Jon. 2015. "The Role of the International Prosecutor." *The Oxford Handbook of International Adjudication*. Edited by Cesare P. R. Romano, Karen J. Alter, and Yuval Shany, 669–690. Oxford: Oxford University Press.

Henderson, Carol M. 1981. "Prosecutorial Comments and Tactics: Another Look at a Continuing Problem." *Criminal Justice Quarterly* 8(1): 6–18.

Herrmann, Joachim. 1996. "Models for the Reform of the Criminal Trial in Eastern Europe: A Comparative Perspective." *St. Louis-Warsaw Transatlantic Law Journal* 1996: 127–151.

Howell, K. Babe. 2014. "Prosecutorial Discretion and the Duty to Seek Justice in an Overburdened Criminal Justice System." *Georgetown Journal of Legal Ethics* 27(2): 286–334.

Hungerford-Welch, Peter. 2019. *Criminal Procedure and Sentencing*. 9th ed. New York: Routledge.

In re Freeman. 2006. 38 Cal.4th 630.

Ingraham, Barton L. 1987. *The Structure of Criminal Procedure*. New York, Westport, CT, and London: Greenwood Press.

J.E.B. v. Alabama ex rel. T.B. 1994. 511 U.S. 127.

Jackson, John D., and Sarah J. Summers. 2012. *The Internationalisation of Criminal Evidence: Beyond the Common Law and Civil Law Traditions*. Cambridge: Cambridge University Press.

Jehle, Jörg-Martin. 2006. "The Function of Public Prosecution within the Criminal Justice System." In *Coping with Overloaded Criminal Justice Systems*. Edited by Jörg-Martin Jehle and Marianne Wade, 3–25. Berlin and Heidelberg: Springer.

Jehle Jörg-Martin. 2013. "Was und wie häufig sind Fehlurteile?" *Forensische Psychiatrie, Psychologie, Kriminologie* 7: 220–229.

Kadish, Sanford H., et al. 2012. *Criminal Law and its Processes*. New York: Wolters Kluwer.

Kant, Immanuel. 1785. *Grundlegung zur Metaphysik der Sitten*. Riga: Johann Friedrich Hartknoch. Translated by Allen W. Wood, 2002. *Groundwork for the Metaphysics of Morals*. New Haven: Yale University Press.

Kemme, Stefanie, and Barbara Dunkel. 2020. "Strafbefehl und Fehlurteil – Erkenntnisse zu einer wenig beachteten Verbindung." *Strafverteidiger* 2020: 52-59.

Kirchengast, Tyrone. 2010. *The Criminal Trial in Law and Discourse*. New York: Palgrave Macmillan.

Kokott, Juliane. 1998. *The Burden of Proof in Comparative and International Human Rights Law*. The Hague, London, and Boston: Kluwer Law International.

Kubicek, Theodore L. 2006. *Adversarial Justice: America's Court System on Trial*. New York: Algora.

Langbein, John H. 1974. "Controlling Prosecutorial Discretion in Germany." *University of Chicago Law Review* 41(3): 439–467.

Langer, Máximo. 2005. "The Rise of Managerial Judging in International Criminal Law." *American Journal of Comparative Law* 53(4): 835–909.

Laudan, Larry. 2006. *Truth, Error, and Criminal Law*. Cambridge: Cambridge University Press.

Laufer, William S. 1995. "The Rhetoric of Innocence." *Washington Law Review* 70(2): 329–421.

Lempert, Richard O. 1991. "Telling Tales in Court: Trial Procedure and the Story Model." *Cardozo Law Review* 13(2–3): 559–573.

Ligeti, Katalin. 2019. "The Place of the Prosecutor in Common Law and Civil Law Jurisdictions." In *The Oxford Handbook of Criminal Process*. Edited by Darryl Brown, Jenia I. Turner, and Bettina Weisser, 139–163. Oxford: Oxford University Press.

Lippke, Richard L. 2014. "The Prosecutor and the Presumption of Innocence." *Criminal Law and Philosophy* 8(2): 337–352.

Markovits, Daniel. 2010. *A Modern Legal Ethics: Adversary Advocacy in a Democratic Age*. New York: Princeton University Press.

Mayer, Gregg. 2007. "Prosecutors in Books." *Law & Literature* 19(1): 77–101.
McClelland, Gregory A. 2002. "A Non-Adversary Approach to International Criminal Tribunals." *Suffolk Transnational Law Review* 26(1): 1–38.
McCord, James W. H., Sandra L. McCord, and C. Suzanne Bailey. 2012. *Criminal Law and Procedure*. 4th ed. Boston: Cengage.
McNaughton, David, and Piers Rawling. 2006. "Deontology." In *The Oxford Handbook of Ethical Theory*. Edited by David Copp, 424–458. Oxford: Oxford University Press.
Mégret, Frédéric. 2012. "International Prosecutors: Accountability and Ethics." In *International Prosecutors*. Edited by Luc Reydams, Jan Wouters, and Cedric Ryngaert, 416–487. Oxford: Oxford University Press.
Miller-El v. Dretke. 2005. 545 U.S. 231.
Mittermaier, Carl Joseph Anton. 1845. *Die Mündlichkeit, das Anklageprinzip, die Öffentlichkeit und das Geschworenengericht*. Stuttgart: Cotta.
Murphy, Dean E. 2005. "Case Stirs Fight on Jews, Juries and Execution." *The New York Times*, March 15, 2005.
Nicolson, Donald. 2005. "Making Lawyers Moral? Ethical Codes and Moral Character." *Legal Studies* 25(4): 601–626.
Norris v. Alabama. 1935. 294 U.S. 587.
Onions, C. T. 1973. *The Shorter Oxford English Dictionary*, vol. 2. Oxford: Clarendon Press.
Pakes, Francis. 2019. *Comparative Criminal Justice*. 4th ed. London and New York: Routledge.
Panzavolta, Michele. 2004. "Reforms and Counter-Reforms in the Italian Struggle for an Accusatorial Criminal Law System." *North Carolina Journal of International Law & Commercial Regulation* 30(3): 577–623.
Partington, Martin. 2019. *Introduction to the English Legal System 2019–2020*. 14th ed. Oxford: Oxford University Press.
People v. McClellan. 1969. 71 Cal.2d 793.
Perrodet, Antoinette. 2002. "The Italian System." In *European Criminal Procedures*. Edited by Mireille Delmas-Marty and John R. Spencer, 348–412. Cambridge: Cambridge University Press.
Peters, Karl. 1985. *Strafprozeß*. Heidelberg: C. F. Müller.
Pizzi, William. T. 1999. *Trials without Truth*. New York and London: New York University Press.
Posner, Richard A. 2009. *Law and Literature*. 3rd ed. Cambridge, MA, and London: Harvard University Press.
Powers v. Ohio. 1991. 499 U.S. 400.
Pradel, Jean. 2000. "France." In *Criminal Procedure Systems in the European Community*. Edited by Christine van den Wyngaert, 105–136. 2nd ed. London: Butterworths.
R. v. Balmforth. 1992. Crim LR 825.
R. v. Chandler [No. 2]. 1964. 2 QB 322.
R. v. Nugent. 1977. 1 WLR 789.
R. v. Oliva. 1965. 1 WLR 1028.
Reinhard, Jakob. 2002. "Der Rechtsreferendar als Sitzungsvertreter der Staatsanwaltschaft." *Juristische Schulung*: 169–173.
Roxin, Claus, and Bernd Schünemann. 2017. *Strafverfahrensrecht*. 29th ed. Munich: C. H. Beck.
Ruckaberle, Axel. 2006. *Lexikon der Weltliteratur*, vol. 1. Stuttgart, Weimar: J. B. Metzler.
Samaha, Joel. 2018. *Criminal Procedure*. 10th ed. Belmont: Cengage.
Scheb, John M., and John M. Scheb, Jr. 2013. *Criminal Law and Procedure*. 8th ed. Belmont: Cengage.

Schmitt, Bertram. 2020. "Introduction." In *Kommentar zur Strafprozessordnung*. Edited by Lutz Meyer-Goßner and Bertram Schmitt. 63rd ed., mn. 19. Munich: C. H. Beck.

Sharpley, Deborah. 2019. *Criminal Litigation 2019/20*. Guildford: College of Law Publishing.

Simpson, J. A., and E. S. C. Weiner. 1989/2002. *The Compact Oxford English Dictionary*. Oxford: Clarendon Press, Oxford University Press.

Sklansky, David Alan. 2016. "The Nature and Function of Prosecutorial Power." *Journal of Criminal Law and Criminology* 106(3): 473–520.

Sklansky, David Alan. 2018. "The Problems with Prosecutors." *Annual Review of Criminology* 1: 451–469.

Slapper, Gary, and David Kelly. 2017. *English Legal System*. 18th ed. London and New York: Routledge.

Smartt, Ursula. 2006. *Criminal Justice*. London, Thousand Oaks, and New Delhi: Sage.

Smith v. Illinois. 1968. 390 U.S. 129.

Soubise, Laurène, and Alice Woolley. 2018. "Prosecutors and Justice: Insights from Comparative Analysis." Fordham International Law Journal 42 (2): 587–626.

Spencer, John R., ed. 1977/1995. *Jackson's Machinery of Justice*. 7th ed., repr. Cambridge: Cambridge University Press.

Spielmann, Alphonse, and Dean Spielmann. 2000. "Luxembourg." In *Criminal Procedure Systems in the European Community*. Edited by Christine van den Wyngaert, 261–278. 2nd ed. London: Butterworths.

Sprack, John. 2015. *Criminal Procedure*. 15th ed. Oxford: Oxford University Press.

State v. Dunkerton. 1929. 128 Kan. 374.

State v. Green. 1973. 275 So.2d 184 (La.).

State v. Mathis. 1966. 47 N.J. 455.

State v. Stewart. 1978. 162 N.J. Super. 96.

Statistisches Bundesamt, *Rechtspflege Strafgerichte 2019*, Fachserie 10, 2020, pp. 14, 24. https://www.destatis.de/DE/Themen/Staat/Justiz-Rechtspflege/Publikationen/_publikationen-innen-gerichte-straf-anwaltschaft.html.

Swain v. Alabama. 1965. 380 U.S. 202.

Thaman, Stephen C. 2007. "Plea-Bargaining, Negotiating Confessions and Consensual Resolution of Criminal Cases." *Electronic Journal of Comparative Law* 11: 1–54.

Turner, Jenia I. 2016. "Plea Bargaining and Disclosure in Germany and the United States: Comparative Lessons." *William & Mary Law Review* 57(4): 1549–1596.

Turner, Jenia I., and Thomas Weigend. 2019. "Negotiated Case Dispositions in Germany, England and the United State." In *Core Concepts in Criminal Law and Criminal Justice*, Vol. 1. Edited by Kai Ambos, Antony Duff, Julian Roberts, and Thomas Weigend, 389–427. Cambridge: Cambridge University Press.

UK Ministry of Justice, *Criminal court statistics quarterly, England and Wales, January to March 2019*, https://www.gov.uk/government/statistics/criminal-court-statistics-quarterly-january-to-march-2019.

United States v. Gallagher. 1978. 576 F.2d 1028 (3d Cir.).

Vasiliev, Sergey. 2012. "Trial." In *International Prosecutors*. Edited by Luc Reydams, Jan Wouters, and Cedric Ryngaert, 700–796. Oxford: Oxford University Press.

Vogler, Richard. 1996. "Criminal Procedure in France." In *Comparative Criminal Procedure*. Edited by John Hatchard, Barbara Huber, and Richard Vogler, 14–95. London: British Institute of International & Comparative Law.

Volk, Klaus, and Armin Engländer. 2018. *Grundkurs StPO*. 9th ed. München: Beck.

von Feuerbach, Anselm. 1821. *Betrachtungen über die Öffentlichkeit und Mündlichkeit der Gerechtigkeitspflege*. Gießen: G. F. Heyer.

Vriend, Koen. 2016. *Avoiding a Full Criminal Trial*. The Hague: Asser, Springer.

Wade, Marianne. 2006. "The Power to Decide—Prosecutorial Control, Diversion and Punishment in European Criminal Justice Systems Today." In *Coping with Overloaded Criminal Justice Systems*. Edited by Jörg-Martin Jehle and Marianne Wade, 27–126. Berlin and Heidelberg: Springer.

Waltoś, Stanisław, and Piotr Hofmański. 2018. *Proces Karny* [Penal Proceedings]. 14th ed. Warsaw: Lexis Nexis.

Ward, Richard, and Amanda Akhtar. 2011. *Walker and Walker's English Legal System*. 11th ed. Oxford: Oxford University Press.

Weigend, Thomas. 2012. "A Judge by Another Name? Comparative Perspectives on the Role of the Public Prosecutor." In *The Prosecutor in Transnational Perspective*. Edited by Erik Luna and Marianne Wade, 377–391. Oxford: Oxford University Press.

Zacharias, Fred C. 1991. "Structuring the Ethics of Prosecutorial Trial Practice: Can Prosecutors Do Justice?" *Vanderbilt Law Review* 44(1): 45–114.

Zila, Josef. 2006. "The Prosecution Service Function within the Swedish Criminal Justice System." In *Coping with Overloaded Criminal Justice Systems*. Edited by Jörg-Martin Jehle and Marianne Wade, 286–311. Berlin and Heidelberg: Springer.

CHAPTER 7

PROSECUTORS AND SENTENCING

NORA V. DEMLEITNER

7.1 Introduction

DESPITE warnings about the immense authority of U.S. prosecutors going back to the 1920s, in subsequent decades scholars, legislators and the media instead focused their attention on other actors within the criminal justice system. Prosecutors attracted comparatively little study despite their vast authority and the discretion inherent in their power.[1] That did not even change during the massive build-up of the criminal justice system that began in the 1980s. As the proliferation of mandatory sentences and the adoption of sentencing guidelines contributed to longer sentences and mass incarceration, reformers laid blame at the door of legislatures and sentencing commissions. Yet, prosecutors have played a crucial role in the growth of the criminal justice system. As judicial discretion at sentencing decreased, their discretion increased concomitantly.[2] All of their decisions, from case processing to parole recommendations, factor into sentencing, directly or indirectly.

Even though it is almost universally true now that "[p]rosecutors are among the most powerful actors in any criminal justice system" (Britton 2018, 377), American prosecutors remain "unique in the world and in an important sense lawless" (Tonry 2012, 5). The primary difference between U.S. and foreign prosecutors is the way in which state prosecutors get selected. In the United States local prosecutors are elected, which makes them political in a sense in which prosecutors in other countries are not. As accountability runs to the local electorate rather than a central bureaucracy,[3] the *zeitgeist* affects prosecutorial decisions. Public opinion may impact a prosecutor's sentencing decisions most directly in high-profile cases, especially when those occur temporally close to an election. Yet, wider changes in public opinion will also affect prosecutorial approaches. For example, with the changing public attitude toward marijuana, a number of urban prosecutors in states that have not opted for legalization declared that possession for personal use no longer triggers criminal prosecution (Fair and Just Prosecution 2017, 4–6; Office of the State's Attorney for Baltimore City 2019, 10, 13). Some prosecutors in states that have legalized marijuana have expressed support for the expungement or sealing of such criminal records, which would allow individuals to deny that they have a conviction (Tchekmedyian 2019).

Effectively, prosecutorial decisions taken at a much earlier point foreshadow the final result. Systemic decisions on the types of crimes to prosecute provide the first inflection point. In cases that are brought to the prosecution's attention or in which they initiate investigations, they must determine whether to levy criminal charges, what types of charges and in what court. For charges that carry mandatory minimum sentences, that decision drives much of the further process such as the defendant's decision whether to proceed to trial. Much of the research into prosecutors focuses on charging practices. After all, only a conviction will lead to a sentence.

Prosecutor impact on sentencing extends throughout the entire system. Therefore, sentencing should be "more broadly understood to encompass a criminal justice system actor's ability to influence the penalty imposed on an offender in response to an offence." After all, prosecutorial "discretion flows back and forth through the criminal justice process, and extends to all decision-making points" (Britton 2018, 379). Prosecutors exert their influence over the sentence at many points throughout the process as well as directly at sentencing (Simons 2009).

First, prosecutors provide the entrée to diversion programs.[4] Those may take the form of sentence suspensions or alternatives to the traditional criminal courts process. Prosecutors have been instrumental in developing—or blocking—specialized courts, such as drug or mental health courts, and back-end re-entry courts. The entrance criteria they set provide the key to admission.[5]

Since trial outcomes threaten a higher sentence than a plea, the vast majority of defendants plead guilty. The negotiations leading up to the bargain usually focus on the type and scope of the criminal sentence though the parties may also consider the impact of the conviction and sentence on potentially attendant civil and administrative consequences (Love, Roberts, and Logan 2018; Demleitner 2020).

The increase in prosecutorial influence on sentencing, however, is no longer solely an American phenomenon. It has been observed in other common law countries and in Continental Europe as well where prosecutors have enlarged their charging discretion and ability to bargain (Fionda 1995; Bachmaier 2015).

As defendants serve their sentence, the prosecution often retains some control over them. Supervision violations require a prosecutor to determine whether to proceed against the individual. In deciding on early release, parole boards allow for the prosecution's input or even require a prosecutorial recommendation. Similarly should the individual ask for clemency from the governor or president, the prosecution will weigh in, formally or informally. Sometimes prosecutors even get to recommend whether a criminal record should be sealed or expunged, so that the convicted person would be legally permitted to deny its existence. The prosecutor's authority over the sentence determination, therefore, extends much longer than that of any other official.

7.2 In the Shadow of Sentencing: Charging and Diversions

The potential sentence looms large throughout the entire criminal justice process and dominates a prosecutor's decisions. What offenses to charge and later whether to bargain or try a case are pivotal determinations. The charging decision sets the parameters for the entire case. It provides the framework for how to categorize the offense, what label to attach to it, and what the sentence exposure will be.

U.S. criminal law encompasses a broad set of federal and state statutes that continues to grow. Legislatures often criminalize actions or enhance sentences upon the commission of high profile offenses or with the advent of new technology that is being misused to obtain illegal ends. The panoply of criminal statutes has led to overlap and duplication, though without raising judicial concern (Stuntz 2001). The disarray is most palpable with respect to federal crimes which are strewn across the federal code (O'Sullivan 2006). Rarely is a criminal statute taken off the books though many languish in obscurity. Studies on federal prosecutions indicate that cases tend to get prosecuted under a limited set of criminal statutes (U.S. Sentencing Commission 2019). As criminal law has turned from a more objective to a substantive approach, it has expanded its reach ever earlier into inchoate offenses. That change expanded the number of individuals within the purview of the criminal law (Chiesa 2018). The scope and breadth of criminal statutes and the incoherence of the criminal codes have dramatically enlarged prosecutorial discretion over time.

After an investigation indicates sufficient proof to charge, the prosecution then details the offenses of which an individual is accused. Often the charge is not singular as one act may violate a host of criminal statutes. It is then the prosecutor's decision, how many statutory charges and which to levy in the charging documents, with grand juries operating usually as a tool to affirm those selections. The prosecution also determines the system in which the case is to be prosecuted—juvenile, state, federal, military, or tribal. With these decisions, prosecutors set the sentence parameters. Prosecutors, for example, may request that a court refer a juvenile for trial into the adult system where prison sentences are substantially lengthier and have moved away from the rehabilitative goals dominant in the juvenile system. Yet, prosecutors do not have untrammeled authority. Under some states' laws they are mandated—or prohibited—to transfer cases into the adult system, based on the offender's age and alleged offense.[6]

Prosecutors may set priorities with respect to the types of cases they prosecute and the sentences for which they ask. That implies they have the authority not to prosecute select types of cases even if sufficient evidence for a conviction exists. In the last few years, that has been a salient issue with respect to possession of marijuana for personal use. While many urban jurisdictions and voters welcomed prosecutorial decriminalization, in other parts of the country prosecutors ran into opposition from police and the judiciary.[7]

Federal and state prosecutors may collaborate or compete for cases. In many localities federal and state prosecutors have standing agreements on who will prosecute those cases over which they have concurrent jurisdiction. In firearms cases, for example, the potential sentence often drives the allocation of responsibility. Federal sentencing data indicates the role mandatory minimums play in these cases and in drug sentencing (Schmitt and Syckes 2019, 16, 19). The minimums as well as enhancements based on prior criminal convictions guarantee a certain sentence level in federal court that drives selection of cases and choice of court. They also drive bargaining, which will be discussed further later in this chapter. Sometimes those negotiations occur in individual cases, granting prosecutors discretion to select the sentence exposure. Since the 1990s joint federal-state task forces have proliferated, investigating together offenses in which both have jurisdiction. These teams permit prosecutors to choose the venue based on the potential sentence, substantive law, and procedural advantages for the prosecution.

Prosecutorial charging practices also impact police actions. For example, law enforcement may attempt to manipulate venue to achieve longer sentences. This is most likely to occur when geographically adjacent prosecutor's offices have different charging practices for the same type of offense.

Definitions of crimes generally include sentence parameters. While crimes with mandatory sanctions set out a sentence floor, guidelines will provide a more nuanced prediction, though one courts can generally exceed. In the case of capital charges, however, the prosecutor demands a particular sentence, death. Generally that limits negotiations to the question whether both sides are willing to accept a life-without-parole sentence. Capital charges are singular in their specificity. Generally, prosecutors seek a particular sentence within a broader set of choices.

Some European countries subscribe to the principle of mandatory prosecution whenever sufficient evidence exists. In recent decades, however, prosecutors there have gained increasing power to divert cases from the criminal system. Often those have been a result of caseload pressures. Some of these diversions are highly structured, depending solely on the type of case at issue. Others are individualized. In some countries the legislature has given prosecutors the right to impose specific sanctions in select cases (Tak 2001, 157). In others, courts retain the sanctioning prerogative though they rarely oppose a prosecutor's request (Fionda 1995, 173–179).

In the United States, a host of alternatives to the traditional criminal justice process have developed. Some of these avoid a conviction and therefore also a formal criminal sentence as long as the accused cooperates with the condition(s) imposed. Sometimes a case gets dismissed in exchange for a payment. That practice has raised concerns about wealthy defendants effectively being able to buy themselves out of the criminal justice system while poorer defendants will be convicted and formally sentenced. Over time, however, many diversion programs changed so as to require entry of a conviction, which would be sealed or expunged upon sentence completion.

These diversion programs are an outgrowth of either prosecutorial or judicial initiative though in the latter case they would only succeed with prosecutorial support. Prosecutors control access to alternative courts, pioneered in the United States but now exported globally.

Even in the development of such courts, prosecutors have substantial input into their parameters, restricting the types of offenses and limiting the offenders who may be diverted. Despite initial efforts to structure such diversions as deferred prosecutions, prosecutors ultimately converted them into convictions that may be dismissed if the offender successfully complies with all requirements. Still these alternatives are far removed from the traditional adversarial system. They require prosecutors to relinquish much of their independence to work cooperatively with the defense and the court and focus on the defendant successfully completing the requirements. Should a defendant fail to comply, it is the prosecutor who holds the authority to prosecute. Yet, in this setting those decisions are a collaborative venture rather than based on the prosecution's unilateral exercise of power.

U.S. prosecutors are not the only ones whose power has grown over the last few decades through alternative processes. Continental European prosecutors, who used to be perceived as bureaucrats who solely executed higher-level orders, have also increased their ability to divert ostensibly criminal cases. Alternative systems have developed because of crushing caseloads. The prosecution's decision to refer a case into the alternative system effectively determines its outcome. Only if someone were to challenge either the charge or the proposed sanction would a formal case be opened. Instead most of these cases end in a payment, which implicitly acknowledges guilt. Only if the stakes are high, should processing in the formal criminal justice system be expected. In addition to these highly structured and automatic diversions, in common law and Continental European countries deferred prosecution agreements have arisen in the context of corporate prosecutions (Bronitt 2019). The same is true in the United States.

On both sides of the Atlantic prosecutors have used the threat of criminal prosecutions to force corporate compliance and civil settlements. They agree to divert corporations from the criminal process in exchange for punitive payments, long-term supervision, and new internal compliance guidelines and structures (Garrett 2011). In Europe, corporations have often been asked to make substantial payments into public coffers in exchange for non-prosecution agreements. In the federal system concern about the reputational and financial consequences of an indictment and potential sentence exposure under the federal sentencing guidelines, has made corporations more willing to agree to often expensive and onerous long-term oversight (Beale 2016).

The availability of alternative and additional non-criminal sanctions also play an increasing role in the prosecutorial toolbox. Federal prosecutors whose offices combine civil and criminal departments use non-criminal sanctions as additional bargaining chips in select cases. Some state prosecutors also consider these in plea deals.

7.3 Isn't Plea Bargaining Effectively Sentencing?

Despite the emphasis on (criminal) trials, mythologized in U.S. popular culture, literature, and movies, the American criminal justice system has long relied on plea bargaining rather than trials. In some states the felony jury trial rate has now fallen below 1 percent though the trial figures vary substantially between the states. In fiscal year 2018, 97.4 percent of all sentenced federal offenders pled guilty (U.S. Sentencing Commission 2019, table 11). Those few who go to trial are generally found guilty.

In a system focused on processing cases to address their relentless stream and limit backlog, trials take up an immense amount of resources. They also infuse uncertainty for both sides. Defendants are often deterred from going to trial as a conviction will almost always carry a longer sentence than a bargain would—the so-called "trial penalty." In addition to being denied a lower sentence range, the defendant will also lose the discount traditionally associated with pleading guilty. Whether that discount is effectively a reward for pleading guilty and showing remorse or rather a penalty for insisting on one's trial right, is irrelevant for this discussion. In light of the incentives the prosecution is able to offer—or deny—in most cases a guilty plea is a defendant's rational, and perhaps only possible, response.

Embedded in the charges rests the prosecution's bargaining leverage. Prosecutors can agree to drop some of multiple charges in exchange for a plea, or they can agree to drop a charge down to a lower level. For example, they may drop a felony to a misdemeanor charge, or select a charge that carries a lower maximum sentence or a lesser guideline range.

Prosecutors have their peak bargaining power with charges that carry mandatory minimums or mandatory sentence enhancement either based on the defendant's criminal history or an offense element. That means mandatory sanctions provide prosecutors with additional leverage if they can offer bargains to avoid such. Research indicates that prosecutors exercise more power over charging and bargaining when severe sanctions in the form of mandatory minimums exist (Engen 2008, 84). In cases of debilitating sanctions the prosecution is unable or unwilling to consider in its offer, defendants may be inclined to opt for a trial as that at least holds out the (minimal) chance of avoiding a conviction.

The most discussed mandatory sanctions are mandatory minimum sentences, applied frequently in drug and firearms cases. The highest mandatory penalties, which range from five up to 30 years, apply when the defendant is charged with possessing, brandishing, or discharging a gun in the course of committing a drug offense. Similarly, the Armed Career Criminal Act penalizes weapons possession for an offender with at least three prior drug trafficking or violent felony convictions. Once the offender pleads to a crime that carries such a sentence, a court is bound to impose the required sentence. For a very narrow category of federal drug offenders, judges have the opportunity to go below the guidelines. The only other possibility for a defendant to escape a mandatory sanction in this situation is to obtain from the prosecutor a substantial assistance motion. Only based on that motion does the court gain discretion to sentence the defendant below the otherwise mandatory sentence. That motion, however, rests solely in the hands of the prosecution and appears to be exercised unevenly across the country.

Mandatory sanctions come also in the form of sentence enhancements, based on the offender's prior criminal record. The well-known three strikes laws fall into that category. The most draconian of those was California's law, which went into effect in 1994. It mandated that the court impose a term of at least twenty-five years to life for any felony conviction when the defendant had two prior convictions for a serious felony. A later referendum changed the requirements so that the new felony has to be serious or violent. Even though that change restricted prosecutors as to the triggering offense, it left intact another important aspect of prosecutorial discretion. Until California's Supreme Court allowed trial judges limited opportunities to disregard certain prior convictions for sentencing purposes, prosecutors alone controlled the sentence. They had the discretion whether to bring prior convictions to the court's attention.

Federal prosecutors control so-called 851 enhancements that enhance the minimum and maximum sentence exposure of a defendant in a drug trafficking case if the person has a prior conviction for a felony drug offense. A study indicated that most of the 851 informations provided to the court were ultimately withdrawn. Federal prosecutors use that enhancement apparently frequently to strengthen their hand in plea bargaining and to compel cooperation. Both the filing and withdrawal of 851 informations vary substantially between different judicial districts, making it subject to the influence of potential biases. African-American offenders were the ones most likely subject and the most likely to receive the sentence enhancement (U.S. Sentencing Commission 2018).

Whether to select the particular charges that carry mandatory minimums or whether to inform the judge about a defendant's priors if those trigger a mandatory enhancement, remain solely in the prosecutor's discretion. The number of cases in which such charges are lowered or the judicial information is dropped indicate how prosecutors employ these to enhance pressure in plea negotiations.

Even discretionary sanctions may present a sufficient threat that the defendant may be more willing to enter a plea or to agree to specific conditions to avoid them. Some defendants, of course, will reject any plea bargain that would require them to admit to an offense they did not commit. Other defendants may consent to an extrajudicial sanction to avoid a harsher criminal penalty. For example, to avoid a prison term, defendants may consent to surrender their medical license, a sanction that would be outside the prosecutor's purview otherwise. Other defendants may instead choose a short prison stint in exchange for having the opportunity to make their case to the licensing board. The proliferation of punitive collateral sanctions and consequences, therefore, has substantially increased the power of prosecutors.

Collateral sanctions range from exclusions from government contracting to removal from the United States. Some follow automatically from certain types of convictions;

others rest in the discretion of extra-judicial bodies, such as administrative agencies or licensing authorities. Studies have indicated that defendants are highly motivated to bargain about inclusion in the sex offender registry and prosecutors often agree to accept a guilty plea to offenses that avoid such inclusion. Such bargains, driven by a collateral consequence that exposes the offender to various other restrictions, may camouflage the underlying offense.

The collateral sanction the U.S. Supreme Court has declared the most impactful is deportation. It is concern about removal from the United States that drives some defendants to gamble on a trial when any deal the prosecution offers leaves them exposed to immigration consequences. Some prosecutors consider the likelihood of deportation in their plea offers. They may, for example, agree to recommend a lower sentence because the defendant will be deported. On the other hand, they may structure a plea agreement so that the defendant at least will not be subject to mandatory deportation but instead has the opportunity to make her case to an immigration judge.

With only a small percentage of criminal cases—between two and ten percent—going to trial, the focus has shifted fully to the plea and the ultimate outcome, the sentence (Leipold 2018, 179). Prosecutorial discretion in charging and plea bargaining have impeded the promise of uniformity which sentencing guidelines and mandatory sanctions held out. The 1984 Sentencing Reform Act was a response to two different problems. Conservatives bemoaned lenient sentences and largely held federal judges responsible. Unwarranted sentence disparities, blamed primarily on federal judges, raised the concern of liberals. After all, the federal system was national, with inmates serving time all around the country, and so sentences should be uniform. These two strands resulted in the creation of the federal sentencing guidelines and supported the rise of mandatory minimums. With the focus on judicial discretion, legislators paid little attention to prosecutors.

Federal prosecutors escaped attention and managed to preserve discretion. Their initial decisions cement the sentence guideposts long before judges impose the actual sentence. Prosecutorial decisions may have mitigated the punishment enhancements included in the sentencing guidelines but they also maintained or even increased racial and gender disparity (Engen 2008; Rehavi and Starr 2014; Davis 2017, 196–206). Sentence enhancements based on prior criminal record reinforce disparate policing between neighborhoods that result in African Americans being more likely to have a criminal record. Especially an extensive prior criminal record makes the defendant appear more of a risk to public safety, justifying prosecutorial insistence on sentence enhancements. Research on the precise prosecutorial contribution to disparity, however, remains challenging. Yet, it is undisputed that even prosecutorial charging guidelines in the federal system and sentencing directives in some European countries have not had much of an impact on unwarranted disparities (Tak 2001, 176–177).

Plea bargains may take different forms: charge bargains, fact bargains, or sentence bargains. Charge bargaining occurs when prosecutors dismiss some charges, which some refer to as count bargaining, or allow a plea to a lesser charge than originally in the indictment. The latter usually implies a decrease in the potential sentence. The dismissal of charges prevents the sentencing judge from imposing consecutive sentences. Yet, depending on the charges, the dismissal of counts may not directly translate into a lesser sanction. In states with sentencing guidelines, the conviction offense is most crucial in setting sentence parameters, which enhances the relevance of charge bargaining. Neither legislatures nor the courts have regulated plea bargaining even as it has come to replace public trials in many states. Prosecutors are almost entirely unconstrained in their ability to structure the type of deal they consider fitting, knowing that they hold great sentence leverage.

In fact bargains, both sides agree to certain facts that may be sentence determining. For example, agreement on a certain drug quantity could allow an offender to avoid a mandatory minimum. Such agreements effectively manipulate the sentence. In controlled-drug-buy cases those decisions should be seen in light of the fact that law enforcement agents often artificially increase the drug amount that provides the basis for the charge and sentence exposure. Yet, those fact bargains also occur in other areas, often to avoid collateral sanctions (Johnson 2019).

Both of these types of bargains impact the sentence, and with the emergence of more guided sentencing these types of pleas are focused more closely on the ultimate sentence (Reitz 2001, 252). Judges have come to deem these agreements effectively binding rather than mere sentence recommendations, which they are. Technically it should be sentence bargains that have the greatest direct impact. Many judges bristle at those but most are usually willing to follow the sentencing set out in charge and fact bargains. For reasons of economy and respect for the parties, judges tend to adopt party agreements that detail a specific sentence.[8]

Even though prosecutors may set the parameters through a multitude of pre-sentence decisions, at sentencing they get an opportunity to detail the specific sentence the state considers appropriate in that specific case.

7.4 Sentencing

While state court misdemeanor and felony sentencing can be fast-paced and hurried, with the exception of mass sentencings for immigration offenses, conducted at the southern border, in federal court sentencing tends to be a more formal process.

With respect to a sentence agreement, federal plea bargains come in two forms. If the parties present a joint sentence recommendation to the court and the judge accepts the agreement, the court will be bound by the sentence. Alternatively, based on the plea agreement, prosecutors may recommend—or not oppose—a sentence range. They may also indicate that specific guideline provisions (not) apply. Prosecutorial sentence recommendations may come in writing or orally at a sentencing hearing. Alternatively, the prosecution may consent to remain silent and not oppose the defense's sentence request. In rarer cases a defendant may plead guilty without an agreement as to the sentence. In those cases both sides will make their argument to the court.

Mandatory sanctions are binding on the judge subject to some exceptions. In the federal system, prosecutors may petition the court to sentence below such a mandatory minimum sentence. That "safety valve," which is available only for lower-level drug offenders with a limited prior criminal record, provides the prosecutor with another tool for leverage. More generally applicable is the prosecutor's power to make a substantial assistance motion based on the defendant's help in the investigation and prosecution of others. That motion provides the judge with the opportunity to sentence the offender below the mandatory minimum.

During the decade and a half when the federal guidelines were mandatory and appellate courts closely reviewed district court decisions to sentence outside the range, a prosecutorial request for a downward departure effectively shielded the court from reversal. Prosecutors may also ask for below guideline sentences though that power became less important after the guidelines were no longer binding.[9] Even though federal judges had the authority to depart prior to the Supreme Court's guideline ruling, compliance was high. Under the current regime, compliance has declined though most non-guideline sentences remain based on prosecutorial request, which reinscribes the authority of federal prosecutors.

Research indicates that demographic disparity did not disappear while the guidelines were mandatory. The Sentencing Commission has found rising racial disparity since the guidelines have lost their mandatory character (Divine 2018). There is disagreement both as to the magnitude of that effect and whether these differences are in fact unwarranted (Starr 2013). It seems clear that both judges and prosecutors independently are sources of sentence disparity though prosecutorial disparity appears larger. The specific judge-prosecutor dynamic independently also affects sentence disparity (Kim, Spohn, and Hedberg 2015).

Sentences are statutorily circumscribed though judicial decisions may limit prosecutors from selecting certain sentences. The Supreme Court, for example, declared death sentences in non-homicide cases unconstitutional, outlawed mandatory life-without-parole sanctions for juveniles, and limited their imposition on juveniles to homicides only.[10] Still adult non-death sentences remain largely unfettered, subject only to a very loose proportionality analysis. Some states have adopted a more vibrant proportionality review, which restrict prosecutors' decisions to slightly greater extent.

Sentence hearings may be perfunctory or elaborate, depending on the court and the type of case. For the vast majority of routine criminal cases, courts, as well as prosecutors, have a "going rate." In federal court and more serious state cases, both parties may call witnesses and argue for a specific sentence during the sentencing hearing. Sentencing hearings are particularly extensive in capital cases where they, rather than the guilt phase, may constitute the crux of the case. Even though victims, or in homicide cases their family members, are permitted to testify at sentencing, sentence recommendations are left to the prosecution. Often those are aligned with the victim's desires. Yet, especially in domestic violence and death cases, disagreements can arise between the prosecution and the victim, as the former sees itself as the representative of the people with potentially conflicting goals.

The influence of prosecutors on the sentence may have special import as judges and defense counsel anchor their thinking around prosecutorial sentence recommendations. The prosecutor's initial sentence demand sets the starting point for discussion (Roberts and Wright 2016, 1483). In the United States, there has been relatively little critique of direct prosecutorial involvement in sentencing, likely because sentencing is now considered a part of the adversarial process.

In other common law countries, the role of prosecutors at sentencing itself has also increased. In the past, English and Australian prosecutors played little role after conviction (Humphreys 1955, 747; Tonry 2012, 25). Today they are required to assist courts at sentencing, in part to prevent "appealable error." Prosecutors are expected to discuss aggravators and mitigators and inform the court about applicable guidelines and precedents. They are also to note community sentiment and ancillary aspects of a sentence, both considerations well outside a typical U.S. sentencing (Britton 2018, 386). This information will provide the court a more holistic account of the full impact of the conviction on the defendant. The growing role of the parties at sentencing in all common law countries may be due to an increased belief in the adversarial process, where the parties are in the best position to provide relevant information to the court. Alternatively, it may be merely a function of a more complicated regime in which judges are dependent on input from the parties.

Still the role of prosecutors in countries like England appears more restrained than in the United States. English prosecutors can indicate their "view as to the appropriate sentence range or tariff" but cannot ask for a specific sentence (Britton 2018, 387). Crown prosecutors are deemed to be disinterested in the outcome.

New Zealand's prosecutors, on the other hand, are more assertive at sentencing and recommend specific sentences. They are not government employees but rather private attorneys who operate in a decentralized manner with little regulatory oversight. Their recommendations often seem infused with populist opinion. Yet, in light of the funding model, they are unlikely to pursue sentence campaigns in the legislature, in contrast to U.S. prosecutors.[11]

In Australia courts have preserved even more of their independence. In 2014 the Australian High Court held that the prosecution is not permitted to express an opinion even on the sentence range unless the court specifically asks for it. The prosecution is allowed to argue for a specific sentencing approach but not an outcome, to assure consistency and individualization.[12] The stated rationale for this nuanced approach is the protection of democratic values and legal legitimacy (Britton 2018, 390).

In the United States the public has long regarded lengthy sentences as a prosecutorial victory and equated them with enhanced public safety. With little data available, voters consider high-profile convictions as a stand-in for public safety. Internally, reputations and rewards often hinge on conviction numbers and sentences imposed (Bibas 2009). As research challenges the connection between public safety and sentence length and the public has come to understand the cost of mass incarceration, the public's assessment of what a prosecutorial victory means may become more nuanced.

Yet, the system built over the last few decades and ongoing concerns about public safety continue to contribute to an expansion of the prosecutorial role. Prosecutorial authority remains influential even long after the formal sentencing process is complete.

7.5 "It Ain't Over 'Til It's Over": The Ongoing Prosecutorial Hold over an Offender

Even after formal imposition of a sentence, the prosecutor's impact continues to be felt. Common law prosecutors are not permitted to appeal an acquittal but retain the power to appeal a sentence for legal error. Such appeals are rare in discretionary sentencing systems unless the judge imposed a potentially illegal sanction. Under mandatory sentencing guidelines, prosecutorial sentence appeals are a more regular occurrence though their import will depend on the standards for reviewing sentence appeals.[13] To prevent the defendant from appealing a conviction and sentence, prosecutors, especially in the federal system, regularly demand appeal waivers to be included in plea agreements (Klein, Remis, and Elm 2015). Courts have generally upheld such waivers but affirmed that certain constitutional rights will survive.

Even after the sentence is final, prosecutorial involvement may not be over. Those under supervision, whether in lieu of an incarcerative term or following it, remain subject to the probation office's oversight. Violations, when serious enough for the probation officer to bring to the court's attention, can lead to sentence revocation and (re-) incarceration. The decision whether to prosecute a probation violation rests with the prosecution. Also, prosecutors may choose to support or oppose probation's recommendation for probation or parole modification after a violation. The widely disparate percentage of probation violators in state prisons across the country bears witness to the different approaches probation and prosecution offices take. These differences are most dramatically reflected in the number of technical offenders behind bars who have violated supervision rules but not committed a new criminal offense. For example, in Rhode Island only about a fifth of all those admitted to prison for a supervision violation committed a technical violation only. In Tennessee, on the other hand virtually all such prison admissions are triggered by technical violations. Yet the percentage of prison admissions due to violations of supervision conditions is virtually identical. The composition of the group differs substantially, however (Justice Center 2019).

Prosecutors, formally or informally, also participate in parole decisions, which, if available in a state system, determine the release date of an offender. Many states permit prosecutors to submit background information on the offense, an assessment of the offender's dangerousness, or even a recommendation regarding early release. In some high-profile cases prosecutors even appeared in person in front of the parole board. In most cases prosecutors base their input entirely on the crime committed even if it occurred decades earlier (Cassidy 2019, 296–300). Because parole decisions have become highly politicized in many of the states that still have parole, prosecutors often hold the key to release.[14] If the prosecution actively opposes release, the board will not grant it. At least under some circumstances, prosecutors therefore exercise substantial influence over the actual term an offender serves.

In continental Europe, on the other hand, prosecutors play no role in such release decisions. Presumptions in favor of early release are strong, and such decisions are often left to specialized judicial tribunals, with the inmate retaining the right to appeal a denial of release (van Zyl Smit and Corda 2018, 450–457).

The role of U.S. prosecutors is also often substantial in clemency requests, such as sentence commutations and pardons. With the politicization of such requests in all U.S. jurisdictions, the role of prosecutors appears to have increased. In many cases, they can effectively prevent a release or a pardon, appealing to concerns for public safety or the heinousness of the crime.[15]

The clemency process put in place during the Obama administration that allowed for the early release of select drug offenders, for example, subjected release recommendations to Department of Justice review and veto. Some commentators sharply criticized that set-up for permitting prosecutors to reject clemency decisions (Love 2015). Generally, the president and governors elicit the opinions of their attorneys general and local prosecutors, especially on sentence commutations or for pardon requests for relatively recent convictions.

Although not formally part of the sentence, many convictions carry collateral consequences relating to housing, employment, or other activities. Early prosecutorial decisions, including charging and bargaining, often set the parameters for such consequences. Since collateral sanctions, however, are not deemed criminal punishment, they can and have been imposed retroactively. Prosecutors do not control such impact. With the recent focus on easing re-entry, some prosecutors have worked with individuals to help them remove convictions from their record. Some have supported erasing earlier arrest records and convictions for marijuana possession and, in states with more generous expungement laws, actively assisted those with even more serious felonies. Other offices, however, have displayed no institutional interest in helping with these efforts, which then fall onto community organizations and the private bar (Murray 2018).

The innocence movement has further highlighted the outsized role of prosecutors. Prosecutors' rejection of testing of crime-related evidence impedes fact-finding, and in many cases makes it effectively impossible to ascertain a convict's factual innocence. Even more difficult are cases in which prosecutors are reluctant to turn over materials that may indicate, for example, investigatory malfeasance, negligence, or incompetence. Prosecution objections to release are frequent even in cases of substantial evidence that an innocent person was convicted (Medwed 2004). Presumably such prosecutorial opposition is based on a belief in the accuracy of the process in the individual case. Alternatively, office culture and political calculus may lead prosecutors to oppose exoneration efforts. Not all prosecution offices have responded in this way, however.

An increasing number of larger offices have created investigatory teams and been willing to look into questionable convictions (Rice 2018).[16] So far at least opposition to exoneration efforts appears to undermine an office's credibility only in high-profile cases where innocence seems blatant. Still offices that have been willing to explore innocence claims have frequently gained praise.

7.6 Conclusion

A focus on individual aspects of prosecutorial power may underestimate the overall impact of such decisions on the sentence ultimately imposed and served. The process begins with the prosecution's decision to charge or offer a pre-charge diversion and then turns to the plea bargaining process. A formal sentencing hearing is ultimately only one element in this process that can last throughout the term of the sentence imposed and even beyond. Prosecutors retain the power to sanction probation violations, may weigh in on parole decisions, and often have a say in executive clemency. That systemic perspective provides a better lens into prosecutorial authority and impact on sentencing than a narrow consideration of the procedure itself.

In the United States and many European countries, over the last few decades prosecutorial power has expanded. Yet, only in the United States has the impact on the growth of the criminal justice system been dramatic. Prosecutorial elections, lack of central oversight or guidance, limits on judicial sentencing discretion without concomitant restrictions on prosecutorial charging or bargaining power, and the impact of the tough-on-crime rhetoric on office culture, have strengthened the adversarial approach to sanctioning and undermined the role of prosecutors as ministers of justice. Whether that role can be reinvigorated remains to be seen. Despite studies that the public prefers less punitive and prison-focused sentences, in many jurisdictions prosecutors appear to pay no price for continuing existing approaches or restricting change largely to the prosecution of low-level drug offenses.

Notes

1. An important exception was Joan Jacoby's study of prosecutors (Jacoby 1980).
2. Prosecutors' role in securing these longer sentences—sometimes with the explicit purpose of increasing prosecutorial power in plea bargaining—is addressed by Russell M. Gold in Chapter 16.
3. Voter accountability is limited as prosecutorial elections are rarely competitive, with incumbent prosecutors only occasionally facing an electoral challenge, especially in rural America (Hessick and Morse 2020; Wright 2009).
4. Prosecutors' role in diversion and accountability courts is addressed by Salmon Shomade in Chapter 9.

5. One example of such a prosecutor-driven initiative is the Brooklyn Drug Treatment Alternative to Prison (Belenko, Sung, Swern, and Donhauser 2008).
6. Prosecutorial power over juveniles is addressed in more detail by Kristin Henning in Chapter 22.
7. Prosecutors in Philadelphia, Houston, and New York City have decided to no longer prosecute such cases. The district attorney in Norfolk, Virginia, however, faced local judges who refused to drop the cases (Demleitner 2020). Recent legislation now mandates Virginia judges dismiss cases when prosecution and defense agree.
8. A high-profile example of such an agreement is the bargain between the U.S. government and John Walker Lindh who was captured in Afghanistan and stood accused of collaborating with the Taliban in killing a CIA officer (*United States v. Lindh* 2002).
9. In *Booker v. United States* (2005), the Supreme Court declared mandatory federal sentencing guidelines unconstitutional but retained them as a recommended sentencing framework.
10. In *Coker v. Georgia* (1977), the U.S. Supreme Court declared the death penalty disproportionate to the rape of an adult woman. In *Roper v. Simmons* (2005), the Court found the Eighth Amendment a bar to the imposition of death for crimes committed when the offender was under 18. That ruling was expanded in *Graham v. Florida* (2010), to prohibit a life-without-parole sentence to be imposed on a juvenile for a non-homicide offense. In *Miller v. Alabama* (2012), the Supreme Court struck down mandatory life-without-parole sentences for those under 18.
11. For more on the U.S. political dynamic regarding sentencing, see Russell M. Gold in Chapter 16.
12. In *Barbaro v. The Queen* (2014), the High Court rejected the defendants' argument that the lower court should have allowed the prosecution to submit sentence ranges.
13. State sentencing guidelines come in many different forms. Some allow for sentence appeals when the sentence does not fall into the prescribed range though others do not (Mitchell 2017, 35–36).
14. One California study indicates that prosecutor's support for parole does not impact the board's decision. A prosecutor's opposition, however, carries substantial weight (Young, Mukamal, and Favre-Bulle 2016).
15. One example is Pennsylvania where lifers can only gain release through clemency. Those discretionary releases have slowed to a trickle (Center on the Administration of Criminal Law 2019, 2, 10). The sole exception to this rule appears to be the Trump administration. In contrast to his predecessors, President Trump bypassed formal processes, including the Department of Justice, in his clemency decisions. Failure to consider prosecutorial input tends to be more likely at the end of a presidential or gubernatorial term.
16. Prosecutors' role post-conviction including their efforts to assist with or oppose exoneration is addressed in more detail by Brandon L. Garrett in Chapter 8.

References

Bachmaier, Lorena. 2015. "The Principle of Legality, Discretionary Justice and Plea Agreements: The Practice in Spain." In *Discretionary Criminal Justice in a Comparative Context*. Edited by Michele Caianiello and Jacqueline S. Hodgson, 89–115. Durham: Carolina Academic Press.

Barbaro v. The Queen. 2014. 253 CLR 58 (Austl.).

Beale, Sara Sun. 2016. "The Development and Evolution of the U.S. Law of Corporate Criminal Liability and the Yates Memo." *Stetson Law Review* 46(1): 42–69.

Belenko, Steven, Hung-En Sung, Anne J. Swern, and Caroline R. Donhauser. 2008. "Prosecutors and Treatment Diversion: The Brooklyn (NY) Drug Treatment Alternative to Prison Program." In *The Changing Role of the American Prosecutor*. Edited by John L. Worrall and M. Elaine Nugent-Borakove, 111–137. Albany: State University of New York Press.

Bibas, Stephanos. 2009. "Prosecutorial Regulation versus Prosecutorial Accountability." *University of Pennsylvania Law Review* 157(4): 959–1016.

Booker v. United States. 2005. 543 U.S. 220.

Britton, Andrew. 2018. "Pressing for Sentence? An Examination of the New Zealand Crown Prosecutor's Role in Sentencing." *Criminal Law Forum* 29(3): 377–433.

Bronitt, Simon. 2019. "Deferred Prosecution Agreements: Negotiating Punishment Before Conviction?" In *The Evolving Role of the Public Prosecutor: Challenges and Innovations*. Edited by Victoria Colvin and Philip Stenning, 45–59. New York and London: Routledge.

Cassidy, R. Michael. 2019. "Undue Influence: A Prosecutor's Role in Parole Proceedings." *Ohio State Journal of Criminal Law* 16(2): 293–305.

Center on the Administration of Criminal Law. 2019. "The Demise of Clemency for Lifers in Pennsylvania."

Chiesa, Luis. 2018. "The Model Penal Code, Mass Incarceration, and the Racialization of American Criminal Law." *George Mason Law Review* 25(3): 605–652.

Coker v. Georgia. 1977. 433 U.S. 584.

Davis, Angela J. 2017. "Prosecutors, Democracy, and Race." In *Prosecutors and Democracy: A Cross-National Study*. Edited by *Máximo Langer* and *David Alan Sklansky*, 195–226. Cambridge and New York: Cambridge University Press.

Demleitner, Nora V. 2020. "The Imperial Prosecutor: Increasing Prosecutorial Power Accompanies Criminal Justice Reforms." In *Can They Do That? Demystifying Prosecutorial Discretion*. Edited by Melba Pearson. Chicago: American Bar Association Publishing.

Divine, Joshua M. 2018. "*Booker* Disparity and Data-Driven Sentencing." *Hastings Law Journal* 69(3): 771–834.

Engen, Rodney L. 2008. "Have Sentencing Reforms Displaced Discretion over Sentencing from Judges to Prosecutors?" In *The Changing Role of the American Prosecutor*. Edited by John L. Worrall and M. Elaine Nugent-Borakove, 73–90. Albany: State University of New York Press.

Fair and Just Prosecution. 2017. "Issues at a Glance: Marijuana Policy Reform." September 25, 2017.

Fionda, Julia. 1995. *Public Prosecutors and Discretion: A Comparative Study*. Oxford: Clarendon Press.

Garrett, Brandon L. 2011. "Globalized Corporate Prosecutions." *Virginia Law Review* 97(8): 1775–1875.

Graham v. Florida. 2010. 560 U.S. 48.

Hessick, Carissa Byrne, and Michael Morse. 2020. "Picking Prosecutors." *Iowa Law Review* 105(4): 1537-1590.

Humphreys, Christopher. 1955. "The Duties and Responsibilities of Prosecuting Counsel." *Criminal Law Review* 1955: 739.

Jacoby, Joan. 1980. *The American Prosecutor: A Search for Identity*. Lexington: D. C. Heath and Company.

Johnson, Thea. 2019. "Fictional Pleas." *Indiana Law Journal* 94(3): 855–900.

Justice Center, The Council of State Governments. 2019. "Confined and Costly: How Supervision Violations Are Filling Prisons and Burdening Budgets."

Kim, Byungbae, Cassia Spohn, and E. C. Hedberg. 2015. "Federal Sentencing as a Complex Collaborative Process: Judges, Prosecutors, Judge-Prosecutor Dyads and Disparity in Sentencing." *Criminology* 53(4): 597–623.

Klein, Susan R., Aleza S. Remis, and Donna Lee Elm. 2015. "Waiving the Criminal Justice System: An Empirical and Constitutional System." *American Criminal Law Review* 52(1): 73–130.

Leipold, Andrew D. 2018. "Criminal Dockets, Sentencing, and the Changing Role of Federal Prosecutors." *Federal Sentencing Reporter* 30(3): 177–185.

Love, Margaret Colgate, Jenny Roberts, and Wayne Logan. 2018. *Collateral Consequences of Criminal Conviction: Law, Policy and Practice*. 2018–2019 edition. Eagan, MN: Thomson Reuters.

Love, Margaret Colgate. 2015. "Justice Department Administration of the President's Pardon Power: A Case Study in Institutional Conflict of Interest." *University of Toledo Law Review* 47(1): 89–107.

Medwed, Daniel S. 2004. "The Zeal Deal: Prosecutorial Resistance to Post-Conviction Claims of Innocence." *Boston University Law Review* 84(1): 125–183.

Miller v. Alabama. 2012. 567 U.S. 460.

Mitchell, Kelly Lyn. 2017. "State Sentencing Guidelines: A Garden Full of Variety." *Federal Probation* 81(2): 28–36.

Murray, Brian M. 2018. "Unstitching Scarlet Letters? Prosecutorial Discretion and Expungement." *Fordham Law Review* 86(6): 2821–2871.

Office of the State's Attorney for Baltimore City. 2019. "Reforming a Broken System: Rethinking the Role of Marijuana Prosecution in Baltimore City."

O'Sullivan, Julie R. 2006. "The Federal Criminal 'Code' is a Disgrace: Obstruction Statutes as Case Study." *Journal of Criminal Law & Criminology* 96(2): 643–726.

Rehavi, M. Marit, and Sonja B. Starr. 2014. "Racial Disparity in Federal Criminal Sentences." *Journal of Political Economy* 122(6): 1320–1354.

Reitz, Kevin R. 2001. "The Disassembly and Reassembly of U.S. Sentencing Practices." In *Sentencing and Sanctions in Western Countries*. Edited by Michael Tonry and Richard S. Frase, 222–258. Oxford and New York: Oxford University Press.

Rice, Josie Duffy. 2018. "Do Conviction Integrity Units Work?" *The Appeal*. March 22, 2018. https://theappeal.org/do-conviction-integrity-units-work-a718bbc75bc7/.

Roberts, Jenny, and Ronald F. Wright. 2016. "Training for Bargaining." *William and Mary Law Review* 57(4): 1445–1504.

Roper v. Simmons. 2005. 543 U.S. 551.

Simons, Michael A. 2009. "Prosecutors as Punishment Theorists: Seeking Sentencing Justice." *George Mason Law Review* 16(2): 303–355.

Schmitt, Glenn R., and Cassandra Syckes. U.S. Sentencing Commission. 2019. "Overview of Federal Criminal Cases: Fiscal Year 2018."

Starr, Sonja. 2013. "Did *Booker* Increase Sentencing Disparity? Why the Evidence Is Unpersuasive." *Federal Sentencing Reporter* 25(5): 323–326.

Stuntz, William J. 2001. "The Pathological Politics of Criminal Law." *Michigan Law Review* 100(3): 505–600.

Tak, Peter J. 2001. "Sentencing and Punishment in The Netherlands." In *Sentencing and Sanctions in Western Countries*. Edited by Michael Tonry and Richard S. Frase, 151–187. Oxford and New York: Oxford University Press.

Tchekmedyian, Alene. 2019. "Prosecutors Move to Clear 54,000 Marijuana Convictions in California." *Los Angeles Times*. April 1, 2019.

Tonry, Michael. 2012. "Prosecutors and Politics in Comparative Perspective." *Crime & Justice* 41(1): 1–33.

U.S. Sentencing Commission. 2019. "2018 Annual Report and Sourcebook of Federal Sentencing Statistics."

U.S. Sentencing Commission. 2018. "Application and Impact of 21 U.S.C. § 851: Enhanced Penalties for Federal Drug Trafficking Offenders."

United States v. Lindh. 2002. Eastern District of Virginia. https://www.justice.gov/archives/ag/plea-agreement.

Van Zyl Smit, Dirk, and Alessandro Corda. 2018. "American Exceptionalism in Parole Release and Sentencing: A European Perspective." In *American Exceptionalism in Crime and Punishment*. Edited by Kevin Reitz, 410–486. New York: Oxford University Press.

Wright, Ronald F. 2009. "How Prosecutor Elections Fail Us." *Ohio State Journal of Criminal Law* 6(2): 581–610.

Young, Kathryne M., Debbie A. Mukamal, and Thomas Favre-Bulle. 2016. "Predicting Parole Grants." *Federal Sentencing Reporter* 28(4): 268–277.

CHAPTER 8

PROSECUTORS POST-CONVICTION

BRANDON L. GARRETT

8.1 Introduction

"He's just not connected to this particular incident," said the prosecutor after DNA testing cleared James Bain in Florida in 2009. From prison, Bain had written numerous hand-written letters to the judges, proclaiming his innocence and asking for DNA testing. The prosecutor had opposed the tests, and despite a 2001 law providing access to post-conviction DNA testing, state judges had all sided with the prosecutor. After years of appeals, and the involvement of the Florida Innocence Project, Bain finally obtained DNA testing, the results cleared him, and he was exonerated (Garrett 2011, 215). Such stories are not uncommon. Other people cleared by DNA have faced retrials, where prosecutors contested innocence in the face of powerful evidence. However, most exonerations happen through a far more cooperative process. Indeed, prosecutors are increasingly leaders in seeking to reopen and investigate closed cases. The longstanding adversarial approach of prosecutions towards post-conviction matters more generally has begun to change.

The prosecutor's duty to seek justice formally continues after a conviction. As the American Bar Association Standards (ABA) put it: "The prosecutor has a duty to defend convictions obtained after fair process." That statement reflects the traditional view, but the ABA Standards go on to say: "This duty is not absolute, however, and the prosecutor should temper the duty to defend with independent professional judgment and discretion." The ABA Standards add that a prosecutor "should not defend a conviction if the prosecutor believes the defendant is innocent or was wrongfully convicted, or that a miscarriage of justice associated with the conviction has occurred" (American Bar Association 2016, Standard 3-8.1; Green 1999). Nineteen states have now adopted some version of ABA Model Rule 3.8(g) and (h) that imposes ethical obligations on prosecutors post-conviction, including to promptly disclose evidence of innocence (ABA Model Rules 2013, R. 3.8[g]-[h]; Ch. 15). While legal ethics scholars have proposed an affirmative obligation of prosecutors to do justice by identifying and correcting wrongful convictions, in the past, few prosecutors meaningfully invested in that role, even if they did occasionally support efforts to reverse convictions (Green and Yaroshefsky 2009, 481; Medwed 2009, 55–57).

Traditionally, the connection between prosecutors and post-conviction proceedings was fairly indirect. Local prosecutors played no role in proceedings following the trial. Typically, state attorney general's offices handle both appeals and any post-conviction proceedings that follow in state or federal court. Moreover, few criminal cases result in post-conviction proceedings. Habeas corpus specialists handled such matters, predominantly in death penalty cases, which raise particularly complex issues and result in protracted litigation. As a general matter, that is still true.

However, that distant and adversarial posture has begun to change in recent years. More prosecutors' offices have taken the responsibility on themselves to investigate new matters post-conviction. A growing number of exonerations occur because prosecutors themselves agree to review new evidence of innocence or locate it themselves. As a result, the prosecution function has become more tied to review of cold cases and reinvestigation and reconsideration of convictions. Prosecutors have done more. They have created specialized conviction integrity units (CIUs) tasked with reviewing cold cases. They have created units to conduct other types of audits and reviews to investigate systemic issues, including regarding forensic evidence and police misconduct. They have even, in some offices, conducted investigations of their own conduct. The post-conviction role of prosecutors has never been more robust, and although most offices may follow a traditional model in which work largely consists in defending final convictions, the clear trend is towards a reconception of the post-conviction role. This chapter describes each of those changes and describes their implications for post-conviction criminal procedure.

8.2 Specialized Appeals Units

Traditionally, state attorney general offices or specialist appeals and post-conviction units handle criminal cases for the government post-trial (Criminal Appeals Division 2018). The ABA Standards recommend that any prosecutor's office designate prosecutors with special expertise in appellate law and procedure (American Bar Association 2016, Standard 3-8.2). Those groups may not communicate closely with trial prosecutors and their work has often been highly procedural and technical, particularly during state and federal habeas proceedings. The separation of such appellate and post-conviction groups, however, can permit expertise in the often-technical rules surrounding such litigation. That separation can also permit review by different actors.

The rise of plea bargaining, structured sentencing, and other changes in criminal adjudication, have accompanied a decline in criminal trials in state and federal systems in the United States. As a result, trials are no longer the primary way that evidence and fairness are tested. Appeals and post-conviction review have also been reduced in importance, as plea agreements typically include waivers of rights to pursue those options (King and O'Neill 2005). Exceptions may exist for ineffective assistance of counsel in the negotiation of those plea bargains, or where certain avenues are preserved for claims of innocence or involuntariness in the negotiation of that plea.

Thus, one area in which a review by separate prosecutors is particularly important is where ineffective assistance of defense counsel is concerned. While prosecutors are adverse parties to the inmate, they owe a duty to seek justice and ensure that a conviction is valid. The ABA Standards note the duty to ensure that claims regarding ineffective assistance of defense counsel are preserved (American Bar Association 2016, Standard 3-8.4). The ABA Standards also highlight that: "The prosecutor need not . . . invoke every possible defense to a collateral attack, and should consider potential negotiated dispositions or other remedies, if the prosecutor and the prosecutor's office reasonably conclude that the interests of justice are thereby served" (American Bar Association 2016, Standard 3-8.5).

8.3 New Evidence of Innocence

New evidence of innocence raises pressing questions for prosecutors, particularly when it comes to light after a conviction is final. Traditionally, as described, a final conviction would end the work of a local prosecutor's office, and a state attorney general would then handle defense of post-conviction challenges. However, the ABA Standards emphasize that a prosecutor "should not defend a conviction if the prosecutor believes the defendant is innocent or was wrongfully convicted, or that a miscarriage of justice associated with the conviction has occurred" (American Bar Association 2016, Standard 3-8.1). By the end of 2019, nineteen states had adopted some version of ABA Model Rule 3.8(g) and (h) that imposes affirmative obligations on prosecutors post-conviction, including to promptly disclose evidence of innocence (see Bruce A. Green in Chapter 15 of this volume). Courts have often assumed that prosecutors may not intervene to correct errors.

Take the example of a Virginia case, that of Thomas Haynesworth, in which a writ of actual innocence was granted based on new DNA evidence; the prosecutor and state attorney general both joined in the motion to vacate the conviction. The state appellate court agreed, but a number of dissenting judges suggested that prosecutors were not even authorized to join such a writ and could not concede the question of innocence (*Haynesworth v. Commonwealth*, 2011 [Elder, J., dissenting]). To clarify that prosecutors are permitted to agree that a person deserves relief on grounds of innocence, lawmakers in 2015 subsequently amended the statute to provide that "The Attorney General may join in a petition for a writ of actual innocence made pursuant to § 19.2-327.10" (Va. Code Ann. § 19.2-327.10:1).

It is common for prosecutors to join in efforts to exonerate inmates, in the United States, including in post-conviction DNA cases. In practice, DNA exonerations have typically proceeded with the consent of prosecutors. In the first 250 DNA exoneration cases in the United States, prosecutors consented to DNA testing in 81 percent of cases in which information was obtained on the subject and opposed it in 19 percent (Garrett 2011, 227). To be sure, in some of those cases, prosecutors may have initially opposed the motion, but in each, they eventually did join. The experience of such high-profile exonerations may have helped to change the attitudes of prosecutors towards requests to reexamine evidence generally. The innocence revolution has changed the roles of prosecutors in other ways, including regarding the creation of conviction integrity units.

Further, it has long been common for executive clemency to involve prosecutors in the process. Informally, it is often crucial whether local prosecutors support an application for clemency. Formally, in many states, the attorney general initially reviews clemency applications and makes recommendation to the governor or to a board of pardons. Whether clemency is granted or denied may formally or informally hinge on the position taken by prosecutors at the local and state level. With the advent of conviction integrity units, discussed next, the role of prosecutors in such processes has shifted, and increasingly one sees prosecutors taking the lead in efforts to review and overturn convictions, rather than taking the lead in opposing such efforts.

8.4 Conviction Integrity Units

New evidence of innocence places prosecutors at the center of the question how to appropriately do justice after a final conviction. The ABA Guidelines note that a prosecutor's office "should develop policies and procedures to address such [newly discovered] information, and take actions that are consistent with applicable law, rules, and the duty to pursue justice" (American Bar Association 2016, Standard 3-8.3).[1]

In over thirty jurisdictions, including some of the largest prosecution offices in the country, prosecutors have created groups designed to identify, remedy, and prevent wrongful convictions. They are commonly called conviction integrity or conviction review units, but they have different names in different jurisdictions, and they have operated quite differently from each other. In the early 2000s, these were novel, and there were just a handful in operation in the United States. By 2015 there were more than twenty such units and by 2017 there were over thirty, according to a report by the National Exoneration Registry (National Registry of Exonerations 2017). A growing share of exonerations are the result of such units. These conviction review efforts are concentrated in large urban counties. The units responsible for the most exonerations have been Harris County, Texas (Houston); Dallas, Texas; Cook County, Illinois (Chicago); and Kings County, New York (Brooklyn) (National Registry of Exonerations 2017, 2; Scheck 2017, 713–714; Ware 2011–2012, 1037).

Many of these offices have been created when new chief prosecutors have assumed office. New prosecutors may be more willing to reexamine cases resolved by their predecessors. The first large such unit, in Dallas, Texas, was created by a newly elected District Attorney Craig Watkins, the first black district attorney elected in Texas, who brought in a former innocence project lawyer to head the group in 2007 (Ware 2011–2012). In the past, Dallas prosecutors had viewed innocence claims and requests for DNA testing with "skepticism, cynicism, and, sometimes, open disdain" (Ware 2011–2012, 1037). Under Watkins, the unit began as a collaborative, with the public defender's office, and cooperation of area innocence projects (Ware 2011–2012, 1040). They were able to secure funding from the country to create the unit, including where an exoneree spoke "passionately and eloquently" to the city council about the deep need for such an office (Ware 2011–2012, 2041). Since its creation, a series of DNA and non-DNA exonerations have resulted, as well as actual culprits identified (Ware 2011–2012, 2014).

Other units have been expanded by a newly elected prosecutor. The Brooklyn unit was created by longstanding District Attorney Charles Hynes, but it took new life under then newly elected district attorney Ken Thompson, who vastly expanded its staff and budget, making it the largest in the country, with nine full-time prosecutors (Wilber 2016). Another part of the story is response to crisis or scandal; in Brooklyn, a large number of convictions were reversed in the wake of a scandal involving fabricated evidence by a Brooklyn detective.

In recent years, these conviction review units have become well known enough that they have been the subject of election campaigns. Thus, the ACLU of Missouri wrote a letter to the newly elected district attorney in St. Louis on behalf of a reform coalition, stating "Within your first 100 days, we seek public opportunities to vet potential policies for your proposed conviction integrity unit" (ACLU of Missouri 2019).

In Harris County, Texas, such an effort was responsible for over a hundred exonerations in cases involving field drug screening results. The Brooklyn unit has reversed over twenty convictions. Other prosecution units have not been as active, and quite a few have never experienced an exoneration (National Registry of Exonerations 2017, 4). The only such federal unit was created by the U.S. Attorney's Office for the District of Columbia.

The policies and practices used by such units are typically not public, although the ABA counsels that policies and procedures should be put into place (not necessarily that they be made public, however) (Hollway n.d.). Best practices have been recommended for such units, including the independence of the re-investigation and review function within an office (Center on the Administration of Criminal Law's Conviction Integrity Project 2012, 4–5). Thus, these units can create an independent and internal review unit within a prosecutor's office. Such an approach is very different from the hands-off approach of traditional offices that delegated post-conviction functions to attorney general's offices, and that ceased factual investigation after a conviction. These offices are far better situated to conduct investigations of new evidence of innocence than a state attorney general, or an independent innocence project for that matter, since they can access police and prosecution files and employ investigators. That said, these review groups have been uneven in their implementation and their resources; time will tell how effective they will become.

8.5 Sentence Review Units

A similar reinvestigation role is becoming more prominent in the area of sentencing. Far more cases involve questions regarding fairness and accuracy of sentences than claims of new evidence of innocence, and many jurisdictions are currently reconsidering lengthy sentences imposed over the past few decades. California is the first state to enact legislation permitting prosecutors to reopen sentences as no longer in the interests of justice. In January 2019, the law went into effect, and it allows the court to recall and resentence a defendant upon the recommendation of the district attorney (an act to amend Section 1170 of the Penal Code). A statewide Sentencing Review Project works with prosecutors to identify cases for resentencing (Sentence Review Project 2018). About two dozen prosecutors' offices are considering opening sentence review units nationally (Hager 2018).

A project of that type in the King County (Seattle) District Attorney's Office has involved a group of prosecutors reviewing life sentences, and signing clemency petitions, on behalf of the office, where they believe that such lengthy sentences were not warranted (Hager 2018). This sentencing review model may spread just as the conviction review model has begun to do so. If so, it will again place prosecutors in the central position to revisit claims that outcomes should be reconsidered.

8.6 Special Inquiries and Audits

Prosecutors also serve an important role as administrators and reformers of the criminal justice system, who are well positioned to intervene to identify and respond to systemic problems.[2] Internal audits can review cases, as well as more broadly, compliance with office policies and procedures as well as with constitutional criminal procedure rules and ethics rules. The Department of Justice has long engaged in such efforts, both internally focused, and designed to assess larger systemic issues.

Attorney General Janet Reno's Commission on the Future of DNA Evidence, in many respects set the stage for future engagement by prosecutors with the problem of error in criminal cases (National Institute of Justice 2018). That Commission extensively documented the then-new phenomenon of convictions reversed by DNA testing post-conviction and it made a series of important recommendations for improving the accuracy of criminal investigations and adjudication.

Some of these reviews have been extremely large-scale efforts. For example, the Department of Justice, in response to revelations regarding testimony by FBI agents in hair microscopy cases, led an audit of thousands of old hair cases. The FBI conducted this review collaboratively with the Innocence Project and the National Association of Criminal Defense Lawyers (NACDL) (Reimer 2013, 16). This effort resulted in the review of 2,900 cases involving hair comparison testimony. The FBI concluded that 96 percent of 2,900 cases reviewed involved flawed hair testimony, including thirty-three of thirty-five death penalty cases (FBI 2018a, 2018b). Among the death penalty cases, nine defendants had already been executed and five died of other causes on death row. The FBI also announced that twenty-six of twenty-eight agents either gave testimony or submitted lab reports with erroneous statements.

In response to the FBI and DOJ audit, many other states, including Florida, Massachusetts, New York, North Carolina, Texas, and Virginia, began to review hair cases as well. A similar large-scale review was conducted in Massachusetts by the attorney general, in response to misconduct uncovered at two state crime laboratories (Office of the Attorney General Commonwealth of Massachusetts 2016, 22–23).

Local level efforts have also been prominent. In addition to the thirty-three CIU's currently in operation, other prosecutor's offices have set up one-time inquiries in response to specific problems. For example, Wayne County, Michigan, set up a project to review firearms evidence in the wake of a scandal and closure of the firearms unit at the Detroit Police crime lab. The Colorado Justice Review Project was a joint Colorado Attorney General and Denver District Attorney effort to use DNA testing post-conviction, supported by a federal grant (Hollway n.d., 18). State district attorney's associations have also created best practices committees to study potential procedural changes (Hamann 2013, 18).

More informally, prosecutors have conducted reviews following criminal convictions to make recommendations for improvements in criminal procedure. The Suffolk County, Massachusetts, district attorney's office convened a task force and adopted eyewitness procedure reforms in response to DNA exonerations. The New Jersey Attorney General's Office issued a memorandum making changes to eyewitness identification procedures in 2001, years before many states began to adopt best practices in the area (State of New Jersey, Department of Law and Public Safety, Office of the Attorney General 2001). The Department of Justice issued memoranda making changes to eyewitness identification procedures and to require videotaping of interrogation procedures by federal agencies (Yates 2017).

In a more long-term effort, the Department of Justice convened in 2013 a National Forensic Science Commission, including scientists, forensic practitioners, judges, and lawyers, as an advisory body to examine forensic sciences and make policy recommendations to the Attorney General, as part of a collaboration with the National Institute of Standards and Technology (NIST). The Commission's mission was to "enhance the practice and improve the reliability of forensic science" (National Commission on Forensic Science 2014). A large number of the Commission's recommendations were adopted during the time that the Commission served (National Commission on Forensic Science 2014). However, the new Administration permitted the term of the Commission to expire in 2017. One recommendation, in fact, of the important 2009 National Academy of Sciences Report on the future of forensic evidence in the United States, was that the regulation and standards function in forensics be vested outside of the Department of Justice and law enforcement, in an independent scientific agency (National Research Council 2009). While that has not occurred, these efforts do involve collaboration between DOJ and a scientific agency. The same DOJ/NIST collaboration also created Organization for Scientific Area Committees (OSAC), which focuses on improving forensic science practice through developing standards; that OSAC process is ongoing.[3]

8.7 Special Investigation Units

Other prosecutor's offices contain units to conduct special investigations, including into closed cases and investigative conduct. The Department of Justice Office of Inspector General (OIG) plays such a role, with broad authority to investigate questions concerning waste, fraud, abuse, and misconduct within the Department (U.S. Department of Justice 2018a). The DOJ's Civil Rights Division investigates law enforcement violations of civil rights, both bringing prosecutions and seeking consent decrees against local police (U.S. Department of Justice 2018b). Some local prosecutor's offices contain a similar function and have expanded such functions in recent years. For example, the San Francisco District Attorney's office created a unit to conduct investigations of police misconduct (Sabatini 2018). However, it is rare for prosecutors to investigate misconduct or impose consequences when police misconduct comes to light.[4] Prosecutors could impose internal office discipline, for example, if *Brady* violations come to light. They could also waive defenses to claims concerning such violations if they agree that errors were made.

8.8 Conclusion

Changes in the prosecution role post-conviction have implications for rules that traditionally envisioned prosecutors in a purely adversarial and defensive role. A wide range of rules impose finality-based limits and defaults on appeals and post-conviction petitions. They typically do not speak to the situation in which a prosecutor seeks to reopen a case and review new facts, and some federal defenses have been deemed as jurisdictional and cannot be waived by a judge (although they are not in fact part of the subject matter jurisdiction of the court). Some such rules do not permit a prosecutor to waive defenses.

This has been a real obstacle to reopening old cases. The FBI audit into hair evidence, for example, resulted in hundreds of letters sent confessing error in closed cases. The letters stated that should habeas petitions be filed in the cases, the FBI would waive any procedural defenses. But some are non-waivable (FBI 2018a).[5] Thus, as occurred in Virginia, the new roles adopted by prosecutors may require that post-conviction procedure be revisited.

These changes in the role of prosecutors suggest new non-adversarial roles post-conviction and a more robust role in reinvestigation of closed cases: a systematic approach to detecting, preventing, and correcting errors (Scheck 2017).[6] As Attorney General Eric Holder put it, "If we truly hope to get to the bottom of errors and reduce the chances of repeating them, then it is time we explore a new, systemwide, way of responding, not by pointing fingers, but by forthrightly assessing our processes, looking for weaknesses in our methods, and redesigning our approach so that the truth will be more attainable" (Cutino 2016, 1071; Holder 2014). Much of this work has occurred outside of judicial process. Perhaps judges could be more closely involved in reviews of old cases, or claims of newly discovered evidence, or review of lengthy sentences. Prosecutors can particulate more actively in the clemency process. It speaks to the power of prosecutors in the United States that prosecutors can be more effective in reviewing closed cases than any other actor in the criminal system. It will also remain to be seen whether more searching post-conviction review can provide feedback and improve processes for handling cases in the first instance. That was the ambition of the National Commission for Forensic Science.

As the role of prosecutors post-conviction shifts, rules of finality may also continue to change. A system focused on final plea bargains and uncommon trial-events may evolve towards a more flexible administrative system with periodic review of sentences, convictions, and other outcomes. If prosecutors continue to move towards such a system, the post-conviction phase may be less distinct and defined apart from the pre-trial and conviction phases. We may see less formal separation between phases of criminal proceedings and less adversarial litigation. We may see prosecutors taking a more active role in reviewing closed cases, and in remedies ranging from reopening investigations, sentence-correction, vacatur, and clemency. The result may be a more flexible and functional approach towards the prosecution role in criminal cases.

Notes

1. Further, prosecutors should comply with ABA Model Rules of Professional Conduct 3.8(g) and (h) (American Bar Association 2016, Standard 3-8.3).
2. The ABA Standards note: "The prosecutor should seek to reform and improve the administration of criminal justice, and when inadequacies or injustices in the substantive or procedural law come to the prosecutor's attention, the prosecutor should stimulate and support efforts for remedial action" (American Bar Association 2016, Standard 3-1.2).
3. The MOU between DOJ and NIST can be found at https://www.justice.gov/ncfs/file/761051/download.

4. See Stephen Rushin in Chapter 24 of this volume.
5. The FBI stated that "DOJ will not raise procedural objections, such as statute of limitations and procedural default claims, in response to defendants' petitions seeking a new, fair trial because of the faulty evidence. But the majority of the FBI examiner testimony was provided in state court prosecutions, and it will be up to the individual states to determine if they will follow DOJ's leading in permitting these cases to be litigated" (FBI 2015).
6. Scheck describes conviction integrity as part of a broader "just culture" approach towards the prosecution function (Scheck 2017).

References

ACLU of Missouri, Letter to Prosecutor Bell from St. Louis Reform Coalition. 2019. https://www.aclu-mo.org/en/news/letter-prosecutor-bell-st-louis-reform-coalition.

American Bar Association. 2016. *Criminal Justice Standards for the Prosecution Function.* 4th ed.

American Bar Association (ABA). 2013. *Model Rules of Professional Conduct.* An act to amend Section 1170 of the Penal Code, relating to recall of sentencing, Assembly Bill No. 2942 (2017th–2018 Sess.).

Center on the Administration of Criminal Law's Conviction Integrity Project. 2018. *Establishing Conviction Integrity Programs in Prosecutors' Offices.*

Committee on Identifying the Needs of the Forensic Science Community National Research Council. 2009. *Strengthening Forensic Science in the United States: A Path Forward.*

"Criminal Appeals | Office of the Attorney General." 2018. https://www.texasattorneygeneral.gov/divisions/criminal-justice/criminal-appeals.

Cutino, Josh. 2016. "Continuous Quality Improvement: Increasing Criminal Prosecution Reliability through Statewide Systematic Improvement Procedures." *Lewis & Clark Law Review* 20(3): 1065–1092.

Federal Bureau of Investigation. 2018a. "FBI/DOJ Microscopic Hair Comparison Analysis Review."

Federal Bureau of Investigation. 2018b. "FBI Testimony on Microscopic Hair Analysis Contained Errors in at Least 90 Percent of Cases in Ongoing Review."

Garrett, Brandon L. 2011. *Convicting the Innocent: Where Criminal Prosecutions Go Wrong.* Cambridge, MA: Harvard University Press.

Green, Bruce A. 1999. "Why Should Prosecutors 'Seek Justice.'" *Fordham Urban Law Journal* 26(3): 607–644.

Green, Bruce A., and Ellen Yaroshefsky. 2009. "Prosecutorial Discretion and Post-Conviction Evidence of Innocence Symposium: Prosecutorial Discretion." *Ohio State Journal of Criminal Law* 6(2): 467–518.

Hager, Eli. 2018. "The DAs Who Want to Set the Guilty Free." *The Marshall Project*, March 20, 2018.

Hamann, Kristine. 2013. "Statewide Best Practices Committees for Prosecutors: Leveraging Experience and New Evidence to Benefit the Criminal Justice System." *PROSECUTOR*, October–December 2013.

Haynesworth v. Commonwealth. 2011. 717 S.E.2d 817 (Va. Ct. App.).

Holder, Eric H., Jr. 2014. National Institute of Justice, U.S. Department of Justice. *Mending Justice: Sentinel Event Reviews*, September 2014.

Hollway, John. n.d. *Conviction Review Units: A National Perspective*, Quattrone Center for the Fair Administration of Justice, University of Pennsylvania Law School.
King, Nancy J., and Michael E. O'Neill. 2005. "Appeal Waivers and the Future of Sentencing Policy." *Duke Law Journal* 55(2): 209–262.
Medwed, Daniel S. 2009. "The Prosecutor as Minister of Justice: Preaching to the Unconverted from the Post-Conviction Pulpit Symposium—The Prosecutorial Ethic: A Tribute to King County Prosecutor Norm Maleng." *Washington Law Review* 84(1): 35–66.
National Commission on Forensic Science. 2017. "Reflecting Back—Looking toward the Future." *U.S. Department of Justice.*
National Institute of Justice. 2018. "National Commission on the Future of DNA Evidence." *National Institute of Justice.* https://www.nij.gov:443/topics/forensics/evidence/dna/commission/pages/welcome.aspx.
National Registry of Exonerations. 2018. "Professional Exonerators." https://www.law.umich.edu/special/exoneration/Pages/about.aspx.
Office of the Attorney General Commonwealth of Massachusetts. 2016. "Investigative Report Pursuant to Commonwealth v. Cotto, 471 Mass. 97 (2015)," April 1, 2016.
Reimer, Norman L. 2013. "The Hair Microscopy Review Project: An Historic Breakthrough for Law Enforcement and a Daunting Challenge for the Defense Bar." *The Champion*, July 2013.
Sabatini, Joshua. 2018. "Budget Committee Weighs Cuts to DA's Special Police Investigation Unit, Citywide Internet Project." *S.F. Examiner*, June 22, 2018.
Scheck, Barry C. 2017. "Conviction Integrity Units Revisited." *Ohio State Journal of Criminal Law* 14(2): 705–752.
"Sentence Review Project." *Sentence Review Project.* 2018. https://www.sentencereview.org/ab-2942/.
State of New Jersey, Department of Law and Public Safety, Office of the Attorney General. 2001. "Attorney General Guidelines for Preparing and Conducting Photo and Live Lineup Identification Procedures." April 18, 2001.
U.S. Department of Justice. 2018a. "Office of the Inspector General." https://oig.justice.gov/.
U.S. Department of Justice. 2018b. "The Civil Rights Division's Pattern and Practice Police Reform Work 1994–Present." https://www.justice.gov/crt/file/922421/download.
Virginia Code Annotated. 2018. § 19.2–327.10:1.
Ware, Mike. 2011–2012. "Dallas County Conviction Integrity Unit and the Importance of Getting It Right the First Time I. Exonerating the Innocent: Pretrial Innocence Procedures." *New York Law School Law Review* 56(3): 1033–1052.
Wilber, Del. 2016. "How these Brooklyn prosecutors work to get innocent convicts out of prison." *Los Angeles Times*, Aug. 5, 2016.
Yates, Sally Q. 2017. "Eyewitness Identification: Procedures for Conducting Photo Arrays." *U.S. Department of Justice.*

CHAPTER 9

ACCOUNTABILITY COURTS AND DIVERSION PROGRAMS

SALMON SHOMADE

9.1 Introduction

Prosecutors are part of the movement that has fueled a rapid expansion of accountability courts and diversion programs both in and out of the United States. In this chapter, I discuss the roles prosecutors played in the creation of these courts and programs, explain their gatekeeping responsibilities, address ethical issues raised by their participation, and conclude that prosecutors, especially in the United States, are likely to continue their support for these courts.

The first U.S. specialized criminal court was the Miami Drug Court created in 1989. Other specialized criminal courts such as mental health courts, veterans courts, domestic violence courts, teen courts, and similar others have since been established. There are now more than 4,300 specialty courts in the United States and several more operating outside of the United States in Australia, Canada, Jamaica, United Kingdom, and other nations.

There are several guiding principles utilized by court practitioners operating these specialized courts. When these courts were initially created, prosecutors were part of the efforts and actively participated in crafting these guiding principles. One of these principles is directed toward prosecutors by asking prosecutors and defense counsel operating in these courts to use a non-adversarial approach for promoting public safety while protecting the defendant's due process rights.

Initially, a few prosecutors had difficulty adjusting to their new roles as members of a non-adversarial court team collaborating together to resolve human and social problems in a courtroom setting. However, in part because of support by national prosecutors such as Janet Reno (who served as U.S. Attorney General in the Clinton administration) and others, many prosecutors have adjusted to this new arrangement of conducting criminal court proceedings in these specialized courts. Janet Reno, prior to becoming the U.S. Attorney General, was the state prosecutor for the Miami area when the first drug court was established. Reno maintained her support for drug and other specialized courts when she became the nation's top prosecutor and ensured that efforts to create these courts on the state level were adequately funded.

Furthermore, criminal justice reform in the United States has recently become very popular; many bipartisan initiatives have been launched throughout the nation. Many of these initiatives directly call for expanding usage of diversion programs and accountability courts. It is the case that prosecutors will continue to be a part of this collaborative effort to continue utilizing these specialized courts to address social problems. In the first section of this chapter, I focus on the foundation and history behind Accountability Courts and Diversion Programs. Because of drug courts' prominence among specialized criminal courts, I provide details about their creation and machinations, followed by a brief discussion of veterans courts. Next, the chapter details the roles of prosecutors in specialized courts, addresses their functions as gatekeepers to these courts, and discusses potential ethical challenges they face participating in these courts' settings. Then the chapter briefly introduces the reader to courts operating outside of the United States and the prosecutors' roles within them. The chapter ends by explicating the roles of prosecutors in the future of specialized courts.

9.2 What Are Accountability Courts and Diversion Programs?

Accountability Courts and Diversion Programs in the United States are specialized criminal courts designed to address the underlying causes of criminal defendants' criminal behaviors. The focus of accountability courts is on increasing the defendant's accountability to the victim(s) of the defendant's criminal behavior (Collins 2017). As Erin Collins rightly notes, "Because accountability is such an amorphous goal, the category of accountability courts encompasses a wide range of specialized courts that scholars tend to distinguish, including, most prominently, domestic violence courts and community courts, but also sex offense courts and gun courts" (2017, 1491). Nonetheless, the underlying organizing principle common to accountability courts is that offenders committing some offenses, especially misdemeanors or low-level felonies such as domestic violence or quality of life crimes, were not being held accountable for the harm they were causing their victims under the prevailing criminal justice system. As a result, certain offenders have escaped the system and further made their victims either insufficiently protected or much more vulnerable (Collins 2017). Hence, accountability courts are created, in part, with the twin goals of offender accountability and victim protection.

Collins emphasizes that inasmuch as some accountability courts offer treatment for offender rehabilitation, "the treatment often supplements, but does not replace, a formal sanction—increasing victim safety and offender accountability takes precedence" (2017, 1491).

In diversion programs, offenders or defendants meeting certain eligibility requirements are admitted into the programs prior to pleading to a specific charge. Thus, these offenders are not required to plead guilty and if they successfully complete the diversion program, they are not prosecuted for the actual crimes for which they were initially arrested. Diversion programs (unlike accountability courts) focus on treating the defendant for the problems that are believed to have either led or contributed to the defendant's criminal behavior (Collins 2017; Kennedy 2015). The most common diversion programs are drug courts, mental health courts, juvenile courts, and driving while impaired (DWI) courts. As discussed below, many of these diversion courts also have post-adjudication programs wherein the offender is required to first plead guilty, participate in the treatment program, and then have his/her sentence either waived or removed from the criminal records. I also note here that accountability courts and diversion programs are both more commonly referred to as "problem-solving courts" or "specialized courts."

To be certain, there are various categories or typologies of specialized criminal courts that scholars have ascribed to these problem-solving courts. Collins (2017), for example, deems some specialized courts focusing on girls and veterans as "status courts." She maintains that these courts should be categorized as such because the organizational principle behind their creation is that the defendants are part of certain status groups with unique needs that the existing criminal justice system is not fulfilling but ought to be. Citing Judge Robert Russell (who is credited with leading the veterans court movement in 2008 based on his observations that "veterans are a niche population with unique needs" who require "tailored care"), Collins explains that "veterans' needs are said to derive from the impact of military service, in particular the traumatic and potentially criminogenic impact of combat" (2017, 1492). Thus, veterans courts focus on the criminal offenders who have served in the U.S. military, and as an alternative to incarceration, these veterans are offered intensive supervision, coordinated social services, and treatment. Meanwhile, the typical "girl court" is a juvenile, non-criminal court that adjudicates juvenile delinquency charges against young female offenders.

Others classify specialized courts in accordance with the theoretical justifications for creating them. For example, Allegra McLeod (2012) utilizes four criminal law reformist models to explain specialized courts: a therapeutic jurisprudence model; a judicial monitoring model; an order maintenance model; and a decarceration model. While providing in great details the bases, aspirations, risks, and limitations of each model, McLeod insists, "The models are distinct from, though often overlapping with, the self-definitions and names of the courts" (2012, 1596). McLeod explains that she composed the models based on legal institutional and ideological features, her research observations and analyses, and her reviews of empirical studies, but "not exclusively, or even primarily, in reference to the self-descriptions of the various courts" (2012, 1596).

She further notes, "So while a drug court might conform to an order maintenance model or a therapeutic jurisprudence model, in either instance the court may still be called simply a drug court" (2012, 1596). But McCleod admits that while multiple models may be at play in any given specialized criminal court, only one of these four models above will be dominant in the court.

In addition to these two legal scholars' typologies, problem-solving courts can also be categorized as deferred prosecution courts (referred to as "diversion programs" above) or post-adjudication courts. For post-adjudication programs, the defendant must first plead guilty before being admitted into the program. But the sentence is suspended or deferred while the defendant participates in the program. Upon successful completion, the sentence is either waived or completely expunged from the criminal records. Of course, if a defendant fails to complete the program or violates numerous program rules, the defendant is returned to the criminal court for sentencing for the original crime.

I also note here that in the United States, there are both state and federal specialized criminal courts. While the specialized court movement originated in a state court, U.S. federal courts have created their own network of specialty courts such as drug and veterans courts. As former U.S. Attorney James Kennedy of the Western District of New York attested in 2015, "reentry courts" are one of the most popular specialized courts. Reentry courts focus on helping those offenders released from prisons avoid becoming recidivists. Unlike the defendants in diversion or post-adjudication courts, reentry courts' defendants have already served some incarceration time and are on supervised release. But they might still be grappling with drug or mental health issues.

Specialized criminal courts should not be confused with non-criminal specialized courts. Non-criminal specialized courts, which exist both on the state and federal levels in the United States, tend to have a functional orientation. For example, these courts have jurisdiction over disputes involving economic or regulatory control such as the U.S. Tax Court or Court of International Trade, with the U.S. government commonly being the defendant, and the courts reviewing the decisions made by government regulatory agencies (Unah and Williams 2017).

As for the rapid increase in the number of specialized criminal courts, regardless of whether they are drug, mental health, or veterans courts, some scholars maintain that these courts became popular in part because of the criminal justice systems' inability to address public frustration with human, legal, and social problems such as drug addiction and mental illness confronting society (Feinblatt, Berman, and Denckla 2002; Shomade 2007, 2010). Others insist that these courts, especially the drug courts, were initially created to address the systems' incapability to resolve persistent problems related to backlog of drug cases awaiting trials, drug arrestees passing through prison revolving doors, "crack" cocaine emergence, and related issues (Hora 2002; Nolan 2001; Shomade 2010). Regardless of the rationales for their creation or growth, these courts remain popular. According to the Bureau of Justice Statistics in the U.S. Department of Justice (2016), in 2012 there were 3,052 problem-solving courts in the United States. While the Bureau has not updated the total number of problem-solving courts since, scholars and commentators (Collins 2017; Ray 2014) observed that the total number as of June 2014 is above 4,200, including about 3,000 drug courts. Separately, the Bureau of Justice Statistics reports that the number of drug courts alone to be over 3,100 as of May 2018, thus making the total number of problem-solving courts in the United States to be more than 4,300. Because drug courts (which embody charge-based diversion programs) are the most commonly known specialized courts, in the next section I focus more on their history, structures, and operations.

9.3 Drug Courts

The first drug court in the United States was created in Miami, Florida in 1989 (Hora, Schma, and Rosenthal 1999; Terry 1999). In 1994 when President Clinton signed a crime bill that for the first time included grants for drug courts (Armstrong 2008), the number of drug courts was forty-one. As indicated above, there are now more than 3,100 drug courts in the United States (Bureau of Justice Statistics 2016). As has been widely reported, the Miami Drug Court was created by local judges looking for ways to help drug offenders while searching for alternative strategies to address their enormous caseloads, case backlogs, and prison overcrowding, all engendered by the 1980s so-called "War on Drugs" (Goldkamp 2003; Nolan 2001). The then-presiding judge Gerald Wethering of Miami's Eleventh Judicial Circuit Court and another judge, Herbert Klein, created a court strategy that emphasized treatment as a major part of helping drug offenders (Goldkamp 2003). However, others (including colleagues), believing that the judiciary's role as a neutral arbiter might be compromised, were skeptical of the new court-based treatment strategy. They felt that judges acting as social workers might undermine the professional detachment expected of them to fairly dispense with their caseloads. This skepticism was somewhat diminished because only offenders with less serious crimes were eligible. Skeptics were also reassured that offenders who failed in the program could still be held accountable and sentenced for their original crimes.

Among the key supporters of this first drug court was Janet Reno, who was the State Attorney for Miami-Dade County then and later became the U.S. Attorney General under President Clinton (Nolan 2001; Olson, Lurigio, and Albertson, 2001). Attorney General Reno was a major champion of these courts during the Clinton administration and provided seed money for their establishment nationwide (Dorf and Fagan 2003). She was also influential in forming the U.S. Drug Courts Program Office, now a part of the U.S. Department of Justice (Goldkamp 1999).

As mentioned in the previous section, drug courts were established for a number of reasons (Shomade 2007, 2010). First, the number of drug arrests in the United States skyrocketed during the 1980s, which led to a huge jail backlog of people awaiting trial. Second, crack cocaine emerged as a popular drug in the 1980s. Third, the re-arrest rate for previously convicted drug offenders became alarmingly higher during the same decade (Harrison and Scarpitti 2002).

While scholars consider these three reasons as the main rationales for the rise of drug courts' popularity in the early days (Hora 2002; Nolan 2001; Shomade 2010), there might have been other reasons too. In fact, James Nolan (2001) notes that the idea of a drug court as an alternative way to deal with the drug scourge did not truly emerge in Miami. Programs such as Treatment Alternatives to Street Crimes (TASC), established in the 1970s, were implementing programs that attempted to combine drug treatment and criminal justice case processing. However, the federal government funding of TASC programs was eliminated in the 1980s (Harrison and Scarpitti 2002). Plus, TASC programs differed from drug court programs because, unlike drug courts, TASC separated the treatment and the adjudicative process (Nolan 2001). With TASC, the offender went through the treatment program and then returned to the court for a legal decision. But with drug courts, both treatment and the adjudicative process are integrated, and the offender goes back and forth between the two.

The structure of a typical U.S. drug court embodies its governing principles. Comprehending the structure of a typical drug court necessitates that one understands these underlying governing principles used in operating many drug courts. Referred to as the "Ten Key Components," these principles are performance standards created in 1997 by a group of drug court professionals, including judges, prosecutors, defense counsel, court administrators, and treatment providers (Shomade 2010). Some of the professionals who created these components were members of the National Drug Court Professional Association or representatives from the Drug Court Office of the U.S. Department of Justice. Former Judge Peggy Hora noted that these components drew on information about addiction, treatment, and recovery and have been adopted by many states, the Conference of Chief Justices, and the American Bar Association (Hora 2002, 1472).

The Ten Key Components, which were first issued by the Drug Court Office of the U.S. Department of Justice in January 1997 and reissued in October 2004, are:

1. drug courts integrate alcohol and other drug treatment services with justice system case processing;
2. using a non-adversarial approach, prosecution and defense counsel promote public safety while protecting participants' due process rights;
3. eligible participants are identified early and promptly placed in the drug court program;
4. drug courts provide access to a continuum of alcohol, drug, and other related treatment and rehabilitation services;
5. abstinence is monitored by frequent alcohol and other drug testing;
6. a coordinated strategy governs drug court responses to participants' compliance;
7. ongoing judicial interaction with each drug court participant is essential;
8. monitoring and evaluation measure the achievement of program goals and gauge effectiveness;

9. continuing interdisciplinary education promotes effective drug court planning, implementation, and operations;
10. forging partnerships among drug courts, public agencies, and community-based organizations generates local support and enhances drug court program effectiveness.

Many of today's drug courts are structured on the basis of these Ten Key Components (Shomade 2010).

Although frequently referred to as a drug court, a typical drug court is in fact a "drug court team." The drug court team works together in a coordinated case-management approach and subjects offenders to graduated sanctions when offenders violate program rules (Olson, Lurigio, and Albertson 2001; Turner et al. 2002). Each member, while collaborating with other team members, represents an organization or clients with different interests. The judge represents the criminal bench and court administrators, the prosecutor the county or applicable prosecutor's office, and the defense counsel the defendant's interests. Meanwhile, the probation officers represent the probation department. Drug treatment centers have their own representatives also participating as members of the team. In some jurisdictions, drug courts work closely with a network of social services organizations operating outside the criminal justice system such as drug testing centers, employment offices, housing agencies, and educational agencies, with all these organizations sponsoring their own representatives when needed to appear in drug courts or in pre-trial hearings (Shomade 2010).

Many drug court programs include treatment referrals right after arrest for drug use; judicial supervision of rewards for treatment progress and sanctions for treatment lapses; regular status hearings of offender progress and compliance with program requirements; mandatory drug testing; and dismissal of charges or sentence reduction post successful program completion (Olson, Lurigio, and Albertson 2001; Terry 1999). The court operates with the judge and the team holding a "staffing session" before the court hearing with the offenders (Hora, Schma, and Rosenthal 1999). The decisions that judges render at these hearings are mostly determined at staffing by consensus. The team's close collaboration makes drug courts distinct from typical criminal courts, but also raises concerns about potential due process violations and the drug court becoming more like an assembly line. I note here that in the initial years of drug courts' creation, prosecutors were the primary gatekeepers to these courts as they determined the eligibility criteria of who was or not accepted into these courts. However, and as further discussed below, that role has evolved to become a de facto team's decision with prosecutors acting as active collaborators in making decisions about eligibility criteria (Koozmin 2017).

Unlike in conventional U.S. criminal courts whereby case disposition is conducted by the traditional adversarial legal system, in drug courts, the adversarial approach still exists, but it is neither predominant nor visible (Turner et al. 2002). In the conventional criminal court, prosecutors and defense counsel follow an objective set of rules before a neutral judge or jury with clear winners and losers. Conversely in drug courts, both sides work with the judge and the team to achieve the optimal recovery plan for offenders. While the face of the court is the judge, the decisions are mostly made by team consensus, with prosecutors dutifully cooperating with other team members as equal partners, and neither being over-aggressive nor submissive in the team's decisions.

The drug court's non-adversarial approach is very evident at staffings and in courtroom proceedings. During staffings, the judge seems to be an equal partner in this meeting whereby decisions regarding offender punishment are mostly and frequently decided. The judge mostly serves as a facilitator at these meetings relying extensively on the team members' recommendations (Shomade 2010). In courtroom proceedings, the judge freely interacts verbally with offenders, equally encouraging them when they reach success benchmarks and chastising them when they fail drug tests or violate program rules (Hora, Schma, and Rosenthal 1999; Nolan 2001). As many scholars who have written about drug court operations indicate, the courtroom scene is indeed different from the typical criminal courtroom scene (Nolan 2001). Because veterans courts exemplify offender-based programs in the United States, I next briefly discuss their characteristics.

9.4 Veterans Courts

Veterans courts in the United States were created as part of the larger criminal justice system's efforts in finding solutions for veterans' struggles with various problems such as mental illness, drug addiction, post-traumatic stress disorder (PTSD), or other psychological issues (Holbrook and Anderson 2011; Lucas and Hanrahan 2016; Perlin 2013). Rather than rely on the conventional alternatives of conviction and incarceration, veterans courts use a range of tools to address the specific needs of the individual veteran by treating his underlying problems that resulted in criminal activities. These courts seek to prevent the individual veteran from being incarcerated and also from committing future crime.

Although the veterans court movement credits the Buffalo Veterans Treatment Court started in 2008 by Judge George Russell as its inspiration, the first veterans court started in Anchorage, Alaska in 2004 (Holbrook and Anderson 2011; Perlin 2013). Alaska District Court Judges Sigurd Murphy and Jack Smith became alarmed by the increasing number of veterans appearing in their courtrooms who had behavioral, medical, and other social-economic challenges connected with their military service (Holbrook and Anderson 2011). They then decided to utilize alternative sentencing arrangements for these veterans by combining judicial monitoring with rehabilitative treatment services supplied by community service providers. In 2008, Judge Russell, who had previously served as a city court judge and encountered increasing numbers of military veterans as defendants, decided to create the Buffalo Veterans Treatment Court (Holbrook and Anderson 2011).

Judge Russell noticed that veterans appearing in both the Buffalo Drug Treatment Court and Buffalo Mental Health Court responded favorably to other veterans. He thus designed the Buffalo Veterans Treatment Court to pair veteran offenders with veteran mentors while also linking the offenders with service providers who specialize in treating veterans' unique problems and challenges. As Judge Russell himself wrote, "The mission driving the [court] is to successfully rehabilitate veterans by diverting them from the traditional criminal justice system and providing them with the tools they need to lead a productive and law-abiding lifestyle" (Russell 2009, 364). Judge Russell noted that the court seeks to achieve this goal by providing veterans struggling with substance abuse, alcoholism, mental health, and other related issues not only with treatment, but with academic and job training tailored for each individual veteran.

When the Buffalo court's success in addressing veteran defendants' unique needs became known, other jurisdictions quickly created similar courts (Holbrook and Anderson 2011). According to the Bureau of Justice Statistics (2016), as of 2012 there were 133 veterans courts throughout the United States. As specialized criminal courts, veterans courts are similar to drug courts. Many veterans courts similarly focus on the treatment-rehabilitate criminal justice model. They likewise rely on therapeutic jurisprudence as the theoretical justification for their creation or existence (Perlin 2013). Veterans courts also adopted the ten key drug court components mentioned above and modified them to create their own ten key components (similar to those of drug courts) which serve as their guideposts.

As Holbrook and Addison report, veterans courts consist of both pre-conviction diversion programs, with charges dismissed upon successful completion or treatment, and post-conviction programs which focus on veteran defendants who have already pled guilty but need treatment plans to help them avoid future misconduct. Many veterans courts accept only non-violent misdemeanor cases while a few take low-level felony cases. Some veterans courts specialize in veterans with brain trauma or PTSD while others concentrate on those with substance abuse or mental illness. Similar to results of effectiveness studies of drug courts, assessment results of veterans courts' effectiveness are either incomplete or inconclusive. While there are many reports of individual veterans court achieving similar rehabilitation and recidivism rates as other specialized treatment courts', there are very few comprehensive studies that capture their overall efficacy (Holbrook and Addison 2011).

As for what happens in a veterans court, the court's organizational structure is similar to a drug court's. The court's participants operate as a team or workgroup with representatives from the U.S. Veteran Affairs Office, various social service agencies, probation officers, prosecutors, defense counsel, and the judge chairing the pre-trial meeting as well as presiding over the courtroom proceeding. During this meeting featuring all the team members, cases are discussed with each defendant's progress assessed and decisions made about next steps. Because of the collaborative spirit of the pre-trial meeting, the team is usually in agreement about next steps for each defendant, including those found violating program rules. A consistently errant veteran defendant could either be recharged, dropped from the program, or resentenced, depending on pre-program status. Thus, the team (including the prosecutor and judge) decides each veteran's case prior to the formal courtroom hearing (Lucas and Hanrahan 2016).

In court, each veteran is called before the judge and the judge speaks directly to the defendant while the defense lawyer acts in a supporting role only when necessary. The judge usually engages the defendant in a friendly and personal manner, commenting on the defendant's health, progress, or challenges going through the program (Lucas and Hanrahan 2016). During this interaction, the judge usually dispenses the team's decision on next steps including sanctions or punishment that the team endorses during pre-trial meetings. Of course, that means occasionally the veteran defendant is sentenced and taken directly to jail from the courtroom.

There are other U.S. specialized criminal courts that might not be as numerous as drug courts but are equally prominent. For example, mental health courts (MHCs) are specialized criminal courts which "utilize a designated judicial, legal, and clinical treatment team in lieu of traditional case processing and sentencing in order to divert individuals from the criminal justice system into community-based treatment" (Castellano 2017, 398). The movement behind their creation resulted equally from judges' frustration with the increasing number of mentally ill offenders and the failure of the conventional system to connect these offenders with treatment or social services that address the underlying causes of their criminal behavior (Castellano 2017; Kubiak et al. 2013). Also relying on therapeutic jurisprudence as its guiding principle, the standard MHC focuses on rehabilitating the offender without sacrificing the offender's rights and the interests of the community and justice systems (Kubiak et al. 2013). The typical MHC is structured as a drug court with court participants operating as a team and ensuring that the twin goals of the offender's treatment and public safety are achieved. There are more than three hundred MHCs operating in some form or other today. While space does not permit more detailed discussions of other specialized criminal courts, the list includes domestic violence courts, driving while intoxicated (DWI) courts, prostitution courts, homeless courts, teen courts, gambling courts, and re-entry courts. Next is an explanation of prosecutors' roles in these specialized courts.

9.5 Prosecutors' Participation in Accountability Courts and Diversion Programs

The role of a prosecutor in a U.S. specialized criminal court, regardless of the type or jurisdiction, tends to be collaborative and rarely adversarial as it might sometimes be in a conventional criminal court. Given that prosecutors joined the court movement at the very beginning and have remained strong advocates, this should not be surprising. Specifically, the second component of the Ten Key Components states that in a drug court, "using a non-adversarial approach, prosecution and defense counsel promote public safety while protecting participants' due process rights." As discussed above, Janet Reno, who later became the U.S. Attorney General under President Clinton, was the State's Attorney when the Miami drug court was established in 1989. She participated in and actively supported its formation. Her enthusiasm for drug courts continued under the Clinton Administration as the nation's chief law enforcement official. She funded the creation of many drug courts and was influential in establishing the U.S. Drug Courts Program Office. Likewise, former General Barry McCaffery, who served as the director of the Office of National Drug Control Policy and in a cabinet-level position from 1996 to 2001, gave his full blessings. He remains a champion and advocate of these courts today.

Because prosecutors represent the position of the state, "most prosecutors' attitudes toward problem solving courts are shaped by their bosses' attitudes" (Wolf 2008, 81). Hence, support of these national prosecution leaders in the early days of the specialty court movement filtered and remained through the ranks of prosecutors on various levels. As former U.S. Attorney James Kennedy—who served in several prosecutorial lower level jobs and prosecuted many high-profile narcotics and violent crime cases—wrote in 2015, "Specialty courts provide us with another tool that we as prosecutors can use to help us do our jobs more intelligently" (Kennedy 2015, 55). Kennedy explained that these courts provide prosecutors with the option of avoiding charging offenders when they have "serious reservations about whether the circumstances of the offender or the offense warrant prosecution and punishment to the fullest extent of the law" (Kennedy 2015, 55). He added that these courts provide opportunities for prosecutors to reconsider charging decisions in cases they initially decide to charge but subsequently obtain additional information about the offender or offense that creates sufficient doubt for reconsideration. He concluded, "I do not view specialty courts as necessarily undermining our adversarial system. Rather, they give us another option to deal with the vast array of situations with which we are presented. Neither a panacea nor a poison, specialty courts simply present another possibility" (Kennedy 2015, 55).

Ordinarily, we would assume that prosecutors serve as the primary gatekeepers to specialty courts and determine defendants' eligibility criteria. That was indeed the case when these courts were first being established, but that role has evolved to become a de facto team's decision with prosecutors participating as active collaborators in these decisions (Koozmin 2017). That the role has shifted should not be surprising as advocacy groups such as the National Drug Court Institute (or "NDCI," a non-profit, government-funded, advocacy organization) has issued guidelines for prosecutors working in problem-solving courts. NDCI, which billed itself as the "definitive authority on the latest research, best practices, and cutting-edge innovations to treat offenders facing substance use and mental health disorders" (NDCI 2019), has a *Core Competencies Guide* for prosecutors working in a drug court that states the following (Koozmin 2017):

1. Participates fully as a drug court team member, committing him or herself to the program mission and goals and works as a full partner to ensure their success.

2. The prosecutor, while in drug court, participates as a team member, operating in a non-adversarial manner, promoting a sense of a unified team member.
3. As part of the drug court team, in appropriate non-court settings (i.e. staffing), the prosecutor advocates for effective incentives and sanctions for program compliance or lack thereof.
4. Ensures community safety concerns by maintaining eligibility standards while participating in a non-adversarial environment which focuses on the benefits of therapeutic program outcomes.
5. Monitors offender progress to define parameters of behavior that allow continued program participation and suggests effective incentives and sanctions for program compliance.
6. Is knowledgeable about addiction, alcoholism and pharmacology generally and applies that knowledge to respond to compliance in a therapeutically appropriate manner.
7. Is knowledgeable of gender, age and cultural issues that may impact the offender's success.
8. Contributes to the team's efforts in community education and local resource acquisition.

That NDCI has influence over the operations of specialty courts is demonstrated by many states' judicial or prosecutors' websites having direct links to the *Core Competencies Guide*. How closely prosecutors adhere to these competencies in actual practice is debatable, but the guidelines reinforce the notion that prosecutors do not solely control events (including gatekeeping decision-making) in the specialty courtroom.

Besides prosecutors offering support for the specialized court movement, scholars have also written about prosecutors' collaborative participation in courtroom hearings. In a recent study of a community court and how it negotiates its dual mission of punishment and treatment in order to maximize its organizational legitimacy, Christine Zozula (2018) found the prosecutor to be an active and willing actor in the court's deliberations. In one court session featuring an anti-underage drinking docket whereby the court wanted to demonstrate the negative consequences of underage drinking to its mostly student defendants (yet uncharged), the judge firmly declared that the city takes underage drinking seriously. Next, the prosecutor methodically explained the consequences the students would face if charges were to be filed: being fined, losing their driving licenses, possibly being jailed for five years because of fake IDs, and potentially losing their federal financial aid or student loans. Although the prosecutor dispensed with these charges, s/he willingly collaborated to threaten the students with their actions' negative consequences. Zozula argues that by having such a docket devoted to the ills of underage drinking, the court gained legitimacy on its dual mission of punishment and treatment, a task seemingly made possible by the prosecutor's full support, collaboration, and participation. Again, given the discussion of the core competencies regarding prosecutors' roles above and the Ten Key Components relied upon by court practitioners operating in specialty courts, this prosecutor's role should be expected. This prosecutor is actively contributing to community education and assisting in making the community a safer place.

In James Nolan's (2001) ground-breaking and oft-cited book on the drug court movement, *Reinventing Justice: The American Drug Court Movement*, he details prosecutors' participation in various drug courts and summarizes his observations on the prosecutor's role in these settings. First, and quoting other drug court scholars, Nolan argues that prosecutors have to abandon their mostly adversarial courtroom role and accept offenders' treatment in specialized courts as part of their responsibility to provide justice. Second, he attests, given the prominence of treatment and judicial monitoring in drug courts, prosecutors must be willing to "abdicate" this traditional responsibility and defer more to the judge and treatment providers. Third, Nolan concedes, some prosecutors seemed to have difficulty accepting their different responsibilities in these contexts and end up creating problems for these courts' operations. This resistance is very similar to prosecutors' behavior, as some scholars have found (Levine 2005), when resisting the reorientation required of them to lead non-traditional efforts for curbing social problems.

Nolan cited several examples of prosecutors trying to solely dictate court participants or sanctions without consultation with other team members, fighting with the judge on court operations, and going as far as getting a judge transferred away from the drug court. Notably, very few scholars apart from Nolan have written about this initial resistance by prosecutors working in drug courts. Rather, one can easily surmise from the extant literature that these are but growing pains behind the drug court movement. Overall, as Nolan rightly notes, many prosecutors end up being supportive of these courts even if they have initial reservations. As a result of this support, he claims, prosecutors end up trying to convince other law enforcement authorities, especially police officers, to accept specialized criminal courts' roles in dispensing justice.

Separately, Jennifer Kelly Wilson et al. (2011), studying prosecutor pre-trial attitudes towards veterans with PTSD and their plea bargaining behavior, found that prosecutors were more lenient towards veterans with PTSD. These scholars found that prosecutors offered more diversion programs to veterans with PTSD as compared to those offered to veterans without PTSD or non-veterans with PTSD. The authors concluded that their study seemed to indicate that prosecutors perceived veterans as less blameworthy for their low-level offenses, empathized more with veteran defendants, and found them to be less criminally culpable than non-veterans. They speculated that these prosecutors, besides their empathy toward veteran defendants with PTSD, might have also surmised that juries are unlikely to punish veterans with or without PTSD as severely, and thus decided to resolve many of the cases at the pre-trial stages.

It has long been established that several factors influence the prosecutor's decision to charge and plea.[1] To mention a few: caseloads, police action or inaction, relationship with court stakeholders (especially the judge and defense counsel), institutional constraints, and public pressure. Because judges in many specialized courts were actively involved in their creation, one would expect that the prosecutor's individual charging or plea decision (if necessary or when the team is unable to coalesce around a consensus decision) would or should be heavily influenced by the relationship with the judge. However, that does not appear to be the case. While judges do have some influence, prosecutors tried to retain their own independent decision-making judgment even while operating as equal partners on events happening in specialized courts (Nolan 2001). Inasmuch as judges are strong advocates of these courts, they treat prosecutors and other court stakeholders as equal allies in these courts' operations.

As earlier mentioned, Janet Reno, as a state prosecutor, was active in the creation of the Miami court. In many jurisdictions, prosecutors not only had seats at the table, they actively contributed to these courts' development, operations, and growth. Depending on the context, once it gives its blessings to the court's creation or operation, the prosecutor's office sometimes does not actively participate in the court's proceedings. In certain specialized courtrooms, especially those equipped with a full-time specialty court manager or dominated by probation officers, the prosecutor is occasionally absent even if it is a pre-trial diversion program (Shomade 2007). In my research of drug courts over the years, I found that the prosecutor's occasional absences are generally reflective of the prosecutor's office concluding that the drug court is in "good hands" and its presence might not be a great use of its time resources. Of course, I note here that these absences do not adhere to the *Core Competencies Guide* discussed above. I also note that when I observed these absences, the prosecutor always seemed to have "official and unavoidable reasons" for doing so.

Separately but relatedly, some concerns have been raised about the defendant's due process rights and whether they are adequately protected in these courts (see, e.g., Lane 2002). As Eric Lane (2002) noted, two pertinent questions arise: (1) How does the collaborative approach impact the defendant's right to effective counsel? and (2) Does the judge's active role affect judicial impartiality or supposed neutrality? While these questions center on defense counsel's and judges' roles, the prosecutor, as an active collaborator in the specialized court setting, is part of the "team" that decides applicable punishment and sanctions when the defendant goes errant. Moreover, the American Bar Association (ABA)—the largest organization representing U.S. lawyers—requires, as part of its ethical guidelines, that prosecutors adequately protect defendants' rights. Specifically, Part I of its comments to Model Rule 3.8 on the *Special Responsibilities of a Prosecutor* states, "A prosecutor has the responsibility of a minister of justice and not simply that of an advocate. This responsibility carries with it specific obligations to see that the defendant is accorded procedural justice, that guilt is decided upon the basis of sufficient evidence, and that special precautions are taken to prevent and to rectify the conviction of innocent persons." Thus, prosecutors could be rightly accused of being willing participants in potential violation of due process rights.

But while these concerns are legitimate, there are adequate safeguards in place for prosecutors not to encroach on defendant's due process rights. For example, advocacy organizations representing defendants' interests such as the National Legal Aid and Defender Association ("NLADA") have issued ethical guidelines for lawyers practicing in problem-solving courts. Many of the provisions in the NLADA's *Ten Tenets of Fair and Effective Problem-Solving Courts* mandate that court practitioners adequately protect defendants' rights (Meekins 2007). While some scholars have criticized the provisions as inadequate in preventing potential defense attorneys' ethical violations, there is an acknowledgment that prosecutors seem better protected against such violations (Meekins 2007). One, defendant's due process rights in a pre-adjudicative specialized court are unlikely to be violated because the defendant has not pled guilty or waived those rights. Two, in the post-adjudicative specialized court, the prosecutor is also protected because the case has already been decided and the defendant has already pled guilty to the charges. Hence, in this situation, the prosecutor's traditional role as the state representative has been concluded prior to the defendant subjecting himself/herself to the jurisdiction of the specialty court. However, as part of the court's team, prosecutors could still be held responsible for the team's decisions that negatively affect the defendant's due process rights. Fortunately for these prosecutors, defense counsel tend to be among the most active team members by being very vocal and serving as the oppositional voice when occasion demands, which frequently are times when the defendant's due process rights are threatened (Nolan 2001; Shomade 2007; Wolf 2008).

9.6 Prosecutors in Non-U.S. Specialized Criminal Courts

James Nolan, a leading authority on the global problem-solving court movement, documents that the first specialized criminal court created outside the United States was a drug court in Toronto established in 1998. Judge Paul Bentley, who presided, understood that the U.S. model had to be initially adapted, but was adamant about trying to tailor it for the Canadian context (Nolan 2009, 2012). Roughly a year later, England formally established two drug courts after some British officials visited the Miami Drug Court and were mesmerized by Judge Stanley Goldstein. According to Nolan (2009), about the same time, both England and Scotland launched Drug Treatment and Testing Orders which were probation-based court orders with many features resembling the U.S. drug court model. For Australia, which created its first drug court in Sydney around the same period, their efforts were based on legislative directives. Nolan (2012) reports that there are now drug courts fully operating in Ireland, Scotland, Bermuda, and Norway. Apart from drug courts, there are other non-U.S. specialized courts. For example, there is the Liverpool Community Justice Centre in England, which is modeled after the U.S.-based Red Hook Community Justice Center in Brooklyn, New York. The Toronto mental health court in Canada was started in 1998, soon followed by other mental health courts in other Canadian provinces. Calgary, Alberta is home to one of Canada's growing number of domestic violence courts, which was launched in 2000 and modelled after the British and U.S. courts.

Comparing U.S. courts with courts in these five nations—England, Ireland, Scotland, Australia, and Canada—Nolan asserts that unlike U.S. specialized courts "characterized by enthusiasm, boldness, and pragmatism," courts in these nations can be qualified as "one of moderation, deliberation, and restraint" (2012, 156). In the U.S. context, "so enthusiastic are problem-solving court practitioners that they sometimes come across as salespersons or religious zealots in their promotion of these courts" (Nolan 2012, 156). Moreover, U.S. specialized court judges tend to be "bold" both inside and outside the courtroom. In the U.S. courtroom, judges speak directly with defendants, asking them personal questions and offering encouraging words, but chastising them when necessary. Outside the courtroom, these judges meet with community leaders and members, lobby Congress and other government officials for support, give frequent interviews to the media, solicit help from social services working with defendants, and interact with anyone or any organization that will enable them to promote the "good work of the court."

Overall, prosecutors' roles in many of these non-U.S. specialized courts are not that significantly different from those of their U.S. counterparts. As in the United States, the structure of a non-U.S. specialized court as a haven of team effort features a prosecutor collaborating with other court practitioners to achieve the court's goals. For example, Canadian drug and other problem-solving courts similarly utilize the Ten Key Components provided by the National Association of Drug Court Professionals and discussed above (Holst 2010; Patenaude 2013). Hence, the prosecutor is a member of the drug court team and participates in the pre-court or staffing session while collaborating with other team members in reaching decisions on each defendant's next steps. In Australian problem-solving courts, including drug courts, staffing sessions are held with the prosecutors similarly collaborating with other court practitioners to restore conflicts and issues prior to formal court sessions (Jeffries 2005; Moore 2012).

However, one scholar who recently observed drug court proceedings in two Canadian drug courts and one Australian one (which utilizes a post-adjudicative process) surmises that the role of the prosecutor differs in both nations (Wilson 2014). In the Canadian courts, which largely use the pre-adjudicative model, the prosecutors or the Crown (Canadian prosecutors are alternatively referred to as the Crown) "played a significant role in drug court proceedings. In fact, in one Court, it was the Crown who directed the proceedings and assumed the role of a pseudo judge—dictating sanctions and disciplining the participants. The Crown in the Canadian Courts also took on a central role in the pre-court team meetings that were observed, whereas in the Australian Drug Court, the judge led both the drug court proceedings and the pre-court team meetings" (Wilson 2014, 1196). Clearly, this is just one study and seems atypical given the extant literature, but it might be the case that the prosecutor in this Canadian court had demonstrated to team members her/his capabilities of leading the sessions.

Meanwhile, in the United Kingdom, prosecutors do not appear to be active in the problem-solving courts (Nolan 2009). Again, this is due in part to the structure of the U.K. criminal justice system. For example, in British specialized courts, British lay magistrates, serving in three-judge panels on a rotating basis, manage the drug courts and many other minor criminal charges (Nolan 2009). Besides having less power than their U.S. colleagues (who single-handedly manage their own courts), British magistrates also have to defer more to probation officers, who are more prominent in directing the activities of the drug courts. Again, this is not surprising because of the structure of these specialty courts under the British criminal justice system.

9.7 The Role of the Prosecutor in the Future of Accountability Courts and Diversion Programs

As polarized as the United States is politically, both sides do agree on criminal justice reform that adds more specialized courts. Progressive politicians are readily seen as being supportive of criminal justice reform. But conservative ones are equally supportive of reform. One public demonstration of such support came from Ken Cuccinelli, the former Virginia Attorney General (deemed to be one of the most conservative attorneys general), when he addressed the Conservative Political Action Conference on March 14, 2013. He received loud ovation for claiming that Obamacare is unconstitutional, the national debt is too high, and the Environmental Protection Agency is a job killer (Reddy and Levin 2014). Reddy and Levin write that Cuccinelli sustained this applause when he said, "How many times have I seen my fellow tough-on-crime conservatives be not merely willing, but excited, to lock up every convict and throw away the key? If we really believe that no one is beyond redemption, we need to stop throwing away that key! Conservatives should lead in changing the culture of corrections in America" (2014, 232). The authors note that Cuccinelli's support of prison reform should not be surprising because many prominent Republican or conservative lawyers—Edwin Meese (former U.S. Attorney General under President Reagan), Asa Hutchinson (former U.S. Attorney and Administrator of the Drug Enforcement Administration), Bill Bennett (former director of Office of National Drug Control Policy under Reagan) and several others—have articulated positions supporting criminal justice reform. Reddy and Levin contend, "The idea that conservatives are ideologically committed to mass incarceration is—and always was—a caricature. American incarceration rates increased significantly in recent decades, and many on the right supported this increase, but conservative support for increased incarceration was linked to unique historical circumstances, not to any philosophical commitment" (2014, 233).

U.S. politicians of all stripes mention having the criminal justice system rely more on alternative programs to incarceration. Since specialized courts prominently represent one of those alternative ways, they are likely to increase. The figures already bear themselves out. Just six years ago, the number of specialized courts was about 3,000, now more than 4,300, and it might easily surpass 5,000 in a couple of years. As the movement spreads, different specialty courts are likely to find innovative or just different ways of practice or operation. For example, the Deputy Attorney General of D.C., Mina Malik, was brought in to lead an initiative for combating juvenile crime (Winston 2018). The initiative, Alternative to Court Experience (ACE) is a diversion program that enables the D.C. office (which shares jurisdiction for criminal matters with the U.S. Attorney's Office) to partner with the D.C. Department of Human for certain specialized courts; grants prosecutors more flexibility to encourage more individuals to participate in pre-trial diversion programs; and provides first-time drug offenders with less punishment, more reform opportunities, and the ability to obtain jobs and receive food stamps after completing designated rehabilitation programs. In Georgia, for example, the shifting of power to judges for designing the "Under the Influence" Court Divisions' establishment criteria and providing on-going support for such divisions is particularly interesting because it recognizes in part how judges have become more influential in the movement to expand specialized courts. Because many of these changes to Georgia law received huge bipartisan legislative support, one can surmise that Georgia prosecutors are definitely in support of these measures, which although aimed at reducing incarceration rates, will ultimately result in utilizing more specialized criminal courts.

9.8 Conclusion

Despite the political polarization in the United States and partisan bickering in Washington, D.C., the U.S. Congress came together in 2018 and passed what is officially known as "The Formerly Incarcerated Reenter Society Transformed Safely Transitioning Every Person Act," commonly referred to as "The First Step Act" (Lopez 2019). The federal law, which was signed into law by President Trump on December 21, 2018, lowers the total number of people in U.S. prisons even though it applies only to the federal judicial system. The First Step Act specifically aims to reduce the prison population by enabling thousands of prisoners to earn an earlier release from prison, and the law could further result in shrinking prison sentences in the future. With support by groups from both the right and the left on the U.S. political spectrum, and including the National District Attorneys Association (an organization representing thousands of U.S. criminal prosecutors), the First Step Act passed by overwhelming bipartisan support in both the U.S. House and the U.S. Senate. Among other provisions, the law gives federal judges more discretion in sentencing drug offenders and encourages prisoners to earn "good time" credits by participating in rehabilitative programs, which presumably includes diversion programs and accountability courts.

In its letter to President Trump prior to the First Step Act's passage into law, the National District Attorneys Association's President Jonathan Blodgett (2018) stressed, "Tasked with the constitutional duty of protecting the communities we serve from bad actors while seeking justice for victims of crime and protecting the innocent, our members are acutely aware of the need for reforms to our criminal justice system." He continued, "Absent meaningful sentencing reform, where the truly dangerous are locked up for an appropriate period of time and those with addiction or mental health issues have the chance for treatment and rehabilitation, rising recidivism rates will continue to persist." Blodgett concluded, "Our members continue to call for a new commission to explore issues across the criminal justice system to ensure law enforcement and prosecutors can protect the communities they serve and respond to emerging issues in the field." This letter represents the breadth and depth of U.S. prosecutors' support for a different approach to the U.S. criminal justice system already championed by many advocates of specialty courts. As discussed above, it seems likely that prosecutors will continue to support ongoing efforts to expand the usage of accountability courts and diversion programs in addressing some previously intractable causes of crime in the United States.

Note

1. For more, see Matt Barno and Mona Lynch in Chapter 2 and Brian D. Johnson and Raquel Hernandez in Chapter 4 of this volume.

References

American Bar Association. 2018. "Rule 3.8 Special Responsibilities of a Prosecutor – Comment."

Armstrong, Edward. G. 2008. "The Drug Court as Postmodern Justice." *Critical Criminology* 16(4): 271–284.

Blodgett, Jonathan. 2018. Letter to President Donald J. Trump, dated November 13, 2018. https://www.judiciary.senate.gov/imo/media/doc/2018-11-13%20-%20National%20District%20Attorneys%20Association%20Support%20Letter%20First%20Step%20Act.pdf.

Bureau of Justice Statistics, Office of Justice Programs in the U.S. Department of Justice. 2016. "Census of Problem-Solving Courts, 2012."

Castellano, Ursula. 2017. "The Politics of Benchcraft: The Role of Judges in Mental Health Courts." *Law & Social Inquiry* 42(2): 398–422.

Collins, Erin R. 2017. "Status Courts." *Georgetown Law Journal* 105(6): 1481–1528.

Dorf, Michael C., and Jeffrey A. Fagan. 2003. "Problem-Solving Courts: From Innovation to Institutionalization." *American Criminal Law Review* 40(4): 1501–1511.

Feinblatt, John, Greg Berman, and Derek Denckla. 2002. "Judicial Innovation at the Crossroads: The Future of Problem-Solving Courts." In *The Improvement of the Administration of Justice*. Edited by G. M. Griller and E. K. Stott, Jr. 7th ed. Chicago: American Bar Association.

Goldkamp, John S. 1999. "The Origin of the Treatment Drug Court in Miami." In *The Early Drug Courts: Case Studies in Judicial Innovation*. Edited by W. Clinton Terry, III. Thousand Oaks, CA: Sage Publications.

Goldkamp, John S. 2003. "The Impact of Drug Courts." *Criminology & Public Policy* 2(2): 197–206.

Harrison, Lana D., and Frank R. Scarpitti. 2002. "Introduction: Progress and Issues in Drug Treatment Courts," *Substance Use and Misuse* 37(12–13): 1441–1467.

Holbrook, Justin G., and Sara Anderson. 2011. "Veterans Courts: Early Outcomes and Key Indicators for Success." *Widener Law School Legal Studies Research Paper* No. 11–25. https://ssrn.com/abstract=1912655.

Holst, Kimberly Y.W. 2010. "A Good Score: Examining Twenty Years of Drug Courts in the United States and Abroad." *Valparaiso University Law Review* 45(1): 73–106.

Hora, Peggy Fulton, William G. Schma, and John T. Rosenthal. 1999. "Therapeutic Jurisprudence and the Drug Treatment Court Movement: Revolutionizing the Criminal Justice System's Response to Drug Abuse and Crime in America." *Notre Dame Law Review* 74(2): 439–538.

Hora, Peggy. F. 2002. "A Dozen Years of Drug Treatment Court: Uncovering Our Theoretical Foundation and the Construction of a Mainstream Paradigm." *Substance Use and Misuse* 37 (12–13): 1469–1488.

Jeffries, Samantha. 2005. "How Justice 'Gets Done': Politics, Managerialism, Consumerism, and Therapeutic Jurisprudence." *Current Issues in Criminal Justice* 17(2): 254–268.

Kennedy, James P., Jr. 2015. "Specialty Courts: Expanding Possibilities for Prosecutors." *United States Attorneys' Bulletin* 63: 52–59.

Koozmin, Anna. 2017 "The Role of Prosecutors in Drug Treatment Courts." *Justice Programs Office*, American University, Washington, D.C.

Kubiak, Sheryl, Liz Tillander, and Bradley Ray. 2013. "Assessing the Role of Legal Actors Across Eight Mental Health Courts." *Michigan State University Journal of Medicine and Law* 17(2): 301–326.

Lane, Eric. 2002. "Due Process and Problem-Solving Courts." *Fordham Urban Law Journal* 30(3): 955–1026.

Levine, Kay L. 2005. "The New Prosecution." *Wake Forest Law Review* 40(4): 1125–1214.

Lopez, German. 2019. "The First Step Act, Explained." *Vox*, February 5, 2019. https://www.vox.com/future-perfect/2018/12/18/18140973/state-of-the-union-trump-first-step-act-criminal-justice-reform.

Lucas, Paul A., and Kathleen J. Hanrahan. 2016. "No Soldier Left Behind: The Veterans Court Solution." *International Journal of Law and Psychiatry* 45(1): 52–59.

McLeod, Allegra M. 2012. "Decarceration Courts: Possibilities and Perils of a Shifting Criminal Law." *Georgetown Law Journal* 100(5): 1587–1674.

Meekins, Tamar M. 2007. "Risky Business: Criminal Specialty Courts and the Ethical Obligations of the Zealous Criminal Defender." *Berkeley Journal of Criminal Law* 12: 75–126.

Moore, Liz. 2012. "Measures of Success: Capturing the Impact of Drug Courts." Thesis. https://ssrn.com/abstract=2236482.

National Drug Court Institute Website (NDCI). 2019. https://www.ndci.org/about-ndci/.

Nolan, James L., Jr. 2001. *Reinventing Justice: The American Drug Court Movement*. Princeton: Princeton University Press.

Nolan, James L., Jr. 2009. *Legal Accents, Legal Borrowing: The International Problem-Solving Court Movement*. Princeton: Princeton University Press.

Nolan, James L., Jr. 2012. "Problem-Solving Courts: An International Comparison." In *The Oxford Handbook of Sentencing and Corrections*. Edited by Joan Petersilia and Kevin R. Reitz, 150–172. Oxford: Oxford University Press.

Office of Justice Programs in the U.S. Department of Justice. 2016. "Drug Courts." https://www.ncjrs.gov/pdffiles1/nij/238527.pdf.

Olson, David, Arthur Lurigio, and Stephanie Albertson. 2001. "Implementing the Key Components of Specialized Drug Treatment Courts: Practice and Policy Considerations." *Law & Policy* 23(2): 171–196.

Patenaude, Allan L. 2013. "Intermediate Sanctions and Community-Based Corrections." In *Adult Corrections in Canada: A Comprehensive Overview*. Edited by John Winterdyk and Michael Weinrath, 225–248. North York, Canada: de Sitter Publications.

Perlin, Michael L. 2013. "John Brown Went off to War: Considering Veterans Courts as Problem-Solving Courts." *Nova Law Review* 37(3): 445–478.

Ray, Bradley. 2014. "Problem-Solving Courts." In *The Encyclopedia of Criminology and Criminal Justice*. Edited by Jay S. Albanese, 1–5. Hoboken: Wiley-Blackwell.

Reddy, Vikrant P., and Marc A. Levin. 2014. "Right on Crime: A Return to First Principles for American Conservatives." *Texas Review of Law & Politics* 18(2): 231–254.

Russell, Robert T. 2009. "Veterans Treatment Court: A Proactive Approach." *New England Journal on Criminal & Civil Confinement* 35(2): 357–372.

Shomade, Salmon A. 2007. "Case Study of the Structures of Criminal and Drug Courts." PhD diss., University of Arizona.

Shomade, Salmon A. 2010. "Case Disposition in the Drug Court: Who Is the Most Central Actor?" *Justice System Journal* 31(1): 74–96.

Terry III, W. Clinton. 1999. "Judicial Change and Dedicated Treatment Courts: Case Studies in Innovation." In *The Early Drug Courts: Case Studies in Judicial Innovation*. Edited by W. Clinton Terry, III, 1–18. Thousand Oaks, CA: Sage Publications.

Turner, Susan, Douglas Longshore, Suzanne Wenzel, Elizabeth Deschenes, Peter Greenwood, Terry Fain, Adele Harrell, et al. 2002. "A Decade of Drug Treatment Court Research." *Substance Use & Misuse* 37(12–13): 1489–1527.

Unah, Isaac and Ryan Williams. 2017. "What Is So Special about Specialized Courts in the United States?" In *Routledge Handbook of Judicial Behavior*. Edited by Robert M. Howard and Kirk A. Randazzo, 541–583. New York: Routledge.

Wilson, Amanda. 2014. "Putting Therapeutic Jurisprudence on Edge: A Gendered Engagement." *UBC Law Review* 47(3): 1185–1217.

Wilson, Jennifer Kelly, Stanley L. Brodsky, Tess Neal, and Robert J. Cramer. 2011. "Prosecutor Pretrial Attitudes and Plea-bargaining Behavior toward Veterans with Posttraumatic Stress Disorder." *Psychological Services* 8(4): 319–331.

Winston, Erika. 2018. "Karl A. Racine & Mina Malik: Reforming D.C.'s Juvenile Justice System." *Washington Lawyer*, April/May: 12–13.

Wolf, Robert V. 2008. "Breaking with Tradition: Introducing Problem Solving in Conventional Courts." *International Review of Law, Computers & Technology* 22(1–2): 77–93.

Zozula, Christine. 2018. "Courting the Community: Organizational Flexibility and Community Courts." *Criminology & Criminal Justice* 18(2): 226–244.

PART II

WORKING ENVIRONMENTS AND RELATIONSHIPS

CHAPTER 10

HIRING AND LEARNING STRATEGIES IN PROSECUTION SERVICES

RASMUS H. WANDALL

10.1 Introduction

Prosecutorial decision-making requires continuously updated skills in law, evidence, and procedure and deep knowledge in specialized areas of law. Prosecutors need to reflect the society in which they practice and to have skills in collaboration and communication across institutional boundaries. Furthermore, bolstering prosecutorial decision-making from political and economic pressures requires a professional culture around law and rational criminal justice policy. In recent decades the prosecutor has come to be the most important decision-maker in criminal justice systems, which amplifies the significance of these qualifications (Pizzi 2012; Weigend 2012). For all of these reasons, there is a clear expectation in nations across the globe that persons appointed as public prosecutors should be appropriately qualified, and that the selection process be objective and impartial.[1]

The chapter provides an overview of the strategies of hiring and learning by prosecution services that exist in a variety of countries. Strategies to hire and to train prosecutors reflect the particular legal and political culture of each jurisdiction. While there are convergences in the methods and strategies applied across borders, strategies continue to vary profoundly. Consequently, there is an important comparative dimension to understanding hiring and training strategies, informed by a number of distinctions (Damaska 1986; Glenn 2010; Jehle and Wade 2006; Luna and Wade 2012; Nelken 2013; Tonry 2012; Wandall 2014; Weigend 2012). The first distinction is between *inquisitorial and adversarial* legal traditions, through which prosecution services are more or less aligned with the judiciary and the roles that follow. The second issue concerns the relative weight of *the legality principle* and *the principle of expediency* in criminal procedure, which determines or reflects how much emphasis we place on legal unity as an organizing principle in the prosecution service. Third, jurisdictions and prosecution services vary in the degree to which they allow space for *political and public accountability* in the work of the prosecution service with significant consequences for the hiring practices of prosecutors. Fourth, distinctions can be made between *different structural locations of prosecution services* and thus the structures of accountability that inform the prosecution service. Fifth, a distinction can be made between *national organization* and *local organization* of prosecution services.

The following sections give a comparative overview of strategies of hiring chief prosecutors and frontline prosecutors, and strategies and methods of learning applied to entry-level prosecutors. Differences in legal and political cultures make for very different organizations of prosecution services and thus very different conditions under which hiring and learning strategies develop. The comparison also shows that some jurisdictions have gone much further than others in ensuring high quality prosecution (both through hiring and through learning), and that some of the most important methods of learning continue to be left in the hands of local offices with little integration at the national or regional level.[2]

10.2 Hiring Chief Prosecutors

The chief prosecutor leads the prosecution service towards its ideals of legality and efficiency and is the face of the organization to the outside world. Historically, an essential challenge for the chief prosecutor has been to balance the organizational leadership with the public and political legitimacy necessary to run the organization—without becoming a tool of political control. Particularly in the hiring process, these mixed requirements are put to the test.

Across jurisdictions, the chief prosecutor is required to have an adequate legal education and (if relevant) to have passed a Bar exam. It is also normal to require citizenship.[3] Some jurisdictions also require a minimum number of years practicing law before one can qualify as chief prosecutor. Normally in jurisdictions with civil law traditions and in newer democracies, candidates cannot be politically affiliated or active.[4] Other than these foundational components, minimum requirements vary between jurisdictions as do the processes of selecting and hiring chief prosecutors.

When it comes to how chief prosecutors are hired, there are fundamentally two different strategies we can observe in nations around the world: direct public elections or appointments.

10.2.1 Direct Public Elections

In the vast majority of jurisdictions in the United States, the chief prosecutor is elected (this position is commonly called "the district attorney"). The elections are political and create a direct relationship of accountability between the district attorney and the local constituency (Miller and Caplinger 2012; Tonry 2012; Wright 2012). The fact that district attorneys are routinely re-elected without contest does not affect this description as a formal matter (Wright 2009). In a legal landscape where prosecution is organized locally, the population is characterized by significant diversity, and many people express a comparatively low level of confidence in state and legal institutions, it is not surprising that the office of the local chief prosecutor relies on the local public for its legitimacy (Wright 2014).

10.2.2 Appointments

In countries where the prosecution is part of the executive bureaucracy, the chief prosecutor holds a professional appointment; he or she is a civil servant and political accountability comes from the process of the appointment and re-appointment. There is significant variation among nations as to the ways in which the executive power to appoint is curtailed. In the United States, for example, the President appoints U.S. Attorneys for the ninety-four federal judicial districts for a fixed term of four years. The appointments require the Senate's approval, but all attorneys serve at the pleasure of the President (Gilliéron 2014, 65). In continental Europe, the appointments are ideally non-political. This is the case in Sweden, for instance, where the chief prosecutor is appointed by the Minister of Justice in an open hiring process (Asp 2012); the same is the case in the Netherlands (Tak 2012). In some German states, the State Minister of Justice appoints the chief prosecutor in collaboration with a judicial committee (Gilliéron 2014, 264). In France, prosecutors are magistrates and are part of the judiciary; however they are subjected to the Ministry of Justice for their appointment and career advancement (Hodgson and Soubine 2016). In Portugal, the Prosecutor General is appointed by the President based on the nomination of the Government.[5] In Canada, three provinces have their Minister of Justice appoint the chief prosecutor, while another three have a committee that selects the candidates and puts forward a selection for approval by the Minister of Justice.

10.2.3 Curtailing Political Influence

Across continents and jurisdictions, curtailing the influence of politics in the selection of the chief prosecutor is a ripe issue. In jurisdictions with elected officials, political influence is an obvious reality during the election cycle, but this concern also looms large in jurisdictions with executive appointments of civil servants, including France, Germany, and throughout Eastern and Central Europe.[6]

There are four typical strategies to curtail political influence in the appointment process. First, some jurisdictions involve the independent judiciary. In Italy, for example, prosecutors are appointed by the Higher Council of the Judiciary (Caianiello 2012, 255), while in Spain the government consults with the General Council of the Judiciary prior to appointment (Aebi and Balcells 2008). Second, some jurisdictions elevate the appointment of the Chief Prosecutor to the President with nominating powers with the executive; this is the model in Portugal.

Third, some jurisdictions have curtailed the power of the executive by requiring parliamentary approval or by giving a different institution the power to nominate. In Hungary, for instance, the President nominates and the Parliament appoints the chief prosecutor.[7] In the federal German prosecution system, the chief prosecutor is appointed by the President following nomination by the Minister of Justice and approval by the *Bundesrat*. The hiring of the Federal Prosecutor General of Switzerland and the Chief Prosecutor of some of the cantons require the acceptance of the parliament (Gilliéron and Killias 2008). In Serbia, the Chief Prosecutor is elected by parliament after nomination. In South Korea, the President appoints the Prosecutor General upon the proposal of the Minister of Justice, and furthermore the Prosecutor General must undergo personal hearings by the National Assembly.[8] A Legislative proposal in the Quebec province suggests that approval by a two-thirds majority of the parliament is required for appointment. This requirement of a qualified majority continues to be advocated internationally as a tool to prevent political control of a government by a single party that controls a simple majority of parliament.[9] (While this may be an effective strategy it does not prevent the issue from becoming a political bargaining chip in parliament.)

Fourth, and perhaps most importantly, some jurisdictions have developed different forms of councils—most often in the shape of prosecution councils—that bring together key professional and political interest groups in the appointment. This approach effectively secures legitimacy but limits the power of the political system to control the appointment process. For example, in Albania, the High Prosecutorial Council—a body consisting of eleven members, six of which are elected by all levels of the prosecution service and five by the Assembly—selects and ranks three candidates based on "an open and transparent procedure." The criteria for selection include "highly qualified jurists with no less than fifteen years of professional experience as jurists," graduation from the magistrates school and no political post or leadership position in the past ten years.[10]

A different but equally important example is Ireland, in which the parliament is not part of the panel. The Director of Public Prosecutions is appointed by the Government based on selection by a committee consisting of the Chief Justice, the Chairman of the General Council of the Bar of Ireland, the President of the Incorporated Law Society, the Secretary of the Government, and the Senior Legal Assistant of the Attorney General. The government cannot appoint a Director who has not been put forward by the committee. Selection panels have also been used on the African continent. In the recent process to appoint a new Director of the National Prosecution Authority of South Africa, for example, a panel procedure was applied to avoid politization of the hiring process and to counter a historically low level of public confidence in the office. Accordingly, the President departed from previous practice and had a selection panel of eight representing the key stakeholders and interest groups to recommend suitable candidates. From this list, the President appointed the new National Director of Public Prosecutions.[11]

10.3 Hiring of Frontline Prosecutors

Strategies to hire frontline prosecutors are as much a reflection of different functional roles of prosecutors as of managerial capacities. For the many jurisdictions with nationally organized prosecution services, hiring entry-level prosecutors is not only about hiring high quality or ethical prosecutors but also about hiring legal officers who can ensure legal unity within a national justice system. Hiring criteria are established, and the process and selection take place on a national level, not on a local office level. This is the case, for example, in France, Germany, England, Denmark, Netherlands, Bulgaria, Republic of Korea, Japan, Kenya, and Ethiopia. Entry-level prosecutors enter a hierarchy of bureaucratic culture that ideally shields them from political pressure and stimulates a coherent legal rational analysis and practice. The quintessential example is found in the civil legal traditions in continental Europe (Luna and Wade 2010).

Depending on the legal tradition, the selection process may be integrated with the judicial branch, integrated with the executive branch, or be fully independent within the prosecution service. In France, for instance, judges and prosecutors are selected from the same class of candidates who passed the exam to attend the national school of magistrates. The self-perception of prosecutors is that they belong to the national judiciary together with trial judges and investigation judges (Hodgson and Soubise 2016). This self-perception can be found also in other jurisdictions with inquisitorial traditions, such as Portugal and Belgium. In Japan, any person who wishes to enter the legal profession—judges, prosecutors, and lawyers alike—must pass the national Bar exam. After that, he or she must undergo one year as a "legal apprentice" within a legal institution and then pass the final exam under the auspices of the Legal Research and Training Institute, which is placed under the auspices of the Supreme Court of Japan. In England and Wales and in Canada, the centrally organized Public Prosecution Service appoints entry-level prosecutors based on written applications and subsequent interviews.

In some jurisdictions the hiring is carried out in collaboration with the Ministry of Justice. For example, in the Republic of Korea, the President appoints prosecutors based on proposals by the Ministry of Justice. In Denmark, the appointment is done by the Office of the Director of Public Prosecutions in collaboration with the Ministry of Justice. Entry-level prosecutors are appointed within the field of the Ministry of Justice. The strategy is to ensure that prosecutors are civil servants within the state bureaucracy.

With centralized appointment, prosecutors are hired into the national organization and not by a local office; they are expected to rotate between offices to ensure consistency. For example, this is the case in France, in the Netherlands, in Sweden and in Japan. However, across jurisdictions, it is increasingly difficult to get prosecutors to move offices, except between offices in the major cities. The consequence of this difficulty is likely to be an increase in variation among office cultures and practices, despite the centralized governance of the organization.

In jurisdictions where prosecution services are localized, national consistency in hiring strategies yields to a more distinctive local focus. For example, in the U.S. Attorneys' offices the local U.S. Attorney hires the Assistant U.S. Attorneys. This process does take place within the guidelines and in coordination with the Justice Department, but it is the U.S. Attorney who hires his or her staff. In the more than 2,300 local district attorney offices, the district attorney hires line prosecutors to handle the office caseload (Wright 2012). The strategies of hiring depend on the organizational resources of the elected district attorney.

With vast differences between offices, we can observe significant variation in hiring strategies and practices even within the same state. For example, in Arizona, the largest number of prosecution offices have five or fewer prosecutors (Miller and Caplinger 2012, 270). These smaller offices have comparatively few resources available to manage strategic outreach to preferred candidates, to conduct a screening process and to engage in strategic decision-making. This makes the need for diversity and quality in hired staff more challenging (Bies et al. 2016). Larger offices, such as the Manhattan District Attorney's Office in New York, the Maricopa County Office in Arizona or the Milwaukee County District Attorney's Office in Wisconsin, have access to human resource departments to manage outreach, screening, and professionalized decision-making; they process hundreds of applications annually and manage qualified screening processes. At the Manhattan District Attorney's Office, for example there are more than one thousand applicants for each of fifty positions each year. Each applicant goes through a written application procedure and four consecutive interviews before final appointment by the district attorney.

10.3.1 Selection Criteria

Jurisdictions across the world set minimum requirements for who can become entry-level prosecutors. It is normal to require citizenship and residency and it is customary to require a legal education. Some countries require a Master of Law degree from a university. This is the case in Netherlands, France, Norway, and Sweden. Others merely require a Bachelor of Law or other equivalent higher education in the field of law. Where Bar exams apply to lawyers generally, these are required for prosecution candidates too. In the Republic of Korea, persons who have qualified as attorneys at law may also become prosecutors.[12] In some jurisdictions it is also normal to set minimum standards for intellectual proficiency and psychological stability. For example, in Sweden applicants must pass a personality test and an intellectual proficiency test to be considered; in the Netherlands, a psychological test applies (Tak 2012).

Some jurisdictions also require practical experience in the legal field before a person can become a prosecutor. In Sweden, the Netherlands and in Poland, for instance, applicants are required to have two or more years of relevant work experience. In Germany, judicial and prosecutorial candidates must undergo two years of training followed by an exam (Gilliéron 2014, 265). In Bulgaria, applicants are required to have passed a legally mandated internship. Similarly, in Canada, applicants need to have completed the "articling programme," providing practical experience of ten months normally. In France, attendants of the magistrate school go through a thirty-one-month combination of theoretical and practical training, ending with a practical tutelage in a court different from the one in which they will be placed upon graduation.

10.3.2 The Process for Hiring Entry-Level Prosecutors

The process for selecting candidates tends to be dominated by two different strategies. One strategy echoes a normal hiring procedure: Positions are advertised, candidates apply and the proper authorities screen documents and perform an evaluation of the candidates. The challenges are to attract suitable candidates and to administer a proper selection process that reflects the required diversity and organizational needs of the prosecution service. This is the case in the local district attorneys' offices across the United States. In Denmark, which has a national prosecution service, the Human Resource department of the Office of the Director of Public Prosecutions screens the written applications, conducts interviews, and selects candidates to commence the program for aspirant prosecutors.

The other strategy requires candidates to complete a written and/or oral examination along with other tests and thereby creates a class of potential candidates for the prosecution service. One example is the Republic of Korea, where candidates submit documents, take a written test, and then must be interviewed. Following this process, the Ministry of Justice submits recommended appointments to the President. Another example is France, where three thousand to five thousand applicants each year take the national test—the *concour*—to apply to the national school of magistrates. The test is highly competitive and only about three hundred and fifty persons pass each year. Candidates are well known to belong to the top tier of their university classes and to be highly qualified lawyers. Entering the school, the candidates go through a thirty-one-month program. At the end of the school all candidates are ranked by an independent jury. Provided a list of vacant offices in the country's Prosecutor General Offices, they choose according to their rank at the school. Similarly, in Bulgaria the Supreme Judicial Council organizes yearly centralized competitions for candidates who desire positions as judges, prosecutors, and investigative magistrates. Following screening of documents, applicants perform a written test. If they score above a required minimum, they take an oral examination. Those who pass are ranked for the available positions. In the Netherlands, both judge candidates and prosecutor candidates have to pass the judicial selection process conducted by the National Committee for the Judiciary. Afterwards they will have to follow a six-year-long training program, which integrates internships and theoretical education (Tak 2012).

Whereas the process in local jurisdictions is distinctly local, in national systems of prosecution services the process is centralized. This allows the organization to choose from among a wider selection of candidates and to be more strategic in its outreach and selection. Furthermore, it allows for an internal ranking of candidates to take positions within the organization—depending on one's rank out of the school (France) or where one's first placement is (Republic of Korea, Sweden, Denmark, England and Wales).

10.4 Learning Strategies

Across jurisdictions, prosecution services share the ideal of developing prosecutors who can successfully handle a caseload and who can meet the goals of the organization. The strategies and techniques jurisdictions employ to that effect differ with the legal culture of the individual prosecution service, the organizational design of it and the available resources. From a comparative perspective it is useful to make a distinction between three main approaches: learning with the judiciary, learning in the civil service, and learning in local jurisdictions. Each makes use of and combines key learning techniques in different ways.

10.4.1 Learning with the Judiciary

In many nations with inquisitorial traditions, training of prosecutors is organized as a part of a national education of both judges and prosecutors, as the two professions share judicial status. A strong example of this in practice is found in the European Commission's report on "Judicial Training—Study on Best Practices in training of judges and prosecutors" (2012). In both Germany and in France, prosecutors are subjected to the executive power and not the judiciary. Nevertheless, in Germany, prosecutors are required to be qualified to hold judicial office; they undergo the same training and pass the same exams (Gilliéron 2014, 265). In France, they undergo the same education and enjoy the status as magistrates (Hodgson 2010, 1363). In France the education is organized by the École Nationale de la Magistrature (ENM). The program for those admitted to the school lasts thirty-one months over three years. The first two years are shared by judges and prosecutors and combine course-based education at the school in Bordeaux and practical training in the different institutions in the legal system. In the final year the candidates are schooled and trained practically as prosecutors. They end the program with a tutelage at a local prosecution office, different from the one in which they will work once appointed as a magistrate. Course-based training is mostly performed by prosecutors and judges. After commencing their work as magistrates, prosecutors continue to have five days per year of funded training at the national school. It falls upon the individual magistrate to complete the training upon appointment.

Non-attendance does not have consequences in the short term but will have long-term consequences for a person's career. Prosecutors are expected to rotate between offices in four to five years intervals; in between, they learn through the local office.

A newer version of this education approach is found in Japan. Like in the United States of America and in Canada, candidates in Japan are required to pass a Bar exam, which is a substantial challenge (Johnson 2012). But unlike in the United States candidates are also required to undergo course-based training and apprenticeship together with future judges and lawyers. The apprenticeship takes place under the auspices of the Legal Research and Training Institute under the Supreme Court of Japan. Like in France, it is highly competitive, and admitted candidates distinguish themselves from other practitioners.

In other jurisdictions, the training of prosecutors occurs after the entry-level appointment. In Bulgaria, appointed junior prosecutors commence their position with a nine-month mandatory training course under the National Institute of Justice, which is under the combined management of the Ministry of Justice and the Supreme Judicial Council. After enduring two years of training at a regional prosecution office, they must pass an exam before receiving their final appointment as public prosecutor. In the Netherlands, training and career management have judicial connections (van de Bunt and van Gelder 2012, 121–122). Appointed prosecutors undergo a program from eighteen months to four years long, depending on their skills and the requirements in the office. The learning and development program integrates practical experience, course-based training, and mentoring. Initial training lasts three to fifteen months, followed by two to six months in the prosecution office of the court of appeal, and then six to thirty-six months of practical training in the prosecutor's office, the court, and a traineeship outside the judiciary.

10.4.2 Public Prosecutors as Part of the National Executive Power

In jurisdictions with national prosecution services organized as independent bodies or as part of the executive branch, learning programs commence after initial appointment and typically produce some form of integration between practical experience, mentoring, and course-based training. Design and management of programs take place centrally under (or in collaboration with) the chief prosecutor; they allow for learning activities to be nationally standardized and integrated. This is an approach that transcends legal cultures and can be found on all continents.

Sweden offers a good example of this approach. Swedish prosecutors progress over a three-year period from "aspirants" to "assistants" to "public prosecutors" through a combination of practical experience, personal mentorship, and formal course-based training programs structured through individual consultations and evaluations. Each year, fifty to seventy-five new assistants commence the program. Prosecutors are "aspirants" for nine to twelve months. It is a trial period, during which the aspirant can appear in court after two months (in simple cases). The aspirant has a practical stage with the police and spends a week with the Prosecutor General's Office. The perception is that given the major distances between local offices in the country, it is vital for organizational unity for each prosecutor to have significant time with the Prosecutor General and his office. The aspirants are evaluated every three months, laying the foundation for progressing to the stage of "assistant prosecutors." This stage lasts two years. It is still a training position and is meant to ensure that those who are finally appointed as public prosecutors are good fits for pursuing long careers with the prosecution service. The two-year period includes fifteen weeks of work-related course-based training focusing on skills and on character. The training sessions bring together teams of thirteen to twenty-five assistant prosecutors from all over the country—also resulting in strong communities among them. After final evaluation assistant prosecutors are appointed as public prosecutors. There is no exam but not all assistants continue as public prosecutors.

The Public Prosecution Service of Canada has implemented a "standardized framework for learning and career progression" through which prosecutors go through a four-year learning program as "counsel (entry level)" to be appointed as "counsel (working level)."[13] It is national and managed by the Office of the Director of Public Prosecution. The program has four stages and integrates a personalized work plan adjusted to regional requirements, mandatory centralized training, on-the-job training, a mentoring program, portfolio work, and evaluations and assessments to determine the prosecutor's preparedness to progress to "working level." The development program has become a central tool in connecting hiring, training, and career priorities into an overall strategy of professionalization of the organization. There are about thirty-five lawyers per course. The course modules are designed to meet the requirements of the Canadian Bars.

Also in Denmark, the learning-by-doing philosophy informs the three-year training and career program for entry-level "deputy" prosecutors. The program integrates actual practice, learning activities, individual development, and career planning. The Office of the Director of Public Prosecutions monitors overall performance and manages the national learning activities. The local chief prosecutor is directly responsible for the progress and education of each new prosecutor. This includes management (and written documentation) of the individual prosecutor's practical experience, development plan, and progress, as well as the assignment of a personal mentor in the office, the nine modules of education and the final exam. The formal campus training is centralized and takes place with the offices of the Director of Public Prosecutors—ensuring a national standard in the coursework. All the twenty-five to thirty new deputy prosecutors each year take part in creating nationwide communities of deputy prosecutors. The practical consequence of the integrated program is that each of the nine modules encompasses real daily case-handling, interaction with local mentors, and campus training. The three-year personal development plan managed by the local chief prosecutor keeps the activities integrated with the ongoing progress of the deputy prosecutor. The three years end with a written and practical exam.

In South Korea prosecutors are appointed to their positions in a local office and only then commence national training under the auspices of the Institute of Justice. The Institute of Justice is an integrated educational and research institution that provides training for public officials under the Ministry of Justice. Prosecutors go through training programs developed for each stage of the prosecutorial career and hierarchy. There is a one-year program for the newly appointed prosecutors. The program covers topics including investigation practice, trial practice, supervision and control on police investigation practice, and basic legal and public interest skills and character. Furthermore, for career prosecutors, branch directors, senior prosecutors, deputy chief prosecutors, and chief prosecutors, programs from two to four weeks cover a variety of subjects to cultivate specialized expertise, leadership, communication skill, and national management. Ad hoc courses of two to three days supplement specialized training in fields such as public security, antitrust, environment, economy, traffic accidents, and trials.

10.4.3 Training Prosecutors in Regional and Local Jurisdictions

A number of countries have prosecution services with local or regional jurisdictions. Germany, Switzerland, Canada, Pakistan, India, Ethiopia, South Africa, Brazil, and the United States of America are examples. Whether independent, part of the executive or the judiciary, the regional and local condition has significant consequences for training approaches. Consider, for example, the more than two thousand three hundred local district attorneys' offices in the United States, where each local office provides (or limits) opportunities for training its employees.

Strategies vary between states and between district offices. There is no national standard for training or early career development, and no standard length of such activity where it occurs. Course-based training is structured by continuous state Bar requirements, but comparatively, learning activities are less informed by a strategy to ensure legal unity and consistency across local jurisdictions than by a desire for local accountability and wise use of available resources. Large offices normally have an official learning program for entry-level prosecutors. For example, the Manhattan District Attorney, one of the largest in the United States, has an introduction program of six weeks followed by continuous specialized skills training and informal mentoring. Smaller offices rarely have the capacity to maintain such programs; they rely on actual practice and interaction in the office, and on the resources made available through national and state professional association resources. Some states offer course-based training of prosecutors, and since the 1970s an increasingly strong coordinating and training network has emerged through the National Association of Prosecutor Coordinators (NAPC), through the National District Attorneys Association (NDAA), and the National Association of Attorneys General (NAAG). Standardized courses and syllabi have emerged over time and today district attorneys have access to both state and national training offers. The NDAA, for example, has developed curricula for specialized areas of prosecution and has put together entry-level learning programs offered to districts nationwide.

10.5 The Individual Learning Methods

Three methods make up the core of learning strategies in the field of prosecution: practical experience, mentorship, and course-based training.

10.5.1 Practical Experience

Subjecting prosecutors to actual practice in all its diverse aspects is the key to training in any prosecution office. Nevertheless, actual practice often stands alone as learning method, it is rarely articulated as a strategy or integrated in formal programs, and almost always its role in strategic learning is underestimated. Nevertheless, it is through practice that entry-level prosecutors learn and career prosecutors develop. In Quebec, Canada, prosecutors are expected to have significant practical experience before they attend the annual introductory training camp. Likewise, in district attorneys' offices across the United States, it is not uncommon for prosecutors to go more than six months before attending even the minimum course-based training. It is not uncommon for entry-level prosecutors to engage in investigation, charge-bargaining, trial advocacy, or criminal sentencing from the first day in office despite having no prior experience or professional training.

Even where official course-based programs and mentorships apply from day one, practical experience from handling one's own cases and questions is critical for a prosecutor's professional development. Actual practice centers around the colleagues, work groups, the office cultures, and internal hierarchies that prosecutors are part of. Empirical research has consistently shown that the daily interaction and the communities through which legal practitioners routinely interact are instrumental to the institutionalization of norms through which police officers, prosecutors, and judges normalize their practice (Church 1985; Eisenstein, Flemming, and Nardulli 1988; Eisenstein and Jacobs 1977; Feeley 1979; Holmberg 2003; Rock 1993; Sudnow 1965; Wandall 2008).

This is not a static process. It evolves over time, is constantly reinforced by experienced practitioners relying on established ways of doing things, and constantly modified and developed by new inputs and experiences. This focus on institutionalization of the roles and the normative frameworks in which prosecutors learn echoes Levine and Wright's (2012) description of office cultures and their importance to prosecutorial practice. It also matches what Wright and Levine (2014) and Stemen and Frederick (2013) describe about the socialization of prosecution through practice over time. How to use one's discretion, how to interpret legal statutes, how to examine witnesses, how to decide what constitutes sufficient evidence, and how to decide what sentences to pursue are all informed through established office cultures and workplace communities.

The power of office cultures is significant. A junior prosecutor faced with a clash between office culture and central prosecution guidelines is caught in a real challenge. In much the same way, course-based learning, internships, and centralized evaluation mechanisms face real challenges when they conflict with office cultures. The consequence is that individual office cultures and communities dramatically inform what entry-level prosecutors learn and believe. It therefore matters what practical experience entry-level prosecutors are subjected to, if the prosecutor rotates between offices, and if offices are part of a larger hierarchy of organizational standards and evaluation. Moreover, it matters if practical experience is strategically combined with other forms of external learning.

10.5.2 Mentoring

Official or not, most if not all entry-level prosecutors turn to experienced prosecutors for institutional knowledge. Mentoring may concern individual case strategies, career planning, communication strategies, and legal and practical knowledge. The mentor may be senior in rank or may simply have more experience. In most places, mentorship is not formalized. For example, in the Crown Prosecution Service in England and Wales it is normal to have a mentor, but it is not part of the institutional design. In other jurisdictions, mentorship is integrated in the formal training program. In Sweden, mentorship is part of the training strategy for all prosecutors. In Bulgaria as well as in Netherlands, mentors are appointed, and training is organized for the mentors. From the observation that entry-level prosecutors learn from their colleagues and through established office cultures, formalizing mentorships has the potential of making more transparent what and whose interpretation of institutional knowledge the organization wants to see reproduced. In prosecution services undergoing organizational change or reform, controlling the reproduction of institutional knowledge is significant to the success of the reform. At the same time, just as with practical experience, mentoring is normally limited to office experience and so in terms of structural location, it gives priority to local rather than national knowledge and standards.

10.5.3 Course-Based Training

Course-based training programs differ from practical experience and mentoring in that they take the prosecutor out of his or her individual office culture and subject him or her to a regional, national, or international level of learning. Course-based training has become an increasingly integrated part of learning programs for prosecutors and other professional groups alike. Jurisdictions vary as to when, how and how much training prosecutors are offered and are expected to undertake. Prosecutors are trained prior to appointment, at the entry-level, and through progressive learning programs that last from one to six years. Prosecutors are also trained as part of their specialization. Furthermore, it is increasingly recognized that both prosecutorial and executive leadership requires education and training. Training of frontline prosecutors, administrative staff, mentors, and trainers alike is an integral part of reforms of prosecution services, whether they are spearheaded domestically or internationally. Training of prosecutors covers a wide variety of topics:

- ethics and professional conduct;
- cultural sensitivity;
- investigation;
- audit, supervision, and control of investigation;
- legal decision-making including charging;
- case management;
- trial and trial advocacy;
- legal and statutory drafting;
- organizational management;
- communication;
- training and mentoring;
- executive skills;
- political leadership;
- specialized areas of prosecution (e.g., juvenile justice, psychiatry, cybercrime, financial crime, environmental crime, cross-border legal assistance, areas of regulatory control, and audit).

Entry-level training of prosecutors typically focuses on character and what is perceived to be the proper role of a prosecutor, but is otherwise mainly focused on providing prosecutors with the skills required to practice. For example, in the Canadian Public Prosecution Service, the overall training program integrates seven areas of competencies: specialized skills and knowledge, professionalism (conduct, fortitude, service-mindedness, self-assessment), judgment, practice management (including file management), communications, interpersonal relationships, and leadership.[14] In Denmark, the nine modules of the three-year development program for prosecutors brings together prosecutors nationwide for class-based training in the role of the prosecutor, methods of prosecution, basic prosecution practice I-II, legality control and supervision with police conduct, case management, communication, and organizational knowledge. In the Republic of Korea training is adapted to each hierarchical level of prosecutor status. For entry-level prosecutors, the training program lasts one year and covers practical knowledge and skills in areas of investigation practice, trial advocacy, supervision of police, as well as organizational and societal understanding. In Sweden, assistant prosecutors go through two years of practice including fifteen weeks of work-related training. Coursework includes investigatory steps and directing investigation, criminal procedure, forensics, criminology, mass media training, rhetoric, and interrogation techniques.

Course-based training programs have also become an instrument to tackle the increasing and rapidly changing technological, legal, and international areas of practice in which prosecutors are expected to deliver. In jurisdictions with centralized learning programs and institutions, prosecutors are offered one- to two-day courses in specialized areas. In jurisdictions with no training program, access to ad hoc courses is gained through networks of prosecution services and through national and international learning institutions. For example, most local jurisdictions in the United States rely on NDAA and other professional associations to offer entry-level bootcamps or ad hoc courses. For countries with no such networks, access is gained through international training networks and organizations.

10.5.4 Integrating Learning Activities

The individual learning methods are practiced side by side in all organizational forms of prosecution services. However, for prosecution services with a central organization of human resource management and performance, it has become more the norm in the past two decades to integrate the methods into overall plans for organizational performance and individual career development. The Public Prosecution Service of Canada has developed such an integrated approach, combined with extensive evaluation tools and practices.[15] The same is the case in Public Prosecution of Denmark, where prosecutors over the course of five to six years develop their competences to align their expectations of a future career as either executive or specialized prosecutor with the competence needs of the organization.[16] Examples are also found in the Netherlands and other jurisdictions. In these integrated learning environments, the different agencies—the individual prosecutor, the mentor, the office chief, and the human resource department—all have responsibilities to ensure that learning, ongoing evaluation, career development of the individual prosecutor and the overall goals and resources of the organization go hand in hand.

10.6 Conclusions

Prosecutors play an increasingly central role in criminal justice systems. They are subject to political and economic pressures, and are expected to keep up with professional standards and rapidly evolving specialized knowledge. The risks of not equipping prosecution services accordingly are real and carry significant consequences. This chapter has provided a comparative overview of the current strategies of hiring and training prosecutors.

The first important observation is that there is no single strategy to hire or train prosecutors that dominates across the globe. Prosecution services across continents differ significantly in their strategies. This is a reflection of differences in levels of professionalization and shows some jurisdictions to be departing from shared global standards of what can be expected from a public prosecution service. At the same time it also reflects differences in the ideals, roles, and functions that drive prosecution services in different societies. The comparison suggests a close connection between the legal cultures under which prosecution services are organized and the strategies of hiring and training.

From a comparative perspective, the most centralized and elaborate hiring and training strategies are found in countries with continental European legal traditions, where statutory law, national state authority, and ideals of legal unity are closely aligned. Prosecutors are hired, trained, and advanced in national hierarchical organizations advancing organizational consistency and legal uniformity in criminal justice and beyond. Training programs are comparatively longer and practical experience, mentoring, and course-based training is integrated the furthest into the plans for both organization and individual prosecutors. In particular in countries with strong inquisitorial traditions prosecutors are educated and appointed in roles of judicial officers, rather than civil servants or adversarial trial attorneys. It is also in these jurisdictions that the more robust uniform testing, education, and training takes place prior to appointment, creating a distinct class of legal officers. A version of this is also seen in Japan.

The contrast to jurisdictions with strong common law traditions is remarkable. For example, the main strategies for who to hire, how to hire and with what methods to train prosecutors in local United States district attorneys' offices are primarily associated with the local office politics and the state Bars. Hiring takes place locally and the dominant learning strategies are local practical experience and local mentoring. Cross jurisdictional training is organized in networks, not through central or hierarchical organizations. Comparatively, there is little emphasis on cross-jurisdictional legality and uniformity, and little emphasis on organizational consistency across jurisdictions. It is noteworthy that England and Wales over the past thirty years have moved from a decentralized design with few governance structures to have a national Crown Prosecution Service with centralized regulatory governance, hiring procedures, training and career programs. The Federal jurisdiction in Canada is another example.

A second important topic that emerges is that learning through actual practice is essential in all prosecution services. The difference between prosecution services is to what extent actual practice is strategically integrated with training, mentoring, career planning, and other exposures to national or regional good practices and standards. From a comparative perspective, the many offices in jurisdictions with little integration of training programs or national or regional good practices, face significant challenges by letting the local office culture dominate the learning strategy (Wright, Levine, and Miller 2014). The consequence is likely a stronger variation between offices in the substantive legal and practical knowledge on how to handle individual cases, when to charge, when to close cases, and how to handle suspects, victims, witnesses, and others. Furthermore, what follows is a lack of cross-jurisdictional consistency and an institutional difficulty in maintaining a healthy balance between politics and legal accountability.

Third, the comparative overview serves to show how differently jurisdictions arrange the balance between political legitimacy and legal accountability when hiring chief prosecutors to lead prosecution services. At the one end of the spectrum are the many United States jurisdictions that elect chief prosecutors through direct local public elections. It is a model that prioritizes local political authority over legal and professional qualifications and one which is characterized by lack of trust in national and state authorities and legal institutions. At the other end of the spectrum are jurisdictions in which chief prosecutors are appointed by the national state through sometimes transparent procedures, ideally leading to the appointment of the best qualified candidate. It is a model in which the political legitimacy relies solely on public confidence in the national state authority's hiring process. While this does hold true in a number of countries, it has proven not to in others. As a result, a number of solutions have been introduced. Parliamentary approval to nominations is one. Another, the Irish model, curtails the appointing power of the executive by having a panel, representing the key interest groups of the legal societies, with exclusive power to put forward nominations. However, the most interesting solutions are found in newer democracies in Central and Eastern Europe, where prosecution councils, bringing together the executive, the parliament, and the representatives of the prosecution service, are empowered to select and rank nominations among the applicants. There are mixed experiences with these councils and new reforms of them continue to make adjustments. However, they do address a significant challenge of political influence in the hiring process, which has proven a real issue in all prosecution services regardless of legal culture.

NOTES

1. See The U.N. Guidelines on the Role of Prosecutors states under the headline: "Qualifications, selection and training," Standards of Professional Responsibility and Statement of the Essential Duties and Rights of Prosecutors, International Association of Prosecutors, 1999, article 6, Recommendation Rec (2000)19 of the Committee of Ministers of the Council of Europe on the role of public prosecution in the criminal justice system, adopted by the Committee of Ministers on October 6, 2000, at the 724th meeting of the Ministers' Deputies, European Commission for Democracy through Law (The Venice Commission), Report on European standards as regards the independence of the judicial system; Part II: The Prosecution System (Study No. 494/2008, CDL-AD[2010]040, and the National District Attorneys' Association standards 1–5.3).
2. In researching for the chapter, I have carried out interviews with the Director of Human Resources of the Swedish Prosecution Service, the Director of Human Resources, and the Director of Training of the Canadian Public Prosecution Service, the former Chief Prosecutor of Quebec, Canada, the Deputy Director of the French National School of Magistrates, the Director of Training of the Crown Prosecution Service of England and Wales, the Director of Development and Training of the Danish Director of Public Prosecutions, the Chief of External Affairs and Training Division, Republic of Korea,

representatives of the National District Attorneys' Association, a senior prosecutor in the Manhattan District Attorney's Office, and a representative of the National Association of Prosecutor Coordinators.

3. See for example Portugal, Statute of the Public Prosecution Service, art. 114.
4. See for example Portugal, Statute of the Public Prosecution Service, art. 82.
5. Constitution of Portugal, art. 133 (m).
6. About France, see also Hodgson and Soubise (2016).
7. See CoE SG/Inf (2016) 3rev "Challenges for the Judicial Independence and Impartiality in the Member States of the Council of Europe." See also Róth (2008).
8. Korean Prosecutors' Office Act, art. 34 (2).
9. See for example The Venice Commission Report.
10. Constitution of Albania, art. 148 (a).
11. See https://www.gov.za/speeches/president-cyril-ramaphosa-appointment-national-director-public-prosecutions-4-dec-2018-0000 (visited October 25, 2020).
12. Korean Prosecutors Act, art. 29.
13. Federal Prosecutor Development Program. Framework. Public Prosecution Service of Canada. May 15, 2013, page 2.
14. Federal Prosecutor Development Program. Framework. Public Prosecution Service of Canada. May 15, 2013.
15. Federal Prosecutor Development Program. Framework. Public Prosecution Service of Canada. May 15, 2013.
16. *Kompetenceudviklingsstrategi* for *anklagemyndigheden*, 2017.

References

Aebi, Marcelo F., and Marc Balcells. 2008. "The Prosecution Service Function within the Spanish Criminal Justice System." *European Journal of Crime Policy Research* 14(2–3): 311–331.

Asp, Peter. 2012. "The Prosecutor in Swedish Law." In *Crime and Justice—Prosecutors and Politics: A Comparative Perspective*. Edited by Michael Tonry, vol. 41, 141–165. Chicago: University of Chicago Press.

Bies, Katherine J., Darryl G. Long, Jr., Megan S. McKoy, Jimmy S. Threatt, and Joshua D. Wolf. 2016. *Diversity in Prosecutors' Offices: Views from the Front Line*. Stanford Criminal Justice Center, Stanford Law School.

Boylan, Richard T., and Cheryl X. Long. 2005. "Salaries, Plea Rates, and the Career Objectives of Federal Prosecutors." *Journal of Law and Economics* 48(2): 627–651.

Bulenda, Teodor, Beata Gruszczynska, Andrzej Kremplewski, and Piotr Sobota. 2006. "The Prosecution Service Function within the Polish Criminal Justice System." In *Coping with Overloaded Criminal Justice Systems: The Rise of Prosecutorial Power across Europe*. Edited by Jörg-Martin Jehle and Marianne Wade, 257–284. Heidelberg: Springer.

van de Bunt, Henk, and Jean-Louis van Gelder. 2012. "The Dutch Prosecution Service." In *Crime and Justice—Prosecutors and Politics: A Comparative Perspective*. Edited by Michael Tonry, vol. 41, 117–140. Chicago: University of Chicago Press.

Caianiello, Michele. 2012. "The Italian Public Prosecutor. An Inquisitorial Figure in Adversarial Proceedings?" In *The Prosecutor in Transnational Perspective*. Edited by Erik Luna and Marianne Wade, 250–267. New York: Oxford University Press.

Church, Thomas W., Jr. 1985. "Examining Local Legal Culture." *American Bar Foundation Research Journal* 10(3): 449–518.

Damaska, Mirjan R. 1986. *The Faces of Justice and State Authority: A Comparative Approach to the Legal Process*. New Haven and London: Yale University Press.

Eisenstein, James, Roy B. Flemming, and Peter Nardulli. 1988. *The Contours of Justice: Communities and Their Courts*. Boston: Little, Brown, and Company.

Eisenstein, James, and Herbert Jacob. 1977. *Felony Justice: An Organizational Analysis of Criminal Courts*. Boston: Little, Brown, and Company.

European Commission. 2014. *Study on Best Practices in Training of Judges and Prosecutors: Final Report*. Luxembourg: Publications Office of the European Union.

Feeley, Malcolm M. 1979. *The Process Is the Punishment: Handling Cases in a Lower Criminal Court*. New York: Russell Sage Foundation.

Gilliéron, Gwladys. 2014. *Public Prosecutors in the United States and Europe: A Comparative Analysis with Special Focus on Switzerland, France, and Germany*. Heidelberg: Springer.

Gilliéron, Gwladys, and Martin Killias. 2008. "The Prosecution Service Function within the Swiss Criminal Justice System." *European Journal of Crime Policy Research* 14: 333–352.

Glenn, Patrick. 2010. *Legal Traditions of the World*. Oxford: Oxford University Press.

Hodgson, Jacqueline. 2010. "The French Prosecutor in Question." *Washington and Lee Law Review* 67(4): 1361–1411.

Hodgson, Jacqueline. 2012. "Guilty Pleas and the Changing Role of the Prosecutor in French Criminal Justice." In *The Prosecutor in Transnational Perspective*. Edited by Erik Luna and Marianne Wade, 116–134. New York: Oxford University Press.

Hodgson, Jacqueline, and Laurène Soubise. 2016. "Prosecution in France." In *Oxford Handbooks Online*. Oxford University Press.

Holmberg, Lars. 2003. *Policing Stereotypes: A Qualitative Study of Police Work in Denmark*. Berlin: Galda + Wilch Verlag.

Jehle, Jürg-Martin, and Marianne Wade, eds. 2006. *Coping with Overloaded Criminal Justice Systems: The Rise of Prosecutorial Power Across Europe*. Heidelberg: Springer.

Johnson, David T. 2002. *The Japanese Way of Justice: Prosecuting Crime in Japan*. Oxford and New York: Oxford University Press.

Johnson, David T. 2012. "Japan's Prosecution System" In *Crime and Justice—Prosecutors and Politics: A Comparative Perspective*. Edited by Michael Tonry, vol. 41, 35–74. Chicago: University of Chicago Press.

Levine, Kay L., and Ronald F. Wright. 2012. "Prosecution in 3-D." *Journal of Criminal Law and Criminology* 102(4): 1119–1179.

Levine, Kay L., and Ronald F. Wright. 2014. "The Cure for Young Prosecutors' Syndrome." *Arizona Law Review* 56(4): 1065–1128.

Luna, Erik, and Marianne Wade. 2010. "Prosecutors as Judges." *Washington and Lee Law Review* 67(4): 1413–1532.

Luna, Erik, and Marianne Wade, eds. 2012. *The Prosecutor in Transnational Perspective*. New York: Oxford University Press.

Miller, Marc L., and Samantha Caplinger. 2012. "Prosecution in Arizona: Practical Problems, Prosecutorial Accountability and Local Solutions." In *Crime and Justice—Prosecutors and Politics: A Comparative Perspective*. Edited by Michael Tonry, vol. 41, 265–310. Chicago: University of Chicago Press.

Miller, Marc L., and Ronald F. Wright. 2012. "Reporting for Duty: The Universal Prosecutorial Accountability Puzzle and an Experimental Transparency Alternative." In *The Prosecutor in*

Transnational Perspective. Edited by Erik Luna and Marianne Wade, 392–407. New York: Oxford University Press.

Nelken, David. 2013. "Can Prosecutors Be Too Independent?" In *European Penology?* Edited by Tom Daems, Dirk van Zyl Smit, and Sonja Snacken, 249–270. Oxford: Hart Publishing.

Pizzi, William T. 2012. "A Perfect Storm: Prosecutorial Discretion in the United States." In *The Prosecutor in Transnational Perspective*. Edited by Erik Luna and Marianne Wade, 190–199. New York: Oxford University Press.

Rock, Paul. 1993. *The Social World of an English Crown Court: Witness and Professionals in the Crown Court Centre at Wood Green*. Oxford: Clarendon Press.

Róth, Erika. 2008. "The Prosecution Service Function within the Hungarian Criminal Justice System." *European Journal of Criminal Policy and Research* 14: 289–309.

Stemen, Don, and Bruce Frederick. 2013. "Rules, Resources, and Relationships: Contextual Constraints on Prosecutorial Decision-Making." *Quinnipiac Law Review* 31(1): 1–84.

Sudnow, David. 1965. "Normal Crimes: Sociological Features of the Penal Code in a Public Defender Office." *Social Problems* 12(3): 255–276.

Tak, Peter J. 2012. "The Dutch Prosecutor. A Prosecuting and Sentencing Officer." In *The Prosecutor in Transnational Perspective*. Edited by Erik Luna and Marianne Wade, 135–155. New York: Oxford University Press.

Tonry, Michael. 2012. "Prosecutors and Politics in Comparative Perspective." In *Crime and Justice—Prosecutors and Politics: A Comparative Perspective*. Edited by Michael Tonry, vol. 41, 1–34. Chicago: University of Chicago Press.

Tonry, Michael, ed. 2012. *Crime and Justice—Prosecutors and Politics: A Comparative Perspective*, vol. 41. Chicago: University of Chicago Press.

Turner, Jenia Iontcheva. 2012. "Prosecutors and Bargaining in Weak Cases: A Comparative View." In *The Prosecutor in Transnational Perspective*. Edited by Erik Luna and Marianne Wade, 102–115. New York: Oxford University Press.

Wandall, Rasmus H. 2008. *Decisions to Imprison*. Aldershot: Ashgate Publishing.

Wandall, Rasmus H. 2014. "Comparative Courts and Sentencing." In *Encyclopedia of Criminology and Criminal Justice*. Edited by Gerben Bruinsma and David Weisburd, 442–451. New York: Springer.

Weigend, Thomas. 2012. "A Judge by Another Name? Comparative Perspectives on the Role of the Public Prosecutor." In *The Prosecutor in Transnational Perspective*. Edited by Erik Luna and Marianne Wade, 377–391. New York: Oxford University Press.

Wright, Ronald F. 2009. "How Prosecutor Elections Fail Us." *Ohio State Journal of Criminal Law* 6(2): 581–610.

Wright, Ronald F. 2012. "Persistent Localism in the Prosecution Services of North Carolina." In *Crime and Justice—Prosecutors and Politics: A Comparative Perspective*. Edited by Michael Tonry, vol. 41, 211–264. Chicago: University of Chicago Press.

Wright, Ronald F. 2014. "Beyond Prosecutor Elections." *SMU Law Review* 67(3): 593–616.

Wright, Ronald F. 2017. "Prosecutor Institutions and Incentives." *Criminology, Criminal Justice, Law & Society* 18(3): 85–100.

Wright, Ronald F., Kay L. Levine, and Marc L. Miller. 2014. "The Many Faces of Prosecution." *Stanford Journal of Criminal Law and Policy* 1(1): 27–47.

CHAPTER 11

THE NECESSITY OF PERFORMANCE MEASURES FOR PROSECUTORS

LAUREN-BROOKE EISEN AND
MIRIAM ARONI KRINSKY

11.1 Introduction

11.1.1 The Current Landscape and Critical Role of Prosecutors

The United States has less than 5 percent of the world's population, but nearly one-quarter of its prisoners. Around 2.1 million people are incarcerated in the United States, with a little over 150,000 in federal prison and 2 million in state and local facilities.

The national crime rate today is about half of what it was at its height in 1991 (Federal Bureau of Investigation [FBI] 2017, table 1). Violent crime has fallen by 46.5 percent since 1991, and property crime by more than 54 percent (FBI 2010, table 1). In 2014, the violent crime rate was the lowest since 1970 (Friedman, Grawert, and Cullen 2017, 1). Yet even with these reduced crime rates, the United States remains a global outlier in rates of incarceration. And there is increasing evidence that incarceration often has criminogenic effects—it increases the propensity of incarcerated individuals to commit crimes.

The racial disparities in enforcement and prosecution are also troubling. On any given day, one in every ten black males in his 30s is in prison or jail. African Americans make up roughly 13 percent of the U.S. population (United States Census Bureau [USCB] n.d., for 2018) but 37 percent of the nation's incarcerated individuals (Carson 2015, 15). If current trends continue, one in three black males born today and one in six Latino males will serve time behind bars (Kutateladze et al. 2014).

Against that backdrop, there has been a growing recognition of the important role prosecutors play in moving beyond incarceration-driven policies, shrinking the size of the justice system, and promoting fair and equitable processes.

These concepts are resonating among voters and communities. And seven in ten victims prefer that prosecutors focus on solving neighborhood problems and stopping repeat crimes through rehabilitation, even if it means fewer convictions and prison sentences (Alliance for Safety and Justice [ASJ] 2016, 5).

Commentators have emphasized that meaningful reductions in incarceration will not be possible without prosecutorial reform (Watkins 2018). Some have focused on how "mandatory sentences and restrictions on early release have shifted much of the control over the length of incarceration from judges and parole boards to prosecutors because the charges filed often determine the sentence served" (Sklansky 2018, 454).

It is clear that changing the behavior of state and local prosecutors could substantially reduce incarceration and ensure a more fair, just, and accountable system. With local prosecutors responsible for 95 percent of criminal cases in the United States, today's more than 2,400 elected local prosecutors (including state, county, and district attorneys) wield immense discretion, and through their decisions impact individuals in every town, city, and state.

11.1.2 The Value of New Metrics

Traditionally, prosecutors have been evaluated by metrics narrowly focused on increasing enforcement, such as numbers of indictments, trials, and convictions. By creating new metrics, prosecutors can be incentivized to think more broadly about their role and to incorporate and emphasize a more holistic and forward-looking vision of "success." In this chapter, we discuss performance metrics that elected or chief prosecutors might use to carry out a broader vision of the prosecutor's job: one that promotes public safety and community trust, while also moving away from rewarding carceral and punitive responses.

Why, generally, do metrics and performance measures matter, and why is this topic one of importance as we think about changing paradigms and reforming the field? The old adage rings true: It is often what gets measured that gets done (Chettiar et al. 2013, 4).[1] Moreover, metrics serve as a statement of values and a way to reimagine the field and reset the narrative. They connect the prosecutor's vision for the future with tangible actions. What is measured is a proxy for what matters to leadership and therefore what attorneys should prioritize. Incentives and metrics also often drive fiscal investment and resources—and can thus serve as a doorway to propelling change. Finally, performance measures are a way to achieve transparency and better educate the public at large around what prosecutors do—and should be doing. They allow prosecutors to track progress, and measure and improve performance. This applies to the office as a whole in addition to individuals within the office.

In recent elections, voters have put in office a more diverse and innovative group of prosecutors who better reflect the communities they serve, and who promised to do their part to move away from policies that perpetuate mass incarceration. In order to truly transform their offices and the justice system, however, these leaders will need to design (or redesign) key features of the system to make it more accountable, equitable, and just. And they will need new metrics to help them, and others, assess and promote change.

By way of analogy, statistics have always been an important aspect of sports. More recently a particular sub-genre of statistics—advanced metrics—has revolutionized baseball and other sports. Now even the most casual sports fans, immersed in fantasy sports leagues or just gathered for a big game, are conversant in metrics that gauge players' efficiency, effectiveness, and even relative monetary value.

It's hard to imagine now given their widespread adoption, but advanced sports metrics were once the exclusive province of a select few "policy wonks" in the sports arena, individuals who ended up driving a metric-fueled revolution that has radically altered the field. Author Michael Lewis's 2003 book "Moneyball: The Art of Winning an Unfair Game" detailed how the Oakland A's use of an analytical, evidence-based approach to creating a more efficient baseball team worked despite Oakland's small budget. By using data and analysis to snap up undervalued players, the under-resourced Oakland A's achieved greater success than their budget alone predicted, and thus changed how team owners and managers traditionally assembled baseball teams. Now, most teams in every sport utilize data for all aspects of game preparation, and many employ entire teams of people devoted solely to analytics-based work (Lewis 2003). The lesson for prosecutor offices is clear, particularly for offices with fewer resources: performance measures can help to use scarce dollars and resources more effectively and wisely.

Prosecutors who truly want to transform how they operate their offices should embrace new and public performance measures. By doing so, they can make better decisions, get better results, and create more transparent information to share with their constituents.

It can be difficult to develop and implement good performance measures tailored to the nuances of each office. Prosecutors need to invest in software such as case management programs that track performance across the office, build capacity to collect and clean data, hire and empower staff with data analytic skills, and learn how to use data to guide office practices and policies. Another hurdle prosecutors face lies in how to make this new data available to the public—whether through reports, press conferences, or simply allowing access to the data on the office's website. Smaller offices also typically face the challenge of limited resources and capability to track and implement sophisticated performance measures. And data is often severely siloed amongst stakeholders, with prosecutors, sheriffs, police, courts, and public defenders having separate and rarely shared information.

Despite these obstacles, there is a growing recognition that well thought out performance measures are integral to improving outcomes. In fact, the John D. and Catherine T. MacArthur Foundation is supporting a partnership between prosecutors in Chicago, Jacksonville, Milwaukee, and Tampa to collaborate with researchers at Florida International University and Loyola University Chicago to examine prosecutorial performance and decision-making (Ellis 2018). The project also reflects how newly elected prosecutors are embracing the need for revised metrics to promote more effective, just, and transparent decision-making in prosecution. Melissa Nelson, State Attorney for the Fourth Judicial Circuit in Florida, acknowledged the value of better performance metrics in describing her enthusiasm for the MacArthur initiative: "The project helps us translate our vision for greater transparency and accountability into practice through robust data and strategic analysis" (Kutateladze et al. 2018, 5).

11.2 The Criminal Justice System's History of Performance Metrics

11.2.1 The Evolution of Metrics in Policing

The history of how police departments have shifted the nature and use of data and metrics over time provides prosecutors' offices with an innovative model of how redefining performance metrics has the power to realign institutions with their communities as well as their long-term strategic goals.

For three decades, police departments in both rural counties and large, urban cities experimented with performance measures. They used metrics to combat crime and better target resources; to track community trust in their offices; and in some cases, to detect officers who violate rules and regulations of their departments. Proponents of adopting performance measures believed that "what gets measured could be improved," and police departments began closely collecting and analyzing data on crime (Shane 2008, 8). Police departments have historically relied on statistics about reported serious crime rates, arrests, clearance rates, and response time to measure police performance, most notably with the New York Police Department's (NYPD) CompStat system.

However, a preoccupation with these numbers encouraged policing tactics that were at odds with addressing the needs of the community, and caused some to lose confidence in the system (Alpert and Moore 1993, 111).[2] As former NYPD Assistant Commissioner Ronald J. Wilhelmy acknowledged in November 2013, reliance on reported crime rates overlooked "what may be our highest priority: public satisfaction," as well as quality of life, integrity, and community relations (Sparrow 2015, 5).

Against the backdrop of the 1960s civil rights movement and a push to improve relations between the police and the communities they served, police departments recognized the importance of transparent performance metrics to improve community trust in their work (Maguire 2003). Law enforcement began to recognize a disconnect between the data collected on lower-level activities and higher-level departmental goals, which left many agencies with performance evaluation models that were arbitrary, inconsistent, and provided no guidance on how to improve even if the organization wanted to (Shane 2010, 10).[3] In the 1980s, Harvard University and the National Institute of Justice convened an executive session that brought together practitioners and academic professionals to discuss police reforms, ultimately producing a series of papers that "revolutionized" policing (National Institute of Justice 2009). This research shaped early thinking about community policing and propelled a problem-solving approach that encouraged police to build relationships with members of their communities. The concept revolved around police collaborating with the community to address public safety challenges. Techniques varied from hosting community meetings to implementing foot patrols or neighborhood watch programs.

By the 1990s, the philosophy of community policing motivated hundreds of departments, from Grand Rapids and Madison to Houston, Dallas, and Newark, to rethink their management and performance systems (Oettmeier and Wycoff 1994, 22). Many departments adopted new metrics that moved away from arrest rates and instead prioritized values like community engagement, restoring crime victims, and professionalism (Alpert and Moore 1993, 122).[4] For example, police departments have been encouraged to reward officers with awards, promotions, or merit increases if they show exemplary service to the community or avoid the use of force when possible (Alpert and Moore 1993, 128). New metrics also include tracking the number of cases dismissed because of police misconduct, resources allocated to crime prevention programs, and law enforcement attendance at school or community events (Alpert and Moore 1993, 133–135).

Former New York City Police Commissioner Lee Brown recognized that a "command and control" approach to performance management, wherein workforces are organized in a strictly hierarchical manner and lower-ranked employees often have little input into, or understanding of, higher-level strategic decisions "doesn't treat officers as intelligent, creative, and trustworthy people" (Shane 2010, 11). This approach pressured the rank and file to keep their heads down to try to just "get through the day," leading to demoralized employees and oppressive leaders (Shane 2010, 11–12). New performance metrics helped change this dynamic by increasing transparency and understanding of individuals' roles.

11.2.2 Metrics in Prosecution

Prosecutors now face a similar inflection point, as public sentiment has shifted in favor of reducing mass incarceration and community harms from overuse of probation and community supervision. New performance measures that are focused on fairness, improving community relations, and promoting safer and healthier communities provide effective institutional means for reorienting prosecutors.

This reorientation—and the accompanying need to shift past thinking and culture—will be a process. As Stanford Law School Professor David Sklansky writes, "Prosecutors' offices . . . still operate, in the main, the way they did fifty years ago" (Sklansky 2018, 460).

Why is it that prosecutors have not embraced performance measures the way police departments have? Sklansky points out that perhaps one reason stems from prosecutors' offices not knowing what sorts of behaviors and decisions to even measure. Additionally, questions swirl around what to do with the data once measures are determined and assessed.

To be clear, many offices have utilized some measurements to assess performance. Yet these metrics are typically focused on past habits of "counting" indictments, convictions, and trials, and pay too little attention to fairness, public safety, and community well-being.

These past notions of how to measure a D.A.'s "success" resulted in prosecutors sending an increasing number of people to jail and prison. For example, a former Cook County State's Attorney was perceived to be "prosecuting too many low-level cases," thereby playing a role in Cook County's stubbornly high jail population (Dumke 2015). Similarly, there have been concerns raised in regard to state attorneys throughout Florida who translated a "tough-on-crime" mentality into a practice of prosecuting large numbers of children as adults, taking advantage of Florida's statutory grant of broad discretion to prosecutors to "direct file" these cases in adult criminal court. A 2011 Department of Justice report found Florida's direct file rate to be disproportionately high as compared to other states (Sago 2017). More than ten thousand minors have been sent to adult court since 2011, and 98 percent of decisions to send children to adult court in 2015 and 2016 were made without any judicial review (Gomes 2018). This approach resulted in disparate results for young people of color; in 2016, 64 percent of youths referred to adult court were African American (Sago 2017).

Over past decades, prosecutors have focused on limited measures that counted punitive contact with the system. As noted above, offices tend to track the number of cases processed, indictments, guilty plea rates, convictions, and sentence lengths. Fiscal incentives based on volume of cases exacerbated this starting point. Budgets have traditionally been based on these numbers, effectively rewarding prosecutors for charging more cases and increasing caseloads, numbers which are used to justify requests for more staff.

Beyond office-level statistics, individual performance evaluations—when conducted at all—are often very limited, examining trial skills and court performance, with little focus on community engagement, efforts to promote the integrity and fairness of the process, or diversion and prevention endeavors. Success is defined by numbers of trials and convictions, with promotional opportunities often limited to those with high numbers of trials. Historically, there has been no reward for promoting system shrinkage or advancing innovation.

Prosecutors also see future professional success tethered to securing convictions and lengthy sentences. According to one study, federal prosecutors who secure longer prison sentences in their cases are more likely to become federal judges and partners in private law firms (Boylan 2005, 396).

Offices traditionally offered little transparency to their constituents concerning how they made decisions. The proverbial "prosecutorial black box" has become an increasing concern due to the lack of information these offices traditionally shared with the public.

These norms are beginning to shift. A new blueprint for elected prosecutors delineates "21 Principles" to transform reform-minded prosecutors' offices as well as the broader criminal justice system. These principles are predicated on the twin pillars of reducing incarceration and enhancing fairness. Newly elected prosecutorial leaders are increasingly embracing these concepts and exploring how to redefine their roles around the growing consensus that the country can simultaneously protect public safety and reduce incarceration (Bazelon and Krinsky 2018; FJP 2018). As this shift plays out, the development of new officewide metrics of success, as well as recalibrated individual performance tools, should be a priority.

11.3 A New Vision: Voices Aligning Around the Need for Change

Conservatives and progressives alike agree that the nation has far too many people behind bars. And voters across the country are casting their ballots for reform-minded district attorneys. In 2016 alone, candidates vowing to shrink the correctional footprint were voted into office in Florida, Louisiana, Texas, Colorado, and Illinois, among other places (Miller 2018; Satterberg and Krinsky 2017). The New York Times observed that these new prosecutors "don't talk about locking up the bad guys and throwing away the key. They talk instead about a justice system that jails too many people at the expense, they say, of common sense, public safety and even humanity" (Robles 2017). And they are "promising less incarceration and more fairness" (Bazelon and Krinsky 2018).

This new agenda is supported by what constituents agree is important. Opinion polling shows that the public is willing to support and invest in system shrinkage and crime prevention. Republican pollster Robert Blizzard found that 87 percent of Americans agree that non-violent offenses should be sanctioned with alternatives to incarceration (Blizzard 2018). And a recent poll conducted by the American Civil Liberties Union in partnership with the Benenson Strategy Group found that 71 percent of Americans believe it is important to reduce the prison population in America, including 87 percent of Democrats, 67 percent of Independents, and 57 percent of Republicans (American Civil Liberties Union [ACLU] 2017).

It's not just voters who seek this change. Academics have wrestled with how to change incentives and craft performance measures. For example, Temple University Law School Professor Lauren Ouziel recently explored why the intent behind many of our criminal laws does not translate into the desired outcomes. She studied federal drug enforcement as a case study through which to explore this mismatch. In particular, Ouziel examined why federal drug enforcement has resulted in the imprisonment of low-level individuals with no prior criminal history (Ouziel 2017). Ouziel notes that while high-profile cases targeting heads of illegal drug operations may be a better focus for federal prosecutors, they don't easily satisfy volume-based or success-based performance metrics (Ouziel 2017).

Judge Stephanos Bibas has written that chief prosecutors can shift practices of their line assistants by tying improved behavior to compensation and rewards (Bibas 2009). Bibas wrote that these metrics and measures would eliminate the perception that only conviction rates matter in prosecutors' offices and would make prosecutors more accountable to the community. Bibas has suggested that line assistant salaries should be tied to outcomes chief prosecutors want to see, suggesting offices collect feedback from myriad stakeholders, including colleagues, supervisors, judges, defense counsel, victims, defendants, and the constituents they serve (Bibas 2009).

Significantly, elected prosecutors are also clamoring for new paradigms, supported by new metrics. During one recent set of research interviews, former and current prosecutors stated that "the metrics for measuring the performance of prosecutors were far too narrow." Trial skills were valued extremely highly, along with an ability to move to trial quickly (Wald 2018).

Rethinking performance measures—both officewide and for individuals—allows chief prosecutors to create clear priorities and incentives to move practices toward a redefined vision. By shifting priorities and measuring incremental changes towards those goals, prosecutors can move the dial toward smarter, more effective, and more fair-minded practices.

Part of the cultural shift underway also requires this new generation of reform-minded prosecutors to be accountable to their constituents. Performance measures allow prosecutors to measure their success and convey their progress (or lack thereof) to those who voted them into office.

Given that the pendulum is swinging toward focusing on new prosecutorial priorities, what should new metrics look like? Most prosecutors did not learn how to create performance measures, let alone how to measure them, in law school. Tackling these challenges will be integral to promoting new paradigms in the field of prosecution as well as the criminal justice system more broadly.

11.4 Twenty-First-Century Priorities and Applicable Metrics

Twenty-first-century prosecutors should focus on the twin goals of enhancing fairness and promoting a safe reduction of incarceration. These principles should serve as the backbone of prosecutors' offices (Eisen, Fortier, and Chettiar 2014; FJP 2018). Although each jurisdiction will have its own challenges, offices that want to embrace transformative change should create performance measures that promote this new vision.

Set forth below are some examples of potential metrics to consider and suggestions on objectives and actions that can anchor these metrics. Some of these metrics will drive ways to assess office-level performance; others will guide the performance evaluation of individual members of the office.[5] Both are important, and while they are distinct processes, they should reflect the same values and may at times have common metrics. For purposes of this discussion, we have not sought to separate these two categories. And, as with all metrics, efforts should be made to use them with care and keep a close eye on any unintended consequences or impacts that may result.[6]

11.4.1 Reduce Incarceration

Although prosecutors have not traditionally thought of their role as reducing the numbers of people in jails and prisons, a new generation of prosecutors is increasingly focused on preventing the harm that incarceration exacts on defendants, their families, and their communities. Changing prosecutorial priorities to reduce the number of people sent to prison and the length of incarceration for those individuals can begin to make dents in the national prison population and improve both the safety and well-being of communities.

11.4.2 Stop People from Entering the Justice System

Elected prosecutors are increasingly examining how to improve the efficiency of justice and prevent individuals and cases from being brought into the justice system unnecessarily.

Professor Adam Gershowitz recently wrote an article exploring how to ensure needless arrests do not clog the criminal justice system and harm defendants, given that prosecutors across the country eventually dismiss about 25 percent of criminal charges (Gershowitz 2019). Gershowtiz surveyed forty prosecutors' offices finding that, with the exception of one office that required pre-screening of domestic violence cases, none of the offices required any prosecutorial involvement in warrantless misdemeanor arrests. He argues the lack of prosecutorial pre-screening leads to unnecessary arrests for charges the prosecutors would never have brought (Gershowitz 2019).[7]

Prosecutors are similarly recognizing that they need to play a role in ensuring that some people avoid the justice system entirely. For example, the Law Enforcement Assisted Diversion (LEAD) program in Seattle has successfully steered hundreds of individuals out of the justice system and is being replicated across the country with the enthusiastic support of prosecutors. LEAD diverts those arrested for low-level drug offenses or prostitution into community-based services at the pre-booking stage. The program was designed by a wide range of stakeholders—including police, prosecutors, public defenders, and community members—with the goal of redirecting individuals out of the justice system (LEAD King County n.d.).

Prosecutors are responding to evidence that even short-term incarceration can increase future criminal behavior, and are seeking to prevent the entry of individuals into the justice system in the first instance. For example, upon taking office in 2018, Philadelphia District Attorney Larry Krasner made clear his decision not to charge certain non-violent crimes (e.g., marijuana possession, prostitution for those with up to two prior convictions) (King 2018). Nueces County, Texas, District Attorney Mark Gonzalez similarly instructed his prosecutors not to prosecute marijuana offenses (Gass 2017). In Mississippi, District Attorney Scott Colom also stopped prosecuting low-level drug offenses. In Massachusetts, Suffolk County District Attorney Rachael Rollins instituted an office policy to decline to prosecute a list of fifteen common low-level crimes, absent unusual circumstances, and instead divert those individuals into community-based services. The list includes shoplifting, drug possession, drug possession with intent to distribute, and disorderly conduct (Rollins n.d.a). And in Chicago, Cook County State's Attorney Kim Foxx stopped prosecuting people arrested for driving with suspended licenses, if they were suspended for financial reasons (Connolly 2018). Resources previously spent prosecuting these offenses were shifted to pursue more important cases.

Potential metrics include:

- Collect data regarding how prosecutorial resources were reallocated in lieu of spending time on specific cases offices have declined to prosecute, measured over time.
- Partner with a university or research team to collect qualitative data from individuals who were not prosecuted to learn how that decision impacted their lives (see discussion of desistance measures below).
- Measure court filing changes over time for certain designated categories of crime where the office is attempting to reduce prosecutions.

11.4.3 Prioritize Diversion and Alternative Non-punitive Responses

Many prosecutors are embracing non-punitive responses to "criminal" behavior by individuals whose conduct is the manifestation of mental illness or a substance use disorder. Prioritizing diversion or alternative responses for these individuals when they come into contact with the justice system are decisions within the prosecutors' control that can safely reduce incarceration. These goals can also be measured through redesigned metrics.

For example, in January 2018, Brooklyn District Attorney Eric Gonzalez launched the Justice 2020 Initiative. D.A. Gonzalez convened a committee of criminal justice experts from a variety of disciplines to develop recommendations to "create a national model of what a truly progressive prosecutor's office can be" (Brooklyn District Attorney's Office [BDA] 2018). Based on these recommendations, Gonzalez has started to develop office guidelines that find "new ways to hold accountable those who can safely be diverted or deflected entirely from the criminal justice system" (BDA 2018).

Similarly, Boulder County District Attorney Michael Dougherty instituted the Mental Health Diversion Program in partnership with the local sheriff and public defenders' office. Under the program, everyone arrested for certain low-level offenses is given a mental health evaluation. Those that qualify are given the option to enroll in treatment and have their charges deferred and ultimately dropped upon completion of the program (Dougherty 2018).

Dallas County District Attorney John Creuzot also recently announced a number of reforms that aim to reduce incarceration and promote public health (Young 2019). His new policies include declining to prosecute activities that criminalize people who are homeless or mentally ill, including misdemeanor possession of marijuana, certain instances of criminal trespass, and theft of items less than $750. Creuzot additionally instructed prosecutors not to ask for jail time for failure to pay fees and fines, and adopted guidelines when recommending bail amounts that avoid monetary conditions and require ability-to-pay assessments (Creuzot 2019). These policies seek to promote wiser application of the justice system, as well as address troubling racial disparities.

And in a recent radio interview, King County, Washington, Prosecuting Attorney Dan Satterberg expressed support for expanding the LEAD program to the rest of his county. He stated that the county is trying to build a "system that's going to offer help to people on the first day, and not wait a year to convict them and give them no help" (Jennings 2018).

Potential metrics include:

- Measure percentage of individuals charged versus diverted.
- Measure percent of alternatives to incarceration recommended versus incarceration sanctions.
- Assess percent of defendants on docket who are sentenced to incarceration compared to previous year. This measure encourages prosecutors to opt, whenever appropriate, for lower charges or incarceration alternatives.

11.4.4 Implement Restorative Justice Programs

Restorative justice programs provide prosecutors with another tool to move away from purely punitive responses and reduce jail and prison populations. They focus on the accountability and rehabilitation of defendants through reconciliation with victims and the wider community.

As victims become more vocal, they have expressed a desire for shorter prison sentences and rehabilitation over punishment. One survey found that by a margin of three to one, victims prefer holding people accountable through options beyond prison and punishment, such as rehabilitation, mental health treatment, drug treatment, community supervision, or community service (ASJ 2016). Illustrative of this wider movement, more and more communities are engaging with restorative justice practices.

Ideally, communities and non-profit organizations will build and promote restorative justice models. Elected prosecutors should encourage these efforts and consider other ways to promote these approaches if others fail to engage. For example, in late 2016, the Marin County District Attorney, in partnership with the probation department, launched the Marin County Restorative Justice Program (MCRJ), which recently expanded to include adult and juvenile defendants. Out of the thirty-five people who completed the program, thirty-four have not committed a new offense (Marin County Probation Department n.d.; Mento 2018). Also in 2016, District of Columbia Attorney General Karl Racine implemented an in-house restorative justice program, focusing on young people. At restorative justice conferences, victims meet with those who have caused them harm. More than one hundred cases have been referred, and more than 80 percent of the young people who completed the program have avoided re-arrest (Racine 2017, 10).

In October 2013, District Court Judge Timothy Connors spearheaded the launch of the Washtenaw County Peacemaking Court (WCPC). Located in Ann Arbor, Michigan, WCPC is the first state court to adopt the use of tribal and community court peacemaking principles to resolve cases.[8] The WCPC incorporates peacemaking values in the way the judge relates to litigants, including out-of-court referrals for peacemaking circles. Instead of adversarial proceedings, lawyers, social workers, and family members work together to resolve conflicts (The Waverly Group-Midwest LLC 2016; Washtenaw County Trial Court n.d.). The WCPC's methods are derived from many of the same goals and missions as the restorative justice movement.

Potential metrics include:

- Track the number of cases referred to restorative justice programs per year.
- Track the number of cases accepted into restorative justice programs per year.
- Track the success of these cases per year including: victim satisfaction, trajectory, and desistance of defendants who participated—including education, employment, and other measures of successful pathways, and also whether people who previously committed serious offenses aren't engaging in equally or more serious new conduct (Butts and Schiraldi 2018; Loebler and LeBlanc 1990).
- Measure individual prosecutor case referrals to these programs.

11.4.5 Promote Proportionate and Fair Sentencing and Charging

There are other metrics that prosecutors should think about tracking to avoid overincarceration and to promote fair and equitable practices:

Potential metrics include:

- In order to ensure that sentences are proportional with the harm caused and that individuals are not unfairly penalized for exercising their right to a trial by jury, prosecutors should keep track of sentence lengths they agree to in plea bargain decisions, sentences in plea bargain deals that they offer but are not accepted, and sentences imposed after trials.

- To reduce overcharging, offices should develop metrics to keep track of initial charges and final case dispositions, which would allow for a comparison of the initial charge with the ultimate outcome of the case.
- Finally, offices should look at metrics that track the role and advocacy of individual prosecutors in challenging or agreeing to parole and clemency decisions.

11.4.6 Avoid Excessive Community Supervision

Reform-minded offices should also seek to reduce the number of people under community supervision and the length of time defendants spend on probation or parole. Excessive supervision increases the likelihood that those who are otherwise at low risk of reoffending will end up incarcerated for technical violations that have little to do with public safety.

Potential metrics include:

- Track individuals initially sentenced to incarceration versus those who are initially placed on probation but later end up incarcerated due to probation violations, including tracking the types of violations.
- Track the length of parole/probation sought by the office and the frequency of reincarceration based on technical violations.

11.4.7 Develop New Measures Predicated on Desistance and Positive Outcomes

Criminologists, sociologists, and those who work with justice-impacted populations are starting to rethink how they measure the success of criminal justice programs and interventions. Traditionally, recidivism rates have served as the vehicle to track these successes or failures. Recidivism, although a complicated measure, tends to refer to the reconviction of someone within three years of release from prison. It is a binary measure: one succeeds or fails.

A more nuanced way to track whether programs and interventions are working is to also measure desistance factors. In the criminal justice context, desistance refers to a "sometimes instant, more often gradual, termination of criminal behavior" (Klingele 2019, 775). Under this framework, crime reduction is viewed as a nuanced process where people learn to comply with laws over time, even if they trip up along the way. Although some desistance measures may require qualitative follow-ups, prosecutors can partner with research universities to develop these types of measures to move away from traditional recidivism metrics that show little about whether incremental change is occurring. In contrast, the focus of desistance measures is on promoting positive outcomes and building strengths that can help individuals avoid future criminal conduct (Butts and Schiraldi 2018).

Careful attention should be given to measuring whether individuals channeled to diversion and alternatives to incarceration are experiencing positive outcomes.

Potential metrics include:

- Track if individuals are making realistic, measurable progress in areas such as using drugs at a lesser rate, using alcohol at a lesser rate, and relapsing less.
- Track individuals' improved education, housing, and employment outcomes.
- Track if individuals are reoffending at a lower rate and/or committing less serious offenses.

11.4.8 Improve Fairness and Justice

Reform-minded prosecutors have committed not simply to moving beyond past incarceration-driven approaches and reducing incarceration, but also to developing policies and practices that promote a fair and more equitable justice system (FJP n.d.). To ensure that this movement is not fleeting, metrics are needed to track progress in advancing these goals as well.

11.4.9 Reduce Pre-trial Detention and Address the Poverty Penalty

Most of the 722,000 people in local jails have not been convicted and are in jail because they are either too poor to make bail, or because they have just been arrested and will make bail in the next few hours or days (Wagner 2015). Many of these individuals pose little risk and are detained pre-trial, while higher risk individuals who can pay bail are released. There is also a troubling correlation between pre-trial detention and *increased* prison time and recidivism (Arnold Ventures n.d.).

Prosecutors can play an important role in reducing the number of people who are in pre-trial detention as well as addressing the criminalization of poverty. For example, Philadelphia D.A. Larry Krasner ended cash bail for low-level offenses in early 2018. This policy led to an immediate decrease in defendants who spent at least one night in jail, and an immediate increase in defendants eligible to be released on their own recognizance without bail or other conditions. Notably, there has been no adverse change in recidivism or defendants failing to appear in court (Ouss and Stevenson 2019). Krasner stated, "There is absolutely no reason why someone who will show up for court, is not a flight risk, and is no threat to their neighbors and community, needs to sit in jail for days because they can't post a small amount of bail" (Lozano 2018).

Prosecutors can also urge diversion programs run by their offices to waive fees for indigent defendants. In Cook County, Illinois, the State's Attorney's Office runs a diversion program that handles five thousand defendants a year and collects no fees. In fact, the notion of charging for diversion strikes many prosecutors as absurd. "That would be a complete failure here in Cook County," said Robert Groebner, Jr., a felony prosecutor. "These defendants, they don't have $50 in their pocket" (Dewan and Lehren 2016).

Potential metrics include:

- Measure reduction or increase in percentage of defendants sent to jail pre-trial.
- Measure change in percentage of bail requests.
- Measure compliance with office bail policies.
- Measure individual attorney's requests to waive, or agreement to defense request for waiver of, applicable fees and fines.
- Measure number of defendants who can't afford to participate in diversionary programs who received fee waivers.

11.4.10 Create Conviction Integrity Units and Review Processes

Prosecutors are increasingly aware of the need to lead the way to ensure that miscarriages of justice do not occur. In fact, 2,410 exonerations have occurred across the country since 1989 (The National Registry of Exonerations 2019).

One significant way to make sure individuals have not been unjustly convicted is to create conviction review processes or conviction integrity units. In 2007, there were only two conviction integrity units in the United States, compared with thirty-three in 2017 and even more since then. Overall, these units have helped secure 269 exonerations from 2003 through 2017 (The National Registry of Exonerations 2018). "CRUs provide helpful mechanisms for revisiting cases which an office previously believed to be justly prosecuted but which, in fact, may be materially flawed" (FJP 2018). When prosecutors come across new facts or evidence that a "defendant has a reasonable claim of actual innocence," they have a duty to investigate these claims (Center on the Administration of Criminal Law 2012, 5; FJP 2017b; Krinsky 2017).

Jacksonville State Attorney Melissa Nelson recently created Florida's first conviction integrity review unit (Pantazi 2018). In Wyandotte County, Kansas, District Attorney Mark Dupree fought for and secured funding to establish a conviction integrity unit. Dupree stated that the unit would have a full-time senior attorney, two part-time support staff, and work in partnership with Kansas law schools to identify eligible cases (Schwers and Rizzo 2018). And Philadelphia District Attorney Larry Krasner recently expanded resources and staffing for his conviction review unit. In addition to claims of actual innocence, his unit reviews cases with concerns about the integrity of the process, including allegations of prosecutorial misconduct, police corruption, or flawed forensics, that are not contingent on actual innocence (Moraff 2018).

Potential metrics include:

- Measure how many cases are investigated through a conviction review process and how many of those result in a recommendation for reconsideration of the conviction.
- Measure length of time from referral of case for conviction review to completion of that review.
- Measure number of cases individual prosecutors have referred for conviction review or sought correction of past convictions.
- Measure steps taken to learn from problems identified through conviction review process—including trainings initiated, new policies crafted, or other systemic changes put in place.

11.4.11 Reduce Racial Disparities in the Criminal Justice System

One of the larger and more troubling concerns arising from vast prosecutorial discretion stems from stark racial disparities in how Black and Latino defendants are treated in the justice system. More targeted performance measures—plus analyses of, and transparency in regard to, this data—can shed light into the decision-making patterns of line prosecutors in their day-to-day roles that may result in the racial disproportionality evident in the justice system.

African Americans and Latinos are overrepresented in the criminal justice system. Almost one in three people arrested for drug crimes are African American, even though drug use rates do not differ significantly by race or ethnicity (ACLU 2013; Borden 2016; Drug Policy Alliance n.d.). African Americans and Latinos are also significantly overrepresented in jails. While together these groups represent 30 percent of the general population, they account for 51 percent of the jail population. In particular, African Americans make up roughly 13 percent of the U.S. population (USCB n.d.) but 37 percent of the nation's prisoners (Carson 2015, 15) and are jailed at almost four times the rate of white people (Subramanian et al. 2015, 11).

Decades of research indicate that these disparities are the result of concerning practices including selective policing in urban, heavily minority neighborhoods (FJP 2018).[9] Prosecutors are beginning to recognize the need to right past wrongs, and voters should hold them accountable for reducing racial biases in charging and prosecution decisions.

In 2005, the Vera Institute of Justice partnered with then Mecklenburg District Attorney Peter Gilchrist (Vera Institute of Justice 2014, 14–16). Vera found that Black defendants referred to the D.A.'s office were more likely to be arrested and charged than white defendants, a higher percentage of Black defendants were charged with eight of the most serious drug offenses, and Black defendants were more likely to be offered pleas in the form of prison or jail sentences, not probation.

As a result of these findings, the Mecklenburg District Attorney's office made key changes: it appointed new supervisory staff and required prosecutors to screen cases more carefully; it implemented more rigorous initial screening processes for drug cases, resulting in a greater than 10 percent decrease in drug-case prosecutions and dismissals; it directed resources to more meritorious cases relying on a data analysis tool; and it developed a comprehensive disparity assessment report, presenting case-outcome statistics organized by race for two discretionary decision points: (1) initial screening and (2) plea offers.

Potential metrics include:

- Collect and analyze data on racial disparities at key decision points.
- Track trends in the incarceration rate and changes in the raw number of people incarcerated by racial and ethnic group.

11.4.12 Improve Diversity of Office Line Staff and Managers

As noted in "21 Principles for the 21st Century Prosecutor," research has shown that across disciplines, incorporating staff members from a wide swath of racial, ethnic, and religious backgrounds makes organizations more effective and open to new ideas. In the context of prosecutors' offices, a diverse staff enhances community trust in the office and its decisions.

In 2014, Manhattan District Attorney Cyrus Vance set out to improve the racial and ethnic diversity of his staff. This was prompted by the release of a Vera study examining racial disparities in the Manhattan criminal justice system (Kutatladze et al. 2014). D.A. Vance believed that a more diverse staff would reduce the possibility of inherent bias. He also appointed a Chief Diversity Officer and a Diversity Committee, composed of attorneys and support staff from all divisions in the D.A.'s office. The D.A.'s office required all A.D.A.s to attend implicit bias training as part of this initiative (Manhattan District Attorney's Office 2014).

While these steps are critical, more can and should be done to promote proximity to impacted communities and to deepen prosecutors' understanding of—and willingness to discuss and own—racial inequities.

Potential metrics include:

- Measure office outreach efforts to recruit and attract more diverse staff.
- Measure changes in diversity hiring, retention, and promotion, and measure success in increasing diversity at all levels.
- Measure staff satisfaction broken down by race, gender, and type of position.

11.4.13 Improve Procedural Fairness

Research shows that when defendants, litigants, and other court participants (including victims and witnesses) perceive the court process to be fair, they are more likely to believe the legal process is legitimate, comply with court orders, and follow the law in the future, regardless of whether they "win" or "lose" their case (FJP 2017a; Tyler 2006).

Every prosecutor's contact with individuals involved with a case—whether that individual is a defendant, victim, or witness—is an opportunity to improve perceptions and build public trust in the criminal justice process (FJP 2017a).

There are multiple ways that prosecutors can aim to improve the procedural fairness of their offices. Innovative prosecutors have started to reach out to members of their communities after high profile incidents. As noted in a report by Fair and Just Prosecution, prosecutors in San Joaquin County, California, go out into the community to speak to residents after a shooting, providing community members access to prosecutors and a way to voice their concerns and ask questions about the incident (FJP 2017a, 2–3).

Some prosecutors have started to underscore the need to improve and address victim satisfaction. Recently, Suffolk County District Attorney Rachael Rollins included improving victim services as part of her campaign platform, promising: "We will respond to victims in a timely fashion, value their feedback, and continually improve our victim services. . . . We will meet with crime victims personally prior to the victim's testifying. This will not only be the role of the Victim Witness Advocates, the ADA will also meet with the victim prior to testifying" (Rollins n.d.b.).

Only 10 percent of victims nationwide reported receiving assistance from a district attorney or prosecutor's office (ASJ 2016, 11). Not surprisingly, polls have found that victims want to be heard. Moreover, their perspectives aren't commensurate with the demand for long sentences some would presume: "Six in 10 victims prefer that prosecutors consider victims' opinions on what would help them recover from the crime, even when victims do not want long prison sentences" (ASJ 2016, 5). Research also indicates that victims of domestic violence who turn to the criminal justice system for intervention may be so disappointed with the outcome that they refrain from calling the police if they need law enforcement assistance in the future (Hotaling et al. 2006, 253). With these concerns in mind, the non-profit group Alliance for Safety & Justice has recommended that states collect more information on who crime victims are and their experiences with the justice system, crime reporting, the impact of repeat victimization and trauma, and access to services and treatment for victims (ASJ 2016, 27).

Some offices have begun to issue surveys to victims. The Snohomish County, Washington, County Prosecuting Attorney's Office created a victim satisfaction survey to "look for ways in which we can improve our services or better tailor them to meet the needs of the County's criminal prosecution needs" (Snohomish County n.d., 1). One of the survey questions focuses on the respect and sensitivity shown to the victim by staff at the County Prosecuting Attorney's Office. The DeKalb County Prosecuting Attorney's Office in Maysville, Missouri, also uses a victim survey. One of their questions asks whether the victim's needs were recognized and addressed (DeKalb County Prosecuting Attorney's Office n.d.).

Prosecutors are often the face of the justice system to the community. Treating people with respect extends beyond victims and community members to those who are charged with violating criminal codes. For example, explaining the reasons surrounding decision-making can make defendants and their families feel they were treated fairly and with respect. Charging and seeking consequences proportional to the harm done can also improve perceptions of legitimacy of prosecutors and the broader justice system. Although challenging to implement, there is value in capturing defendants' perceptions of the justice system and the way they were treated throughout their case.

Potential metrics include:

- Work with external partners to measure whether victims feel they were dealt with fairly and efficiently.
- Work with public defender's offices and/or court personnel to track defendants' experiences with prosecutor's offices.

11.4.14 Improve Community Engagement and Promote Community Trust and Well-Being

Prosecutors should be evaluated on their ability to keep neighborhoods safe, ensure community well-being, and improve trust in the justice system. This requires that they build trust with community members they engage with in their offices as well as those in the community who benefit from improved public safety.

11.4.15 Improve Prevention and Promote Education

Historically, law enforcement resources did not prioritize prevention and education, as resources went to combatting crime after it occurred. Prosecutors similarly have viewed their role as reactive, responding after the fact to crimes and individuals who come into the criminal justice system. Today, twenty-first-century prosecutors have started to reimagine that starting point, and a new conversation is starting to take hold in their offices, as well as in D.A. elections.

When she was on the campaign trail in a 2018 district attorney election in San Diego, Genevieve Jones-Wright stumped on the need for prosecutors to focus on prevention: "I do understand that it's humans who are affected by decisions and policies that come out of D.A. offices, and when someone is justice-involved, how that can affect generations to come. And so we talk about preventing crime, but we also have to talk about preventing harm" (Ciaramella 2018).

More than five years ago, King County Prosecuting Attorney Dan Satterberg established a Truancy Dropout Prevention Unit in the King County Prosecuting Attorney's Office (Satterberg 2013a). Instead of focusing on prosecuting students, the office works with school districts throughout the county to host workshops designed to understand why students are not going to school. The school, the student, and parents or guardians sign an agreement designed to re-engage the student with an educational track (Satterberg 2013b).

11.4.16 Improve Community Partnerships

In order to improve relationships with the communities that prosecutors serve, community partnerships can provide additional resources and reduce the intimidation that community members may feel about speaking to law enforcement. For example, the Brooklyn District Attorney's office partners with churches to give those with open warrants an opportunity to speak to free legal counsel. The office's "Begin Again" program allows those with summons warrants—which are issued when people fail to answer a ticket for minor quality of life offenses, such as drinking alcohol in public or being in a park after closing—to resolve these warrants and other lingering legal issues (BDA n.d.). A partnership like Begin Again restores the trust of defendants, their families, and wider community members in their local prosecutor's office. Such partnerships also positively impact defendants and their families. For example, of the 3,248 Begin Again participants, none have been arrested, and each attendee received consultation with attorneys from Legal Aid to resolve their warrants on other legal issues (BDA n.d.).

Other outreach activities can include: participating in town hall meetings, partnering with schools, developing relationships with churches and faith-based organizations, and engaging with underrepresented populations, such as Native Americans and many urban neighborhoods (Eisen, Fortier, and Chettiar 2014). By involving educators, clergy, and other public service agencies in these efforts, communities will benefit.

Potential metrics include:

- Measure prevention and education activities by collecting data regarding prosecutors speaking at schools or community groups to educate the broader public on the role of prosecutors and the function of the criminal justice system. Also track individual prosecutors' engagement.
- Track feedback received at town halls and through other means, as well as any changes implemented as a result of that feedback.
- Examine yearly data to see if these community partnerships are increasing and improving.
- Collect data on the number of complaints made by victims, defendants, and members of the community against the prosecutor's offices, as well as changes in complaint rates.
- Collect data on the community's feelings of confidence and trust in prosecutor offices.

11.4.17 Focus on Collateral Consequences and Reentry

Prosecutors have traditionally focused their attention on the front end of the criminal justice system: charging and sentencing. Generally, what happens post-sentencing, particularly after a defendant is locked up, has not been viewed as within a prosecutor's purview. However, this approach is changing as prosecutors who are concerned with overincarceration look to back-end reforms focusing on removing barriers to reentry to reduce recidivism and more effectively promote public safety.[10]

Reentry is often conceived of as a back-end reform. Traditionally, correctional agencies, other government agencies, or non-profits assist the formerly incarcerated with reentry programs and services. Yet prosecutors can also play a critical role in thinking about potential collateral consequences of criminal justice involvement on defendants, ensuring that defendants receive help obtaining expungements where appropriate, and partnering with businesses and employers to assist formerly incarcerated individuals obtain jobs.

Among those modeling this reform was former San Francisco District Attorney George Gascón, who explained that prosecutors should also aim "to facilitate [individuals] coming out and not going back again" (Oliva 2018). Starting in 2012, D.A. Gascón led regular forum meetings with prosecutors and inmates at San Quentin State Prison to give prosecutors a better understanding of life in prison and discuss steps toward reentry into society (Office of the San Francisco District Attorney [SFDA] n.d.a). The San Francisco D.A.'s office plans to make this forum a mandatory part of training for new felony prosecutors (SFDA n.d., 6). Gascón also established the Formerly Incarcerated Advisory (FIA) Board in 2016. Comprised of formerly incarcerated individuals and prosecutors, the FIA Board "works to enhance social inclusion by creating clearer pathways for formerly incarcerated men and women to rejoin the workforce, the housing market, educational environments, and community-based organizations" (SFDA n.d., 3).

Prosecutors have also focused on expungement and clearing old convictions or warrants to facilitate reentry for people convicted of felonies. Under the leadership of Stephanie Morales, the Commonwealth Attorney's Office for the City of Portsmouth, Virginia hosts a monthly seminar to assist residents in removing crimes from their records and restoring other rights lost due to criminal involvement (Portsmouth Commonwealth's Attorney n.d.). More recently, Gascón (when he was D.A.) and other D.A. offices launched exciting partnerships with Code for America to use new technology to automatically clear eligible convictions, starting with marijuana convictions (SFDA 2018). Brooklyn D.A. Eric Gonzalez, expanding on a program launched by his predecessor, has given residents the opportunity to clear misdemeanor marijuana convictions (BDA n.d.). More than 3,600 people have participated so far and more than 2,240 warrants have been cleared (BDA n.d.).

"Clean Slate" programs have also been started in Sedgwick County, Kansas (Wichita Bar Association n.d.),[11] and Albany County, New York (Albany County District Attorney's Office n.d.),[12] among other jurisdictions. Vermont Attorney General T. J. Donovan is partnering with Vermont Legal Aid to host a series of record expungement clinics across the state. At these clinics, attorneys from both offices assist individuals to file expungement petitions as well as fee waivers when applicable. Without clearing these convictions, individuals returning to the community would face lasting barriers to housing, employment, loans, and more. As one public defender noted, these types of programs are "a good way for her clients to get on with life—to 'be able to then go on, apply for jobs, go to school, drive cars, without worry that the police may stop them and incarcerate them because of these warrants'" (Roth 2015).

As part of a push to be "smarter on crime," prosecutors are increasingly cognizant of the "collateral consequences" of criminal charges when making decisions on charging and plea deals. Dominating the discussion are immigration-related consequences of being arrested. Undocumented immigrants face heightened risks of deportation if they are convicted of certain offenses, while convictions may jeopardize legal status for visa and green card holders and block future citizenship (Thompson 2017).

As early as 2011, Santa Clara County D.A. Jeffrey Rosen directed that collateral consequences be considered in each case, regardless of the defendant's legal status. For example, U.S. citizens may lose custody of their children, employment, state-funded scholarships, or public housing if detained or convicted (Thompson 2017). D.A. Rosen implemented a policy providing that in cases involving non-serious, non-violent offenses "where the collateral consequences are significantly greater than the punishment for the crime itself, it is incumbent upon the prosecutor to consider and, if appropriate, take reasonable steps to mitigate those collateral consequences" (Rosen 2011).

More recently, Baltimore City State's Attorney Marilyn Mosby instructed her prosecutors to "utilize our prosecutorial discretion as we do in every case by considering the unintended collateral consequences that our decisions have on our immigrant population," including by ensuring minor crimes face only minor consequences (Office of the State's Attorney for Baltimore City 2017).

Brooklyn D.A. Eric Gonzalez implemented a similar policy and hired two immigration attorneys to train his staff on immigration issues and consult on cases involving non-citizen defendants "in an effort to avoid disproportionate collateral consequences" (BDA 2017). Under the new policy, "if an appropriate disposition or sentence recommendation can be offered that neither jeopardizes public safety nor leads to removal or to any other disproportionate collateral consequence—the ADA should offer that disposition or make that recommendation" (BDA 2017). The policy also recognizes that "[i]n certain instances, it may be appropriate to offer a non-citizen defendant a plea for a lesser offense in light of the disproportionate immigration consequences a higher-level offense may result in" (BDA 2017). A senior staff attorney at Brooklyn Defenders noted that prosecutors and defense attorneys have taken a more collaborative approach to cases with immigration implications and "have been able to negotiate misdemeanor cases down to violations that do not jeopardize the immigration status of the defendant and do not jeopardize public safety" (Ryan 2017).

Recently, Contra Costa County District Attorney Diana Becton enacted an office policy to minimize the adverse immigration consequences of criminal convictions. The policy requires prosecutors to consider potential immigration consequences during the plea negotiations process, and includes alternative considerations, such as guidelines for crafting a plea that avoids exposing defendants' immigration status (Becton 2019).

And in Suffolk County, Massachusetts, District Attorney Rachael Rollins joined a lawsuit seeking to end Immigration and Customs Enforcement officers' practice of making arrests at local courthouses. She also requires employees to notify her of any federal ICE officers patrolling the Suffolk County courthouse (Rios 2019).

Potential metrics include:

- Collect data on reentry efforts, such as programming the office supports, reentry assistance the office gives, and number of individuals assisted.
- Track number of people the office has worked with to expunge past convictions.
- Track immigration-related work that is done to assist families and defendants.
- Track employment statistics of individuals the office has worked with to clear warrants, expunge cases, or on broader job readiness or employment-related opportunities. (Collateral Consequences Resource Center 2018).[13]

11.5 Changing Incentives and Promotion Practices to Align with New Priorities

As noted earlier, changing culture requires offices to change incentives to ensure that staff align their goals with the direction the office is headed. One example of a way to change incentives is to shift how prosecutors are promoted, which is often the engine driving prosecutorial behavior.

In some prosecutors' offices, promotions have been driven by numbers of trials and convictions line attorneys secured. Yet these measures of performance simply reward those who take cases to trial, prioritizing trials in lieu of supporting alternatives to incarceration and diversionary programs. It also incentivizes prosecutors to charge more severe crimes if they think they can win at trial, assuring them a sure win instead of charging a crime that is more appropriately calibrated to the alleged crime.

If prosecutors are rewarded for reducing prison populations, enhancing trust in the community, improving victims' experiences, and ensuring more fair and just outcomes, practices will follow.

Elected prosecutors should reward their staff for promoting new paradigms around prosecution. For example, promotional decisions should take into account community engagement; defendants' and victims' perceptions of fair treatment; and time spent promoting efforts to advance alternatives to incarceration, deflection from the criminal justice system, and racial equity.

Additionally, chief prosecutors should recognize staff in office meetings, officewide communications, and public settings for demonstrating these types of efforts, while also moving away from trial "war stories" and pats on the back for winning cases. Instead, chief prosecutors should highlight work that their staff does to promote a fair, measured, and just system. Supervisors should also regularly remind their teams about their priorities and values, stress that performance will be regularly reviewed, and that these metrics will serve as bases for course correction as needed.

11.6 Implementation of New Performance Measures: Melding Data with Policy

Performance measures and metrics merely provide a place to start the conversation and the work, not the work itself. They are a diagnostic tool and should be seen as a foundation for change. It's important to recognize that performance measures can play a critical role in driving incentives, yet offices still need to roll up their sleeves to implement changes once the performance measures point out where a change in course is necessary.

Realistically, it is difficult to implement performance measures, track them, and continually adjust for how the staff is or is not inputting information into the case management system. The Urban Institute recently surveyed 158 prosecutor's offices of varying sizes to determine if and how prosecutors use data in informing their decision-making. The report found that most prosecutor's offices collect data on screening, alternative approaches, or sentencing, and almost all use some kind of electronic case management system. However, the report also found that many offices either did not have the resources or expertise to use data more extensively (Olsen et al. 2018). And overall, less than half of even large and medium-sized offices currently use data-driven management systems to track staff performance (Olsen et al. 2018).

Prosecutor's offices need to invest in critical infrastructure such as case management systems and software that allows for tracking of court-based work and day-to-day decision-making by the staff. Offices need to hire those with specializations in implementing case-management systems for large public agencies.

Offices that have started to pilot new measures commonly work with outside consultants to troubleshoot and then plan the rollout of tracking these metrics. For example, as noted earlier, researchers at the Florida International University (FIU) and Loyola University Chicago are implementing a research and policy project with four prosecutor's offices in Chicago, Jacksonville, Milwaukee, and Tampa to assist these offices to become more data-driven and evidence-based.

Additionally, smaller offices such as those with twenty-five attorneys or fewer may face their own challenges in implementing new metrics. It is expensive, time-consuming, and often not something within their capacity to implement. Yet small or mid-sized offices should look at implementing some of the measures detailed in this report and can create less complex dashboards to track progress.

11.7 Conclusion

Crafting new performance measures for prosecutor's offices is challenging work. It will require strong resolve and assistance from external partners.

While creating more nuanced metrics may seem outside the purview of the work that prosecutors have traditionally done, reform-minded prosecutors have a unique opportunity to push the envelope and spearhead a new way of holding themselves and their offices accountable to their communities. Some of these measures may indicate that diversionary programs run by prosecutors are not being robustly utilized or seeing the success rates that they hoped for, while other measures may indicate inherent biases within their offices that need to be addressed. Yet these markers should not be deemed failures by the prosecutors or the communities who elected them. Offices and communities should view these metrics through a rubric of change, as the public and criminal justice leaders work together to create more equitable systems.

Notes

1. This quote is usually attributed to management expert Peter Drucker. See generally Drucker Institute n.d. There is consensus among experts around the benefits of performance measurement to achieve results. For example, Kaplan and Norton (2004) advocate for incorporation of outcome-based performance measurements into strategic planning. Managing by results receives attention in many other sources (Kaplan and Norton 1996; Management By Objectives 2009; Melkers and Willoughby 2005).
2. Controversy arose in 2010 when secret recordings revealed that NYPD captains were imposing ticket-writing quotas on officers and possibly manipulating crime statistics to meet data-driven goals (Baker and Rivera 2010).
3. For example, a 1972 report from the Dallas Police Department found that "[i]n the past, performance evaluation in the police department has been a largely meaningless biannual exercise in numerically grading employees with little thought to the true purpose of performance evaluation" (Oettmeier and Wycoff 1994, 21).
4. Oettmeier and Wycoff (1994) discuss different community engagement strategies and performance measurement systems that police departments around the country considered.
5. Performance management is a public exercise done at the executive and team levels and is about decision-making—it is a non-punitive exercise focused on learning and improvement (the data collected through this process are also used as communications tools). Individual performance evaluation, in contrast, is a confidential process used to develop employees. It can (and should be) punitive at times.
6. Of particular concern is Campbell's Law, a premise developed by social psychologist Donald Campbell, which states that "the more any quantitative social indicator is used for social decision-making, the more subject it will be to corruption pressures and the more apt it will be to distort and corrupt the social processes it is intended to monitor" (Campbell 1979, 85). This phenomenon occurs in education, health care, and other fields. As such, those designing prosecutorial performance measures must discern what sorts of behaviors they might incentivize, whether those are actually the intended goals, and if not, how to adjust the measure accordingly.
7. Gershowitz (2019) argues that prosecutors should have the authority to approve or reject all warrantless arrests. Beyond spending unnecessary judicial resources on these arrests, arrestees face significant harm in the form of the permanent existence of arrest records, loss of employment due to inability to post bail, wrongful convictions, immigration issues, and emotional trauma.

8. The only other non-tribal court known to use tribal court practices this way is the community court in Red Hook, New York. Unlike Red Hook, which refers cases to an internal court-annexed program, the WCPC is institutionalized within the state system.
9. Alexander (2012, 16) puts it this way: "The fact that more than half of the young black men in many large American cities are currently under the control of the criminal justice system (or saddled with criminal records) is not—as many argue—just a symptom of poverty or poor choices, but rather evidence of a new racial caste system at work." Similar observations appear throughout the social science literature (Greenwald and Krieger 2006, 966 ("[I]mplicit race bias is pervasive and is associated with discrimination against African Americans"); Richardson 2012, 1145 (arguing that "[i]mplicit social cognition research demonstrates that implicit biases can affect whether police interpret an individual's ambiguous behaviors as suspicious")).
10. See Blinder 2018 ("[A]lthough law enforcement officials have traditionally opposed such measures for an array of reasons . . . a growing number of them have begun to recognize that criminal records can be enduring obstacles to self-sufficiency and even help trap people in cycles of crime"); King 2018 ("[S]ome effective re-entry programs have failed to attract more candidates due to rewards and incentives of the program that are minor compared with the major effort required of re-entering Philadelphians. Effective re-entry programs prevent crime and should apply to more re-entering Philadelphians").
11. "The Wichita Bar Association's Clean Slate Day, held on March 4, 2016, allowed hundreds of people to obtain expungements at no cost."
12. "Those who successfully complete the program can avoid the life-altering consequences of a felony conviction when the District Attorney consents to the dismissal of the felony charge in the interest of justice."
13. An empirical study by Sonja Starr and J. J. Prescott shows that setting aside an individual's record of conviction is associated with "a significant increase in employment and average wages," and with a low recidivism rate (Prescott and Starr 2019).

References

Albany County District Attorney's Office. n.d. "Reclamation." Accessed March 14, 2020. http://www.cleanslate.albanycountyda.com/redirection.

Alexander, Michelle. 2012. *The New Jim Crow: Mass Incarceration in the Age of Colorblindness.* New York: The New Press.

Alliance for Safety and Justice (ASJ). 2016. *Crime Survivors Speak: The First-Ever National Survey of Victims' Views on Safety and Justice.*

Alpert, Geoffrey, and Mark H. Moore. 1993. "Measuring Police Performance in the New Paradigm of Policing." In *Performance Measures for the Criminal Justice System*, 108–141. Washington, D.C.: Bureau of Justice Statistics.

American Civil Liberties Union (ACLU). 2013. *The War on Marijuana in Black and White.*

American Civil Liberties Union (ACLU). 2017. *Smart Justice Campaign Polling on Americans' Attitudes on Criminal Justice.*

Arnold Ventures. n.d. "Pretrial Justice." Our Work. Accessed March 14, 2020. https://www.arnoldventures.org/work/pretrial-justice/.

Baker, Al, and Ray Rivera. 2010. "Secret Tape Has Police Pressing Ticket Quotas." *New York Times*, September 9, 2010.

Bazelon, Emily, and Miriam Krinsky. 2018. "There's a Wave of New Prosecutors. And They Mean Justice." *New York Times*, December 11, 2018.

Becton, Diana. 2019. "Immigration Policy." Office of the District Attorney Contra Costa County. Last modified May 8, 2019. https://www.contracosta.ca.gov/DocumentCenter/View/60282/Contra-Costa-DA-Immigration-Policy-2019-PDF.

Bibas, Stephanos. 2009. "Rewarding Prosecutors for Performance." *Ohio State Journal of Criminal Law* 6(2): 441–452.

Blinder, Alan. 2018. "Convicts Seeking to Clear Their Records Find More Prosecutors Willing to Help." *New York Times*, October 7, 2018.

Blizzard, Robert. 2018. *Key Findings from a National Survey of 800 Registered Voters*. Justice Action Network. January 25, 2018.

Borden, Tess. 2016. *Every 25 Seconds: The Human Toll of Criminalizing Drug Use in the United States*. Human Rights Watch.

Boylan, Richard T. 2005. "What Do Prosecutors Maximize? Evidence from the Careers of U.S. Attorneys." *American Law & Economics Review* 7(2): 379–403.

Brooklyn District Attorney's Office (BDA). n.d. "Begin Again Continues in 2018." Accessed March 14, 2020. https://web.archive.org/web/20200812115943/http://brooklynda.org/begin-again/.

Brooklyn District Attorney's Office (BDA). 2017. "Acting Brooklyn District Attorney Eric Gonzalez Announces New Policy Regarding Handling of Cases against Non-Citizen Defendants." Press Release. Last modified April 24, 2017.

Brooklyn District Attorney's Office (BDA). 2018. "DA Eric Gonzalez Announces Justice 2020 Initiative." Press Release. Last modified January 24, 2018.

Butts, Jeffrey A., and Vincent Schiraldi. 2018. *Recidivism Reconsidered: Preserving the Community Justice Mission of Community Corrections*. Papers from the Executive Session on Community Corrections. Last modified March 2018.

Campbell, Donald T. 1979. "Assessing the Impact of Planned Social Change." *Evaluation and Program Planning* 2(1): 67–90.

Carson, E. Ann. 2015. *Prisoners in 2014*. Washington, D.C.: Bureau of Justice Statistics.

Center on the Administration of Criminal Law, New York University School of Law. 2012. *Establishing Conviction Integrity Programs in Prosecutors' Offices*.

Chettiar, Inimai M., Lauren-Brooke Eisen, Nicole Fortier, and Timothy Ross. 2013. *Reforming Funding to Reduce Mass Incarceration*. Brennan Center for Justice.

Ciaramella, C. J. 2018. "A Public Defender Is Shaking Up the Race for San Diego D.A." *Reason*, May 16, 2018.

Collateral Consequences Resource Center. 2018. "Michigan Set-Asides Found to Increase Wages and Reduce Recidivism." Last modified February 27, 2018.

Connolly, Christopher. 2018. "National Advocacy Groups Back Candidates to Challenge Local Prosecutors." *NPR*, April 10, 2018.

Creuzot, John. 2019. "To the People of Dallas County." Dallas County District Attorney's Office.

DeKalb County Prosecuting Attorney's Office. n.d. "Survey." Accessed April 3, 2019. https://web.archive.org/web/20191022081013/http://www.dekalbcountyprosecutor.com/survey.html.

Dewan, Shaila, and Andrew W. Lehren. 2016. "After a Crime, the Price of a Second Chance." *New York Times*, December 12, 2016.

Dougherty, Michael. 2018. "Improving the Justice System's Response to Mental Health Issues." *Times-Call*, June 29, 2018.

Drucker Institute. n.d. "About Peter Drucker." Accessed March 14, 2020. https://www.drucker.institute/perspective/about-peter-drucker/.
Drug Policy Alliance. n.d. "Race and the Drug War." Accessed March 14, 2020. http://www.drugpolicy.org/issues/race-and-drug-war.
Dumke, Mick. 2015. "Is State's Attorney Anita Alvarez Protecting Public Safety—Or an Obstacle to Justice?" *Chicago Reader*, June 15, 2015.
Eisen, Lauren-Brooke, Nicole Z. Fortier, and Inimai M. Chettiar. 2014. *Federal Prosecution for the 21st Century*. Brennan Center for Justice.
Ellis, Amy. 2018. "MacArthur Foundation Awards FIU $1.7 Million to Study Prosecutor Behavior." *FIU News*, March 9, 2018.
Fair and Just Prosecution (FJP). n.d. "Our Work and Vision." Accessed March 14, 2020. https://fairandjustprosecution.org/about-fjp/our-work-and-vision/.
Fair and Just Prosecution (FJP). 2017a. *Building Community Trust Procedural Justice: Enhancing the Legitimacy of the Justice System*.
Fair and Just Prosecution (FJP). 2017b. *Conviction Integrity Units and Internal Accountability Mechanisms*.
Fair and Just Prosecution (FJP). 2018. *21 Principles for the 21st Century Prosecutor*.
Federal Bureau of Investigation (FBI). 2010. "Crime in the United States."
Federal Bureau of Investigation (FBI). 2017. "Crime in the United States."
Friedman, Matthew, Ames C. Grawert, and James Cullen. 2017. *Crime Trends: 1990–2016*. Brennan Center for Justice.
Gass, Henry. 2017. "Meet a New Breed of Prosecutor." *Christian Science Monitor*, July 17, 2017.
Gershowitz, Adam. 2019. "Justice on the Line: Prosecutorial Screening Before Arrest." *University of Illinois Law Review* 2019(3): 833–872.
Gommes, Trimmel. 2018. "Florida Lawmakers Push Bill to Limit Children Tried in Adult Court." *Orlando Weekly*, February 27, 2018.
Greenwald, Anthony G., and Linda Hamilton Krieger. 2006. "Implicit Bias: Scientific Foundations." *California Law Review* 94(4): 945–968.
Hotaling, Gerald T., Eve S. Buzawa, Janine Zweig, Martha R. Burt, and Ashley Van Ness. 2006. "Victim Satisfaction with the Criminal Justice System." *National Institute of Justice Journal*, no. 253 (January): 16–18.
Jennings, Nicole. 2018. "Prosecutor Dan Satterberg Says LEAD Program Expansion Will Get People off Drugs." *KIRO Radio*, September 12, 2018.
Klingele, Cecelia M. 2019. "Measuring Change: From Rates of Recidivism to Markers of Desistance." *Journal of Criminal Law and Criminology* 109(4): 769–817.
Kaplan, Robert S., and David P. Norton. 1996. *The Balanced Scorecard: Translating Strategy into Action*. Cambridge, MA: Harvard Business Review Press.
Kaplan, Robert S., and David P. Norton. 2004. *Strategy Maps: Converting Intangible Assets into Tangible Outcomes*. Cambridge, MA: Harvard Business School Publishing Corporation.
King, Shaun. 2018. "Philadelphia DA Larry Krasner Promised a Criminal Justice Revolution. He's Exceeding Expectations." *The Intercept*, March 20, 2018.
Krinsky, Miriam A. 2017. "Promoting Integrity in Conviction Integrity Review." *Huffington Post*, November 6, 2017.
Kutateladze, Besiki, Ryan Meldrum, Rebecca Richardson, Don Stemen, and Elizabeth Webster. 2018. *Prosecutorial Attitudes, Perspectives, and Priorities: Insights from the Inside*. Florida International University and Loyola University Chicago.
Kutateladze, Besiki, Whitney Tymas, and Mary Crowley. 2014. *Race and Prosecution in Manhattan*. Vera Institute of Justice.

Law Enforcement Assisted Diversion (LEAD). n.d. "About LEAD." Accessed March 14, 2020. http://leadkingcounty.org/about/.

Lewis, Michael. 2003. *Moneyball: The Art of Winning an Unfair Game*. New York: W. W. Norton.

Loebler, Rolf, and Marc LeBlanc. 1990. "Toward a Developmental Criminology." *Crime and Justice* 12: 375–474.

Lozano, Alicia Victoria. 2018. "Philadelphia District Attorney Larry Krasner Ends Cash Bail for Low-Level Offenses." *NBC 10 Philadelphia*, March 19, 2018.

Maguire, Edward R. 2003. "Measuring the Performance of Law Enforcement Agencies." *CALEA Update Magazine* 83.

"Management by Objectives." 2009. *The Economist*, October 21, 2009.

Manhattan District Attorney's Office. 2014. "DA Vance and Vera Institute of Justice Announce The Release of Study Examining Racial Disparities in The Manhattan Criminal Justice System."

Marin County Probation Department. n.d. *Marin County Restorative Justice Program*. Accessed March 14, 2020. https://www.marincounty.org/-/media/files/departments/pb/documents/rj-program_brochure.pdf?la=en.

Melkers, Julia, and Katherine Willoughby. 2005. "Models of Performance-Measurement Use in Local Governments: Understanding Budgeting, Communication, and Lasting Effects." *Public Administration Review* 65(2): 180–190.

Mento, Tarryn. 2018. "Marin, San Diego Counties Work to Keep Offenders from Prosecution Through Restorative Justice." *KPBS*, August 30, 2018.

Miller, Justin. 2018. "The New Reformer DAs." *The American Prospect*, January 2, 2018.

Moraff, Christopher. 2018. "New Philadelphia DA Larry Krasner Hits Reset on the Office's Troubled Conviction Review Unit." *The Appeal*, February 15, 2018.

National Institute of Justice. 2009. "Past Executive Session on Policing."

Oettmeier, Timothy N., and Mary Ann Wycoff. 1994. "Police Performance in the Nineties: Practitioner Perspectives." *American Journal of Police* 13(2): 21–50.

Office of the San Francisco District Attorney (SFDA). n.d. "Partnering with San Quentin: The SFDA/San Quentin News Forum." Accessed March 14, 2020. https://web.archive.org/web/20200812084557/https://sfdistrictattorney.org/partnering-san-quentin-sfdasan-quentin-news-forum.

Office of the San Francisco District Attorney (SFDA). n.d. *Report on the Formerly Incarcerated Advisory (FIA) Board: The Inspiration, Inception, and Impact*. https://web.archive.org/web/20191114034913/https://sfdistrictattorney.org/sites/default/files/Formerly%20Incarcerated%20Advisory%20Board%20Report_1.pdf.

Office of the San Francisco District Attorney (SFDA). 2018. "DA Gascón Teams Up with Code for America to Automatically Reduce Eligible Marijuana Convictions in San Francisco & Beyond." Press Release.

Office of the State's Attorney for Baltimore City. 2017. "States Attorney Marilyn Mosby Instructs Her Office to Strongly Consider Prosecutorial Discretion for Cases Involving Immigrant Defendants, Witnesses, and Victims." Press Release.

Oliva, Courtney. 2018. "Disrupting and Re-imagining the Role of Prosecutors: A New Focus on Re-entry and Rehabilitation." *The Appeal*, January 5, 2018.

Olsen, Robin, Leigh Courtney, Chloe Warnberg, and Julie Samuels. 2018. *Collecting and Using Data for Prosecutorial Decisionmaking*. Urban Institute.

Ouss, Aurélie, and Megan T. Stevenson. 2019. "Bail, Jail, and Pretrial Misconduct: The Influence of Prosecutors." George Mason Legal Studies Research Paper No. LS 19-08.

Ouziel, Lauren. 2017. "Ambition and Fruition in Federal Criminal Law: A Case Study." *Virginia Law Review* 103(6): 1077–1140.

Pantazi, Andrew. 2018. "In a Florida First, Jacksonville's State Attorney Hired Someone to Exonerate Inmates." *The Florida Times-Union*, March 1, 2018.

Portsmouth Commonwealth's Attorney. n.d. "Ctrl+Alt+Del Program." Accessed March 14, 2020. https://www.portsmouthcwa.com/ctrlaltdel-program/.

Prescott, J. J., and Sonja B. Starr. 2019. "Expungement of Criminal Convictions: An Empirical Study." U of Michigan Law & Econ Research Paper No. 19-001.

Racine, Karl A. 2017. *In the Public Interest: Attorney General's Annual Report*. Office of the Attorney General for the District of Columbia.

Richardson, L. Song. 2012. "Police Efficiency and the Fourth Amendment." *Indiana Law Journal* 87(3): 1143–1182.

Rios, Simón. 2019. "DAs Join Lawsuit That Seeks to Bar ICE Arrests at Local Courthouses." *WBUR News*, April 29, 2019.

Robles, Frances. 2017. "5 Prosecutors with a Fresh Approach." *New York Times*, March 30, 2017.

Rollins, Rachael. n.d.a. "Charges to Be Declined." Accessed April 2, 2019. https://rollins4da.com/policy/charges-to-be-declined/.

Rollins, Rachael. n.d.b. "Policy." Accessed April 2, 2019. https://rollins4da.com/policy/.

Rosen, Jeff. 2011. "Memo: Collateral Consequences." Office of the Santa Clara County District Attorney.

Roth, Alisa. 2015. "In a Church Basement, Chipping Away at a Mountain of Minor Crime Warrants." *NPR*, September 13, 2015.

Ryan, Kate. 2017. "Collateral Consequences: Brooklyn DA Seeks to Protect Immigrant Defendants from Deportation." *WNYC*, December 12, 2017.

Sago, Renata. 2017. "Charging Youths As Adults Can Be a 'Cruel Wake-Up Call.' Is There Another Way?" *NPR*, August 15, 2017.

Satterberg, Dan. 2013a. "Keeping Kids in School Is the Best Crime Prevention Policy." *Bellevue Reporter*, December 3, 2013.

Satterberg, Dan. 2013b. "Truancy Prevention Means Crime Prevention." *Federal Way Mirror*, November 9, 2013.

Satterberg, Dan, and Miriam Krinsky. 2017. "Prospective Winds of Change." *Huffington Post*, June 7, 2017.

Schwers, Kaitlyn, and Tony Rizzo. 2018. "Wyandotte Co. DA to Create New Unit for Reviewing Claims of Wrongful Convictions." *The Kansas City Star*, August 31, 2018.

Shane, Jon M. 2008. "Developing a Police Performance Measurement System." *FBI Law Enforcement Bulletin* 77(9): 8–18.

Shane, Jon M. 2010. "Performance Management in Police Agencies: A Conceptual Framework." *Policing: An International Journal of Police Strategies & Management* 33(1): 6–29.

Sklansky, David Alan. 2018. "The Problems with Prosecutors." *Annual Review of Criminology* 1: 451–469.

Snohomish County. n.d. "Victim Satisfaction Survey." Accessed March 14, 2020. https://snohomishcountywa.gov/FormCenter/Prosecuting-Attorneys-Office-53/Victim-Satisfaction-survey-340.

Sparrow, Malcolm K. 2015. *Measuring Performance in a Modern Police Organization*. Harvard Kennedy School and the National Institute of Justice.

Subramanian, Ram, Ruth Delaney, Stephen Roberts, Nancy Fishman, and Peggy McGarry. 2015. *Incarceration's Front Door: The Misuse of Jails in America*. Vera Institute of Justice.

The National Registry of Exonerations. 2018. *Exonerations in 2017*.

The National Registry of Exonerations. 2019. "Exonerations in the United States Map." Interactive Data Display. Last modified March 22, 2019. http://www.law.umich.edu/special/exoneration/Pages/Exonerations-in-the-United-States-Map.aspx.

Thompson, Christie. 2017. "How Prosecutors Are Fighting Trump's Deportation Plans." *The Marshall Project*, May 16, 2017.

Tyler, Tom R. 2006. *Why People Obey the Law*. Princeton: Princeton University Press.

United States Census Bureau (USCB). n.d. "Quick Facts, United States."

Vera Institute of Justice. 2014. "A Prosecutor's Guide for Advancing Racial Equity."

Wagner, Peter. 2015. "Jails Matter. But Who Is Listening?" *Prison Policy Initiative*.

Wald, Johanna. 2018. "What's Inside the Prosecutorial 'Black Box'?" *The Crime Report*, March 22, 2018.

Washtenaw County Trial Court. n.d. "Peacemaking." Court Divisions. Accessed March 14, 2020. https://www.washtenaw.org/1168/Peacemaking.

Watkins, Matt. 2018. "Prosecutor Power #1: John Pfaff on Mass Incarceration." *New Thinking*, March 27, 2018.

The Waverly Group-Midwest LLC. 2016. *An Evaluation of the Peacemaking and Parent Partners Initiative*. Washtenaw County Trial Court and Dispute Resolution Center of Washtenaw County.

Wichita Bar Association. n.d. "Expungement Information." Accessed March 14, 2020. https://www.wichitabar.org/page/CleanSlate?&hhsearchterms=%22clean+and+slate%22.

Young, Stephen. 2019. "Dallas DA Creuzot Takes Heat from Council Members over New Theft Policy." *Dallas Observer*, April 23, 2019.

CHAPTER 12

SPECIALIZED UNITS AND VERTICAL PROSECUTION APPROACHES

CASSIA SPOHN

12.1 Introduction

The "organizational shape" (Levine and Wright 2012, 1136) of prosecutors' offices and the procedures used to assign cases to assistant prosecutors vary from one jurisdiction to another.[1] Some jurisdictions assign assistant prosecutors to cases, based on the attorney's expertise, experience and skill; others assign attorneys to courtrooms, either permanently or for a specified period of time. In many large urban jurisdictions, assistant prosecutors are assigned to courtrooms and cases are prosecuted horizontally; different prosecutors handle the case at each stage in the process. In other jurisdictions, cases are prosecuted vertically; each case is assigned to an assistant prosecutor (sometimes after the decision to charge has been made by the felony review unit), who handles the case as it moves up through the system until final disposition.

Many large jurisdictions combine horizontal and vertical prosecution. Whereas routine felony cases are prosecuted horizontally, targeted cases (e.g., homicides, sex offenses, high-level drug trafficking offenses, white-collar crimes, or cases involving career criminals or gang members) are prosecuted vertically. Typically, targeted cases are assigned to specialized units within the prosecutor's office. In some jurisdictions, the prosecutors assigned to the unit handle all of the case decisions, including the decision to file charges; in others, cases are forwarded to the specialized unit only after a decision to file charges has been made.

Legal scholars and social scientists (Cade 2014; Ensslin and Phillips 2013; Long and Wilkinson 2011; Williams 2006; Wright 2017) contend that both vertical prosecution and assignment of cases to specialized units provide several potential advantages in the processing of cases—such as sexual assaults, domestic violence cases, and cases involving gang members—with reluctant or fearful victims and potentially complex and difficult evidentiary issues. Advocates of vertical prosecution, for example, argue that assigning cases to attorneys (rather than assigning attorneys to stages of case disposition) means that the attorney will have continuous contact with the case as it proceeds through the criminal justice system. As a result, the attorney will have a greater understanding of the evidentiary issues surrounding the case, will be able to develop a consistent legal strategy for handling the case, and will be better able to manage the victims and witnesses whose testimony will be needed to obtain a conviction. The use of one attorney with continuous case responsibility also is beneficial to the victim, as it obviates the need for the victim to discuss his or her allegations with a new prosecutor at each stage in the process; this, in turn, is likely to enhance victim trust in the prosecutor and encourage victim cooperation as the case moves forward. Critics of horizontal prosecution also point out that there is a danger that attorneys who handle only one stage of a case—and especially the newly minted prosecutors typically assigned to handle the pre-trial process—will fail to take ownership of the case (Cade 2014). As Wright (2017, 429) noted, in the horizontal prosecution environment, "the young prosecutor is likely to develop tunnel vision, focusing only on her link in the chain instead of the overall context of the case."

As noted above, many large jurisdictions have implemented specialized units dedicated to prosecuting homicide, adult and child sexual assault, and domestic violence cases, as well as cases involving career criminals, gang members, and hate crimes. The logic behind specialized prosecution units is that they "provide prosecutors with concentrated trial experience, focused training, and the opportunity to work closely with law enforcement and community partners" (Long and Wilkinson 2011, 1). Given that specialized prosecution units typically go hand-in-hand with vertical prosecution, it is not surprising that many of the arguments in favor of specialization are similar to those in support of vertical prosecution (Beichner and Spohn 2005; Long and Wilkinson 2011; Parkinson 2016; Pyrooz, Wolfe, and Spohn 2011; Seelinger 2014). Advocates of specialization argue that routine exposure to a certain type of case may result in accumulated experiences that make the specialized attorney better able to assess the strengths and weaknesses of a case, to anticipate and respond to defense tactics, and to communicate more sensitively and confidently with victims (Beichner and Spohn 2005). Prosecutors who specialize also are able to develop the skills needed to address the evidentiary issues they commonly confront in prosecuting the particular type of crime—for example, the fact that sexual assault victims may not have reported the crime promptly or may have engaged in behavior prior to the incident that could be viewed as risky; the fact that domestic violence victims may not show up for court appearances or, if they do, may recant the allegations or minimize the defendant's behavior; and the fact that victims of gang violence may fear retaliation by the defendant (or by his family or friends) if they testify at trial. As Long and Wilkinson (2011) point out, development of these skills is enhanced through focused multi-disciplinary training on investigative techniques, trial strategies, and victim/witness management.

Those who champion use of specialized units also suggest that having a small group of prosecutors responsible for a certain type of criminal case will minimize disparity in decision-making (Loh 1980). An assumption underlying this assertion is that prosecutors assigned to a specialized unit will make decisions using a common frame of reference and a coherent charging strategy (Jacoby 1980),[2] and that problematic cases will be discussed among the members of the unit. As a result, decisions will be made more consistently and with less reliance on legally irrelevant characteristics of the victim, the suspect, or the incident.

Whereas most commentators tout the advantages of specialized prosecution units, Wright (2017, 429) notes that use of these units creates a risk that more experienced prosecutors will be assigned to handle the more serious homicide, sexual assault, and gang violence cases and that more junior prosecutors "will take leftover positions in the lower-risk bureaus, such as misdemeanors or juvenile courts." Although assigning the most experienced prosecutors to handle the most serious cases makes sense from a case management perspective, doing so has the potential to create a two-tiered hierarchical system in which more junior prosecutors feel undervalued and in which turnover among the junior staff is high.

The assumptions underlying vertical prosecution and specialized prosecution units are largely untested.[3] There is no research comparing the efficacy of horizontal and vertical prosecution and very limited research examining the effectiveness of specialized prosecution units. In the sections that follow, the findings of research on specialized units for handling sexual assault cases, domestic violence cases, and gang-related homicide cases are summarized.

12.2 The Effectiveness of Specialized Sexual Assault Units

There is very limited research on the effectiveness of specialized sexual assault units. There is no research evaluating case outcomes before and after the implementation of a specialized prosecutorial unit for handling sexual assault cases[4] and only one study comparing outcomes in two jurisdictions that used different procedures for screening and prosecuting sexual assault cases. There also are studies that provide descriptive data on the operation of specialized sexual assault units and the perceptions of victims and other stakeholders whose cases were assigned to these units.

The most comprehensive examination of specialized sexual assault units is a study that examined sexual assault charging decisions and subsequent case outcomes in Kansas City, Missouri, and Dade County (Miami), Florida (Beichner and Spohn 2005). The Office of the Prosecuting Attorney for the Sixteenth Judicial Circuit of Missouri (Kansas City) had a specialized sex crimes unit that handled all cases of sexual assault involving children and adults, as well as all cases of child homicide. All arrests for these offenses were referred to the Sex Crimes Unit for screening; one of the prosecutors assigned to the unit reviewed the case, decided whether or not to charge the suspect with a felony, and then handled the case as it moved toward trial. By contrast, the Dade County (Miami) State's Attorney's Office had a specialized sex offense unit, but the unit focused almost exclusively on cases involving children. Sexual assaults involving teenagers and adults were prosecuted vertically by the Felony Division, but only after cases were screened by either the Felony Division (first-degree felonies) or the Felony Screening Unit (second- and third-degree felonies).

Reflecting the assumptions that undergird the use of specialized units, Spohn and Beichner (2005) predicted that charging rates would be higher and that legally irrelevant victim characteristics would be less influential (in terms of charging decisions) in Kansas City than in Miami. These hypotheses were not confirmed. In fact, the authors found that the odds of charging were almost identical in the two jurisdictions; prosecutors filed charges in 57.5 percent of all sexual assault cases in Kansas City and in 58.6 percent of all cases in Miami. Moreover, the authors found that the predictors of charging decisions in each jurisdiction reflected a combination of legally relevant indicators of case seriousness and evidentiary strength and legally irrelevant victim characteristics. In Kansas City, for example, charging was less likely if there was information in the case file to suggest that the victim had engaged in some kind of risk-taking behavior at the time of the incident; similarly, in Miami, information that raised questions about the victim's reputation or character led to a reduction in the likelihood of charging. In each jurisdiction, in other words, a legally irrelevant victim characteristic emerged as a significant predictor of prosecutors' decisions to file charges. Noting that prosecutors in both jurisdictions based their charging decisions on the beyond a reasonable doubt standard of proof, Beichner and Spohn (2005, 491) concluded that "prosecutors' charging decisions, like judges' sentencing decisions, are guided by a set of 'focal concerns'" and that, "regardless of whether decisions are made in a specialized unit or not, victim credibility is a real focal concern of the prosecutor in sexual assault cases."

Although Beichner and Spohn's (2005) hypotheses about the impact of a specialized unit were not confirmed, they did find some differences between the two jurisdictions in final case dispositions. Their analysis of fully prosecuted cases revealed that prosecutors in Kansas City, who were operating under what Jacoby (1980) termed a trial sufficiency model of prosecutorial decision-making, were more likely to take cases to trial, whereas prosecutors in Miami, who followed a system efficiency model of decision-making, were more likely to dispose of cases through plea bargaining. Although the authors of this study did not have data on the sentences imposed on convicted offenders, they speculated that the Kansas City Sex Crimes Unit prosecutors' greater willingness to take cases to trial (rather than settle cases through plea bargaining) would translate into harsher sentences in Kansas City than seen in Miami. As they noted (Beichner and Spohn 2005, 488), "Given that cases taken to trial would be less likely to receive sentence discounts associated with plea negotiation, we would expect conviction charges to be more severe and prison sentences to be longer in tried cases than in those cases disposed through plea bargaining."

A second study used a qualitative approach to identify barriers to the successful prosecution of sexual assault during periods of conflict or political unrest in Kenya, Liberia, Sierra Leone, and Uganda (Seelinger 2014). Interviews with relevant stakeholders disclosed that there were many serious challenges to the investigation and prosecution of sexual violence both during and after periods of conflict and unrest in these four countries. The research, which was conducted by the Human Rights Center at the University of California Berkeley School of Law, also revealed that police departments and, to a lesser extent, prosecutor's offices had implemented specialized units to respond to crimes of sexual and gender-based violence. The researchers found that the directors of public prosecution in Kenya and Uganda had identified specific prosecutors "to act as point persons to advise police prosecutors on cases of sexual and gender-based violence" (Seelinger 2014, 556); Kenya also established a team of prosecutors with experience in handling sexual violence cases who could be called upon on an ad hoc basis. The researchers, who viewed the approaches taken in Kenya and Uganda as only a partial remedy to the challenges identified, noted that Liberia adopted a more comprehensive approach to specialized prosecution by establishing a Sexual and Gender-Based Violence Crimes Unit staffed by four prosecutors and by other professionals tasked with ensuring the welfare of survivors.[5] The authors of the study concluded by noting that the specialized units were relatively new and that their effectiveness was unknown; they suggested that the units be subjected to "rigorous assessment" designed to determine whether they are an "effective strategy to improve accountability" (Seelinger 2014, 564).[6]

Two studies, neither of which was designed to assess the effectiveness of specialization, provide descriptive data on the operation of specialized sexual assault units and the decision rules they use in making charging decisions. For example, Frohmann (1991) examined prosecution decisions in two West Coast jurisdictions with specialized units and vertical prosecution of sexual assault cases. Consistent with Albonetti's (1987) assertions that prosecutors attempt to "avoid uncertainty" by only prosecuting cases where the evidence is strong and the victim credible, Frohmann found that prosecutors in these jurisdictions used a number of techniques to explain away or justify decisions to not pursue charges. Most of the explanations focused on the credibility of the victim and the factors that might have motivated the victim to bring charges against the suspect. Even in these specialized units, case convictability—the likelihood that the prosecutor would be able to secure a conviction at trial—was an important determinant of whether to proceed. As Frohmann (1991, 224) concluded, in making charging decisions in sexual assault cases prosecutors "are orienting to a 'downstream' concern with convictability" and "are constantly 'in dialogue with' anticipated defense arguments and anticipated judge and juror responses to case testimony."

A recent study of policing and prosecuting sexual assault in Los Angeles also provided descriptive data on specialized prosecution of sexual assault cases (Spohn and Tellis 2014). The Los Angeles County District Attorney's Office has a specialized unit, the Victim Impact Unit (VIP), that vertically prosecutes sexual assault, stalking, domestic violence, and hate crimes. Each of the eleven branches of the DA's Office utilizes a VIP team approach, with an experienced deputy district attorney designated as the VIP deputy in charge. The goal of the unit is to ensure that sexual assault and family violence cases are adequately prepared and prosecuted. To facilitate this goal, all prosecutors assigned to a VIP team receive enhanced, ongoing training focusing on legal issues, potential defenses, and trial tactics.

Although all of the prosecutors interviewed for their project affirmed that the VIP is philosophically committed to the notion of vertical prosecution, many noted that the case screening process varied by branch and by the deputy in charge of the VIP team (Spohn and Tellis 2014, ch. 2). In some branches case screening and filing decisions were handled by the deputy in charge, in others there was a designated case screener, and in still others all members of the VIP team participated in case screening and made filing decisions. In branches where "everyone screened cases," if the deputy district attorney screening the case decided to file charges, he/she was assigned to prosecute the case. As one respondent noted, "After filing, we own the case so we take the filing decision very seriously." Another respondent expressed a more cynical attitude, noting that "If you file the dog, you walk the dog." In some branches, the VIP deputy in charge screened cases initially and decided whether the case should be rejected; cases that were not rejected outright were assigned to a member of the VIP team, who conducted the pre-filing interview with the victim and decided whether charges should be filed and, if so, what the charges should be. In other branches, the VIP deputy in charge conducted the interview with the victim and made the filing decision; cases that were filed were then assigned to a member of the VIP team for prosecution. At least in this jurisdiction, then, the charging process varied across the branches of the specialized unit.

12.3 The Effectiveness of Specialized Domestic Violence Units

Like sexual assault cases, domestic violence cases present unique evidentiary challenges that impede their investigation and prosecution: the victim typically has a complicated personal and economic relationship with the offender; victims may be unwilling to cooperate and/or may recant their allegations after reconciling with the offender; and victims often fear retaliation by the offender and may be subjected to threats and intimidation if the case proceeds to trial (Belknap, Hartman, and Lippen 2011). To combat these obstacles, many jurisdictions have established specialized police and prosecution units,[7] as well as specialized domestic violence courts. Specialized prosecution units use several strategies to reduce the likelihood of charge dismissal in domestic violence cases: invoking "no-drop" policies that require the state to prosecute the defendant regardless of whether the victim wants to do so (Davis, Smith, and Davies 2001); instituting vertical prosecution from filing through trial; and using evidence-based prosecution, which relies on physical evidence and witness testimony rather than testimony by the victim (Dawson and Dinovitzer 2001).

Although the effectiveness of domestic violence courts has been addressed in a number of studies (Dawson and Dinovitzer 2001; Gover, MacDonald, and Alpert 2003), there is only one study that evaluated a specialized DV prosecution unit. Regocczi and Hubbard (2018) used a quasi-experimental design to evaluate the components of the Cleveland Domestic Violence Project, which began in 1997 with a goal of increasing the number of investigations, charges, and successful prosecutions in domestic violence cases. One of the components evaluated was the specialized domestic violence unit of the City of Cleveland's Prosecutor's Office, which consisted of three prosecutors who reviewed cases presented by detectives, issued misdemeanor or felony charges, and prosecuted misdemeanor cases using evidence-based strategies. Because the Domestic Violence Project was implemented in only three of the five police districts in the City of Cleveland, the authors were able to use a quasi-experimental design to compare the outcomes of cases handled by the Domestic Violence Project to the outcomes of those handled in the districts that were not part of the Project.

The authors of this study found that domestic violence cases were more likely to be investigated by the police in districts with domestic violence units. However, the prosecutor's domestic violence unit was significantly *less* likely to file charges than were prosecutors not associated with the unit. By contrast, there were no differences between the two prosecutorial approaches in three areas: in the likelihood of dismissal after filing, in the likelihood of conviction, or in sentence length. The authors suggested that the lower likelihood of charging for the domestic violence prosecution unit reflected inadequate staffing of the unit. As they noted (Regoeczi and Hubbard 2018, 18), "A significant challenge for the current system in Cleveland is the overwhelming caseloads shouldered by only a handful of DV prosecutors in the Cleveland Prosecutor's Office." The authors pointed out that during the six-month study period, the prosecutor's office reviewed approximately one thousand cases, about half of which resulted in the filing of charges (and, thus, additional work for the prosecutors assigned to the unit). They concluded (18) that "for jurisdictions considering this type of model for handling domestic violence offenses, sufficient staffing will be critical."

12.4 The Effectiveness of Specialized Gang Units

Gang-related crimes—especially violent crimes involving gang members—raise evidentiary issues that make them especially difficult to prosecute. These cases often include multiple offenders, witnesses who are reluctant to cooperate because of intimidation or fear of retaliation, and victims with disreputable backgrounds or unsavory reputations (Genelin and Naiman 1988; Jackson 2004). Other issues in these cases include the need for gang intelligence and knowledgeable experts to testify and for cooperation between juvenile and adult courtroom workgroups (Genelin and

Naiman 1988; Jackson 2004; Johnson, Webster, and Connors 1995; Natapoff 2009). Prosecutors in filed cases also have to worry about proving a gang motive, proving a gang identity, establishing individual criminal liability, and ensuring that witnesses show up to testify (Jackson 2004). As Miethe and McClorkle (2002, 174) pointed out, in gang-related violent crimes, "victim and witness problems are so acute that many prosecutors are more willing to use a current arrest to revoke a previous probation . . . than to initiate prosecution on a new charge."

To address these problems, district attorney's offices throughout the United States have developed specialized units to prosecute gang-related cases (Johnson et al. 1995). One such unit was Operation Hardcore (now known as the Hardcore Gang Investigations Unit), established by the Los Angeles County District Attorney's Office in 1979, which was tasked with prosecuting serious violent crimes involving hardcore gang members. Prosecutors assigned to the unit were given a reduced caseload and augmented investigative support, and all cases were prosecuted vertically. An early evaluation of Operation Hardcore used an interrupted time series design to compare outcomes before and after the implementation of the specialization unit (Dahmann 1983). This study found that Operation Hardcore resulted in a significant decrease in dismissals, a significant increase in convictions, and a significant increase in the rate of incarceration.

Pyrooz, Wolfe, and Spohn (2011) also evaluated Operation Hardcore, but with a focus on prosecutors' charging decisions in gang-related homicide cases. The study was designed to identify the victim, suspect, and incident characteristics that affected the decision to reject charges in these cases and to determine whether the likelihood of charge rejection was lower for gang-related cases prosecuted by the specialized unit than for similar cases prosecuted by the non-specialized unit. The authors estimated a multivariate model that included victim characteristics, suspect characteristics, incident characteristics, and whether the case was evaluated by the specialized unit. They found that the likelihood of charge rejection was higher if the suspect was a female or if the suspect was gang-affiliated, but the odds of charge rejection were lower for cases with more victims. Importantly, cases evaluated by the non-specialized unit had substantially higher odds of charge rejection than cases evaluated by the specialized unit. In fact, cases screened by the non-specialized unit were more than four times more likely than those screened by the specialized unit to be rejected for prosecution. These results led the authors to conclude (Pyrooz et al. 2011, 17) that "the specialized unit was effective in moving precarious gang homicide cases to the next stage of adjudication."

12.5 Conclusion

Legal scholars and social scientists maintain that there are several advantages to processing certain types of cases—for example, sexual assault, domestic violence, and crimes involving career criminals or gang members—using vertical prosecution and a specialized prosecution unit. The argument is that these types of cases involve complex evidentiary issues and problems with victim and witness management that are more effectively addressed by a specialized unit in which prosecutors have specialized training and continuous case responsibility. Advocates of specialized prosecution also contend that the approach has advantages for victims, who are not required to discuss the case anew with multiple attorneys at each stage of the process and who therefore may be more willing to cooperate as the case moves forward. Prosecutors working in specialized units also accumulate experience and skills in handling a particular type of case. This facilitates case assessment, enhances prosecutors' ability to anticipate and respond to defense tactics, and improves rapport with victims and witnesses.

The assumptions that undergird the use of vertical prosecution and specialized units are largely untested; there is no research comparing the effectiveness of vertical and horizontal prosecution and only limited research examining specialized units. Moreover, the research that has been conducted reveals that there are very few differences in the outcomes of cases prosecuted by attorneys assigned to specialized units and those prosecuted by attorneys not assigned to specialized units. Although one study found that the charging rate in gang-related homicides prosecuted by the specialized unit was substantially higher than the rate for cases prosecuted by the non-specialized unit (Pyrooz et al. 2011), other research found either that there were no differences in the likelihood that charges would be filed (Beichner and Spohn 2005) or that the charging rate for the specialized unit was lower than the rate for the non-specialized unit (Regoczi and Hubbard 2018). These results raise questions about the assumptions regarding the benefits of specialized prosecution units.

One plausible explanation for the finding that specialized units are not more effective than traditional prosecution relates to prosecutors' concerns with convictability (Albonetti 1987) and their belief that charges should not be filed unless they have both proof beyond a reasonable doubt and a reasonable likelihood of conviction. Although it is possible that prosecutors with specialized training and substantial experience handling a particular type of case will be better able to develop evidence, to encourage victims and witnesses to cooperate, and to anticipate defense strategies, like prosecutors in non-specialized units they will nonetheless be looking for evidence that meets the proof beyond a reasonable doubt standard. As Loh (1980, 603) observed more than three decades ago:

> Convictability...is a standard that does not leave much room for the exercise of discretion. So long as the fact patterns of the complainants are essentially the same, and prosecutors rely on these facts to the same extent before and after the reform, the filing outcome can be expected to stay the same.

If, in other words, all prosecutors evaluate cases using a trial sufficiency standard, the implementation of a specialized unit will not necessarily lead to changes in charging practices.

A second interrelated explanation for why the results of research do not reflect the predicted benefits of specialization is that the specialized unit may be largely symbolic in form and function (Edelman 1964). That is, the specialized unit may serve as only a symbolic representation of reform and may not lead to instrumental changes in policies, practices, and outcomes. In fact, the literature on legal impact, which abounds with examples of "the remarkable capacity of criminal courts to adjust to and effectively thwart reforms" (Eisenstein, Flemming, and Nardulli 1988, 296), would lead us to predict that specialized prosecution units would have only limited effects on charging decisions and other case outcomes (see Spohn and Horney's (1992) study of the rape reform movement).

Given the limited amount of research conducted to date, it would be inappropriate to conclude definitively that specialized prosecution units are not more effective than traditional prosecution. As noted above, there is no research comparing case outcomes in offices that use vertical rather than horizontal prosecution and the research on specialized units is both dated and methodologically unsophisticated. There is a need for additional research using experimental or quasi-experimental designs to compare various types of case outcomes before and after changes in prosecutorial policies and practices. Also needed is qualitative research examining the structure, operation, and decision rules of specialized prosecution units and the perceptions of victims, witnesses, and others whose cases are handled by specialized and non-specialized units.

NOTES

1. It is important to point out that most prosecutors' offices are located in small or medium-sized jurisdictions, where specialized units are unlikely to be found. According to the Bureau of Justice Statistics (2011), in 2007 there were about two thousand full-time prosecutors' offices; of these, only forty-three were located in jurisdictions with a population of one million or more and only 211 were located in jurisdictions with a population of 250,000 to 999,999. Although offices in the largest jurisdictions had an average of 187 assistant prosecutors, those in the smallest jurisdictions averaged only three assistant prosecutors.
2. Jacoby and her colleagues (Jacoby 1980; Mellon, Jacoby, and Brewer 1981) assert that prosecutorial decision-making is not a product of individual exercises in discretion, but instead is influenced by factors over which the individual prosecutor has little if any control. More specifically, these authors emphasize the importance of examining case outcomes in the context of departmental policy. They suggest that prosecutors' offices operate within one of four distinct types of charging policies: legal sufficiency, system efficiency, defendant rehabilitation, and trial sufficiency. Prosecutors operating under the legal sufficiency policy accept all cases in which the elements of the crime are present; dispositional patterns include high rates of cases accepted for prosecution and high dismissal rates at preliminary hearings. System efficiency policy, which emphasizes case screening as a way of decreasing office workload, is characterized by two distinctive dispositional patterns: high levels of referrals to diversionary programs and overcharging for the purposes of enhancing plea bargaining power. Defendant rehabilitation policy reflects the notion that the majority of defendants should not be processed through the criminal justice system; the focus of this policy is on early diversion of defendants and the use of

non-criminal justice alternatives. Trial sufficiency policy, which is congruous with the contention that prosecutors' decisions reflect concerns with convictability (Albonetti 1987; Frohmann 1991, 1997), is characterized by a high rejection rate during the initial screening of cases and a high trial conviction rate.

3. Most of the research that does exist is descriptive and/or dated (see Barlow and Layman 1977; Berliner 1981; Blakey, Goldstock, and Rogovin 1978; Chaiken and Chaiken 1990; Greenwood 1980; Johnson, Webster, and Connors 1995; Levine 2005; Los Angeles County Office of the District Attorney 1983).
4. LaFree (1981, 1989) examined sexual assault case processing decisions before and after the creation of a specialized sex offenses unit in the Indianapolis Police Department. Although he found differences in attitudes toward rape and rape victims between officers assigned to this unit and officers assigned to the homicide and robbery unit, he did not find that arrest and felony filing rates increased following the creation of the unit. He also found little support for the hypothesis that extralegal variables would have a reduced effect on decision-making in the post-reform period. LaFree (1989, 88) concluded that "some factors are difficult to change no matter how enlightened or motivated the public official. Arrest and felony screening require elements, such as a reasonable suspect and a victim willing to testify, that are often beyond the control of the police."
5. The research team also found that Liberia established a dedicated court for adjudication of sexual and gender-based violence cases and that Sierra Leone had dedicated "Saturday Courts" for handling these cases.
6. There is some evidence that victims and other participants in the criminal justice system have positive attitudes toward specialized prosecution units (see Parkinson 2016). For example, an evaluation of the Specialist Sexual Offences Unit in Victoria, Australia, found that victims, police, and other professionals generally believed that the unit had been effective in reducing trauma for survivors of sexual assault and enhancing the quality of sexual assault prosecutions (Success Works 2011).
7. A recent study by the Bureau of Justice Statistics (Reaves 2017) found that about half of all state and local law enforcement agencies with one hundred or more sworn personnel operated a full-time domestic violence unit in 2013. There are no estimates of the number of prosecutor's offices that have established domestic violence units.

References

Albonetti, Celeste A. 1987. "Prosecutorial Discretion: The Effects of Uncertainty." *Law & Society Review* 21(2): 291–313.

Barlow, S. R., and M. F. Layman. 1977. *Pierce County Business Fraud/Stolen Paper Property Unit*. (NCJRS No. 41646). Unpublished paper. http://www.ncjrs.gov/App/publications/abstract.aspx?ID=41646.

Beichner, Dawn, and Cassia Spohn. 2005. "Prosecutorial Charging Decisions in Sexual Assault Cases: Examining the Impact of a Specialized Prosecution Unit." *Criminal Justice Policy Review* 16(4): 461–498.

Belknap, Joanne, Jennifer L. Hartman, and Victoria L. Lippen. 2011. "Misdemeanor Domestic Violence Cases in the Courts: A Detailed Description of the Cases." In *Female Victims of Crime: Reality Reconsidered*. Edited by Vanessa Garcia and Janice E. Clifford, 259–279. Upper Saddle River, NJ: Prentice Hall.

Berliner, L. 1981. "King County's Approach to Child Sexual Abuse." In *Innovations in the Prosecution of Child Sexual Assault: A Report to the American Bar Association*. Edited by J. Bulkley, 112–118. Washington, D.C.: National Legal Resource Center for Child Advocacy and Protection.

Blakey, George R., Ronald Goldstock, and Charles H. Rogovin. 1978. *Rackets Bureaus: Investigation and Prosecution of Organized Crime*. NCJRS No. 041953. Washington, D.C.: U.S. Government Printing Office.

Bureau of Justice Statistics. 2011. *Prosecutors in State Courts, 2007*. Washington, D.C.: Bureau of Justice Statistics.

Cade, Jason A. 2014. "The Challenge of Seeing Justice Done in Removal Proceedings." *Tulane Law Review* 89(1): 1–78.

Chaiken, Marcia R., and Jan M. Chaiken. 1990. *Redefining the Career Criminal: Priority Prosecution of High-Rate Dangerous Offenders*. Washington, D.C.: U.S. Department of Justice.

Dahmann, Judith. 1983. *Final Report Evaluation of Operation Hardcore: A Prosecutorial Response to Violent Gang Criminality*. NIJ 19160. Washington, D.C.: National Institute of Justice.

Davis, Robert C., Barbara E. Smith, and Heather J. Davies. 2001. "Effects of No-Drop Prosecution of Domestic Violence upon Conviction Rates." *Justice Research & Policy* 3(2): 1–13.

Dawson, Myrna, and Ronit Dinovitzer. 2001. "Victim Cooperation and the Prosecution of Domestic Violence in a Specialized Court." *Justice Quarterly* 18(3): 593–622.

Edelman, Murray. 1964. *The Symbolic Uses of Politics*. Urbana: University of Illinois Press.

Eisenstein, James, Roy B. Flemming, and Peter F. Nardulli. 1988. *The Contours of Justice: Communities and Their Courts*. Boston: Little, Brown, and Company.

Ensslin, Kelly, and Nicole L. Phillips. 2013. "Best Practices for Investigating and Prosecuting Child Abuse: Applying Lessons Learned from Delaware's Earl Bradley Case." *Widener Law Review* 19(1): 51–72.

Frohmann, Lisa. 1991. "Discrediting Victims' Allegations of Sexual Assault: Prosecutorial Accounts of Case Rejections." *Social Problems* 38(2): 213–226.

Frohmann, Lisa. 1997. "Convictability and Discordant Locales: Reproducing Race, Class, and Gender Ideologies in Prosecutorial Decision-Making." *Law & Society Review* 31(3): 531–555.

Genelin, Michael, and Loren Naiman. 1988. *Prosecuting Gang Homicides*. NIJ 148383. Washington, D.C.: U.S. Department of Justice.

Gover, Angela R., John M. MacDonald, and Geoffrey P. Alpert. 2003. "Combating Domestic Violence: Findings from an Evaluation of a Local Domestic Violence Court." *Criminology & Public Policy* 3(1): 109–132.

Greenwood, Peter W. 1980. "Career Criminal Prosecution: Potential Objectives." *Journal of Criminal Law and Criminology* 71(2): 85–88.

Jackson, Alan. 2004. *Prosecuting Gangs: What Local Prosecutors Need to Know*. Bureau of Justice Assistance Grant 2001-GP-CX-K050. Alexandria, VA: American Prosecutors Research Institute.

Jacoby, Joan E. 1980. *The American Prosecutor: A Search for Identity*. Lexington, MA: Lexington Books.

Johnson, Claire M., Barbara Webster, and Edward Connors. 1995. *Prosecuting Gangs: A National Assessment*. Washington, D.C.: National Institute of Justice.

LaFree, Gary D. 1981. "Official Reactions to Social Problems: Police Decisions in Sexual Assault Cases." *Social Problems* 28(5): 582–594.

LaFree, Gary D. 1989. *Rape and Criminal Justice: The Social Construction of Sexual Assault.* Belmont, CA: Wadsworth.

Levine, Kay L. 2005. "The New Prosecution." *Wake Forest Law Review* 40(4): 1125–1214.

Levine, Kay L., and Ronald F. Wright. 2012. "Prosecution in 3-D." *Journal of Criminal Law & Criminology* 102(4): 1119–1180.

Loh, Wallace D. 1980. "The Impact of Common Law and Rape Reform Statutes on Prosecution: An Empirical Study." *Washington Law Review* 55(3): 543–625.

Long, Jennifer G., and John Wilkinson. 2011. *The Benefits of Specialized Prosecution Units in Domestic and Sexual Violence Cases.* Aequitas Strategies in Brief, Issue 8. Washington, D.C.: Aequitas.

Los Angeles County District Attorney's Office. 1983. *Operation Hardcore (Crime) Evaluation—Los Angeles, 1976–1980.* Los Angeles: Los Angeles County District Attorney's Office.

Mellon, Leonard R., Joan E. Jacoby, and Marion A. Brewer. 1981. "The Prosecutor Constrained by His Environment: A New Look at Discretionary Justice in the United States." *Journal of Criminal Law & Criminology* 72(1): 52–81.

Miethe, Terance D., and Richard C. McCorkle. 2002. "Evaluating Nevada's Antigang Legislation and Gang Prosecution Units." In *Responding to Gangs: Evaluation and Research.* Edited by Winifred L. Reed and Scott H. Decker, 169–195. NCJ 190351. Washington, D.C.: National Institute of Justice.

Natapoff, Alexandra. 2009. *Snitching: Criminal Informants and the Erosion of American Justice.* New York: New York University Press.

Parkinson, Patrick. 2016. *Specialist Prosecution Units and Courts: A Review of the Literature.* Report for the Royal Commission into Institutional Responses to Child Sexual Abuse. Sydney: Commonwealth of Australia.

Pyrooz, David C., Scott E. Wolfe, and Cassia Spohn. 2011. "Gang-Related Homicide Charging Decisions: The Implementation of a Specialized Prosecution Unit in Los Angeles." *Criminal Justice Policy Review* 22(1): 3–26.

Reaves, Brian A. 2017. *Police Response to Domestic Violence, 2006–2015.* Washington, D.C.: Bureau of Justice Statistics.

Regoeczi, Wendy C., and Dana J. Hubbard. 2018. "The Impact of Specialized Domestic Violence Units on Case Processing." *American Journal of Criminal Justice* 43(3): 570–590.

Seelinger, Kim Thuy. 2014. "Domestic Accountability for Sexual Violence: The Potential of Specialized Units in Kenya, Liberia, Sierra Leone and Uganda." *International Review of the Red Cross* 96 (issue 894): 539–564.

Spohn, Cassia, and Julie Horney. 1992. *Rape Law Reform: A Grassroots Revolution and Its Impact.* New York: Springer US.

Spohn, Cassia, and Katharine Tellis. 2014. *Policing and Prosecuting Sexual Assault: Inside the Criminal Justice System.* Boulder, CO: Lynne Rienner Publishers.

Success Works. 2011. *Sexual Assault Reform Strategy: Final Evaluation Report.* Melbourne: Department of Justice.

Williams, David M. 2006. "Children First: National Model for the Vertical Prosecution of Cases Involving Murdered and Physically Abused Children." *Journal of Aggression, Maltreatment and Trauma* 12(3–4): 131–148.

Wright, Ronald F. 2017. "Reinventing American Prosecution Systems." *Crime and Justice* 46: 395–439.

CHAPTER 13

COURTROOM WORKGROUPS

"A Prosecutor, a Defense Attorney, and a Judge Walk into a Bar..."

MILTON HEUMANN, RICK KAVIN, AND ANU CHUGH

13.1 INTRODUCTION

"COURTROOM workgroups" is a descriptive term that James Eisenstein and Herbert Jacob coined in their influential 1977 study of courts in three American cities (Eisenstein and Jacob 1977). Their study was of a comparative nature and focused on case processing criminal courts in Detroit, Baltimore, and Chicago. The authors defined "courtroom workgroups" as the ongoing relationships among the three main parties in case processing: judges, prosecutors, and defense attorneys. It was deceptively easy, though wrong, to believe that the workgroups inherently *caused* important case outcomes, and indeed, the authors were careful to note that the picture was complex. Additionally, their efforts to explain outcomes based on the workgroup differences depended on the outcome being examined, as well as on a host of external variables (Eisenstein and Jacob 1977, 62–63, 173–287). Nevertheless, it was also easy to understand why some would embrace the explanatory value of courtroom workgroups, for they offered a tempting and parsimonious explanation of the ways that courts operated.

We stress at the outset that simply because "workgroups" are the topic for our chapter, we will not rush to tout the robustness of the concept for *explaining* court dynamics. Rather, we contend that while workgroups are a piece of the puzzle that explains what goes on in local courts, so are a variety of other factors. The workgroups play a role, but they may serve as more of a host entity to deliver other factors to the trial process than as influential entities in their own right. Unraveling these other factors—or at least putting them into the explanatory pot—will be a theme for the chapter.

As we delve into the relationships between the various members of the courtroom workgroup, we note the central role the prosecutor plays. Of course, this varies by jurisdiction, but generally, despite assumptions regarding the strength of a judge's position, it is often the prosecutor who wields the most power among our triumvirate. At all stages of the trial process, it is the prosecutor who is in the driver's seat, and he or she enjoys wide discretion (Hall 2002; Skolnick 1967). Within the constraints of the trial process, the prosecutor possesses some means of regulating the flow of cases to the court (Cole 1970). Prosecutors not only decide the severity, type, and number of charges filed against a defendant (or ultimately whether to charge at all), but also hold much of the leverage for plea bargaining (Alschuler 1968; Heumann 1977). Prosecutors offer recommendations both for pre-trial bail and post-trial sentencing, including whether sentences should run consecutively or concurrently. Prosecutors can choose to be more lenient as well, using their discretion to circumvent mandatory minimum or so-called "three strikes" laws (Bjerk 2005). They may even have the right to determine the court before which a case is heard, as state laws are sometimes also violations of a city ordinance (Cole 1970). Though each of our three major players—the judge, the prosecutor, and the defense attorney—have particular strengths and weaknesses associated with their position in the workgroup, the prosecutor looms large because of these unique powers.

13.2 Methodology

Before the 1970s, political science research on courts overwhelmingly adhered to the approach of law schools. Constitutional law, especially that of the United States, characterized most of the "public law" scholarship. But with the advent of the behavioral revolution in political science, scholars turned their attention to trial courts as well as appellate courts. Simultaneously, they moved from a doctrinal approach to a more empirical one. These changes, in turn, led to a substantial number of studies, both of our criminal courts in general and of more specific criminal court practices. These include (among many others) bail, plea bargaining, sentencing, and the differences between felony and misdemeanor courts.[1] Workgroup research was embedded in this early period of "discovering law in action."

In this chapter, we begin with the vast literature on criminal courts to address the place of workgroups among the myriad factors at play in the court process. We then venture beyond the body of extant research and report the results of our own interviews with informed practitioners in the courts. It was not our intent to interview a random or representative sample from any one jurisdiction. Instead, we opted for a small number of intensive interviews with experienced practitioners from all three roles in courts in several states as well as in the federal system. Generally, the three principal investigators jointly conducted the interviews, allowing for multiple summaries of these interviews and a comparison of our individual impressions from each session. In all, we conducted twelve interviews. In each, we asked the respondents to reflect on workgroup relationships in the past and present. Indeed, our goal was to explore workgroup issues utilizing not just an already extensive trial court literature, but also by incorporating the current perspectives of experienced prosecutors, public defenders or private defense attorneys, and judges.

Notably, we often had to explain the concept of "workgroups," since this descriptive term is seldom used in the courts and has not become a familiar characterization of work patterns to the participants it ostensibly describes. Still, while the term may not reflect actual courtroom jargon, all interviewees were familiar with such relationships. We asked them to speculate about whether, how, and why workgroup structures ought to change in the future. In short, we wanted to infuse and enliven the summary of the literature with new and informed empirical observations from the field. Just as Eisenstein and Jacob warn about the representativeness and generalizability of their own study, we similarly make no claim about the representativeness of our own study (Eisenstein and Jacob 1977, 12–16).

In the sections that follow, we first paint with a broad brush to discuss the accepted working definitions of workgroups. We then raise three concerns and questions about workgroups that were implied in the literature and then highlighted by our interviews. Finally, we conclude with several suggestions for future research and offer observations about workgroups in the grand scale of criminal court case processing. We appreciate that this is an ambitious agenda and that, in some cases, we will be outlining arguments rather than fully developing them. Our goal is to survey the understandings of workgroups from the literature while assessing the implications of insider conceptions about why, how, and to what degree workgroups affect criminal court dispositions. In short, we hope to provide modern insight into an aspect of the courtroom long taken at face value.

13.3 Workgroups: What They Are, Aren't, and Could Be

As noted earlier, "workgroups" is not a term familiar to court personnel. Often, though, as we explained how the term was defined in the literature, our interviewees nodded, cutting us off and demonstrating a clear understanding of the concept as one that concerns the relationships among the central court figures. Eisenstein and Jacob formally defined the workgroup concept in *Felony Justice*, and that definition has subsequently appeared in the academic literature (though rarely in any real-world court):

> In our view, what judges, prosecutors, defense counsel and others do depends heavily on how they interact with one another. None works alone. Rather they are interconnected through an intricate system of countervailing powers. Thus, courtrooms are small but nevertheless complex organizations.
>
> (Eisenstein and Jacob 1977, vi)

Later, others would offer their own similar definitions. Neubauer and Meinhold, for example, describe the courtroom workgroup as representing "a complex network of ongoing social relationships" (Neubauer and Meinhold 2017, 272).

It is important to stress that Eisenstein and Jacob reject a conspiratorial model of these relationships, and we wholeheartedly share in this assessment. In contrast to some earlier arguments that emphasized how the court players necessarily put their own interests ahead of those of the defendants, and worked toward case resolution in an almost conspiratorial fashion, Eisenstein and Jacob instead focus on patterns that reappear in these relationships. Eisenstein and Jacob do not impose a necessarily pejorative or conspiratorial explanation for why these patterns exist or their consequences.[2]

We unpack the workgroup concept by relying on decades of research on criminal courts and on the discussions with our interview respondents. Courtroom workgroups are primarily composed of incumbents of three roles: a judge, a prosecutor, and a public defender or private defense attorney. Others who may participate in proceedings and have impacts on these three main players include bailiffs, prison officials, diversion program officials, and probation officers, though the key players of the workgroup are the core "Big Three"—judges, prosecutors, and defense attorneys, with prosecutors sitting as the first among equals.

Several considerations are necessary to understand the dynamics of any courtroom workgroup. First must be the nature of the day-to-day relationships among the Big Three. Our interviews repeatedly surfaced the assignment of cases (vertical or horizontal) as a major structuring factor. Because this chapter shies away from a focus on any particular state's practices, we discuss "vertical" in the multiple ways it was described in our interviews. In some systems, cases are vertically assigned to prosecutors, and the same prosecutor follows the case from arraignment or grand jury all the way through to trial. This stands in contrast to a horizontal system, in which different prosecutors are responsible for different stages of the case's processing. Similarly, some systems are arranged around "person-to-person" defense models: As with prosecutors, a private defense attorney or public defender sometimes follows a case through all steps of the trial courts. In other systems, different attorneys from the same office are responsible for different stages. There is also a judge-centric model, with one judge responsible for all aspects of a case rather than different judges handling different stages. For example, one set of judges may oversee plea bargains, and if these deals do not materialize, the cases are assigned to other judges for trial.

Further complicating these alternative approaches are the various methods by which a case can be assigned to a judge. In one of the states we studied, two prosecutors and two public defenders are assigned to a particular judge by their respective offices for at least one year, in what is called a "trial team." This system represents the workgroup at its most intimate. Cases are assigned to different judges, and the assignment of prosecutors and defense attorney thus depends on which judge gets the case. The workgroup consists of an ongoing team processing all of the judge's cases (except, of course, for those not represented by a public defender). In other systems, there is no such ongoing assignment to judge. Judges get cases by random assignment, and prosecutors and public defenders follow "their" case to a judge.

Echoing Eisenstein and Jacob's important caveat that their three cities do not represent the total range of variation, we too note that ours is not an exhaustive list of models (Eisenstein and Jacob 1977, 11). The spectrum of the courtroom workgroup model ranges from a permanent and formalized team in some states to a much more fluid arrangement in others. It is also significant that many of our respondents contrasted state systems, particularly the permanent assignment of prosecutors and public defenders to a judge, with the federal system, which never uses such an ongoing formal structure. Even on this single dimension, our interviews revealed, variations are differences in degree, not kind. In the most "separated" system, respondents acknowledged the inevitability of some natural closeness among the three actors and indeed the possibility that the relationships could have some beneficial results. This familiarity is not without a potential downside, which we will discuss shortly. But first, we note the potential benefits one defense attorney ascribes to these close relationships:

> Defendants might think it good if a public defender has a good relationship with a judge, [and] might feel he has insights into what works for the judge.... The reality [is] that you work frequently with the people involved...and it could benefit the client.... (Interview #7)

Delving more deeply into the benefits of such proximity, this attorney discussed at length the many professional functions that courts sponsor and how attorneys frequently attend these conferences at least in part to develop relationships with their workgroup counterparts.

If we probe into this core courtroom workgroup, we see variations in the nature of the actors on each leg of the triad. The most notable differences are on the defense side. Defendants can be represented by public defenders, by private attorneys who may be retained by defendants for a fee (or who are assigned to defendants because of potential conflicts with co-defendants represented by public defenders), and, in some states, by organizations that represent indigents in a way similar to public defender systems. These organizations are typically smaller than the public defender's office and are perceived as providing a more aggressive defense for their clients, though limited funding enables them to represent only a small number of defendants. Prosecutors are more homogeneous, though during our interviews a major distinction emerged between elected and appointed prosecutors. In the United States, forty-five states elect their prosecutors locally; Alaska, Connecticut, Delaware, New Jersey, and Rhode Island, along with the District of Columbia, appoint the prosecutors who lead local offices.

Similar points were raised regarding differences between elected and appointed judges, and also about whether the judges had yet obtained tenure in their position (Interview #3).[3] Methods of judicial selection, however, vary even more widely than those of prosecutors. Data compiled by the National Center for State Courts show that processes of obtaining judgeships in trial courts (and also state courts of appeals and state supreme courts) vary widely across and even within states (National Center for State Courts 2015). These methods include elections (partisan in some jurisdictions and non-partisan in others) as well as gubernatorial appointments (whether unilateral or assisted by a third party such as a nominating committee), while some localities use a combination. Each method has been praised and criticized for reasons too numerous to delve into here, though it is easy to imagine how the pressures and considerations of one means of selection could differ from another.

Other variables can be associated with the interactions of our Big Three courtroom actors. The following are but a few examples. First, career ambitions of each of the actors—promotions they might like to obtain, future job prospects, private practice aspirations, etc.—can affect his or her decision-making process. Relatedly, prior career roles of the actors affect their workgroup interactions, a notion that remains largely unexplored in the literature. For example, how might two judges differ if, before ascending to the bench, one served as a prosecutor and the other a public defender? Or, perhaps more pertinent for this volume, how might a prosecutor who had previously worked as a defense attorney behave differently from one without defense experience (and vice versa)?

The policies of what Eisenstein and Jacob call "sponsoring organizations" can also influence case outcomes. Depending in part on the policies of his or her office, each member of the courtroom workgroup may approach the process with either substantial or narrowly circumscribed discretion. Consider a prosecutor office's policy, for example, that no assistant prosecutor can offer a plea deal in a case in which a gun was involved; or perhaps that of a public defender's office precluding guilty pleas without supervisory approval; or that of a judge whose ability to participate in plea bargaining is forbidden without exception. There are innumerable examples, and we feature but a few to demonstrate that each of these policies could significantly affect workgroup interactions.

Additionally, the goals of the criminal justice system as felt in the courtroom trenches affect the overall process of moving a case through the court. Eisenstein and Jacob write of four such coexisting goals, each no doubt receiving different weights in different courts for different reasons. Their goals: (1) reducing uncertainty; (2) disposing of cases; (3) doing justice; (4) maintaining group cohesion. Weight attached to the importance of each of these goals could similarly alter the nature of courtroom activities, and it should be stressed that there is no easy way to determine how these goals are weighted in any courtroom.

Further, there are other largely unexplored goals that a prosecutor may prioritize that could alter the relationships of the Big Three, particularly between a prosecutor and a defense attorney, a notion that Skolnick explores (Skolnick 1967). If a prosecutor chooses, for example, to focus on earning, maintaining, or restoring public trust, one might expect some friction with a defense attorney seeking a favorable plea deal. Similarly, individual policies instituted by a prosecutor, such as a prohibition on offering a plea agreement in any case involving a firearm, can end negotiations before they ever begin. The effects of an individual prosecutor's office policies on relationships among workgroup members are discussed in our "Concluding Thoughts" section, with a brief exploration of how a newly elected prosecutor's goals altered the longstanding workgroup organization in Philadelphia. Other goals, such as addressing an overburdened prison system, can originate from the prosecutor or surface as an external pressure applied by the courts or even prison wardens themselves (Cole 1970). On the other hand, prosecutors are also "shaped by the communities in which they serve," perhaps creating an amplification effect for the commonly accepted values of that jurisdiction (Hall 2002). The ways in which an office's existing culture influence an incoming prosecutor can also influence his or her relationships with other workgroup members (Levine and Wright 2012).

Finally, weights assigned to public opinion and/or media coverage (or even merely the perceptions of what public opinion and media coverage may be) also affect the behavior of actors in the workgroup. Workgroup members in some courtrooms may perceive more scrutiny than those in other courtrooms when subjected to a kind of constant media visibility. While this sort of scrutiny may be real or imagined, it nonetheless can result in differences in courtroom dealings.

We will not (and likely, we *could* not) flesh out how any of these factors, holding all others constant, singularly shape courtroom interactions. We have simply alluded to the relationships among the host of variables and the final outcome. A few examples help illustrate this point. The most obvious output of the workgroup is resolution of a defendant's case and a subsequent sentence if necessary, but the workgroup may have additional consequences for bail decisions, for screening cases out of the system before adjudication, for the length of time it takes to reach a disposition, and so on.

In short, to understand workgroups even in the very direct way we have addressed them thus far, we can easily identify a host of variables and outcome measures with which interactions can be associated. Were we to simply stop here, the table would be set for further study of workgroups, ideally controlling as much as possible for some of the variables while explaining how one attribute or another affects one or more of the outcomes. However, before turning more directly to our reflections about this bigger picture, we stop to surface some concerns that must be distilled from the complex mélange of factors just reviewed.

13.4 Workgroup Concerns

Three critical issues emerge from our interview data. Two of these are policy-oriented and related to each other: first, the matter of a "too close" or "too cozy" relationship between courtroom participants, and second, the resulting effects such relationships could have on defendant perceptions of the process. The third critical issue is more theoretical, and it centers around *efficiency* as a justification for particular workgroup patterns.

The first issue involves the degree of intimacy among members of the workgroup. One of the systems we encountered actually functions by means of a "trial team." This is a formalized set of two to four prosecutors and public defenders assigned to a particular judge for at least a year (barring any irreparable personality conflicts or other such issues). In each judge's courtroom, a permanent team processes cases. These teams often had regular weekly meetings. We were told by many members of such teams that concerns about efficiency dictated this kind of organization. Striking to us were responses from the interviewees who had no experience with such a team. This was especially true for those who were more familiar with the federal system, which is very different in structure. We report just a few of these responses:

- When first hearing [that an individual was "judge so-and-so's prosecutor], it made me cringe. (Interview #10)
- I found [the formalized team approach] shocking. (Interview #9)
- When I was a public defender, I was worried about getting too cozy as a result of the team. Maybe defendants pled when they shouldn't have. And this is the problem with the [state's] team approach. (Interview #4)
- Though sometimes participants don't get along, all things being equal, [the team arrangement] fosters a kind of chumminess. (Interview #3)
- I can't understand the idea of defense attorney and prosecutor assigned to a judge ... way too much danger [that the main goal becomes] to get along. (Interview #7)

Even without the formalized team structure, concerns about too close a familiarity do not go unmentioned in the literature. Amy Bach, for example, uncovers a level of geniality that she paints as the result of, at best, laziness and, at worst, something more sinister (Bach 2010). Neubauer and Meinhold illustrate the bigger point well: "Every day, the same courthouse regulars assemble in the same courtroom, sit or stand in the same places, and perform the same tasks.... Only the names of the victims and the defendants vary from day to day. Thus, although defendants and their cases come and go, the judges, prosecutors, and defense attorneys work together daily" (Neubauer and Meinhold 2017, 272). In a recent study on workgroups in criminal courts, Christi Metcalfe attempted to determine whether "higher levels of familiarity and similarity between the judge, prosecutor, and defense attorney in a case will induce greater cooperation" (Metcalfe 2016). Metcalfe interviewed a judge who told her:

> I think when they don't get along, it has an impact on the overall resolution of their cases, which impacts me. In other words, if they're not able to come to a negotiation on any of their cases, all of a sudden we have a bunch of cases that have to go to trial and frankly the system can't handle everything being tried. We just don't have time to do that.

Similarly, a public defender she interviewed explained that it is important to "play nice" with prosecutors, as it does not do the client any good "to get into a pissing match with the prosecutors" (Metcalfe 2016). In the same vein, one of our own interviewees, a private attorney, told us he would "do battle in court and then grab a drink with the other guy after," further stressing the importance of maintaining these day-to-day relationships despite the adversarial nature of the courtroom setting (Interview #2).

While the first of our concerns addresses the structure of the workgroup, our second more directly relates to the effects of those structures. As outsiders to the "trial team" court, we were particularly curious about how this arrangement affected defendants' attitudes toward how their cases were resolved. Of course, it is impossible to definitively address this without careful systematic study, but our interview results were nonetheless instructive (see Casper 1972, 51–99).[4] Respondents did not always simply embrace the impressions that seemed so evident to us, such as the notion, for example, that defendants might not feel properly represented in a system in which the defense attorney, prosecutor, and judge were part of an apparent "team." This is a central argument of a foundational work by Blumberg, who asserts that the back-and-forth between a defendant and a prosecutor is all part of a "confidence game" to persuade a defendant (and his or her family) to accept a plea offer as the best deal possible (Blumberg 1967). Some of our respondents, as noted, considered the possibility that familiarity could lead to better deals for defendants because close relations afforded opposing sides better insight into how to structure their case to please a particular court actor. But more interviewees expressed their concerns about how defendants viewed the justice system in light of the close relationships between prosecutors and defense attorneys. The observations of a prominent defense attorney reflected these conflicting views. This attorney works in an environment with a less structured relationship than the team model, but still one in which the parties frequently interacted and were quite comfortable with each other. When we asked directly about defendants' perceptions, his answer was:

> Fantastic question. It could work in different ways. Defendants might think it good that a public defender has a good relationship with a judge. He might feel he [the public defender] has insights into what works for the judges. But the flip side is that the defendant feels the public defender will pull punches. I am not sure how it washes out. (Interview #7)

Similarly, a prosecutor noted:

> I am not saying [workgroup members] shouldn't know each other, but [I want] to counter the [notion] that workgroups lead to laziness, [prosecutors and defense attorneys simply become] assembly line disposition machines.... [it is important to have] credibility before judges.... but not [to be] so chummy [with judges and defense attorneys] that you get backroom deals. (Interview #6)

And finally, another defense attorney, formerly a prosecutor, echoed these themes:

> From the clients' perspective, some feel public defenders [are] colluding with prosecutors. You do develop relationships, but [hope] they remain professional and zealous. But at the same time [you are] collegial when not on trial, and even during trial.... Defendants can feel everyone is in this together, and I've heard defendants vocalize this in court. (Interview #5)

As our data so strongly indicate, a general discussion of workgroups must then confront concerns about this degree of familiarity among workgroup members. Some degree of familiarity is inevitable in light of repeated interactions and might be viewed as a positive by defendants. On the other hand, concerns about the "costs" of too much familiarity are real, whether they are defendant perceptions of excessive chumminess among the courtroom actors that then lead to a less adversarial approach than ought to be taken, or in fact a reality of a less adversarial position being pursued than would be optimal. This core concern of over-familiarity is central to any discussion of workgroups.

The third concern about workgroups raised in our interviews speaks to a more theoretical matter. Specifically, workgroup patterns were almost always associated with the courts' concerns for the *efficient* resolution of cases. When discussing the starkest example of the formalized "team" approach—the permanent assignment of specific prosecutors and public defenders to a particular judge for no less than one year—we were told repeatedly that this model was necessitated by the large number of cases that the court had to process. This is a common claim, echoing Skolnick's interviews from decades earlier (Skolnick 1967). One judge noted that the design was required to "move the business, move cases... which is the judge's main priority... and with the assignment to his court it works efficiently as long as the prosecutor and public defender get along. If they don't, nothing moves; if they get along the system hums" (Interview #3). Another judge echoed this view: "[I] want to be able to reach out and touch [the members of "his" team].... I think [our state] has the most efficient way, all the attorneys are before you... not true of private attorneys, but they are a very small part of the criminal case business" (Interview #4). Several respondents were skeptical of this more formal model, but believed that what animated the choice was an emphasis on efficiency and an indifference to effects on defendants, whether real or perceived: "I can't understand the idea of a defense attorney and prosecutor assigned to a judge—way too much danger [that the main goal becomes] to get along.... Proponents of the system argue that it is more efficient, [but to me it seems that] everything that screws our clients [as a public defender] is 'more efficient'" (Interview #7).[5]

Our comparative, though admittedly limited, analysis of several jurisdictions from which interview subjects were selected fostered even more skepticism. A number of subjects came from a jurisdiction in which we were told that heavy caseloads necessitated the "team" approach to workgroup structure. They maintained that without such a team approach, chaos would rule and cases simply could not be processed in any reasonable way. However, other respondents came from jurisdictions in another state with comparatively heavy caseloads. Yet in these jurisdictions, the team approach was viewed as indefensible. Different organizational structures linked the three players (and some brought them closer than others), but the kind of permanent assignment defended as being *necessary* in some jurisdictions was rejected out of hand in others with even far more demanding caseloads. In one set of jurisdictions a particular workgroup arrangement was considered *necessary*; in another set, it was entirely *unthinkable*. Whether actors in the first set of jurisdictions were implicitly less concerned about defendants' claims (as implied by a respondent who indicated "efficiency" is often trotted out with at best an indifference to defendants) or because "this is the way it's always been done" is a question beyond the scope of this chapter. But just like falsely claiming that case pressure drives plea bargaining or that case volume in civil courts explains the length of time it takes to resolve cases, "efficiency" as the explanation for specific workgroup designs is simplistic, lacks nuance, and at its core is simply wrong.[6]

13.5 Workgroups Exist . . . So *What?*

We have learned much about criminal courts during the past fifty years. Myths have been debunked, simplistic explanations have been rejected, and many intriguing hypotheses about what drives court disposition processes have been developed in the literature. However, there remains a risk that when given a piece of the courtroom puzzle—in our case, workgroups—we might be overcome by something we call "concept hagiography." By this we mean that there may be an inclination to give undue credit to the concept under study and its explanatory value for the dependent variables being explored. So, courtroom workgroups, even when accounting for the nuance and variations described earlier, might appear to have significant explanatory power with respect to bail outcomes, or plea rates, or sentences, etc. But as a research team, we remain skeptical of the explanatory power of workgroups, standing alone.

Even in *Felony Justice*, the seminal book on workgroups, we find an ambivalence regarding the amount of variance explained by workgroups. For example, early in the work the authors note that "[t]he severity of sentences *may* also reflect workgroup organization" (Eisenstein and Jacob 1977, 63). And more centrally, in the second part of their study they explicitly attempt to compare the explanatory power of case-specific variables (the crimes, defendants' attributes, etc.) to the explanatory power of workgroups with respect to a number of dependent variables. At best, they find workgroup structures to be of limited explanatory value. For example, they marveled: "Courtroom workgroups in the three cities produced remarkably similar dispositions, although the methods they used to reach their dispositions differed substantially" (232).

Noting mixed results about the independent effects of the differing workgroup models, they stressed that courtroom norms could trump the case-specific attributes in explaining outcomes in some courts across their three sites (258). But, in our view, even when these norms are significant independent variables, it is problematic to assume that these norms surface because of the workgroup structure in these courts. It seems more plausible to us that norms may explain the workgroup structure (or possibly even that both derive from some other exogenous variable), and, more important, that they directly define the seriousness of cases. This is evident in the variation of local "going rates" for certain charges in plea bargains (Heumann 2018). Where these norms originate is itself an intriguing question well beyond what we have discussed, though others have attempted such a study, with Eisenstein, Flemming, and Nardulli, for example, likening the courtroom to a "community" composed of interdependent actors (1988). Perhaps one of our most insightful and experienced interviewees phrased it best: When asked to account for differences in court outcomes across states or between state and federal courts, he concluded that the best explanation is simply "that it is different because that's the way it has been . . . so much is cultural, not in [any] rules of procedure" (Interview #10).

In Metcalfe's recent workgroup study, she also finds mixed, muddled, and sometimes even conflicting claims about the consequences of workgroup familiarity. We already reported on an interview she conducted with a judge who noted the importance of informal negotiations in resolving disputes (Metcalfe 2016). However, in the same study she reports that other respondents make claims that both familiarity and lack of familiarity can lead to an increased likelihood of trial, depending on which members of the group are indeed familiar with one another. While familiarity between the judge and prosecutor may increase the odds of a plea, familiarity with the defense attorney may be more likely to lead to trial. She further contends that while familiarity between judges and prosecutors or prosecutors and defense attorneys seemed to facilitate a more efficient case processing system, familiarity between a judge and a defense attorney actually impeded the plea process. She posits that this could be a result of less familiar defense attorneys behaving more collegially than those who may know the other players well. In the study, she focused on four factors that might influence the actors' familiarity with each other: having attended the same law school, being of the same race, being of the same sex, and their years of experience. Metcalfe explains that generally dissimilar workgroups in terms of race, sex, and law school were more likely to proceed to trial as well. Interestingly, she also finds that cases handled by workgroups composed of members of the same sex "had greater odds of being resolved by a plea of guilt or no contest." "Sex similarity," she finds, "consistently emerged as a significant predictor, such that it increased the likelihood of a plea and decreased the time to case disposition." In sum, Metcalfe finds that the effect of workgroup familiarity is at least partially dependent on which members are familiar with one another, as well as the makeup of the group itself (Metcalfe 2016).

To be sure, we are not dismissing the reality that workgroups can have a number of effects, attitudinal and otherwise, nor are we suggesting that study of such workgroups is without value. We do raise the possibility, however, based on our own interviews and the contributions of others, that the effects of workgroup structures on court outcomes may be minimal.[7] The major contributions of these structures—translating court norms into decisions—are most likely reflections of the workgroups being shaped by other variables rather than the workgroups themselves accounting for the outcomes. The workgroups are more the means of delivery for a particular culture rather than the mechanism by which it is created. They do have more than a simple spurious relationship to outcomes, insofar as there probably *are* some independent effects for which workgroup relationships account. But it is arguable that most of what goes on in the courts is better understood through other variables, as well as by the staying power of long-standing practices and the cultural factors mentioned.

"Concept hagiography" is alluring, but in the literature generally—and even in Eisenstein and Jacob's "discovery" of workgroups, and in our own interviews—there is much to suggest caution. Standing alone, it is not the workgroup that explains the variance in outcome; the workgroups themselves may be reflections of these more general variables.

13.6 Concluding Thoughts

Our workgroup-centric foray into the world of criminal courts (coupled with an appreciation from the literature for the host of variables that affect court outcomes) has highlighted several problems that together could constitute an important agenda for further social science research and subsequent policy formulation.

First, an examination of jurisdictions that experience dramatic changes from past practices would be incredibly valuable. "Reflecting state and local values" is commonly recognized as a core responsibility of any prosecutor (Heumann and Pinaire 2002). One might imagine that as these values change, so too might the policies of the prosecutor's office. A before-and-after setting could help tease out the variables that are most significant in understanding court outputs, while holding other environmental factors constant.

One ideal locale for precisely this kind of study is Philadelphia. There, in May 2017, Larry Krasner, a former public defender considered an "anti-establishment" liberal, won a seven-way primary with nearly 40 percent of the vote and almost twice the vote tally of his nearest challenger. In a city like Philadelphia, the "real race" is often the Democratic primary, and Krasner steamrolled over his Republican opponent in the general election with just shy of 75 percent of the vote (Philadelphia Votes 2017). Since his swearing in to the prosecutor's office on New Year's Day 2018, he has changed many charging policies and replaced an unusually large number of attorneys in the office. With these arguable changes in the culture, of course, came changes in the operation of the workgroup (Ewing 2018; King 2018). We need not discuss these here other than to note that this dramatic shake-up of long-standing practices affords scholars a unique opportunity to learn more about what can (and cannot) be changed, how things will be changed, and what will remain when the innovation dust settles.

Though the Philadelphia setting presents the most dramatic "interrupted time series" opportunity for research, we were surprised to learn during our interviews that a number of other sites during the past decade presented valuable opportunities, albeit more limited ones, for before-and-after research. In one instance, a newly elected prosecutor "ruled" that vertical, not the long-standing horizontal, prosecution would be the new norm in his office. In another, a state chief justice unilaterally decreed that his state courts would process cases just as the federal courts did (a short-lived experiment). This remains an ongoing discussion, and a recent op-ed in the *New York Times* highlighted reforms initiated by newly elected prosecutors in Philadelphia as well as Chicago and Kansas City (Bazelon and Krinsky 2018).

A second method to explore inner workgroup operations is to look at how outsiders to the court manage their cases (Mather 1974).[8] A common practice in many jurisdictions is for an outside attorney to hire an insider familiar with local norms. This ensures at least some level of understanding of the culture and the relationships between the players who already know each other well. To the extent that the workgroup is based on the interactions between repeat players, an outsider likely begins at a disadvantage, especially an outsider who eschews retaining local counsel (Galanter 1974). Our guess is that this phenomenon varies by court. But in studying the experiences of how outsiders fare in courts, novel perspectives on process and outcomes could emerge.

Finally, we end with the small- and big-picture takeaways of the courtroom workgroups. The small picture envisions tripartite interactions within the criminal court, typically conducted by prosecutors, defense attorneys (usually public defenders), and judges with varying degrees of formal and informal interactions and with a number of simultaneous goals. Variations in methods of case assignment, such as whether such assignment is vertical or horizontal, distinguish the workgroups. These differences may have attitudinal effects on consumers (both defendants and victims) and may result in divergent outcomes for the different stages of case processing. These workgroups operate within what we may call a zone of indifference: an area that outsiders such as the media rarely penetrate. Of course, the zone varies across communities (and so too do its effects on comparable workgroups), perhaps in major ways, but more likely just manifests in the form of effects at the proverbial margins.

But there is also a bigger picture here, which was suggested in our earlier discussion of what explains the variance in court outcomes. Were we to import variables to address these outcomes, we would include the nature of the case, defendant characteristics, "going rates" in a jurisdiction, statutory rules, court decisions, and, on a more general level, local political and legal culture and traditions, and maybe even jail and prison resources. We note these only to emphasize once again why we conclude that courtroom workgroups *can* matter, but in all likelihood more on the margins. Many variables contribute to the kind of rich explanation needed to understand issues such as bail, time to dispose, plea bargaining, trials, sentences, and the myriad other aspects of the criminal justice system. Workgroups, with varying consequences depending on their specific form, constitute just a piece of the puzzle of why criminal courts do what they do. Further studies of workgroups, as suggested above, will be useful in illuminating the differences they do make in case outcomes, but we reiterate that we believe these will probably just be differences at the margin. Both the literature and our interviews suggest that understanding the mélange of factors explaining the inner workings of criminal courts is complex, and cannot be subject to a tempting, parsimonious, and ultimately too narrow set of courtroom workgroup explanations.

Notes

1. Recent overviews of criminal justice dynamics include Pfaff (2017) and Stuntz (2011). For a fascinating recent discussion on misdemeanor court, see Kohler-Hausmann (2018).
2. For the classic description of a conspiracy-like workgroup world, see Blumberg (1967).
3. The disdain that some judges held for an elected judiciary was apparent when one judge noted, "I'm eternally grateful for appointments. I would not be here [as a judge] if we elected judges."
4. In the seminal study of defendants' attitudes towards the criminal justice system, Casper (1972) finds by conducting a series of interviews that defendants negatively view their public defenders. On the other hand, in a quantitative follow-up to his book, Casper (1978) finds, somewhat to his surprise, that when the time attorneys spend with their clients is controlled, most of the differences in defendant evaluations of public and private attorneys disappears.
5. This calls to mind Herbert Packer's two models of criminal process, pitting the obstacle course against the assembly line: the "due process" model or, as we see here, the "crime control" model. While the due process model emphasizes the rights-based procedure as we know it, the crime control model centers around efficiency. In the latter model, needs to address crime issues inspire workgroup actors to resolve cases quickly (Packer 1964). Perhaps Packer's pitting of the more efficiency-based model as opposite "due process" speaks for itself.
6. For a discussion exploring and rejecting the contention that case pressure explains plea bargaining, see Heumann (1977). On local legal culture being a better explanation for civil case disposition than is civil caseload see Church (1985).
7. Indeed, in Metcalfe's attempt to expand on the Eisenstein and Jacob arguments, she finds that only some configurations of workgroup interactions seem to have some effect on plea bargaining and trial outcomes. Even these, we think, need to be viewed with great caution given that her study was limited to a single site and her qualitative data were limited to three interviews, one for each position.
8. Here we refer to real outsiders and not, for example, insiders who don't carry their load or are seen as irresponsible. Their treatment is a different matter, including consequences (unspecified by a respondent judge) who, when he encounters the "derelict in his duties" attorney, stamps his file: DDS. This is the judge's shorthand for "Didn't Do Shit!!"

References

Alschuler, Albert. 1968. "The Prosecutor's Role in Plea Bargaining." *University of Chicago Law Review* 36(1): 50–112.

Bach, Amy. 2010. *Ordinary Injustice: How America Holds Court.* New York: Harry Holt & Company.

Bazelon, Emily, and Miriam Krinsky. 2018. "A Wave of New Prosecutors Means Justice." *New York Times*, December 13, 2018: A29.

Bjerk, David. 2005. "Prosecutorial Discretion: Making the Crime Fit the Penalty." *Journal of Law & Economics* 48(2): 591–625.

Blumberg, Abraham S. 1967. "The Practice of Law as Confidence Game: Organizational Cooptation of a Profession." *Law & Society Review* 1(2): 15–39.

Casper, Jonathan D. 1972. *American Criminal Justice: The Defendant's Perspective*. Upper Saddle River: Prentice-Hall.

Casper, Jonathan D. 1978. *Criminal Courts: The Defendant's Perspective*. Washington, D.C.: U.S. Department of Justice.

Church, Thomas W., Jr. 1985. "Examining Local Legal Culture." *Law & Social Inquiry* 10(3): 449–510.

Cole, George F. 1970. "The Decision to Prosecute." *Law & Society Review* 4(3): 313–343.

Eisenstein, James, and Herbert Jacob. 1977. *Felony Justice: An Organizational Analysis of Criminal Courts*. Boston: Little, Brown, and Company.

Eisenstein, James, Roy Flemming, and Peter Nardulli. 1988. *The Contours of Justice: Communities and Their Courts*. Boston: Little, Brown, and Company.

Ewing, Maura. 2018. "Philadelphia's New Top Prosecutor Is Rolling Out Wild, Unprecedented Criminal Justice Reform." *Slate Magazine*, March 14, 2018.

Galanter, Marc. 1974. "Why the 'Haves' Come Out Ahead: Speculations on the Limits of Legal Change." *Law & Society Review* 9(1): 95–160.

Heumann, Milton. 1977. *Plea Bargaining: The Experiences of Prosecutors, Judges, and Defense Attorneys*. Chicago: University of Chicago Press.

Heumann, Milton. 2018. "Plea Bargaining: Lessons Learned, Issues Outstanding." *Harvard Law & Policy Review*. http://harvardlpr.com/2018/07/24.

Heumann, Milton, and Brian K. Pinaire. 2002. "Prosecutor." In *The Oxford Companion to American Law*. Edited by Kermit L. Hall, David S. Clark, James W. Ely, Jr., Joel Grossman, and N. E. H. Hull, 675–677. Oxford: Oxford University Press.

Interview #2. June 25, 2018. State County Prosecutor. Conducted in person.

Interview #3. July 25, 2018. Assignment Judge, State Court. Conducted in person.

Interview #4. July 30, 2018. Retired Judge, State Court. Conducted by phone.

Interview #7. August 6, 2018. Federal Public Defender. Conducted by phone.

Interview #9. August 6, 2018. Former Employee of Judge's Chambers and State Prosecutor's Office. Conducted by phone.

Interview #10. August 14, 2018. Former Bureau Chief, District Attorney's Office. Conducted in person.

King, Shaun. 2018. "Philadelphia DA Larry Krasner Promised a Criminal Justice Revolution. He's Exceeding Expectations." *The Intercept*, March 20, 2018.

Kohler-Hausmann, Issa. 2018. *Misdemeanorland: Criminal Courts and Social Control in an Age of Broken Windows Policing*. Princeton: Princeton University Press.

Levine, Kay L., and Ronald F. Wright. 2012. "Prosecution in 3-D." *Journal of Criminal Law and Criminology* 102(4): 1119–1180.

Mather, Lynn. 1974. "The Outsider in the Courtroom: An Alternative Role for the Defense." In *The Potential for Reform of Criminal Justice*. Edited by Herbert Jacob, 263–289. Thousand Oaks: Sage Publications.

Metcalfe, Christi. 2016. "The Role of Courtroom Workgroups in Felony Case Dispositions: An Analysis of Workgroup Familiarity and Similarity." *Law & Society Review* 50(3): 637–673.

National Center for State Courts. 2015. "Methods of Judicial Selection."

Neubauer, David W., and Stephen Scott Meinhold. 2017. *Judicial Process: Law, Courts, and Politics in the United States*. Boston: Cengage Learning.

Packer, Herbert L. 1964. "Two Models of the Criminal Process." *University of Pennsylvania Law Review* 113(1): 1–68.

Pfaff, John. 2017. *Locked In: The True Causes of Mass Incarceration*. New York: Basic Books.

Philadelphia Votes. 2017. "2017 Primary District Attorney-Dem." https://www.philadelphiavotes.com/en/resources-a-data/ballot-box-app.
Skolnick, Jerome H. 1967. "Social Control in the Adversary System." *Journal of Conflict Resolution* 11(1): 52–70.
Stuntz, William. 2011. *The Collapse of American Criminal Justice*. Boston: Harvard University Press.

CHAPTER 14

LAW ENFORCEMENT ORGANIZATION RELATIONSHIPS WITH PROSECUTORS

DANIEL C. RICHMAN

14.1 Introduction

WHILE other chapters in this volume consider case-specific decision-making by prosecutors and law enforcement officers,[1] this one explores the organizational dynamics that structure those retail engagements. Unquestionably, prosecutorial interactions with police officers, at both the retail and wholesale level, will significantly affect the nature and quality of criminal justice within a county, district, or other jurisdictional unit.

The chapter starts with the horizontal and non-hierarchical relationship between police and prosecutors that is characteristic of the American system. Then it explores the prosecutorial gatekeeping role within this organizational architecture and its promise of the better decision-making that generally occurs when culturally and perhaps politically distinct organizations are required to collaborate across a shared boundary. But collaboration is not the only possibility, and I will consider the nature and sources of institutional conflicts between prosecutors and police with respect to arrest and charging decisions and police tactics.

I will also consider other promising sites of police-prosecutor interaction, made possible by prosecutors' privileged ability to disseminate information to and collect it from the police. The chapter will look at how prosecutors can help monitor and train the police, and how they can leverage their constitutional disclosure obligations—which oblige them to consider derogatory reports that go to a testifying officer's credibility—to address police misconduct. Yet prosecutors may not always be up to taking a magisterial perspective on officer misconduct. And the final section in the chapter will explain how the risk that prosecutors won't be able to maintain that stance is particularly great when they inquire into and determine whether to bring charges in police shooting cases.

14.2 Horizontal Alignment and Coordinate Powers

Foundational to the American criminal justice system is what Mirjan Damaška characterized as the "coordinate mode of organization" (1984, 44). Organizational alignment is horizontal rather vertical, with police and prosecutorial units working as equal partners, and neither having hierarchical power over the other. Indeed, in most cases, police and prosecutors have separate lines of political accountability. Deputy sheriffs reporting to elected sheriffs (Tomberlin 2018, 113), or police officers reporting to police chiefs appointed by elected mayors, will bring cases to District Attorney's offices headed by an elected D.A. Even in the U.S. federal system, where, at least in theory, all criminal enforcement units could be in a single department, they aren't. Most investigation and apprehension units are in the Justice Department, but others are in Homeland Security, Treasury, or elsewhere in the Executive Branch. And even though the U.S. Attorney General and the Deputy Attorney General sit atop an organizational chart that includes all Justice Department special agents and all federal prosecutors, they are the only two federal officials with hierarchical authority crossing the police-prosecutor divide. Fragmented authority reigns here as well (Richman 2003, 755–756). As a general matter, American prosecutors simply lack the formal authority to order the police to investigate and bring them a case, and the police lack formal authority to require that prosecutors take any particular case or type of case.

One can easily imagine a variety of more hierarchical models and can easily find them abroad now or in the past. In one model, the police could dominate. Prior to the establishment of the Crown Prosecution Service in 1985, the police in England and Wales "were responsible for criminal prosecutions, which they brought either in person, or through locally instructed prosecuting solicitors" (Gattrell 1990, 262; Godfrey 2008, 171; Hodgson 2017, 76, 83). Alternatively, prosecutors could be in charge from the start. In France, the *procureur* is understood to have direct authority over the police investigation of a case (Hodgson 2010, 1368). In Japan, prosecutors "strongly and frequently direct police investigations" (Johnson 2012, 42). In China, at least in theory, prosecutors "are accorded a supervisory function which enables them to oversee all the law enforcement agencies, including the courts and the police" (Mou 2017, 621). The United States, because of some combination of path dependence and ideological commitment to separation of power principles, has not gone in either of these directions.

One caveat: although the practice often eludes scholarly attention, a "surprising number" of U.S. jurisdictions allow police officers (notwithstanding their lack of a license to practice law) to directly file and prosecute criminal cases (Horwitz 1998, 1306). Arguments have been made that such an arrangement violates the Due Process Clause, in part because an arresting officer often acts as both witness and prosecutor (Frye 2012, 339). Yet the practice can still be found in underfunded jurisdictions or where the minimization of legal personnel (since the judge may not be a lawyer either) is deemed a virtue (New York City Bar Task Force on Town and Village Courts 2007).

14.3 Prosecutors as Gatekeeper

As a general matter then, prosecutors are gatekeepers for all criminal charges, and have a monopoly on their being brought. When a police officer presents a case and asks for charges to be filed, a prosecutor thus has a decision to make, not a duty to comply with. Indeed, gatekeeping at this critical juncture lies at the heart of the prosecutorial role. Reasons for declining to file may be technical in nature—like "insufficient evidence" or a "bad search"—but they may also be "office policy." Assessments of evidentiary strength may themselves reflect views of the zeal with which a case should be pursued, since case files are artifacts of enforcer effort (Richman 2003, 762–763). They too may reflect some mix of an individual screener's discretion and office policy.

Such decisions might be routinized and unilateral. Indeed, the norm in most cases, especially at the county level, has police officers presenting arrests that they have made on their own initiative to prosecutors who, seeing the case for the first time, will quickly decide whether to accept or decline. The roles played in this set-piece can reinforce regrettably narrow perspectives (Griffin 2017, 326). Police officers or agents will all too often believe their job stops with an arrest and will think of themselves as having little stake in the disposition of a case (Richman 2003, 774–775). Such an attitude will be reinforced by agency performance metrics that don't consider adjudicative concerns (Richman 2003, 763), and by the readiness of the police to use an arrest as a regulatory tool in its own right, irrespective of the adjudicative outcome (Feeley 1979; Jain 2015, 809). Prosecutors too might have a limited conception of their role and think of themselves as passive recipients of a file created by the police. Yet, there are plenty of agents and officers who look beyond such a narrow conception of their job and have considered views on what happens to a case. (Richman 2017, 68). Similarly, there are many prosecutors who embrace their repeat-player status and seek to shape police behavior in future cases.

Even when the police have unilaterally investigated a case without prosecutorial input, they could be encouraged or even required to preliminarily consult with prosecutors before actually making an arrest (Gershowitz 2019). Such consultations can help ensure that weak or otherwise inappropriate cases get weeded out expeditiously, saving many an arrestee from unnecessary transport and booking hardships. Canvassing practices around the nation, Adam Gershowitz reports that in Harris County, Texas, "police officers cannot make any warrantless arrest without first calling the 'intake hotline' and receiving approval from a prosecutor" (2019, 28). He also offers evidence that other counties adopting this ostensibly resource-intensive system have actually saved money (2019, 34).

Moreover, prosecutors will regularly work closely with cops or agents to make a case, particularly where prosecutors are gatekeepers over needed investigative techniques—e.g., grand juries, search warrants, electronic surveillance, cooperation agreements (Richman 2003, 781–782).[2] Each of these tools requires a level of prosecutorial engagement, preparation, and, for most, sponsorship with bureaucratic hierarchies and judicial authorities that tend to make a prosecutor a partner, or at least reviewer, in investigative decision-making. When an investigation can be pursued only with the help of an accomplice witness, the prosecutor who will have to negotiate a cooperation agreement and guilty plea will have an influence on how the investigation develops that a colleague who simply sits in the complaint room and reviews arrests lacks. And the prosecutor who has spent weeks calling fact witnesses into the grand jury and negotiating subpoena compliance will be far more prepared to suggest new avenues of inquiry to the investigating agency than the prosecutor who simply presents a "fully" investigated case to the grand jury for an indictment.

Whether arising out of investigative exigencies or simply a deliberative process at the charging stage, productive interactions between police officers and prosecutors have considerable promise. As I've suggested elsewhere, the engagement of diverse professionals answering to separate organizations with separate lines of political accountability and distinct cultures allows, at least potentially, for mutual monitoring and "can promote depolarization and more thoughtful decision making" (Richman 2003, 810).[3] Anchored in a legal culture that connects them to other professionals, including defense lawyers, and tasked with defending police tactics and investigative adequacy in court, prosecutors might be tempted to worry about "cowboy" or "street-oriented" cops. However, a shared commitment to broad public safety, legality and even justice goals, coupled with the erosion of professional boundaries natural in high-pressure worksites, can lead to "knowledge transfer" (Abbott 1988, 65; Richman 2003, 792) and mutual respect. These interactions therefore ought to be embraced at the case level, and even formalized.

The nature and extent of police-prosecutorial collaboration will affect not only the quality of investigations and prosecutions but the very kind of cases that get pursued. To be sure, divergent enforcement priorities can lead prosecutors to disfavor certain kinds of cases. Yet their distinct perspective may lead them to promote others. "The pressures on police forces with crime control and patrol responsibilities are indefeasible," and often "come at the cost of the intensive police work needed to investigate crimes not in plain view" (Richman 2017, 55). Many such crimes, entailing some of the most grievous exercises of illegitimate power—domestic violence, organized crime, or corruption—can be pursued only if prosecutors get involved early and intensively. Working closely with police officers, prosecutors can ensure that evidence is developed that withstands changes in a domestic violence victim's readiness to implicate her assailant (Nelson 2012, 526; Richman 2017, 56). In cases involving more organized criminal conduct, prosecutors' unique competence lies in their ability to deploy the adjudicative process itself as an investigative tool, striking the cooperation deals that allow the targeting of those who would otherwise enjoy impunity (Richman 1995, 69; Richman 2017, 55). Whether prosecutors will actually pursue matters that draw on their unique competencies depends on their readiness to take an active role in case development and on their interest in pursuing more than the "usual suspects."

Yet close cooperation between prosecutors and police officers in developing a case also has its downsides. "Prosecutors who have helped call the shots in an investigation will be hard pressed to retain their magisterial perspective not just about the tactics used in the investigation, but about whether charges should be pursued thereafter" (Richman 2003, 803; see Barkow 2009, 896). Early involvement can only heighten the risks of prosecutorial "tunnel vision," "the confirmation bias and selective information processing" that can lead investigators "to search out and recall information that tends to confirm one's existing beliefs, and to devalue disconfirming evidence" (Bandes 2006, 475; Burke 2007, 517; Findley and Scott 2006, 291; Godsey 2019). Moreover, integral membership in the investigative team can make prosecutors prone to conforming to consensus and not undercutting the "team" (Simon 2012, 28–29).

At best, however, there will be productive and enriching interaction across institutional roles, with the "structured interaction of enforcers drawn from two relatively distinct cultures" promoting "depolarization and more thoughtful decision making" (Richman 2003, 810). The goal ought to be the "team" valorized in the organizational literature, which means a

> set of individuals (1) whose agencies' contributions are thought to be mutually complementary in their productive capacities and (2) whose individual characteristics—including such matters as their knowledge and skills, their access to resources and to status within their home agencies, their aspirations and beliefs, their personal strengths and weaknesses—are taken into account by those, including the team members themselves, who organize their respective activities. (Bardach 1998, 117)

Police-prosecutor interactions can continue after the charging decision to include decisions as to disposition. As Feeley and Lazerson observed: "Because prosecutors are the dominant members of the police-court transaction, they often attempt to make the police feel part of the legal process by soliciting officers' advice about the appropriate plea or sentence" (1983, 216). One way to do this is through the "boundary-spanning institutions" (Feeley and Lazerson 1983, 216) that jurisdictions have established over the years. In Charlotte, North Carolina, for instance, the detectives on a homicide case are formally included in prosecutorial deliberations on what position to take in plea negotiations (Abel 2017, 1748–1749). This arrangement was designed to address

> a recurring conflict between prosecutors and police, a conflict that had grown acute under a prior district attorney's regime. Previously, prosecutors and police were at each other's throats, publicly blaming each other for settling too many cases too cheaply. Police blamed prosecutors for pleading out murder cases that could have

> received stiffer penalties at trial, and claimed these lenient plea agreements were making it harder to enforce the law on the street. Prosecutors replied that the cases could not go to trial because the police had performed such shoddy investigative work. (Abel 2017, 1749)

The Charlotte prosecutor who fails to consult with interested police officers on a case disposition and takes a position at odds with their strong preferences might find herself the subject of a complaint to her superiors (Abel 2017, 1763). Officers can also "derail a plea by leaking word that the prosecutor is considering a lenient offer and did not consult with police first. If the plea offer has already been made, officers may go on the record to voice their dissatisfaction with the plea and make clear that they were not consulted" (Abel 2017, 1746). In some jurisdictions, the prosecutor might even suffer the disruptive intervention of the police as a separate actor in the adjudicative process. While there is disparate state case law on whether the police are bound by the prosecutor's position, "[g]iving the defendant the ability to claim breach and withdraw his plea" when the police argue for a harsher punishment than the prosecutor has agreed to would be both "a spur to [police]-prosecutor collaboration" and "a matter of simple fairness" (Richman 2003, 829; see Abel 2017, 1765–1769). Optimally, however, the risk of such interventions will simply lead to better communication and internalization of police perspectives into prosecutorial decision-making.

14.4 Organizational Conflicts over Charging

Prosecutorial gatekeeping will not always promote collaborative interaction with police officers. Sometimes it will lead to organizational conflict, with the priorities and tactics that shape a police department's or law enforcement agency's supply of cases at odds with the policy preferences of the prosecutor's office. The conflict can usefully be seen in market terms, with prosecutorial control over access to the adjudication process generally mirrored by a police monopoly over the supply of materials for the bringing of cases.

An important qualification: An ordinarily stark bilateral monopoly might be qualified when jurisdictions overlap. For example, when an investigation spans two boroughs, the New York Police Department might be able to play one county D.A.'s office against another. Even when multiple counties are not involved, a department might be able pursue the local U.S. Attorney's office to take a case federally. For its part, a D.A.'s office might not be wholly reliant on the local police and might take cases from federal or state agencies. At the federal level, the multiplicity of enforcement agencies and the flexibility of district venue rules allow for similar games that marginally reduce what otherwise would be monopoly power of prosecutors and agencies (Richman 2003, 759–761).

Does prosecutorial monopoly power mean that the police will internalize prosecutorial preferences in order to achieve their own goals? Not necessarily, and the consequences of their failing to do so can be disastrous. For example, the New Orleans District Attorney—in a laudable effort to reduce plea bargaining incentives—required his prosecutors to increase the rigor with which they screened cases before charging (Wright and Miller 2002). The New Orleans Police Department might have responded by bringing stronger cases, but it did not. It simply accepted the rejection of an extraordinarily high number of its serious felony arrests, with predicable public safety consequences (Richman 2006, 2058–2060).

Disjunctions between police and prosecutorial decision-making may be rooted less in institutional dysfunction than in varying political preferences or policy judgments. Elections or the political appointment process for prosecutors are highly imperfect mechanisms for capturing public sentiments (Gold 2011; Wright 2009). Neither, given party dynamics and the broad range of issues in play during mayoral elections, can one expect police leadership necessarily to reflect broad community preferences. Nonetheless, the responsiveness, however attenuated, of both prosecutor's offices and police departments to their respective mechanisms of democratic accountability (and to the interest groups that exploit those mechanisms) will regularly put them on different pages with respect to enforcement priorities, strategies, and tactics.

The likelihood that this will happen gets far greater when one extends the model to consider the "mesh of networked institutions" (Richman 2016, 68) in which police and prosecutors do their work. Police tactics often respond to public safety concerns, officer-protection needs, community relationships or the lack thereof, and performance metrics—which are sometimes poorly chosen, like the number of street stops (Baker 2017; Mummolo 2018). At its heart, a great deal of police work is spatially oriented: neighborhoods to patrol, property to protect, information sources to cultivate in a particular area. A prosecutor's office may also respond to those concerns, but its obligation to navigate the legal and equitable demands of courts, juries, and defense counsel may dramatically affect its perspective, requiring it to wrestle with issues of equality, due process, community norms, and moral desert that sometimes get short shrift in the policing project.

Such demands, as well as a distinct professional perspective, may make prosecutors look askance at the steady stream of low-level misdemeanor arrests that will inevitably accompany a police department's pursuit of an order maintenance strategy. Experienced prosecutors screening these arrests may weed quite a few out, deeming them unworthy of a full adjudication, and perhaps questioning the need for the suspect to have a criminal record (Bowers 2010, 1693–1703; Natapoff 2018, 68–71). As Natapoff notes, however, "[t]he combination of enormous caseloads and inexperienced prosecutors" will leave police officers with "de facto prosecutorial authority" in the misdemeanor world (Natapoff 2018, 70–71).

Disjunctions between police and prosecutor policy preferences are not merely a feature of a mutual monitoring model but offer a promise of a broader accountability for both institutions that goes beyond this mesh of inside actors. It generally won't take long before serious conflicts spill out into the public arena, with local (or even national) media outlets eagerly disseminating the on- or off-the-record complaints of each side, trying to mobilize or curry favor with voters or funders or both. As I've noted elsewhere:

> Iterated interaction between police and prosecutors is not unique to liberal democracies. The same creative tensions presumably arise in authoritarian states, without necessarily contributing to democratic accountability. What distinguishes the interactions in a liberal democracy is the nature of the institutions involved, with the possibility that police and prosecutors there have diverse political anchors that bring a dialogic richness (perhaps with expletives) to their conversations. What also distinguishes them is that, in an open society and a media interested in crime news, these arguments easily spill into public discourse. (Richman 2017, 68)

The resulting discourse can provide an important source of accountability for institutions whose decisional processes are generally all too opaque. To be sure, there is also a risk that the public dialogue may be skewed in one direction, as can occur when the electoral power of police unions has an outsized influence in the election of a local prosecutor. Abel reports that "unions sometimes see it as their duty to speak up when their members are upset about the way prosecutors are handling cases" (2017, 1763). Given the variable and often inadequate mix of information available to voters in prosecutorial elections (Medwed 2004; Wright 2014, 593), the absence of voices of moderation to balance police union critiques (and votes) can lead to regrettable electoral consequences.

Even where interactions are not productive in the narrow sense, leaving, say, the police aggrieved at what they believe is an unduly risk-averse prosecutorial decision, the resulting tension at the police-prosecutor fault line can promote prosecutorial accountability with respect to specific cases. This is certainly what occurred when police dissatisfaction with the Manhattan D.A.'s decision not to prosecute famed producer Harvey Weinstein in 2015 spilled onto the front pages in 2017 (McKinley 2017) and sparked further inquiries that led to serious felony charges against him in 2018. How the continued cross-organizational finger-pointing in this case will play out remains to be seen (Rose and Friedman 2018).

Broader differences about the handling of offense classes can also spill into public discourse. When Baltimore State's Attorney Marilyn Mosby announced that her office would no longer prosecute any marijuana possession cases, "regardless of the quantity or the person's criminal history," the city's police commission responded that his force "will continue to make arrests for illegal marijuana possession unless and until the state legislature changes the law regarding marijuana possession" (Prudente 2019). Disagreement between Manhattan D.A. Vance and New York City's police department and mayor over the handling of subway fare evaders has spiraled into a sustained debate about the disproportionate effects of enforcement and prosecution on communities of color (Flagg and Nerbovig 2018).

Whether the differences between prosecutors and police reflect policy preferences or legal compliance may itself be a matter of disagreement. Reacting in 2012 to the level and nature of the New York Police Department's "stop and frisk" tactics, the Bronx D.A. refused to prosecute arrests from housing projects in the absence of an interview with the arresting officer "to ensure that the arrest was warranted" (Goldstein 2012). Did the D.A. affirmatively intend to reduce the nature of the police footprint in the projects or would any such reduction have simply been an unintended result of punctilious case preparation? Either way, it's hard to imagine that the D.A.'s view of the underlying policing project did not color the intensive scrutiny she mandated for the tactics used therein (Howell 2014, 304).

Other times, the policy differences will be quite clear. Perhaps the most transparent airing of differences has occurred as jurisdictions struggle to reconcile changing public attitudes toward marijuana usage with the frequency with which police stops (often with a racialized distribution) end in marijuana possession arrests (Mueller 2018; Rice 2018). Lauren Ouziel has nicely highlighted how the distinct ways each criminal justice bureaucracy refracts public preferences will lead to particularly constructive (or problematic) dialogues between criminal justice institutions during a period of policy flux (Ouziel 2020).

14.5 Prosecutorial Role in Monitoring and Training Police

In their role as adjudicative gatekeeper, and particularly when they do not see a case until they need to make a charging decision, prosecutors will inevitably act on their assessments of police conduct: Did the police gather sufficient evidence? Did the gathering of the evidence comply with constitutional and sub-constitutional requirements? Police internalization of prosecutorial decisions in this regard may have an educative and disciplinary effect. Yet, prosecutors can do much more to promote compliance with evidentiary standards and the rule of law, both in specific cases and broader interventions.

As David Sklansky explains:

> Prosecutors present and defend the work of the police in court, but they also explain and legitimize the law to the police, and—in varying degrees—supervise the police to ensure they comply with the law. They are envoys—"culture-brokers"—between the realm of the judges and the domain of law enforcement, between the courtroom and the squad room. (2017, 503–504)

Prosecutors can play the role of "translators and organizational intermediaries" (Sklansky 2017, 504) in a number of ways. At the very least, they can ensure that police officers fully understand why evidence found to have been illegally seized has been suppressed. Not only can every suppression decision be a teaching moment, but so too can the preparation for every suppression hearing. When doing the latter, prosecutors must take care to avoid presenting the relevant legal standard as a target the officer should tailor his testimony to fit. Indeed, a prosecutor is particularly well placed to ensure that officers should testify truthfully (Williams 2001, 836–837), in part by assuring officers that she is perfectly prepared to work with any true set of facts. Prosecutors in specialized units, who develop relationships with a group of officers, can also share legal expertise and institutional knowledge beyond context of a specific case (Levine and Wright 2012, 1176–1177).

Prosecutors might go even further than working to get the police to internalize judicial rulings. The Fourth Amendment's exclusionary rule doctrine has found any number of exceptions—scenarios when unconstitutionally obtained evidence can nonetheless be introduced against a defendant. Russell Gold has suggested that prosecutors have an executive and ethical obligation to avoid using evidence that they deem unconstitutionally obtained even when a court would allow its use—"a duty of administrative suppression" (2014, 1595). Were prosecutors to take this duty seriously, he reasons, the police, to avoid this suppression

> would be incentivized to consult prosecutors for their Fourth Amendment expertise, which would allow prosecutors to serve their intended role as an intra-executive-branch check. Police would more frequently ask prosecutors to approve warrant applications—as ethical standards already recommend—and prosecutors would have reason to make that review as stringent as possible. (2014, 1596)

Moreover, after the fact, were prosecutors to tell officers not just of their decision to suppress but of the rationale for doing so, officers would gain a far better understanding of the constitutional duties that judicial suppression decisions under-enforce (Gold 2014, 1596). Gold's assumption that the public safety effects of prosecutors accepting this extrajudicial role would be minimal is contestable. But he is quite right to focus on the promise of the prosecutorial role in promoting constitutional policing.

Prosecutors can similarly turn their dismissal of a case against a person the police have arrested without a warrant into a "teachable moment" (Gershowitz 2019). Adam Gershowitz urges prosecutors' offices to adopt a formal policy in that regard and suggests the possibility of a database that could identify officers who regularly bring in weak cases. Surveying a variety of offices, he found wide variation in the degree to which prosecutors tried to communicate dismissal information to police officers (2019, 9). Prosecutorial feedback has been found particularly useful in promoting police compliance with evidentiary collection protocols that lead to stronger cases against domestic abusers (Nelson 2013, 8).

Efforts by prosecutors to educate police officers (and perhaps vice versa, since good teachers always learn from their students) will often occur in more formal settings. The ABA Criminal Justice Standards for the Prosecution Function recommend that prosecutor offices

> promote compliance by law enforcement personnel with applicable legal rules, including rules against improper bias. The prosecutor's office should keep law enforcement personnel informed of relevant legal and legal ethics issues and developments as they relate to prosecution matters and advise law enforcement personnel of relevant prosecution policies and procedures.
>
> (ABA Standards 2017, 3-3.2; Logan 2011, 108)

Even where the prosecutor's office does not have a formal role in police training, as in Atlanta, police academy "instructors consult with the D.A.'s Office about specific problem areas in which the District Attorneys would like to see the recruits receive more training" (Fleming Hirokawa 2000, 322).

Just as prosecutors can provide much needed information about legal compliance to the police, so too can their failure to do so risk systemic dysfunction. Such appears to be the recent lesson from Orange County, California, where, presented with evidence that the Sheriff's Department had used a network of jailhouse informants to exact illegal confessions, an appellate court condemned the D.A.'s office (OCDA) for allowing its "loyalty to the Sheriff [to] interfere[] with its ability to discharge its constitutional and statutory obligations":

> Not only did the OCDA intentionally or negligently ignore the Sheriff's violations of targeted defendants' constitutional rights, but the OCDA on its own violated targeted defendants' constitutional rights through its participation in the CI program.
>
> (*People v. Dekraai* 2016, 1145)

14.6 Disclosure as a Site of Police-Prosecutorial Interaction across Cases

Police-prosecutor interaction, and the possibility of enhanced police accountability, can involve police conduct separate from the investigative activity that generated the interaction. Such is the case when the constitutional obligation on a prosecutor to disclose "material" exculpatory or impeachment evidence to defense counsel (often referred to as the *Brady* obligation)[4] requires inquiry into the disciplinary records of police officers whose past abusive or deceitful actions might constitute evidence of just this sort. In deference to this obligation and spurred by its interaction with defense lawyers pressing for such disclosure, a prosecutor's office might use its leverage over a police department to press for disciplinary records and investigative reports that the department is averse to sharing (McKinley 2018). Many offices do not, however, leaving the compliance with the constitutional mandate to police departments, or to defense counsel diligence (when records are publicly available) (Abel 2015, 743; Levine 2019).

A prosecutor's office, should it press forward, may use its privileged access to information about officer conduct not merely to ensure disclosure and adjudicative fairness but to deter and sanction illegal or improper conduct. Such efforts can be informal and invisible to outsiders, such as a conversation between a supervisory prosecutor and a police supervisor or commander about a problematic officer. Yet a prosecutor trying to send—perhaps to the public or even to the entire police force—a broader message that she will not tolerate certain behavior or practices can go further. In 2018, for example, the Circuit Attorney for St. Louis delivered an "exclusion list" to the police department naming twenty-eight officers from whom her office would henceforth not accept cases. She spoke only generally about the "responsibility" of prosecutors to "defend the integrity of the criminal justice system," and how any "breach of trust" on the part of an officer, when it came to the "veracity" of his word, "must be approached with deep concern." In response, an official from the police union complained that some officers were on the list because they had "asserted their Fifth Amendment right against self-incrimination in cases where [the prosecutor]'s office was simultaneously reviewing an officer's conduct in a police shooting and pursuing charges against the person shot" (Byers 2018). That same year, a Texas county's chief prosecutor's refusal to accept cases from one local department's officer—whom she accused of "unethical" and "untrustworthy" behavior—spiraled into her refusal to take any cases from the entire police department for more than a year (O'Rourke 2018).

When a police officer's disciplinary record is serious enough to lead a prosecutor's office to avoid calling him as a witness—lest his credibility be undermined with such impeachment material—the officer's value to his department will likely suffer. The prospect of this happening can itself lead to troubling strategic acting within the shared workspace, with prosecutors putting officers on the "*Brady* list" for trivial or otherwise unjustified reasons, perhaps even at the behest of a police chief seeking to punish a disfavored officer (Abel 2015, 781–782). The possibility of misuse, however, ought not deter a prosecutor's office from carefully considering, and disclosing, *Brady* material and appreciating the institutional consequences of doing so. Moreover, prosecutors can and should draw on their own experiences with testifying officers—particularly those they suspect of "testilying" (Williams 2001, 834)—when choosing witnesses and communicating concerns to police commands.

14.7 Police Shootings

While prosecutorial disclosure obligations can be a source of tension with police rank and file and perhaps police leadership, that tension pales beside that arising when the police-prosecutor interaction occurs not in the context of charges against a civilian defendant but when prosecutors consider criminal charges against an officer.

As Kate Levine notes:

> [T]he same skills and relationships that effectuate a functioning system when prosecuting civilian defendants make local prosecutors the least objective adversaries when it comes to prosecuting law enforcement. When prosecuting an officer, the prosecutor must switch from her reliance on the police as allies to the position of an adversary, questioning the credibility and judgment of a police officer, charging the officer with crimes that often carry stiff prison sentences, and pursuing the case against the officer as vigorously as she would against a civilian defendant.
>
> (Levine 2016, 1470)

Whatever internal conflict a prosecutor feels by virtue of her position will likely be exacerbated by external forces when she needs to decide whether to charge an officer. Now the police union likely to have played a part in the prosecutor's election will often have strong views (Levine 2016, 1476), as will interest groups whose expressions of views will not necessarily be proportionate to their knowledge of the actual facts of the case. Police leadership might steer officers away from an oppositional stance, but they cannot be counted on to do so. Because of these "cognitive biases and political pressures," Levine would bar local prosecutors from handling these cases, leaving them to a prosecutor from a different county, the state attorney general, or federal prosecutors, even as she acknowledges the drawbacks of each alternative. Suffice it to say that jurisdictions around the nation are still working through how best to handle these cases (Institute for Innovation in Prosecution 2019).

Although cases involving police misconduct occupy but a small part of a prosecutor's docket, they have, as Rachel Harmon observes, "substantial symbolic and normative importance."

> No other form of remedy so clearly expresses the government's condemnation of specific police violations of law, and none shows as much respect for the victims of police misconduct, especially with respect to police violence. Prosecutions also build public confidence in the government's commitment to lawful policing and fair application of criminal justice. (Harmon 2017, 43)

14.8 Conclusion

Although police departments and prosecutor's offices cannot function without a high degree of collaboration, their organizational roles and networks, coupled with the distinctive perspectives of their personnel, will inevitably and regularly lead to forceful dialogue and occasionally disruptive friction over the range of their interactions. Within the frame of an individual case, those involved might fairly worry that such friction will undermine thoughtful deliberation about public safety, the rule of law, and democratic responsiveness. Viewed more broadly, however, these interactions are a critical source of just such deliberation, which will become even healthier and more valuable when the dialogue breaks out of the closed world of criminal justice bureaucracies and includes the public to which these bureaucracies are ultimately responsible.

Notes

1. See Chapters 2, 9, 12, 18, 21, 22, and 25 in this volume.
2. But see Russell M. Gold (2014, 1646), noting that police have authority, in most jurisdictions, to obtain a warrant without prosecutorial approval.
3. I've also noted how the organizational literature on team production can help "reconcile us to the doctrinal oddity of thinking in separation of power terms within the executive branch" (Richman 2003, 810). For further discussions of how separation of power principles can be implemented within a prosecutor's office, see Barkow 2006, 989; Barkow 2009, 897; Green and Roiphe 2017, 510–511.
4. See *Kyles v. Whitley* 1995, 421.

References

American Bar Association. 2017. *Standards for Criminal Justice: Prosecution Function*. 4th ed. Chicago: American Bar Association.

Abbott, Andrew. 1988. *The System of Professions: An Essay on the Division of Expert Labor*. Chicago: The University of Chicago Press.

Abel, Jonathan. 2015. "*Brady*'s Blind Spot: Impeachment Evidence in Police Personnel Files and the Battle Splitting the Prosecution Team." *Stanford Law Review* 67(4): 743–808.

Abel, Jonathan. 2017. "Cops and Pleas: Police Officers' Influence on Plea Bargaining." *Yale Law Journal* 126(6): 1730–1787.

Baker, Al. 2017 "Police Evaluations Should Focus on Lawfulness of Stops, Monitor Says." *New York Times*, October 20, 2017.

Bandes, Susan A. 2006. "Loyalty to One's Convictions: The Prosecutor and Tunnel Vision." *Howard Law Journal* 49(2): 475–494.

Bardach, Eugene. 1998. *Getting Agencies to Work Together: The Practice and Theory of Managerial Craftsmanship*. Washington: Brookings Institution Press.

Barkow, Rachel E. 2006. "Separation of Powers and the Criminal Law." *Stanford Law Review* 58(4): 989–1054.

Barkow, Rachel. 2009. "Institutional Design and the Policing of Prosecutors: Lessons from Administrative Law." *Stanford Law Review* 61(4): 869–922.

Bowers, Josh. 2010. "Legal Guilt, Normative Innocence, and the Equitable Decision Not to Prosecute." *Columbia Law Review* 110(7): 1655–1726.

Burke, Alafair. 2007. "Neutralizing Cognitive Bias: An Invitation to Prosecutors." *New York University Journal of Law & Liberty* 2(3): 512–530.

Byers, Christine. 2018. "St. Louis Prosecutor Says She Will No Longer Accept Cases from 28 City Police Officers." *St. Louis Post-Dispatch*, August 31, 2018.

Damaška, Mirjan R. 1984. *The Faces of Justice and State Authority*. New Haven: Yale University Press.

Feeley, Malcolm M. 1979. *The Process Is the Punishment: Handling Cases in a Lower Criminal Court*. New York: Russell Sage Foundation.

Feeley, Malcolm M., and Mark H. Lazerson. 1983. "Police-Prosecutor Relationships: An Interorganizational Perspective." In *Empirical Theories about Courts*. Edited by Keith O. Boyum and Lynn Mather, 216–243. New York: Longman.

Findley, Keith A., and Michael Scott. 2006. "The Multiple Dimensions of Tunnel Vision in Criminal Cases." *Wisconsin Law Review* 49(2): 291–398.

Flagg, Anna, and Ashley Nerbovig. 2018. "Subway Policing in New York City Still Has a Race Problem." *Gothamist.com*, September 12, 2018.

Fleming Hirokawa, Corey. 2000. "Making the Law of the Land the Law on the Street: How Police Academies Teach Evolving Fourth Amendment Law." *Emory Law Journal* 49(1): 295–372.

Frye, Nikolas. 2012. "Allowing New Hampshire Police Officers to Prosecute: Concerns with the Practice and a Solution." *New England Journal of Criminal & Civil Confinement* 38(2): 339–358.

Gattrell, V. A. C. 1990. "Crime, Authority and the Policeman State." In *Cambridge Social History of Britain, 1750–1950*. Edited by F. M. L. Thompson, 243–310. Cambridge: Cambridge University Press.

Gershowitz, Adam. 2019. "Justice on the Line: Prosecutorial Screening Before Arrest." *University of Illinois Law Review* 2019(3): 833–873.

Godfrey, Barry. 2008. "Changing Prosecution Practices and Their Impact on Crime Figures: 1857–1940." *British Journal of Criminology* 48(2): 171–189.

Godsey, Mark. 2019. *Blind Injustice: A Former Prosecutor Exposes the Psychology and Politics of Wrongful Convictions*. Berkeley: University of California Press.

Gold, Russell M. 2011. "Promoting Democracy in Prosecution." *Washington Law Review* 86(1): 69–124.

Gold, Russell M. 2014. "Beyond the Judicial Fourth Amendment: The Prosecutor's Role." *U.C. Davis Law Review* 47(5): 1591–1666.

Goldstein, Joseph. 2012. "Prosecutor Deals Blow to Stop-and-Frisk Tactic." *New York Times*, September 25, 2012.

Green, Bruce A., and Rebecca Roiphe. 2017. "Rethinking Prosecutors' Conflicts of Interest." *Boston College Law Review* 58(2): 463–538.

Griffin, Lissa. 2017. "Ministers of Justice and Mass Incarceration." *Georgia Journal of Legal Ethics* 30(2): 301–335.

Harmon, Rachel H. 2017. "Legal Remedies for Police Misconduct." In *Reforming Criminal Justice: Policing*. Edited by Erik Luna, vol. 2, 27–50. Phoenix, AZ: Academy for Justice.

Hodgson, Jacqueline S. 2010. "The French Prosecutor in Question." *Washington & Lee Law Review* 67(4): 1361–1411.

Hodgson, Jacqueline S. 2017. "The Democratic Accountability of Prosecutors in England and Wales and France: Independence, Discretion and Managerialism." In *Prosecutors and Democracy: A Cross-National Study*. Edited by Máximo Langer and David Alan Sklansky, 76-108. Cambridge: Cambridge University Press.

Horwitz, Andrew. 1998. "Taking the Cop Out of Copping a Plea: Eradicating Police Prosecution of Criminal Cases." *Arizona Law Review* 40(4): 1305–1378.

Howell, K. Babe. 2014. "Prosecutorial Discretion and the Duty to Seek Justice in an Overburdened Criminal Justice System." *Georgia Journal of Legal Ethics* 27(2): 285–334.

Institute for Innovation in Prosecution. 2019. *The Prosecutor's Role in Addressing Officer-Involved Fatalities and Critical Incidents*. New York: John Jay College of Criminal Justice.

Jain, Eisha. 2015. "Arrests as Regulation." *Stanford Law Review* 67(4): 809–867.

Johnson, David T. 2012. "Japan's Prosecution System." *Crime and Justice* 41(1): 35–74.

Kyles v. Whitley. 1995. 514 U.S. 419.
Levine, Kate. 2016. "Who Shouldn't Prosecute the Police." *Iowa Law Review* 101(4): 286–334.
Levine, Kate. 2019. "Discipline and Policing." *Duke Law Journal* 68(5): 839–905.
Levine, Kay, and Ronald F. Wright. 2012. "Prosecution in 3-D," *Journal of Criminal Law & Criminology* 102(4): 1119–1180.
Logan, Wayne A. 2011. "Police Mistakes of Law." *Emory Law Journal* 61(1): 69–110.
McKinley, James C., Jr. 2017. "Cy Vance Defends Decision Not to Pursue Case Against Harvey Weinstein." *New York Times*, October 11, 2017.
McKinley, James C., Jr. 2018. "Manhattan District Attorney Demands Access to Police Records." *New York Times*, July 9, 2018.
Medwed, Daniel S. 2004. "The Zeal Deal, Prosecutorial Resistance to Post-Conviction Claims of Innocence." *Boston University Law Review* 84(1): 125–184.
Mou, Yu. 2017. "Overseeing Criminal Justice: The Supervisory Role of the Public Prosecution Service in China." *Journal of Law & Society* 44(4): 620–645.
Mueller, Benjamin. 2018. "Two District Attorneys May Stop Prosecuting Most Marijuana Arrests." *New York Times*, May 14, 2018.
Mummolo, Jonathan. 2018. "Modern Police Tactics, Police-Citizen Interactions, and the Prospects for Reform." *Journal of Politics* 80(1): 1–15.
Natapoff, Alexandra. 2018. *Punishment Without Crime*. New York: Basic Books.
Nelson, Eric L. 2012. "Police Controlled Antecedents Which Significantly Elevate Prosecution and Conviction Rates in Domestic Violence Cases." *Criminology & Criminal Justice* 13(5): 526–551.
Nelson, Eric L. 2013. "The Relationship Between Individual Police Officer Work Habits and the Stated Reasons Prosecutors Reject Their Domestic Violence Investigations." *SAGE Open* (October-December 2013): 1–11.
New York City Bar Task Force on Town and Village Courts. 2007. *Recommendations Relating to Structure and Organization*. New York: Association of the Bar of the City of New York.
O'Rourke, Ciara. 2018. "The Prosecution Rests." *Texas Observer*, September 14, 2018.
Ouziel, Lauren M. 2020. "Democracy, Bureaucracy, and Criminal Justice." Boston College Law Review 61(2): 523–589.
People v. Dekraai. 2016. 5 Cal.App.5th 1110 (4th Dist.).
Prudente, Tim. 2019. "Baltimore Will Stop Prosecuting Marijuana Possession, Mosby Announces." *Baltimore Sun*, January 30, 2019.
Rice, Rachel. 2018. "St. Louis Circuit Attorney's Office Will Dismiss Some Smaller Marijuana Possession Cases." *St. Louis Dispatch*, June 13, 2018.
Richman, Daniel. 1995. "Cooperating Clients." *Ohio State Law Journal* 56(2): 69–152.
Richman, Daniel. 2003. "Prosecutors and Their Agents, Agents and Their Prosecutors." *Columbia Law Review* 103(4): 749–832.
Richman, Daniel. 2006. "Institutional Coordination and Sentencing Reform." *Texas Law Review* 84(7): 2055–2074.
Richman, Daniel. 2017. "Accounting for Prosecutors." In *Prosecutors and Democracy: A Cross-National Study*. Edited by Máximo Langer and David Alan Sklansky, 40–75. Cambridge: Cambridge University Press.
Rose, Joel, and Rose Friedman. 2018. "Weinstein Seeks Dismissal of Sexual Assault Case in Possible#MeTooSetback." *NPR*, December 17, 2018.
Simon, Dan. 2012. *In Doubt: The Psychology of the Criminal Justice Process*. Berkeley: University of California Press.

Sklansky, David Alan. 2017. "The Nature and Function of Prosecutorial Power." *Journal of Criminal Law & Criminology* 106(3): 473–520.
Tomberlin, James. 2018. "'Don't Elect Me': Sheriffs and the Need for Reform in County Law Enforcement." *Virginia Law Review* 104(1): 113–156.
Williams, Gary C. 2001. "Incubating Monsters: Prosecutorial Responsibility for the Rampart Scandal." *Loyola of Los Angeles Law Review* 34(2): 829–842.
Wright, Ronald F. 2009. "How Prosecutor Elections Fail Us." *Ohio State Journal of Criminal Law* 6(2): 581–610.
Wright, Ronald F. 2014. "Beyond Prosecutor Elections." *Southern Methodist University Law Review* 67(3): 593–616.
Wright, Ronald, and Marc Miller. 2002. "The Screening/Bargaining Tradeoff." *Stanford Law Review* 55(1): 29–118.

CHAPTER 15

BAR AUTHORITIES AND PROSECUTORS

BRUCE A. GREEN

15.1 Introduction

THIS chapter examines how institutions of the legal profession (i.e., Bar associations) influence the professional work of U.S. prosecutors. For the most part, the Bar's influence is indirect, arising out of Bar associations' informal role in the lawyer regulatory processes overseen by state supreme courts. To a large extent, prosecutors regard the legal profession's influence as unwelcome, leading prosecutors to resist it, often successfully. Consequently, the lawyer regulatory processes have occasionally become a battleground between institutions of the organized Bar, on one hand, and prosecutors' offices and representatives, on the other.

15.2 Professional Regulation of Prosecutors

U.S. prosecutors are not regulated independently from other lawyers. There is no separate track for educating and licensing U.S. prosecutors, no separate body of rules governing their professional conduct, and, with rare exceptions in some jurisdictions, no separate disciplinary mechanism for investigating their alleged wrongdoing or for sanctioning them for professional misconduct.[1]

The regulation of U.S. lawyers is primarily the responsibility of the courts, not of Bar associations. In the case of U.S. advocates, including prosecutors, courts regulate through two different processes—first, through state courts' adoption of professional conduct rules and their enforcement of these rules through disciplinary processes; and second, in the course of overseeing individual civil and criminal cases in which trial or appellate courts may sanction lawyers for misconduct or issue opinions expressing their normative expectations for lawyers' work:

> The processes by which courts develop and propound enforceable norms to govern US advocates' work are unusual, if not unique, in that courts proceed down two separate tracks, which occasionally converge, occasionally diverge and occasionally run parallel. A US lawyer must comply with a formal set of professional conduct rules adopted by the judiciary of the state in which the lawyer is licensed to practice law.... But US lawyers' work in the course of litigation is defined not only by rules but also by other standards of conduct that courts develop on an ad hoc basis in common law fashion [in the course of adjudication].
>
> (Green 2013b)

The standards adopted and applied in these different contexts are not necessarily consistent (Zacharias and Green 2009a). This chapter focuses on the regulation of prosecutors through disciplinary rules and processes, not on judicial regulation in the course of criminal adjudication.

While the institutions within which prosecutors work (e.g., District or County Attorneys' Offices) may also oversee prosecutors, judicial regulation of U.S. prosecutors is a practical necessity, in part, because prosecution in the United States is decentralized. Unlike in countries such as Japan where all prosecutors are employed by a centralized Ministry of Justice (Johnson 2002), prosecutors in the United States work in a range of different autonomous offices, some quite small, at different levels of government. While federal prosecutors serving under the auspices of the U.S. Department of Justice ("DOJ") are subject to formalized, internal regulation (Green 1995; 2009), elected prosecutors in rural counties may work independently or with a handful of subordinates within an institutional framework that affords little or no meaningful oversight.

The organized Bar's influence over U.S. prosecutors arises primarily out of its role in the adoption and interpretation of professional conduct rules, which are sometimes referred to colloquially as ethics rules. For over a century, the American Bar Association ("ABA"), a voluntary membership association speaking on behalf of all U.S. lawyers, has sought to influence the development of the professional conduct rules adopted and enforced by state courts. In 1908, thirty years after its founding, the ABA adopted *Canons of Professional Ethics* ("Canons") with the aim of influencing judicial decisions concerning lawyers' conduct. Eventually, state courts exercised their rule-making authority, as afforded by state constitutions or statutes, to adopt professional conduct rules. The ABA's 1970 *Model Code of Professional Responsibility* became the basis of almost all state rules until 1981 when the ABA adopted the *Model Rules of Professional Conduct* ("Model Rules") (ABA 2018).

As of today, every state judiciary has a set of professional conduct rules that is based significantly on the Model Rules. State judiciaries have declined to adopt some provisions proposed by the ABA, have supplemented the proposed rules, and have occasionally re-worded them. But there is nevertheless significant state judicial agreement on the substance of lawyers' professional obligations as a result of the ABA's efforts to harmonize the professional conduct rules among the state courts. For the most part, the rules apply to all lawyers, including prosecutors, insofar as relevant to their work; however, there is an additional rule, Model Rule 3.8, titled "Special Responsibilities of a Prosecutor," containing eight provisions applicable to prosecutors specifically.

The ABA periodically amends the Model Rules, and this provides it an opportunity to propose new rules in response to newly perceived problems of professional conduct. Additionally, the ABA has a Standing Committee on Professional Ethics (known as its ethics committee) which issues opinions interpreting the Model Rules in the context of particular problems lawyers face. Although the ABA's interpretations are not binding on state courts, they are intended to influence courts in their interpretation of the state rules that correspond to the Model Rules. State and local Bar associations play a role in promoting the adoption of versions of the Model Rules in the individual states, and sometimes they propose new rules that have no counterpart in the Model Rules. Many state and local Bar associations also have ethics committees that interpret their states' professional conduct rules.

Although the focus of this chapter is on the Bar's regulatory influence, the legal profession seeks to exert influence on prosecutors in at least three other ways. First, Bar associations, and particularly the ABA, publish writings expressing normative expectations for prosecutors that are not necessarily meant to be judicially enforced; rather, these writings are primarily meant to influence prosecutors' offices and individual prosecutors as a matter of self-governance. For example, the ABA has adopted sets of *Criminal Justice Standards* ("Standards") that offer guidance, and express the ABA's position, regarding various aspects of the criminal justice process. These include Standards on "The Prosecution Function" that focus on prosecutors' conduct (ABA 2015; Green 2011b). Guidance is also offered to prosecutors in the writings of voluntary "specialty" Bar associations that have been formed exclusively to serve as organizational representatives of prosecutors both locally and nationally (DAASNY 2011; NDAA 2009). Prosecutors' publications sometimes reflect disagreement with the views expressed by the ABA or by state Bar associations (Green 1999).

Second, Bar associations take positions on legislation and in court cases, including on issues regarding prosecutorial conduct. For example, some Bar organizations, including both the ABA and the National District Attorneys Association ("NDAA"), file legal briefs as *amicus curiae* in U.S. Supreme Court cases or other cases, including sometimes cases relating to prosecutorial conduct (Green 2012). Both the ABA and the National Association of Criminal Defense Lawyers ("NACDL"), which principally represents members of the criminal defense Bar, lobby for law reform relating to criminal justice, including law reform relating to prosecutors' disclosure obligations or other aspects of their work (Green 2013a).

Third, Bar associations sometimes call perceived problems directly to the attention of prosecutors, in an effort to influence prosecutors to change their practices on their own. Typically, the Bar's efforts at persuasion are more effective when they are accompanied by the possibility of legislative or judicial reform. An illustration is the effort of the ABA, together with other organizations, to persuade the DOJ to change its practice of rewarding corporations for waiving the attorney-client privilege. A 1999 DOJ memorandum encouraged white-collar prosecutors investigating and prosecuting corporate crime to provide leniency to a corporation that assisted the government's investigation, in part, by waiving its attorney-client privilege in order to provide information acquired by the corporation's lawyers in interviewing corporate employees. Successor memoranda failed to assuage the ABA's concern about how pressure and inducements from federal prosecutors and regulators were eroding the protections of the attorney-client privilege. The ABA engaged DOJ "in a public dialogue in an attempt to coax [it] into modifying [its] policies" while at the same time working with other organizations to lobby for legal reform (McFadyen 2007).

15.3 The Professional Codes' Limited Impact on Prosecutors' Work

The state courts' professional conduct codes have limited practical significance for prosecutors because they are not very stringent. They contain few provisions dealing exclusively with prosecutors, with aspects of prosecutors' work that differ from the work of advocates for private clients, and with ways in which prosecutors' professional expectations differ from those of other lawyers (Green 2017).

One could envision the Bar developing a separate prosecutorial ethics code with the objective of encouraging state courts to adopt it and enforce it in the disciplinary process. The code could address the full range of prosecutors' work and give expression to the courts' recognition that prosecutors' distinct role gives rise to distinctive professional obligations—a "duty to seek justice" (Green 1999; Zacharias 1991). However, Model Rule 3.8, concerning prosecutors' "special responsibilities," brings together only a handful of provisions that state courts have adopted selectively (Green 2003). A Comment accompanying Rule 3.8 acknowledges prosecutors' unique role:

> A prosecutor has the responsibility of a minister of justice and not simply that of an advocate. This responsibility carries with it specific obligations to see that the defendant is accorded procedural justice, that guilt is decided upon the basis of sufficient evidence, and that special precautions are taken to prevent and to rectify the convictions of innocent persons.
>
> (ABA 2018)

However, with an eye toward preserving a "unified Bar," the ABA has declined to adopt and promote specialized sets of professional conduct rules for lawyers, such as prosecutors, who work in specialized areas of legal practice (Green 2016c). Further, the ABA has rejected the idea of significantly expanding Rule 3.8 to fully elaborate prosecutors' special obligations (Green 2003).

Many of the existing professional conduct rules have no application at all to prosecutors. For example, provisions regulating lawyers in their business role, such as those governing marketing and legal fees, are irrelevant to government lawyers such as prosecutors. Further, the provisions regulating lawyers' relationship with clients have only limited significance for prosecutors. A defining normative expectation for prosecutors—albeit, one not specifically addressed in the ethics codes—is their "professional independence" from external influences, including other public officials (Green and Roiphe 2018). Prosecutors do not interact with, advise, or take direction from, an individual client or a representative of an institutional client. Rather, prosecutors, as public officials, themselves make decisions in a legal representation analogous to the decisions that a private client would make in an ordinary lawyer-client relationship. Therefore, provisions concerning such subjects as the lawyer's role in counseling clients, the scope of the representation and the allocation of decision-making are inapplicable to prosecutors.[2]

Other provisions "are far less significant for [prosecutors] than for other lawyers"—in particular, those codifying lawyers' fiduciary duties of confidentiality, loyalty, and competence (Green and Zacharias 2000). While the provision on client confidentiality is highly significant in an ordinary representation, it has minimal importance for prosecutors, who are subject to other legal restrictions, such as criminal procedure rules on grand jury secrecy, which establish their obligations of confidentiality. Similarly, although prosecutors, like other lawyers, must avoid conflicts of interest, the standards regarding prosecutors' impermissible conflicts of interest are principally established by court decisions and law apart from the professional conduct rules (Green and Roiphe 2017).

In theory, the duty of competence might be interpreted to require reasonable care to prevent convictions of the innocent, and as so interpreted, might "regulate much of the conduct currently left to prosecutorial discretion." However, disciplinary authorities and courts have neither endorsed a broad interpretation of the competence rule nor applied the rule rigorously to prosecutors (Zacharias and Green 2009).

For prosecutors, the most significant of the generally applicable professional conduct rules are those regulating the work of advocates, including their interactions with the court, defendants, opposing counsel, and witnesses. Most of these provisions are uncontroversial and add little to other law. Some ethics provisions subject advocates, including prosecutors, to professional discipline for violating existing legal obligations such as court rules, case law, and statutes governing disclosure to the opposing party, and criminal law forbidding suborning or exploiting perjurious testimony. Various others incorporate judicial and professional expectations that have prevailed for over a century. By incorporating other law and codifying conventional understandings, the rules give disciplinary authorities a basis for sanctioning lawyers who violate well-accepted professional norms.

Notwithstanding the ordinary assumption that prosecutors' special role as "ministers of justice" subjects them to more rigorous ethical demands than other lawyers (Green 1999; 2016b), some professional conduct rules have been interpreted and applied even less restrictively with respect to the work of prosecutors than with respect to the analogous work of other advocates (Zacharias and Green 2000). For example, with limited exception, neither private lawyers nor private investigators acting at their direction are permitted to deceive others in order to obtain admissions or gather other evidence, but these restrictions on deceitful conduct are generally considered inapplicable to police and other investigative agents with whom prosecutors work. Similarly, although private lawyers may not compensate witnesses for agreeing to testify, prosecutors may give witnesses a substantial inducement—namely, leniency from prosecution.

The organized Bar has largely acceded to prosecutors' assumption that, in these respects, the relevant professional conduct rules should apply differently and less demandingly to prosecutors' work in light of the importance and particular challenges of criminal investigations.

Additionally, the Bar's ability to influence prosecutors indirectly through the professional conduct rules potentially depends on the courts' willingness not only to adopt the Bar's proposed rules and interpretations but to enforce the rules either through the formal disciplinary process or in individual criminal cases. Some prosecutors may ignore professional conduct rules if they do not perceive a serious risk that disciplinary authorities or courts will punish them for rule breaking. At least until recently, however, "the conventional wisdom has been that disciplinary authorities do not effectively regulate prosecutors" and "in the rare cases of discipline, courts typically let prosecutors off too lightly" (Green and Levine 2016). Critics point both to the scarcity of cases in which prosecutors are publicly disciplined and to the seemingly high number of cases in which a trial court found that the prosecutor engaged in misconduct but no discipline followed (Green 1995; 2010; Sullivan and Possley 2015; Zacharias 2001):

> Courts and scholars have identified a wide array of prosecutorial misconduct that violates a variety of disciplinary rules. For example, courts have documented numerous violations of prosecutors' discovery obligations, which defense lawyers and some courts assume to be the tip of the iceberg. Courts have identified frequent improprieties in prosecutors' jury arguments, typically finding that the improprieties were "harmless error." Prosecutors have been found to commit various other improprieties, both in and out of court. In contrast, studies suggest, prosecutors have relatively rarely faced public discipline.
>
> (Green and Levine 2016)

The apparent lack of serious disciplinary enforcement might be explained by the ordinary selectivity of disciplinary authorities, who reserve their resources for "instances of misconduct that are intentional, recurring, and/or extremely prejudicial," but critics perceive "that disciplinary authorities have overlooked even serious prosecutorial wrongdoing, as long as the conduct falls short of criminal law breaking" (Green 1995; Green and Levine 2016).[3] Although prosecutors are assumed to have a professional commitment to complying with professional conduct rules, among other law, it seems unlikely that their commitment is significantly reinforced by the perceived disciplinary risk (Yaroshefsky and Green 2012).

Perhaps the Bar's most successful effort to influence prosecutors through the regulatory process has been its work to discourage all trial lawyers, including prosecutors, from discussing their cases outside of court. The ABA's efforts led to both Model Rule 3.6, which restricts advocates from discussing ongoing cases in the public media, and a set of Criminal Justice Standards (ABA 2013). The ABA's efforts originated in the 1908 Canons but truly began in earnest in the late 1960s in response to concerns that advocates' quotes in newspapers or their appearances on radio or television would have an inordinate impact on jurors and prospective jurors in high-profile cases (Matheson 1990). Because of countervailing concern for constitutionally protected speech, the rule does not forbid all extrajudicial comments about lawyers' pending cases but only extrajudicial statements that "will have a substantial likelihood of materially prejudicing" the trial by bringing improper considerations to the jury's attention. If anything, as a practical matter, Rule 3.6 imposes less restraint on prosecutors than on defense lawyers because it allows lawyers to discuss matters that are already in the public record. This means that prosecutors, who place more information in the public record than defense lawyers, have substantial leeway to hold press conferences or issue press releases recounting matters that appear in their indictments and other public filings. Rule 3.6 has been adopted by the state supreme courts, which share the ABA's disapproval of trial lawyers' efforts to try their cases in the media. Prosecutors have not opposed the rule because it does not interfere with their core function of investigating and prosecuting criminal conduct, it does not single them out or uniquely disadvantage them, and, to the contrary, they benefit from the reciprocal restraint imposed on criminal defense lawyers. Although prosecutors occasionally violate the rule (Levenson 2010), and are rarely disciplined for doing so, trial judges have sometimes responded to prosecutors' transgressions with public expressions of disapproval. Particularly in the internet era, it seems likely that without the rule, some prosecutors would be substantially less restrained in discussing their cases in the media.

15.4 Adoption and Interpretation of Professional Conduct Rules: Areas of Controversy

The organized Bar is not limited to proposing professional conduct rules that simply codify existing law or deeply rooted professional understandings. The Bar can propose new rules, or promote interpretations of existing rules, that would restrain lawyers' conduct in order to promote professional values such as the integrity of the profession, the preservation of attorney-client relationships and the fairness of adjudicative proceedings. In recent decades, the organized Bar has in fact sought to influence prosecutors through the adoption or interpretation of professional conduct rules with respect to several areas of prosecutorial conduct. But the Bar has not been as influential as it has hoped.

The Bar's lengthiest and most contentious conflict with prosecutors over professional regulation concerned criminal investigations. The conflict centered around Rule 4.2, a professional conduct rule forbidding all lawyers from communicating directly with represented individuals without the permission of the individuals' counsel. The "no-contact" rule found expression in an 1836 treatise and then in the 1908 Canons. At its inception, it may have been intended less to protect represented clients from opposing lawyers' overreaching than to promote courtesy among lawyers (Hazard and Irwin 2009; Leubsdorf 1979). But courts came to take the rule seriously in civil litigation, sometimes sanctioning lawyers or suppressing evidence when it was violated, in order to protect attorney-client relationships from intrusion and to ensure represented clients the benefit of legal advice in their interactions with opposing counsel (Flamm 2014).

In the 1980s, criminal defense lawyers began to invoke the rule "as a ground for suppressing admissions made by represented defendants in the course of undercover investigations and interviews by investigators and informants acting under prosecutors' direction" (Green 2012). The defense lawyers argued in individual criminal cases that the no-contact rule, applicable to prosecutors no less than other lawyers, effectively established restraints in criminal investigations that were more stringent than those imposed by constitutional case law and legislation. Prosecutors initially countered that courts should interpret the rule to be coextensive with other law (Cramton and Udell 1992; Green 1996; Zacharias and Green 2000).

Although the effort to give meaning to the no-contact rule was driven primarily by defense lawyers, the ABA was not entirely a bystander. It sought unsuccessfully to find common ground with prosecutors around an interpretation or revision of Rule 4.2 that would have some significance without seriously impeding criminal investigatory efforts. Failing that, the ABA's ethics committee sought to placate prosecutors by publishing an interpretive opinion in 1995 which acknowledged that the rule had limited applications to criminal investigations (ABA 1995). However, at the same time, the ABA would not abide prosecutors' fundamental position "that professional conduct rules were an illegitimate vehicle for regulating areas of [prosecutors'] practice that are already addressed by statutes and constitutional case law" (Green 2012). The ABA committee's opinion stated:

> [I]n criminal cases, Rule 4.2 is not simply coextensive with the Fifth and Sixth Amendments. While the Fifth and Sixth Amendments provide protections to individuals in the context of a criminal case, the Constitution establishes only the "minimal historic safeguards" that defendants must receive rather than the outer limits of those they may be afforded. Ethics rules, on the other hand, seek to regulate the conduct of lawyers according to the standards of the profession quite apart from other laws or rules that may also govern a lawyer's actions. Consequently, by delineating a lawyer's duties to maintain standards of ethical conduct, ethical rules like Rule 4.2 may offer protections beyond those provided by the Constitution.
>
> (ABA 1995)

In response to concerns about how courts might apply Rule 4.2, in 1998 the DOJ adopted an administrative regulation that was meant to supersede the professional conduct rule in federal criminal cases. Lower federal courts were skeptical of the DOJ regulation, but before a case challenging it could reach the Supreme Court, Congress adopted legislation in 2000 that had the effect of overturning the regulation and subjecting federal prosecutors to the professional conduct rules of the states in which they practiced. The law, known as the McDade Amendment, reinforced courts' view that prosecutors, like all other lawyers, are subject to professional conduct rules. But at the same time, prosecutors were comforted by judicial decisions rejecting defendants' argument that the no-contact rule should be interpreted broadly (Green 2012, 2017).

Another effort to restrain prosecutors at around the same time fueled antagonism between prosecutors, particularly federal prosecutors, and the organized Bar. In 1990, following the lead of the Massachusetts state Bar, the ABA added a controversial provision to Rule 3.8, the rule identifying prosecutors' "special responsibilities." Until then, Rule 3.8 was generally regarded as undemanding and uncontroversial. The first two provisions, dating to the ABA's 1970 Model Code, required prosecutors to refrain from prosecuting criminal charges without probable cause and to disclose evidence known to negate the guilt of the accused. Both provisions were widely assumed at the time merely to codify prosecutors' constitutional obligations and, in any event, they were largely ignored by prosecutors and disciplinary authorities. The other two provisions, dating to 1981, were also overlooked. The first required prosecutors to give defendants a chance to retain counsel and the other forbade prosecutors from seeking waivers of certain pretrial rights from unrepresented defendants (but not including the right to remain silent) (Green 2017).[4]

The new provision addressed prosecutors' growing "practice of issuing grand jury subpoenas to lawyers for testimony concerning their current or past clients" (Green 2017). The Bar's concern was that by turning criminal defense lawyers into witnesses against their clients, prosecutors eroded defendants' trust in their lawyers and frightened defendants from confiding in them. Prosecutors, however, saw this as a legitimate measure to gather proof that higher-ups in criminal conspiracies were financing underlings' legal fees. The ABA's model rule imposed restraint on prosecutors in situations where other law, such as the law governing the attorney-client privilege, did not (Zacharias 1992). Many states did not adopt the provision and federal prosecutors brought successful constitutional challenges to it in some states where it was adopted, with the result that "it is questionable whether the provision has an impact in the federal grand jury investigations at which it was principally directed" (Green 2017).

The Bar's efforts to interpret existing Model Rule 4.2 and to amend Model Rule 3.8 to restrain prosecutors' investigative efforts undermined relations between the organized Bar and prosecutors, who perceived that "the ABA had been captured by the criminal defense bar" (Green 2017). "For example, a 1991 press release jointly issued by the DOJ, the National District Attorneys Association, and the National Association of Attorneys General, accused the ABA of lending 'aid and comfort' to the defense bar in its 'attempt[] to use rules of professional conduct to stymie criminal investigations and prosecutions'"

(Green 2012). The ABA, which has an interest in collaborating with the DOJ on initiatives outside the area of professional regulation, responded with conciliatory efforts. An ABA advisory committee issued a series of recommendations in 1992 "meant to strengthen prosecutors' voice in the Association and avoid 'us[ing] the ethical rules that govern the profession to establish rules of criminal procedure that are more properly the province of judicial rulemaking or legislative action'" (Green 2012). For the next fifteen years, the ABA studiously avoided reviving tensions with prosecutors over the content of professional regulation. Consequently, when it "set to work from 1997 to 2002 to comprehensively review and amend the Model Rules, it essentially left Rule 3.8 untouched" (Green 2003; 2017).

Eventually, however, the need for the Bar to take at least a modest stand on potentially controversial questions of prosecutorial conduct began to seem more imperative. Several high-profile cases of prosecutorial misconduct, including one involving a federal prosecution of a U.S. Senator, led to judicial expressions of concern about prosecutors' disclosure violations. The exoneration cases demonstrated that prosecutorial misconduct can lead to wrongful convictions (Joy 2006). Fueled in part by social media, the public became increasingly aware of prosecutorial misconduct. Law reform organizations made prosecutors' conduct a target of criminal justice reform. In response to forces such as these, the Bar undertook three noteworthy efforts to influence the professional regulation of prosecutors (Green and Yaroshefsky 2016). Although these efforts, individually and collectively, were modest, they each met resistance.

First, in 2008, the ABA added two new provisions to Rule 3.8—sections (g) and (h)—to address the remedial steps a prosecutor must take after securing a criminal conviction when confronted with evidence of a clear miscarriage of justice.[5] "Building on prior judicial pronouncements, [these provisions] propose that when a prosecutor learns of new exculpatory evidence that is 'material' and 'credible,' and that establishes 'a reasonable likelihood' that a convicted defendant is innocent, the prosecutor should disclose the new evidence to the court and to the defendant and conduct a reasonable investigation to determine whether a miscarriage of justice in fact occurred. Further, the model [provisions] would call on the prosecutor to attempt to set the conviction aside if the investigation leads to 'clear and convincing' evidence of the defendant's innocence" (Green and Yaroshefsky 2009). The post-conviction provisions of Rule 3.8 were uncontroversial within the ABA, where prosecutors had a substantial role in developing them (Green 2012).

The new provisions were not meant to significantly burden or restrain prosecutors but to codify normative obligations arising out of prosecutors' role as ministers of justice and grounded in defendants' right to fair process. It was assumed that seasoned prosecutors almost universally accepted these obligations, but codifying them was intended to help in educating new and future prosecutors and in promoting prosecutorial cultures which value preventing and rectifying convictions of the innocent as much as convicting the guilty. By the end of 2018, nineteen states, including New York and California, had adopted some version of the post-conviction provisions. But occasionally when state courts considered adopting these provisions, federal and/or state prosecutors opposed them. Prosecutors' objections, which courts found unpersuasive, included that the provisions would expand defendants' rights beyond those afforded by other law, and that the disciplinary authorities enforcing the rules would interfere with prosecutors' legitimate work (Green 2012). Although prosecutors' expressed concerns may be insincere and are surely overstated, "[t]he *in terrorem* effect of prosecutors' hostility conceivably goes beyond discouraging courts from adopting these particular rules; it discourages bar associations from promoting any new ethics rules for prosecutors" (Green 2012).

Second, and potentially more significant, was the ABA's effort to breathe life into Model Rule 3.8(d), the provision on prosecutors' disclosure obligations. For years, the provision had essentially been hiding in plain sight. Every state ethics code includes a version of this provision, which requires prosecutors to "make timely disclosure to the defense of all evidence or information known to the prosecution that tends to negate the guilt of the accused or mitigates the offense." Legal academics have long recognized that, on its face, Rule 3.8(d) expresses obligations that are more demanding than constitutional case law and, in many jurisdictions, more demanding than legislation and criminal procedure rules. But the Bar long overlooked the rule.

Constitutional decisions require prosecutors to disclose evidence or information that could be used to exonerate the accused or impeach prosecution witnesses only if the evidence or information is "material" in the sense that, given its significance or the general weakness of the prosecution's proof, it is reasonably likely to lead to an acquittal. Many courts hold that at least some "material" evidence may be withheld until the trial is underway and, if the defendant is inclined to plead guilty, withheld altogether. Criminal justice reform efforts have specifically targeted prosecutors' disclosure obligations with the result that a handful of states have liberalized their disclosure laws, typically in response to revelations of misconduct by local prosecutors. But the defense Bar has been unsuccessful in its attempts to persuade the Supreme Court to expand constitutional protections, to persuade federal judges to liberalize the criminal procedure rules governing discovery, or to persuade Congress to expand prosecutors' disclosure obligations legislatively (Green 2013a).

In 2009, the ABA's ethics committee published an opinion calling the attention of the bench and Bar to the requirements of Rule 3.8(d). The opinion emphasized that favorable evidence and information must be disclosed under the rule regardless of whether it is "material" in the constitutional sense. Further, the requirement of "timely" disclosure means that prosecutors cannot withhold favorable evidence until trial or withhold it altogether from defendants who are disposed to plead guilty (ABA 2009; Green 2011a). In 2016, a local Bar association issued an opinion similarly interpreting New York's version of Model Rule 3.8(d) (New York City Bar 2016). These opinions provide a basis for disciplinary authorities to bring charges against prosecutors who willfully withhold favorable information, regardless of whether they violate constitutional law in doing so. The opinions would also support court orders requiring prosecutors to make disclosure in accordance with the plain language of the professional conduct provision (Green and Yaroshefsky 2020).[6]

The ABA opinion was initially viewed as a harbinger of change (McMunigal 2010), but as of the end of 2018, its impact was modest though not insignificant. Some state prosecutors accepted the ABA's interpretation. Others, however, argued that, despite the language of the rule, prosecutors may be disciplined only for violating their obligations under constitutional case law, statutes and procedural rules. In the handful of cases where the question was litigated, courts split, with some adopting the ABA's interpretation and others endorsing the prosecutors' argument (Ricciuti, Conti, and Corso 2018; Schimpff 2012).

The third noteworthy effort to influence prosecutors' conduct through professional regulation was driven by state Bar associations, not the ABA. The effort was directed at a small, but troubling, plea bargaining practice adopted principally by federal prosecutors. As the Supreme Court has recognized, most criminal cases are resolved by plea bargains, not by trials. Often, in exchange for leniency, prosecutors require defendants to waive procedural rights in addition to the trial rights that are automatically relinquished by a guilty plea. In particular, prosecutors have conditioned leniency on waivers of the right to challenge one's conviction on appeal or in other post-conviction proceedings. Except when defendants can show that their consent to this condition was itself procedurally defective, one effect of this waiver is to foreclose defendants from correcting illegal sentences. Another effect, which several Bar associations' ethics committees found particularly concerning, is that if the waiver is given effect, it forecloses defendants from arguing that their lawyer rendered constitutionally ineffective representation that affected their decision to plead guilty or their sentence. A succession of state and local Bar ethics committees interpreted professional conduct rules to forbid prosecutors from including such broad waivers in their plea agreements. In general, they reasoned that the prosecutors' waiver demands were "prejudicial to the administration of justice" because defense lawyers might encourage clients to accept prosecutors' offer not because it was in the defendant's best interest but to protect the defense lawyers from accusations of incompetence.

Prosecutors might simply have ignored the Bar associations' opinions, which do not have the force of law. Defense lawyers were not objecting to the waiver provisions in court; judges, who were aware of the terms of plea bargains, were not striking these waivers on their own initiative; and disciplinary authorities were not initiating charges against prosecutors whose plea agreements were accepted by judges. But, perhaps in a burst of overconfidence, federal prosecutors in Kentucky decided to take advantage of their state's relatively unusual procedure allowing for judicial review of the state Bar's ethics opinions. In 2014, the Kentucky Supreme Court rejected prosecutors' challenge and upheld the state Bar association's interpretation. In response, the DOJ "change[d] its plea-bargaining policy to cease the waiver practice nationally" (Green 2017).

15.5 Unfulfilled Promise

The Bar has been highly selective in attempting to adopt new Model Rules and in propounding new interpretations of existing rules to address prosecutorial obligations and restrictions. As the battles over the no-contact rule and the attorney-subpoena rule revealed, the Bar's regulatory efforts can generate prosecutors' ill-will while accomplishing little. Even seemingly uncontroversial initiatives, such as the ABA's post-conviction rules, generate opposition: "prosecutors can tick off more than a dozen reasons why the ABA should not be trusted to propose rules of prosecutors' ethics, and why virtually any proposed rule is inadequate, sight unseen, even if one accepts the underlying normative premise, as in the case of Rules 3.8(g) and (h)" (Green 2017).

The Bar's hesitance to urge courts to strengthen the professional regulation of prosecutors reflects the Bar's awareness of its limited political influence and its interest in preserving good relations with prosecutors.

> It would be virtually futile for the ABA to propose special rules of prosecutorial ethics over the opposition of prosecutors, especially federal prosecutors. And opposition would be almost inevitable. The thirty-year review of prosecutorial ethics is largely a story about federal prosecutors' obstruction of ethics regulation at every turn[.]
> (Green 2017)

While the ABA might not worry about other lawyers' uncooperativeness, prosecutors are not just any lawyers. They are politically powerful public officials who have the ear and sympathy of the judiciary. It is unlikely that state judiciaries will adopt comprehensive rules for prosecutors if prosecutors do not actively participate in the drafting process and endorse the rules. Moreover, the ABA works closely with prosecutors on other aspects of criminal justice reform and cannot afford to antagonize them by proposing wholesale reform of prosecutors' ethics over their objection (Green 2017).

One consequence is that, even when professional conduct rules address the behavior of lawyers in general, these rules are often considered inadequate to address prosecutors' conduct in particular. For the most part, the rules fail to identify normative standards governing advocacy that should be more stringent for prosecutors than for other trial lawyers (Zacharias 1991). For example, professional conduct rules generally forbid trial advocates from introducing evidence they "know" to be false but allow advocates to rely on evidence and testimony that they "reasonably believe" to be false. For trial lawyers representing private clients, the fiduciary duty of loyalty to the client and to preserve the client's trust, and the ordinary obligation to attempt to achieve the client's objectives through lawful means, might counterbalance their duty to promote the integrity of the truth-seeking process. But the rules are inadequate for prosecutors, who should have a greater duty than other lawyers to ensure the reliability of their evidence, both to protect the fairness of the criminal process and to prevent wrongful convictions (Green 2016a; Zacharias and Green 2009b). The ABA has acknowledged that the normative expectation for prosecutors should be more demanding; a Prosecution Function Standard provides: "When a prosecutor has reason to doubt the truth or accuracy of particular evidence, the prosecutor should take reasonable steps to determine that the evidence is reliable, or not present it." But the Standard, unlike a professional conduct rule, is not enforceable, and prosecutors may therefore ignore it. The problem of prosecutors' use of potentially false evidence is compounded because the professional conduct rules do not meaningfully restrain how prosecutors interview witnesses and prepare them to testify. The rules do not stop prosecutors from employing highly suggestive, if not coercive, methods (Flowers 1998; Gershman 2002).

Likewise, courts have recognized that, as a general matter, prosecutors' duty of candor to the court should be more demanding than that of other advocates (Green 2016b). The ABA acknowledges this in a Prosecution Function Standard titled, "The Prosecutor's Heightened Duty of Candor," which states that: "In light of the prosecutor's public responsibilities, broad authority and discretion, the prosecutor has a heightened duty of candor to the courts and in fulfilling other professional obligations" (ABA 2015). But the Model Rules do not codify and elaborate on this higher duty.

At the same time, the professional conduct rules leave a vast swath of prosecutorial conduct virtually untouched, including, most significantly, prosecutors' exercise of charging, plea bargaining and sentencing discretion. Increasingly, "the public and the media are coming to understand that prosecutors' decisions about whom to charge, what plea bargain to offer, or what sentences to pursue may not be simply unwise, but abusive, reflecting wrongdoing in an ordinary, if not legal, sense" (Green and Yaroshefsky 2016). Among the targets of concern are abusive plea-bargaining tactics (Alkon 2017), and the use of charging power arbitrarily, too harshly, or in a discriminatory manner (Davis 2007; Green and Yaroshefsky 2016).

Particularly in light of "[p]rosecutors' limited public accountability," it would be useful for them to have "well-established normative standards governing [their] discretionary decision-making" (Green and Zacharias 2004). The Model Rules, however, include only two rules expressly constraining prosecutors' exercise of discretion: Model Rule 3.8(a) codifies the constitutional requirement of "probable cause" to prosecute a charge; Rule 3.8(g) and (h) requires investigative measures when new evidence shows that prosecutors probably convicted someone who was innocent, and remedial measures when "clear and convincing evidence" confirms that they in fact did so. In one limited respect, Bar association ethics committees sought to constrain prosecutors' power in plea bargaining by publishing opinions condemning plea agreements containing waivers of the right to competent representation. One can envision the adoption of additional rules, or more creative interpretation and enforcement of existing rules, to restrict prosecutors' discretion in far more substantial ways (Green and Levine 2016; Levine 2017).

15.6 Conclusion

In theory, the organized Bar could influence prosecutors' work by persuading state courts to adopt and enforce professional conduct rules that constrain prosecutors' most controversial and troublesome decisions and behaviors. In practice, the Bar's influence has been limited. The organized Bar acknowledges that prosecutors should have different and, in some respects, more demanding obligations than other lawyers, given prosecutors' unique professional role. But unless it can win prosecutors' approval, the organized Bar hesitates to propose professional conduct rules that give expression to prosecutors' special obligations. That is in part because the Bar has been scarred by its occasional confrontations with prosecutors and in part because its ability to influence the courts is counterbalanced by that of prosecutors.

Notes

1. Federal prosecutors are subject to regulatory oversight by an office, the Office of Professional Responsibility, within the U.S. Department of Justice. Because its work is not transparent, it is difficult to assess how meaningful its oversight is (Green 2009). Additionally, in late 2018, New York passed a law establishing a state agency to investigate allegations of prosecutorial misconduct. State prosecutors immediately filed a lawsuit challenging the law's constitutionality.
2. Although prosecutors often communicate with crime victims and have a statutory obligation to do so in some jurisdictions, prosecutors do not represent crime victims as clients. Consequently, the professional conduct rules governing lawyers' communications with clients, and other rules governing the lawyer-client relationship, are inapplicable to prosecutors' relationship with victims. Rather, prosecutors' interactions with victims are governed by the rules regulating lawyers' dealings with third parties.
3. Disciplinary processes differ from state to state. Some rely on volunteer lawyers or on a Bar association to conduct investigations, prosecute charges, and/or conduct hearings, while others rely primarily on professional staff to investigate and prosecute and/or on judges to conduct hearings (Curtis 2011). The majority of disciplinary cases are brought against private practitioners in small firm and solo practice.
4. The ABA later added a provision, Model Rule 3.8(f), which supplements Model Rule 3.6, governing extrajudicial communications. The most significant requirement of Rule 3.8(f) is that "except for statements that are necessary to inform the public of the nature and extent of the prosecutor's action and that serve a legitimate law enforcement purpose, [a prosecutor must] refrain from making extrajudicial comments that have a substantial likelihood of heightening public condemnation of the accused . . . ." Although prosecutors did not seriously contest this addition, there have been notable occasions when they ignored it (Malanchuk 2008).
5. Prosecutors' post-conviction role is addressed in more detail by Brandon L. Garrett in Chapter 8 of this volume.
6. Prosecutors' disclosure obligations are addressed in more detail by Darryl K. Brown in Chapter 5 of this volume.

References

Alkon, Cynthia. 2017. "Hard Bargaining in Plea Bargaining: When Do Prosecutors Cross the Line?" *Nevada Law Journal* 17(2): 401–428.

American Bar Association. 1995. Standing Committee on Ethics and Professional Responsibility, Formal Opinion 95-396.

American Bar Association. 2009. Standing Committee on Ethics and Professional Responsibility, Formal Opinion 09-454.

American Bar Association. 2013. *Criminal Justice Standards, Fair Trial and Public Discourse.*

American Bar Association. 2015. *Criminal Justice Standards for the Prosecution Function.*

American Bar Association. 2018. *Model Rules of Professional Conduct.*

Cramton, Roger C., and Lisa K. Udell. 1992. "State Ethics Rules and Federal Prosecutors: The Controversies Over the Anti-contact and Subpoena Rules." *University of Pittsburgh Law Review* 53(2): 291–391.

Curtis, Deborah Moss. 2011. "Attorney Discipline Nationwide: A Comparative Analysis of Process and Statistics." *Journal of the Legal Profession* 35(2): 209–337.

Davis, Angela J. 2007. "The Legal Profession's Failure to Discipline Unethical Prosecutors." *Hofstra Law Review* 36(2): 275–310.

District Attorneys Association of the State of New York ("DAASNY"). 2011. "'The Right Thing': Ethical Guidelines for Prosecutors."

Flamm, Richard E. 2014. *Lawyer Disqualification—Disqualification of Attorneys and Law Firms.* 2nd ed. Berkeley: Banks & Jordan Law Publishing.

Flowers, Roberta K. 1998. "What You See Is What You Get: Applying the Appearance of Impropriety Standard to Prosecutors." *Missouri Law Review* 63(3): 699–766.

Gershman, Bennett L. 2002. "Witness Coaching by Prosecutors." *Cardozo Law Review* 23(3): 829–863.

Green, Bruce A. 1995. "Policing Federal Prosecutors: Do Too Many Regulators Produce Too Little Enforcement?" *St. Thomas Law Review* 8(1): 69–95.

Green, Bruce A. 1996. "Whose Rules of Professional Conduct Should Govern Lawyers in Federal Court and How Should the Rules Be Created?" *George Washington Law Review* 64(3): 460–531.

Green, Bruce A. 1999. "Why Should Prosecutors 'Seek Justice'?" *Fordham Urban Law Journal* 26(3): 609–643.

Green, Bruce A. 2003. "Prosecutorial Ethics as Usual." *University of Illinois Law Review* 2003(5): 1573–1604.

Green, Bruce A. 2009. "Regulating Federal Prosecutors: Let There Be Light." *Yale Law Journal Pocket Part* 118: 156. http://yalelawjournal.org/forum/regulating-federal-prosecutors-let-there-be-light.

Green, Bruce A. 2010. "Beyond Training Prosecutors About Their Disclosure Obligations: Can Prosecutors' Offices Learn from Their Lawyers' Mistakes." *Cardozo Law Review* 31(6): 2161–2186.

Green, Bruce A. 2011a. "Prosecutors' Ethical Duty of Disclosure: In Memory of Fred Zacharias." *San Diego Law Review* 48(1): 57–91.

Green, Bruce A. 2011b. "Developing Standards of Conduct for Prosecutors and Criminal Defense Lawyers." *Hastings Law Journal* 62(5): 1093–1110.

Green, Bruce A. 2012. "Prosecutors and Professional Regulation." *Georgetown Journal of Legal Ethics* 25(4): 873–904.

Green, Bruce A. 2013a. "Federal Criminal Discovery Reform: A Legislative Approach." *Mercer Law Review* 64(3): 639–682.

Green, Bruce A. 2013b. "Judicial Regulation of US Civil Litigators." *Legal Ethics* 16(2): 306–321.

Green, Bruce A. 2016a. "Access to Criminal Justice: Where Are the Prosecutors?" *Texas A&M Law Review* 3(3): 515–536.

Green, Bruce A. 2016b. "Candor in Criminal Advocacy." *Hofstra Law Review* 44(4): 1105–1125.

Green, Bruce A. 2016c. "Should There Be a Specialized Ethics Code for Death-Penalty Defense Lawyers?" *Georgetown Journal of Legal Ethics* 29(3): 527–558.

Green, Bruce A. 2017. "Prosecutorial Ethics in Retrospect." *Georgetown Journal of Legal Ethics* 30(3): 461–483.

Green, Bruce A., and Samuel Levine. 2016. "Disciplinary Regulation of Prosecutors as a Remedy for Abuses of Prosecutorial Discretion: A Descriptive and Normative Analysis." *Ohio State Journal of Criminal Law* 14(1): 143–182.

Green, Bruce A., and Rebecca Roiphe. 2017. "Rethinking Prosecutors' Conflicts of Interest." *Boston College Law Review* 58(2): 463–538.

Green, Bruce A., and Rebecca Roiphe. 2018. "Can the President Control the Department of Justice?" *Alabama Law Review* 70(1): 1–75.

Green, Bruce A., and Ellen Yaroshefsky. 2009. "Prosecutorial Discretion and Post-conviction Evidence of Innocence." *Ohio State Journal of Criminal Law* 6(2): 467–517.

Green, Bruce A., and Ellen Yaroshefsky. 2016. "Prosecutorial Accountability 2.0." *Notre Dame Law Review* 92(1): 51–116.

Green, Bruce A., and Ellen Yaroshefsky. 2020. "Should Criminal Justice Reformers Care About Prosecutorial Ethics Rules?" *Duquesne Law Review* 58(2): 249-278.

Green, Bruce A., and Fred C. Zacharias. "The Uniqueness of Federal Prosecutors." *Georgetown Law Journal* 88(2): 207–261.

Green, Bruce A., and Fred C. Zacharias. 2004. "Prosecutorial Neutrality." *Wisconsin Law Review* 2004(3): 837–904.

Hazard, Geoffrey C., Jr., and Dana Remus Irwin. 2009. "Toward a Revised 4.2 No-Contact Rule." *Hastings Law Journal* 60(4): 797–851.

Johnson, David T. 2002. *The Japanese Way of Justice: Prosecuting Crime in Japan*. Oxford: Oxford University Press.

Joy, Peter A. 2006. "The Relationship Between Prosecutorial Misconduct and Wrongful Convictions: Shaping Remedies for a Broken System." *Wisconsin Law Review* 2006(2): 399–429.

Leubsdorf, John. 1979. "Communicating with Another Lawyer's Client: The Lawyer's Veto and the Client's Interest." *University of Pennsylvania Law Review* 127(3): 683–710.

Levenson, Laurie L. 2010. "Prosecutorial Sound Bites: When Do They Cross the Line?" *Georgia Law Review* 44(4): 1021–1061.

Levine, Samuel J. 2017. "The Potential Utility of Disciplinary Regulation as a Remedy for Abuses of Prosecutorial Discretion." *Duke Journal of Constitutional Law & Public Policy* 12(1): 1–12.

Malanchuk, Peter Andrew. 2008. "The Court of Public Opinion: Did Former Attorney General John Ashcroft Violate Ethics Rules Regarding Extrajudicial Statements and If So, Why Was He Not Sanctioned?" *Journal of the Legal Profession* 32: 237–257.

Matheson, Scott M., Jr. 1990. "The Prosecutor, the Press and Free Speech." *Fordham Law Review* 58(5): 865–938.

McFadyen, Rebecca C. E. 2007. "The Thompson Memo: Its Predecessors, Its Successor, and Its Effect on Corporate Attorney-Client Privilege." *Journal of Business and Securities Law* 8(1): 23–58.

McMunigal, Kevin C. 2010. "The (Lack of) Enforcement of Prosecutor Disclosure Rules." *Hofstra Law Review* 38(3): 847–865.

National District Attorneys Association ("NDAA"). 2009. *National Prosecution Standards.* Washington, D.C.: National District Attorneys Association.

New York City Bar. 2016. "Formal Opinion 2016-3: Prosecutors' Ethical Obligations to Disclose Information Favorable to the Defense."

Ricciuti, Michael D., Caroline E. Conti, and Paolo G. Corso. 2018. "Criminal Discovery: The Clash Between *Brady* and Ethical Obligations." *Suffolk University Law Review* 51(3): 399–437.

Schimpff, Kirsten M. 2012. "Rule 3.8, The Jencks Act, and How the ABA Created a Conflict Between Ethics and the Law on Prosecutorial Disclosure." *American University Law Review* 61(6): 1729–1782.

Sullivan, Thomas P., and Maurice Possley. 2015. "The Chronic Failure to Discipline Prosecutors for Misconduct: Proposals for Reform." *Journal of Criminal Law and Criminology* 105(4): 881–945.

Yaroshefsky, Ellen, and Bruce A. Green. 2012. "Prosecutors' Ethics in Context." In *Lawyers in Practice: Ethical Decision Making in Context.* Edited by Leslie C. Levin and Lynn Mather, 269–292. Chicago: University of Chicago Press.

Zacharias, Fred C. 1991. "Structuring the Ethics of Prosecutorial Trial Practice: Can Prosecutors Do Justice?" *Vanderbilt Law Review* 44(1): 45–114.

Zacharias, Fred C. 1992. "A Critical Look at Rules Governing Grand Jury Subpoenas of Attorneys." *Minnesota Law Review* 76(4): 917–956.

Zacharias, Fred C. 2001. "The Professional Discipline of Prosecutors." *North Carolina Law Review* 79(3): 721–778.

Zacharias, Fred C., and Bruce A. Green. 2009a. "Rationalizing Judicial Regulation of Lawyers." *Ohio State Law Journal* 70(1): 73–139.

Zacharias, Fred C., and Bruce A. Green. 2009b. "The Duty to Avoid Wrongful Convictions: A Thought Experiment in the Regulation of Prosecutors." *Boston University Law Review* 89(1): 1–59.

CHAPTER 16

PROSECUTORS AND THEIR LEGISLATURES, LEGISLATURES AND THEIR PROSECUTORS

RUSSELL M. GOLD

16.1 Introduction

THE textbook story of American prosecutors and legislatures[1] would find two sets of actors working in different branches of government checking each other as a means of protecting liberty.[2] But a better standard account of American prosecutors and legislatures is one of "pathological politics"—legislatures are happy to provide prosecutors with as much authority as possible (Stuntz 2001). In so doing, legislatures appear tough on crime, which, at least until quite recently, was undoubtedly good for their reelection prospects. If prosecutors use that authority to its maximum extent and do something that voters dislike, legislatures can blame that decision on prosecutorial overreach and come out scot-free. If prosecutors decline to use the full breadth of their authority, so too can legislatures blame prosecutors for that choice. "Where prosecutors can be selective, legislators will tend to see criminal law as a one-way ratchet" (Stuntz 2001, 547). At bottom, when it comes to institutional incentives, prosecutors and legislators are "natural allies. Both need to please voters in order to survive, and for both, pleasing voters means essentially the same thing: punishing people voters want to see punished" (Stuntz 2001, 534). That has meant creating an extraordinary web of broad and deep criminal law backed by harsh sentences, often in the form of mandatory minimums or sentencing enhancements over which prosecutors maintain control—a distinctively American creation (Barkow 2019; Luna 2005; Stuntz 2004; Tonry 2012). Whether the recent smart on crime and progressive prosecutor developments have staying power and whether they will lead to widespread change or are merely momentary reactions to highly publicized police shootings of Black men or other scandals in prosecutors' offices remains to be seen.

Prosecutors are not merely passive recipients of power delegated by legislatures but are also a powerful lobbying force, as no shortage of scholars has taught us (see, e.g., Barkow 2005, 2019; Stuntz 2001). Prosecutors have powerful representation in national organizations such as the National District Attorneys' Association ("NDAA") and the National Association of Assistant United States Attorneys ("NAAUSA"). "Prosecutors' associations are often the leading obstacles to reform legislation that would lower sentences, provide diversionary programs, or stop treating juveniles as adults" (Barkow 2019, 112). And perhaps most importantly, they work against politically unpopular adversaries—criminals and lawyers who defend "those people."[3] I do not mean to suggest that prosecutors are *always* successful in such efforts though. They aren't. Cost poses their biggest obstacle, particularly in sentencing law.

Prosecutors have secured from legislatures extraordinary power, unrivaled elsewhere in the administrative state because of the lack of meaningful external checks (Barkow 2019; but see Bellin 2019). Prosecutors have secured extraordinarily deep and broad criminal law across jurisdictions in what Rachel Barkow calls an "endless cycle" where "no other institutional actor is currently positioned or willing to stop this dynamic" (Barkow 2019, 132).[4] The depth and breadth means that a wide swath of conduct is criminal and that the numerous different relevant crimes that could apply to any fact pattern form an extensive "menu" from which prosecutors may order in any particular case (Stuntz 2004). Deep and broad codes afford the potential for widely different sentences (perhaps mandatorily at prosecutors' option) and for widely different collateral consequences upon conviction. The Supreme Court has proven itself wholly unwilling to regulate or allow lower courts to regulate these bludgeons (e.g., *Bordenkircher v. Hayes* 1978; *Brady v. United States* 1970). Ordinary judicial sentencing discretion does not exist in many instances because of mandatory minimums. Neither do parole boards provide a back-end check on sentence length as they once did.

Unlike substantive criminal law where state legislatures across the United States seem largely content to give prosecutors whatever they desire, the political dynamics of sentencing law work somewhat differently because changes to sentencing law can be expensive and sentencing commissions may increase the salience of cost concerns. Indeed, cost concerns sometimes lead state legislatures to override prosecutors' objections and reduce sentences. The U.S. Congress, however, because it need not balance the federal budget, had very little hesitation to continually increase sentences between the 1970s and the early 2000s.

Criminal procedure protections for defendants have come largely from courts rather than legislatures. But a new trend may be emerging at least in some places because of some locally elected prosecutors that may help pave a path for statewide reform. Some prosecutors, for instance, have gotten ahead of their state legislatures on moving away from money bail or providing more and earlier discovery than state law or Supreme

Court precedent requires of them. On a statewide basis, some states have substantially curtailed their use of money bail, and New York recently substantially increased prosecutors' discovery obligations—seemingly empowered at least in part by Brooklyn already affording broader discovery without a parade of horribles. Some of these statewide reforms may simply be grounded in legislatures' concern about costs—such as curtailing widespread pre-trial detention—but others such as discovery reform cannot be driven by cost concerns.

This chapter proceeds in three parts. They discuss the relationship between legislatures and prosecutors in substantive criminal law, sentencing law, and criminal procedure, respectively. This chapter then closes with a cautious note of optimism as to whether the standard paradigm of American criminal law's increasing punitiveness may be beginning to break.

16.2 Substantive Criminal Law

The standard account of separation of powers in American law would find a legislature that thoughtfully calibrates the scope of substantive criminal law and passes statutes that strike to balance the people's various policy interests. Police officers would then monitor violations of those laws and refer those violations to prosecutors. Prosecutors would be responsible for faithfully implementing legislatures' policy choices and the will of the people by deciding how aggressively to pursue each potential crime by weighing complex competing interests. Only when the legislative and executive branches concur—the legislature has authorized a prohibition, the police have detected a particular violation, and the prosecutor has decided that that violation is worth pursuing—should we have a prosecution (Barkow 2006). That separation of powers is often thought to be liberty protecting. This section first considers the primary challenge to that account—the pathological politics of criminal law—and one critique of the pathological politics dynamic. It then articulates courts' unwillingness to regulate in this sphere.

16.2.1 The Pathological Politics

Legislatures' and prosecutors' institutional incentives provide substantial cause for skepticism of the standard model of separation of powers in criminal law, as William Stuntz's account of the "pathological politics of criminal law" explains (Stuntz 2001). Legislators want to stay in office and thus need to please their constituents. To do so, legislators need to produce the outcomes that the median voter seeks and take symbolic stands that the median voter finds attractive. Although there is no reason to think that the public knows or cares much about the scope of substantive criminal law in its own right—questions such as whether crime *x* should have element *c* or only elements *a* and *b*—reducing the requirements of substantive law empowers prosecutors to decide for themselves when a law has been violated and makes it easier for them to obtain convictions. Passing a largely redundant statute that criminalizes already-criminal conduct but offers a different potential sentence and collateral consequences affords prosecutors another tool (Seigel and Slobogin 2005). Similarly, even when a new law is completely unnecessary, legislatures might wish to respond to a high-profile case by passing a new law to appear tough on crime.

Unlike in much of the world, in the United States chief prosecutors are elected at a local level in the vast majority of states (Wright 2009). Prosecutors in many countries—such as Sweden—are appointed and work for a national prosecution service rather than a local one (Asp 2012; Tonry 2012). Like elected legislators, American prosecutors need to please the public so that the lead prosecutor in the office is re-elected; perhaps the elected chief prosecutor or even the line prosecutors wish to pursue higher office. Accordingly, prosecutors and legislators are "natural allies" (Stuntz 2001, 534). The public wants not only prosecutions but convictions; some evidence of this desire comes from the frequency with which conviction statistics arise in prosecutor campaign discourse (Wright 2009). Because of their natural interest alliance, prosecutors provide an important voice on criminal law issues, and the separation of powers between defining and enforcing crime becomes far less meaningful than one might think.[5]

Legislators' and prosecutors' interest alignment, coupled with prosecutorial discretion, allows legislators to treat substantive criminal law as a one-way ratchet because it affords them a "heads I win, tails you lose" scenario. In theory, legislators run two potential risks—sweeping in too much conduct or sweeping in too little. But prosecutorial discretion eliminates risk for legislators.[6] If a statute sweeps in too much conduct, legislators can rely on prosecutors to under-enforce it to avoid unpopular outcomes. If prosecutors fail to do so, legislators can blame prosecutorial overreach. By contrast, legislators who sweep in too little conduct might face public blowback. Thus, the choice is easy: sweep as broadly and as deeply as possible and divert any blame toward prosecutors.[7] The remaining risk is that salaried prosecutors may prosecute too little, but there too legislators can blame prosecutors and can seek to avoid this scenario ex ante by making prosecutions as cheap as possible (Stuntz 2001). Making prosecution more efficient serves legislators' goals in potentially two different ways: it allows prosecutors to bring more cases with the same resources—what some call net-widening—or save money for the public fisc (Brown 2004). Legislators are thus well served when prosecutors possess maximum plea leverage, and they can provide such leverage through broad and deep criminal codes as well as harsh sentencing ranges. These dynamics yield an extensive menu of crimes and corresponding potential punishments from which a prosecutor may "order" in any given case (Stuntz 2004). This confluence of prosecutorial discretion and sizable plea leverage through charge-based control over sentencing is a peculiar arrangement not known outside the United States (Tonry 2012).

One important factor in legislatures' willingness to continue to embrace ever broader and deeper substantive criminal law is the one-sided nature of interest group pressure. Public choice theory aptly explains this dynamic. Although there is some recent reason to question this idea, it has long been true that "[a] variety of groups may seek to broaden criminal liability[,] . . . [b]ut organized interest group pressure to *narrow* criminal liability is rare" (Stuntz 2001, 553; see also Dripps 1993; Luna 2005). Criminal law seems like an instance where the benefits are diffuse to the public at large—such as public safety through deterrence and incapacitation—and the costs fall on a concentrated group of people (Wright 2004). Diffuse benefits and concentrated costs would suggest as a matter of public choice theory that legislatures would *not act*. But criminal law defies that conventional wisdom because prosecutors or prosecutor associations provide a prominent mouthpiece on the benefits-side of the ledger and because the costs fall disproportionately on a marginalized group: most criminal defendants are poor people of color who lose their right to vote, perhaps forever (Barkow 2019; Wright 2006; see also Forman 2010).[8] And for some criminal laws, the benefits run not to the public at large but to a more concentrated group such as business owners who have suffered property losses; in that scenario public choice theory ably explains why prosecutors would act (Robinson and Cahill 2004).

The most important assumption underlying Stuntz's analysis of the institutional incentives regarding substantive criminal law reform is that the public always desires more law enforcement.[9] Appearing tough on crime is thus safe for legislators, but opposing a criminal law bill risks a legislator's job (Beale 1997; Robinson and Cahill 2004). Politicians contribute to those public desires as they "pander[] to public anxiety" about crime and public safety and stoke implicit or explicit racial biases (Barkow 2019, 5). Most famously and perhaps most importantly from the perspective of future candidates' risk aversion, during the 1998 U.S. presidential race George H. W. Bush ran ads featuring Willie Horton—a Black man who committed a brutal rape and murder while on a prison furlough in Governor Dukakis's home state of Massachusetts. Politicians continue to want to avoid the risk of a "Willie Horton moment." Ostensibly a Willie Horton moment means seeming soft on crime. But it can hardly be an accident that the ads ran *photos* of Willie Horton to stoke stereotyping of the dangerous Black man (Potts 1997). Anxieties about crime and safety run especially high because public information about crime in America is quite poor and coverage largely focuses on particular, sensational crimes rather than broader statistical trends. Thus, as one scholar puts it, "Politicians fear endorsing any position that an opponent can characterize as 'soft on crime' in a 30-second television commercial" (Alschuler 1991, 932). In the Conclusion this chapter will briefly return to consider whether Stuntz's assumption about the public continuing to desire more law enforcement remains a fair one.

Darryl Brown challenges the pathological politics account, arguing that state legislatures have indeed repealed some criminal laws, that tough on crime legislative proposals fail at the same rate as other bills, and that other unpopular laws are rarely enforced (Brown 2007). For these reasons, Brown concludes that "criminal law's substantive scope is almost surely *narrower* in most respects than in the past, at least in its effect on most citizens" (Brown 2007, 226). Brown provides important pushback to the prevailing Stuntzian view. But legislative inertia and the lack of public salience of criminal law also explain failed legislative action (Stuntz 2001, 549). And the move to discount laws on the books that prosecutors rarely enforce gives away too much. Such laws may nonetheless be enforced disparately against minority groups and provide a basis on which police can hassle citizens; so too may rarely enforced laws provide potential leverage for prosecutors even if charges are never filed or are not pursued to conviction. Police need probable cause to conduct an automobile stop or obtain a warrant to search a home, but the broader the substantive law the less protection that probable cause requirement affords (Stuntz 1997). And charging decisions have no bearing on that phenomenon.

Although it is hard to know precisely what to make of the numbers, statistics on the expansion of criminal codes are nonetheless striking in their general trend: since 2008, Michigan has created an average of forty-five new criminal laws every year (Barkow 2019). Forty years of changes to Illinois's criminal code created hundreds of new crimes, many of which cover the same conduct but offer different punishment levels as the crimes previously on the books (Robinson and Cahill 2004). North Carolina's criminal code nearly doubled between 1943 and 2011 (Welty 2014). There are more than four thousand federal criminal laws—more than four hundred of which were added between 2008 and 2013. More than 300,000 federal regulations subject individuals to criminal penalties; for example, advertising beer using taste test results without divulging the taste tester's name and address is a federal crime (@CrimeADay, 2019).

This American dynamic of prosecutors seeking and obtaining what they want from the legislative branch is quite different from the primary concern with prosecutors in Poland, for instance, which has a history of politicians influencing decisions in individual cases for political reasons (Krajewski 2012). Poland made structural changes to combat that concern in 2010. By contrast, Sweden explicitly bars other government actors from influencing case-level decisions (Asp 2012).

16.2.2 Lack of Judicial Intervention

The breadth and depth of criminal law allows prosecutors to charge multiple nearly identical counts in a single case, and the judiciary has done nothing to regulate such behavior (Seigel and Slobogin 2005). Although there is certainly a conceivable role for courts to stop prosecutors from piling on redundant charges that may intimidate a defendant into waiving her constitutional rights, courts have abdicated any such role. The Fifth Amendment's Double Jeopardy clause could play a meaningful role here, but two charges are considered not "the same offense" so long as "each provision requires proof of an additional fact which the other does not" (*Blockburger v. United States* 1932). Similarly, unless a jurisdiction's law says otherwise, that same test applies to whether a judge should run the sentences on each count concurrent or consecutive—which can have a sizable effect on the total amount of time served. Moreover, even if the sentences would ultimately run consecutively, the lack of judicial regulation of multiple, largely overlapping counts can intimidate defendants into pleading guilty because it makes acquittal seem less attainable and makes the potential sentence seemingly quite long (Gold, Hessick, and Hessick 2017). For cases that actually go to trial, multiple largely redundant counts afford juries opportunities to reach a compromise verdict, which, if the counts are going to run simultaneously in any event, provides a complete victory to the government.

16.3 Sentencing Law

Scholarly wisdom varies about prosecutorial influence over sentencing reform. As with substantive criminal law, prosecutors continue to push harsh policies. And as with substantive law, they score a substantial number of victories. But unlike with substantive criminal law, increasing sentences is expensive (Butler 2009), and there are actors in the system such as sentencing commissions who can and do raise that concern, thereby standing in the way of the one-way ratchet of increasing sentences. For federal sentencing law, however, cost concerns are not particularly meaningful and thus have not frequently halted the one-way ratchet that has afforded prosecutors immense power to prod defendants to plead guilty (Gold, Hessick, and Hessick 2017; Wright 2005; see also *United States v. Kupa* 2013). Somewhat surprisingly, however, from this position of immense prosecutorial power Congress has modestly decreased sentences of late. The first part of this section explains the leverage that discretionary-mandatory-sentencing provisions afford prosecutors in securing plea bargains and prosecutors' lobbying efforts to secure such sentencing provisions in criminal statutes. The next part examines federal "discretionary mandatories" in more detail and their racially disparate effects. Lastly, this section discusses how cost concerns make sentencing law's political dynamics different from substantive criminal law.

16.3.1 Harsh Sentencing and Prosecutors' Leverage

American prosecutors have lobbied hard to create harsher sentences—often in the form of mandatory minimums, three-strikes laws, or other sentencing enhancements[10]—and have similarly lobbied hard to oppose efforts to reduce sentences or eliminate mandatory sentencing (Barkow 2019; Tonry 2012). Prosecutors' lobbying efforts on this score should be unsurprising. Such laws transfer sentencing power from judges to prosecutors (Simons 2009) and afford prosecutors massive leverage to induce guilty pleas (Gold, Hessick, and Hessick 2017). When criminal codes are broad and deep and some available charges carry mandatory minimum sentences, prosecutors can threaten to levy the charge with a mandatory minimum or sentencing enhancement if the defendant does not acquiesce immediately and plead guilty to the charge that does not carry a harsh mandatory sentence (Schulhofer 1993; *United States v. Kupa* 2013). "Bargained for" outcomes reached by affording prosecutors massive charge-based sentencing hammers that they can trade away through offers "too good to be refused" are unknown outside the United States (Tonry 2012; see also Gold, Hessick, and Hessick 2017). Other countries do not have laws comparable to three-strikes laws, lengthy mandatory minimums, or repeat offender statutes; foreign prosecutors cannot unilaterally dismiss some charges in exchange for a guilty plea to others in cases involving serious crimes. Such a system makes the prosecutor the "central adjudicator of facts"—the person to whom equitable arguments about particular defendants are best directed (Lynch 2003).

To offer a few examples of prosecutors' discretion over sentencing and the resulting plea leverage, when a heroin dealer declined a plea deal with a ten-year sentence, prosecutors levied sentencing enhancements that yielded a mandatory life sentence (Barkow 2019). Orville Wollard too had the temerity to refuse a guilty plea carrying a five-year sentence after he fired his handgun into a wall to scare his daughter's boyfriend; prosecutors responded by charging an offense carrying a twenty-year mandatory minimum (Oppel 2011). That is the system that prosecutors and legislatures have created—one where prosecutors hold all the cards and a defendant gets to decide whether to exercise her constitutional right to trial with the sword of Damocles hanging above.

Federal prosecutors gained further control of sentencing power by pushing the Feeney Amendment, which tightened the appellate standard of review for sentencing guideline departures—making lenient judicial sentencing even less likely (Richman 2009, 2098). Because of the harsh and sometimes-mandatory sentencing structures, prosecutors and defense lawyers can "bargain" about the facts—sometimes outright lie to the court—to secure a deal that both sides think is more sensible than the sentence that the legislature has actually provided (Bowman and Heise 2001; Johnson 2019). To help preserve all of this authority, legislatures authorize sentences that presumably no one would think appropriate if actually imposed. Leandro Andrade, for example, received a fifty-year sentence for stealing video tapes from K-Mart (*Lockyer v. Andrade* 2003).

Prosecutor organizations have sometimes been transparent that their desire to preserve leverage drives much of their opposition to sentencing reform (Barkow 2005, 728n25; Barkow 2019; Gold, Hessick, and Hessick 2017; Drug Mandatory Minimums 2000). When the U.S. Attorney General sought to reduce mandatory minimum sentences to free up money for other law enforcement needs, the NAAUSA responded that mandatory minimums are "an indispensable tool" to "secure offender cooperation" and described such sentences as "the leverage, the hammer we have" (Marimow 2015). In 2013, an effort by the U.S. Department of Justice to reduce mandatory minimums for non-violent drug offenses prompted opposition from the NAAUSA, explaining that the law would "prevent[] [prosecutors] from obtaining benefits gained through concessions during [plea] bargaining" (Barkow 2019, 7; Letter from Dennis Boyd, 2014). Similar dynamics occur at the state level. Nebraska prosecutors, for example, opposed reductions to mandatory minimum sentences because they would reduce the leverage that "will help you wrap up a case" (Barkow 2019, 7).

Other times prosecutors defend the more traditional ground, claiming that longer sentences are always better or articulating the need for more punishment to fight crime. The head of the NAAUSA opposed reducing federal sentences in 2016 on the simple (although empirically flawed) premise that "when you put criminals in jail, crime goes down" (Satterfield 2016). While formal prosecutor organizations have doggedly pursued harsher sentences and mandatory minimums, ad hoc groups of former prosecutors have occasionally argued against such harsh sentences in particular cases (Luna and Cassell 2010).

Harsh sentencing laws, like substantive criminal law, find significant interest alignment between prosecutors and legislators. Not only are harsh sentencing laws opportunities for politicians to appear tough on crime, but sentencing makes for better applause lines in a campaign than, for instance, substantive law changes such as narrowing the *actus reus* in a statute (Stuntz 2001). Candidates can quite comfortably and easily talk about being tough on crime when they are touting mandatory minimum sentences and three-strikes laws that ensure that judges will not be too lenient.

Lobbying efforts by prosecutors for harsh mandatory sentencing paid huge dividends. Between 1970 and 1996, forty states adopted mandatory minimums for recidivists (Murakawa 2014). From 1993–1995, twenty-four states adopted three-strikes versions of such mandatory laws. On the federal level, Congress passed 207 new mandatory minimum sentencing laws between 1980 and 2000.[11] And these efforts have been put to significant use. In fiscal year 2018, 16,228 cases in the federal system carried a mandatory minimum, and 14.2 percent of all federal criminal defendants remained subject to mandatory minimums at sentencing (United States Sentencing Commission 2019).

Widespread mandatory minimum sentencing was not always the American way. Before 1975, mandatory minimums were rare and added little to sentences (Tonry 2012). Judges imposed indeterminate sentences, and parole boards ultimately decided on the timing of defendants' release. Under federal law, in 1970 Congress repealed virtually all mandatory minimums in drug cases (United States Sentencing Commission 1991). In so doing, Congress recognized that mandatory minimums were so harsh that they led prosecutors to decline more cases.[12] As discussed in more detail in the next sub-section, "discretionary mandatories" allowed Congress to appear tough on crime and give prosecutors heavy hammers without usurping prosecutors' discretion in ways that might make them hesitant to file charges.

16.3.2 Federal "Discretionary Mandatories" and Race

Federal sentencing law provides numerous "discretionary mandatories" or "bargaining-chip mandatories" that afford prosecutors with "hammer[s]" that they can invoke when they so choose to obtain more favorable guilty pleas (Schulhofer 1993, 202). Let us consider each hammer in more detail. For defendants with prior drug convictions, prosecutors can charge a sentencing enhancement that would be mandatory on the judge if charged—the so-called § 851 enhancement (Bowman and Heise 2001). Prosecutors can also choose whether to add a weapon enhancement—increasing a defendant's sentence by as much as twenty-five years per instance (18 U.S.C. § 924(c)). So too can they decide whether to charge engagement in a continuing criminal enterprise, which carries a mandatory minimum of twenty years' imprisonment or more (21 U.S.C. § 848).

By contrast to these hammers, prosecutors also have release valves. In non-violent, low-level drug cases where defendants have only minor criminal history, prosecutors can certify that the defendant provided the government with whatever information she had about a drug operation and thus permit judges to sentence below a mandatory minimum—the so-called safety valve. If prosecutors agree that a federal criminal defendant has provided substantial assistance, the defendant's guidelines sentence decreases, often by quite a lot: one-fifth of federal criminal convictions included such a substantial assistance downward departure, and half of the defendants who received such a departure had their sentence reduced by half or more. As Frank Bowman and Michael Heise explain, prosecutorial and judicial discretion account for much of the decrease in federal drug sentence lengths during the 1990s. That aggregate decrease masks widespread variation during that time across federal districts, however, which highlights the extent to which Congress conferred prosecutorial discretion to largely control sentencing (Bowman and Heise 2002). That decrease is attributable to many factors, including prosecutors using the leverage that legislatures have afforded them to secure guilty pleas in as many cases as possible and likely prosecutors employing their discretion to reduce federal drug sentences that they recognize are too long.[13]

Prosecutors' discretionary power over sentencing through mandatory minimums and sentencing enhancements provides a channel for race and class to affect sentence length. Prosecutors exercise discretion not to file mandatory minimums or enhancements in many eligible cases, but that discretion has been wielded disproportionately to the detriment of Black offenders—a group already disproportionately represented among those charged with drug crimes. In the federal system, more than 51 percent of the drug enhancements filed in Fiscal Year 2016 were filed against Black defendants, and so too were nearly 58 percent of the enhancements actually levied at sentencing (United States Sentencing Commission 2018). Indeed, prosecutorial decisions about whether to file a charge carrying a mandatory minimum explain most of the large racial disparity in federal sentences for Black versus White defendants (Rehavi and Starr 2014). The odds of a Black defendant facing a mandatory minimum are nearly double that of a White defendant. Some of that disparity, however, reflects differences in criminal history caused by prior racial disparities in policing and prosecution.

And the disparate *use* of mandatory minimums in drug cases is hardly the extent of the racial story behind mandatory minimums. Congress passed massive new mandatory minimums in the 1980s by ramping up the drug war in response to a crack "epidemic" that had been deeply racialized through portrayals of "crack whores" and "gangbangers," building on "racial stereotypes of black women as irresponsible, selfish 'welfare queens,' and black men as 'predators'—part of an inferior and criminal subculture" (Alexander 2012, 52). The war on drugs is no small part of America's mass incarceration—what Michelle Alexander refers to as "The New Jim Crow."

The mandatory minimum sentences that American prosecutors wield in drug cases are far higher than comparable sentences in other countries. Possession with intent to distribute 28 grams of crack in America yields a five-*year* mandatory-minimum sentence of imprisonment whereas five kilograms—178 times the amount—would yield a likely sentence of six *months'* imprisonment in Britain (Mauer 2006; 21 U.S.C. § 841(b)(1)(B)(iii)). Until 2010, the threshold necessary to trigger that same five-year mandatory minimum was a mere five grams—one-thousandth of the amount that would yield a six-month sentence in Britain (Fair Sentencing Act of 2010).

As with substantive law, although the judiciary could have regulated this pathological dynamic between legislators and prosecutors through the unconstitutional conditions doctrine or the Eighth Amendment, it hasn't (Barkow 2019, 130). To the contrary, the Supreme Court has blessed it by holding that prosecutors may threaten the death penalty against a defendant for refusing to plead guilty (*Brady v. United States* 1970). So too may a prosecutor charge a defendant with a crime carrying a mandatory life sentence if he refuses to plead guilty and accept the five-year sentence as part of a plea offer for the heinous crime of forging an $88 check (*Bordenkircher v. Hayes* 1978). Those are simply the (somehow-acceptable) costs of exercising one's constitutional rights in America.

16.3.3 Cost Considerations

As with substantive criminal law, prosecutors lobby for harsh sentences and politicians benefit from giving prosecutors the tools that they seek. But cost considerations and the existence of sentencing commissions to raise the salience of those concerns make the politics of sentencing law different than those of substantive criminal law (Tonry 1998). Lengthening sentences is expensive (Brown 2007; Wright 2002). As state legislatures or Congress pass more mandatory minimums, sentencing enhancements, or three-strikes laws, so too do they increase corrections costs. And at least in some states, these cost concerns in the past decade have prompted legislatures to eliminate mandatory minimums or reinstitute parole (Alexander 2012; Demleitner 2005; Wright 2011).

There are several relevant system actors and interest groups who can and do raise to legislatures concerns about the financial costs of lengthy sentences. Officials in charge of prisons (and potentially jails) may raise these concerns because it is their budgets that feel the pinch of longer sentences (Wright 2004). So too can sentencing commissions provide an important voice and specific data about cost. Let us consider the latter in more detail.

The public choice account in the substantive law section above described prosecutors as an organized group pit against a lack of powerful interests on defendants' side. But with respect to sentencing law, sentencing commissions can provide a system-level voice that provides systemic cost information that can work against prosecutors' requests (Barkow 2005; Wright 2006). Sentencing commissions provide valuable information to legislatures about costs, particularly through resource impact statements that articulate the fiscal effect of particular sentencing policies. Without this source of information, however, legislatures may be blissfully unaware of the costs of ratcheting up criminal sentencing, at least in a specific way. Sentencing commissions not only provide data to politicians but also "political cover" to "temper . . . soft-on-crime attacks" (Barkow 2005, 811). Without such system actors there is little public pressure to decrease cost in criminal sentencing because the public has no real sense of how much money the government spends on criminal law or how it spends it (Brown 2004; Gold 2011).

Occasionally, at least on a state level, legislatures themselves raise cost concerns that halt more punitive turns in sentencing law. In North Carolina in 1992, for instance, the legislature rejected a plan from the state's sentencing commission that called for modest increases in prison costs, and only then did the commission come up with a plan that did not require more prison resources (Wright 2002).[14] North Carolina ultimately increased prison terms for serious felons while decreasing terms for less serious crimes to achieve neutrality in prison costs. Thus, although it is often sentencing commissions that temper politicians' punitive instincts, so long as sentencing commissions afford the relevant information cost pressure come from legislatures themselves.

When sentencing commissions' and legislatures' interests align, the commissions provide a useful institutional voice (Barkow 2005). But sentencing commissions are only as powerful as legislatures allow them to be, and their greatest tool is simply providing information. Sometimes legislators simply choose not to pay attention to cost pressures.[15] Minnesota, for instance, employed a "credit-card-sentencing policy" from 1989–1992 whereby legislators simply chose not to care whether the state could then or in the future pay for increased sentences (Frase 1993, 367–377). If legislation has a long latency period before the expenses accrue—such as three-strikes laws—legislators are more likely able to ignore those costs (Wright 1995). California, for instance, passed the country's most sweeping three-strikes law that did not require the third strike to be a serious, let alone violent, offense (Barkow 2019). The California law swept so broadly that it required a sentence of twenty-five years' imprisonment to life imprisonment for stealing a slice of pizza (Leonard 2010).

Unlike the federal government, states cannot simply pass longer and longer sentences with impunity. "States . . . care about the costs of sentencing policies in a way the federal government does not" (Barkow 2005, 811). Corrections make up too large of a share of any state's budget to ignore the estimated effects of a legislative change (Wright 2006). And the vast majority of states must balance their budgets. In the federal system, by contrast, corrections make up such a small slice of the overall budget that Members of Congress can indeed ignore cost estimates of criminal sentencing laws if they are so inclined; moreover, the federal budget need not and does not balance. That difference in cost concerns helps explain why, until the Obama administration, Congress made no similar moves to reduce sentences or relieve pressure from some mandatory minimums as states have. Indeed, the Fair Sentencing Act in 2010 was the first time Congress had repealed a mandatory minimum since the Nixon Administration (Luna and Cassell 2010).

16.4 Criminal Procedure

In criminal procedure, legislative records are largely pro-prosecutor. But localism may play an important role if that one-way ratchet is to break. Some progressive prosecutors recently have protected defendants' rights where legislatures have not, and state-local federalism may thus facilitate important experimentation.

16.4.1 State and Federal Legislative Efforts

As a matter of theory, Donald Dripps explains anti-defendant criminal procedure outcomes from a public choice perspective that quite resembles the Stuntzian story of substantive criminal law: questions about whether to afford more criminal procedure protections ultimately turn on balancing the risks of false negatives and false positives (Dripps 1993). Most of the public views itself as more likely to be the victim of a crime than an accused perpetrator. Accordingly, the public fears false negatives much more than false positives. Why much of the public, particularly those with political power, views themselves as more likely to be victims than defendants relates closely to race and class in American criminal law. Policing is often heavily concentrated in poor neighborhoods of color, as are arrests (see, e.g., Gold 2020; U.S. Department of Justice n.d.; Heath 2014).[16] It is thus hardly surprising then that the vast majority of criminal defendants are poor people of color (Forman 2011; Natapoff 2012; see also Valdes, Culp, and Harris 2002). But that means that the burdens of the criminal legal system and the lack of meaningful procedural protections are concentrated on a marginalized group, and the ostensible benefits of avoiding false negatives accrue to White wealthy people. With that allocation of burdens and benefits, public choice theory helps explain legislatures' hesitance to afford procedural protections for defendants.

Meaningful criminal procedure protections have come largely from the judiciary rather than from legislatures or prosecutors (Dripps 1993). And legislators have undermined (or sought to undermine) even some of those defendant victories. For instance, even though the Supreme Court held that defendants have a right to appointed counsel if they cannot afford to pay a lawyer, legislatures across the country have failed to adequately fund indigent defense services and have indeed assessed defendants fees for that representation regardless of *Gideon*'s promise (Colgan 2014; Joe 2016). Prosecutors sometimes facilitate that lack of funding for indigent defense. The Executive Director of the Louisiana District Attorneys Association, for example, argued that New Orleans indigent defense is *too well funded*—a laughable claim when judges were dismissing cases because of the lack of defense counsel (Pishko 2017). And Louisiana is not alone (Marshall 2004; Richman 2017). But other times prosecutor organizations have been largely quiet or even supported increases to indigent funding. New York provides a good example. Manhattan's District Attorney Robert Morgenthau was noticeably silent during litigation over funding for appointed defense counsel, and prosecutors widely supported rate increases for appointed counsel in New York in the late 1990s (Wright 2004).

Prosecutors and legislators have worked together (at least to some extent) seeking to eliminate some criminal procedure protections. For instance, Congress attempted to repeal by statute the Supreme Court's *Miranda* decision. When a challenge to the

Miranda-repealer statute was eventually litigated in the Supreme Court, the NDAA supported the law (Biskupic 2000).[17] Interestingly, the U.S. Department of Justice took the opposite position.

Prosecutors have also halted plenty of potential criminal procedure reforms. To pick a few examples, New York's bail reform efforts were initially thwarted, due in no small part to the District Attorney's Association of the State of New York (Rice 2018). Alabama seemed poised to substantially reform asset forfeiture law on a bipartisan basis until the Alabama District Attorneys Association blocked it. New York prosecutors had successfully thwarted discovery reform between 1979 and 2018 (Schwartzapfel 2019). In 2019, however, the legislature enacted sweeping discovery reform over the objections of most of the state's prosecutors (Southall and Ransom 2019).[18] Those reforms in their full breadth were short lived, however; a few months after they took effect, the legislature curtailed New York's bail and discovery reforms with the vocal support of some prosecutors (Bazelon and Rahman 2020; McKinley 2020; McKinley and Mays 2020).

16.4.2 Localism

Recently, some progressive prosecutors have curtailed discriminatory practices without legislative involvement (see Cassidy 2014). Money bail systems are a prime example. In Durham, North Carolina, for instance, after judges had recently rewritten bail procedures, District Attorney Satana Deberry announced that her office would undertake even broader reforms (Killian 2019). Durham now presumes release solely on a written promise to appear without monetary conditions except for those facing charges "involving physical harm or threats of physical harm to another person." In Houston, District Attorney Kim Ogg directed her prosecutors to recommend release on recognizance as the default in most misdemeanor cases—at least those where defendants do not present a clear public safety risk (Tolan and McCray 2017). In Chicago, State's Attorney Kimberly Foxx campaigned on a promise to reform bail, and the initial returns show modest progress ("In Pursuit of Justice for All: An Evaluation of Kim Foxx's First Year in Office" 2018). Foxx's support was an important driver behind the Chief Judge's general order that prohibits judges from setting money bail in amounts that a defendant cannot afford, which has reduced the local jail population ("In Pursuit of Justice for All: An Evaluation of Kim Foxx's First Year in Office" 2018).[19]

Aside from policy decisions by progressive prosecutors in their own counties, current and former prosecutors have written important amicus briefs in bail litigation siding with criminal defendants. Those briefs have explained that the public is poorly served by a rigid system of money bail that does not account for defendants' ability to pay (e.g., "Brief of Amici Curiae Current and Former District and State's Attorneys in Support of Plaintiffs-Appellees, *ODonnell v. Harris County*" 2017). Such amicus briefs, like the actions of progressive prosecutors, thwart the potential for state prosecutors' associations to claim to speak with a single voice as tough on crime. In so doing, they complicate the political forces that politicians face such that ever-greater enforcement is no longer the only sensible resolution as a matter of politics.

Policy changes have come from progressive county prosecutors. To the extent that the preferences of the voting public on criminal justice issues indeed depart from the conventional desire for ever-greater enforcement, it makes sense that reform would begin with county officials who are closer to the people than are state or federal officials (Ouziel 2019). Moreover, county-level governance may help bring together a more homogenous constituency than does larger state-level governance. And as with federalism generally, progressive prosecutors can experiment with different approaches and demonstrate positive consequences that can then serve as an example for other (and perhaps more widespread) reforms. Some statewide reforms were able to advance after individual counties had paved the way. Discovery reform in some states fits that mold. For instance, the Brooklyn District Attorney's Office has shared broad discovery with defendants in many cases since well before statewide discovery reform was enacted in April 2019 (Abruzzese 2019). Before North Carolina enacted open-file discovery statewide in 2004—a bill that prosecutors have periodically sought to have repealed—the larger cities in North Carolina already had similar policies (Wright 2012).

Cost remains an important source of pressure to restrain criminal law enforcement by providing more defendant-protective procedures. Bail reform, like sentencing law, can be seen as a story about controlling costs; after all, prosecutors typically work at the county level, which is the same level of budget that operates the jails. When the financial incentives are properly aligned rather than externalized onto a different level of government, we should expect to see more concern about costs.

Perhaps there is reason to think that community organizing and tensions between law enforcement and local communities have become so bad in many places that some prosecutors have a mandate to at least pick the low-hanging fruit in their reform efforts even when they are not driven by costs. But those incentives would tend toward reform regarding the "non, non, nons"[20] rather than prompting change in violent crime cases.

16.5 Conclusion

Although the pathological politics of criminal law continue to enable America to be the world's leading prison warden, recent developments have offered reason to think that perhaps there is some prospect for modest change. As mass incarceration has reached what one can hope is its peak in America during the twenty-first century, interest groups have begun to gain traction pushing back on the scope of substantive criminal law and its extraordinarily racist manifestations (Barkow 2019). Cell phone and body camera videos showing White police officers fatally shooting Black men in cities across the country have laid bare a truth that had been too easily ignored. Police choking Eric Garner to death on Staten Island or police asphyxiating George Floyd with a knee to his neck are but a few prominent examples of the politics in America around criminal law perhaps beginning to shift. Groups like the NAACP and grassroots efforts like Black Lives Matter have at least succeeded in making police-involved shootings of Black men important and potentially decisive campaign issues in prosecutor elections. Their efforts have led to at least some reform at the local level by progressive prosecutors, particularly in criminal procedure.[21] The push for criminal justice reform touched off by these high-profile shootings has sparked broader conversations about the ballooning of criminal law and our current state of mass incarceration. Those efforts have converged with efforts by libertarian groups such as the Koch Foundation to bring small-government principles to criminal law.[22] And interest convergence seems quite important for the prospects of reform (see Gold and Wright 2020).[23]

Indeed, perhaps because there is plenty of low-hanging fruit to be picked in reining in the scope of American criminal law, legislatures have even been involved in some recent pro-defendant reforms. Some jurisdictions have decriminalized (or indeed legalized) possession of marijuana as a matter of state law (e.g., McKinley and Wang 2019). New York decriminalized possession of gravity knives (Slattery 2019). So too have there been movements to decriminalize fare evasion on the New York subway—a crime that the Manhattan District Attorney has announced that he will not prosecute. And in states like California and Arizona with strong traditions of governing in part through the initiative process, perhaps there is further room for optimism through processes where legislators need not fear being tagged as soft on crime.

These reform efforts may have begun to slightly chip away at mass incarceration and the one-way ratchet of American criminal law, but it remains to be seen how far and long these reforms will go. Since 2009, the total number of incarcerated people in American jails and prisons has begun to decline (Barkow 2019, 119). Yet the declines have been quite minimal given the scope of the carceral state in America. It will take seventy-five years to cut our prison population in half at the current pace. And indeed even our current pace may appear deceptively fast compared to what one might project forward because it was sparked in large part by a Supreme Court decision requiring California to alleviate prison overcrowding and the resulting realignment efforts that California undertook.[24] In sum, there is some reason to hope that cost concerns will (and perhaps) have finally begun to halt the one-way ratchet of American criminal law and so too that localism and community sentiment may enable interest convergence that generates modest reforms. But how much hope to hold out for a new dynamic different from one of pathological politics limited by cost constraints or what shape that new dynamic may take is far from clear. Localism may, however, provide an important piece of a path forward.

Notes

1. The title of this chapter is based on Daniel Richman's article (2003). I would like to thank Anna Matejcek for excellent research assistance.
2. In France, by contrast, "prosecutors are judges" insofar as they share the same educational background, civil service status, office space, budget, staff, and can move between the two

positions (M. Cohen 2017, 109, emphasis removed). Such a structure is quite different than the formal notion of separation of powers in American criminal law across the three branches of government (Barkow 2006).

3. The quotation marks here are meant to evoke the standard cocktail party question asked of criminal defense attorneys, "how can you defend those people?" So too are they meant to evoke the treatment of criminal defendants as "other."
4. For those seeking a steady stream of examples, there is a Twitter feed dedicated to pointing out obscure federal crimes. See @CrimeADay. It is, for instance, "a federal crime to sell mozzarella cheese made with a mixture of cow milk and water buffalo milk." @CrimeADay, Twitter, June 14, 2019, 8:01 p.m.
5. Jeffrey Bellin argues that prosecutors are not in fact a powerful lobbying force because legislators already share prosecutors' interests on most matters (Bellin 2019). He thus contends that prosecutors are not exercising "power" because they are not overcoming other system actors' resistance but rather giving those system actors what they both want. Regardless of whether one labels that "power"—as Bellin does not—prosecutors end up securing quite favorable outcomes.
6. Many European countries have ostensibly mandatory prosecution policies under the so-called "legality principle" (Asp 2012; Jescheck 1970; Krajewski 2012).
7. Cost concerns complicate this picture somewhat for legislatures, as discussed below.
8. Forman 2010 ("Prison . . . is the province of the poor and the uneducated . . ."). In forty-six states and the District of Columbia prisoners lack the right to vote, and in some jurisdictions the loss of the franchise is lifelong (Barkow 2019, 116). Even after Florida voters recently amended their constitution to restore felons' voting rights, elected officials gutted that effort (Gardner 2019). And, at least as of the time of this writing, the federal courts have permitted them to do so (*Jones v. Governor of Florida* 2020).
9. This is not to say that a fully informed public would always wish for more criminal law enforcement if it understood the issues and corresponding costs (Gold 2011) but only that the public is now seen to hold that preference.
10. Mandatory minimum sentences provide a floor on the sentence that the judge can impose following a conviction on a particular crime. They typically afford prosecutors substantial discretion, however, because it is the prosecutor who decides whether to charge that crime. Three-strikes laws are a form of repeat offender penalty that impose a severe sentence—typically mandatory life imprisonment—the third time that a particular defendant is convicted of certain crimes. Because three-strikes laws encompass some convictions but not others, prosecutors' ability to decide what crimes to charge affords them significant power over sentencing. Sentencing enhancements refer to a variety of sentence increases that prosecutors can levy against repeat offenders on top of the underlying charge.
11. Congress added a net of seventy-two mandatory minimums under the twelve years of the Reagan and George H. W. Bush administrations, while it added 116 during Clinton's eight years (Murakawa 2014).
12. In New York state courts under the Rockefeller drug laws, harsh sentences where prosecutors had no discretion to avoid them caused prosecutors to indict vastly fewer drug cases (J. Cohen and Tonry 1983; Schulhofer 1993).
13. Although mandatory minimums may be good politics and they afford prosecutors a good deal of leverage, they can hardly be thought to be good policy (Tonry 1998).
14. For more detail on these sentencing reforms, see (Wright 2002).

15. Because states pass criminal laws and operate prisons, there is no correctional free lunch problem as we see in other aspects of criminal law such as when counties fund prosecution but states operate the prisons that house convicted defendants (Bierschbach and Bibas 2017; Gershowitz 2016; Gold 2020; Zimring and Hawkins 1991).
16. One recent study found that a suspect's race and the racial makeup of a neighborhood were more strongly correlated with police use of the "high crime area" basis for a stop than was the actual crime rate in the neighborhood (Grunwald and Fagan 2019).
17. The Supreme Court ultimately held that Congress could not overrule *Miranda* through ordinary legislation because it was a rule of constitutional origin (*Dickerson v. United States* 2000).
18. That same bill also curtailed New York judges' ability to impose money bail (Schwartzapfel 2019).
19. These are not the only examples in the bail reform space. Other progressive prosecutors such as Larry Krasner in Philadelphia or Rachael Rollins in Boston have also trumpeted bail reform (Covert 2019; Wulthmann 2019).
20. "Non, non, nons" refers to non-serious, non-violent, non-sexual offenders (Gottschalk 2014).
21. Even there, the pace of progress has been slower than many might wish because of complex factors regarding the interrelation between democracy and bureaucracy (Ouziel 2019).
22. Prominent libertarian Grover Norquist testified to Congress against mandatory minimums, for instance (Mandatory Minimums Hearing 2009).
23. Bell 1980, 523 ("[T]his principle of 'interest convergence' provides: The interest of blacks in achieving racial equality will be accommodated only when it converges with the interest of whites").
24. Realignment is itself a promising strategy because it helps combat some of the ways that criminal law is made too cheap, but such a strategy may not be politically popular (Gold 2020).

References

@CrimeADay, Twitter, June 30, 2019, 8:36 p.m.

18 U.S.C. § 924.

21 U.S.C. § 841.

21 U.S.C. § 848.

Abruzzese, Rob. 2019. "Brooklyn DA Pushes Major Reform in Evidence Disclosure." *Brooklyn Daily Eagle*, March 4, 2019.

Alexander, Michelle. 2012. *The New Jim Crow: Mass Incarceration in the Age of Colorblindness*. New York: The New Press.

Alschuler, Albert W. 1991. "The Failure of Sentencing Guidelines: A Plea for Less Aggregation." *University of Chicago Law Review* 58(3): 901–952.

Asp, Petter. 2012. "The Prosecutor in Swedish Law." In *Prosecutors and Politics: A Comparative Perspective*. Edited by Michael Tonry, vol. 41, 141–165. Chicago: University of Chicago Press.

Barkow, Rachel E. 2005. "Administering Crime." *UCLA Law Review* 52(3): 715–814.

Barkow, Rachel E. 2006. "Separation of Powers and the Criminal Law." *Stanford Law Review* 58(4): 989–1054.

Barkow, Rachel E. 2019. *Prisoners of Politics: Breaking the Cycle of Mass Incarceration*. Cambridge, MA, and London: The Belknap Press of Harvard University Press.

Bazelon, Emily, and Insha Rahman. 2020. "There's a Strong Case for Sticking with Bail Reform." *New York Times*, January 24, 2020.

Beale, Sara Sun. 1997. "What's Law Got to Do with It: The Political, Social, Psychological and Other Non-Legal Factors Influencing the Development of (Federal) Criminal Law." *Buffalo Criminal Law Review* 1(1): 23–66.

Bell, Derrick A., Jr. 1980. "*Brown v. Board of Education* and the Interest-Convergence Dilemma." *Harvard Law Review* 93(3): 518–533.

Bellin, Jeffrey. 2019. "The Power of Prosecutors." *N.Y.U. Law Review* 94(2): 171–212.

Bierschbach, Richard A., and Stephanos Bibas. 2017. "Rationing Criminal Justice." *Michigan Law Review* 116(2): 187–246.

Biskupic, Joan. 2000. "Court Urged to Repeal 'Miranda': Police Groups Target 1966 Rights Ruling." *Washington Post*, April 9, 2000.

Blockburger v. United States. 1932. 284 U.S. 299.

Bordenkircher v. Hayes. 1978. 434 U.S. 357.

Bowman, Frank O., III, and Michael Heise. 2001. "Quiet Rebellion—Explaining Nearly a Decade of Declining Federal Drug Sentences." *Iowa Law Review* 86(4): 1043–1136.

Bowman, Frank O., III. 2002. "Quiet Rebellion II: An Empirical Analysis of Declining Federal Drug Sentences Including Data from the District Level." *Iowa Law Review* 87(2): 477–562.

Brady v. United States. 1970. 397 U.S. 742.

"Brief of Amici Curiae Current and Former District and State's Attorneys in Support of Plaintiffs-Appellees, *ODonnell v. Harris County*" 2017.

Brown, Darryl K. 2004. "Cost-Benefit Analysis in Criminal Law." *California Law Review* 92(2): 323–372.

Brown, Darryl K. 2007. "Democracy and Decriminalization." *Texas Law Review* 86(2): 223–276.

Butler, Paul. 2009. *Let's Get Free: A Hip-Hop Theory of Justice*. New York: The New Press.

Cassidy, R. Michael. 2014. "(Ad)ministering Justice: A Prosecutor's Ethical Duty to Support Sentencing Reform." *Loyola University Chicago Law Journal* 45(4): 981–1026.

Cohen, Jacqueline, and Michael H. Tonry. 1983. "Sentencing Reforms and Their Impacts." In *Research on Sentencing: The Search for Reform*. Edited by Alfred Blumstein, Jacqueline Cohen, Susan E. Martin, and Michael H. Tonry, vol. 2, 305–459. Washington, D.C.: National Academy Press.

Cohen, Mathilde. 2017. "The French Prosecutor as Judge: The Carpenter's Mistake?" In *Prosecutors and Democracy: A Cross-National Study*. Edited by Máximo Langer and David Sklansky, 109–137. Cambridge: Cambridge University Press.

Colgan, Beth A. 2014. "Paying for *Gideon*." *Iowa Law Review* 99(5): 1929–1950.

Covert, Bryce. 2019. "Progressive Philly D.A. Larry Krasner's Bail Reform Plans Seem Stalled, Advocates Say." *The Appeal*, June 25, 2019.

Demleitner, Nora V. 2005. "Is There a Future for Leniency in the U.S. Criminal Justice System?" *Michigan Law Review* 103(6): 1231–1272.

Dickerson v. United States. 2000. 530 U.S. 428.

Dripps, Donald A. 1993. "Criminal Procedure, Footnote Four, and the Theory of Public Choice; Or, Why Don't Legislatures Give a Damn about the Rights of the Accused?" *Syracuse Law Review* 44(4): 1079–1102.

Drug Mandatory Minimums: Are They Working?: Hearing Before the Subcomm. on Criminal Justice, Drug Policy, and Human Resources of the H. Comm. on Gov't Reform, 106th Cong.

62 (2000) (statement of John Roth, Chief, Narcotic and Dangerous Drug Section, Criminal Div., Dep't of Justice).

Fair Sentencing Act of 2010, Pub. L. No. 111-220, 124 Stat. 2372 (August 3, 2010).

Forman, James, Jr. 2010. "Why Care About Mass Incarceration?" *Michigan Law Review* 108(6): 993–1010.

Forman, James, Jr. 2011. "The Black Poor, Black Elites, and America's Prisons." *Cardozo Law Review* 32(3): 791–806.

Frase, Richard S. 1993. "The Role of the Legislature, the Sentencing Commission, and Other Officials Under the Minnesota Sentencing Guidelines." *Wake Forest Law Review* 28(2): 345–380.

Gardner, Amy. 2019. "Florida Legislators Agree to Limit Felons' Voting Rights. Critics Call It a New Poll Tax." *Washington Post*, May 3, 2019.

Gershowitz, Adam M. 2016. "Consolidating Local Criminal Justice: Should the Prosecutors Control the Jails?" *Wake Forest Law Review* 51(3): 677–704.

Gold, Russell M. 2011. "Promoting Democracy in Prosecution." *Washington Law Review* 86(1): 69–124.

Gold, Russell M. 2020. "Paying for Pretrial Detention." *North Carolina Law Review* 98(6): 1255–1295.

Gold, Russell M., Carissa Byrne Hessick, and F. Andrew Hessick. 2017. "Civilizing Criminal Settlements." *Boston University Law Review* 97(5): 1607–1660.

Gold, Russell M., and Ronald F. Wright. 2020. "The Political Patterns of Bail Reform." *Wake Forest Law Review* 55(4): 743–756.

Gottschalk, Marie. 2014. *Caught: The Prison State and the Lockdown of American Politics.* Princeton: Princeton University Press.

Grunwald, Ben, and Jeffrey Fagan. 2019. "The End of Intuition-Based High-Crime Areas." *California Law Review* 107(2): 345–404.

Heath, Brad. 2014. "Racial Gap in U.S. Arrest Rates: 'Staggering Disparity.'" *USA Today*, November 18, 2014.

"In Pursuit of Justice for All: An Evaluation of Kim Foxx's First Year in Office." 2018. https://www.chicagoreader.com/general/201712/Equal_Justice_for_All_-_A_Report_on_Kim_Foxx_s_First%20Year-ForWeb.pdf.

Jescheck, Hans-Heinrich. 1970. "Principles of German Criminal Procedure in Comparison with American Law." *Virginia Law Review* 56(2): 239–253.

Joe, Irene Oritseweyinmi. 2016. "Systematizing Public Defender Rationing." *Denver Law Review* 93(2): 389–430.

Johnson, Thea. 2019. "Fictional Pleas." *Indiana Law Journal* 94(3): 855–900.

Jones v. Governor of Florida. 2020. No. 20-12003 (11th Cir.).

Killian, Joe. 2019. "Durham Prosecutors No Longer Seeking Cash Bail in Most Cases." *The Progressive Pulse*, May 29, 2019.

Krajewski, Krzysztof. 2012. "Prosecution and Prosecutors in Poland: In Quest of Independence." In *Prosecutors and Politics: A Comparative Perspective*. Edited by Michael Tonry, vol. 41, 75–116. Chicago: University of Chicago Press.

Leonard, Jack. 2010. "'Pizza Thief' Walks the Line." *Los Angeles Times*, February 10, 2010.

Letter from Dennis Boyd, Executive Director, National Association of Assistant U.S. Attorneys, to Patti B. Saris, Chair, U.S. Sentencing Commission. July 2, 2014.

Lockyer v. Andrade. 2003. 538 U.S. 63.

Luna, Erik. 2005. "The Overcriminalization Phenomenon." *American University Law Review* 54(3): 703–746.

Luna, Erik, and Paul G. Cassell. 2010. "Mandatory Minimalism." *Cardozo Law Review* 32(1): 1–84.

Lynch, Gerard E. 2003. "Screening Versus Plea Bargaining: Exactly What Are We Trading Off." *Stanford Law Review* 55(4): 1399–1408.

Mandatory Minimums Hearing. 2009. Mandatory Minimums and Unintended Consequences: Hearing before the Subcomm. on Crime, Terrorism, and Homeland Security of the H. Comm. on the Judiciary, 111th Cong. 34–66 (2009) (Statement of Grover Norquist, President, Americans for Tax Reform).

Marimow, Ann E. 2015. "Softening Sentences, Losing Leverage." *Washington Post*, October 31, 2015.

Marshall, Lawrence C. 2004. "Gideon's Paradox." *Fordham Law Review* 73(3): 955–968.

Mauer, Marc. 2006. *Race to Incarcerate*. Rev. ed. New York: The New Press.

McKinley, Jesse. 2020. "The Bail Reform Backlash That Has Democrats at War." *New York Times*, February 14, 2020.

McKinley, Jesse, and Jeffery C. Mays. 2020. "After Anti-Semitic Incidents, New Bail Law in N.Y. Comes Under Attack." *New York Times*, January 8, 2020.

McKinley, Jesse, and Vivian Wang. 2019. "Marijuana Decriminalization Is Expanded in N.Y., but Full Legalization Fails." *New York Times*, June 20, 2019.

Murakawa, Naomi. 2014. *The First Civil Right: How Liberals Built Prison America*. Oxford and New York: Oxford University Press.

Natapoff, Alexandra. 2012. "Misdemeanors." *Southern California Law Review* 85(5): 1313–1376.

Oppel, Richard A., Jr. 2011. "Tough Sentences Help Prosecutors Push for Plea Bargains." *New York Times*, September 25, 2011.

Ouziel, Lauren. 2019. "Democracy, Bureaucracy, and Criminal Justice Reform." *Boston College Law Review* 61(2): 523–589.

Pishko, Jessica. 2017. "Prosecutors Are Banding Together to Prevent Criminal-Justice Reform." *The Nation*, October 18, 2017.

Potts, Randolph G. 1997. "The Social Construction and Social Marketing of the 'Dangerous Black Man.'" *Journal of African American Men* 2(4): 11–24.

Rehavi, M. Marit, and Sonja B. Starr. 2014. "Racial Disparity in Federal Criminal Sentences." *Journal of Political Economy* 122(6): 1320–1354.

Rice, Josie Duffy. 2018. "Prosecutors Aren't Just Enforcing the Law—They're Making It." *The Appeal*, April 20, 2018.

Richman, Daniel. 2003. "Prosecutors and Their Agents, Agents and Their Prosecutors." *Columbia Law Review* 103(4): 749–832.

Richman, Daniel. 2009. "Political Control of Federal Prosecutions: Looking Back and Looking Forward." *Duke Law Journal* 58(8): 2087–2124.

Richman, Daniel C. 2017. "Accounting for Prosecutors." In *Prosecutors and Democracy: A Cross-National Study*. Edited by Máximo Langer and David Sklansky, 40–75. Cambridge University Press.

Robinson, Paul H., and Michael T. Cahill. 2004. "The Accelerating Degradation of American Criminal Codes." *Hastings Law Journal* 56(4): 633–656.

Satterfield, Jamie. 2016. "Knoxville Federal Prosecutor Battling in Congress Against Sentencing Reform." *Knoxville News Sentinel*, April 22, 2016.

Schulhofer, Stephen J. 1993. "Rethinking Mandatory Minimums." *Wake Forest Law Review* 28(2): 199–222.

Schwartzapfel, Beth. 2019. "'Blindfold' Off: New York Overhauls Pretrial Evidence Rules." *The Marshall Project*, April 1, 2019.

Seigel, Michael L., and Christopher Slobogin. 2005. "Prosecuting Martha: Federal Prosecutorial Power and the Need for a Law of Counts." *Penn State Law Review* 109(4): 1107–1132.

Simons, Michael A. 2009. "Prosecutors as Punishment Theorists: Seeking Sentencing Justice." *George Mason Law Review* 16(2): 303–356.

Slattery, Denis. 2019. "Cuomo Signs Legislation Legalizing Gravity Knives." *New York Daily News*, May 30, 2019.

Southall, Ashley, and Jan Ransom. 2019. "Once as Pro-prosecution as Any Red State, New York Makes a Big Shift on Trials." *New York Times*, May 2, 2019.

Stuntz, William J. 1997. "The Uneasy Relationship between Criminal Procedure and Criminal Justice." *Yale Law Journal* 107(1): 1–76.

Stuntz, William J. 2001. "The Pathological Politics of Criminal Law." *Michigan Law Review* 100(3): 505–600.

Stuntz, William J. 2004. "Plea Bargaining and Criminal Law's Disappearing Shadow." *Harvard Law Review* 117(8): 2548–2569.

Tolan, Casey, and Rebecca McCray. 2017. "Making Freedom Free." *Slate*, March 29, 2017.

Tonry, Michael. 1998. *Sentencing Matters: Studies in Crime and Public Policy*. Oxford and New York: Oxford University Press.

Tonry, Michael. 2012. "Prosecutors and Politics in Comparative Perspective." *Crime and Justice* 41(1): 1–33.

United States Sentencing Commission. 1991. "Special Report to the Congress: Mandatory Minimum Penalties in the Federal Criminal Justice System."

United States Sentencing Commission. 2018. "Application and Impact of 21 U.S.C. 851: Enhanced Penalties for Federal Drug Trafficking Offenders."

United States Sentencing Commission. 2019. "Quick Facts, Mandatory Minimum Penalties."

United States v. Kupa. 2013. 976 F. Supp. 2d 417 (E.D.N.Y.).

U.S. Department of Justice, Bureau of Justice Statistics. n.d. "2017 Crime in the United States." FBI. Accessed August 13, 2019. https://ucr.fbi.gov/crime-in-the-u.s/2017/crime-in-the-u.s.-2017/topic-pages/persons-arrested.

Valdes, Francisco, Jerome M. Culp, and Angela P. Harris, eds. 2002. *Crossroads, Directions, and a New Critical Race Theory*. Philadelphia: Temple University Press.

Welty, Jeff. 2014. "Overcriminalization in North Carolina." *North Carolina Law Review* 92(6): 1935–2026.

Wright, Ronald F. 1995. "Three Strikes Legislation and a Sinking Fund Proposal." *Federal Sentencing Reporter* 8: 80–83.

Wright, Ronald F. 2002. "Counting the Cost of Sentencing in North Carolina, 1980–2000." *Crime and Justice: A Review of Research* 29: 39–112.

Wright, Ronald F. 2004. "Parity of Resources for Defense Counsel and the Reach of Public Choice Theory." *Iowa Law Review* 90(2): 219–268.

Wright, Ronald F. 2005. "Trial Distortion and the End of Innocence in Federal Criminal Justice." *University of Pennsylvania Law Review* 154(1): 79–156.

Wright, Ronald F. 2006. "The Power of Bureaucracy in the Response to *Blakely* and *Booker*." *Houston Law Review* 43(2): 389–414.

Wright, Ronald F. 2009. "How Prosecutor Elections Fail Us." *Ohio State Journal of Criminal Law* 6(2): 581–610.

Wright, Ronald F. 2011. "Portable Minimalism in Sentencing Politics." *Cardozo Law Review* de Novo 2011: 9.

Wright, Ronald F. 2012. "Persistent Localism in the Prosecutor Services of North Carolina." *Crime and Justice: A Review of Research* 41: 211–264.

Wulthmann, Walter. 2019. "Rachael Rollins, 100 Days In: What Has Changed, and What Hasn't, Under The Reformer DA." WBUR, April 12, 2019.

Zimring, Franklin, and Gordon J. Hawkins. 1991. *The Scale of Imprisonment*. Chicago: University of Chicago Press.

CHAPTER 17

THE RELATIONSHIP BETWEEN PROSECUTORS AND DEFENDERS

ELLEN YAROSHEFSKY

17.1 Introduction

PROSECUTORS and defenders have unique roles in criminal justice systems throughout the world and their relationship is critical to how those systems function. Fundamentally, the difference in power dynamics is the driving force that defines the relationship between prosecution and defense counsel. No matter the country or culture, criminal justice systems are a structurally tilted playing field where the prosecutor wields power and the defense has a limited role (Fish 2018). The extent of that differential largely defines the relationships between counsel, with the United States yielding the greatest disparity in power dynamics among common law countries.

Whether in an adversarial or inquisitorial system, that relationship depends not only on the power differential, but also on a range of other significant variables that include professional and office culture, experience, age, race, ethnicity, gender, and the personalities of the individual lawyers. These and other factors lead to significant differences that make generalizations difficult (Eisenstein and Jacob 1977). There is limited research on the relationship between counsel, especially research with any national scope and existing studies are typically based upon interviews with all system stakeholders (Levine and Wright 2012).

This chapter relies upon those studies and recent interviews by this author to examine the interrelated factors that affect the relationship between prosecutors and defenders in the United States, and in some other common law countries and civil law countries. First, it discusses the respective roles of prosecutors and defenders and the attitudes that often result from these roles. It then considers the most significant factor in all countries: the power of prosecutors and differences in how different prosecutors exercise that power. Other factors that affect the relationship between these lawyers are discussed in turn. These are social architecture of the offices, the reward structures and the lawyer's individual characteristics. It discusses structural changes in the past decades that have changed or may change those relationships. The article then addresses the comparable relationship in common law and civil law countries.

Overall, the relationship between prosecutors and defenders differs to some extent by the distinct differences between adversarial and inquisitorial systems. All systems can be viewed on a continuum, as "mostly shaped by the inquisitorial or adversarial tradition" (Brants 2012). At one end of the continuum, in inquisitorial systems, the emphasis is upon investigative pre-trial procedure largely lead by the prosecutor, with the defender's role limited to pointing the prosecutor and the court to facts favorable to the defendant and requesting additional avenues for investigation. The relationship between the lawyers is perceived to be relatively collaborative until the trial phase, when the facts can be tested by cross examination and often by judicial examination. By contrast, the adversarial system is partisan from the start and purports to seek truth through an adversarial contest where each side investigates the facts. While the system requires lawyers on both sides to have effective negotiation skills, it is necessarily an adversarial practice, even where cooperation and collegiality may best serve the client and the criminal justice system. Despite these overall differences between common law and civil law systems, the power dynamic and tilted playing field in all countries is the key factor that influences the relationships between counsel.

17.2 The United States

17.2.1 Overview of the System and the Lawyers' Roles

In the United States adversarial process, the prosecutors' and defense attorneys' perceptions of their own role has a significant impact on the relationship between them. The prosecutor's stated role is to seek justice and not merely to seek convictions (ABA Model Rules of Professional Conduct 2020). The minister of justice role imposes ill-defined and wide-ranging obligations to the victim, the defendant, the community, and the criminal justice system. Prosecutors are granted wide-ranging discretion to accomplish these goals.

To be sure, all prosecutors define their role as enhancing public safety, but they may have different approaches to that fundamental task. Those who see their role as maximizing convictions or punishments use their discretion in charging and plea-bargaining discretion to secure guilty pleas and lengthy sentences. On the other hand, prosecutors with a more expansive justice mission often use their discretion to limit excessive sentences and to engage in various alternative programs and approaches to public safety (Lantigua Williams 2016).

The defense lawyer, by contrast, has only one role and owes her duty solely to the client to be a zealous advocate within the bounds of ethical constraints. Defense lawyers proudly call themselves "liberty's last champion" in the defense of constitutional rights and individual clients (NACDL n.d.). They embrace this role for a range of reasons from making a difference in the lives of their individual clients, to representing underdogs, upholding the constitutional rights of those charged with crimes, and fighting the good fight against power to the broader social justice mission of ending mass incarceration and combatting racism. Most defenders are motivated to keep clients out of a "soul crushing" system (Smith 1995).

The often-complicated relationship between prosecutors and defenders is typified by the classic difference at any gathering. Defenders are asked versions of "How can you represent those people?" Prosecutors are rarely if ever asked, "How can you prosecute those people?" (Smith and Freedman 2013). The recent attention to mass incarceration in the United States has altered that dynamic somewhat in some jurisdictions, but fundamentally the prosecutor is perceived as enhancing public safety and doing justice. The prosecutor wears the "white hat." The defender stands in the way of just results to "get people off on a technicality" and is thought of as manipulative (Nardulli, Eisenstein, and Flemming 1988; Smith 2012). At least this is the perception in popular culture in the United States. It often has a profound effect on the relationship between the lawyers.

Although both prosecutors and defenders may all view themselves as engaged in social justice through different lenses, defenders readily challenge the notion that prosecutors who "put people of color in cages" are acting to enhance social justice (Davis 2018). The defender often views the prosecutor as undermining the dignity and respect of her clients. She believes that the prosecutor is not "moved by the whole person" but by the client's commission of a crime (Smith 2001). By contrast, the prosecutor views her social justice role as protecting the community; she believes that the defendant undermines the dignity and respect of the victim and harms the community.

Within this dynamic, the extent to which the adversaries understand and appreciate their differing roles and perceive their opponents as engaging in fair play has an important impact upon their relationship. For instance, sometimes, at trial, the prosecutor may claim that the defense lawyer is "hiding the ball" about certain facts when it is contrary to the defense lawyer's obligation to present the information (Interview Notes 2018). On the other hand, when the prosecutor is perceived as engaging in fair play, the relationship will work most effectively.

To promote a sense of fairness, a lead prosecutor in the Midwest notes the importance of collaboration with the defense: "We work collaboratively. We fight tooth and nail in the courtroom and advocate for our positions but at end of day, for the most part, we treat each other with civility and respect. We train our lawyers to respect the fact that it not worth it, in the long run, to take undue advantage in any given case, because you will be interacting with the lawyers across the aisle in many future cases. We 'work together for justice and fairness'" (Interview Notes 2018). A highly regarded defense lawyer in the Southwest expresses similar sentiments and points out the importance of working well together: "Don't make enemies. Try to get along with prosecutors. Because the courthouse is a community with repeat players, it is good to have a relationship with prosecutors, cops, and probation officers. Reputation matters. The major issue is, 'Can I trust your word?' I am in a better position to negotiate if I trust you as competent, passionate, and ethical" (Interview Notes 2018; Maine 2000).

Even where prosecutors are perceived to engage in fair play in individual cases, trust between the adversaries is often tenuous because of the power dynamic. In both the federal and state systems, prosecutors have virtually unilateral power to affect lives by their discretionary choices. The prosecutor, and not the judge, decides upon the charges that will determine the range of punishment. Thus, properly understood, prosecutors are more adversary adjudicators than solely adversaries" (Barkow 2014; Fish 2018).

Over the years, the federal prosecutor has achieved even greater power because of mandatory minimum sentences and other laws, enacted in the 1990s (Rakoff 2014). Such laws encouraged, if not compelled, individuals to accept prosecutorial plea offers to avoid harsher punishment. Comparably, prosecutors in state systems are responsible for significantly increased felony sentences since the 1990s, as a result of increased funding to hiring significant numbers of them during the era of the "war on drugs" (Pfaff 2017). Consequently, it is now widely acknowledged that the United States has the largest percentage of people imprisoned in the world, that prosecutors drove this process (Pfaff 2017), and that our system has disproportionately singled out and punished people of color (Alexander 2010).

This increased prosecutorial power results in a "guilty plea system" in lieu of one where defendants exercise the right to a trial (Rakoff 2014). In both state and federal systems between 95 and 97 percent of defendants plead guilty.[1] Defendants plead guilty at such a high rate because of the significantly increased sentence that follows if found guilty after a trial.

In state systems, the high rate of guilty pleas is not only because of disparate sentencing if found guilty after trial but also because of bail policies and court processing delays. In the United States, 90 percent of cases are in state court and the overwhelming majority are misdemeanors against indigent defendants (Lee 2018). In 2009, there were 10.5 million misdemeanor filings in the United States (Boruchowitz, Brink, and Domino 2009). State systems vary across the United States, but there is often an "assembly line" system of what is termed "case processing" where most defendants enter guilty pleas in misdemeanor cases early in the process, oftentimes on the date that they are formally charged with a crime. They do so to avoid spending time in jail awaiting a trial or often to avoid numerous pre-trial court appearances that may interfere with employment or family responsibilities (Natapoff 2018). In both misdemeanors and felonies, even though the defense lawyer is provided with limited information from the prosecutor about the case and cannot adequately counsel a client, the significant punitive effects of asserting a right to trial are too onerous to contest the charges (Kim 2015; NACDL 2018; Wright 2005). Thus, clients plead guilty after a plea-bargaining process that defenders describe as begging, pleading, or groveling rather than an actual negotiation session to obtain a reasonable plea bargain from the prosecutor (Lee 2004; Smith 2012).

The tensions caused by the guilty plea system are exacerbated by the lack of funding for defense counsel. Even in jurisdictions where the state provides monies for defender offices, the offices are notoriously underfunded despite the more than fifty years of the constitutional requirement to provide effective counsel for indigent defendants (ABA Standing Committee on Legal Aid and Indigent Defendants 2004; Justice Policy Institute 2011). This is consistently described as a crisis (Justice Policy Institute 2011; Lee 2004). Public defenders lack the capacity to turn away clients despite the inability to adequately represent them (Lee 2004). Prosecutors also often have punishing caseloads and clamor for additional funds, but the disparity in funding is typically severe. The reality of seriously underfunded counsel, massive caseloads, the paucity of trials, and lack of information sharing is the context to understand the often tension-filled relationships between the defense and prosecution. All of these tensions must be viewed in the larger context of the disproportionate charging and punishment of people of color. Mass incarceration is the lens through which to view all of the other tensions between prosecutor and defender.

Prosecution in the federal system differs in some significant ways, including better funding for indigent defendants, but the underlying power dynamic produces the same guilty plea system and its attendant tensions. Relationships among counsel are typically characterized by civility more often than in state systems, but the underlying dynamic mirrors that in state court.

17.2.2 Organization and Ethic of Prosecutors' Offices

Factors beyond the power dynamic contribute to the relationship between prosecutors and defenders. A significant one is the "social architecture" of the prosecutor's office (Levine and Wright 2012), that is, its organization and ethos as a professional office. This includes leadership, training, supervision, hiring practices, accountability mechanisms, and informal practices. A good leader sets the tone and establishes effective training, supervision, and accountability programs. Offices that emphasize conviction rates produce line prosecutors who are more likely to cut corners and hide or ignore contrary evidence (Fish 2018). Lawyers in such offices are perceived to be aggressive often with a "win at all costs" mentality and are not trusted by the defense community. Even in offices where the newly elected leader may espouse notions of justice beyond conviction rates, the line prosecutors who have been in that office for some years under a different leader may not readily adapt without significant training, supervision, and oversight.

Office cultures have varying cultural norms. Some are aggressive and adversarial. Others are more balanced and moderate (Bibas 2004; Meares 1995; Miller and Wright 2008; Yaroshefsky and Green 2012). Nevertheless, there is a culture of competitiveness within most prosecutors' offices that is nurtured not only by the prosecutors in the office, but by the police. Office cultures that are known to celebrate convictions and death sentences with festivities and rewards promote a conviction mentality. These offices historically offer the line prosecutor little incentive to dismiss cases for innocent defendants or to consider a fair result short of a guilty verdict at trial (Fish 2018). This conviction culture is difficult to alter (Fish 2018; Levine and Wright 2012; Miller and Wright 2008; Wright and Levine 2014). "The moral and political climate in an agency can foster a 'conviction psychology' more powerfully than can any specific policy basing promotions on an assistant's conviction rate" (Fisher 1988). As one former prosecutor said "[O]ne ought not underestimate the unifying influence of a shared commitment to 'getting the bad guys,' hardened by the adversarial process, nurtured by mutual respect and need, and on occasion lubricated by alcohol" (Richman 2003).

Such conviction culture is perceived to be inevitable although there may be some changes in offices that emphasize pre-trial exonerations and dismissal of charges. But in general, "In view of the institutional culture of prosecutor's offices and the culture of the adversary system generally, it is perhaps inevitable that the overriding interest of prosecutors would be winning" (Smith 2001).

The most significant source of tension between prosecutors and defenders is the exercise of the prosecutor's power to share information. Laws require the prosecutor to provide the defense with information that may cast doubt upon the guilt of the person charged with a crime. Flowing from the Supreme Court's 1963 decision in *Brady v. Maryland*, prosecutors have a constitutional obligation to provide both exculpatory and impeachment information to the defense. Termed "*Brady* obligations" as a shorthand for the discovery obligations, they continue to lead to fierce disputes, tensions, and discord between prosecutors and defenders in many jurisdictions. These laws vary significantly in states and federal courts (Yaroshefsky 2011). In some jurisdictions with limited discovery, the defense lawyer is not provided with names of witnesses and their prior statements until extremely late in the process, often during trial when the witness is called to testify. These laws in "narrow compliance" jurisdictions encourage the aggressive prosecutor to withhold information. Defenders call it a "cat and mouse game" (Yaroshefsky and Green 2012). It breeds mistrust.

In some jurisdictions, prosecutors provide more information than required by statute or other law. This often occurs in white-collar cases with there is voluminous material and where the prosecutors trust the defender. Offices with more generous discovery practices and norms perceived to be less punitive have better relationships with defense lawyers (Levine and Wright 2012).

Other jurisdictions, known as "open file" discovery jurisdictions, provide virtually all of the non-privileged information to the defense early in the case. In such jurisdictions, the relationship between prosecutors and defenders is improved although still contingent on other factors such as defense funding and methods of discovery compliance (Grunwald 2017). But offices that espouse broad discovery practices but informally promote shoddy discovery and lack accountability for lawyers who flaunt the law promote a lack of trust among defense lawyers (Grunwald 2017; Yaroshefsky and Green 2012).

There is a longstanding and ongoing dispute as to whether *Brady* violations are an epidemic or are episodic. Prosecutors complain that they are unfairly accused of *Brady* violations and defenders complain that such violations are far more common than acknowledged by courts and prosecutors' offices. Empirical data cannot be gathered because failure to disclose *Brady* is inherently a hidden problem (Green and Yaroshefsky 2016). Even in jurisdictions where prosecutors are overworked and negligently fail to provide required information, the culture is often toxic, with many prosecutors accused of intentionally "hiding the ball."

Tensions about discovery compliance are often exacerbated because of other prosecutorial policies and practices. For example, most jurisdictions have speedy trial rules that require cases to be brought to trial within certain time periods. Prosecutors are accused of skirting these requirements by making marginally untruthful representations of readiness for trial that courts accept as normative practice. Other practices that generate hostility include seeking onerous guilty plea waivers of the right to appeal, misuse of search and seizure waivers, and increased restrictions upon defendants (Hopwood 2014). Overall, the perceived lack of accountability—either by judicial sanctions or within the office—for prosecutors who have engaged in sharp practices to win their cases, and even for those who have violated the law (Sullivan and Possley 2016), results in cynicism and undermines trust between counsel. "[M]y experience showed me that prosecutors are strongly influenced to disregard and minimize rights by the culture that surrounds them. Disciplining or firing miscreants may be necessary, but it's not enough: It doesn't address the root causes of fearful culture and bad incentives" (White 2016).

A defender in a small Midwest city recounts: "The Midwest is generally a polite place and people are friendly but the relations between our offices are not friendly. Mostly the prosecutors do everything they can to win, not to serve justice. They accuse us all of hiding the ball. My job requires me to 'hide the ball' and I do it ethically. I don't lie. I am seeking justice. They just don't understand my role. They are haughty and not trustworthy.... They don't write down when a victim recants. I used to believe them. Maybe I have just been around longer, but if the prosecutor says the victim is cooperative, I don't believe them."

Another long-term highly regarded defender in a large city says, "they have to give me a reason to trust them. I have had too many years of experiences of mistrust" (Interview Notes 2018).

Another recalls a plea-bargaining practice that may be accepted within many offices, but nevertheless causes mistrust:

> There is a plea offer of 20 years on the record. After much hand wringing, the defendant does not take the offer. The next day, the prosecutor dismisses the case because they cannot prove it. This happens too often so that I no longer believe the prosecutor's representations. How can a case be worth 20 years on Monday and dismissed on Tuesday? (Interview Notes 2018)

17.2.3 Defender Social Architecture

Unlike prosecutors who all work in an institutional setting, defense counsel in the United States may be in individual or larger law firm practice, or in an institutional public defender office. Lawyers in private practice may be retained, but many of them represent indigent clients pursuant to local or state programs that pay relatively low hourly fees for their services (Lee 2004). White-collar lawyers retained to represent corporate or other well-heeled clients often work within medium to large-size law firms and have significant resources for effective client representation. These lawyers tend to have the best relationships with prosecutors because many of them are former federal prosecutors and the white-collar cases do not present traditional public safety concerns. There is variation by locale.

Institutional defenders generally aspire to provide quality defense, but they are often hampered by crushing caseloads and disrespect by the courts and prosecutors (ABA Standing Committee on Legal Aid and Indigent Defendants 2004). Many of the institutional defenders across the country provide quality defense and are deserving of the mantle as "liberty's last champion." The good defense lawyers are empathetic, respect their clients, and attempt to maximize their clients' dignity and autonomy. Respect means "taking clients seriously, acknowledging that they have lived a life, recognizing that there is more to them than their current predicament. Every client has a life story and the defender must learn and embrace the whole person" (Smith 2004).

A recent innovation is the holistic defender model pioneered by the Bronx Defenders and adapted by other organizations. That model recognizes that a client charged with a crime may have a myriad of other legal issues in family, civil, immigration, or other courts. The holistic defender works in a team of lawyers, social workers, community outreach workers, and others in a collaborative assistance model. This model is a social justice one that inspires many young defenders but also exacerbates tensions where prosecutors do not recognize the social justice mission and are only "processing cases" (Bronx Defenders n.d.).

Some institutional defender offices with a robust defense ethic are confrontational and accused of incivility, often more frequently than private counsel. Prosecutors and some judges accuse zealous defenders of going "over the line" on behalf of clients by, for example, continuing to assert their client's rights even when the court and the prosecutor starkly reject the defender's position. The defenders, often beleaguered, say that they are doing their job. Zealous defenders may compromise with prosecutors less often than private counsel do and their offices train young lawyers to assume an uncompromising stance in defense of their clients (Bronx Defenders n.d.; Gideon's Promise n.d.). Such intransigence may work, and they often find daily reminders that neither they nor their clients are treated with respect. This hardens their views and increases zealous advocacy as well as adversarialness. A supervisor in a mid-sized urban office says:

> The courthouse culture is disturbing, and they don't even know it. The prosecutors and judges do not respect our role. Many of the judges were formerly in the prosecutor's office and form bonds that affect their role as judge.... Sometimes I get to court and they [prosecutors] are parked in the judge's chambers. Most judges are former prosecutors. I think the judges and prosecutors believe that we represent garbage clients and we are the garbage men. (Interview Notes 2018)

Not all institutional defender offices have such a robust ethic of client representation. They are beset by structural issues including gaps in effective leadership, training, supervision, and a culture that undermines quality representation. These lawyers are often accused of compromising with prosecutors when it does not benefit the client (Nardulli, Eisenstein, and Flemming 1988). They do not remain vigilant and diligent in client representation. Some fail to do good work either because the caseload is simply too overwhelming despite best intentions or because the lawyer becomes cynical, tired, and lazy. That lawyer is responsible for the view of many clients who disparage public defenders saying, "you get what you pay for" (Hartley, Miller, and Spohn 2010).

Some defense lawyers are former prosecutors. Their past experience is a factor in representation, sometimes to the detriment of the client. A prosecutor notes: "Some former prosecutors who have become defense lawyers . . . see their job as being a broker between the government and their client. They act as if their job is to plead people guilty. They are terrible lawyers." He notes:

> Prosecutors usually think in terms of guilty pleas. They think in terms of victims and they are used to working hand in hand with law enforcement. Some look down on criminal defendants with disdain. They have been conditioned to see the defendant as the bad guy, to assume guilt, and in private practice that can translate to seeing the defendant/bad guy as dollar signs without much in the way of compassion. But generalizations are difficult. "Some former District Attorneys are the best lawyers. The best of them are not the best because they used to work for the government. They are the best despite the fact that they used to work for government."
>
> (Bennett and Kennedy 2012)

The organization and structure of the varying defender and prosecutor offices foster levels of competence that affects the interaction between the lawyers. Although not universal, highly competent ethical lawyers on both sides of the aisle tend to work well together with an understanding of the limits of their respective roles. Or at least they understand the role of civility and their advocacy is strategic and tactical. Prosecutors know the competency of defense lawyers more often than defense colleagues do. Good prosecutors want the defendant to be represented by competent counsel. They also want defenders to help move along the case and caseload, and competent counsel is usually a help in doing so. Unfortunately, there are far too many defense lawyers who consistently engage in ineffective assistance of counsel (Bernard 2017). They are lazy, not competent, and do not particularly care about their clients. Prosecutors describe them as the "go along get along" or "cop out artists" (Nardulli, Eisenstein, and Flemming 1988). They do not engender respect and they are often the ill-prepared lawyers who treat prosecutors with some measure of contempt. Sometimes these are the lawyers who get along best with prosecutors at the expense of their clients. A study of prosecutors' offices demonstrated that most of these defenders are the lawyers who are not familiar with the court or criminal practice (Wright and Levine 2014). "These are the defense attorneys that I think are idiots" (Wright and Levine 2014). Prosecutors view part of their role as keeping these defense lawyers within bounds of acceptable conduct in court.

17.2.4 Geographical Factors

In addition to structure and organizational differences, geographical variations play somewhat of a role in the relationship between adversaries. It is reported that prosecutors and defenders in small rural areas get along well because they necessarily interact in a range of non-lawyering settings such as their children's schools, sporting events, religious settings, and in community groups (Weisheit, Falcone, and Wells 2006; Interview Notes 2018). They learn to be cooperative and some lawyers report that there is less discord than in urban areas. Others, however, challenge such a notion unless there is a robust defender attitude in the community. As a lead defender who had been tasked with evaluation of such offices noted in response, "Yes, these prosecutors and defenders may get along better because they erode justice together. They violate people's rights together" (Interview Notes 2018). Once again, the power dynamic and a range of factors that define office culture determine the extent to which such claims have validity in any given locale (Bibas 2009).

17.2.5 Individual Factors

Numerous personal factors also affect the relationship between counsel. This includes age, experience, race, ethnicity, and gender. "I think a lot of people, particularly younger people when they start [practicing], they want to, they're all fired up and they just think that, go to the wall with these people and you're going to fight with them and hate each other. That's not the way it is. A lot of young prosecutors, and a lot of young defense lawyers, they really get 'it's us against them' mentality, and I don't think that's healthy for our profession. I think we need to be able to respect each other" (Wright and Levine 2014). That is difficult because the adversarial incentives have a strong effect on young and risk-averse prosecutors and are reinforced by the day-to-day operation:

> Most cases first appear as a file that the police hand off detailing what the police claim the defendant has done. The prosecutor conducts little independent investigation in most cases and is conditioned to be skeptical of new information that the defense attorney provides. They are thus often in a position of uncertainty regarding key facts in the case and considering this uncertainty they default to a presumption that the defendant is culpable. This default is reinforced by the conveyor-belt nature of prosecutors' job. They have many cases at once, they see the same charges over and over, many of the fact patterns are similar, and the local criminal justice system usually sets a market rate for guilty pleas to common offenses.... Prosecutors also must often get approval from their bosses for more lenient dispositions, which they may consequently be reluctant to seek. This daily reality creates an adversary case-processing system where prosecutors receive a file, assume it is correct, resolve uncertainties in favor of guilt, and treat discussions with the defense lawyer as a strategic game to secure a guilty plea at market rates. In other words, the defense lawyer's word and information is not worth a great deal.
>
> (Fish 2018)

17.2.6 Necessarily, This Creates Tensions and Distrust

The relationship among counsel is not only dependent upon age and experience, but upon personality, politics, individual characteristics, and the moral compass of the individual. Studies show that a lawyer's original ethnic, religious, and socioeconomic community are relevant to the lawyer's place in the profession (Heinz and Laumann 1982) and are also likely to have had an impact upon the relationship between counsel (Smith 2012).

More prosecutors tend to be conservative, vote Republican, and be religious as compared with defenders. They are more likely to be on the punitive end of the scale for conduct rather than rehabilitative. Defenders on the other hand, tend to be more liberal politically and have rehabilitative attitudes towards those who engage in criminal conduct. Political party preference, and job experience, have been found to be significantly related to attitudes about punishment and courthouse reputation (Heinz and Laumann 1982).

Students who choose prosecution are "more conventional, judgmental, and professionally ambitious" than those who choose defense (Smith 2012). In a study of fifty defenders across the country, a common—although not universal—conclusion was that the prosecutors were self-important, lacking in imagination, and moral absolutists. A smaller number of prosecutors were "humble, modest, fair, open-minded, and compassionate, as well as excellent trial lawyers. The best of them understand that they are operating in an imperfect system. Even better are those who understand the context in which crime occurs and the gravity of criminal punishment" (Smith 2012).

The anticipated rewards of their respective positions also affect the relationship among lawyers. First, the prosecutor receives greater respect than defenders from the other players in the system, as well as from the public. Even if the individual prosecutor does not feel particularly powerful, that lawyer is often treated with respect by the court and others while the defender has to earn that respect. Many judges are former prosecutors and can readily identify with those who occupy their former role.

Defenders, on the other hand, generally represent the underdogs and may have limited individual and community support for their role. Their difficult job has few societal rewards except when a defender may have participated in an exoneration or an occasional publicly supported "not guilty" verdict in a highly publicized or political case (NACDL n.d.; Sarat and Sheingold 2006). Often there is an inverse correlation between the defender's success on behalf of her clients and respect by the court and adversaries. For defenders, this disparate reward structure of respect is yet another source of tension. Additionally, the prosecutor is rewarded with greater opportunities for advancement in the profession. That reward structure is not dependent primarily upon differing degrees of skill and competence but by role. Prosecutors are more likely to be selected for judgeships and they have a more direct path to become politicians or join prestigious law firms (Lee 2004). The long-term career paths and opportunities have an impact as to how the adversaries interact.

There are also numerous reports and articles about the role that race and gender play for prosecutors and defense lawyers (Pratt 2012; Scheindlin et al. 2017; Williams

Pinder 1993). However, there is insufficient data about the numbers of lawyers of color and women advocates in the criminal justice system, no less studies of the role that race and gender assume in the relationships between adversaries. Nevertheless, it is apparent that race and gender affect those relationships. A prominent example is that African American attorneys experience overt discrimination and more subtle forms of bias in many interactions both inside and outside the courtroom (Rachlinski et al. 2009; Pratt 2012). When both the prosecutor and the defender are African American and mutually recognize racial bias by others in court, there is an implicit, if not explicit, understanding and perhaps a bond formed between these adversaries even though they each continue to advocate within the boundaries of their roles. Similar dynamics exist for Latinx, Asian, and other lawyers of color. It is not obvious how these dynamics interact with the other factors that cause tension in the relationship between prosecutors and defenders. The power dynamic differential remains the critical factor.

Gender differences may have a similar effect when both the prosecutor and defender are women and treated dismissively or with other forms of disrespect. Lesbian, queer, or transgender lawyers may experience unique forms of discrimination and can bond despite differences in role.

Because of their fundamentally different roles, perspectives, and individual characteristics, prosecutors and defenders do not often engage outside the court or office arena. Indeed, many on both sides of the aisle say "I would not be caught dead socializing" with the other. There is a perspective in some defender offices that getting along with prosecutors shows disloyalty to one's clients. An experienced leader of a large defender office said "My heart and soul are in this work, so I will not and cannot engage with prosecutors. It would make work too difficult." Others say, "I can go drinking with adversaries, but my loyalty has to be to client" (Bennett and Kennedy 2012). Older lawyers indicate that things have changed significantly. A former state prosecutor in a large urban office said "Years ago we used to socialize outside the office and still do battle in the courtroom. Now the environment seems toxic" (Interview Notes 2018).

All told, the environment in state and federal courts in the United States produces widely different views by prosecutors and defenders as to their relationships. Prosecutors have a more positive view of their relationship with defense lawyers than vice versa. A widely respected national leader and office director in the federal defender system makes the observation:

> By and large, the relationships between federal prosecutors and the lawyers in my office, myself included, are polite and professional. But that doesn't mean we don't often think poorly of our adversaries. I imagine they feel the same about us. But even when we think a prosecutor is acting inappropriately, we often have to bite our tongues and play nice because we have no other option. I think prosecutors probably have a rosier view of our relationships than we do. If we've been perfectly nice to them to try to get what we need for our client, they often think we're genuinely fond of them. (Interview Notes 2018)

This stark view of the interaction echoes across state and federal defenders.

Prosecutors find these attitudes discouraging. "Defense lawyers in this era of mass incarceration have a negative view of the system and put prosecutors in the center of it. We take an extreme hit for what the legislature did. It is depressing because we encourage our young assistants to be collaborative and to weed out innocent people as well as to find the right disposition for the guilty" (Interview Notes 2018).

17.3 Structural Changes

17.3.1 Collaborative Models

A structural change in criminal justice systems that has fostered differing relationships between prosecutor and defenders is the innovation of problem-solving courts. Beginning in 1989, jurisdictions established drug courts that promised treatment for the underlying conditions that caused drug addictions in lieu of a traditional criminal court process. These courts "fundamentally altered the traditional adjudication process" (Nolan 2001).

Over the decades, this model spread to other types of "problem-solving courts" including domestic violence courts, integrated family courts, and veterans' courts. The model has been exported internationally (Nolan 2001). Although there are many variations in the structure and culture of these courts, they alter the relationship between counsel. The process is no longer adversarial and the defense lawyers "must get rid of the adversarial attitude." The traditional defense lawyer's role to protect constitutional rights and liberties and serve as a "protective counterforce against the formidable law enforcement and prosecutorial resources of the State" does not operate in these courts" (Nolan 2001). Lawyers also play a less prominent role. Therapeutic concerns dominate. The judge has a more prominent role and the demands on the client are more onerous than in a traditional court. This model is critiqued by many defenders as insufficiently protective of the client's rights (Zeidman 2002).

The military justice system is another less-contentious model of criminal justice in United States. Although the military process is adversarial, and the roles of prosecutor and defender are comparable to civilian ones, lawyers are required to rotate between roles as prosecutors and defenders (Luban 2008). They thus develop a nuanced appreciation for the adversary's role and its challenges, and less distrust (Luban 2018). Trust is also enhanced by the robust disclosure of information by the prosecution. "[I]n all cases, the military prosecutor's bargaining position is weaker than that of his civilian counterpart because of the more thorough investigation performed before the guilty plea and the reduced information asymmetry in the military system" (Note 2010). The military lawyers operate with civility and respect for the adversary's role. This is greatly influenced, of course, by the fact that the military is a closed system.

17.3.2 New Reform Prosecutors

Recent elections of reform prosecutors may shift the tension-filled dynamic between prosecutions and defenders. It is conventional wisdom that, because they are elected, most state chief prosecutors are punitive and focused on conviction statistics (Wright and Levine 2014). More than twenty-five reform prosecutors have been elected around the country each with a mission to change that perspective and to adopt new roles and policies for their offices. The traditional adversarial relationship with defenders will change, to some extent, where such prosecutors can implement new policies and practices. The expectation is that although the reform prosecutor and the defender have different missions, they will work collaboratively to help defendants, victims, and their communities and to minimize the severity of the criminal justice system. But prosecutors who desire to develop a true minister of justice model to get beyond conviction rates and "law and order" models of prosecution have a difficult path.

Their ability to carry out such a different mission will depend to a great extent on the ability to change office culture. It will also depend on the competence of the defense bar. Reform prosecutors understand the necessity to promote funding for effective defense (Bogira 2018; Gonnerman 2018). Calling for such assistance for the defense community is a relatively new phenomenon for prosecutors in the United States although many recognize that a healthy system requires competent, ethical defense counsel.

17.4 International

Lawyers in countries outside the United States operate in criminal justice systems that vary by structure, laws, the country's history, geography, demographics, and socio-political evolution. There are significant differences among common law and civil law countries, but in general, the relationship among lawyers outside the United States is less adversarial and partisan. To some degree, this may be attributed to cultural and social norms in countries where courteous conduct is a paramount societal value and people are more reserved. It is also attributable to structural differences in the criminal processes themselves, in role definition and in power dynamics. Significantly, in every country, there is comparatively less plea bargaining and there is no starkly punitive trial penalty such as the one that exists in the United States. However, the power dynamics of a structurally tilted playing field exists internationally and produce a defense bar with comparable complaints about prosecutors. There is a nearly universal perspective among defense lawyers in all countries that the system often produces unfair results for their clients and that defenders and their clients deserve better treatment from the courts and prosecutors.

In other common law countries including England and Canada, the professional community is different than that in the United States (Soubise and Woolley 2018). There are longstanding formal traditions as to how lawyers express themselves in court. The community is smaller, and the significance of reputation is paramount. Structural differences in the prosecution role also reduce partisanship. For example, in Canada, prosecutors have a significant degree of political independence. They are not elected but are civil servants, the vast majority of whom work for the Attorney General of the province or for the federal Public Prosecution Service. Moreover, while Canadian prosecutors exercise discretion akin to those in the United States about the nature and extent of prosecution, their exercise of discretion is aided by published guidelines that affirm the overarching duty of Canadian prosecutors to be ministers of justice. Plea bargaining is an authorized part of the process, although there is no significant trial penalty as in the United States (Soubise and Woolley 2018). Canada does not have a right to counsel akin to the United States, and only provides legal aid monies to provinces for counsel in serious cases and other select matters. Consequently, funds for defense counsel are limited and complaints abound. As one Canadian commentator noted, "criminal defense lawyers have always been second class citizens" (Spratt 2016).

Although there are instances of alleged prosecutorial misconduct in Canada, notably for failure to disclose evidence, the prevalence of such claims pale by comparison to the United States (Soubise and Woolley 2018). In general, the relationships between adversaries is less partisan and accusatory although the underlying power dynamics are akin to that in the United States.

England has a similar, less partisan dynamic between prosecutors and defenders. Institutional prosecution in England did not begin until the 1990s when the Crown Prosecutor Service was established. Prior to that time, the police prosecuted lesser crimes in the pre-trial phase and would hire barristers to prosecute cases in court (Hughes 1984). Now these cases are all handled by the Crown Prosecutor and, as in Canada, there are publicly available written standards for prosecutorial conduct. Significantly, the profession is divided between solicitors and barristers and barristers represent both the prosecution and the defense in different cases. Barristers are not as closely identified with their clients as are defense lawyers in the United States. Courtroom architecture makes this evident: the defendant's barrister sits at counsel's table with the solicitor behind him. The defendant is in the "well." Also, there are statutory limits on plea bargains so that prosecutors have less discretion in the plea process. This has changed to some degree since the advent of the Crown Prosecutor with the increasingly common practice of charge bargaining, but there is still no sentencing bargaining (Griffin 2001). Reportedly, partisanship is on the rise because of the institutional prosecution service, but the level of it does not compare to the United States (Interview Notes 2018).

South Africa, on the other hand, is a notable exception to the prosecutorial power dynamics in other common law countries. Although it has a national system of well-trained prosecutors, they are burdened with a highly politicized office where the head prosecutor is appointed by the President and the police and clerks make prosecution difficult (Cartwright and Shearling 2009). The police are extremely under resourced, often incompetent or corrupt, and cannot produce evidence in competent fashion.

The police or the clerks lose files. It is difficult to ensure that witnesses will come to court and even if they do, there are constant continuances that make prosecution difficult (Interview Notes 2018). The conviction rate is extremely low by comparison to any other country (Cartwright and Shearling 2009). Although plea bargaining is permitted, it is rare because the defendant has few incentives to plead guilty when there is a significant likelihood that the case will be dismissed. South Africa public defenders in the past decade have developed a robust system where the lawyers are relatively well paid and engender respect. These dynamics produce a less contentious relationship between public defenders and prosecutors in most cases although it can vary markedly, depending on whether or not the individuals have a reputation as ethical advocates. "In many cases there is a healthy relationship, but in others there can also be a hateful one" (Interview Notes 2018). Both sides are aware of their respective high caseloads and the need to resolve matters relatively amicably.

Private lawyers, who are not repeat players in the system nor burdened by caseload pressures, have a more adversarial relationship with prosecutors (Phipps 2014).

By contrast to common law adversarial systems, inquisitorial systems such as France, Germany, Italy, and the Netherlands are premised upon a lengthy and objective investigative phase as the truth-seeking process. These civil law systems have educational and structural aspects in common that afford more power to judges and magistrates. Prosecutors are generally considered civil servants and typically viewed as quasi-administrators. The prosecutor's power derives from their control over the pre-trial investigation, during which they are charged to be neutral truth-seekers (Fish 2018). "[T]he state directs career bureaucrats, not to function as parties, but rather to serve in a quasi-judicial role investigating the facts for and against the defendant. Indeed, this vision of the law is introduced and reinforced in law school where law faculties instruct students that an objective truth exists, and most legal problems have only one 'solution'" (Boyne 2015). Concepts of cognitive bias, which inevitably affect the police and prosecution's view of a case, are more prominent concerns primarily of defense lawyers who frequently complain that prosecutors have a limited view of the evidence and do not readily pursue alternative facts and theories (Kantorowicz-Reznichenko 2015).

During the investigative phase, the defense's role is limited to asking the prosecutor to investigate information favorable to the defendant; the prosecutor has a duty to investigate. After the investigative phase, the prosecution produces a dossier with all relevant charges, transcripts of witness statements, and facts and has little discretion in charging the crimes in the dossier (Brants 2012; Fish 2018).

At trial, inquisitorial judges play a prominent role not only in orders to produce evidence, but in questioning defendants and witnesses, the defense is not permitted to ask questions outside the dossier presented to the court. The defense lawyer has a limited role and is often viewed unfavorably: "The legal tradition in most civil law countries does not recognize a role for strong, pro-active defence lawyers. Instead, the defence lawyer's role is premised on dialogue and compromise, which discourages lawyers from engaging in active and zealous defence" (Cape et al. 2010).

Sweden, unlike other civil law systems, is more akin to the American and English criminal justice systems. It treats the investigatory state of criminal proceedings as inquisitorial but the trial as more adversarial. In Sweden, plea bargains are not permitted, and all cases go to trial. However, the Swedish criminal trial process is not completely analogous to an adversarial model as the judge plays a much more active and direct role in the case in Swedish criminal proceedings (Ortwein 2002). Judges and a professional lay panel of three people, not juries, hear the cases. The defendant is a source of information and there is no right not to testify.

The defense lawyers handle large caseloads and many clients are held on bail pending trial. Thus, the pressures to try cases without adequate preparation often results in tension, especially when prosecutors fail to produce information until shortly before trial.

Both prosecutors and defenders in some inquisitorial systems express frustration because judges, and not the lawyers, play a significant role at trial in asking questions. This occurs less in France. Despite these and other differences in France, Germany, Italy, and Sweden, their systems result in similar lessened levels of partisanship and tensions between prosecutors and defenders than in the United States.

Beyond discussion of degrees of partisanship, it is difficult to generalize about criminal justice systems in various countries and the relationships between prosecutors and defenders because there are often significant structural differences throughout the criminal process (Frase 1990). There are also significant differences in the training and supervision of police, prosecutors, and judges, the relationship between the police and the prosecutor, the structure of prosecutors' offices, and the stated and actual role of the defense lawyer. European systems are described as hierarchical with police, prosecutors, and judges required to undergo nationwide bureaucratic selection, training, promotion, and supervision (Frase 1990). There is a national hierarchy and those who become prosecutors do so as a career choice rather than as a stepping-stone to other office. It is unlikely that a prosecutor will choose to be a defense lawyer later in his or her career. But all inquisitorial systems have similar power dynamics with the defense lawyer having a limited role and not being a major factor in the way in which the systems view case resolution. Primarily, the cases are resolved by judges and prosecutors. "In many cities, there is a strong norm of cooperation between the prosecution office and the judiciary.... In cities where close, tight-knit relationships exist, there is a potential to resolve cases more quickly because the prosecutor and judge have had the time to trust each other's judgment" (Boyne 2015).

The most significant difference in the power dynamics between the United States and all other countries is with respect to plea bargaining. By law, in countries such as Germany, France, and Italy, there are sharp restrictions on that practice. But over the last decades, informal versions of plea-bargaining practices have grown throughout criminal justice systems in the world, even where not legislatively authorized (Turner 2009). Even though charge or sentencing bargaining have become relatively more common in these countries, they do not approximate that of the United States (Langbein 1979). These are not plea-bargaining systems. The process is not "a glorious Turkish rug market," as in the United States (Luna and Wade 2010).

Nevertheless, these plea bargaining practices often suffer from the same problems as in the United States. Prosecutors in German, Italy, and France engage in "tacit bargains" in which defendants expect and receive leniency in return for waiving full "due process" procedures. Prosecutors and police have significant discretion in the filing of charges, and judicial supervision of the investigatory and adjudicatory stages is largely absent (Goldstein and Marcus 1977).

Despite differences between adversarial and inquisitorial systems, defense lawyers in inquisitorial ones report the same dynamics and tensions between prosecutors and defenders for the same reasons: notably failure to obtain necessary information from the police and prosecutor to defend a case, pressures to try cases on a punishing schedule, and the judges' failure to consider evidence and charges other than that presented by the prosecution. Prosecutors dispute these claims of failure to disclose information and, overall, share the belief that their criminal justice systems function relatively well.

A highly regarded defense lawyer who has represented clients not only throughout Sweden, but in France, Germany, and the United States, reports that "it is the same in all of these countries" (Interview Notes 2018). Defense lawyers have similar mindsets and face the same problems of not receiving the necessary information to adequately investigate a case. "It is interesting to go around the world. When I talk with criminal defense lawyers, we think the same way. We understand one another. We talk about difficulties in getting information, the fact that prosecutors assume our clients are guilty and that they have significant cognitive biases. The relationship with prosecutors may not be as contentious as in the United States but the underlying dynamics are similar. All cases are about politics. Prosecutors want to win. Politicians are tired of crime and want to see people get convicted and go to jail so the pressure is on prosecutors and the police to convict. People think it is a solution to problems."

17.5 Conclusion

Prosecutors throughout the world operate in systems with significant structural differences between their roles and powers and that of defense lawyers. It is this differential power dynamic that is the fundamental factor in the relationship between prosecutors and defenders. Prosecutors around the world have common approaches and mindsets. Defenders do as well. The tensions are universal no matter whether in common law or inquisitorial systems and their manifestation differs by degree only. Thus, although there is less partisanship in inquisitorial systems than in the United States, the tensions that exist are often dependent upon many of the same factors as evidenced in the United States including power dynamics, exercise of discretion, politics, structure, locale, personality, and other individual characteristics of the individual lawyers.

Note

1. In the federal system, ninety-seven percent of convicted defendants plead guilty. The author calculated this number using the data obtained from Bureau of Justice Statistics (2011, tbl.5.22.2010).

References

Alexander, Michelle. 2010. *The New Jim Crow*. New York: The New Press.

American Bar Association (ABA). 2018. *Model Rules of Professional Conduct*.

American Bar Association, ABA Standing Committee on Legal and Indigent Defendants. 2004. *Gideon's Broken Promise: America's Quest for Equal Justice*.

Barkow, Rachel E. 2014. "Criminal Law as Regulation." *N.Y.U. Journal of Law & Liberty* 8(2): 316–342.

Bennett, Mark, and Paul Kennedy. 2012. "Why It Matters if Your Defense Lawyer Used to Be a Prosecutor." *Trial Theory Blog*.

Bernard, Adele. 2017. "Ineffective Assistance of Counsel and the Innocence Revolution." In *Wrongful Convictions and the DNA Revolution*. Edited by Daniel S. Medwed. Cambridge: Cambridge University Press.

Bibas, Stephanos. 2004. "Plea Bargaining Outside the Shadow of Trial." *Harvard Law Review* 117(8): 2463–2547.

Bibas, Stephanos. 2009. "Prosecutorial Regulation Versus Prosecutorial Accountability." *University of Pennsylvania Law Review* 157(4): 959–1016.

Bogira, Steve. 2018. "The Hustle of Kim Foxx." *The Marshall Project*, October 29, 2018.

Boruchowitz, Robert, Malia Brink, and Maureen Domino. 2009. "Minor Crimes: Massive Waste." *National Association of Criminal Defense Lawyers*.

Boyne, Shawn Marie. 2015. "Procedural Economy in Pre-Trial Procedure: Developments in Germany and the United States." *Southern California Interdisciplinary Law Journal* 24(2): 329–368.

Brants, Chrisje. 2012. "Wrongful Convictions and the Inquisitorial Process: The Case of the Netherlands." *University of Cincinnati Law Review* 80(4): 1069–1114.

Bronx Defenders. n.d. Accessed December 21, 2020. https://www.bronxdefenders.org/.

Bureau of Justice Statistics, U.S. Department of Justice. 2011. *Sourcebook of Criminal Justice Statistics Online*.

Cape, Ed, Zaza Namoradze, Roger Smith, and Taru Spronken. 2010. *Effective Criminal Defence in Europe: Executive Summary and Recommendations*.

Cartwright, John, and Clifford Shearling. 2009. "Introduction." In *Criminal (In)justice in South Africa: A Civil Society Perspective*. Edited by Chandré Gould. Pretoria, South Africa: Institute for Security Studies.

Chambliss, Elizabeth, and Bruce A. Green. 2008. "Some Realism About Bar Associations." *DePaul Law Review* 57(2): 425–446.

Davis, Angela. 2018. "The Progressive Prosecutor: An Imperative for Criminal Justice Reform." *Fordham Law Review Online* 87: 8–12.

Eisenstein, James, and Herbert Jacob. 1977. *Felony Justice*. Maryland: University Press of America.

Fish, Eric. 2018. "Against Adversary Prosecution." *Iowa Law Review* 103(4): 1419–1482.

Fisher, Stanley Z. 1988. "In Search of the Virtuous Prosecutor: A Conceptual Framework." *American Journal of Criminal Law* 15(3): 197–262.

Frase, Richard. 1990. "Comparative Criminal Justice as Guide to American Law Reform: How The French Do It, How We Can Find Out and Why Should We Care." *California Law Review* 78(3): 539–683.

Gideon's Promise. n.d. Accessed Nov. 18, 2018. https://www.gideonspromise.org/about.

Goldstein, Abraham, and Martin Marcus 1977. "The Myth of Judicial Supervision in Three Inquisitorial Systems, France, Italy and Germany." *Yale Law Journal* 87(2): 240–283.

Gonnerman, Jennifer. 2018. "Acts of Conviction." *New Yorker*, October 23, 2018.

Griffin, Lissa. 2001. "The Correction of Wrongful Convictions: A Comparative Perspective." *American University International Law Review* 16(5): 1241–1308.

Green, Bruce A., and Ellen Yaroshefsky. 2016. "Prosecutorial Accountability 2.0." *Notre Dame Law Review* 92(1): 51–116.

Grunwald, Ben. 2017. "The Fragile Promise of Open-File Discovery." *Connecticut Law Review* 49(3): 771–836.

Hartley, Richard, Hilly Miller, and Cassia Spohn. 2010. "Do You Get What You Pay For: Type of Counsel and Its Effect on Criminal Court Outcomes." *Journal of Criminal Justice* 38(5): 1063–1070.

Heinz, John P., and Edward Laumann. 1982. *Chicago Lawyers: The Social Structure of the Bar*. Russell Sage Foundation.

Hopwood, Shon. 2014. "The Not So Speedy Trial Act." *Washington Law Review* 89(3): 709–746.

Hughes, Graham. 1984. "English Criminal Justice: Is It Better than Ours?" *Arizona Law Review* 26(3): 507–614.

Jackson, Robert H. 1940. "The Federal Prosecutor." *Journal of the American Institute of Criminal Law and Criminology* 31: 3–6.

Kantorowicz-Reznichenko, Elena. 2015. "Cognitive Biases and Procedural Rules: Enhancing the Use of Alternative Sanctions." *European Journal of Crime, Criminal Law and Criminal Justice* 23(3): 191–213.

Kim, Andrew Chongseh. 2015. "Underestimating the Trial Penalty: An Empirical Analysis of the Federal Trial Penalty and Critique of the Abrams Study." *Mississippi Law Journal* 84(5): 1195–1256.

Langbein, John H. 1979. "Land Without Plea Bargaining: How the Germans Do It." *Michigan Law Review* 78(2): 204–225.

Lantigua Williams, Juleyka. 2016. "Are Prosecutors The Key To Justice Reform?" *The Atlantic*, May 18, 2016.

Lee, Kyung M. 2004. "Reinventing *Gideon v. Wainwright*: Holistic Defenders, Indigent Defendants, and the Right to Counsel." *American Journal of Criminal Law* 31(3): 367–432.

Levine, Kay L., and Ronald F. Wright. 2012. "Prosecution in 3-D." *Journal of Criminal Law and Criminology* 102(4): 1119–1180.

Luban, David. 2018. *Lawyers and Justice: An Ethical Study*. Princeton, New Jersey: Princeton University Press.

Luban, David. 2008. "Lawfare and Legal Ethics in Guantanamo." *Stanford Law Review* 60(6): 1981–2026.

Luna, Erik, and Marianne Wade. 2010. "Prosecutors as Judges." *Washington and Lee Law Review* 67(4): 1413–1532.

Maine, Jeffrey A. 2000. "The Importance of Ethics and Morality in Today's Legal World." *Stetson Law Review* 29(4): 1075–1090.

Meares, Tracey L. 1995. "Rewards for Good Behavior: Influencing Prosecutorial Discretion and Conduct with Financial Incentives." *Fordham Law Review* 64(3): 851–920.

Miller, Marc, and Ronald F. Wright. 2008. "The Black Box." *Iowa Law Review* 94(1): 125–196.

Nardulli, Peter, James Eisenstein, and Roy B. Flemming. 1988. *The Tenor of Justice: Criminal Courts and the Guilty Plea Process*. Chicago: University of Illinois Press.

Natapoff, Alexandra. 2018. *Punishment Without Crime*. New York: Basic Books.

National Association of Criminal Defense Lawyers (NACDL). n.d. https://www.nacdl.org/Default.aspx.

National Association of Criminal Defense Lawyers (NACDL). 2018. "The Trial Penalty: The Sixth Amendment Right to Trial on the Verge of Extinction and How to Save It."

Note, "Prosecutorial Power and the Legitimacy of the Military Justice System." 2010. *Harvard Law Review* 123(4): 937–958.

Nolan, James L., Jr. 2001. *Reinventing Justice*. Princeton: Princeton University Press.

Ortwein II, Bernard Michael. 2002. "The Swedish Legal System: An Introduction." *Indiana International & Comparative Law Review* 13(2): 405–446.

Pfaff, John. 2017. *Locked In*. Philadelphia: Basic Books.

Pratt, Carla D. 2012. "Sisters in Law: Black Women Lawyers' Struggle for Advancement." *Michigan State Law Review* 2012(5): 1777–1796.

Rakoff, Jed R. 2014. "Why Innocent People Plead Guilty." *New York Review of Books*, November 20, 2014.

Rachlinski, Jeffrey J., Sheri Lynn Johnson, Andrew J. Wistrich, and Chris Guthrie. 2009. "Does Unconscious Racial Bias Affect Trial Judges?" *Notre Dame Law Review* 84(3): 1195–1246.

Richman, Daniel. 2003. "Prosecutors and Their Agents, Agents and Their Prosecutors." *Columbia Law Review* 103(4): 749–832.

Sarat, Austin, and Stanley Sheingold. 2006. *Cause Lawyering and Social Movements*. Palo Alto: Stanford University Press.

Scheindlin et al., Hon. Shira A. 2017. "If Not Now When? Achieving Equality for Women Attorneys in the Courtroom and in ADR." *New York State Bar Association*, November 2017.

Smith, Abbe. 1995. "Carrying On in Criminal Court: When Criminal Defense is Not So Sexy and Other Grievances." *Clinical Law Review* 1(3): 723–748.

Smith, Abbe. 2001. "Can You Be a Good Person and a Good Prosecutor?" *Georgetown Journal of Legal Ethics* 14(2): 355–400.

Smith, Abbe. 2004. "Too Much Heart and Not Enough Heat: The Short Life and Fractured Ego of the Empathetic, Heroic Public Defender." *U.C. Davis Law Review* 37(5): 1203–1266.

Smith, Abbe. 2012. "Are Prosecutors Born or Made?" *Georgetown Journal of Legal Ethics* 25(4): 943–960.

Smith, Abbe, and Monroe Freedman, eds. 2013. *How Can You Represent These People?* New York: Palgrave Macmillan Press.

Soubise, Laurène, and Alice Woolley. 2018. "Prosecutors and Justice: Insights from Comparative Analysis." *Fordham International Law Journal* 42(2): 587–626.

Spratt, Michael. 2016. "Canadian Defense Counsel Hit Hardest by Antiquated Defence System." *Canadian Lawyer*, October 17, 2016.

Sullivan, Thomas, and Maurice Possley. 2016. "The Chronic Failure to Discipline Prosecutors for Misconduct: Proposals for Reform." *Journal of Criminal Law and Criminology* 105(4): 881–946.

Taylor, Kate. 2011. “System Overload: The Cost of Under-Resourcing Public Defense.” *Justice Policy Institute.*

Turner, Jenia I. 2009. *Plea Bargaining Across Borders.* New York: Aspen Publishers.

wiesheit, Ralph A., David N. Falcone, and L. Edward Wells. 2006. *Crime and Policing in Rural and Small-Town America.* Waveland Press.

White, Ken. 2016. “Confessions of an Ex-Prosecutor.” *Reason,* June 23, 2016.

Williams Pinder, Wilma. 1993. “When Will Black Women Lawyers Slay the Two-Headed Dragon: Racism and Gender Bias.” *Pepperdine Law Review* 20(3): 1053–1070.

Wright, Ronald F. 2005. “Trial Distortion and the End of Innocence in Federal Criminal Justice.” *University of Pennsylvania Law Review* 154(1): 79–156.

Wright, Ronald F., and Kay L. Levine. 2014. “The Cure for Young Prosecutors’ Syndrome.” *Arizona Law Review* 56(4): 1065–1128.

Wright, Ronald, and Marc Miller. 2002. “The Screening/Bargaining Tradeoff.” *Stanford Law Review* 55(1): 29–118.

Yaroshefsky, Ellen. 2011. “Prosecutorial Disclosure Obligations.” *Hastings Law Journal* 62(5): 1321–1348.

Yaroshefsky, Ellen, and Bruce A. Green. 2012. “Prosecutor’s Ethics in Context: Influences on Prosecutorial Disclosure.” In *Lawyers Ethical Decision Making in Practice.* Edited by Leslie C. Levin and Lynn M. Mather. University of Chicago Press.

Zeidman, Steven. 2002. “The Impact of Problem Solving on the Lawyer’s Role and Ethics.” *Fordham Urban Law Journal* 29(5): 1892–1924.

CHAPTER 18

VICTIMS AND PROSECUTORS

AMANDA KONRADI AND
TIRZA JO OCHRACH-KONRADI

18.1 Introduction

Social science research on victims and prosecutors is varied. Some investigations explore whether statutes and procedural developments related to victims are implemented and significantly alter justice outcomes, such as the number of cases charged, the number of convictions obtained, or sentence lengths. Following Tom Tyler (Tyler 1990; Tyler and Huo 2002), other research seeks to determine if participation in the system produces procedural as well as substantive justice for crime victims, leaving them satisfied with its fairness and outcomes (Fisher 2015; Kunst, Popelier, and Varekamp 2015). These investigators believe that victims' individual experiences transfer outward to the community, reinforcing or undermining the legitimacy of the system. Studies also are concerned with understanding how victimized individuals make meaning of their experience and engage the criminal justice process, drawing on their varied social resources to maneuver through an alien institution (Konradi 2007). Research focuses on understanding the impact that participation has on the emotions and well-being of crime victims so as to produce a sense of therapeutic jurisprudence (Freckelton 2008; Winick 2009). These studies explore whether and how prosecutors' and defense attorneys' interactions with victims can help them overcome the trauma of crime and reduce secondary victimization by the criminal justice process (Cattaneo and Goodman 2010; Erez, Ibarra, and Downs 2011; Finn 2013; Pemberton and Reynaers 2011; Walther 2011). Investigators may engage more than one of these concerns in individual projects.

This chapter draws on literature from a variety of areas, as well as on legal analysis, to explore the development and current status of victims' rights legislation, prosecutorial responses to it, and how both legislation and response can impact victims. While the United States is at the center of the discussion, we introduce research from other countries with adversarial and inquisitorial justice systems to illustrate the operation of practices that have therapeutic or procedural justice potential.[1]

18.2 Victims' Rights Legislation (VRL)

VRL developed over the last four decades and has become a key element of the environment in which prosecutors carry out their work. Broad rights encompass "the victims' rights to fairness, respect, dignity, privacy, freedom from abuse, due process, and reasonable protection" (Beloof 2007, 1148). Specific rights include the right "to be notified, present and heard' at critical stages of the criminal process; to speak at pretrial release, plea, sentencing and parole hearings; to confer with the public prosecutor; to a prompt disposition (also known as a victims' speedy trial); and to attend the trial" (Beloof 2007, 1149). The provision of these rights is intended to avoid causing secondary harm to victims (Beloof 2007) and to achieve a level of procedural justice and victim satisfaction that can reinforce the legitimacy of the criminal justice process. Prosecutors' discretionary decisions determine whether victims' rights are actualized.

Since 1980, all U.S. states have passed legislation to protect crime victims' rights. Between 2008 and 2016, thirty-five states established constitutional guarantees for victims' rights for greater permanence, visibility, and enforceability (Erez and Roberts 2013; Howley and Dorris 2013). In the 2018 mid-term elections, voters passed victims' rights amendments in five more states: Georgia, Kentucky,[2] Nevada, North Carolina, and Oklahoma.

Victims' capacity to enforce their rights is limited. Multiple states grant victims a right to fair treatment and respect that extends to the protection of their privacy and dignity, which might serve as a basis for standing (Schlam 2015).[3] However, the majority of states do not provide victims with adequate tools to hold prosecutors accountable for enforcing their participatory rights. In fact, most explicitly specify that victims have no cause for damages or that there is no cause of action at all (Howley and Dorris 2013). For example, the 2018 North Carolina amendment prohibits victims from challenging court decisions made without their input (Ballotpedia 2018). Some states—Arizona, Texas, Florida, and Indiana—only provide places for victims to lodge complaints (Howley and Dorris 2013). In Maryland, victims can petition the Court of Special Appeals; in Louisiana, North Carolina, and Utah, they can file for a writ of mandamus (Howley and Dorris 2013). Yet, appellate courts have not shown a willingness to extend mandamus and overturn decisions made when victims' rights were abrogated. The 2015 Illinois Constitutional Amendment progressively granted victims standing and allowed them to seek injunctive relief; however, it precluded victims from securing damages from prosecutors for failing to enforce their rights (Schlam 2015).

The U.S. Congress first introduced an explicit victims' right to be present and be heard in federal court proceedings in the Victim and Witness Protection Act of 1982. This was followed by the Victims of Crime Act (1984) and the Victim's Rights and Restitution Act of 1990, which provided victims with rights to be compensated for their crime-related losses, to confer with U.S. attorneys, and to be informed about the offender's changes in status (Erez and Roberts 2013; Levine 2010). The Violent Crime Control and Law Enforcement Act of 1994 and the Crime Victims' Rights Act (CVRA) of 2004 (Erez and Roberts 2013) followed. Under the 2004 CVRA, victims may file motions with the district court to ensure provisions of the CVRA are followed (Kirchengast 2013). Victims unhappy with district court rulings may appeal for a writ of mandamus to reopen plea bargains and sentences. The text of the CVRA specifies that the law should not be "construed to impair prosecutorial discretion" and that the assertion of a right must pass a "test of reasonableness" (Levine 2010, 345). Debate currently pertains to the level of review that appellate courts should apply; the Second and Ninth Circuit Courts of Appeal review victim petitions for "legal error or abuse of discretion," but the Fifth and Tenth Circuits hold victim petitions to a higher mandamus standard (Levine 2010).

Several years ago, a Victims Rights Amendment to the U.S. Constitution was introduced that encompasses much of what is currently in federal statutes, but also requires courts to consider "victims' interests" when receiving requests for delays and to consider victim safety when imprisoned convicts seek parole (Erez and Roberts 2013). It would also "give crime victims standing to assert and enforce their rights" (The National Center for Victims of Crime 2018). To date, the amendment has not received substantial support.[4]

18.3 Who Is Protected by VRL?

VRL in the United States universally covers victims of violent felonies. In some states it is extended to victims of misdemeanors, but only 40 percent of states provide full rights to victims of all crimes committed by adults (Howley and Dorris 2013). About half of states extend some, if not all, victims' rights to cases involving juvenile defendants (Howley and Dorris 2013).[5] In most states the parent or survivor of a murder victim is extended victim status. In some states participatory rights are not fully extended to those who are incarcerated (Howley and Dorris 2013). The 2004 CVRA defined "victim" in general terms: "a person directly and proximately harmed as a result of the commission of a federal offense" (Doak 2008, 20). The Sixth Circuit Court of Appeals narrowed "proximate" to individuals who can demonstrate a strong connection between the acts of the accused and the harms they experienced (*United States v. Sharp* 2006).

18.4 What Rights Are Encompassed by VRL?

This section will explore those victims' rights that significantly shape the prosecution context.

18.4.1 Right to Privacy

Legislation to protect rape survivors from the introduction of their past sexual history exists in some form in all U.S. states, Canada, and Australia. Protecting victims requires the law to be invoked by the prosecutor, but the judge has discretion to determine the relevance of information the defense wants to introduce. Studies show that U.S. prosecutors do not raise objections and invoke the laws and that U.S. judges interpret them narrowly (Konradi 2007). VRL also protects clinical relationships between crime victims and crisis counselors or mental health professionals. For example, New Jersey appellate courts have limited a defendant's ability to force a victim to be examined by a physician specified by the defendant or to secure a photograph of a victim without her consent, and an Arizona appellate court has upheld a victim's right to prevent the defendant from reviewing her counselor's notes (Schlam 2015). Rights to privacy create a victim expectation that they generally have control over their personal information and that the prosecutor will support them. However, this may be at odds with the narrative of victimization the prosecutor is building and the emotional affect they seek to draw from the victim at trial (Konradi 2007), as well as with the prosecutor's obligation to divulge exculpatory evidence before trial (Pokorak 2007).

18.4.2 Right to Information and Notification

VRL commonly promises victims access to general information about the steps of the process, crime victims' compensation programs, victims' resources, and notice of case-specific information, such as when court proceedings will take place. Howley and Dorris (2013) summarize the status of state notification requirements as follows: some states specify victims be given notice about "all critical stages" and others about "important criminal justice hearings." Not all states give victims the right to be informed if court events are cancelled or rescheduled. Most states grant victims a right to information about a defendant's pretrial release or a convict's transfer, escape, or parole. Most recently legislation has required victims be informed if criminal cases are reopened, DNA evidence is retested, or defendants seek to expunge their records. Prosecutors generally have responsibility to ensure victims receive general and case-specific information, a task they may shift to crime victim advocates. Local jurisdictions have varied systems for informing victims; some now allow for email notification. In 2011, forty-two states had automated systems to inform victims of circumstances related to the department of corrections (Howley and Dorris 2013).

The 1984 Victims' of Crime Act and the Violence Against Women Act and its reauthorizations have provided funding for crime victims' advocates (CVA) across the United States. In their support role, these various non-legal personnel intercede in the relationship between prosecutors and victims (Zweig and Yahner 2013). However, CVA are not readily available in all jurisdictions and may be limited by law to working with certain types of victims. For the most part, prosecutors hold positive views of advocates who assist in cases; they highlight advocates' ability to provide a sense of consistency for victims as the case progresses, to provide general information about the process, and to build rapport with victims (Erez, Ibarra, and Downs 2011).

Advocates may be housed within the criminal justice system or in non-profit NGOs. The former arrangement allows advocates to access information and to build relationships with prosecutors, which may enable them to better represent victims' wishes. On the other hand, advocates may limit their advocacy for individual victims to protect their long-term relationships with prosecutors when physically located in proximity to them (Englebrecht 2011; Konradi 2007; Zweig and Yahner 2013).

18.4.3 Right to be Present

As of 2013, victims had the right to attend criminal justice proceedings in forty states and the District of Columbia "consistent with the rules of evidence" or the "rights of the accused" (Howley and Dorris 2013). Half the states allow victims to attend trial after they have testified, while seventeen exempt victims from sequestration (Thompson 2014). For the most part, courts have rejected defense arguments that the mere presence of a victim is prejudicial to defendants (Howley and Dorris 2013). This victim right may conflict with prosecutorial trial strategy, given that they are invested in how judges and jurors interpret the demeanor of crime victims.

18.4.4 Right to Be Heard

Beloof (2007) argues that victims' interests are part of the public interest, with which the court should be concerned, and that this provides grounds for victims to speak and share their views with discretionary decision-makers. There are several "distinct modes of participation beyond the right to be informed that are embedded in VRL: a right to confer with the prosecutor, a mandatory consultation requirement, a right to address the court (in person or in writing), and the federal right to appeal for a writ of mandamus where these rights have been breached" (Pugach and Tamir 2017, 49). As discussed above, most victims have little recourse if state prosecutors do not involve them. While a federal writ of mandamus can force a trial court to "re-open a plea or sentence," there is a significant cost to the victim to hire an attorney (Pugach and Tamir 2017). Appealing is much more likely when the victim is a corporation or wealthy individual (Pugach and Tamir 2017).

The victim's right to be heard is supported by legislation directed at employers. More than thirty states prohibit employers from penalizing or terminating victims of crime who miss work due to subpoenas. Some extend protection to victims who attend hearings or consult with prosecutors. A very few extend protections to victims to attend any hearing that serves their interests. These employment protections are enforceable through criminal and civil sanctions (Howley and Dorris 2013).

The first victim impact statement (VIS) was created in 1976 by a Fresno County California probation officer (Howeley and Dorris 2013). Since then, the opportunity to submit written or oral statements to the court before sentencing has been extended to direct-victims of crime and to bereaved victims (family members of murder victims). All states grant crime victims a right to speak or submit a written VIS before offenders are formally sentenced. These statements can be subject to cross-examination and some states have acted to limit that practice. Victims are also generally granted a right to contribute written and/or oral input to parole boards (Howley and Dorris 2013).

Arguments for VIS focus on treating victims with dignity, acknowledging their harms and accurately representing them in sentences, and fostering emotional and psychological recovery (Konradi and Burger 2000). VIS enable a direct confrontation between victims and offenders, in which the victims can feel empowered, assert their reality, share their anguish, and also convey righteous anger or concern for their victimizer (Erez, Ibarra, and Downs 2011; Konradi 2007; Konradi and Burger 2000). Research shows that victim participation varies across jurisdictions and varies for personal reasons (Konradi 2007; Roberts 2009). Pemberton and Reynaers's (2011) review of research suggests most victims are motivated to have a voice, although many wish to participate also to influence sentences.

There is some debate about what is permissible in a VIS: which victims may speak and what they may say, and how VIS may impact sentencing (Erez and Roberts 2013). Arguments against VIS focus on the victim's status as a non-party in adversarial proceedings, the possibility of disproportionate or disparate sentences motivated by emotion, the time VIS adds to already overtaxed courts, the potential that VIS do not lead to desired outcomes and will increase victim resentment, and the potential that victims will feel responsible and obligated to speak even though they would rather not (Erez and Roberts 2013). *Payne v. Tennessee* (1991) held that crime victims could relate their own specific harms in impact statements (Pugach and Tamir 2017). In *Kenna v. District Court*, the Ninth Circuit Court of Appeals confirmed victims have a right to read their impact statements in court. The U.S. Supreme Court has declined to weigh in further on the scope of permissible victim impact statement content although relevant cases have been presented to it (Kirchengast 2013).

VIS are relevant to prosecution and prosecutors in several ways. They can provide detail of harm to support prosecutors' arguments for specific sentences, giving an advantage in plea negotiations. They can provide victims who lose their ability to tell their story via a plea agreement an opportunity to go "on the record." They also provide a space within which victims can openly emote. VIS are also a site of tension for prosecutors and may be a site of victims' secondary victimization. A plea may create conditions where the crime to which the defendant admits guilt is significantly different from aspects of victimization that are central to the victim's experience. Thus, a prosecutor may feel a need to assert editorial control over the victim's public statements. Even victims' expression of emotions when delivering VIS in court may be of concern to prosecutors, if they anticipate the defendant's family may be inflamed (Booth 2012). Adult sexual assault victims have reported anger and frustration with prosecutors who have pressured them to limit the content of their VIS or strongly urged them to participate in allocution when they had not previously chosen to actively participate (Konradi and Burger 2000, 2007).

In the present, researchers suggest that jurisdictions are doing a better job of informing victims about their rights than when VIS were new. However, all eligible victims are still not informed (Erez and Roberts 2013) and all who desire to speak may not have an opportunity to do so (Englebrecht 2012). There is also some recent evidence that prosecutors and judges manage victims with the cooperation of defense attorneys, to ensure both that the VIS experience is positive and not disruptive to the decorum of the court or the flow of work.

Booth's (2012) ethnographic study of the implementation of VIS legislation in New South Wales (Australia) courts revealed that prosecutors and judges sought to restrict the expression of inappropriate emotions or an excess of emotions in the courtroom from bereaved victims. The VIS statute in NSW circumscribes what victims may say in court. In pre-court sessions, Crown Prosecutors described the statutorily allowed content in VIS, preparing family members for the fact that their "voice" in the process was limited (Booth 2012). What prosecutors did not communicate to victims was the fact that their statements were simply symbolic, the NSW Supreme Court having previously ruled that VIS may not influence the penalty imposed on a defendant (Booth 2012). After the pre-court meetings prosecutors transmitted written copies of family members' VIS to defense counsel for review. In court, defense attorneys rarely objected to the written documents they received, and many oral statements contained prohibited content (Booth 2012). However, Booth noted that defense attorneys, prosecutors and the judge spoke in legal shorthand during the court event to acknowledge their shared understanding that VIS were irrelevant to the sentence (Booth 2012). When VIS were delivered, judges watched and empathized with speakers, offered tissues and water, and urged them to speak slowly to be understood, even acknowledging the content of their statements. When the defense objected to sections of the VIS, judges took time to explain that "the law" required the excision of content. In short, Booth concluded that empathy displayed in pre-court preparation and sentencing hearings functioned to "cool out" bereaved victims, to enable them to accept the court outcomes and their limited place in the process.

In re Dean, the United States Fifth Circuit Court of Appeals held that victims are entitled under the CVRA to conference "meaningfully" with prosecutors before they reach a plea agreement. State statutes variously offer victims a right to be "consulted," to "confer," or to have the prosecutor "obtain their views." As of 2013, more than half of states required prosecutors to engage victims before plea agreements are finalized, and many of them extend consultation to pretrial release or diversion, declining charges, or dismissing charges (Cassell, Mitchell, and Edwards 2014; Howley and Dorris 2013; Thompson 2014). Less than half of the states permit victims to submit oral or written statements at plea hearings, yet in some, like Mississippi and Arizona, a plea cannot be accepted without the prosecutor confirming that "reasonable efforts" have been made to confer with victim(s) and inform them of their allocution right (Howley and

Dorris 2013). Ten states grant crime victims the right to submit information at bail-related hearings (Howley and Dorris 2013). Case law has not established whether victims' rights apply before or after charges have been formally filed against defendants (Cassell, Mitchell, and Edwards 2014; Howley and Dorris 2013). No states have given victims a right to veto a prosecutor's decision to file or dismiss charges or to make plea agreements with defendants (Erez and Roberts 2013).

18.5 Can Victims Participate Meaningfully?

The relationships between prosecutors and victims, in which the dynamic of consultation plays out, have been captured over several decades in qualitative interview and observational studies. Most have focused on the experiences of victims of gendered violence (Frohmann 1991; Holmstrom and Burgess 1983; Konradi 2007; Martin and Powell 1994; Regehr et al. 2008). They have brought attention to the emotional demands of prosecution work (Martin 2005), the ways in which prosecutors' actions before and during court events are and are not supportive of victims, the conflict over pleas (Konradi 2007)—in particular, whether they accurately represent victims' experiences of victimization and adequately sanction it (Dylan, Regehr, and Alaggia 2008)—and the link between victims' ability to participate in the guilt phase and their use of VIS opportunities (Konradi and Burger 2000). Ethnographic studies of prosecution have captured how the organization of work (vertical or horizontal) shapes relations with victims before charging (Frohmann 1991), preparation of victims for court, and involvement of victims in plea offers (Konradi 2007).

Recently, qualitative investigators have focused on the specific ways in which prosecutors respond to victims' needs in the context of VRL and also seek to guide their behavior to meet prosecutorial ends. Several of these studies explore prosecutors' relationships with bereaved victims, family members of homicide victims who have gained recognition by virtue of VRL (Englebrecht 2011; Goodrum 2013; Goodrum and Stafford 2003).

Englebrecht (2011) found that prosecutors she studied in New York believed that bereaved victims should have input into case development. The majority reported "consulting" with bereaved families "before accepting a plea deal or before moving forward with a trial" (2011, 136) and having frequent interactions by telephone or in person. However, some prosecutors may intentionally limit contact in spite of their positive attitudes towards victims' involvement. Goodrum and Stafford (2003) found that prosecutors in an unnamed location felt burdened by bereaved victims' intense sadness. While they felt a social obligation to respond with sympathy, pursuing opportunities to communicate it interfered with their ability to maintain a dispassionate approach to the case. Thus, they maneuvered to create distance and discouraged victims from contacting them on the basis of the importance of their work on the case. These prosecutors also shifted the burden of victim contacts to victim witness advocates, using their organizational position as a shield. In short, Goodrum and Stafford (2003) reported that in order to shield themselves from unwanted emotions, emotionally burdened prosecutors sought to maintain an illusion of approachability while intentionally avoiding victims. In contrast, in a study of a jurisdiction with a "national reputation of being an innovator in victim services," Goodrum (2013) found that prosecutors generally went beyond what was required by VRL in the way that they emotionally related with many victims, suggesting "substantive change" brought about by VRL. However, she also discovered that prosecutors offered circumstantial sympathy; they withheld emotionally from bereaved victims whose loved ones had criminal histories and from others in a pattern that suggested racial and/or class bias (2013).

Prosecutors actively worked to influence what victims thought and felt to produce courtroom behavior that would reinforce their message to the judge and jury. When victims' views about plea bargains and sentences differed from their own, prosecutors in Englebrecht's study (2011) said they would do what they thought was best for the case. However, in these situations, prosecutors made attempts to bring bereaved victims' perspectives into alignment with their orientation to the case, to "get victims on board." This was important from the standpoint of being able to tell judges that victims agreed with pleas and to protect their professional reputations. Similarly, Erez, Globokar, and Ibarra (2014) found that prosecutors shared information to equip victims to fulfill their participatory obligations and to strategically guide them to accept plea bargains as logical. This served prosecutors' interests in efficiency and their perceptions of justice.

Goodrum and Stafford (2003) found that prosecutors controlled bereaved victims' access to information to prevent them from manifesting intense negative feelings at inappropriate times. They explained the adversarial nature of trials to prepare bereaved victims to encounter negative portrayals of their loved ones. Yet they sometimes suppressed details about the murder to minimize the likelihood that bereaved victims would display intense anger in the courtroom, where their demeanor might damage the prosecution case. The upside of asserting emotional control over victims was the degree that prosecutors could use it to enhance the success of cases; the downside was the possibility that bereaved victims would be disillusioned, disappointed, and frustrated (2003).

The prosecutors studied by Erez, Globokar, and Ibarra (2014) also managed victims' emotions to increase their willingness to testify and to produce compelling testimony. They sought to increase victims' feelings of support by displaying empathy verbally and behaviorally, and they directed victims to display a demeanor that conformed to court decorum and also adhered closely with emotional expressions of sympathetic victims. This latter strategy included guiding victims to exert control over their emotions and specifically to suppress displays of anger that could turn off jurors.

Bereaved families who recalled being consulted by prosecutors also reported having a positive relationship with them (Englebrecht 2011). However, those who reported that they received no notification or information, even if they called the district attorney's office, felt illegitimately excluded and were frustrated. Some victims also expressed disappointment and frustration when they discovered that their input into plea decisions was not determinative (Englebrecht 2011). Similarly, Erez, Globokar, and Ibarra (2014) found that when prosecutors selectively complied with VRL requirements—not always appointing victims' advocates, providing education and preparation late, and conveying information without relevant detail—victims were more likely to be disappointed by the process. Victims were also disappointed to be told not to attend court events when they were legally entitled to be present (Erez, Globokar, and Ibarra 2014). Goodrum (2013) reported that when prosecutors shared emotions with victims, victims' sense of satisfaction improved, independent of the case outcome, and helped both the bereaved victims and prosecutors accomplish their objectives. Specifically, bereaved victims were able to influence decisions about pleas when they made emotional connections with prosecutors, and prosecutors gained their trust through connection and were able to convey difficult outcomes without being blamed for them (2013). Goodrum concluded that despite the need to protect themselves from burnout, prosecutors who relegate emotion work to advocates will not address victims' needs and will not gain the benefits that could insulate their reputations from negative outcomes.

Pokorak (2007) argues that two issues underlie the "problem" that victims have with prosecutors about pleas. The first is that they take on the witness role unaware that pleas are the normal way of doing justice. This fact is obfuscated by cultural representations of the adversarial system. The second is that prosecutors and investigators engage in a lot of co-identity language or "we talk" to build rapport and trust and commitment to the prosecution case that strongly implies a representative relationship when one legally does not exist. In short, a lack of transparency about the amount of discretionary power prosecutors have in the criminal justice process, in combination with treatment that implies a vested interest in victims' needs, results in victims' dissatisfaction.

18.5.1 Moving toward More Meaningful Involvement: Guidelines and Nudges

O'Hear (2007) recommends local development of plea guidelines for standard charges to complement and structure consultation with victims. Guidelines would make clear that plea bargaining is the normal method for resolving cases, that the prosecutor does not represent the victim, and that decision-making is not random but driven by precedent. The prosecutor would characterize the case to the victim after charges are filed and explain associated punishment, as specified in the guidelines. The victim would then have an opportunity to contest it and offer alternatives before a plea agreement was reached. At the plea hearing the prosecutor would present how they arrived at the charge and if the victim's position was different, why it was not accepted. The victim could also address the court and argue for their position. However, O'Hear notes that guidelines could be drafted to maximize prosecutor discretion and so become useless or be overly harsh.

With respect to the CVRA, Pugach and Tamir (2017) suggest "nudges" that preserve the prosecutor's and judge's discretion but push both actors "not to go directly to the default position," to seal plea agreements rapidly (2017, 48). The "nudges" Pugach and Tamir propose consist of a requirement that prosecutors document the process of victim consultation and file a certification with the judge. Information in the certification would include when contacts occur between prosecutor and victim, whether the victim has been informed of a right to express concerns, what the victim's view is about a plea bargain, and whether the victim's perspective has been taken into consideration. Pugach and Tamir argue that the process of documentation would push prosecutors to work more actively with victims, and that judges would be pushed to weigh the information and make a decision, not simply sign off. The authors acknowledge that the strength of contrary preferences can work against nudges and it ought to be piloted and studied.

18.5.2 Do Prosecutors Help Victims Produce Meaningful Testimony?

Being able to convey what one means effectively in court is an important aspect of being heard. Thus, improving the quality of witness testimony matters apart from the emotional burden of the act of testifying. How prosecutors and defense attorneys elicit witnesses' contributions matters.

Studies of defense attorneys' cross-examinations of child witnesses showed that they contain legal terms that are unfamiliar to children, double negatives, and tag questions that are grammatically complex (Evans, Lee, and Lyon 2009). Zajac, Gross, and Hayne (2003) reported that defense attorneys' constructions influence how accurately children testify. Comparative analysis of prosecutors' and defense attorneys' questioning of children conducted in the United States (Andrews, Lamb, and Lyon 2015; Evans, Lee, and Lyon 2009), New Zealand (Zajac, Gross, and Hayne 2003), and Scottish courts (Andrews and Lamb 2017) revealed that both types of attorneys used a level of wordiness and linguistic complexity that was age inappropriate. Andrews, Lamb, and Lyon (2015) reported that prosecutors in California favored closed ended prompts (Did *x* happen?) and frequently used option-posing prompts (Did *x* or *y* or *z* happen?) rather than inviting children to narrate their reality. Also, California prosecutors' questions produced at least one contradiction in the testimony of 85 percent of children, although defense produced 90 percent (2015, 258). Andrews and Lamb's (2017) analysis of Scottish trial transcripts from 2009 to 2014 revealed that question complexity increased the likelihood that children would be unresponsive, express uncertainty, and (to a non-significant extent) contradict themselves. These outcomes may well result in "deleterious effects on the evaluation of children's testimony" (2017, 190) and may also contribute to secondary victimization. On the other hand, Evans, Lee, and Lyon (2009) found that complex defense questions followed by "I don't know" answers were associated with convictions. They suggested that jurors assign competence and honesty to children who admit their lack of knowledge or that defense attorneys increase question complexity hoping to mislead when the prosecution case is particularly strong.

Pre-court preparation has been largely focused on decreasing victims' anxiety and stress. Yet this has done little to compensate for victims' encounters with cross-examination, during which they feel blamed and often bullied. An alternative approach to preparation might focus more directly on cross and specifically on improving the quality of witnesses' responses. Researchers have begun to explore this matter with child witnesses. Two recent studies found that providing children with feedback after requiring them to answer cross-examination types of questions resulted in more accurate answers, regardless of age, when they later participated in an unrelated cross-examination scenario (O'Neill and Zajac 2013; Righarts, O'Neill, and Zajac 2013). Children seemed to learn and later be able to apply principles from the preparation session: "e.g., *disagree when the interviewer gets it wrong*" (O'Neill and Zajac 2013, 315). However, the timing of training matters; when testing occurred one day or one week after training, there was significant improvement. After a month no improvement was reported (O'Neill and Zajac 2013). These studies also show that training by a third-party (who is not associated with direct or cross-examination) produces positive results, suggesting that children's testimony may be improved without involving prosecutors, who might be accused of coaching.

England and Wales have adopted an intervention to ensure that children understand what is being asked in the courtroom. Before trials, speech and language experts assess children's communication competency, advise the court about how to question, and monitor the progress of questioning in court. It is also now common for attorneys to "draft questions ahead of time to check for wording, sequencing and relevance *before* trial" to facilitate children's testifying (Hanna and Henderson 2018, 422). Studies of court personnel in England and Wales show the majority of counsel and judges are highly positive about the involvement of non-questioning intermediaries (Hanna and Henderson 2018). Conversations with British judges and barristers revealed that none thought the involvement of intermediaries jeopardized a fair trial (Hanna et al. 2013).

On the basis of her analysis of sexual assault survivors' experiences with cross examination, Konradi (2007) proposed the possibility of using intermediaries with adults. However, she notes that such an approach has limitations, because it would reduce the ability of the prosecutor to behave as a courtroom ally and could result in witnesses juggling yet another interaction dynamic (in addition to those with the defendant, supporters, and the prosecutor).

18.6 Protecting Victims in Court

VRL typically grants victims protections from harassment by defendant(s) or their representatives via no contact orders. Forty states provide victims with private waiting rooms in courthouses (Howley and Dorris 2013). A number of accommodations, including shielding and support animals, are also intended to reduce the traumatic quality of testifying. But in order for victims to gain access to them, prosecutors must request them.

18.6.1 Shielding

The practice of shielding arises from social science research that indicated the experience of testifying, in particular exposure to the defendant, both traumatized children and reduced the competency and accuracy of their testimony (Dennis 2011). As children's fear of the defendant increased, the number of prosecutor's questions they answered dropped (Dennis 2011). Legislation followed to reduce the trauma experienced by children. It allowed for courtroom supports, physical screens, or realignment of courtroom furniture that limited eye contact between witnesses and the defendant, and technology to allow remote televised testimony (Erez and Roberts 2013).

Video-testimony strategies used in U.S. jurisdictions include closed circuit television (CCTV), remote, and taped. CCTV testimony involves the victim-witness giving live testimony from a room of the courthouse separate from the courtroom. The prosecuting and defense attorneys are with the victim-witness, while the defendant, judge, and jury remain in the courtroom. Two-way CCTV involves the courtroom and victim-witness receiving video of each other; one-way CCTV involves only video of the victim-witness being projected into the courtroom. Attorneys in a courtroom can also use two-way CCTV to ask questions of a victim-witness who is in a remote geographic location. Depositions taped in the presence of a judge, as well as interviews taped by law enforcement, may be introduced in court in the absence of a victim (as testimonial hearsay) (Lyon and Dente 2012).

In *Coy v. Iowa* in 1988, the U.S. Supreme Court ruled that a trial court must make an individual determination that a witness requires shielding from a defendant. Two years later, in *Maryland v. Craig*, the Court held that when shielding was necessary to "further important public policy" or the "reliability of testimony," a face-to-face confrontation was not required (quoted by Dennis 2011, 353). Shortly following the *Craig* decision, Congress passed the Child Victims' and Child Witnesses' Rights Act (CVCWRA 1990, 18 U.S.C. § 3509) that instructed federal courts to use two-way CCTV with child witnesses and defined conditions for use. The statute also permitted introduction of prerecorded depositions and exclusion of the defendant from the deposition to protect a child's ability to testify.

A nationwide survey of 153 prosecutors conducted by Goodman et al. (1999) after the *Craig* decision explored their attitudes toward, and use of, shielding technologies. They found that shielding practices were infrequently deployed with child witnesses. The minority of prosecutors who had experience with shielding rated it as "moderately useful" to reduce the trauma of testifying for children. Prosecutors reported that judges denied their requests to use shielding, they feared defense appeals based on use of shields, and they simply did not have the appropriate technology to use CCTV because of its cost. Dennis summarizes: prosecutors view shielding as "infeasible, needless, ineffective, and impermissible" (2011, 357) despite its constitutionality.

Subsequent to *Maryland v. Craig* and passage of the CVCWRA, federal appellate decisions reasserted that the potential for trauma, not fear of the defendant, needed to be established (*Lomholt v. Iowa* 2003) to implement shields and upheld use of CCTV in the absence of a state statute addressing the subject (*Hicks-Bey v. United States* 1994; Tluczek 2008). In 2012, courts also determined two-way CCTV was constitutional because one-way was permissible (*Roadcap v. Commonwealth* 2007) and extended access to two-way CCTV to child witnesses who are not victims (*People v. Lujan* 2012) (National Crime Victim Law Institute 2008). By 2012, only four states lacked a statute that addressed CCTV (National Center for Prosecution of Child Abuse 2012).[6] States with statutes extended usage of CCTV to all child victims (NCPCA 2012), although the age limits varied from 10 in Georgia (Ga. Code Ann. § 17-8-55) to 18 in Vermont (Vt. Rule 807). Some states extended shielding to all child witnesses (Dennis 2011).

A small minority of states extend the CCTV option to mentally retarded adult victims (NCPCA 2012). Hawaii allows any adult to testify with two-way CCTV (Garvin, Wilkinson, and LeClair 2011). Case law has further extended use of CCTV to adult victims with mental disabilities (Michigan), intimidated witnesses (Ohio), those prone to anxiety (South Carolina), and to all adult witnesses (in federal courts and Wyoming).[7]

Video testimony is in wide use in other countries. Canadian law allowed the usage of videotaped evidence beginning in 1988, and Britain allowed video taped and CCTV testimony after 1991 (Perry and McAuliff 1993). In England and Wales, victims can request remote CCTV (Wade, Lewis, and de Cavarlay 2008). Depending on the nature of the crime, children can be cross-examined on videotape before trial or cross-examined by live link (Doak 2008). Those adults suffering from "mental disorder or impairment of intelligence or social functioning" or "physical disability" are also eligible for accommodation (Doak 2008). In Germany, video recordings of witnesses under 18 may be used even if the witness is available. They may also be used in cases in which there is a heavy psychological burden, such as sex crimes, crimes against life, or crimes against dependents (Walther 2011). German victims who do not wish to confront the defendant in court can also be accommodated with closed circuit technology (Walther 2011). Scandinavian countries have been using pre recorded testimony of children since the 1960s (Perry and McAuliff 1993).

18.6.2 Emotional Support: Facility Dogs

Federal law and many states allow an adult attendant to accompany children to court. The child may hold the attendant's hand or sit on her/his lap (Cowan 2013). The use of facility dogs as an accompaniment to calm child victims, in the absence of an adult, is the most recent advancement in courtroom support. Research has shown that a service dog can significantly reduce systolic and mean arterial pressure, heart rate, and behavioral distress in children ages 3 to 6 (Nangegast et al. 1997). Anecdotal evidence from specific cases indicates a service animal can help children open up in court (Cowan 2013).

The dog is positioned close to or touching the witness while they are on the stand; the dog's leash may be held by the witness or a handler (Glazer 2018). Facility dogs have been employed in the United States since 2012, when one assisted a pair of California sisters testifying against their father in sexual abuse case (*People v. Spence* 2012). Florida passed Statute 92.55 allowing facility dogs the same year. As of 2018, there were 178 facility dogs spread across thirty-eight states (Courthouse Dogs Foundation n.d.).[8]

Detractors argue that use of facility dogs infringes upon defendants' rights, because the presence of a facility dog makes the witness appear more sympathetic (Gerkey 2016). Advocates argue dogs pose less of a risk of bias than the adults whom child witnesses are legally allowed to have as accompaniment. The animal does not understand the court dialog and will not react to the content of the trial (Gerkey 2016). Steps can also be taken to minimize the impact of facility dogs, including walking them in and out of the courtroom when the jury is absent, keeping them outside of the jury sight line, and having the judge present limiting instructions to the jury (Ensminger 2016; Gerkey 2016).

Case law has supported the use of facility dogs for children in New York (*People v. Tohom* 2013) and California (*People v. Spence* 2012) (NCVLI 2014). Case law has also extended the use of facility dogs to disabled adults in Washington state (*State v. Dye* 2013) and to non-victim witnesses in Arizona (*State v. Millis* 2017) (NCVLI 2017). Research should be conducted to explore U.S. prosecutors' current access to and attitudes towards court animals and to determine the impact of facility dogs on jurors and witnesses.

18.7 Enforcement of Rights: Legal Representation

Legal representation can ensure that victims' rights are recognized and protected. For example, in the United States, sexual assault victims may employ private legal representation for matters of privacy, specifically to introduce motions to keep medical and counseling records out of the hands of the defense (Kirchengast 2015). In New Hampshire, Wisconsin, and West Virginia, private attorneys may represent victims to limit introduction of sexual history evidence (Braun 2014). Costs generally limit victims' use of legal representatives. However, research suggests that where representation exists, it can have broad impacts.

18.7.1 Attorneys Provided through Legal Clinics

The Office of Victims of Crime of the DOJ funded a demonstration project from 2002 to 2009 that grew to encompass eight state clinics: Arizona, Idaho, Maryland, New Jersey,

New Mexico, South Carolina, and Utah and a federal clinic in Arizona (Davis et al. 2012). The clinics were focused on providing attorneys to directly serve clients and on selectively bringing cases through the appellate level to push for written decisions that expanded or clarified victims' rights. Initially, "all clinics pushed for victim standing to enforce victim rights within their jurisdiction" (Davis et al. 2012, 4). The clinics were free to structure themselves to accommodate local conditions. The RAND Corporation completed a process evaluation in 2009 and Davis et al. (2012) completed an impact evaluation thereafter. Ultimately, the impact study focused on four clinics in Maryland, Utah, South Carolina, and Colorado.

Prior to clinic implementation in Colorado, criminal justice personnel and victim advocates revealed that their knowledge of victims' rights was uneven and particularly inaccurate about the events about which victims were entitled to be informed, who decides a victim can give oral or written input at sentencing, and what conditions required restitution. After the clinic had been in operation for a year, researchers found significant increases in positive attitudes and support for victim rights, but no increase in knowledge and significant differences by profession for both time periods.

Surveys conducted with legal personnel in Maryland, Utah, and South Carolina showed a statistically significant positive shift in attitudes towards victims' rights and perceived compliance with victims' rights legislation across all professions and that contact with victims' attorneys significantly increased favorability towards them. However, use of clinic attorneys did not increase prosecutors' compliance with VRL. In combination, the clinic cases were less likely to be dismissed and more likely to result in a plea. Victims represented by clinic attorneys reported more of their rights were protected than those without attorneys; however, they were also less satisfied with the criminal justice process. It is unclear if unsatisfied victims sought out legal representation because they had problems or increased their expectations as a result of working with attorneys. In sum, the impact analysis conducted by Davis et al. (2012) did not demonstrate that clinic attorneys produced an overall compliance effect, although individual sites had positive results in some areas. Further, they determined clinic sustainability to be tenuous, because the clinics were funded entirely through federal and private grants and they never made it into the presidential budget.

18.7.2 State-Funded Attorneys for Sexual Assault Victims

Recent military justice reforms specific to sexual assault include the creation of a Special Victims Counsel (SVC), a Judge Advocate Corps attorney assigned to a victim who makes a restricted or unrestricted report (Garvin and Beloof 2015).[9] The SVC provides information to the restricted reporter and "attorney-client privileged representation" through the entire process to the unrestricted reporter (2015, 73). These attorneys help victims protect their private materials and ensure that rape shields are properly applied (Goewert and Dilworth 2013). In the first eleven months of the program, SVCs provided 18,919 hours of representation to sexual assault victims (Goewert and Dilworth 2013).

The Air Force conducted satisfaction surveys of victims and found "92% were 'extremely satisfied' with the support they received during the Article 32 hearing and court martial" and "98% would recommend that other victims request an SVC" (Garvin and Beloof 2015, 74). Positive attitudes toward the SVC persisted with acquittals (2015). On-going research of SVC is needed.

Since 2011 in New South Wales, rape and sexual assault victims have been able to secure state-funded legal representation to assist with preventing or restricting access to their private communications about sexual assault (Braun 2014). Similar provisions for sexual assault victims exist in the Republic of Ireland (Braun 2014). In Switzerland, Germany, Hungary, Poland, and Sweden, victims are entitled to legal representation when they appear as witnesses (Wade, Lewis, and de Cavarlay 2008), see below.

18.8 Victim Direction of Prosecution

18.8.1 Private Prosecution in the United States

Presently, a "handful of states," including Kentucky, Mississippi, Missouri, and Oklahoma, allow victim-initiated and -funded prosecution (Fairfax 2009, 423).[10] These "victim-retained private prosecutors generally are authorized only to assist the public prosecutor or, in rare circumstances, to step in and perform the prosecutorial role when the government declines to do so in a given case" (Fairfax 2009, 426). California allows private attorneys to be appointed by the district attorney "to enforce a state anchorage ordinance" (O'Neill 2010, 693). Delaware law allows attorneys to be "deputized" to prosecute cases under the supervision of the Attorney General, while New York allows private prosecution under the supervision of the state prosecutor (O'Neill 2010). New Jersey statutes limit private prosecution to cases where there are "cross complaints" and a conflict exists for the municipal prosecutor (O'Neill 2010).

In 1996, the U.S. Supreme Court let stand without review a Fifth Circuit decision about a capital murder case (*Faulder v. Johnson* 1996) that was prosecuted by an attorney hired by the victim's son (O'Neill 2010). However, on grounds of a conflict of interest, several state statutes forbid paid attorneys from representing clients in both criminal and civil cases, and state appellate courts in other states have ruled similarly (O'Neill 2010). Courts in New Hampshire have limited private attorneys to prosecuting cases not involving imprisonment (O'Neill 2010).

One of the problems faced by victim witnesses in domestic violence cases is defendants' violation of civil protection orders. Prosecutors can enforce them, but the time lag is significant and defendants pose a threat to the participation of the victim in the original abuse case. Some victims have, with judicial encouragement, brought criminal contempt cases forward. The U.S. Supreme Court supported the practice, holding in *Young v. United States ex rel. Vuitton et Fils* that district courts had the power to appoint private prosecutors to pursue contempt citations (1987). However, in a series of decisions culminating in *In re Taylor* in 2013, the D.C. Court of Appeals narrowed the conditions under which criminal charges for violation of civil protection orders may be pursued by parties other than the public prosecutor, to the point of ending the practice (Cross 2015).

18.8.2 Private Prosecution Internationally

Private prosecution, carrying a full trial independently, is available in some adversarial systems of justice—Sweden, Denmark, Norway, and Portugal, for example—and in some that are inquisitorial—Austria, Germany, Turkey, and Poland, to name a few (Wade, Lewis, and de Cavarlay 2008; Wolhuter 2010). However, pursuing this option requires victims to take on the costs of the trial in many cases. In England and Wales, the private prosecutor may also be limited in their[11] ability to access materials from the investigation or the prosecutor's files, and the Director of Public Prosecutions or the Attorney General may order the proceedings be discontinued in the public interest (Doak 2008; O'Neill 2010). Doak (2008) argues the obstacles to complete private prosecution in England and Wales make it of little practical value and essentially a symbolic right.

18.8.3 Accessory Prosecution Internationally

Accessory prosecution has been adopted in some countries with inquisitorial systems of justice, such as Germany, Switzerland, Croatia, and Turkey (Wade, Lewis, and de Cavarlay 2008). In 1986, the German Victim Protection Act guaranteed victims of crime "an assured procedural position," allowing them to participate in the trial process as joint plaintiffs on par with the public prosecutor. This gave them access to case files, assignment of an attorney, the ability to protect themselves from questions that invaded their privacy, and the right to ask for the public to be excluded from the courtroom or the defendant to be temporarily removed. However, the fact that under the law victims remained responsible for all the costs (including those of the attorney) unless the defendant was convicted resulted in few exercising their right as accessories. In 2004, the German Victims' Rights Amendment created the position of a state-paid "privileged victim attorney" for victims of sex crimes, attempted homicide, some other personal felonies, youths under 16 years of age, and bereaved victims who were eligible for accessory prosecution. Access to a paid attorney was therefore extended. In 2009, the Second Victims' Rights Act expanded accessory prosecution to a wider range of victims of personal injury crimes and individuals under 18 years of age (Kury and Kilchling 2011).

Under the inquisitorial system, the state determines which charges will be filed and the victim "joins" the state prosecutor as an "accessory" (Walther 2011, 104). By joining early as an accessory, the accuser can ask for discovery and thereby influence the specific accusation the state makes, but they cannot appeal to amend the prosecutor's filed accusation (Walther 2011). At trial, the victim has a separate and parallel relationship with the judge. They can exercise their rights alone or through their attorney, have a desk in the courtroom, and have access to all evidence. The accessory prosecutor may file a motion to hear any witness, including themselves, at trial (Walther 2011). The victim can ask questions and cross-examine witnesses, have the last opportunity to speak in the case, and can appeal the results (Kury and Kilchling 2011). Although the accessory prosecutor can propose sentences, they may not appeal for a harsher sentence (Walther 2011). The accessory prosecutor has a right to be informed about important procedural decisions (Walther 2011); however, should the prosecutor and defense discuss a plea bargain, neither the victim nor the accessory attorney has a right to be heard in advance (Kury and Kilchling 2011).

18.9 Conclusion

The reviewed literature suggests that the full potential of VRL—to offer meaningful participation opportunities for victims in the criminal justice process and thereby to provide therapeutic outcomes and procedural justice for them—is yet to be realized. Prosecutors have not fully implemented legal practices to protect victims' rights due to career incentives that punish innovation, reward efficiency, and promote resource conservation. Prosecutors also struggle to reconcile their own emotional needs with the demands of individuals who have experienced trauma and are personally invested in cases.

This literature also suggests that prosecutors developing an evidence-based orientation toward their practice would be advantageous for victims. Such an orientation will work against generalizing about their needs and desires and about juror expectations, which contribute to resistance to innovation. It might even improve outcomes. For example, evidence is mounting that measures to protect child victims from trauma also yield testimony of greater accuracy. Additionally, studies in countries with adversarial systems show that prosecutors can implement measures in ways that are acceptable to defense attorneys and judges. When jurisdictions in the United States commit to innovation, they should also conduct evaluation research. For example, the military CVA system should be studied to determine its transferability to the states and federal systems. The use of facility dogs should be documented and examined for its impact on victim well-being, quality of testimony, and juror bias. Studies of private attorneys provided by legal clinics should continue. Pilot programs can also be undertaken to determine whether evidence supports extending supports, deemed acceptable for children, to adults.

Evaluation is likely to rely heavily on quantitative strategies. However, this review underscores the importance of ethnographic work to expose prosecutors' investments and incentives. These studies also highlight the boundary between guidance and manipulation that prosecutors sometimes cross when they construct themselves as serving the interests of victims in a legal context, where the victim is effectively a "tool" for building a legal case against the defendant. This brings us to a final concern.

This literature suggests the need for greater transparency with victims, so they are able not only to exercise their right to participate, but also to choose not to. If new legislation or case law negates the instrumental effect of victims' participation under VRL, victims must be informed. Prosecutors should not, with or without the aid of the judiciary, make decisions about what is in the best emotional interests of victims.

Notes

1. See Salmon Shomade in Chapter 9 of this volume for a discussion of specialized and diversionary courts. See Cassia Spohn in Chapter 12 for a discussion of specialized organizational structures for processing specific kinds of victimization. This chapter does not explore human rights literature, war crimes prosecution or post sentencing restorative justice.
2. A circuit court judge almost immediately blocked certification of the vote on grounds the question put to voters was misleading. In June 2019, the Kentucky State Supreme Court upheld the decision (Lovan 2019).
3. Fifteen states have granted victims standing according to Schram: Arizona, Idaho, Illinois, Indiana, Louisiana, Michigan, Mississippi, New Jersey, New Mexico, Ohio, Oklahoma, South Carolina, Texas, Utah, and Virginia.
4. See Cassell (2012) for a clause-by-clause analysis of the legislation and Seiden and Twist (2012) for a discussion of the arguments advanced for and against a constitutional amendment.
5. Most state laws allow judges to order restitution from juveniles. Some states, such as Nevada, give judges discretion to allow victims to be present at juvenile hearings (Howley and Dorris 2013).
6. Interpreting their state constitutions literally, the Supreme Courts of Illinois, Massachusetts, and Pennsylvania required face-to-face confrontation between defendant and witnesses (Dennis 2011).
7. *People v. Burton* 1996, *Horn v. Quarterman* 2007, and *State v. Johnson* 2011.
8. Facility dogs are also used in seven Canadian provinces and in a nationwide Family Crime program in Chile (O'Neill-Stephens 2010).
9. Restricted reports do not initiate legal proceedings but enable victims to access medical treatment and counseling.
10. O'Neill reports thirteen states "allow private counsel to participate in criminal prosecution in some way"—"Alabama, Georgia, Indiana, New Jersey, New York, Ohio, Pennsylvania, Tennessee, Vermont, Virginia, West Virginia, and Wisconsin" (2010, 689).
11. We have used "they" as a gender inclusive pronoun instead of she/he. The position of accessory is not limited to women or men.

References

18 U.S.C. § 3509

Andrews, S. J., M. E. Lamb, and T. D. Lyon. 2015. "Question Types, Responsiveness and Self-Contradictions when Prosecutors and Defense Attorneys Question Alleged Victims of Child Abuse." *Applied Cognitive Psychology* 29(2): 253–261.

Andrews, Samantha J., and Michael E. Lamb. 2017. "The Structural Linguistic Complexity of Lawyers' Questions and Children's Responses in Scottish Criminal Courts." *Child Abuse & Neglect* 65(3): 182–193.

BallotPedia. 2018. "Georgia Amendment 4, Marsy's Law Crime Victim Rights Amendment (2018)." https:// ballotpedia. org/ Georgia_Amendment_4,_Marsy%27s_Law_Crime_Victim_Rights_Amendment_(2018).

Beloof, Douglas E. 2007. "Weighing Crime Victims' Interests in Judicially Crafted Criminal Procedure." *Catholic University Law Review* 56(4): 1135–1170.

Booth, Tracey. 2012. "'Cooling Out' Victims of Crime: Managing Victim Participation in the Sentencing Process in a Superior Sentencing Court." *The Australian and New Zealand Journal of Criminology* 45(2): 214–230.

Braun, Kerstin. 2014. "Legal Representation for Sexual Assault Victims—Possibilities for Law Reform?" *Current Issues in Criminal Justice* 25(3): 819–837.

Cassell, Paul G. 2012. "The Victims' Rights Amendment: A Sympathetic, Clause-By-Clause Analysis." *Phoenix Law Review* 5(2): 301–340.

Cassell, Paul G., Nathanael J. Mitchell, and Bradley J. Edwards. 2014. "Crime Victims' Rights During Criminal Investigations? Applying the Crime Victims' Rights Act Before Criminal Charges are Filed." *Journal of Criminal Law & Criminology* 104(1): 59–103.

Cattaneo, Lauren B., and Lisa A. Goodman. 2010. "Through the Lens of Therapeutic Jurispudence: The Relationship Between Empowerment in the Court System and Well-Being for Intimate Partner Violence." *Journal of Interpersonal Violence* 25(3): 481–502.

Courthouse Dogs Foundation. n.d. "Program Standards." Courthouse Dogs Foundation. Accessed March 20, 2018. https://courthousedogs.org/getting-started/best-practices/.

Cowan, Maj. Bradley M. 2013. "Children in the Courtroom: Essential Strategies for Effective Testimony by Child Victims of Sexual Abuse." *Army Lawyer* 2013(2): 4–16.

Coy v. Iowa. 1988. 487 U.S. 1012.

Crime Victims' Rights Act, 18 U.S.C. § 3771.

Cross, Courtney. 2015. "Civil Protection Orders: Increased Access and Narrowed Enforcement." *University of the District of Columbia Law Review* 18(2): 191–200.

Davis, Robert C., James M. Anderson, Susan Howley, Carol Dorris, and Julie Whitman. 2012. *No More Rights Without Remedies: An Impact Evaluation of the National Crime Victim Law Institute's Victims' Rights Clinics*. Santa Monica, CA: RAND Corporation.

Dennis, Andrea L. 2011. "Prosecutorial Discretion and the Neglect of Juvenile Shielding Statutes." *Nebraska Law Review* 90(2): 341–387.

Doak, Jonathan. 2008. *Victims' Rights, Human Rights and Criminal Justice: Reconceiving the Role of Third Parties*. Portland: Hart Publishing.

Dylan, Arielle, Cheryl Regehr, and Ramona Alaggia. 2008. "And Justice for All? Aboriginal Victims of Sexual Violence." *Violence Against Women* 14(6): 678–696.

Englebrecht, Christine M. 2011. "The Struggle for 'Ownership of Conflict': An Exploration of Victim Participation and Voice in the Criminal Justice System." *Criminal Justice Review* 36(2): 129–151.

Englebrecht, Christine M. 2012. "Where Do I Stand? An Exploration of the Rules That Regulate Victim Participation in the Criminal Justice System." *Victims and Offenders* 7(2): 161–184.

Ensminger, John. 2016. "Cases and Statutes on the Use of Dogs by Witnesses While Testifying in Criminal Proceedings: A Periodically Updated Online Article." Animal Legal & Historical Center, Michigan State University. https://www.animallaw.info/article/recent-cases-use-facility-dogs-witnesses-while-testifying.

Erez, Edna, and Julian Roberts. 2013. "Victim Participation in the Criminal Justice System." In *Victims of Crime*. Edited by Robert C. Davis, Arthur J. Lurigio, and Susan Herman, 251–270. Thousand Oaks, CA: SAGE Publications.

Erez, Edna, Julie L. Globokar, and Peter R. Ibarra. 2014. "Outsiders Inside: Victim Management in an Era of Participatory Reforms." *International Review of Victimology* 20(1): 169–188.

Erez, Edna, Peter R. Ibarra, and Daniel M. Downs. 2011. "Victim Welfare and Participation Reforms in the United States: A Therapeutic Jurisprudence Perspective." In *Therapeutic Jurisprudence and Victim Participation in Justice*. Edited by Edna Erez, Michael Kilchling, and Jo-Anne Wemmers, 15–40. Durham: Carolina Academic Press.

Evans, Angela, Kang Lee, and Thomas D. Lyon. 2009. "Complex Questions Asked by Defense Lawyers But Not Prosecutors Predicts Convictions in Child Abuse Trials." *Law and Human Behavior* 33(3): 258–264.

Fairfax, Roger A., Jr. 2009. "Delegation of the Criminal Prosecution Function to Private Actors." *U.C. Davis Law Review* 43(2): 411–456.

Faulder v. Johnson. 1996. 81 F.3d 515 (5th Cir.), cert. denied, 519 U.S. 995.

Finn, Mary A. 2013. "Evidence-Based and Victim-Centered Prosecutorial Policies: Examination of Deterrent and Therapeutic Jurisprudence Effects on Domestic Violence." *Criminology & Public Policy* 12(3): 443–472.

Fisher, Cortney. 2015. "What Matters: An Analysis of Victim Satisfaction with the Criminal Justice System in a Procedural Justice Framework." Ph.D. diss. University of Maryland. ProQuest Dissertations Publishing, 2015.3711224.

Freckelton, Ian. 2008. "Therapeutic Jurisprudence Misunderstood and Misrepresented: The Price and Risks of Influence." *Thomas Jefferson Law Review* 30(2): 575–596.

Frohman, Lisa. 1991. "Discrediting Victims' Allegations of Sexual Assault: Prosecutorial Accounts of Case Rejections." *Social Problems* 38(2): 213–226.

Garvin, Meg, Alison Wilkinson, and Sarah LeClair. 2011. "Allowing Adult Sexual Assault Victims to Testify at Trial via Live Video Technology." *Violence Against Women Bulletin*, September. National Crime Victim Law Institute, Lewis & Clark Law School.

Garvin, Margaret, and Douglas E. Beloof. 2015. "Crime Victim Agency: Independent Lawyers for Sexual Assault Victims." *Ohio State Journal of Criminal Law* 13(1): 67–88.

Gerkey, Loric. 2016. "Legal Beagles, a Silent Minority: Therapeutic Effects of Facility Dogs in the Courtroom." *International Journal of Therapeutic Jurisprudence* 1: 405–430.

Glazer, Melissa. 2018. "Assessing the Perceptions of the Use of a Courthouse Facility Dog Program with Child and Youth Witnesses." University of Western Ontario, Electronic Thesis and Dissertation Repository, 5265. https://ir.lib.uwo.ca/etd/5265.

Goewert, Maj. Christopher J., and Captain Seth W. Dilworth. 2013. "The Scope of a Victim's Right to Be Heard Through Counsel." *Military Justice Reporter* 40(3): 27–31.

Goodman, Gail S., Jodi Quas, Josephone A. Buckley, and Cheryl Shapiro. 1999. "Innovations for Child Witnesses: A National Survey." *Psychology Public Policy and Law* 5(2): 255–281.

Goodrum, Sarah. 2013. "Bridging the Gap Between Prosecutors' Cases and Victims' Biographies in the Criminal Justice System Through Shared Emotions." *Law & Society Review* 38(2): 257–287.

Goodrum, Sarah, and Mark C. Stafford. 2003. "The Management of Emotions in the Criminal Justice System." *Sociological Focus* 36(3): 179–196.

Hanna, Kirsten, and Emily Henderson. 2018. "'[Expletive], That Was Confusing, Wasn't It?' Defense Lawyers' and Intermediaries' Assessment of the Language Used to Question a Child Witness." *International Journal of Evidence & Proof* 22(4): 411–427.

Hanna, Kirsten, Emma Davies, Emily Henderson, and Linda Hand. 2013. "Questioning Child Witnesses: Exploring the Benefits and Risks of Intermediary Models in New Zealand." *Psychiatry, Psychology and Law* 20(4): 527–542.

Hicks-Bey v. United States. 1994. 649 A.2d 569 (D.C. Ct. App.).

Holmstrom, Lynda Lytle, and Ann Wolbert Burgess. 1983. *The Victim of Rape: Institutional Reactions*. New Brunswick, NJ: Transaction Publishers.

Horn v. Quarterman. 2007. 508 F.3d 306 (5th Cir.).

Howley, Susan, and Carol F. Dorris. 2013. "Legal Rights for Crime Victims in the Criminal Justice System." In *Victims of Crime*. Edited by Robert C. Davis, Arthur J. Lurigio, and Susan Herman, 271–292. Thousand Oaks, CA: SAGE Publications.

In re Dean. 2008. 527 F.3d 391 (5th Cir.).

In re Taylor. 2013. 73 A. 3d 85 (D.C. Ct. App.).

Kenna v. U.S. District Court. 2006. 435 3d 1011 (9th Cir.).

Kirchengast, Tyrone. 2013. "Victim Lawyers, Victim Advocates, and the Adversarial Criminal Trial." *New Criminal Law Review* 16(4): 568–594.

Kirchengast, Tyrone. 2015. "Enforceable Rights for Victims of Crime: Shifting the State/Offender Paradigm in Adversarial Systems of Criminal Law and Justice." *Pandora's Box*: 25–35.

Konradi, Amanda. 2007. *Taking the Stand: Rape Survivors and the Prosecution of Rapists*. Westport, CT: Greenwood.

Konradi, Amanda, and Tina Burger. 2000. "Having the Last Word: An Examination of Rape Survivors' Participation in Sentencing." *Violence Against Women* 6(4): 351–395.

Kunst, Maarten, Lieke Popelier, and Ellen Varekamp. 2015. "Victim Satisfaction with the Criminal Justice System and Emotional Recovery: A Systematic and Critical Review of the Literature." *Trauma, Violence, & Abuse* 16(3): 336–358.

Kury, Helmut, and Michael Kilching. 2011. "Accessory Prosecution in Germany: Legislation and Implementation." In *Therapeutic Jurisprudence and Victim Participation in Justice*. Edited by Edna Erez, Michael Kilchling, and Jo-Anne Wemmers, 41–66. Durham: Carolina Academic Press.

Levine, Danielle. 2010. "Public Wrongs and Private Rights: Limiting the Victim's Role in a System of Public Prosecution. *Northwestern University Law Review* 104(1): 335–362.

Lomholt v. Iowa. 2003. 327 F.3d 748 (8th Cir.).

Lovan, Dylan. 2019. "Kentucky Supreme Court Voids Victim's Rights Amendment." *Associated Press*, June 13, 2019.

Lyon, T. D., and J. A. Dente. 2012. "Child Witnesses and the Confrontation Clause." *Journal of Criminal Law & Criminology* 102(4): 1181.

Martin, Patricia Yancey. 2005. *Rape Work: Victims, Gender, and Emotions in Organizational and Community Context*. New York: Routledge.

Martin, Patricia Yancey, and Marlene Powell. 1994. "Accounting for the 'Second Assault': Legal Organizations' Framing of Rape Victims." *Law & Social Inquiry* 19(4): 853–888.

Maryland v. Craig. 1990. 497 U.S. 836.

Mattox v. United States. 1895. 156 U.S. 237.

Nangegast, S. L., M. M. Baun, M. Megel, and M. Leibowitz. 1997. "The Effects of the Presence of a Companion Animal on Physiological Arousal and Behavioral Distress in Children During a Physical Examination." *Journal of Pediatric Nursing* 12(6): 323–330.

National Center for Prosecution of Child Abuse. 2012. "Closed-Circuit Televisions Statutes." *National District Attorneys Association* (August).

National Center for Victims of Crime. 2018. "Issues: Constitutional Amendments." Accessed Fall 2018. http://victimsofcrime.org.

National Crime Victim Law Institute. 2008. "Practical Tips and Legal Strategies for Easing Victims' Concerns About Testifying." *NCVLI News* (Winter).

O'Hear, Michael M. 2007. "Plea Bargaining and Victims: From Consultation to Guidelines." *Marquette Law Review* 91(1): 323–347.

O'Neill, Michael Edmund. 2010. "Private Vengeance and the Public Good." *University of Pennsylvania Journal of Constitutional Law* 12(3): 659–750.

O'Neill, Sarah, and Rachel Zajac. 2013. "Preparing Children for Cross-Examination: How Does Intervention Timing Influence Efficacy?" *Psychology, Public Policy, and Law* 19(3): 307–320.

O'Neill-Stephens, Ellen. 2010. "Courthouse Dogs Expand to Chile." *Wayback* June-August: 44–47.

Payne v. Tennessee. 1991. 501 U.S. 808.

Pemberton, Anthony, and Sandra Reynaers. 2011. "The Controversial Nature of Victim Participation: Therapeutic Benefits in Victim Impact Statements." In *Therapeutic Jurisprudence and Victim Participation in Justice*. Edited by Edna Erez, Michael Kilchling, and Jo-Anne Wemmers, 229–248. Durham: Carolina Academic Press.

Perry, Nancy W., and Bradley D. McAuliff. 1993. "The Use of Videotaped Child Testimony: Public Policy Implications." *Notre Dame Journal of Law, Ethics, and Public Policy* 7(2): 387–422.

People v. Burton. 1996. 556 N.W.2d 201 (Mich. Ct. App.).

People v. Lujan. 2012. 150 Cal. Rptr. 3d 727 (Cal. Ct. App.).

People v. Spence. 2012. 212 Cal.App.4th 478 (Cal. Ct. App.).

People v. Tohom. 2013. 109 A.D.3d 253 (N.Y. App. Div.).

Pokorak, Jeffrey J. 2007. "Rape Victims and Prosecutors: The Inevitable Ethical Conflict of De Facto Client/Attorney Relationships." *South Texas Law Review* 48(3): 695–731.

Pugach, Dana, and Michal Tamir. 2017. "Nudging the Criminal Justice System into Listening to Crime Victims in Plea Agreements." *Hastings Women's Law Journal* 28(1): 45–72.

Regehr, Cheryl, Ramona Alaggia, Liz Lambert, and Michael Saini. 2008. "Victims of Sexual Violence in the Canadian Criminal Courts." *Victims & Offenders* 3(1): 99–113.

Righarts, Saskia, Sarah O'Neill, and Rachel Zajac. 2013. "Addressing the Negative Effect of Cross-Examination Questioning on Children's Accuracy: Can We Intervene?" *Law and Human Behavior* 37(5): 354–365.

Roadcap v. Commonwealth. 2007. 653 S.E.2d 620 (Va. Ct. App.).

Roberts, Julian V. 2009. "Listening to the Crime Victim: Evaluating Victim Input at Sentencing and Parole." *Crime and Justice* 38(1): 347–412.

Schlam, Lawrence. 2015. "Enforcing Victims' Rights in Illinois: The Rationale for Victim 'Standing' in Criminal Prosecutions." *Valparaiso University Law Review* 49: 597–658.

Seiden, Daniel, and Steven J. Twist. 2012. "The Proposed Victims' Rights Amendment: A Brief Point/Counterpoint." *Phoenix Law Review* 5(2): 341–378.

State v. Dye. 2013. 309 P.3d 1192 (Wash.).

State v. Johnson. 2011. 958 N.E.2d 977 (Ohio Ct. App.).

State v. Millis. 2017. 391 P.3d 1225 (9th Cir.).

Thompson, Greg J. 2014. "Victims' Rights in the Military: Empowering Sexual Assault Victims with a Meaningful DOD Victims' Bill of Rights." *Virginia Journal of Social Policy and the Law* 21(3): 423–470.

Tluczek, Claire. 2008. "Traumatic Testimony: Easing Stress on Testifying Children While Protecting the Confrontation Rights of the Accused." *Michigan Child Welfare Law Journal* 11(4): 25–37.

Tyler, Tom. 1990. *Why People Obey the Law*. Princeton: Princeton University Press.

Tyler, Tom, and Yuen J. Huo. 2002. *Trust in the Law: Encouraging Public Cooperation with the Police and Courts*. New York: Russell Sage Foundation.

United States v. Sharp. 2006. 463 F. Supp. 2d 556 (E.D. Va.).

Wade, Marianne, Christopher Lewis, and Bruno Aubusson de Cavarlay. 2008. "Well-Informed? Well Represented? Well Nigh Powerless? Victims and Prosecutorial Decision-Making." *European Journal on Criminal Policy and Research* 14(2–3): 249–261.

Walther, Susanne. 2011. "Victims' Rights: Procedural and Constitutional Principles for Victim Participation in Germany." In *Therapeutic Jurisprudence and Victim Participation in Justice*. Edited by Edna Erez, Michael Kilchling, and Jo-Anne Wemmers, 97–111. Durham: Carolina Academic Press.

Winick, Bruce J. 2009. "Therapeutic Jurisprudence Perspectives on Dealing with Victims of Crime." *Nova Law Review* 33(3): 535–543.

Wolhuter, Lorraine. 2010. "German and Swedish Procedures as Models for the Empowerment of Racial Minority Women in Rape Trials." *International Journal of Law, Crime and Justice* 38(1): 1–16.

Young v. United States ex rel. Vuitton et Fils. 1987. 481 U.S. 787.

Zajac, Rachel, Julien Gross, and Harlene Hayne. 2003. "Asked and Answered: Questioning Children in the Courtroom." *Psychiatry, Psychology and Law* 10(1): 199–209.

Zweig, Janine, and Jennifer Yahner. 2013. "Providing Services to Victims of Crime." In *Victims of Crime*. Edited by Robert C. Davis, Arthur J. Lurigio, and Susan Herman, 325–348. Thousand Oaks, CA: SAGE Publications.

CHAPTER 19

PROSECUTORS AND VOTERS

CARISSA BYRNE HESSICK

19.1 INTRODUCTION

THE relationship between prosecutors and voters is complicated. As a formal matter, chief prosecutors in the United States are democratically accountable: they are either directly elected, or they are appointed by officials who are themselves democratically accountable. But in practice the accountability may be more apparent than real. Prosecutor elections are rarely contested. And even when voters have more than one candidate to choose from, they rarely have the information that they need to make an informed choice.

The question whether prosecutors ought to be democratically accountable—and if so, how much—is contested. On the one hand, prosecutors are extremely powerful. They have significant discretion in executing and enforcing the law. That discretion requires them to make important policy decisions—such as which crimes to prioritize and the circumstances under which to enforce the law. This policy power suggests that American prosecutors ought to be accountable—either directly or indirectly—to voters.

But, at the same time, there is a widely shared belief that individual criminal prosecutions should not be "political." And much of the discretion that prosecutors wield allows them to act not only as advocates, but also as the judge and jury. To the extent that prosecutors often act as adjudicators, rather than advocates, that suggests we ought to prioritize the independence of prosecutors above their accountability.

Other countries have struck a different balance. Many have limited prosecutorial discretion through their criminal codes or bureaucratic controls. And electoral control is, with few exceptions, far more attenuated outside of the United States. But that is not to say that other countries have not struggled with the question of how to balance independence and democratic control. Several countries have undertaken reforms that are aimed, in part, to adjusting that balance (Hodgson 2017, 85–96).

This essay surveys the complicated relationship between prosecutors and voters. It describes the various ways in which American prosecutors are accountable to voters. It surveys the empirical literature about how often voters hold—or are able to hold—their elected prosecutors accountable, as well as the empirical literature that seeks to measure the effects of elections on prosecutorial behavior. It makes some comparisons between the United States and other countries. And it summarizes the tension between the need for prosecutorial accountability and the need for independence.

19.2 Selecting Prosecutors in the United States

The United States is the only country that elects its chief prosecutors (Brown 2016, 28; Ellis 2012, 1530).[1] Elections make chief prosecutors accountable to voters. But there is variation in how, precisely, that accountability occurs. For example, there is variation in in the length of a chief prosecutor's term. Most states elect chief prosecutors for four-year terms. But some states have longer terms: Alabama, Kentucky, and Louisiana have six-year terms; Tennessee has eight-year terms. New Hampshire has short two-year terms. And Colorado imposes term limits on its prosecutors (Hessick and Morse 2020, 1552).

States also vary in how they deal with prosecutors who run unopposed in elections. Most states require incumbents to appear on the ballot and to obtain a certain percentage of votes in order to be re-elected. But a number of other states do not require candidates to appear on the ballot if they are unopposed; if they face no opposition, then they are simply declared the winner (Hessick and Morse 2020, 1554–1556). The effect of these laws can be quite dramatic. For example, when Louisiana held elections in 2014, twenty-seven of the forty-two district attorneys were unopposed (Hessick and Morse 2020, 1556–1557). As a consequence, more than half of the district attorneys in the state did not appear on the ballot. Obviously, if a race does not appear on the ballot, then voters cannot provide much in the way of accountability. What is more, when the office of prosecutor does not appear on the ballot, its absence may contribute to public misunderstanding about the political accountability of prosecutors. One recent study found that many Americans do not to know that their chief prosecutor is elected (Bazelon 2019, 78).

To be sure, not all chief prosecutors are elected. Most notably, United States Attorneys—the chief prosecutor in each federal district—are nominated by the President and confirmed by the Senate. Some states also appoint their chief prosecutors. In Alaska and Delaware, the elected Attorney General of the state appoints the local district attorneys.[2] New Jersey's appointment system resembles the federal model: the governor appoints chief prosecutors, and those prosecutors are confirmed by the state senate. In Connecticut, chief prosecutors are appointed by a criminal justice commission.

Rhode Island does not have local prosecutors; all criminal cases are prosecuted by the state Attorney General's Criminal Division. And three states—Hawaii, Montana, and North Dakota—employ a hybrid approach; chief prosecutors are either elected or appointed, depending on the county (Hessick and Morse 2020, 1551–1552).

As a general matter, elected chief prosecutors are answerable only to their local voters. State officials are not able to dictate local policies, nor are state officials able to remove local prosecutors. That is not to say that state officials are powerless to counteract decisions of local prosecutors with which they disagree. In New Hampshire, state law notes that locally elected prosecutors are "under the direction of the attorney general." Other states do not formally subordinate their local prosecutors to state officials. They do, however, permit state officials—often the attorney general—to remove a case from the control of a local prosecutor and prosecute it herself. And while some states permit cases to be removed from local prosecutors only under very limited circumstances, other states place essentially no limits on the power of state officials to take over these cases (Yeargain 2018). Importantly, while most states have these laws allowing state officials to supersede the decisions of local prosecutors, those laws are rarely used, and so prosecution remains a largely local affair. Indeed, these laws are used so infrequently that instances of their invocation have garnered national headlines (Berman 2017; Robles 2017).

Even when prosecutors are appointed, they still remain accountable—at least indirectly—to voters. Take, for example, federal prosecutors. The primary democratic check on federal prosecutors is the presidential election. The president can select the individuals he or she wants to appoint as U.S. Attorney, and the president has the ability to fire the U.S. Attorney. To be sure, the President's power to appoint the U.S. Attorney is limited by the Senate's power to confirm. But Senators are also elected, and so their confirmation power is another indirect democratic check on federal prosecutors.

19.3 Measuring Democratic Control through Elections

American prosecutors are, as a formal matter, democratically accountable. But that accountability may be more apparent than real. Incumbent prosecutors are almost always reelected. And voters rarely have the information they would need to make informed choices in those elections. As for appointed prosecutors, once they are appointed, they are rarely removed. What is more, once appointed, they are often insulated from the wishes of the elected officials who appointed them.

Several empirical studies of prosecutor elections tell us that, as a practical matter, voters do not exercise their control over prosecutors very often. For example, in a study of fifteen states over multiple election cycles, Professor Ronald Wright documented that incumbent prosecutors rarely face challengers in elections, and are usually reelected even when they do face challengers (Wright 2009; 2014). In particular, Wright found that approximately 80 percent of incumbent prosecutors ran for reelection unopposed and that approximately two-thirds of incumbent prosecutors won reelection when challenged (Wright 2014, 601). Importantly, because so few prosecutors ran in contested elections, the reelection rate for incumbents was almost 95 percent.

Sam Krumholz also found that most prosecutor elections were uncontested. Krumholz collected data on 6,620 separate local prosecutor elections from multiple election cycles; his data set included at least one election return for 84 percent of the counties that elect chief prosecutors. He found that 75 percent of those races were uncontested (Krumholz 2018).

A study by the Prosecutors and Politics Project at the University of North Carolina confirmed both that prosecutor elections are rarely contested and that incumbents usually win (Hessick and Morse 2020). The PPP study collected data about every prosecutor election in the country for a single election cycle. It found that 70 percent of all local prosecutor elections were uncontested in both the primary and general elections and that incumbents were reelected 95 percent of the time that they ran. It also found that elections for open seats—that is, elections in which no incumbent was running—were unopposed 47 percent of the time.

Prosecutor elections are least likely to be contested in rural areas and districts with small populations (Hessick and Morse 2020, 1566; Wright 2014, 601–602). Indeed, some small counties are unable to identify even a single eligible candidate to run for local prosecutor. Those jurisdictions have to appoint a prosecutor (Hessick and Morse 2020, 1575).

Wright also studied the media coverage of prosecutor elections (Wright 2009). He found that election coverage largely focused on the candidates' individual qualifications, rather than the performance of the office (Wright 2009, 600–602). And when campaign rhetoric did speak about results, those results were framed almost entirely in terms of the quantity of cases processed rather than "the practices of the office related to plea bargaining or screening of cases that the local police recommend for prosecution" (Wright 2009, 604–605). As Wright notes: "All told, prosecutor elections do not provide voters with meaningful information to evaluate the work of the incumbent," which makes elections "highly imperfect mechanisms to promote accountability" for prosecutors (Wright 2009, 605).

Like their elected counterparts, appointed officials rarely face removal for their decisions. In the federal system, for example, Presidents have the authority to both appoint and remove U.S. Attorneys. But Presidents have rarely chosen to remove U.S. Attorneys that they appointed. What is more, there appears to be a prevailing norm against Presidents removing U.S. Attorneys merely because they insufficiently implement the President's policy priorities. For example, several U.S. Attorneys were asked to resign in 2007, based, in part, on those prosecutors' failure to be "vigorous in challenging voter fraud and in prosecuting immigration violations," "insufficient gun crime prosecution," and "resistance to taking up a death penalty case." Although these would seem to be matters of policy over which elected officials should have control, the firings prompted such a strong backlash that the Attorney General Alberto Gonzales resigned (Driesen 2008, 710–714). Simply put, it is hard to square a norm against removal for policy reasons with democratic accountability of appointed prosecutors.

19.4 Measuring Democratic Control through Prosecutorial Decisions

Despite the paucity of contested elections, voters may nonetheless influence the decisions that prosecutors make. That is because prosecutors may change their behavior in anticipation of an upcoming election. Even if incumbent prosecutors are unlikely to face a challenger or unlikely to lose an election, they might nonetheless perceive a risk of that happening. And thus elections may influence prosecutorial decisions even without any turnover in the office (Wright 2009, 596–597).

There is a small, but growing literature that identifies an "election effect" on prosecutors. That literature documents changes in prosecutorial behavior in the time period leading up to elections. The election effect is premised on the "political business cycle theory" (Dyke 2007, 419). The political business cycle theory tells us that elected officials alter their behavior in advance of an election in order to maximize their chances of reelection.

The election effect literature proceeds from a basic premise: voters evaluate prosecutors based on the convictions they obtain, and a prosecutor will be deemed more successful if she obtains more convictions (Gordon and Huber 2002; Rasmusen, Raghav, and Ramseyer 2009). Prosecutors can dispose of cases in three basic ways: They can convince a defendant to plead guilty, they can dismiss the charge(s), or they can bring a case to trial. Guilty pleas obviously increase convictions—they permit prosecutors to process cases more quickly and efficiently than trials, and they also remove the possibility that the defendant might be acquitted. Dismissing charges obviously reduces convictions—a decision to dismiss charges is necessarily a decision not to obtain a conviction. Bringing cases to trial will result in fewer convictions than guilty pleas, but more convictions than dismissing charges. That is because trials may end in either a conviction or an acquittal.

Even though convictions are less certain following a trial rather than plea bargaining, voters may nonetheless prefer prosecutors who take cases to trial. Prosecutors who take cases to trial may send signals to voters about their competence and quality (Bandyopadhyay and McCannon 2013; 2014). After all, winning a criminal trial is harder than negotiating a plea bargain. Trials often garner more media attention than plea bargaining, helping prosecutors establish or maintain name recognition. And trial success is more consistent with popular culture depictions of prosecutors—who routinely take cases to trial—than is plea bargaining success (Bibas 2006, 924–925). Taking a case to trial may also result in a longer sentence for the defendant. That is because a defendant who is convicted after a trial usually receives a significantly longer sentence than a similarly situated defendant who plea bargains.[3] Prosecutors can point to those long sentences when telling voters that they have worked to protect public safety.

While the election effect theory seems logical, the elections effect studies are somewhat mixed. For example, one study documented a decrease in case dismissals when prosecutors run for re-election (Dyke 2007). Dismissing fewer cases is consistent with the election effect theory because any case that is dismissed cannot result in a conviction. But a separate study showed that prosecutor elections were correlated with an increase in case dismissals (McCannon 2018, 17). And a third study found only a very small reduction in case dismissals (Bandyopadhyay and McCannon 2017, 25). Importantly, there is a relatively small number of studies about the election effects on prosecutorial behavior, especially as compared to the number of studies about election effects on judicial behavior; more studies of additional jurisdictions might indicate clearer trends.

To be sure, there are some studies that have documented an effect from elections. For example, one study documented that prosecutors took a larger number and a higher percentage of cases to trial in the period leading up to elections (Bandyopadhyay and McCannon 2014). And a separate study found that prosecution wins at trial were more likely in years when prosecutors were facing elections (McCannon 2018, 4). But not all findings were consistent with the election effect theory. One study found that prosecutors were less likely to file charges in the time leading up to election. That same study also found that, although convicted defendants were more likely to be admitted to prison in the period leading up to elections, their sentences were shorter. As the study authors noted, although they found an election effect, "the direction of the effect . . . was contrary to initial expectations" (Nadel, Scaggs, and Bales 2017, 858).

The empirical evidence is also mixed regarding changes in prosecutorial behavior for those incumbents who are facing a challenger, as opposed to those who are not. One study found an effect (Nadel, Scaggs, and Bales 2017, 859), while another did not (Bandyopadhyay and McCannon 2013). And a third study found stronger election effects in districts that have historically seen more electoral competition, rather than focusing on whether a particular election involved a challenger (Dyke 2007, 431–434).

Put simply, the currently available studies do not consistently support the theory that prosecutors will seek more convictions and longer sentences in the period leading up to an election.[4] It is certainly possible that future studies might find consistent and sustained effects of elections on prosecutorial behavior. But unless and until that occurs, there are reasons to be skeptical that elections influence prosecutorial decisions to increase convictions and sentences. For example, there are practical reasons to doubt the election effect theory. That is because most cases are handled by assistant prosecutors, rather than by the chief prosecutor. While chief prosecutors must stand for election, assistant prosecutors are not elected; they are permanent employees and they often enjoy civil service protection that shields them from firing for purely political reasons. To be sure, the chief prosecutor can try to control some of the decisions that assistant prosecutors make by issuing office policies and appointing office supervisors. But there are limits to those tactics (Ouziel 2020; Richman 2005), and the elected prosecutor is unlikely to issue an office policy that says, "An election is coming, so let's look tougher on crime."

There are also logical reasons to doubt the election effect theory. The election effect assumes that prosecutors are acting rationally—namely that they are changing their behavior in order to maximize their chances of reelection. But a rational prosecutor would doubtlessly know that their reelection rate is unbelievably high: if a prosecutor runs for reelection, she has a greater than 90 percent chance of being reelected. Given how high that reelection rate is, it seems unlikely that prosecutors are unaware of the fact that they can essentially skate to reelection. And yet the theory does not account for that fact. What is more, those prosecutors who appear to be most likely to face a challenger—prosecutors in large, urban jurisdictions—appear to be less punitive than prosecutors who appear to be least likely to face a challenger—prosecutors is smaller, rural jurisdictions (Hessick and Morse 2020, 1566–1567, 1587).

In sum, although the election effect may be logically appealing, we cannot say with certainty that it exists.

19.5 Democratic Control and Independence

In addition to the empirical literature on prosecutors and elections, there is also a literature on the tension between democratic accountability and professional independence for prosecutors. This literature explains that there is a tradeoff between accountability and independence (Brown 2016, 25–59; Davis 2001, 438; Richman 2017; Tonry 2012). The tradeoff is that we want prosecutors to be democratically accountable, but we also want them to be able to exercise their professional judgment free from political pressure. Take, for example, the recent outcry about prosecutors who have not brought charges against police officers for what appear to be unjustified shootings of civilians. Some prosecutors appear to have lost elections for failure to sufficiently pursue these cases (Levitz 2018). If those electoral losses led prosecutors to bring charges in *all* police shooting cases—even those where the evidence suggested that the officer's use of force was justified—then accountability would have interfered with independence.

Those who value independence over accountability often express the concern that democratic pressures will lead government officials to act more punitively. This concern is based on the assumption that the general public tends to favor punitive criminal justice policy (Beale 1997; Nourse 2004). Some have noted that existing political accountability for prosecutors is skewed by the fact that those who are most impacted by the criminal justice system often have their views underrepresented in elections (Johnson 2016, 450; Michaelson 2015). Some are willing to tolerate elections, but they point to the advantages of placing at least some questions of crime policy in the hands of criminal justice professionals (sentencing commissions, advisory panels, and so on), which are more removed from majoritarian politics (Barker 2009; Lacey 2010). Others have argued that accountability should not trump independence, and thus prosecutors ought not be elected (Tonry 2012, 12). And many note that the United States is unique in the balance that it has struck in the accountability-independence tradeoff: the United States is the only country that directly elects prosecutors, while other Western democracies placed much more value on independence (Brown 2016, 28).

While other countries do not directly elect their prosecutors, some have ensured indirect democratic control. For example, the French prosecution service is hierarchically accountable to the Minister of Justice, a cabinet level official. Thus, while prosecutors themselves are not subject to elections, they are situated within a hierarchy that ultimately depends on voters (Weigand 2012, 390). Prosecutors in Germany are also situated within a hierarchy that culminates with the Minister of Justice (Boyne 2017, 148–149). Bureaucratic hierarchy is not the only way in which democratic control is exercised. In England and Wales, for example, the adoption of new prosecution policies includes a practice of public consultation, which ensures that those policies are shaped, in part, by public opinion (Hodgson 2017, 102).

The precise amount of democratic control in these other countries has been in flux (Di Federico 1998, 373). For example, France has sought to increase independence by requiring the Minister of Justice to give all instructions to prosecutors in writing and by forbidding the Minister of Justice from issuing instructions to French prosecutors in individual cases (Di Federico 1998, 374; Hodgson 2017, 102). Importantly, not all countries provide for democratic control. Italy, for example, has effectively insulated its prosecutors from political influence, eschewing a balance between accountability and independence and instead prioritizing independence at the expense of accountability (Di Federico 1998). And the balance that these other countries have struck must be understood against the backdrop of very different criminal justice system structures—including inquisitorial, as compared to adversarial systems—as well as different understandings of what it means for an official to be independent and what qualifies as democratic accountability (Boyne 2017, 140; Hodgson 2017, 96).

To be sure, the discussion in the United States surrounding accountability and independence does not uniformly favor increased independence. For example, Russell Gold has argued that, because prosecutors "act on the public's behalf, their decisions should reflect their constituents' preferences" (Gold 2011, 71). And Angela Davis, has argued that increased democratic accountability might help to cabin prosecutorial discretion and to curb prosecutorial misconduct (Davis 2001, 438–440). Both Gold and Davis, however, detail the many ways our current system actually fails to supply sufficient accountability in practice.

Striking an appropriate balance between accountability and independence is complicated by the fact that prosecutors perform many roles in the criminal justice system. They not only enforce the laws in particular cases, but they also adopt general enforcement policies (Lemos 2017). In the United States, those general enforcement policies, at least in some respects, function as substantive criminal codes. That is because prosecutors cannot possibly enforce the laws in all situations, and so some prosecutors decide which cases to prioritize through the use of enforcement criteria, rather than deciding which cases to prosecute on an ad hoc basis. Enforcement criteria are especially important when legislatures adopt overly broad laws. Lawmakers do not expect prosecutors to enforce the law as written; and so whatever enforcement policies the prosecutor adopts is, in essence, the "real law" (Hessick 2019, 992–996).

Notably, this broad policy discretion is not necessarily the norm outside of the United States. In England and Wales, for example, prosecution decisions are often split among multiple actors—some of whom are non-lawyers who act in a purely ministerial fashion. This bureaucratic model reduces the power of any single prosecutor, resulting in the standardization of decision-making across cases (Hodgson 2017, 89–90, 103). Even in France, where prosecutors enjoy more discretion, that discretion is ordinarily exercised "in more standardized and pre-determined ways" (Hodgson 2017, 94).

When prosecutors enjoy substantial enforcement discretion, as they do in the United States, then they are, in a very real sense, determining the content of the substantive criminal law through their enforcements policies.[5] Democratic accountability for this policymaking seems desirable. Yet enforcement policies are rarely made public in the United States, and so voters do not know what policies their prosecutors have adopted (Hessick 2019, 997–999).[6]

Modern criminal prosecutors also have a dual role after deciding whether to prosecute an individual. In those situations they function not only as advocates for the state in adversarial litigation, but also as adjudicators (Sklansky 2017, 277). Prosecutors function as advocates when they try cases before juries or argue before a judge in favor of a particular position. But much of the power that prosecutors have is exercised outside of the courtroom in charging and plea bargaining. As other chapters in this volume explain, prosecutors have a lot of discretion in deciding whether to bring charges and the types of charges to bring.[7] And prosecutorial leverage in plea bargaining allows prosecutors to essentially dictate a defendant's sentence in many cases. So, to a great extent, the charging and bargaining power exercised by prosecutors is, at least functionally, the power to convict and the power to sentence—powers that are ordinarily exercised by judges and juries.

To the extent that prosecutors are acting as adjudicators, they resemble judges and juries, and so it may seem appropriate to insulate them from accountability and ensure independence. After all, we often seek to ensure the independence of judges and juries by insulating them from external pressures.

There is a significant literature about the accountability-independence tradeoff for judges (Atchison, Liebert, and Russell 1999), the great majority of which emphasizes the need for independence. And unlike prosecutors—who are overwhelmingly selected as a result of direct elections—judges are often more insulated from political pressure. To be sure, some judges are directly elected in competitive elections; but others are appointed according to a merit selection plan and are subject only to retention elections (Shugerman 2012).[8] Federal judges, of course, enjoy great independence because they have life tenure. And the amount of independence that state judges enjoy depends not only on the state, but also whether the judge serves on the trial court, an intermediate appellate court, or the state supreme court (Brennan Center 2019).

We also take efforts to shield juries from political pressure: they are instructed not to read any news stories or consume any media about the case. That is (at least in part) because we do not want them to be influenced by the opinions of others. We sometimes even withhold the names of jurors from the public—ostensibly because we do not want them to be subject to threats or harassment, but the practice also shields them from informal accountability, such as the potential disapproval of their friends and neighbors.

Importantly, a prosecutor's exercise of charging and bargaining power is not particularly transparent.[9] When prosecutors act as advocates—that is, when they try cases in front of juries or when they argue for certain positions in front of judges—their actions are quite public. Public access to courtrooms is both expected and protected by law. But charging and bargaining decisions are conducted in low-visibility settings. It is difficult for members of the public to know whether a prosecutor has offered a defendant a plea bargaining for the most serious readily provable charge, or whether the defendant has been allowed to plead guilty to a far less serious crime. And, as noted above, charging and bargaining are rarely the subject of discussion in prosecutor campaigns. If voters are unaware of how prosecutors wield their charging and bargaining power, and if it would be difficult for voters to discover that information, then they cannot hold their prosecutors responsible for those decisions. Thus, when it comes to these adjudicatory-like functions, prosecutors enjoy significant independence and almost no accountability.

To be sure, charging and bargaining decisions need not remain opaque. Some prosecutors have released case processing data (Rice 2018; Sernoffsky 2019), and some have permitted researchers to examine their files (Kutateladze, Tymas, and Crowley 2014). Local media, potential challengers, and other stakeholders could ask incumbent prosecutors for more information about their charging and bargaining decisions. And voters could punish prosecutors who fail to provide that information by voting against them in elections. Put differently, because they are accountable, prosecutors could be required to be more transparent.

But more transparency in charging and bargaining decisions brings us back to the accountability-independence tradeoff. If plea bargains are suddenly more transparent, then the public may demand that prosecutors offer less favorable plea terms to defendants. Prosecutors might respond to that pressure by obtaining sentences that are harsher than they deem necessary. Or prosecutors might be less likely to file charges in the first instance. While it is not clear what the result of more transparency might be, the assumption that it is likely to change prosecutorial behavior is, at bottom, an acknowledgment that prosecutors might allow electoral concerns to trump their independent judgment.

There is no consensus about how we ought to strike the balance between accountability and independence for prosecutors. But there is a relatively clear consensus that the accountability mechanisms we currently have are not functioning robustly: because most prosecutor elections are uncontested, voters rarely have the opportunity to exert control at the ballot box. And because important prosecutorial decisions—such as the setting of enforcement policies, the selection of charges, and plea bargaining—are largely shielded from public view, voters do not have enough information to make an informed decision in those elections.

Notes

1. As Ellis notes, "[t]he Swiss cantons of Geneva, Basel-City, and Tessin elect judges who have a prosecutorial function, but they are not public prosecutors in the common-law sense of the office" (Ellis 2012, 1530).
2. In Delaware, the Attorney General is directly elected; whereas in Alaska, the Attorney General is appointed by the Governor.
3. This increase in sentences is often referred to as the "trial penalty," and its existence has been widely documented (Kim 2015).
4. The inconsistency in study results has not necessarily deterred those who conduct these studies from arguing in favor of the existence of the election effect. They have hypothesized that the difference in the cases studied may explain the inconsistent results (Nadel, Scaggs, and Bales 2017, 858). Or they have hypothesized that the effect they expected to observe actually existed, but was not easily observed because of other behaviors (Nadel, Scaggs, and Bales 2017, 858–859).
5. In addition to their power to shape criminal justice policy through enforcement decisions, prosecutors in some jurisdictions are heavily involved in the formal legislative process, lobbying in favor or against particular pieces of legislation. See Russell M. Gold in Chapter 16 in this volume.
6. For a discussion that complicates the relationship between accountability and transparency, see Green (2019).
7. See Matt Barno and Mona Lynch, Nora V. Demleitner, Salmon Shomade, and Cassia Spohn in Chapters 2, 7, 9, and 12 of this volume.
8. Notably, the studies of election effects on judges suggest that judges who must stand only for retention elections, as compared to direct elections, may also decide cases differently as election dates approach (Huber and Gordon 2004). But the effect, to the extent that it exists, appears to be much weaker for judges facing retention elections than those facing competitive direct elections (Gordon and Huber 2007; Levine and Cooke 2015).
9. This lack of transparency surrounding a prosecutor's adjudicatory decisions stands in stark contrast to the transparency of decisions by judges and juries. Judges' decisions are enshrined in opinions or orders, both of which are a matter of public record. Similarly, a jury's decision is always transparent—it is declared in open court whether the jury finds the defendant guilty or not guilty, and that verdict then becomes part of the public record.

References

Atchison, Amy B., Lawrence T. Liebert, and Denise K. Russell. 1999. "Judicial Independence and Judicial Accountability: A Selected Bibliography." *Southern California Law Review* 72(2–3): 723–810.

Bandyopadhyay, Siddhartha, and Bryan C. McCannon. 2013. "Re-election Concerns and the Failure of Plea Bargaining." *Theoretical Economics Letters* 3(5B): 40–44.

Bandyopadhyay, Siddhartha, and Bryan C. McCannon. 2014. "The Effect of the Election of Prosecutors on Criminal Trials." *Public Choice* 161(1/2): 141–156.

Bandyopadhyay, Siddhartha, and Bryan C. McCannon. 2017. "Queuing Up for Justice: Prosecutor Elections and Case Backlogs." https://ssrn.com/abstract=3097736.

Barker, Vanessa. 2009. *The Politics of Imprisonment: How the Democratic Process Shapes the Way America Punishes Offenders*. New York: Oxford University Press.

Bazelon, Emily. 2019. *Charged: The New Movement to Transform American Prosecution and End Mass Incarceration*. New York: Random House.

Beale, Sara Sun. 1997. "What's Law Got to Do with It? The Political, Social, Psychological and Other Non-legal Factors Influencing the Development of (Federal) Criminal Law." *Buffalo Criminal Law Review* 1(1): 23–66.

Berman, Mark. 2017. "After Florida Prosecutor Says She Won't Seek Death Penalty, Governor Reassigns Case of Slain Police Officer." *Washington Post*, March 16, 2017.

Bibas, Stephanos. 2006. "Transparency and Participation in Criminal Procedure." *New York University Law Review* 81(3): 911–966.

Boyne, Shawn. 2017. "German Prosecutors and the Rechtstaat." In *Prosecutors and Democracy: A Cross-National Study*. Edited by Máximo Langer and David Sklansky, 138–174. Cambridge: Cambridge University Press.

Brennan Center for Justice. 2019. "Judicial Selection: An Interactive Map." Accessed October 15, 2019. http://judicialselectionmap.brennancenter.org/?court=Supreme.

Brown, Darryl K. 2016. *Free Market Criminal Justice: How Democracy and Laissez Faire Undermine the Rule of Law*. Oxford: Oxford University Press.

Davis, Angela J. 2001. "The American Prosecutor: Independence, Power, and the Threat of Tyranny." *Iowa Law Review* 86(2): 393–466.

Di Federico, Giuseppe. 1998. "Prosecutorial Independence and the Democratic Requirement of Accountability in Italy." *British Journal of Criminology* 38(3): 371–387.

Driesen, David M. 2008. "Firing U.S. Attorneys: An Essay." *Administrative Law Review* 60(3): 707–728.

Dyke, Andrew. 2007. "Electoral Cycles in the Administration of Criminal Justice." *Public Choice* 133 (3–4): 417–437.

Ellis, Michael J. 2012. "The Origins of the Elected Prosecutor." *Yale Law Journal* 121(6): 1528–1570.

Gold, Russell M. 2011. "Promoting Democracy in Prosecution." *Washington Law Review* 86(1): 69–124.

Gordon, Sanford C., and Gregory A. Huber. 2002. "Citizen Oversight and the Electoral Incentives of Criminal Prosecutors." *American Journal of Political Science* 46(2): 334–351.

Gordon, Sanford C., and Gregory A. Huber. 2007. "The Effect of Electoral Competitiveness on Incumbent Behavior." *Quarterly Journal of Political Science* 2(2): 107–138.

Green, Bruce A. 2019. "Prosecutors in the Court of Public Opinion." *Duquesne Law Review* 57(2): 271–292.

Hessick, Carissa Byrne. 2019. "The Myth of Common Law Crimes." *Virginia Law Review* 105(5): 965–1024.

Hessick, Carissa Byrne, and Michael Morse. 2020. "Picking Prosecutors." *Iowa Law Review* 105(4): 1537–1590.

Hodgson, Jacqueline S. 2017. "The Democratic Accountability of Prosecutors in England and Wales and France: Independence, Discretion and Managerialism." In *Prosecutors and Democracy: A Cross-National Study*. Edited by Máximo Langer and David Sklansky, 40–75. Cambridge: Cambridge University Press.

Huber, Gregory A., and Sanford C. Gordon. 2004. "Accountability and Coercion: Is Justice Blind When It Runs for Office?" *American Journal of Political Science* 48(2): 247–263.

Johnson, Brock A. 2016. "Voting Rights and the History of Institutionalized Racism: Criminal Disenfranchisement in the United States and South Africa." *Georgia Journal of International & Comparative Law* 44(2): 401–450.

Kim, Andrew Chongseh. 2015. "Underestimating the Trial Penalty: An Empirical Analysis of the Federal Trial Penalty and Critique of the Abrams Study." *Mississippi Law Journal* 84(5): 1195–1256.

Krumholz, Sam. 2018. "The Effect of District Attorneys on Local Criminal Justice Outcomes." October 31, 2018. https://ssrn.com/abstract=3243162.

Kutateladze, Besiki, Whitney Tymas, and Mary Crowley. 2014. *Race and Prosecution in Manhattan*. New York: Vera Institute of Justice.

Lacey, Nicola. 2010. "American Imprisonment in Comparative Perspective." *Daedalus* 139(3): 102–114.

Lemos, Margaret H. 2017. "Democratic Enforcement? Accountability and Independence for the Litigation State." *Cornell Law Review* 102(4): 929–1002.

Levine, Dan, and Kristina Cooke. 2015. "Uneven Justice: In States with Elected High Court Judges, a Harder Line on Capital Punishment." *Reuters*, September 22, 2015.

Levitz, Eric. 2018. "Progressive Reformer Ousts Prosecutor Who Didn't Charge Michael Brown Case." *New York Magazine*, August 8, 2018.

McCannon, Bryan C. 2018. "Debundling Accountability: Prosecutor and Public Defender Elections in Florida." https://ssrn.com/abstract=3204623.

Michaelson, Jay. 2015. "95% of Prosecutors Are White and They Treat Blacks Worse." *Daily Beast*, August 17, 2015.

Nadel, Melissa R., Samuel J. Scaggs, and William D. Bales. 2017. "Politics in Punishment: The Effect of the State Attorney Election Cycle on Conviction and Sentencing Outcomes in Florida." *American Journal of Criminal Justice* 42(4): 845–862.

Nourse, Victoria F. 2004. "Rethinking Crime Legislation: History and Harshness." *Tulsa Law Review* 39(4): 925–940.

Ouziel, Lauren M. 2020. "Democracy, Bureaucracy, and Criminal Justice Reform." *Boston College Law Review* 61(2): 523–589.

Rasmusen, Eric, Manu Raghav, and Mark Ramseyer. 2009. "Convictions Versus Conviction Rates: The Prosecutor's Choice." *American Law & Economics Review* 11(1): 47–78.

Rice, Josie Duffy. 2018. "Kim Foxx Just Released Six Years of Data—Most Prosecutors' Offices Remain Black Boxes." *The Appeal*, March 7, 2018.

Richman, Daniel C. 2005. "Institutional Coordination and Sentencing Reform." *Texas Law Review* 84(7): 2055–2074.

Richman, Daniel C. 2017. "Accounting for Prosecutors." In *Prosecutors and Democracy: A Cross-National Study*. Edited by Máximo Langer and David Sklansky, 40–75. Cambridge: Cambridge University Press.

Robles, Frances. 2017. "Lock 'Em Up? Prosecutors Who Say 'Not So Fast' Face a Backlash." *New York Times*, March 30, 2017.

Sernoffsky, Evan. 2019. "SF DA Gascon Launches State's First Website Showing Prosecution Data." *San Francisco Chronicle*, May 29, 2019.

Shugerman, Jed Handlesman. 2012. *The People's Courts: Pursuing Judicial Independence in America*. Cambridge: Harvard University Press.

Sklansky, David Alan. 2017. "Unpacking the Relationship between Prosecutors and Democracy in the United States." In *Prosecutors and Democracy: A Cross-National Study*. Edited by Máximo Langer and David Sklansky, 276–299. Cambridge: Cambridge University Press.

Tonry, Michael. 2012. "Prosecutors and Politics in Comparative Perspective." In *Crime and Justice* 41(1): 1–33.

Weigand, Thomas. 2012. "A Judge by Any Other Name? Comparative Perspectives on the Role of the Public Prosecutor." In *The Prosecutor in Transnational Perspective*. Edited by Erik Luna and Marianne L. Wade, 377–391. Oxford: Oxford University Press.

Wright, Ronald F. 2009. "How Prosecutor Elections Fail Us." *Ohio State Journal of Criminal Law* 6(2): 581–610.

Wright, Ronald F. 2014. "Beyond Prosecutor Elections." *SMU Law Review* 67(3): 593–616.

Yeargain, Tyler Quinn. 2018. "Discretion Versus Supersession: Calibrating the Power Balance Between Local Prosecutors and State Officials." *Emory Law Journal* 68(1): 95–138.

CHAPTER 20

COMMUNITY PROSECUTION AND BUILDING TRUST ACROSS A RACIAL DIVIDE

RONALD F. WRIGHT

20.1 Introduction

For as long as public prosecutor offices have existed, they have struggled over how to include the public in their work. This struggle involves both the people who should influence prosecutors and the timing of that influence. When it comes to the question of who should have influence, the prosecutor does not take direction from a single client as other lawyers do; a prosecutor's client is the entire public. In another sense, the prosecutor's client is the rule of law itself (Bellin 2020). Within that institutional framework, other legal actors can properly influence the prosecutor's work while remaining within their own assigned roles.

As for the timing of public influence, the public prosecutor must enforce criminal statutes that were created through democratic processes across many years. Yet current residents and voters have their own present-day priorities about how the prosecutor should achieve public safety in the local area. Prosecutors can listen to those current public priorities because they have discretion—in some systems more and in some systems less—about which criminal charges to prioritize. To compound the difficulties of the job, the public grants a limited operating budget to the prosecutor's office and the courts, funding something less than full enforcement of the criminal law. Taken together, these conflicting signals, sent from different directions, leave prosecutors with no clear guidance from the public about their office objectives.

This chapter explores what happens when prosecutors try to obtain input from the community about how to carry out their duties. These efforts sometimes take on the title of "community prosecution." The community prosecution philosophy aims to build a relationship of trust between the office and the people it serves, especially in those places where trust is hard to find. Under the community prosecution model, members of the community start to trust prosecutors when they can shape the priorities of the office. The results, hopefully, are greater public safety and stronger legitimacy of criminal justice systems in the eyes of the people who interact most directly with prosecutors, courts, police, and social support agencies.

In many places (particularly in the United States), a history of racial injustice looms over the relationship between the prosecutor's office and the community. Because of repeated bad interactions between prosecutors and police on the one side, and racial minorities and economically stressed neighborhoods on the other side, prosecutors must attempt to cross a chasm of distrust. Thus, any survey of actual experience with community prosecution must address race along with any particular programs or habits that a prosecutor's office might choose.

This chapter begins with a quick review of methods that different legal systems use to hold prosecutors accountable, whether through elections or bureaucratic discipline. After that, I consider why some prosecutors supplement the input they receive from voters during election campaigns through ongoing partnerships with community groups.

My account then turns to the *activities* of community prosecution offices, emphasizing how they differ from those taken by the traditional prosecution office. These activities include those "upstream" from the courtroom to prevent crime or to divert potential criminal defendants out of the criminal courts and into other programs for accountability and restorative justice. Prosecutors also partner with community groups to develop innovative non-incarceration sentences and "downstream" re-entry programs for people who return to the community at the end of their incarceration sentences.

The final sections of this chapter discuss the internal and external *prerequisites* to implementing the community prosecution model. From the external vantage point, I review the options that prosecutors face when they select partners in the community. From an internal perspective, the chapter closes by discussing the changes to office culture, hiring, and organization that can best support strong relationships with community groups. Commitments to collection and use of data, transparency, and accountability are all helpful in the effort to build community trust.

Prosecutors in many places endorse the general goal of a community prosecution philosophy, to increase legitimacy for the prosecutor's work in the most challenged communities. Consultation with community groups delivers the most value where racial inequality and economic injustice have created the deepest distrust of prosecutors. The particular uses of community consultation vary enormously, though, both within the United States and around the world. The design challenge is to match the features of specific community prosecutor programs with local needs.

20.2 Methods of Holding Prosecutors Democratically Accountable

Public prosecutors did not always handle criminal cases. Across many types of legal systems around the world, the victims of crimes brought their own cases into the courts to convince the state to punish those who harmed them. Sometimes the victims represented themselves and sometimes they employed a lawyer to press their claims (Langbein 2003). Eventually, however, governments everywhere created public prosecutors to litigate ordinary criminal claims (Fairfax 2009).

After government-employed prosecutors started acting on behalf of the entire public, legal systems around the world had to develop methods for holding prosecutors accountable to the public (Parrillo 2013; Sklansky 2017). For most state court prosecutors in the United States, local elections keep prosecutors attuned to public sentiment. Chief prosecutors in forty-five of the fifty states in the United States are elected at the local level, while a few leaders of local prosecutor offices—and U.S. Attorneys, the chief prosecutors in the federal courts—are appointed by elected officials.

In legal systems elsewhere in the world, prosecutors remain accountable because they operate within well-drafted codes of criminal law and criminal procedure, passed by democratically elected legislatures. In addition, prosecutors outside the United States work inside large units of the national government and follow regular bureaucratic routines. Elected officials in parliamentary systems, such as the Minister of Justice, determine the general policies and priorities that prosecutors must follow as they enforce the criminal law. These organizational constraints—some bureaucratic, some democratic—keep prosecutors within legal bounds and add to their legitimacy in the eyes of the public (Luna and Wade 2010; Wright and Miller 2010).

20.3 Why Prosecutors Need Input from Community Groups

Sometimes, however, these front-line methods of gaining public trust are simply not enough. Elections send only blunt signals to prosecutors because too often, voters do not learn anything about prosecutor office practices beyond success or failure in a few high-profile cases. This is particularly true when incumbents run unopposed and never have to explain to voters what they have done.[1] Elections also offer little guidance to prosecutors in between electoral cycles (Wright 2014). As for the more bureaucratic national prosecutor services around the world, the organizations and rules that produce national uniformity also fail to account for special local conditions. This leaves local offices of the national prosecutor service unable to address the problems that most concern people (Center for Court Innovation 2009).

These "democracy deficits" among prosecutors create the most intense problems with racial minorities and low-wealth neighborhoods. These groups too often have negative interactions with police, prosecutors, and other criminal justice officials. Their destructive experiences produce a lack of trust and legitimacy (Lanni 2005; Tyler 2007). Because the people most affected by a traumatic experience with one agency (say, the police) do not readily distinguish among different units of government, their distrust and disengagement with that one official or entity can infect their attitude towards all components of criminal justice systems, including the prosecutor.

High levels of distrust can create a public safety disaster, because prosecutors need witnesses of crimes to step forward and to testify in court. But that sort of witness cooperation requires confidence in the system, which is only possible when people believe they will be heard. Instead, police often find people at a crime scene who feel that the police and the courts have never treated them fairly. In response, they refuse to help police solve serious violent crimes in their community (Leovy 2015). Prosecutors must be especially alarmed at the boycott of the criminal courts by so many victims of domestic violence and sexual assault, often in marginalized communities. The victims don't trust that involving the police (or prosecutors or courts) will improve their situation, as bad as it is (Bell 2017).

One strategy a prosecutor might use to address this lack of trust and legitimacy is to build stronger support for individual victims within the office (Holder 2018).[2] But the problem goes beyond the difficulty of finding cooperative witnesses for trial. When members of a racial minority or residents of a stressed community do not trust the police or prosecutors, they are less likely to participate in crime prevention efforts. Alienated groups may hesitate to speak up and exercise the sort of informal social controls that make the biggest difference for safe neighborhoods (Fagan and Meares 2008). Efforts to connect the prosecutor's office to the social capital of community groups must be part of the answer to this deep problem (Alfieri 2002).

In recent years, some prosecutors in the United States have appealed to voters with promises to place less weight on traditional law enforcement, which customarily leads to criminal charges and sentences of incarceration. They commit instead to listen to community groups about the crimes that deserve less emphasis, along with social support programs for those who committed criminal acts in the past to prevent crimes in the future. They seek out and respond to community groups when they face new local threats to public safety. Most important, these prosecutors promise transparency, holding themselves accountable to the public by releasing data about the patterns of outcomes in their own offices.[3] They make choices about new office initiatives based on data about programs with the best records for preventing crime.

Some observers label these candidates as "progressive prosecutors." Others use different titles, such as "modern prosecutors," to prevent a confusing overlap between prosecutorial philosophy and a more general political orientation (Travis, Stewart, and Goldberg 2019). There are certainly examples of candidates who succeed with this electoral strategy in large cities and other jurisdictions where the voters tend to be more progressive in a political sense (Bazelon 2019). But the strategy could apply equally well in other jurisdictions with different political profiles—any place where responsive prosecutors could produce better results by listening to the community and adjusting office priorities based on what they hear from those groups.

20.4 Community Input about Criminal Proceedings

The community prosecution model in the United States grew out of the community policing movement (Green and Burke 2012). During the 1990s, local police departments began to develop and embrace a philosophy that decentralized and democratized the work of police officers. Under this model, the officers became more proactive, consulting community members about ways to prevent crimes and asking about local views on the greatest threats to public safety. Based on some positive experience in the policing realm, a few local prosecutors in the United States began to experiment with similar concepts for their own offices (Thompson 2002).

The earliest versions of community prosecution in the United States involved satellite offices; a few prosecutors created offices away from the courthouse district, both to be more visible to the community and to hear about the priorities of the residents and business owners there (Dickey and McGarry 2006; Wolf and Worrall 2004). The prosecutors based in these satellite offices often heard ideas about special local concerns, such as loitering or property destruction, that residents wanted the office to charge more frequently. Community prosecution also supported a deeper and more interactive relationship with the police (Boland 1998), giving legal advice to support innovative policing that responded to community interests. These early versions of community prosecution programs, therefore, aimed to make prosecution efforts more visible to people in the community and to devote *more* court resources to the enforcement priorities of local community groups (Coles and Kelling 1999; Levine 2005).

Current uses of the community prosecution model call for prosecutors to use input from the community to de-escalate certain criminal charges: they select relatively low-priority cases to charge with a lesser version of the crime traditionally employed in that context. For instance, some prosecutors in the United States—after consulting with community groups—have declared that they will charge theft cases below a threshold amount (say, 1,000 dollars) under the misdemeanor theft statute rather than the felony theft statute that carries heavier criminal penalties (Schmadeke 2016). This de-escalation of charges frees up resources to emphasize other more serious cases that present a greater concern for the community (Gold 2011).

Victims are not clients of the prosecutor. Nonetheless, prosecutors hire staff to support individual victims of crime and to reduce the harm they experience during court proceedings. Outreach to community groups with particular ties to individual crime victims is an extension of this traditional prosecutor relationship with those individual victims (Baker and Anderson 2019). One focal point for community prosecution in some jurisdictions gives particular weight to the views of groups purporting to speak for victims, such as Mothers Against Drunk Driving or labor advocates who press for criminal charges in industrial manslaughter settings or in wage theft situations (Lee 2014; Sarre 2007).

In international tribunals, prosecutors also try to account for the priorities of community groups in their selection and development of cases. They make efforts to get input from victim groups and others not adequately represented in the standard judicial process (Findlay and Henham 2010; Sperfeldt 2017). The point of the consultation is to improve the information available to prosecutors and to the tribunal in identifying and proving formal charges.

Centralized prosecutorial services in various European countries also have experimented with community prosecution, but their efforts typically do not lead to direct consultation with residents or local interest groups. Instead, prosecutors in regional or local offices consult regularly with local government officials, such as the police chief and the mayor, to adjust national policies in light of local conditions (Boutellier 1997; Terpstra and Bakker 2004). Again, the objective of this consultation is to shape the priorities of the government during traditional criminal proceedings, to better align the work of criminal courts with local concerns and problems.

20.5 Community Input about Functions Upstream from the Criminal Courts

As we have seen, the earliest forms of community prosecution gave the prosecutor broader information about charging priorities inside the court system, particularly with regard to crimes that some victims and community residents believed were *under-enforced*. But the logic of community prosecution pushes the prosecutor out of the courtroom. These prosecutors build partnerships in the community to address public safety, both upstream and downstream from the courtroom (Goldkamp, Irons-Guynn, and Weiland 2003). Community partnerships can tell a prosecutor about *over-enforcement* of certain criminal laws as well as under-enforcement.

Upstream, prior to the start of criminal proceedings, prosecutors get involved in prevention and diversion programs. Some prosecutors work with community groups in drug education programs, anti-truancy, and other prevention programs (Gramckow 1997; Levine 2005). For instance, the District Attorney's office in Brooklyn partners with community groups to conduct anti-bullying awareness programs, social worker support for students in school, and programs using instruction in basketball and chess to reduce the risk of juvenile delinquency (Gonzalez 2020). These activities happen in the public schools, in community recreation centers, and other locations far from the courthouse building.

As for diversion programs that operate upstream from the criminal courts, some prosecutors work with law enforcement agencies and local social service agencies to select arrestees who might have been charged and processed in the criminal courts and to divert them into non-criminal programs to address the underlying causes of the conduct. A prominent example of such a program is "Law Enforcement Assisted Diversion" (LEAD), which began as an experiment in Seattle (Collins, Lonczak, and Clifasefi 2017). When the police arrest people for low-level drug sales or prostitution and the arrestees meet the predetermined qualifications, they can avoid criminal charges and are instead assigned to case workers. They receive immediate help, such as a hot meal, a coat, or a place to sleep, followed by longer-term treatment for addiction and other conditions that contributed to their criminal conduct.

In other diversion programs, prosecutors rather than law enforcement officers determine which individuals can enter the program as an alternative to filing criminal charges. Residential drug treatment programs are one common form of prosecutor-led diversion (Dynia and Sung 2000). In a third governance model for diversion programs, the prosecutor files criminal charges but then recommends to the criminal court judge that the defendant be admitted to a diversion program prior to conviction; defendants who succeed in the program see their criminal charges dismissed.[4]

Other diversion programs do not place the individual into treatment; instead, they address outside the criminal courts the harms caused to individual victims and to communities. In a straightforward sense, those who caused an injury might pay restitution to the individual victim or perform community service (outside the supervision of the court system) to address the damage. The legal systems in some countries, such as the Netherlands, allow prosecutors to participate in these programs without invoking the judicial system (van de Bunt and van Gelder 2012).

Some diversion programs promote conversation between crime victims and the people who commit the crime, aiming to restore personal relationships and social order. These discussions reveal to the defendants in more detail the harms they caused the victims; they also promote accountability. Sometimes prosecutors withhold criminal charges when Native peoples in Canada employ these practices, under the rubric of "healing" circles (Braithwaite 2000), and some U.S. prosecutors have partnered with community groups to accomplish similar goals (Bazemore and Umbreit 2001). The prosecutor's role in these programs is to refer appropriate candidates to the program in light of what the prosecutor learns about the person who committed the harmful action and the victim(s) of that action.

The overarching objective for all of these diversion programs is reduction of harm. While drug sales and other low-level crimes are harmful, overuse of the criminal sanction as a one-size-fits-all response can also harm communities. Prosecutors need help from community groups to sort out the big cases from the little cases. With local input, the prosecutor reserves the criminal sanction for the greatest social harms.

In some situations, community input leads a prosecutor to an outright refusal to file charges, without even requiring the person to enter a diversion program. These choices reflect a judgment that the conduct involved presents no real threat to public safety.

Therefore any coercive state program, whether inside or outside the criminal courts, is not likely to benefit the person or the community. This sort of rationale explains why a number of urban prosecutors in the United States have declared that possession of small amounts of marijuana, absent some aggravating circumstances, will not lead to any criminal charges in the state courts (Dewan 2019).

20.6 Community Input about Functions Downstream from the Criminal Courts

Downstream, after criminal proceedings end, prosecutors participate with community partners in programs to ease the re-entry of criminal defendants after they complete their terms of incarceration and return to the community. Some prosecutors arrange meetings with inmates just prior to their release to help them create re-entry plans and to establish contact with relevant social service agencies. Prosecutors also work with community groups to help returnees obtain drivers' licenses and to expunge convictions when allowed under the law (NYU Center on the Administration of Criminal Law 2017). And finally, they sometimes convene other government actors and local groups to create new re-entry programs and to locate funding for them.

The Brooklyn District Attorney's office, for example, uses a variety of re-entry programs. The office partners with public corrections agencies and private non-profit organizations to connect some returning prison or jail inmates to anger management services, job readiness workshops, clothing services, and emergency shelters (Abruzzese 2017). Partnerships between the prosecutor and the police in Boston and in San Diego both emphasized the work of case managers to connect individuals returning to the community with the social services most helpful to them (Braga, Piehl, and Hureau 2009; Mulmat et al. 2010). A variation on this theme appeared in San Francisco, where the District Attorney formed a "Formerly Incarcerated Advisory Board," composed of people who returned to their communities after a term of incarceration (Nonko 2019). The function of the board was to offer feedback to prosecutors about the most effective forms of re-entry support for new returnees.

20.7 The Choice of Community Partners

Prosecutors develop the sorts of programs described above through partnerships with community groups. But sometimes it is not easy to know how to choose the best working partners.

As they develop community partnerships, prosecutors need to remain alert to their own blind spots. Input from their own familiar social groups is easy to hear; other members of the public, however, might be less involved in election campaigns or circulate in different social circles than the prosecutor. It is especially difficult sometimes for a prosecutor to hear messages across a racial or class divide. Those unheard members of the public often experience the largest and most immediate effects from the prosecutor's work. Ultimately, the prosecutor's office should aim to represent all components of the local public, including voters and non-voters, crime victims and criminal defendants (Simonson 2019).

If we think of partnership choices in spatial terms, as a series of concentric circles with the prosecutor in the center, the easiest choices involve the first circle. These would include government officials outside the prosecutor's office, such as public housing authorities, health departments, child welfare agencies, public transportation administrators, court administrators, and others. When prosecutors become leaders in local public safety efforts, they necessarily cross paths with these other units of government. They can learn more about the dimensions of public safety problems and create more effective and multi-pronged responses to the issues when they convene meetings, make introductions, and pool resources. This sort of intra-governmental consultation is a prominent part of community prosecution as practiced by some national governments in Europe (NYU Center on the Administration of Criminal Law 2017; Wright 2012).

In the second circle out from the center, the prosecutor can partner with pre-existing non-governmental organizations (NGOs) in the community. These groups might center their interests around the victims of certain types of crimes, such as drunk driving or domestic violence. Admittedly, some existing advocacy groups might exaggerate or fearmonger about the effects of crime. Prosecutors must ignore counter-productive and short-term public desires that would ultimately waste tax dollars and harm public safety (Barkow 2019). Nevertheless, some NGOs can share genuine expertise about the impact of certain crimes on individuals and the community, and prosecutors can engage positively with those groups.

The existing NGOs might also have a track record of lobbying the legislature or public advocacy on particular issues, such as juvenile justice or homelessness or mental health. Some straightforward partnerships between prosecutors and community groups arise when the group already operates a program to provide services to the people who commit criminal acts, or to the victims of those actions, or both. In that situation, the prosecutor can help with publicity and funding from foundations and other donors, which makes it possible to scale up the existing programs to serve more clients (Satterberg and Wright 2018).

Even further from the center, there are inchoate groups that the prosecutor can identify through social media. In the past, individuals with interest in a particular public safety or justice issue were invisible to one another and to the prosecutor, and they had no way to meet or coordinate their efforts. Technology erodes those barriers. Now a prosecutor can form working groups that take advantage of hidden but real social connections, even where no formal group was operating up until then. The prosecutor's office—or a cooperating entity with community organizing skills—might assemble "focus groups" to gather and discuss local problems and proposals to address them

(Scales and Baker 2000). Alternatively, a prosecutor might poll the public from time to time about current public perceptions of crime and their public safety priorities. In these instances, the prosecutor receives input from individuals who never coalesce into a group.

A final concentric circle of relationships involves NGOs and informal coalitions that do not agree to "partner" with the prosecutor at all. Instead, they pursue their own agendas on public safety questions, sometimes supporting prosecutor office policy and at other times conflicting with the prosecutor. For example, some community groups establish "bail funds" to expand the number of people who are released from local jails during the period between arrest and final disposition of their criminal cases (Simonson 2017). Private donors create the bail fund and distribute money to arrestees who remain in jail because the courts (often at the urging of the prosecutor) set bail at a level too high for them to afford. When bail funds select candidates for release based on local priorities, they can represent a community judgment. In a sense, they push back against judges and prosecutors who overuse the jail to hold people the community itself does not treat as a serious danger.

Similarly, court watching groups provide community critiques of prosecutors. These groups—some with formal organizational structures and others with looser informal affiliations—send observers into criminal courtrooms to record and publicize the practices and outcomes for others to analyze and critique. Sometimes the courtroom observers watch for signs of unjustified leniency; they flag cases involving potentially serious crimes that unexpectedly result in dismissals, charge reductions, or modest sentences. But more recently, other court watching groups have looked for signs of over-enforcement, such as prosecutor requests for unreasonably high bail amounts. Court watchers also concentrate on policy announcements by chief prosecutors that promise fewer charges for low-level crimes and less reliance on jail and prison. The observers publicize examples of line prosecutors who file charges or argue for sentences that appear to conflict with these announced office policies (Simonson 2014). For example, when prosecutors in Brooklyn declared that they would only file charges for low-level marijuana possession in exceptional cases, Courtwatch NYC used twitter accounts to publicize cases that seemed to depart from the policy (Hadley 2018). And when the Manhattan District Attorney's office adopted a policy of declining cases against young people who jumped over turnstiles to enter the subway, court watchers took note that the same declination policy did not apply to riding public buses without paying fares.

Prosecutors sometimes react defensively to the critiques from court watching groups, and at times it is indeed necessary to correct the record when a court watching group publishes a factually erroneous account of what the prosecutor did. Yet there are also times when the prosecutor's silence is prudent. The rules of professional ethics place some limits on the prosecutor's interaction with court watchers and others who raise questions about the actions of the prosecutor's office in particular cases. Ethics rules limit the level of detail about individual cases and the decision-making process that a prosecutor can reveal to the press (Gray 2008).

But when the ethics rules and other aspects of the situation allow a prosecutor to respond and she does so, acknowledging the public critique, a stronger community relationship can result. The lead prosecutor can treat the observers as a source of reform ideas, and even as one method of holding line prosecutors accountable for implementing office policies (Heffernan 2019).

20.8 Implications for Office Values and Structure

The community outreach programs inside the prosecutor's office might remain limited to a few specialists who meet with the public about the operations of their own particular units. The specialist view of community prosecution was prevalent during the early years of experimentation with these programs (Forst 2000; Rainville and Nugent 2002).

But it is also possible that the work of community prosecution transforms the office more fundamentally. It can lead to a reformulation of office values, its sense of mission, and the criteria that leaders use to measure success among attorneys and other staff throughout the office (Thompson 2002). For instance, a deep commitment to community prosecution would mean that an office should put less weight on courtroom milestones—like conviction rates or the severity of sentences imposed—to measure their success.[5] Community prosecutors could instead emphasize their efforts to engage with local groups and to develop program options outside the courtroom to deal with potential crime. In addition to actual improvements in local crime rates, community prosecutors should care about (and measure) local *perceptions* of public safety (Doolan 2001).

Changes in office values could lead to new hiring and training practices. There was a time when chief prosecutors had to reassure the line prosecutors assigned to work on community prosecution initiatives that it would not hurt their career path (Levine 2005; Thompson 2002). Chief prosecutors might now be able to count on idealistic applicants who will join the office precisely because of its emphasis on community input. The relevant skills for new hires in the office would include collaborative and organizational skills, and not just trial court proficiency. At the same time, chief prosecutors who change the objectives of the office need to account for the professional self-image of the veteran line prosecutors and the possibility that they will resist the new direction (Wright and Levine 2018).

Community-oriented prosecutors might also take more care during internal office conversations related to victims and the communities where crime occurs. Prosecutors and support staff sometimes use pejorative language, referring negatively to high-crime neighborhoods or commenting that they would rather work with "true" victims rather than victims who may have committed their own crimes in the past. Disrespectful language sets the tone for disinterested dealings with some victims, which furthers the cycle of community distrust in police and prosecutors (Satterberg and Wright 2018).

Offices that embrace community input stress transparency, both in the internal and external sense (Miller and Wright 2008). For internal purposes, offices could collect and rely on pre-declared performance measures to evaluate and manage the attorneys who work in the office, encouraging them to align their own work with office priorities. Community prosecutors could also ask for statements of reasons to support decisions to file charges more serious than office policy decrees.

For external purposes, community prosecutors would inform the public about their own objectives and performance. External transparency would include data-based evaluations of the programs the office pursued, such as diversions for defendants charged with particular crimes (Miles 2014). The data released to the public also must go beyond aggregate tallies for the entire office, because community groups will need to identify the prosecutor office performance in neighborhoods and for types of crimes that most interest them.

Decentralized use of data is critical to allow for public access to prosecutors (Simon 2017). Giving power to community groups to analyze data for themselves means that prosecutors should release data about office performance that records outcomes at the individual case level—while removing fields that could intrude on individual privacy. Some prosecutor offices already post data about their office performance at the case level (Sernoffsky 2019). A few even sponsor hack-a-thons to invite the insights of data-savvy residents about how to organize and analyze their own office data (Cook County State's Attorney 2018). Prosecutors also need to accept that other sources of data, such as court system records and the observations of court watching groups, will supplement their own databases. Community groups will use all of these data sources to evaluate the prosecutor's office performance.

Finally, a community-oriented prosecutor's office might communicate honestly with the public about the harms that can flow from unwise use of the criminal sanction and the ways that prosecutors and police can sometimes contribute to racial injustice on the local level (Davis, Chisholm, and Noble 2019). This communication could take the form of an apology for past errors. Less provocatively, a statement could acknowledge the harms that flowed from prosecutor decisions in the past, without framing the issue in terms of fault. In this regard, the use of conviction integrity units not only addresses potential error in individual cases, but also signals self-awareness and openness to input that might carry over into community relations more generally.[6]

20.9 Conclusion

Prosecutors do their jobs differently in different places. And that is appropriate, in my view, even when it leads to different charging practices and out-of-court programs among local prosecutors who apply a single criminal code. That inconsistency is a consequence of listening to community input.

In jurisdictions outside the United States, this means granting to local offices within a single national prosecutorial service the authority to emphasize different charges and prevention efforts, depending on local conditions. And in the United States, community prosecution depends on prosecutors who partner with community groups to choose their courtroom priorities and to address public safety upstream and downstream from the courtroom.

Prosecutors who respond to the entire community remain alive to racial differences, knowing that it is essential to hear and respond to marginalized groups. That responsiveness is necessary to build the public trust that eventually creates public safety. It is the first step in making prosecutors effective in the local landscape.

Notes

1. See Carissa Byrne Hessick in Chapter 19 of this volume.
2. See Amanda Konradi and Tirza Jo Ochrach-Konradi in Chapter 18 of this volume.
3. See Lauren-Brooke Eisen and Miriam Aroni Krinsky in Chapter 11 of this volume.
4. See Matt Barno and Mona Lynch in Chapter 2 of this volume. The taxonomy of diversion programs described here deliberately excludes specialized treatment and accountability courts. For further discussion of the variety of diversion programs and specialized courts, see Salmon Shomade in Chapter 9 of this volume.
5. See Lauren-Brooke Eisen and Miriam Aroni Krinsky in Chapter 11 of this volume.
6. See Brandon L. Garrett in Chapter 8 of this volume.

References

Abruzzese, Rob. 2017. "Brooklyn DA and Kings County Criminal Bar Association Make a Difference with Suit Drive." *Brooklyn Eagle*, December 26, 2017.

Alfieri, Anthony V. 2002. "Community Prosecutors Colloquium on Community Policing." *California Law Review* 90(5): 1465–1512.

Baker, Jean Peters, and Lenore Anderson. 2019. "Prosecutors and Crime Survivors: How Can Prosecutors Better Address the Needs of Crime Survivors?" Institute for Innovation in Prosecution. New York: John Jay College of Criminal Justice.

Barkow, Rachel E. 2019. *Prisoners of Politics: Breaking the Cycle of Mass Incarceration*. Cambridge, MA: Harvard University Press.

Bazelon, Emily. 2019. *Charged: The New Movement to Transform American Prosecution and End Mass Incarceration*. New York: Random House.

Bazemore, Gordon, and Mark Umbreit. 2001. *A Comparison of Four Restorative Conferencing Models: Juvenile Justice Bulletin*. NCJ 184738. Washington, D.C.: Office of Juvenile Justice and Delinquency Prevention.

Bell, Monica C. 2017. "Police Reform and the Dismantling of Legal Estrangement." *Yale Law Journal* 126(7): 2054–2151.

Bellin, Jeffrey. 2020. "Theories of Prosecution." *California Law Review* 108(4): 1203–1253.

Boland, Barbara. 1998. "Community Prosecution: Portland's Experience." In *Community Justice: An Emerging Field*. Edited by David L. Karp, 253–278. Lanham, MD: Rowman & Littlefield.

Boutellier, Hans. 1997. "Right to the Community." *European Journal on Criminal Policy and Research* 5(4): 43–52.

Braga, Anthony A., Anne M. Piehl, and David Hureau. 2009. "Controlling Violent Offenders Released to the Community: An Evaluation of the Boston Reentry Initiative." *Journal of Research in Crime and Delinquency* 46(4): 411–436.

Braithwaite, John. 2000. "Restorative Justice and Social Justice." *Saskatchewan Law Review* 63(1): 185–194.

Bunt, Henk van de, and Jean-Louis van Gelder. 2012. "The Dutch Prosecution Service." *Crime and Justice* 41(1): 117–140.

Center for Court Innovation. 2009. "Testing Community Prosecution in England and Wales," December 15, 2009.

Coles, Catherine M., and George L. Kelling. 1999. "Prevention Through Community Prosecution." *Public Interest* 136(1): 69–84.

Collins, Susan, Heather Lonczak, and Seema Clifasefi. 2017. "Seattle's Law Enforcement Assisted Diversion (LEAD): Program Effects on Recidivism Outcomes." *Evaluation and Program Planning* 64(1): 49–56.

Cook County State's Attorney. 2018. "Hacking 4 Justice." August 2, 2018. https://hacking4justice.org/.

Davis, Angela J., John Chisholm, and David Noble. 2019. "Race and Prosecution." Institute for Innovation in Prosecution. New York: John Jay College of Criminal Justice.

Dewan, Shaila. 2019. "A Growing Chorus of Big City Prosecutors Say No to Marijuana Convictions." *New York Times*, January 29, 2019.

Dickey, Walter J., and Peggy A. McGarry. 2006. "The Search for Justice and Safety through Community Engagement: Community Justice and Community Prosecution." *Idaho Law Review* 42(2): 313–382.

Doolan, Devin J., Jr. 2001. "Community Prosecution: A Revolution in Crime Fighting." *Catholic University Law Review* 51(2): 547–582.

Dynia, Paul, and Hung-En Sung. 2000. "The Safety and Effectiveness of Diverting Felony Drug Offenders to Residential Treatment as Measured by Recidivism." *Criminal Justice Policy Review* 11(4): 299–311.

Fagan, Jeffrey, and Tracey L. Meares. 2008. "Punishment, Deterrence and Social Control: The Paradox of Punishment in Minority Communities." *Ohio State Journal of Criminal Law* 6(1): 173–230.

Fairfax, Roger A., Jr. 2009. "Delegation of the Criminal Prosecution Function to Private Actors." *U.C. Davis Law Review* 43(2): 411–456.

Findlay, Mark, and Ralph Henham. 2010. "Activating Victim Constituency in International Criminal Justice." In *Beyond Punishment: Achieving International Criminal Justice*. Edited by Mark Findlay and Ralph Henham, 82–120. London: Palgrave Macmillan.

Forst, Brian. 2000. "Prosecutors Discover the Community." *Judicature* 84(3): 135–141.

Gold, Russell M. 2011. "Promoting Democracy in Prosecution." *Washington Law Review* 86(1): 69–124.

Goldkamp, John S., Cheryl Irons-Guynn, and Doris Weiland. 2003. *Community Prosecution Strategies*. Washington, D.C.: Bureau of Justice Assistance.

Gonzalez, Eric. 2020. "Youth Initiatives of the Brooklyn District Attorney's Office." http://www.brooklynda.org/youth-initiatives/.

Gramckow, Heike. 1997. "Community Prosecution in the United States." *European Journal on Criminal Policy and Research* 5(4): 9–26.

Gray, Kelley Bowden. 2008. "Community Prosecution: After Two Decades, Still New Frontiers." *Journal of the Legal Profession* 32: 199–214.

Green, Bruce A., and Alafair S. Burke. 2012. "The Community Prosecutor: Questions of Professional Discretion." *Wake Forest Law Review* 47(2): 285–318.

Hadley, Megan. 2018. "Can 'Court Watchers' Help Reform America's Flawed Justice Systems?" *The Crime Report*, April 11, 2018.

Heffernan, Olivia. 2019. "A NYC Grassroots Movement Vows to Keep Watch on Prosecutors." *The Crime Report*, August 29, 2019.

Holder, Robyn. 2018. "Co-Producing Prosecution: Old and New Third Party Forms." In *Criminal Justice and Regulation Revisited: Essays in Honour of Peter Grabosky*. Edited by Lennon Y. C. Chang and Russell Brewer, 70–84. London and New York: Routledge, Taylor & Francis Group.

Langbein, John H. 2003. *The Origins of Adversary Criminal Trial*. Oxford: Oxford University Press.

Lanni, Adriaan. 2005. "The Future of Community Justice." *Harvard Civil Rights-Civil Liberties Law Review* 40(2): 359–406.

Lee, Stephen. 2014. "Policing Wage Theft in the Day Labor Market." *UC Irvine Law Review* 4(2): 655–678.

Leovy, Jill. 2015. *Ghettoside: A True Story of Murder in America*. New York: Spiegel & Grau.

Levine, Kay L. 2005. "The New Prosecution." *Wake Forest Law Review* 40(4): 1125–1214.

Luna, Erik, and Marianne Wade. 2010. "Prosecutors as Judges." *Washington & Lee Law Review* 67(4): 1413–1532.

Miles, Thomas J. 2014. "Does the 'Community Prosecution' Strategy Reduce Crime? A Test of Chicago's Experience." *American Law and Economics Review* 16(1): 117–143.

Miller, Marc L., and Ronald F. Wright. 2008. "The Black Box." *Iowa Law Review* 94(1): 125–196.

Mulmat, Darlanne H., Elizabeth Doroski, Lisbeth Howard, Debbie Correia, Sandy Keaton, Kristen Rohanna, and Cynthia Burke. 2010. "Improving Reentry for Ex-Offenders in San Diego County: SB 618 Third Annual Evaluation Report." San Diego Association of Governments.

Nonko, Emily. 2019. "DAs Have This Blueprint for Rethinking Criminal Justice." *Next City*, March 28, 2019.

NYU Center on the Administration of Criminal Law. 2017. "Disrupting the Cycle: Reimagining the Prosecutor's Role in Reentry."

Parrillo, Nicholas R. 2013. *Against the Profit Motive: The Salary Revolution in American Government, 1780–1940*. New Haven: Yale University Press.

Rainville, Gerard, and M. Elaine Nugent. 2002. "Community Prosecution Tenets and Practices: The Relative Mix of 'Community' and 'Prosecution.'" *American Journal of Criminal Justice* 26(2): 149–164.

Sarre, Rick. 2007. "White-Collar Crime and Prosecution for 'Industrial Manslaughter' as a Means to Reduce Workplace Deaths." In *International Handbook of White-Collar and Corporate Crime*. Edited by Henry N. Pontell and Gilbert Geis, 648–662. Boston: Springer US.

Satterberg, Dan, and Ronald Wright. 2018. "Prosecution That Earns Community Trust." Institute for Innovation in Prosecution. New York: John Jay College of Criminal Justice.

Scales, Bob, and Julie Baker. 2000. "Seattle's Effective Strategy for Prosecuting Juvenile Firearm Offenders." U.S. Department of Justice, Office of Justice Programs, Office of Juvenile Justice and Delinquency Prevention.

Schmadeke, Steve. 2016. "Top Cook County Prosecutor Raising Bar for Charging Shoplifters with Felony." *Chicago Tribune*, December 15, 2016.

Sernoffsky, Evan. 2019. "SF DA Gascón Launches State's First Website Showing Prosecution Data." *San Francisco Chronicle*, May 30, 2019.

Simon, William H. 2017. "The Organization of Prosecutorial Discretion." In *Prosecutors and Democracy: A Cross-National Study*. Edited by Máximo Langer and David Sklansky, 175–194.

Simonson, Jocelyn. 2014. "The Criminal Court Audience in a Post-trial World." *Harvard Law Review* 127(8): 2173–2232.

Simonson, Jocelyn. 2017. "Bail Nullification." *Michigan Law Review* 115(5): 585–638.

Simonson, Jocelyn. 2019. "The Place of 'The People' in Criminal Procedure." *Columbia Law Review* 119(1): 249–308.

Sklansky, David A. 2017. "Unpacking the Relationship Between Prosecutors and Democracy in the United States." In *Prosecutors and Democracy: A Cross-National Study*. Edited by Máximo Langer and David Sklansky, 276–299. Cambridge: Cambridge University Press.

Sperfeldt, Christoph. 2017. "The Trial Against Hissène Habré: Networked Justice and Reparations at the Extraordinary African Chambers." *The International Journal of Human Rights* 21(9): 1243–1260.

Terpstra, Jan, and Inge Bakker. 2004. "'Justice in the Community' in The Netherlands: Evaluation and Discussion." *Criminal Justice* 4(4): 375–393.

Thompson, Anthony. 2002. "It Takes a Community to Prosecute." *Notre Dame Law Review* 77(2): 321–372.

Travis, Jeremy, Carter Stewart, and Allison Goldberg. 2019. "Prosecutors, Democracy, and Justice: Holding Prosecutors Accountable." Institute for Innovation in Prosecution. New York: John Jay College of Criminal Justice.

Tyler, Tom R. 2007. *Legitimacy and Criminal Justice: An International Perspective*. New York: Russell Sage Foundation.

Wolf, Robert V., and John L. Worrall. 2004. *Lessons from the Field: Ten Community Prosecution Leadership Profiles*. Washington, D.C.: National District Attorneys Association.

Wright, Ronald F. 2012. "Community Prosecution, Comparative Prosecution." *Wake Forest Law Review* 47(2): 361–372.

Wright, Ronald F. 2014. "Beyond Prosecutor Elections." *SMU Law Review* 67(3): 593–616.

Wright, Ronald F., and Kay L. Levine. 2018. "Career Motivations of State Prosecutors." *George Washington Law Review* 86(6): 1667–1710.

Wright, Ronald F., and Marc L. Miller. 2010. "The Worldwide Accountability Deficit for Prosecutors." *Washington and Lee Law Review* 67(4): 1587–1622.

PART III

PROSECUTION IN SPECIALIZED CONTEXTS

CHAPTER 21

PROSECUTORS AND THE IMMIGRATION ENFORCEMENT SYSTEM IN THE UNITED STATES

JENNIFER CHACÓN

21.1 Introduction

THE deepening interdependence of the criminal enforcement system and the immigration enforcement system in the United States has important implications for prosecutors. Although the linkages between immigration enforcement and criminal law enforcement in the United States are long and deep (Rosenbloom 2016), recent legal and policy developments have made these ties more robust and consequential (Chacón 2012).

The developments that have strengthened these connections can be grouped into four broad categories. First, the most recent three presidential administrations have prioritized the prosecution of immigration crimes, pushing the numbers of federal immigration prosecutions to unprecedented levels. Few new federal migration offenses have been created in this period and unauthorized entrances into the United States are at fifty-year lows, yet the number of federal immigration prosecutions has soared. Federal prosecutors have played a key role in this development, deploying new resources to prosecute immigration crimes as well as shifting existing resources in support of these prosecutions.

Second, Congress amended federal immigration law in 1994 and again, much more significantly, in 1996, to increase the severity of the immigration consequences attached to non-citizens' criminal convictions, to expand substantially the scope of criminal offenses that will generate such consequences, and to severely limit the power of immigration courts and federal judges to alleviate those consequences. The expansion and intensification of the immigration consequences attached to criminal sentences coincided with a cresting wave of criminal prosecutions resulting from the "war on crime" and "war on drugs" waged by police and prosecutors at both the federal and state level. Consequently, hyper-criminalized immigrant communities of color not only were increasingly vulnerable to lengthy prison sentences for relatively minor offenses, but these same individuals were now increasingly likely to lose their right to reside in the United States as a consequence of these criminal offenses. Because prosecutors at the federal and state level possess tremendous discretionary charging authority, these prosecutors have played a critical (and, until recently, an often unwitting) role in shaping immigration outcomes for non-citizen criminal defendants.

This increasing entwinement of criminal convictions and immigration consequences has generated a third development: the intentional reconfiguration of state and local laws and law enforcement policies to shape immigration outcomes. Prosecutors have played an important part in these developments. Although state law enforcement officials play no formal role in the enforcement of federal immigration law, some state prosecutors have used their powers as administrators of state criminal laws to supplement federal immigration enforcement efforts through the prosecution of state offenses that are designed or implemented in ways that target immigrants. Others have developed policies or practices—sometimes responsive to state legal requirements—that leverage prosecutors' charging discretion to mitigate the federal immigration consequences of criminal sanctions.

Fourth, Congress has given greater power to prosecutors and other law enforcement agents at all levels of government to protect non-citizens from immigration enforcement in cases where these non-citizens can assist law enforcement in the prosecution of crimes. With the passage of the Trafficking Victims Protection Act in 2000, Congress created two new visas—the T visa and the U visa—designed, respectively, for the victims of trafficking and of other serious crimes—that could be accessed by non-citizens certified by law enforcement agents (including prosecutors) as cooperating in the related criminal prosecutions. The overall numbers of cases in which T and U visas are issued are not large in the scheme of national prosecutions. Nevertheless, the existence of these programs has heightened awareness in some prosecutors' offices about the vulnerability of immigrant crime victims. Moreover, because these visas are the only available legal mechanism by which some long-term residents can regularize their immigration status, they, too, have become a notable tool through which prosecutors effectively shape immigration law outcomes. As federal legislation has required prosecutors to be more attentive to the plight of immigrant victims of crime, prosecutors have also begun to play a more prominent role in advocating for immigrant victim safety from immigration consequences, including by promoting policies and engaging in litigation to limit federal immigration enforcement efforts in and around state courthouses.

Each of these sets of developments has raised new practical and ethical challenges for prosecutors, but efforts to grapple with these challenges are still in relatively nascent stages. The remainder of this chapter explores the issues that prosecutors face within each of the four categories of developments described above and draws on existing literature to explore the varying responses that prosecutors have designed to meet these challenges.

21.2 Prosecuting Immigration Crimes

One of the most obvious ways that prosecutors play a role in the lives of non-citizens is through the prosecution of immigration-related offenses. Entry without inspection at a place other than a designated port of entry has been a federal misdemeanor offense since 1929 (Hernández 2017, 138). In the early to mid-1980s, Congress criminalized the hiring of unauthorized non-citizen workers, reliance on false documents to evade these employer sanctions, and marriage fraud (Chacón 2009, Medina 1997). In the late 1980s and early 1990s, Congress added felony criminal sanctions for illegal reentry after removal and for various acts of fraud in the immigration process.

As Congress expanded the list of federal immigration crimes, it also authorized greater funding for immigration enforcement. In the years between 1986 and 2012, Congress increased the budget for immigration enforcement fifteen-fold (accounting for inflation), from about $575 million in 1986 to about $18 billion in 2012 (Meissner et al. 2013).

With this significant increase in enforcement resources came a concomitant increase in immigration prosecutions. In 1993, immigration crimes made up about 5.4 percent of the total number of cases investigated and prosecuted by the federal government (Bureau of Justice Statistics 1993). This was consistent with patterns of prosecutions in previous decades. But beginning in the late 1990s, that stable trend changed. By 2014, the Bureau of Justice Statistics reported that immigration crimes made up 49.7 percent of federal prosecutions, with a total of 81,881 prosecutions (Bureau of Justice Statistics 2017 [2014]).

21.2.1 Operation Streamline

A person can be convicted of misdemeanor illegal entry under section 1325 if a federal prosecutor can prove beyond a reasonable doubt that an individual entered the country without inspection—as when an individual enters away from of a port of entry or otherwise evades inspection. Over the past ten years, section 1325 prosecutions have comprised the majority of federal immigration prosecutions and the districts along the southern border account for nearly all of these prosecutions (TRAC Immigration 2018). The bulk of these cases are processed by federal magistrate judges (TRAC Immigration 2018).

To secure a misdemeanor illegal entry conviction, a prosecutor does not need to prove that the individual possessed any particular mental state, so the prosecutions of these crimes are relatively straightforward. Taking advantage of this fact, federal prosecutors began prosecuting immigration crimes en masse in federal district court in Del Rio, Texas, in 2005. The proceedings through which these group prosecutions take place bear the official moniker "Operation Streamline" (Chacón 2009). The Streamline program has expanded during the presidencies of Barack Obama and Donald Trump and is now operational in all states along the United States-Mexico border (Spagat 2018).

In Streamline proceedings, defense counsel typically speaks for a few minutes with their clients—many of whom are wearing the same clothes that they wore in the desert and are shackled in their proceedings. These clients generally accept the plea deal. After discussing the implications of the plea collectively with large groups of defendants assembled before them, judges proceed to enter pleas by asking each defendant whether he wishes to enter the guilty plea. Many defendants wear headphones so they can get a simultaneous translation of a hearing that they otherwise will not understand.

This brief and dehumanizing proceeding represents the sum total of the criminal process in Streamline cases (Chacón 2009). Tens of thousands of cases have been processed in these watered-down procedures over the past decade. In fact, the routinization of these criminal prosecutions has come to affect the prosecution of drug cases along the southern border as well. As Mona Lynch has documented, in a border jurisdiction "the prevailing adjudicatory logic" in drug prosecutions "is concerned with defendants' status as unauthorized outsiders such that these defendants are barely distinguishable from immigration defendants in how their sentences are calculated and rhetorically justified" (Lynch 2017).

21.2.2 Family Separations

During the Bush and Obama Administrations, prosecutors tended to reserve their filing of misdemeanor illegal entry prosecutions in Operation Streamline procedures for immigrants—most commonly men—traveling alone. But during the Trump Administration, a new kind of scenario unfolded. In a memorandum dated April 23, 2018, Department of Homeland Security (DHS) officials recommended that agents separate families at the border to facilitate the criminal processing of the adult family members (McAleenan 2018). Prosecutors began filing criminal immigration charges against immigrants traveling with small children. When this happened, the children were separated from their parents—sometimes to be placed in separate, civil detention facilities (including extended stays in facilities intended only for short-term processing) while their parents were criminally processed and sometimes the children were placed with families in the United States (OIG DHS 2018). The cruelty of imposing family separation in order to prosecute minor offenses of dubious deterrent value sparked a national outcry that led to modifications in the policy, although many families remained separated (Shear, Goodnough, and Haberman 2018). As of October 2020, more than two years after the program was officially discontinued, DHS has reported that they have been unable to find the parents of 545 children that the Department separated from their parents (Spagat 2020).

21.2.3 Felony Reentry Prosecutions

The second most commonly prosecuted immigration offense—and the top lead charge among federal district court judges (as distinct from federal magistrate judges)—is felony reentry as defined in 8 U.S.C. § 1326 (TRAC Immigration 2018). Individuals who have "been denied admission, excluded, deported, or removed" or departed "while an order of exclusion, deportation, or removal is outstanding," can be convicted for this offense if they reenter or attempt to reenter the United States. For a long time, these prosecutions were relatively rare, in part because formal entry of removal orders was the exception rather than the rule. During the 1990s, even though more than a million people were turned away at the southern border each year, most were informally excluded. No formal process was initiated against them and no formal order of removal was entered. Consequently, there was often no basis for charging re-entrants with a felony re-entry count.

This changed under President George W. Bush, who pledged to end what he characterized as an existing policy of "catch-and-release" along the southern border. Under his administration, enforcement agents at the border shifted to a policy of formalizing the removal process, entering removal orders against those who previously might have been returned informally. When those individuals returned, they were sometimes charged with felony reentry. Felony reentry charges peaked during the early portion of President Obama's second term (TRAC Immigration 2016). Since that time, the numbers have fallen slightly but remain high (TRAC Immigration 2018).

Depending on the nature of the underlying removal order, this offense is punishable with sentences of up to twenty years, but actual sentences for this offense vary wildly. For a time, for defendants in particular federal districts designated "Fast Track" jurisdictions (generally, jurisdictions with relative high rates of immigration-related prosecutions), pleas of two to three years were not uncommon. At the same time, for individuals tried in other geographic locations, sentences tended to be three or four times longer, regardless of the underlying offenses—if any—that led to the initial removal (Seigler 2009). The Fast Track program was phased out during President Obama's second term (Chacón 2017), but along the southern border, the felony reentry charge continues to allow for quick and easy convictions in "flip-flop court"—rapid proceedings devoted to border drug and immigration cases (Lynch 2017).

21.2.4 Other Federal Immigration Prosecutions

The remainder of the prosecutions for immigration offenses are comprised of a number of disparate offenses, including serious offenses like human smuggling. Such prosecutions constitute an extremely small portion of the overall number of immigration prosecutions. In 2012, charges for human smuggling, human trafficking, and immigration-related fraud were relatively "few and far between" and "criminal prosecutions of employers who ha[d] violated IRCA's criminal provisions [were] rare" too (Chacón 2012). That continues to be true. Even as the number of immigration prosecutions overall spiked in 2017 and 2018 (a spike that may be partly attributable to better record-keeping among federal magistrate judges), the number of prosecutions for these serious immigration crimes remained at low levels. In the United States, immigration-related prosecutions are largely deployed as a supplement to the parallel, civil system of immigration detention and removal.

21.3 Determining the Immigration Consequences of Criminal Convictions

One of the most significant developments in immigration enforcement over the past twenty years has been the development of an increasingly tight linkage between criminal prosecutions and immigration consequences. It has long been the case that immigration enforcement agents have interacted with state and local police to effectuate their goals. This has been true in the cases of individuals whose criminal record renders them deportable (Rosenbloom 2016) as well as in cases involving mass removals.[1] But since the mid-1990s, these linkages have become thicker and more systematic as a result of three developments.

First, Congress significantly expanded the scope of criminal conduct that will render an otherwise lawfully present foreign national deportable. In 1996, with the passage of the Anti-terrorism and Effective Death Penalty Act (AEDPA) and the Illegal Immigration Reform and Immigrant Responsibility Act (IIRIRA), Congress added a long list of criminal conduct to the list of offenses that could trigger removal, including, in many cases, the mandatory removal and lifelong bar triggered by an "aggravated felony" (at 8 U.S.C. § 1101[a][43]). At the same time that Congress widened the net of immigration consequences, it also greatly reduced immigration courts' discretion to allow otherwise removable immigrants to remain, meaning that prosecutors' charges will often determine immigration outcomes in ways that immigration courts cannot avoid (Morawetz 2000). Since the changes were retroactive, many long-time, authorized immigrant residents became deportable for past convictions that were not deportable offenses at the time of their commission or punishment. Since individuals present without authorization were already subject to removal, some of the harshest effects of the 1996 laws actually fell on immigrants lawfully admitted to the United States. A wide range of charging decisions made by prosecutors now have largely irrevocable immigration consequences for immigrants, including lawful permanent residents.

Second, as previously noted, Congress substantially expanded the resources devoted to immigration enforcement during this period, giving DHS the capacity to remove much larger numbers of individuals with criminal convictions than previously had been the case. This expanded deportation capacity came upon the heels of a period of intense overcriminalization and mass incarceration in the criminal enforcement system, so there are plenty of individuals with low-level criminal offenses on their records who are easy targets for removal. Prosecutors inadvertently paved the way for the current period of mass removal with charging decisions made even before the 1996 immigration laws were enacted. The ability of Congress to impose retroactive immigration consequences to criminal convictions is not commonly understood, but the widespread implementation of such retroactive laws ought to sound a cautionary note to prosecutors charging foreign nationals with crimes.

Third, state and local law enforcement agents increasingly act as immigration enforcement agents or as direct funnels to the immigration system, and prosecutors play a role in amplifying or mitigating these efforts. Congress expressly authorized the formal participation of state and local agents as immigration enforcement agents in 1996 with the addition of Section 237(g) to the Immigration and Nationality Act. This provision allows state and local law enforcement agents who are trained and supervised by federal immigration agents to participate directly in immigration enforcement within the scope of their official agreement. 287(g) agreements have been widely criticized—including by DHS's Inspector General—for lacking sufficient federal oversight and training. Under the Obama administration, many 287(g) agreements were phased out over these concerns, concerns about racial profiling, and other criticisms. But under President Trump, the number of agreements once more expanded, growing from thirty at the beginning of his term to seventy-six by May of 2018 (Capps et al. 2018).

Simultaneously, the federal government operates much more pervasive forms of cooperation in the form of other Immigration and Customs Enforcement (ICE) programs, including joint task forces and, most importantly, the Secure Communities program. Under the Secure Communities program state and local arrestees now have their fingerprints run through Department of Homeland Security databases to ascertain whether they are of potential interest to immigration enforcement agents. If so, DHS contacts local agents and asks them to hold the individual. Some jurisdictions comply, although others have declined to cooperate, citing Fourth Amendment concerns (Capps et al. 2018). Regardless, with thousands of arrests being processed through the DHS database, the overall enforcement net has widened substantially under Secure Communities. But not all state and local law enforcement actors have engaged with these immigration enforcement systems in the same way. Prosecutors, among others, have developed distinctive approaches to respond to the increasing intertwinement of their functions and federal immigration enforcement.

Professor Ingrid Eagly has done the most systematic empirical study to date on the varying approaches that prosecutors have used when processing the cases of defendants who are not U.S. citizens (Eagly 2013). She describes three different models that prosecutors (along with other law enforcement agents) follow in such cases. The first approach is an "alienage neutral" approach. Her case study for this approach is Los Angeles County, California. In "alienage neutral" jurisdictions, investigators decline to ask about immigration status or to report non-citizens to federal immigration enforcement agents during the investigative stage of the proceeding. Prosecutors seek to achieve parity of results between citizen and non-citizen defendants. They structure plea agreements in ways that will allow non-citizen defendants to avoid triggering harsh immigration consequences whenever it is possible to do so without materially reducing the resulting criminal sanction. This might mean offering defendants the opportunity to plead to crimes slightly different from those originally envisioned or by structuring sentences in ways that are deliberately designed to avoid triggering immigration consequences like mandatory removal or lifelong bars to reentry.[2]

The U.S. Supreme Court approved and even encouraged this approach with its 2010 decision in *Padilla v. Kentucky*. Justice Stevens wrote that:

> Informed consideration of possible deportation can only benefit *both the State* and noncitizen defendants during the plea-bargaining process. By bringing deportation consequences into this process, the defense *and prosecution* may well be able to reach agreements that better satisfy the interests of both parties.

(*Padilla v. Kentucky*, 373) (emphasis added). The Court effectively encouraged not only defense attorneys but also prosecutors to craft immigration-safe pleas when doing so serves the interest of justice.

Scholars including Heidi Altman have reasoned that after *Padilla*, prosecutors have a duty to mitigate immigration consequences if possible in cases where doing so will avoid the excessive punishment of non-citizen defendants. Altman argues that prosecutors' "informed consideration of immigration-related penalties during plea bargaining" serves at least three goals identified in 2007 by the American Prosecutors Research Institute, namely: "the pursuit of fair, impartial, and expedient justice," "the stewardship of public safety and the interests of the community," and "the integrity of the prosecution profession, including practice within prevailing norms of professional ethics and the pursuit of the appropriate role of the state prosecutor in light of federalism concerns" (Altman 2012, 8–9; Blout, Cahn, and Aroni Krinsky 2018).

Santa Clara County prosecutors were early adopters of such a policy, making clear that the prosecutors in that office must take "reasonable steps to mitigate . . . collateral consequences" that are "significantly greater than the punishment for the crime itself" (Altman 2012, 26). Following suit, the state of California now requires all state prosecutors to take immigration consequences into account in their plea bargaining (Assemb. Bill 1343, 2015–2016 Reg. Sess. [Cal. 2015]; Eagly 2017), as does the Philadelphia District Attorney's Office (Krasner 2018). In Cook County, Illinois, prosecutors can offer individuals charged with their first offense the ability to participate in diversionary programs that avoid triggering the immigration consequences of a criminal punishment (Blout, Cahn, and Aroni Krinsky 2018, 38). But while adherence to this approach is on the rise in prosecutors' offices, it is still not the dominant approach.

The second approach Eagly identifies in her survey is the "immigration enforcement" model (Eagly 2013). Her example of this approach is taken from Harris County, Texas.

Harris County has unique features that Eagly explains in some detail: police do not inquire into immigration status at the investigative phase; prosecutors rather than police determine whether there is sufficient probable cause to jail a suspect after screening cases brought by police; and once the probable cause determination is made, the County mandates booking. Eagly observes that the Harris County policies taken together "facilitate federal jail-based immigration screening of all felony and misdemeanor defendants, but only after a prosecutor first decides that criminal charges are warranted" (Eagly 2013, 1174). In other words, citizenship status is irrelevant (at least theoretically) at the stage of investigation and during the initial probable cause determination that leads to booking. Prosecutors then play a pivotal role in making the booking determination—and that is the key moment at which information about the arrest is shared with DHS under Secure Communities. From the point of the defendant's appearance before a magistrate onward, non-citizens who lack authorization are treated differently, and more harshly, than other defendants in the Harris County system (1174). Their bail is set higher, prosecutors are prohibited from offering them plea bargains to probation, and they are barred from treatment programs that other defendants are offered as an alternative to incarceration (1176). Prosecutors also generally decline to take into account the immigration consequences of criminal charges during plea negotiations (1178–1179).

Although Harris County has certain procedures that are fairly unique, the "immigration enforcement" model of prosecuting immigrants is not limited to Harris County. In their work in King County, Washington, Katherine Beckett and Heather Evans found that "non-citizens flagged by immigration authorities stay in jail significantly longer than their similarly situated counterparts" (Beckett and Evans 2015). This may be changing, however, as prosecutors in jurisdictions that lean more heavily toward the Democratic Party seek to insulate immigrant defendants from the harshness of President Trump's expanded enforcement activity.

The third approach that Eagly identifies is the "illegal alien punishment" approach (Eagly 2013). In Eagly's study, this approach was typified by prosecutors in Maricopa County, Arizona. It is essentially the opposite approach from the "alienage neutral" approach. The objective of prosecutors in "illegal alien punishment" jurisdictions is to maximize the immigration consequences of criminal enforcement. Police inquire into immigration status during the investigation of criminal activity and communicate with federal immigration officials when they encounter non-citizens (1182). Some defendants are turned directly over to federal immigration enforcement officials before state criminal proceedings even commence (1183). Individuals present without authorization are denied bail (1184). Alienage is actually an element of certain state crimes (1185), meaning that there are some acts that are not criminal for citizens but are criminal for non-citizens. Some offenses are punished more heavily in the case of non-citizens than in the case of citizens. And "county prosecutors may insist on pleas to aggravated felonies or crimes of moral turpitude with the explicit aim of increasing the odds of deportation and application of criminal bars on reentry" (1188). In short, every stage of the process is designed to achieve the most negative immigration outcome possible for the non-citizen interfacing with the criminal enforcement system.

A fourth approach, not taken by the jurisdictions in Eagly's case studies, but characteristic of some prosecutor's offices in the period before *Padilla* and, notwithstanding *Padilla*, still operational in some, is an approach that sits between the approach taken by Harris County and that of Los Angeles County. Perhaps it could be described as "alienage indifferent." Such an approach treats defendants the same regardless of immigration status (including lack of authorization) throughout the criminal process. This means that police do not inquire into immigration status at the investigation phase, nor do they collect information about status when charging. Immigration status is irrelevant in the setting of bail and in determining access to diversionary programs (although lack of work authorization might preclude unauthorized workers from certain kinds of programs). Prosecutors or judges might issue blanket warnings about immigration consequences, but no efforts are made by either to exacerbate or mitigate results. Unlike in the "alienage neutral" jurisdiction, immigration status also is not be taken into account in determining appropriate criminal sanctions, which has decidedly negative consequences for foreign nationals. In 2012, about the same time as Eagly's study, Heidi Altman described policies in several jurisdictions in New York that might be characterized as "alienage indifferent." In 2012, the New York County District Attorney, the Queens County District Attorney, and the Office of the Special Narcotics Prosecutor in New York did nothing beyond issuing a blanket warning to non-citizens that their pleas carried potential deportation risks, with no policy favoring the appropriate mitigation of immigration consequences (Altman 2012). The Kings County (Brooklyn) District Attorney's office also had no formal policy in place to deal with the issue of non-citizen defendants (Altman 2012).

Under this approach, prosecutors approach cases involving foreign nationals in the same way that they would approach any case, offering the same plea deals that they would offer to citizen defendants. In their view, it is up to the immigration enforcement system to mete out immigration consequences. They view their own work in isolation from that system but recognize that their refusal to shape plea agreements with attention to immigration status will trigger harsh removal consequences for many immigrant defendants and will effectively punish these defendants much more severely than their citizen counterparts.

As prosecutors have become increasingly aware of their often dispositive role in determining immigration consequences for immigrant defendants, they are choosing between these models more intentionally. Brooklyn's District Attorney Eric Gonzalez, (Gonzalez 2017), and Philadelphia's District Attorney Larry Krasner, for example, have hired immigration specialists in their offices. These experts consult on cases involving non-citizens and train prosecutors to tailor criminal charges to avoid unwanted immigration consequences. Non-profit organizations like the Immigrant Legal Resource Center, the Immigrant Defense Project and other immigrant-serving organizations also consult with elected prosecutors throughout the country to provide more training and information on the immigration consequences of criminal convictions and contact with the criminal enforcement system.

21.4 Shaping Immigration Consequences through State Criminal Law Enforcement

Given the increasing interdependence between criminal law and immigration enforcement, prosecutors obviously play a substantial role in shaping immigration enforcement through their routine processing of criminal law cases, whether federal or state. But in some cases, prosecutors have also tried to play a more active role in immigration enforcement by targeting immigrant communities for unique prosecutions and punishments. The goal of such efforts has been expressed as helping to effectuate immigration enforcement through attrition. The idea is that the criminal law can be used as a tool to make life so miserable for immigrants that those immigrants, particularly but not exclusively those who lack authorization or are otherwise removable, will simply leave. Failing that, the goal is to create a criminal record that renders the immigrant defendant removable.

One high profile—and ultimately unconstitutional—example of such efforts played out in Arizona during the Obama Administration. In Maricopa County, Arizona, prosecutors began charging immigrants with a state human smuggling offense on the grounds that they had smuggled themselves (Eagly 2011). As Ingrid Eagly noted, "to enhance these self-smuggling prosecutions, a sophisticated procedural system has emerged. This system includes state alienage-based rules for criminal bail, sentencing, material witnesses and jails. It also includes local policies for arresting, charging, detaining and plea bargaining" (1753). As is evident from that description, prosecutors were deeply implicated in establishing the necessary procedures for bringing this problematic charge on a wide scale. Ultimately, a federal court enjoined this use of self-smuggling prosecutions, finding that these prosecutions were preempted by federal immigration policy (Hendley 2013).

But state laws provide an array of tools that prosecutors can and do use to target non-citizens. Some state crimes of general applicability are used exclusively or predominantly against non-citizens. Many state laws prohibiting human trafficking, for example, were also often crafted with immigrant punishment in mind, as is evident in the legislative history of anti-trafficking laws in states like Georgia (Chacón 2017). Under Arizona law, identity theft includes cases where an individual is using a Social Security number that belongs to no one; prosecutors in Maricopa County exclusively charged non-citizens with this offense (Farzan 2017).

Other state laws target non-citizens more directly. More than twenty states have laws that impose unique restrictions and punishments on non-citizens for the possession, carrying, or transporting of firearms (Gulasekaram 2007). A number of states have laws on the books—some enforced, some not—that enhance criminal penalties when the actus reus is performed by a non-citizen (Eagly 2017). The Supreme Court recently upheld the constitutionality of a state's prosecution of tax fraud offenses that targeted immigrants unauthorized to work (*Kansas v. Garcia* 2020).

In short, prosecutors have a host of state law crimes in their toolbox that can be deployed to disproportionately or exclusively target immigrant communities. While some such efforts are arguably preempted by federal law, some have been implemented with little legal pushback.

21.5 Mitigating Harm to Immigrant Victims and Witnesses

Many prosecutors are aware that immigrants are uniquely vulnerable to crime because of their legal vulnerability (Blout, Cahn, and Aroni Krinsky 2018, 38). Immigrant victims of crime may be reluctant to report crimes because of their own lack of legal status or tenuous legal status. Individuals living in immigrant neighborhoods may be faced with the reality that their neighbors and friends who witness crimes will also be unwilling to assist in the prosecution of perpetrators because doing so will open them up to questions about their own immigration status. Indeed, these concerns about immigrants who are victims of crime have animated recent efforts on the part of various state court judges and prosecutors to keep immigration officials out of state courthouses (Cantil-Sakauye 2017; Rios 2019; Satterberg 2017). And as immigration enforcement in the interior of the United States has grabbed national attention since the election of President Trump, some jurisdictions have seen declines in the reporting of crime in immigrant neighborhoods (Engelbrecht 2018).

One tool Congress has used to attempt to mitigate the vulnerability of immigrant crime victims is the creation of special visas available to immigrants who lack legal status but who have been the victim of a serious crime. Beginning in 1994, with the passage of the Violent Crime Control and Law Enforcement Act, prosecutors could seek an S visa for cooperating non-citizen witnesses assisting in criminal prosecutions. But Congress capped the number of S visas available in any given year at two hundred; it was hardly a commonly used prosecutorial device. In 2000, with the passage of the Trafficking Victims Protection Act, Congress created two new visas. The T visas were available to individuals who had been the victim of severe forms of sex or labor trafficking. Congress authorized the issuance of up to five thousand visas per year to individuals who fit this category, provided that the individual was assisting with the investigation or prosecution of the trafficking (Chacón 2006). In the same piece of legislation, Congress also authorized the issuance of up to ten thousand U visas every year for individuals who have suffered mental or physical abuse and are helpful to law enforcement or government officials in the investigation or prosecution of criminal activity (DHS 2019).

In all cases involving the S, T, and U visas, the issuance of the visas is contingent on certification by a law enforcement agent, with certain exceptions for trafficking victims who are minors. These visas have transformative capacity—allowing immigrants to emerge from dangerous and abusive domestic situations, empowering immigrant workers to speak out and organize against exploitative conditions and providing one of the very few pathways to legalization available to many of the nation's unauthorized immigrant residents. But law enforcement agents, including police and prosecutors, have wildly different policies for determining who is eligible for certification, with some adopting hardline policies against certification, including in meritorious cases (Srikantiah 2007). The lack of uniformity in certification policy effectively ensures that an immigrant's ability to avail herself of the laws' protections will vary significantly depending upon on the jurisdiction in which she attempts to achieve certification. These visas are also weak medicine to counteract the powerful subordinating forces generated by the multifaceted criminalization of migrants discussed above.

21.6 Conclusions

Prosecutors play an obvious and direct role in shaping criminal law outcomes for immigrants in the criminal justice system. They also play a less obvious but critical role in determining immigration law outcomes. As immigration enforcement efforts at the federal level expand, state and federal prosecutors have tremendous—if often under-analyzed—power to decide which immigrants will bear the brunt of those enforcement efforts.

Notes

1. The mass removal of Mexicans and Mexican Americans in the 1930s was initiated by state and local law enforcement. The mass removal of Mexican workers in the 1950s—performed by the federal government under the auspices of "Operation Wetback"—also relied heavily on the state and local law enforcement.
2. This is not easy to do. The number of crimes that trigger removal consequences are vast. The Immigration Legal Resource Center's "Quick Reference Chart" for determining the immigration consequences of various offenses under California Law runs to sixty-eight pages with a precatory four pages of definitions. Nevertheless, immigration consequences sometimes can be minimized or avoided all together through careful consideration of the substantive criminal plea, attention to the information contained in the record of conviction, and thoughtful sentencing structures.

References

Altman, Heidi. 2012. "Prosecuting Post-Padilla: State Interests and the Pursuit of Justice for Noncitizen Defendants." *Georgetown Law Review* 101(1): 1-59.

Anti-terrorism and Effective Death Penalty Act, Pub. L. No. 104-132, 110 Stat. 1214 (codified as amended in scattered sections of 8 U.S.C.).

Assemb. Bill 1343, 2015–2016 Reg. Sess. (Cal. 2015).
Beckett, Katherine, and Heather Evans. 2015. "Crimmigration at the Local Level: Criminal Justice Processes in the Shadow of Deportation." *Law & Society Review* 49(1): 241–278.
Blout, Hillary, Rose Cahn, and Miriam Aroni Krinsky. 2018. "The Prosecutor's Role in the Current Immigration Landscape." *Criminal Justice* 32(4): 35–39.
Bureau of Justice Statistics. 1993. *Compendium of Federal Justice Statistics, 1993*. NCJ-160089. Washington, D.C.: U.S. Department of Justice.
Bureau of Justice Statistics. 2017. *Federal Justice Statistics, 2014 Statistical Tables*. Washington, D.C.: U.S. Department of Justice.
Cantil-Sakauye, Tani G. 2017. "Letter to Jeff Sessions, Attorney General, U.S. Department of Justice, and John F. Kelly, Secretary of Homeland Security, U.S. Department of Homeland Security, March 16, 2017."
Capps, Randy, Muzaffar Chishti, Julia Gelatt, Jessica Bolter, and Ariel G. Ruiz Soto. 2018. *Revving Up the Deportation Machinery: Enforcement and Pushback under Trump*. Washington, D.C.: Migration Policy Institute.
Chacón, Jennifer M. 2006. "Mysery and Mypopia: Understanding the Failures of U.S. Efforts to Stop Human Trafficking Stop Human Trafficking." *Fordham Law Review* 74(6): 2977-3040.
Chacón, Jennifer M. 2009. "Managing Migration through Crime." *Columbia Law Review Sidebar* 109: 135–148.
Chacón, Jennifer M. 2012. "Overcriminalizing Immigration." *Journal of Criminal Law and Criminology* 102(3): 613–652.
Chacón, Jennifer M. 2017. "Human Trafficking, Immigration Regulation, and Subfederal Criminalization." *New Criminal Law Review* 20(1): 96–129.
Department of Homeland Security. 2019. "U Visa Law Enforcement Resource Guide."
Eagly, Ingrid V. 2011. "Local Immigration Prosecution: A Study of Arizona before SB 1070." *UCLA Law Review* 58(6): 1749–1818.
Eagly, Ingrid V. 2013. "Criminal Justice for Noncitizens: An Analysis of Variation in Local Enforcement." *New York University Law Review* 88(4): 1126–1223.
Eagly, Ingrid V. 2017. "Criminal Justice in an Era of Mass Deportation: Reforms from California." *New Criminal Law Review* 20(1): 12–38.
Engelbrecht, Cora. 2018. "Fewer Immigrants Are Reporting Domestic Abuse: Police Blame Fear of Deportation." *New York Times*, June 3, 2018.
Farzan, Antonia Noori. 2017. "Mad That Guadalupe Garcia Was Deported Today? Blame Arizona's Aggressive Identity Theft Laws." *Phoenix New Times*, February 9, 2017.
Gonzalez, Eric. 2017. "Press Release, Brooklyn Dist. Attorney's Office: Acting Brooklyn District Attorney Eric Gonzalez Announces New Policy Regarding Handling of Cases Against Non-Citizen Defendants," April 24, 2017.
Gulasekaram, Pratheepan. 2007. "Aliens with Guns: Equal Protection, Federal Power, and the Second Amendment." *Iowa Law Review* 92(3): 893–955.
Hendley, Matthey. 2013. "Joe Arpaio Can't Arrest People for Smuggling Themselves into Country, Judge Rules." *Phoenix New Times*, September 30, 2013.
Hernández, Kelly Lytle. 2017. *City of Inmates: Conquest, Rebellion, and the Rise of Human Caging in Los Angeles, 1771–1965*. Chapel Hill: University of North Carolina Press.
Illegal Immigration Reform and Immigrant Responsibility Act (IIRIRA) Pub. L. No. 104–208, 110 Stat. 3009 (codified as amended in scattered sections of 8 U.S.C.).
Immigration and Nationality Act, 8 U.S.C. § 1101 et seq.
Kansas v. Garcia. 2020. 140 S. Ct. 791.

Krasner, Larry. 2018. "Larry Krasner Announces Appointment of Immigration Counsel for Philadelphia District Attorney's Office," January 25, 2018.

Lynch, Mona. 2017. "Backpacking the Border: The Intersection of Drug and Immigration Prosecutions in a High-Volume US Court." *British Journal of Criminology* 57(1): 112–131.

McAleenan, Kevin K. 2018. *Memorandum from Commissioner, U.S. Customs and Border Protection, et al., to Kirstjen Nielsen, Secretary of Homeland Security, Department of Homeland Security*, April 23, 2018.

Medina, Maria Isabel. 1997. "The Criminalization of Immigration Law: Employer Sanctions and Marriage Fraud." *George Mason Law Review* 5(4): 669–732.

Meissner, Doris, Donald M. Kerwin, Muzaffar Chishti, and Claire Bergeron. 2013. *Immigration Enforcement in the United States: The Rise of a Formidable Machinery*. Washington D.C.: Migration Policy Institute.

Morawetz, Nancy. 2000. "Understanding the Impact of the 1996 Deportation Laws and the Limited Scope of Proposed Reforms." *Harvard Law Review* 113(8): 1936–1962.

Office of the Inspector General, U.S. Department of Homeland Security. 2018. *Special Review—Initial Observations Regarding Family Separation Issues under the Zero Tolerance Policy*. OIG-18-84. Washington, D.C.: U.S. Department of Homeland Security.

Padilla v. Kentucky. 2010. 559 U.S. 356.

Rios, Simón. 2019. "DAs Join Lawsuit That Seeks to Bar ICE Arrests At Local Courthouses." *WBUR News*, April 29, 2019.

Rosenbloom, Rachel E. 2016. "Policing Sex, Policing Immigrants: What Crimmigration's Past Can Tell Us about Its Present and Its Future." *California Law Review* 104(1): 149–200.

Satterberg, Dan. 2017. "Crackdown on Immigrants Undermines Public Safety." *The Seattle Times*, March 24, 2017.

Shear, Michael D., Abby Goodnough, and Maggie Haberman. 2018. "Trump Retreats on Separating Families, but Thousands May Remain Apart." *New York Times*, June 20, 2018.

Spagat, Elliot. 2018. "Zero Tolerance Causes Soar in Immigration Cases, California Adopts Mass Hearings." *Chicago Sun Times*, July 8, 2018.

Spagat, Elliot. 2018. "Parents of 545 Children Separated at Border Can't Be Found." *Washington Post*, October 20, 2020.

Siegler, Alison. 2009. "Disparities and Discretion in Fast-Track Sentencing." *Federal Sentencing Reporter* 21(5): 299–310.

Srikantiah, Jayashri. 2007. "Perfect Victims and Real Survivors: The Iconic Victim in Domestic Human Trafficking Law." *Boston University Law Review* 87(1): 157–212.

TRAC Immigration. 2018. *Immigration Prosecutions November 2018*. January 11, 2019.

TRAC Immigration. 2016. *Immigration Now 52 Percent of All Federal Criminal Prosecutions*. November 28, 2016.

CHAPTER 22

PROSECUTING RACE AND ADOLESCENCE

KRISTIN HENNING

22.1 INTRODUCTION

OVER the last quarter century, research has shown that much of youth crime is the product of normal adolescent development. Adolescents often make impetuous and ill-considered decisions, are susceptible to negative influences and outside pressures, and have limited capacity to identify and weigh the short- and long-term consequences of their choices. Because children and adolescents are more malleable and amenable to rehabilitation than adults, the Supreme Court has recognized youth as a mitigating factor in the disposition of even the most serious criminal behavior by adolescents. Most notably, in *Roper v. Simmons* in 2005, *Graham v. Florida* in 2010, and *Miller v. Alabama* in 2012, the Supreme Court relied upon developmental research to conclude, respectively, that the death penalty is categorically inappropriate for youth under the age of 18, the sentence of life without the possibility of parole is too severe for youth convicted in non-homicide cases, and a mandatory sentence of life without the possibility of parole in homicide cases is impermissible because it denies youth the opportunity to present mitigating evidence concerning their development.

Notwithstanding the Court's recognition of youths' diminished culpability, persistent racial disparities in the treatment of youth at all stages of the juvenile and criminal justice systems suggest that these mitigating principles of adolescent development are not applied equitably across race and class. Although Black youth comprised only 16 percent of all youth in the United States in 2016 (Puzzanchera, Sladky, and Kang 2018), they accounted for 35 percent of all juvenile arrests, 36 percent of juvenile court referrals, 40 percent of detained youth, 40 percent of youth formally processed by the juvenile court, 37 percent of adjudicated youth, 47 percent of youth judicially waived to criminal court (OJJDP 2017c), and 42 percent of youth in residential placements

(Hockenberry 2018, 12). Research suggests that decision-makers in the juvenile and criminal justice systems treat youth of color more harshly than their White peers in part because they are less inclined to recognize their developmental immaturity, particularly in light of racial stereotypes that negatively affect judgments about adolescent culpability, maturity, risk of recidivism, and deserved punishment (Soung 2011, 437).

As gatekeepers of juvenile court jurisdiction, prosecutors have a unique opportunity to reduce racial disparities by filtering out explicit and implicit bias in the system and applying the key principles of developmental psychology to all youth. Although we know more than ever before about the interplay between race, adolescence, and crime, most prosecutors have little practical guidance on how to apply the research at critical stages in a juvenile or criminal case. This chapter draws upon recent findings in adolescent development and implicit racial bias to lay out a framework that will improve prosecutorial decision-making, enhance public safety, and help all youth make a healthy and productive transition to adulthood.

22.2 Prosecutors at the Gate: The Risky Business of Prosecution

A child's transition to a healthy, safe, and productive adulthood is not automatic but instead depends on a number of variables, including the youth's environment and social supports. We have long understood the first three years of life to be among the most important years in a child's development. However, recent neurological research has shown that adolescence (years 10 to 19) presents another critical window when the brain is malleable and subject to change (Steinberg 2014, 37). During adolescence, the brain matures and changes in ways that affect three significant domains of our development: (a) our experience of pleasure (reward system), (b) the ways we think about other people (relationship system), and (c) our ability to exercise self-control (regulatory system). Because the brain continues to evolve through our early to mid-20s, neurologists describe adolescence as a period of heightened plasticity—or malleability—of the brain. It is a time when the brain can change, adapt, and respond to life experiences and the environment (Steinberg 2014, 25). In fact, because the brain will never again be as malleable as it is during those years, developmental psychologist Laurence Steinberg has described adolescence as "our last best chance to make a difference" in the brain's structure and how it operates (Steinberg 2014, 217).

In turn, adolescence is also a time when we can set youth on the *wrong* course in their transition to adulthood. Because adolescence is a time when youth experience significant and rapid growth in their capacities, positive or negative changes in a youth's family, school, or community are likely to have considerable influence on the youth's development (Steinberg and Cauffman 1999, 393; Chung, Little, and Steinberg 2005, 92).

For at-risk youth, decisions within the justice system—including a decision to charge, dismiss, or divert a child from the system—play a significant role in facilitating or undermining a youth's successful development.

Prosecutors have extraordinary influence over outcomes at every stage of a criminal case (Davis 1998, 25, 31). In both juvenile and adult cases, prosecutors have direct authority over whether to charge or divert an accused from the system, what charges to bring, and whether to extend a plea offer. Prosecutors also have tremendous influence on the judge's decisions to detain or release a defendant pending trial, what sentence the judge will impose, and whether the judge will revoke probation if there is a violation. Prosecutorial decision-making in juvenile court is unique, as it is shaped consciously and subconsciously by the prosecutor's understanding of and perspectives on adolescent development. Prosecutors who appreciate a youth's heightened vulnerabilities in police interrogation should inquire more deeply before accepting a child's confession. Prosecutors who understand a youth's diminished psychosocial capacity and poor decision-making skills in the emotionally complex circumstances that lead to crime may be more receptive to mitigating arguments that account for adolescents' susceptibility to duress or diminished capacity to foresee the natural outcome in a felony-murder case and other defenses that affect *mens rea* (Levick and Tierney 2012, 501). Because a chapter of this length cannot explore the impact of adolescent development in every aspect of a juvenile case, this chapter will focus on prosecutorial discretion at the charging and disposition phases. The first section of the chapter will focus on the charging decision and the next section will consider detention, transfer, and sentencing decisions in more serious juvenile cases.

22.2.1 Prosecutorial Discretion at the Charging Phase: Criminalizing Normal Adolescent Behavior

From the inception of the first juvenile court, Child Savers intuitively understood that youth are different from adults and should be "treated" rather than punished for their criminal conduct (Tanenhaus 2005, 107). Those intuitive perceptions are now bolstered by a wealth of developmental and neurological research documenting considerable deficiencies in adolescent decision-making capacities, especially in the fast-paced, emotionally charged settings common to adolescent offending (Albert and Steinberg 2011, 216–220; Steinberg et al. 2009a, 586). Compared to adults, adolescents are more impulsive, more likely to engage in sensation seeking (Steinberg et al. 2008, 1774), less likely to consider the future consequences of their actions (Steinberg et al. 2009b, 39), and more likely to pay attention to the potential rewards—especially the immediate rewards—of a risky decision than to the potential costs (Cauffman et al. 2010, 204; O'Brien et al. 2011, 747–753; Silva et al. 2016, 696–705; Weigard et al. 2014, 71–78).

With MRI technology, researchers have been able to identify a neurobiological basis for the developmental and psychosocial difference between youth and adults

(Durston et al. 2001, 1012–1016). Of particular importance, research reveals that different regions of the brain develop and mature at different times (Gogtay et al. 2004, 8174). Specifically, parts of the brain most associated with risk-taking, sensation-seeking, peer approval, and other incentive-processing functions develop earlier than the parts of the brain most responsible for logical reasoning, planning, and regulating impulses and behavior (Chein et al. 2010, F2). Generally, the capacity to reason and understand develops progressively from preadolescence through the late teen years. Thus, while youth in early adolescence have difficulty conceptualizing future consequences and often lack the knowledge and experience needed to reason through consequences, older teens learn to think ahead and weigh the pros and cons of their choices (Scott 2000). Yet, even as a child's cognitive processes improve, deficiencies in psychosocial development tend to cause youth to underestimate the risks involved in a given course of conduct, focus heavily on the present while failing to consider the future, and encounter difficulty regulating their emotions and controlling their conduct (Cauffman et al. 2010, 206; Halpern-Felsher and Cauffman 2001, 265, 268; Scott and Steinberg 2008, 813–816; Steinberg et al. 2009b, 38–39). Although youth by the age of 15 or 16 often have cognitive abilities similar to adults in controlled settings, psychosocial deficiencies that affect social, emotional, and temporal perceptions and judgments persist well into late adolescence and even early adulthood, ages 18–25 (Arnett 2000; Steinberg 2009, 466–468; Steinberg et al. 2008, 1774–1776; Steinberg et al. 2009a, 586).

Reckless behavior is so common among adolescents that it is virtually a normative characteristic of adolescent development; yet few youth go on to become "life-course-persistent" criminal offenders as adults (Mulvey et al. 2010, 454; Scott and Steinberg 2008, 54–56; Steinberg, Cauffman, and Monahan 2015, 3). Incidents of both minor delinquency and more serious violent crime peak in adolescence and drop precipitously in young adulthood, with most youth aging out of delinquent behavior by late adolescence (Steinberg 2014, 88–89). As youth transition to adulthood, they not only develop the skills they need to process information and think in hypotheticals, but they also develop their own sense of personal identity, learn to resist peer pressure, and begin to understand and control their emotions and impulses.

Of course, the developmental research has its limits. The research cannot tell prosecutors what to do with any one youth in any one case. But prosecutors can draw from the science to construct meaningful and practical insights to guide prosecutorial discretion at all stages of the case. At the charging phase, developmental research may help prosecutors decide whether to charge a youth as an adult or juvenile, whether to charge a juvenile offense as a felony or misdemeanor, and whether to dismiss or divert a child out of the system all together. Armed with evidence that youth naturally age out of criminal behavior, prosecutors may be willing to excuse some adolescent behavior from prosecution and trust that parents, teachers, and other adults will provide discipline and redirection. When those interventions are less certain, prosecutors may refer youth to a diversion program. Consider how adolescent development might affect the charging and diversion decisions in the following examples:[1]

Jaquan: Several boys are sitting outside in a public park. Jaquan, aged 15, finds marijuana in his older brother's room and brings it out to share with his friends. All of the boys try it—each one excited about the opportunity to experiment and afraid of appearing lame in front of his friends. Police arrest all of the boys, and prosecutors charge Jaquan with distribution and the others with possession of marijuana.

James: 15-year-old James is wearing a hoodie sweatshirt in public, a violation of an obscure city ordinance prohibiting such attire. James mouths off at the police officer who tells him to take it off and the encounter escalates into a physical struggle when the officer removes the hood from his head. The officer arrests James. Prosecutors charge James with felony assault on a police officer.

Shannon: 16-year-old Shannon is riding a public bus with five classmates from her special education school when she notices one of the teacher's aides from her school at the back of the bus. Shannon snatches the aide's hat and tosses it to one of her classmates. After playing a game of catch with the hat through peals of laughter, the children drop the hat and get off the bus. Police arrest Shannon at school the next day. Prosecutors charge her with robbery.

Kara: A school resource officer (SRO) observes 17-year-old Kara arguing with her boyfriend, whom she suspects is cheating on her. Kara eventually snatches her boyfriend's phone and walks away while scrolling through his text messages. The SRO arrests her. The prosecutor charges her with robbery.

While each of these examples involves allegations that, if true, meet the statutory elements for the crimes listed, prosecutors have discretion not to act. Prosecutors have long used their discretion to decline prosecution, divert youth from the system, and identify creative alternatives to adjudication. Historically, society has always been able to tolerate some adolescent offending. We expect that youth will test the limits, take risks, and sometimes even break the law. Our role as adults, and more important, as prosecutors, is to respond in ways that promote healthy adolescent development and prevent youth from harming themselves and others. Recognizing that judicial intervention is not always necessary to achieve these goals, prosecutors committed to adolescent-appropriate responses to delinquency will need to be thoughtful about how to incorporate developmental research into charging decisions.

In each of the scenarios above, the prosecutor must decide whether to treat the youth's conduct as "normal" adolescent behavior that can be managed at home, school, or in the community, or as deviant behavior warranting judicial intervention or punishment. Notwithstanding the obvious dangers of drug use and the aide's frustration in losing his hat, few would criticize a prosecutor who exercised her discretion to send Jaquan and his friends home with a warning and referral to a local drug education class or a prosecutor who decided not to charge Shannon for her school bus prank, but instead urged the school to impose their own sanctions. Many would even applaud the prosecutor who refused to prosecute a Black youth who had been confronted for wearing a "hoodie" in public. Yet, despite the availability of these options, cases like these routinely populate juvenile courts across the country—and at rates that disproportionately include youth of color. Developmentally framed charging principles would help prosecutors make more appropriate and equitable charging decisions.

22.2.2 Developmentally Appropriate Responses to Adolescent Offending

In most states, prosecutors have little guidance on how to effectively respond to adolescent offending, and even less guidance on the impact of implicit racial bias in the legal system. Even when statutes and court rules express a preference for diversion or the least restrictive response to adolescent offending, these statutory provisions are often vague and rarely provide specific guidelines for charging and processing youth in juvenile court (Alaska Stat. § 47.12.010; D.C. Code § 16-2301.02(2); Minn. Stat. Ann. § 388.24(2)(1); Neb. Rev. Stat. Ann. § 43-260.04; N.J. Stat. Ann. § 2A:4A-71; Wis. Stat. Ann. § 938.01(2)(e)). Prosecutors have published few internal standards to guide prosecutorial discretion at the youth intake and charging stage, and the standards that do exist do not adequately account for developmental research. For example, even with the most recent 2016 updates, the National District Attorney's Association's (NDAA) National Prosecution Standards include only a brief reference to the adolescent brain and vague references to the youth's age and maturity (NDAA 2016, 64–67).

NDAA standards identify ten criteria prosecutors should consider at the charging and diversion stage: the "seriousness of the alleged offense"; the alleged role of the accused youth in the offense; the "nature and number of previous cases" against the youth and their disposition; the youth's "age, maturity, and mental status"; the availability of appropriate treatment or services through the juvenile court or diversion; the youth's admission of guilt or acceptance of responsibility for involvement in the charged offense; the "dangerousness or threat posed by the juvenile to the person or property of others"; "decision[s] made with respect to similarly situated" youth; the "provision of financial restitution to victims"; and "[r]ecommendations of the referring agency, victim, law enforcement and advocates for the juvenile" (NDAA 2016, 65). Notwithstanding the explicit reference to the youth's age and maturity, these standards differ little from adult charging guidelines and provide virtually no information about the developmental features that contribute to adolescent offending, adolescents' amenability to treatment, and strategies for promoting healthy, positive youth development. The 2016 commentary to these standards offers no additional guidance on the meaning and application of developmental research to these factors.

As a way forward, prosecutors would benefit from internal decision-making guidelines that contextualize charging criteria through the lens of adolescent developmental. In December of 2018, Fair and Just Prosecution released a blueprint, *21 Principles for the 21st Century Prosecutor*, laying out a vision for reducing incarceration, promoting fairness, and ensuring developmentally appropriate responses to delinquency. Although their blueprint does not include a comprehensive discussion of charging standards in juvenile courts, they do urge prosecutors to "treat kids like kids" and specifically recommend that prosecutors "not prosecute kids for typical adolescent behavior such as fist fights, smoking marijuana, disorderly conduct, or other infractions at school that don't result in serious physical harm" (FJP 2018, 9). This fundamental principle provides an important foundation for expanding upon existing NDAA charging criteria with developmental research. A closer examination of NDAA's charging criteria is instructive.

22.2.2.1 *Alleged Role in Offense*

The case examples involving Jaquan and Shannon demonstrate the spontaneous and unplanned roles youth often play in delinquency, as well as the difficulties an adolescent may face when attempting to exit from an escalating criminal event. Developmental research highlights the limits of adolescent cognitive and psychosocial capacity in the heat of a crime, the tendency of adolescents to underestimate the risk of harm in a given situation, and the impact of peer influence on adolescent judgments. Given the gap between cognitive and psychosocial development, it is plausible that a 16-year-old would have the cognitive ability to understand—in a controlled conversation with an adult—that harassing the teacher's aide is wrong, yet impulsively participate in such conduct with a group of friends who snatch the aide's property and run away in the heat of the moment. With susceptibility to peer influence peaking around age 14 and then declining slowly during late adolescence, peer presence makes youth significantly more likely than adults to take risks and engage in antisocial behavior (Gardner and Steinberg 2005, 626–634; Steinberg and Monahan 2007, 1538–1539). The fear of rejection and desire for approval from peers help explain why delinquency is more common in adolescence and why adolescents are more likely than adults to engage in illicit behavior in groups (Scott and Steinberg 2008, 38–39). Understanding this contextual backdrop would help prosecutors navigate difficult decisions by attending to the needs of victims, while avoiding harm to youth who are not a real threat to society.

22.2.2.2 *Dangerousness of the Threat Posed to Others, Seriousness of the Current Offense, and Nature and Number of Prior Offenses*

At face value, James' alleged assault on a police officer and Kara's robbery are serious felonies. Robbery even falls within the FBI's violent crime index. In both instances, victims felt threatened, lost property, and reported the offense to the police. Yet, with thoughtful reflection on principles of adolescent development, prosecutors should recognize Kara's and James' conduct as emotional adolescent outbursts. A fair but developmentally appropriate response to these incidents might involve diversion, an apology, and restitution without a criminal record that interferes with the youths' educational and vocational opportunities.

Charging these behaviors as felonies also creates a record of criminal offending that appears more dangerous than it actually is. Many prosecutors evaluate the risk of future offending by focusing primarily, if not solely, on the nature and number of previous offenses. Unfortunately, this focus may be inadequate in juvenile cases where the misdemeanor and felony labels often mask the true nature and circumstances of the underlying offense. Of course, in some instances the child's prior record may document a history of serious, violent offending, but in many instances a youth who has a record of two "violent felonies" may have engaged in little more than grabbing a boyfriend's phone to check his text messages. When evaluating a child's risk of danger to others, a prosecutor should always delve further to assess the youth's prior criminal contexts from a developmentally appropriate lens.

22.2.2.3 *Youth's Admission of Guilt and Acceptance of Responsibility*

Diversion from formal prosecution is often reserved for those youth who admit involvement early on, are remorseful for their behavior, and demonstrate a capacity for change. Developmental research might expand the category of youth deemed appropriate for diversion by educating prosecutors on the difficulties youth often face in expressing remorse in the hours and days after an offense (Duncan 2002, 1491; Henning 2009, 1148–1153). Youth with limited life experiences, diminished cognitive capacity, or poor language skills may struggle to convey remorse to a police officer, victim, or probation officer shortly after an offense. Other developmental features of adolescence, such as peer influence and teenage bravado, may further block adultlike expressions of grief and remorse. Moreover, because remorse itself is a form of suffering, youth sometimes employ defense mechanisms such as humor, denial, or apparent indifference to avoid it. Given these limitations, empathy and remorse provide a particularly unreliable measure of a youth's amenability to treatment and need for punishment, especially in police interrogation and intake interviews that occur before the youth has had an opportunity to reflect or benefit from counseling. For youth who have not demonstrated remorse, prosecutors may identify restorative justice alternatives that teach youth how to resolve conflict and emphasize the values of empathy, respect, honesty, acceptance, responsibility, and accountability (Ashley and Burke 2010, 7; Center for Restorative Youth Justice 2018).

22.2.2.4 *Recommendations of the Referring Agency, Victim, Law Enforcement, and Advocates for the Youth*

Although victims, witnesses, and police officers often have strong views in the charging and sentencing phases of a criminal case, prosecutors must exercise independent judgment and guard against the rote implementation of police recommendations and victim impact statements. When engaging victims of youth crime, prosecutors should be transparent about the underlying reasons for each charging decision and educate victims on alternatives to prosecution that promote healthy adolescent development and thus better serve the community's interest in public safety. Ultimately, to treat children like children, prosecutors must resist external pressures for harsh responses to adolescent offending and firmly resolve to respond in ways that reflect the key principles of adolescent development and help youth transition to a safe and productive adulthood. As explored in the next section, developmentally tailored charging principles would also promote consistency and equity across race by reminding prosecutors that youth of all races experience the same developmental trajectories and urging prosecutors to resist harmful and inaccurate stereotypes about youth of color.

22.2.3 Prosecution at the Intersection of Race and Adolescence

Although we now have a wealth of research on developmental immaturity and adolescent offending, racial disparities at every stage of the juvenile justice system suggest that state actors do not rely on developmentally appropriate responses for youth of color to the same extent as they do for White youth. Data indicates that youth of color are less likely than White youth to be afforded the benefits of diversion, community-based alternatives to detention, developmental supports, and other rehabilitative programming in the community. As noted at the start of this chapter, although Black youth comprised only 16 percent of all youth in the United States in 2016, they accounted for 40 percent of youth formally prosecuted in juvenile courts that year and 47 percent of youth judicially waived to adult court. Prosecutors who have discretion to dismiss cases altogether or to file charges in juvenile courts rather than criminal courts have direct authority in both of these contexts.

Of course, racial disparities surface in the juvenile justice system long before the charging decision. Police arrest youth of color at rates that far exceed their proportion in society, and school officials who enforce zero-tolerance policies and employ school resource officers to regulate normal adolescent behavior contribute significantly to the disproportionate referral of youth of color to the courts. Once youth are referred to the judicial system, prosecutors evaluate the strength and merits of the delinquency allegation and probation officers review information about the youth's family, neighborhood, and school performance. In many jurisdictions, probation officers also advise prosecutors about whether to file or decline to file a formal complaint. Despite the significant role that probation officers, police, and schools play in contributing to racial disparities in the juvenile justice system, prosecutors serve as the ultimate gatekeepers of juvenile court jurisdiction and are arguably the system's most powerful decision-makers (Davis 1998, 17–18; Henning 2013, 430). Given their enormous power to decline prosecution and divert youth from the system, prosecutors may be in the best position to achieve or lead meaningful and sustainable efforts to reduce racial disparities.

Prosecutors committed to fair and equitable decision-making will benefit from additional guiding principles at the charging phase. The NDAA criteria indicate that prosecutors should consider *decisions made with respect to similarly situated persons*, with an implicit admonition to treat similarly situated persons the same. Unfortunately, that admonition alone is not likely to reduce racial disparities in the juvenile and criminal justice systems. As outlined in this section, prosecutors need better guidance on how to identify and overcome their own biases, as well as strategies to disrupt structural inequities and dismantle policies that disadvantage youth of color.

22.2.3.1 *Understanding Implicit Racial Bias and Perceptions of Adolescent Culpability*

If asked, most prosecutors would say they are committed to racial equity and treat all defendants the same regardless of race. In juvenile cases, most would be able to provide a rational, race-neutral explanation to support each of the charging decisions they make—relying on the dangerousness of the crime, the youth's record of prior offending, the youth's lack of family support, the victim's rights, public safety, and the need to respond to community interests. Yet even these seemingly neutral charging principles are susceptible to distortion by implicit racial bias. Like other state actors, prosecutors are vulnerable to the unconscious effects of negative stereotypes and harmful narratives about youth of color.

All of us rely on cognitive shortcuts and biases to fill in missing data, sort through the vast amount of information we receive, and categorize people and information according to cultural stereotypes (Eberhardt et al. 2004, 877; Richardson and Goff 2012, 297–301). These shortcuts help us manage the many decisions we must make every day, including those in the justice system (Richardson and Goff 2012, 297–301). Implicit racial bias refers to those cognitive shortcuts that involve race and include both "unconscious stereotypes (beliefs about social groups) and attitudes (feelings, either positive or negative, about social groups)" (Richardson and Goff 2013, 2630). People of all races have implicit racial biases that may negatively affect their behavior, even those who actively support racial equality, vehemently reject racism and discrimination, and have positive relationships with people of other races (Kang and Mahzarin 2006, 1514). Implicit bias is often so subtle that we are generally not aware of it and may act on it reflexively without realizing it (Lyon 2012, 759; Richardson 2011, 2043).

The impact of implicit racial bias has been well documented in all phases of the criminal justice system. Researchers have found evidence of implicit bias among police officers (Correll et al. 2007; Graham and Lowery 2004; Plant and Peruche 2005), potential jurors (Levinson 2007; Levinson, Cai, and Young 2010; Levinson and Young 2010), judges (Levinson, Cai, and Young 2010; Rachlinski et al. 2009), probation officers (Graham and Lowery 2004), prosecutors (Berdejó 2018), defense attorneys (Edkins 2011; Lyon 2012), and undergraduate students and the general public who could assume any of these roles (Eberhardt et al. 2004; Hugenberg and Bodenhausen 2003; Todd, Thiem, and Neal 2016). Most important, several studies have explored the unique ways implicit racial bias affects perceptions of childhood innocence and culpability, predictions about adolescent re-offending, and recommendations for punishment or treatment after a juvenile adjudication. Prosecutors will benefit from understanding how bias operates at different stages of the justice system as they evaluate recommendations from other stakeholders and develop strategies to resist biases in their own judgments.

In one of the earliest studies of bias and adolescent culpability, researchers found that probation officers were significantly more likely to attribute crime to internal personality causes, such as lack of remorse, lack of cooperation with the probation officer, and failure to take the proceedings seriously when a Black youth was involved, but more likely to attribute crime to external influences, such as dysfunctional families, drug and alcohol use, difficulties at school, and the influence of delinquent peers when White youth were involved (Bridges and Steen 1998, 564). Even after controlling for the severity of the youth's current and past criminal behavior, probation officers were also much more likely to view Black youth as prone to criminal behavior in the future and to recommend sentences longer than the sentencing guideline range.

A few years later, another team of researchers explored the impact of unconscious racial stereotyping on police officers' and probation officers' perceptions of adolescent culpability, deserved punishment, and likely recidivism (Graham and Lowery 2004, 484–499). Police officers who were primed with words associated with Black Americans perceived young offenders in a factual vignette to be more "adult-like" and more responsible for their behavior than did officers who were not primed with those words. Similarly, probation officers who were primed with words about Black Americans judged the alleged offenders to be more mature, more violent, more culpable, more likely to reoffend, and more deserving of punishment. In both instances, the participants ultimately endorsed harsher punishment for youth perceived to be more violent and culpable. These outcomes were consistent across the ethnicity and gender of the study participants and persisted even when the decision-makers consciously desired to avoid prejudice.

In 2012, researchers studied the impact of race on public support for severe sentences such as life without the possibility of parole for youth under age 18 (Rattan et al. 2012, 2–4). To measure the extent to which the public believed that youth who commit serious crimes should be considered less blameworthy than adults who commit the same crime, researchers provided participants with a factual summary of a recent Supreme Court case involving a violent youth offender along with information in support of and in opposition to life without parole sentences for youth in non-homicide cases. Even when controlling for the participant's political ideology and evidence of racial bias, researchers found that study participants were more likely to favor harsher sentences when they were primed to believe the offender was Black than when they believed the offender was White.

In perhaps one of the most comprehensive and revealing studies of all, a team of researchers conducted a series of experiments in 2014 with university students and police officers to examine the perceived ages and levels of culpability of Black, Latino, and White boys (between the ages of 10 and 17) purportedly engaged in a variety of felony and misdemeanor offenses (Goff et al. 2014). When asked to estimate the age of each child and answer a series of questions related to the "suspect's" culpability for the offense, study participants perceived Black boys as older and less innocent than White boys of the same age. Specifically, the civilian and law enforcement participants perceived Black youth felony suspects as 4.53 and 4.59 years older, respectively, than they actually were, and both groups perceived Black youth felony suspects as significantly more culpable than White or Latino felony suspects for the identified crime. Research has confirmed similar public perceptions of Black girls. In 2017, researchers found that survey participants viewed Black girls—especially in the age range of 5–14—as more likely to appear and behave older than their stated age, more knowledgeable about adult topics, including sex, and more likely to take on more adult roles and responsibilities than would be expected for White girls of their age (Epstein, Blake, and González 2017).

Studies like these help explain racial disparities in juvenile court referrals and the more punitive treatment of Black youth in the juvenile justice system. Although studies have not looked specifically at how race affects prosecutors' perspectives on adolescent culpability, we have every reason to believe that bias operates in similar ways with prosecutors. Research in the adult criminal context shows that prosecutors are vulnerable to racialized perceptions of aggressiveness, violence, and danger (Berdejó 2018, 1198; Davis 1998, 35), and data confirms that prosecutors are more likely to charge Black suspects than Whites (Berdejó 2018, 1190), even when their prior criminal records are the same (Smith and Levinson 2012, 806). Prosecutors and other justice stakeholders who are committed to reducing racial disparities must be attentive to ways in which bias increases referrals from other state actors and consider how their own biases may affect their interpretation of charging criteria such as *dangerousness and threat posed to others.* As prosecutors develop their own internal standards and guiding principles for the charging phase, they should incorporate research on implicit racial bias and highlight developmental research confirming that youth of all ethnicities and socioeconomic status exhibit similar patterns of impulsivity and risk-taking. Prosecutors should also provide feedback to other stakeholders and collaborate in systemic efforts to address structural inequities.

22.2.3.2 *Checking Prosecutorial Bias*

Fortunately, research suggests that well-intentioned actors—like prosecutors—may offset their own implicit bias when they are made aware of the stereotypes and biases they hold, have the cognitive capacity to self-correct, and are motivated to do so. Researchers have found positive results in the simultaneous and long-term implementation of five corrective strategies to reduce implicit racial bias: stereotype replacement (replacing stereotypical responses to stereotyped groups with non-stereotypical responses), counter-stereotypic imaging (imagining a stereotyped group in counter-stereotypic ways), individuation (declining to make judgments without obtaining specific information about each person), perspective-taking (assuming the first-person perspective of a stereotyped group before taking action or making decisions), and increased opportunities for contact with commonly stereotyped groups (Devine et al. 2012, 1270). When implemented in tandem, these strategies increase the actor's prospects of breaking persistent, subconscious bias-induced habits. Prosecutors would benefit from training that exposes them to implicit bias research and provides them with opportunities to practice and apply these strategies in the justice context.

Prosecutors would also benefit from research documenting similar patterns of impulsivity, risk-taking, sensation-seeking, susceptibility to peer influence, and limited future orientation across all socioeconomic and ethnic groups (Cauffman et al. 2010, 200, 204–206; Steinberg and Monahan 2007, 1538–1539; Steinberg et al. 2009b, 36–37; Steinberg et al. 2008, 1775). This research would remind prosecutors that youth of color are not inherently more dangerous than White youth and encourage them to afford all youth the mitigating advantages of adolescence, including opportunities for diversion and other alternatives to prosecution. Prosecutors should also consider two national self-report studies on youth violence and drug use that further document similar patterns of self-reported delinquency and risky behaviors among White, Black, and Hispanic youth (The University of Michigan and the Center for Disease Control [CDC]). Self-reported data supports the conclusion that youth of all races—especially those between the ages of 15 and 19—engage in dangerous, risk-taking behaviors, such as drunk driving, unprotected sex, and drug use. Yet notwithstanding data that Black[2] youth consistently report less drug use than Whites and Hispanics for most types of drugs,[3] Black youth are consistently charged (i.e., "formally petitioned") for drug offenses at significantly higher rates than White youth. For example, in 2015, Black youth accounted for just 14 percent of the total youth population (Puzzanchera, Sladky, and Kang 2018), but represented 59 percent of all youth charged for drug law violations (OJJDP 2017a, 2017b).

Self-report studies also provide evidence that race does not predetermine violent offending. Although Black youth are charged at much higher rates than White youth for weapons offenses, CDC's Youth Risk Behavior Surveillance Study reveals that White youth self-report involvement in weapons offenses at similar or higher rates than Black youth. CDC data from 2015, for example, revealed that White youth were more likely to report carrying a weapon such as a gun, knife, or club than Hispanic or Black youth (CDC 2015); yet Black youth accounted for 70 percent of all youth charged with a weapons offense that year. (OJJDP 2018a). While drug preferences, types of violence, and types of weapon carried may differ across races in self-reporting, these studies confirm that adolescents of all races engage in dangerous, risk-taking behaviors and provide little or no justification for persistent racial disparities in youth arrests and prosecutions.

Recognizing that racial disparities often arise out of structural inequities and other seemingly race-neutral features that are imbedded throughout the juvenile and criminal justice systems, prosecutors should consider how their own practices and policies may contribute to the problem. At the charging phase, prosecutors might revisit office-wide policies that prevent frontline attorneys from diverting drug cases involving "more dangerous" drugs such as crack, crystal meth, or heroin when those policies systemically disadvantage youth of color who live in communities where those drugs are less expensive and more accessible. In 2009, the Vera Institute's Prosecution and Racial Justice Project tracked charging decisions in Milwaukee and found that Milwaukee prosecutors declined to prosecute 41 percent of White adults arrested for possession of drug paraphernalia compared to only 27 percent of non-White adults arrested for the same offense. The project revealed that prosecutors pursued drug paraphernalia charges more aggressively if the paraphernalia was a crack pipe, which was more common among Black defendants, than other types of paraphernalia that were more common among White defendants. Following this revelation, the Milwaukee District Attorney adopted a policy that directed staff to decline all paraphernalia cases "whenever it [is] reasonable to do so and to refer the arrested individuals to drug treatment" (McKenzie et al. 2009, 7).

In the juvenile justice context, prosecutors might also revisit charging criteria and risk assessment tools that distinguish between accused youth on the basis of social factors, such as perceived family stability, parental employment, community support, and school performance, that are closely correlated with race and contribute to the disproportionate incarceration of children of color (Birckhead 2017; Hoytt et al. 2004; Johnson 2007, 412; Moriearty 2008, 304; Roberts 2001, 1020–1027). For example, state actors may presume that parents who work long or non-traditional hours are unable to provide adequate supervision at home. Youth of color, whose parents are more likely to have low-wage jobs with strict leave policies, bear the brunt of these presumptions. Even risk-assessment instruments that use actuarial science to assess an offender's potential risk of criminal activity may rely on racially coded factors, such as the presence or absence of two parents in the youth's home or the arrest record of parents and siblings, to score the child's risk of offending. Risk factors like these ignore the history of disproportionate policing in Black communities and favor the traditional features of a two-parent White American family over single-parent and extended-family structures disproportionately common in Black communities (Moore and Padavic 2011, 852–853).

Finally, as prosecutors begin to think differently about youth of color, they must also learn to speak differently about these youth. Labels like "thug," "wild," "remorseless," and "incorrigible" have demonized and dehumanized youth of color in juvenile courts across the country. Even the term "juvenile," which is rarely used in any context other than crime and delinquency, now carries a negative connotation that has become virtually synonymous in the subconscious mind with youth of color. Through counter-stereotypic imaging and perspective-taking, prosecutors must learn to think about and talk about court-involved youth in the same ways they would talk about their own children. Undoubtedly, overcoming prejudices, especially those arising out of long-held implicit biases, is a protracted process that requires intentionality and commitment.

22.2.3.3 *Identifying Opportunities for Systemic Reform: The School to Prison Pipeline*

Prosecutors have an opportunity to systemically influence public and private agencies that repeatedly and disproportionately refer youth of color to the juvenile justice system. School officials who once addressed normal adolescent misconduct through counseling and other in-school interventions now routinely hire school resource officers to patrol hallways and manage even the least offensive adolescent behavior (Kupchik and Monahan 2006, 620–621). As a result, the school-to-prison pipeline has become a primary source of referrals to the juvenile justice system and increasingly pushes minority students into the courts. A recent analysis of data compiled by the

U.S. Department of Education Office for Civil Rights (OCR) for the 2015–2016 school year reveals that Black students in forty-three states and the District of Columbia are arrested at school at a disproportionately high level (Blad and Harwin 2017). Although Black youth represented only 15 percent of the total student enrollment in the OCR dataset for the 2015–2016 school year, 31 percent of students who were referred to law enforcement or arrested were Black. In twenty-eight states, the share of arrested students who are Black is at least ten percentage points higher than their share of enrollment in schools with at least one arrest. In ten of those states, that gap is at least twenty percentage points.

Unlike school officials and police officers who generally interact with youth in a limited geographic space, prosecutors often screen referrals from across the city and may track and compare patterns of arrest and referral by neighborhood (McKenzie et al. 2009, 1–7). Prosecutors who see that youth of color are routinely referred from one or more schools for low- to mid-level offenses may decline to prosecute and encourage schools and community leaders to identify alternative responses to adolescent offending. As gatekeepers of juvenile court jurisdiction, prosecutors may decline to prosecute school referrals that involve disorderly conduct, trespass, simple drug possession, disregard of police commands, school fights that do not involve serious or repeated injuries, and petty thefts when the victim receives restitution or the benefit of community service (Sherrod, Huff, and Teske 2008; St. George 2011). By declining to prosecute these normal adolescent behaviors, prosecutors set the standard for juvenile court intake and over time may significantly reduce disproportionate minority confinement. To be more transparent at the charging phase, prosecutors may also inform police officers of the reasons for dismissals and explicitly articulate a preference for allowing counselors, teachers, and parents to regulate certain adolescent behaviors. Sharing this information should help officers better decide when to make warrantless arrests and ultimately reduce the number of youth unnecessarily referred to the juvenile justice system (Gershowitz 2018, 1525, 1545).

Prosecutors may assume an even more expansive role in leading systemic efforts to reduce school-based referrals to the juvenile justice system by following the lead of Judge Steven Teske and others who have developed school offense protocols to reverse the trend toward escalating school arrests. Prosecutors may work with local school resource officers to develop a series of graduated sanctions and educational programming before they refer a student to court for specified offenses (Cooperative Agreement 2004, 2–4). Graduated sanctions may involve school social workers and counselors who are often in a better position than courts to prevent and correct misconduct among youth. System-wide efforts like these reduce the steady influx of delinquency referrals from schools and allow states to conserve limited resources for the most serious offenses. School Offense Protocols have also had some success in reducing disproportionate minority contact with the juvenile court. For example, in Clayton County, Georgia between 2003 and 2011, school referrals to juvenile court decreased by more than 73 percent; youth of color referred to court decreased by 60 percent (Status Offense Reform Center 2014, 3).

To avoid potential claims that prosecutors are ignoring or underenforcing criminal laws in communities of color (Kennedy 1997, 19; Meares and Kahan 1998, 199–200; Natapoff 2006, 1716–1718), prosecutors should explain their charging decisions to victims and actively engage the community, legislators, and school leaders in developing alternatives to prosecution. Prosecutors must first correct faulty public perceptions about the nature and scope of youth crime in the community. Despite the media's focus on high-profile youth crime, most adolescent offending involves misdemeanors and low- and mid-level felonies, such as simple assault, drug offenses, property crimes, violations of a public order, technical violations or "status offenses" (OJJDP 2018b). Only a small percentage of detained or adjudicated youth have committed homicide, violent sexual assault, robbery, or aggravated assault. Armed with accurate information about adolescent offending, prosecutors have considerable opportunity to educate others and identify scientifically supported responses that serve public safety and victims' rights while also accounting for the unique features of adolescence and ensuring that the mitigating principles of adolescent development are applied equitably across race and class.

22.3 Serious Adolescent Offending

Much of this chapter has focused on intake and the decision to dismiss or divert a youth from formal prosecution. Of course, not all adolescent offending can or should be excused. Prosecution is sometimes necessary to hold youth accountable, meaningfully acknowledge harm, secure restitution for a victim, or to ensure rehabilitation punishment for a young offender. Research on adolescent development and implicit racial bias are no less important in cases involving more serious adolescent offending. Decisions about what charges to bring and whether to recommend pre-trial detention, transfer to adult court, or a sentence involving incarceration are all vitally important and deeply impacted by what we know about adolescent offending. Decisions that fail to account for adolescent development and implicit racial bias could undermine healthy adolescent development and exacerbate racial inequities in the system.

22.3.1 "Do No Harm"

Just as developmentally appropriate responses to delinquency can increase the chances that adolescents will reach a healthy turning point in their transition to adulthood, developmentally inappropriate interventions by the justice system can derail or impede that transition. Because youth's desire for pleasure is heightened and their self-control is still evolving during adolescence, it is important for adults to limit adolescents' exposure to situations that threaten their health or compromise their brain when it is still malleable (Steinberg 2014, 207). Prosecutors influence youths' short and long-term outcomes with the decisions and recommendations they make at every stage of the juvenile and criminal justice systems.

22.3.1.1 *Harms of Detention and Incarceration*

The social context in which adolescents transition to adulthood has a significant impact on a youth's development of cognitive and psychosocial capacities. Successful interventions help produce healthy and well-adjusted youth by teaching them to make plans and follow them, anticipate the longer-term consequences of their actions, and regulate their behavior, emotions, and thinking (Steinberg 2014, 31). Unfortunately, the repetitive, controlled activities that are common in most detention facilities and prisons rarely provide youth with the experiences and responsibilties that help the youth's brain stay malleable and stimulate the development of higher-order cognitive abilities and self-control and (61–62). Youth fair better in classrooms and with vocational tasks and extracurricular activities with adults who provide them with novel, challenging, and cognitively stimulating activity. Youth in detention rarely participate in activities that give them the opportunity to think critically and independently or to make decisions that have real-world consequences (207).

Incarceration also disrupts important opportunities for proper socialization and may further deteriorate youths' already troubled relationships with their parents, causing them to lose family support when they need it most. Further, because youth are profoundly influenced by the way others view them (Nakkula and Toshalis 2016, 119), the stigma and rejection commonly associated with an out-of-home placement will likely have a significant psychological impact on the self-image and identity of youth who are removed from their communities (Chung, Little, and Steinberg 2005, 82). Adolescent identity development is particularly important for youth of color who often struggle to construct a positive and cohesive identity in the face of racial hierarchies and the legacy of racial and ethnic oppression (Nakkula and Toshalis 2016, 119).

Youth placed in facilities euphemistically named "residential treatment centers" fare little better than youth in more traditional correctional facilities. Notwithstanding their names, these facilities are often poorly equipped to address the needs of youth in the system. System-involved youth often experience trauma, mental health problems, unstable and unsupportive family connections, poverty, crime-ridden neighborhoods, negative peer influences, and poor school performance. (Chung, Little, and Steinberg 2005, 71). Left unaddressed, these conditions can greatly impede the youth's transition to adulthood. Even when youth do obtain services to address these needs, the skills they acquire and other gains they make while in "treatment" are often lost in the difficult transition from institutionalization back to the community (Magellan Health Services 2008, 4–5). Youth in residential treatment programs also risk abuse from other residents or from staff who rely on aggressive behavioral control methods such as seclusion and restraints. Youth returning to the community after these experiences have had little opportunity to develop the psychosocial capacities they need to succeed as adults. Not surprisingly, some incarcerated youth increase antisocial behavior after exposure to and placement with other delinquent youth (Chung, Little, and Steinberg 2005, 81–82).

In their 21st Century blueprint, Fair and Just Prosecution recommends that prosecutors generally should not seek incarceration for teenagers while their cases are pending, and if youth cannot stay home safely, prosecutors should promote alternatives to detention such as community-based day supervision and treatment centers. After conviction or adjudication, prosecutors should continue to seek alternatives to incarceration whenever possible (FJP 2018, 9). These recommendations are well founded given that we know pre-trial detention, incarceration, and secure treatment during adolescence are particularly detrimental to healthy psychosocial development (Chung, Little, and Steinberg 2005, 79, 101; Steinberg, Chung, and Little 2004, 27–28).

22.3.1.2 *Transfer to Adult Court*

Prosecutors have enormous power over whether children will be treated like children in the juvenile justice system or transferred to the criminal justice system for prosecution as adults. In most jurisdictions, prosecutors have statutory discretion to file charges in juvenile court rather than adult court and to elect charges that circumvent mandatory transfer statutes. Criminal prosecution deprives youth of confidentiality protections and the range of rehabilitative sentencing options typically available to youth in juvenile court, as well as the risk of incarceration with adults who may prey on youth physically, sexually, or psychologically (Beale 2009, 521; Henning 2004, 542–560). Recognizing that most young people age out of criminal behavior as they mature and that most youth are substantially better off if they remain in juvenile court, Fair and Just Prosecution recommends that prosecutors should not seek to try children under the age of 18 in adult court, except in very limited circumstances after an evaluation of factors such as the youth's background and the nature and circumstances of the offense. Fair and Just Prosecution also recommends that where a state statute mandates trying a child as an adult for a certain offense, the prosecutor should consider charging the child with a lesser-included crime if possible (FJP 2018, 10).

22.3.1.3 *Harsh and Racially Disparate Sentencing*

In constructing sentencing recommendations for young offenders, prosecutors should consider the impact of harsh punishments and racial inequities on the legitimacy of the criminal justice system and public safety. Although Black youth accounted for only 16 percent of the population of youth under 18 in the United States in 2015, 42 percent of all youth held in juvenile residential facilities on October 28 of that year were Black, 31 percent were White, and 22 percent were Hispanic[4] (Hockenberry 2018, 12). In the adult system, about 77 percent of youth serving a sentence of life without parole in 2014 were Black and Latino, with Black youth serving life without parole at a rate ten times greater than White youth (ACLU 2014, 4). Evidence suggests that these harsh and racially disparate responses to adolescent offending do little to enhance public safety as they ignore the root causes of crime and undermine adolescents' respect for the law and legal institutions (Fagan and Meares 2008, 178–179; Tonry 2010, 274). Severe punishments that remove Black men and youth from their neighborhoods destabilize communities and deprive youth of developmental supports in ways that ultimately increase crime (Fagan and Meares 2008, 173). The unique concentration of families with incarcerated family members in low-income neighborhoods facilitates a downward spiral of poverty and dislodges important social supports that help prevent youth from engaging in risky adolescent behaviors (Pritikin 2008, 1065–1067).

Youth incarcerated in juvenile or adult facilities may also be automatically removed from Medicaid rolls and required to reenroll through a lengthy reapplication process upon release (Acoca, Stephens, and Van Vleet 2014). Other youth become homeless because of laws that make them and their families ineligible to live in Section 8 housing after adjudication. Formerly incarcerated youth also have difficulty finding employment, earning academic credits while in placement or reaching educational goals like attaining a high school diploma or GED. Even when formerly incarcerated youth do secure employment, their earnings are likely to be less than those who have not been incarcerated (Chung, Little, and Steinberg 2005, 72; Nellis 2011, 22–24).

Harsh and racially disparate responses to crime and delinquency contribute to community dissatisfaction and distrust of the legal system. Because adolescence is a critical time during which norms and values (including beliefs about the law and legal institutions) are formed, youths' positive and negative perceptions of justice during adolescence often have a substantial and lasting effect on their attitudes and willingness to obey the law (Henning 2017). When authorities—like prosecutors—enforce rules and make decisions in a way that is fair, youth are more likely to respect and cooperate with legal authorities and ultimately to obey their rules (Penner et al. 2014, 234; Trinkner and Cohn 2014, 608).

22.3.2 Promoting Positive Youth Development

Recognizing that youth have an inherent potential for growth and change, prosecutors can use their power to help youth improve their life outcomes and transition to a successful adulthood. Youth who engage in delinquency in adolescence can reach a "turning point[]" toward responsible law-abiding behavior and healthy psychosocial development with the help of caring and supportive adults who guide and advocate for them in school, work, and the community (Chung, Little, and Steinberg 2005, 77; Scott and Steinberg 2008, 56–57). Prosecutors can help youth reach this turning point by referring them to rehabilitative programs that expose them to role models, prosocial peers, and extracurricular activities; helping them find vocational opportunities that allow them to achieve financial independence; and making sure they have positive adult supports that compensate for deficient family relationships. To capitalize on the brain's malleability during adolescence, prosecutors must work with other stakeholders to ensure youth receive the educational and vocational training they need to succeed in the workforce, as well as the affirmation they need to develop a positive sense of their own worth, independence, and ability to set and achieve their own goals. The justice system can also teach youth to behave responsibly toward the community in which they live by engaging them in structured activities that cultivate social and interpersonal skills, help them understand and appreciate other people's needs, motivations, and intentions, and help them maintain healthy and satisfying intimate relationships (Chung, Little, and Steinberg 2005, 76).

Studies have shown that even serious, violent, and chronic young offenders can benefit from community-based interventions (Scott and Steinberg 2008, 217–219). For example, a number of cost-effective, community-based responses to adolescent offending have been shown to reduce crime across a range of offending patterns. Among them are Functional Family Therapy (FFT), Multisystemic Therapy (MST), Multidimensional Treatment Foster Care (MTFC), Aggression Replacement Therapy (ART), and Trauma Focused Cognitive Behavioral Therapy (TF-CBT). FFT seeks to strengthen the family through therapists who work to improve the emotional connection between youth and their parents and to teach authoritative parenting skills that impose structure and limits on children (Functional Family Therapy 2018). MST, which has been particularly successful with violent and aggressive youth, is a community-based approach that seeks to empower families with the skills and resources they need to cope with family problems, address peer group concerns, and advocate on behalf of their children in the school and community (Multisystemic Therapy 2018). MTFC, which has been effective with high-risk and chronic offenders, separates youth from their delinquent peers, provides them with adult mentoring, heightened supervision, and support in school and the community, and places youth with trained foster parents for six to twelve months while they complete family therapy with their own family (National Institute of Justice 2011a). These programs succeed in part because of their attention to the psychosocial capacities that youth need to prepare for adulthood. ART seeks to develop social skills, emotional control, and moral reasoning among chronically aggressive and violent adolescents (National Institute of Justice 2012), while TF-CBT is designed to help 3- to 18-year-olds overcome serious emotional problems such as post-traumatic stress, fear, anxiety, and depression by teaching children and parents new skills for processing thoughts and feelings arising out of traumatic life events (National Institute of Justice 2011b).

Interventions like TF-CBT are particularly important given the strong link between delinquency and childhood traumas that compromise adolescent decision-making and impulse control over time. Many youth involved with the juvenile justice system report having experienced at least one traumatic incident, such as physical abuse, sexual abuse, domestic violence, community violence, or other personal or community disasters. Prosecutors who understand that arrest and prosecution can exacerbate already-existing trauma may consider using trauma screening instruments that help differentiate between delinquent behaviors and traumatic stress reactions and reduce the re-traumatizing effects of court involvement (Ford et al. 2007, 3–4).

In response to fears that they are being "soft" on crime, prosecutors may educate the community on the key features of adolescent offending and resilience and be transparent about policies and practices that are necessary to address racial disparities in the system. Scientific validation and Supreme Court endorsement of developmental research give much-needed credibility to adolescent-appropriate responses to delinquency and help shield prosecutors from criticism. Research also suggests that many victims prefer rehabilitative alternatives to incarceration for youth. In 2016, the Alliance for Safety and Justice commissioned a National Survey of Victims' Views. The survey revealed that by a two-to-one margin, victims prefer that the criminal justice system focus on rehabilitation rather than punishment (Alliance for Safety and Justice 2016). When specifically asked about youth, the study showed that by a margin of seven to one, victims prefer increased investments in crime prevention and programs for at-risk youth over more investments in prisons and jails. Of the victims surveyed, seven in ten prefer that prosecutors focus on solving neighborhood problems and stopping repeat crimes through rehabilitation, even it means fewer convictions and prison sentences. Even when constituents and victims remain committed to retribution and incarceration for young offenders, prosecutors will have to make hard choices that disappoint some but nonetheless apply principles of diminished culpability more equitably to youth of color and achieve public safety through strategies that promote rehabilitation and positive youth development.

22.4 Conclusion

Notwithstanding the growing body of developmental research demonstrating that much of youth crime and delinquency is the product of normal adolescent development, persistent racial disparities in the treatment of youth in the juvenile and criminal justice systems suggest that mitigating principles of adolescent development are not being applied equitably across race and class. Contemporary narratives portraying youth of color as dangerous and irredeemable lead police, probation officers, and prosecutors to reject the most effective responses to adolescent offending in favor of punitive and institutional approaches to crime that do little to improve public safety. This chapter urges prosecutors to acknowledge the unique developmental status of all youth and develop guidelines for prosecuting youth that adequately account for youths' amenability to treatment and diminished culpability in criminal activity. Prosecutors must learn to recognize implicit bias not only in their own decisions, but also in the decisions of other system stakeholders. As gatekeepers of juvenile court jurisdiction, prosecutors have tremendous power to reduce racial disparities in the system over time and improve life outcomes for all system-involved youth.

Notes

1. Each of these examples comes from the author's own representation of youth in Washington, D.C. The youths' names have been changed the names to protect confidentiality.
2. Although the CDC report uses the term "African American," this chapter uses Black to maintain consistency.

3. In 2016, the CDC reported the annual prevalence of illicit drug use *other than marijuana* in grade 10 as 10.3 percent among White youth, 7.8 percent among Black youth, and 11.1 percent among Hispanic youth, and in grade 12 as 15.5 percent among White youth, 10.3 percent among Black youth, and 13.7 percent among Hispanic youth. Black youth outpace White youth for marijuana use in the 8th and 10th grades, and for crack and heroin use in the 12th grade. The CDC reported the annual prevalence of *any* type of drug use in grade 12 as 38.5 percent among White youth, 35.6 percent among Black youth, and 39.7 percent among Hispanic youth (Johnston et al. 2016; Johnston et al. 2017; CDC 2017).
4. This chapter uses the terms Hispanic and Latino interchangeably to stay true to the essence of each study and report.

References

Acoca, Leslie, Jessica Stephens, and Amanda Van Vleet. 2014. *Health Coverage and Care for Youth in the Juvenile Justice System: The Role of Medicaid and CHIP*. Washington, D.C.: Kaiser Family Foundation.

American Civil Liberties Union. 2014. "Racial Disparities in Sentencing (submitted to the Inter-American Commission on Human Rights 153rd Session, Oct. 27, 2014)."

Alaska Stat. § 47.12.010.

Albert, Dustin, and Laurence Steinberg. 2011. "Judgment and Decision Making in Adolescence." *Journal of Research and Adolescence* 21(1): 211–224.

Alliance for Safety and Justice. 2016. *The First-Ever National Survey of Victims' Views on Safety and Justice*.

Arnett, Jeffrey J. 2000. "Emerging Adulthood: A Theory of Development from the Late Teens through the Twenties." *American Psychologist* 55(5): 469–480.

Ashley, Jessica, and Kimberly Burke. 2010. "Implementing Restorative Justice: A Guide for Schools." *Illinois Criminal Justice Information Authority*.

Beale, Sara Sun. 2009. "You've Come a Long Way, Baby: Two Waves of Juvenile Justice Reforms as Seen from Jena, Louisiana." *Harvard Civil Rights-Civil Liberties Law Review* 44(2): 511–546.

Berdejó, Carlos. 2018. "Criminalizing Race: Racial Disparities in the Plea-Bargaining." *Boston College Law Review* 59(4): 1187–1249.

Birckhead, Tamar R. 2017. "The Racialization of Juvenile Justice and the Role of the Defense Attorney." *Boston College Law Review* 58(2): 379–461.

Blad, Evie, and Alex Harwin. 2017. "Black Students More Likely to Be Arrested at School." *Education Week*, January 24, 2017.

Bridges, George S., and Sara Steen. 1998. "Racial Disparities in Official Assessments of Juvenile Offenders: Attributional Stereotypes as Mediating Mechanisms." *American Sociological Review* 63(4): 554–570.

Cauffman, Elizabeth, Elizabeth P. Shulman, Laurence Steinberg, Eric Claus, Marie T. Banich, Sandra Graham, and Jennifer Woolard. 2010. "Age Differences in Affective Decision Making as Indexed by Performance on the Iowa Gambling Task." *Developmental Psychology* 46(1): 193–207.

Center for Restorative Youth Justice, accessed November 17, 2018.

Centers for Disease Control and Prevention (CDC). 2015, 2017. "High School Youth Risk Behavior Surveillance System."

Chein, Jason M., Dustin Albert, Lia O'Brien, Kaitlyn Uckert, and Laurence Steinberg. 2010. "Peers Increase Adolescent Risk Taking by Enhancing Activity in the Brain's Reward Circuitry." *Developmental Science* 14(2): F1–F10.

Chung, He Len, Michelle Little, and Laurence Steinberg. 2005. "The Transition to Adulthood for Adolescents in the Juvenile Justice System: A Developmental Perspective." In *On Your Own Without a Net: The Transition to Adulthood for Vulnerable Populations.* Edited by D. Wayne Osgood, E. Micheal Foster, Constance Flanagan, and Gretchen R. Ruth, 68–91. Chicago: University of Chicago Press.

"Cooperative Agreement between the Juvenile Court of Clayton County, the Clayton County Public School System, the Clayton County Police Department, the Riverdale Police Department, the Jonesboro Police Department, the Forest Park Police Department, the Clayton County Department of Family and Children Services, the Clayton Center for Behavioral Health Services, Robert E. Keller, District Attorney and the Georgia Department of Juvenile Justice." 2004. 2–4.

Correll, Joshua, Bernd Wittenbrink, Bernadette Park, Charles M. Judd, Melody S. Sadler, and Tracie Keesee. 2007. "Across the Thin Blue Line: Police Officers and Racial Bias in the Decision to Shoot." *Journal of Personality and Social Psychology* 92(6): 1006–1023.

D.C. Code § 16-2301.02(2).

Davis, Angela J. 1998. "Prosecution and Race: The Power and Privilege of Discretion." *Fordham Law Review* 67(1): 13–68.

Devine, Patricia, G., Patrick S. Forscher, Anthony J. Austin, and William T. L. Cox. 2012. "Long-Term Reduction in Implicit Race Bias: A Prejudice Habit-Breaking Intervention." *Journal of Experimental Social Psychology* 48(6): 1267–1278.

Duncan, Martha Grace. 2002. "'So Young and So Untender': Remorseless Children and the Expectations of the Law." *Columbia Law Review* 102(6): 1469–1526.

Durston, Sarah, Hilleke E. Hulshoff Pol, B. J. Casey, Jay N. Giedd, Jan K. Buitelaar, and Herman Van Engeland. 2001. "Anatomical MRI of the Developing Brain: What Have We Learned?" *Journal of the American Academy of Child and Adolescent Psychiatry* 40(9): 1012–1020.

Eberhardt, Jennifer L., Valerie J. Purdie, Phillip Atiba Goff, and Paul G. Davies. 2004. "Seeing Black: Race, Crime, and Visual Processing." *Journal of Personality and Social Psychology* 87(6): 876–893.

Edkins, Vanessa A. 2011. "Defense Attorney Plea Recommendations and Client Race: Does Zealous Representation Apply Equally to All?" *Law and Human Behavior* 35(5): 413–425.

Epstein, Rebecca, Jamilia J. Blake, and Thalia González. 2017. *Girlhood Interrupted: The Erasure of Black Girls' Childhood.* Washigton D.C.: Georgetown Law Center on Poverty and Inequality.

Fagan, Jeffrey, and Tracey L. Meares. 2008. "Punishment, Deterrence and Social Control: The Paradox of Punishment in Minority Communities." *Ohio State Journal of Criminal Law* 6(1): 173–229.

Fair and Just Prosecution. Accessed November 16, 2018.

Ford, Julian D., John F. Chapman, Josephine Hawke, and David Albert. 2007. *Trauma among Youth in the Juvenile Justice System: Critical Issues and New Directions (Research and Program Brief).* Washigton D.C.: National Center for Mental Health and Juvenile Justice.

Functional Family Therapy. Accessed November 16, 2018.

Gardner, Margo, and Laurence Steinberg. 2005. "Peer Influence on Risk Taking, Risk Preference, and Risky Decision Making in Adolescence and Adulthood: An Experimental Study." *Developmental Psychology* 41(4): 625–636.

Gershowitz, Adam. 2018. "Prosecutorial Dismissals as a Teaching Tool (and Database) for the Police." *The George Washington Law Review* 86(6): 1525–1551.

Goff, Phillip Atiba, Brooke A. L. Di Leone, Matthew Christian Jackson, Carmen Marie Culotta, and Natalie Ann DiTomasso. 2014. "The Essence of Innocence: Consequences of Dehumanizing Black Children." *Journal of Personality and Social Psychology* 106(4): 526–545.

Gogtay, Nitin, Tom F. Nugent III, Giedd, David Herman, Anna Ordonez, Deanna Greenstein, Kiralee M. Hayashi, Liv Clasen, Arthur W. Toga, Jay N. Giedd, Judith L. Rapport, and Paul M. Thompson. 2004. "Dynamic Mapping of Human Cortical Development during Childhood through Early Adulthood." *Proceedings of the National Academy of Sciences* 21: 8174–8179.

Graham v. Florida. 2010. 560 U.S. 48.

Graham, Sandra, and Brian S. Lowery. 2004. "Priming Unconscious Racial Stereotypes About Adolescent Offenders." *Law and Human Behavior* 28(5): 483–504.

Halpern-Felsher, Bonnie L., and Elizabeth Cauffman. 2001. "Costs and Benefits of a Decision: Decision-Making Competence in Adolescents and Adults." *Journal of Applied Developmental Psychology* 22(3): 257–273.

Henning, Kristin. 2004. "Eroding Confidentiality in Delinquency Proceeding: Should Schools and Public Housing Authorities Be Notified?" *New York University Law Review* 79(2): 520–611.

Henning, Kristin. 2009. "What's Wrong with Victims' Rights in Juvenile Court?: Retributive versus Rehabilitative Systems of Justice." *California Law Review* 97(4): 1107–1170.

Henning, Kristin. 2013. "Criminalizing Normal Adolescent Behavior in Communities of Color: The Role of Prosecutors in Juvenile Justice Reform." *Cornell Law Review* 98(2): 383–461.

Henning, Kristin. 2017. "Boys to Men: The Role of Policing in the Socialization of Black Boys." In *Policing the Black Man*. Edited by Angela J. Davis, 57–94. New York: Penguin Random House LLC.

Hockenberry, Sarah. 2018. "National Report Series Bulletin: Juveniles in Residential Placement, 2015."

Hoytt, Eleanor H., Vincent Schiraldi, Brenda V. Smith, and Jason Ziedenberg. 2004. "Reducing Racial Disparities in Juvenile Detention." *Pathways to Juvenile Detention Reform* 1–79.

Hugenberg, Kurt, and Galen V. Bodenhausen. 2003. "Facing Prejudice: Implicit Prejudice and the Perception of Facial Threat." *Psychological Science* 14(6): 640–643.

Johnson, Olatunde C. A. 2007. "Disparity Rules." *Columbia Law Review* 107(2): 374–425.

Johnston, Lloyd D., Patrick M. O'Malley, Richard A. Miech, Jerald G. Bachman, and John E. Schulenberg. 2016. "Monitoring the Future: National Survey Results on Drug Use 1975-2016, 2016 Overview Key Findings In Adolescent Drug Use."

Johnston, Lloyd D., Patrick M. O'Malley, Richard A. Miech, Jerald G. Bachman, and John E. Schulenberg. 2017. "Demographic Subgroup Trends among Adolescents in the Use of Various Licit and Illicit Drugs."

Kang, Jerry, and Mahzarin R. Banaji. 2006. "Fair Measures: A Behavioral Realist Revision of Affirmative Action." *California Law Review* 94(4): 1063–1118.

Kennedy, Randall. 1997. *Race, Crime, and the Law*. New York: Random House, Inc.

Kupchik, Aaron, and Torin Monahan. 2006. "The New American School: Preparation for Post-Industrial Discipline." *British Journal of Sociology of Education* 27(5): 617–631.

Levick, Marsha L., and Elizabeth-Ann Tierney. 2012. "The United States Supreme Court Adopts a Reasonable Juvenile Standard in *J.D.B. v. North Carolina* for Purposes of the Miranda Custody Analysis: Can a More Reasoned Justice System for Juveniles Be Far Behind?" *Harvard Civil Rights-Civil Liberties Law Review* 47(2): 501–528.

Levinson, Justin D. 2007. "Forgotten Racial Equality: Implicit Bias, Decisionmaking, and Misremembering." *Duke Law Journal* 57(2): 345–424.

Levinson, Justin D., and Danielle Young. 2010. "Different Shades of Bias: Skin Tone, Implicit Racial Bias, and Judgments of Ambiguous Evidence." *West Virginia Law Review* 112(2): 307–350.

Levinson, Justin D., Huajian Cai, and Danielle Young. 2010. "Guilty by Implicit Racial Bias: The Guilty/Not Guilty Implicit Association Test." *Ohio State Journal of Criminal Law* 8(1): 187–208.

Lyon, Andrea D. 2012. "Racial Bias and the Importance of Consciousness for Criminal Defense Attorneys." *Seattle University Law Review* 35(3): 755–768.

Magellan Health Services. 2008. "Perspectives on Residential and Community-Based Treatment for Youth and Families," 1–14.

McKenzie, Wayne, Don Stemen, Derek Coursen, and Elizabeth Farid. 2009. "Prosecution and Racial Justice: Using Data to Advance Fairness in Criminal Prosecution." *Vera Institute of Justice*, 1–8.

Meares, Tracey L., and Dan M. Kahan. 1998. "The Wages of Antiquated Procedural Thinking: A Critique of Chicago v. Morales." *University of Chicago Legal Forum* 1998(1): 197–214.

Miller v. Alabama. 2012. 567 U.S. 460.

Minn. Stat. Ann. 2012. § 388.24(2)(1).

Moore, Lori D., and Irene Padavic. 2011. "Risk Assessment Tools and Racial/Ethnic Disparities in the Juvenile Justice System." *Sociology Compass* 5(10): 850–858.

Moriearty, Perry L. 2008. "Combating the Color-Coded Confinement of Kids: An Equal Protection Remedy." *New York University Review Law and Social Change* 32(2): 285–343.

"Multisystemic Therapy, Blueprints Rating: Model Plus." Accessed November 16, 2018.

Mulvey, Edward P., Laurence Steinberg, Alex R. Piquero, Michelle Besana, Jeffrey Fagan, Carol Schubert, and Elizabeth Cauffman. 2010. "Trajectories of Desistance and Continuity in Antisocial Behavior Following Court Adjudication Among Serious Adolescent Offenders." *Development and Psychopathology* 22(2): 453–475.

N.J. Stat. Ann. § 2A:4A-71.

Nakkula, Michael, and Eric Toshalis. 2016. *Understanding Youth: Adolescent Development for Educators*. Cambridge, MA: Harvard Education Press.

Natapoff, Alexandra. 2006. "Underenforcement." *Fordham Law Review* 75(3):1715–1776.

National District Attorneys Association. 2016. *National Prosecution Standards* § 4–11 (3rd ed.), 1–82.

National Institute of Justice. 2011a. *Program Profile: Multidimensional Foster Care—Adolescents*.

National Institute of Justice. 2011b. *Program Profile: Trauma Focused Cognitive Behavioral Therapy*.

National Institute of Justice. 2012. *Program Profile: Aggression Replacement Training (ART)*.

Neb. Rev. Stat. Ann. § 43-260.04.

Nellis, Ashley. 2011. "Addressing the Collateral Consequences of Convictions for Young Offenders." *The Champion Magazine*, July/August 2011: 20–27.

O'Brien, Lia, Dustin Albert, Jason Chein, and Laurence Steinberg. 2011. "Adolescents Prefer More Immediate Rewards When in the Presence of Their Peers." *Journal of Research on Adolescence* 21(4): 747–753.

Office of Juvenile Justice and Delinquency Prevention. 2017a. *Statistical Briefing Book (Juvenile Arrests)*. Released on March 27, 2017.

Office of Juvenile Justice and Delinquency Prevention. 2017b. *Statistical Briefing Book (Juvenile Arrest Rate Trends)*. Released on December 6, 2017.

Office of Juvenile Justice and Delinquency Prevention. 2017c. *Statistical Briefing Book (Juvenile Arrests)*. Released on December 6, 2017.

Office of Juvenile Justice and Delinquency Prevention. 2018a. "*Statistical Briefing Book (Case Flow by Detailed Offense)*. Released on August 22, 2018.

Office of Juvenile Justice and Delinquency Prevention. 2018b. *Statistical Briefing Book*. Released on October 22, 2018.

Penner, Erika K., Jodi L. Viljoen, Kevin S. Douglas, and Ronald Roesch. 2014. "Procedural Justice versus Risk Factors for Offending: Predicting Recidivism in Youth." *Law and Human Behavior* 38(3): 225–237.

Plant, E. Ashby, and B. Michelle Peruche. 2005. "The Consequences of Race for Police Officers' Responses to Criminal Subjects." *Association for Psychological Science* 16(3): 180–183.

Pritikin, Martin H. 2008. "Is Prison Increasing Crime?" *Wisconsin Law Review* 2008(6): 1049–1108.

Puzzanchera, Charles, Anthony Sladky, and Wei Kang. 2018. *Easy Access to Juvenile Populations: 1990–2017*.

Rachlinski, Jeffrey J., Sheri Johnson, Andrew J. Wistrich, and Chris Guthrie. 2009. "Does Unconscious Racial Bias Affect Trial Judges?" *Notre Dame Law Review* 84(3): 1195–1246.

Rattan, Aneeta, Cynthia S. Levine, Carol S. Dweck, and Jennifer L. Eberhardt. 2012. "Race and the Fragility of the Legal Distinction between Juveniles and Adults." *PLoS ONE* 7(5): e36680.

Richardson, L. Song. 2011. "Arrest Efficiency and the Fourth Amendment." *Minnesota Law Review* 95(6): 2035–2098.

Richardson, L. Song, and Phillip Atiba Goff. 2012. "Self-Defense and the Suspicion Heuristic." *Iowa Law Review* 98(1): 293–336.

Richardson, L. Song, and Phillip Atiba Goff. 2013. "Implicit Racial Bias in Public Defender Triage." *Yale Law Journal* 122(8): 2626–2649.

Roberts, Dorothy E. 2001. "Criminal Justice and Black Families: The Collateral Damage of Over-Enforcement." *University of California Davis Law Review* 34(4): 1005–1028.

Roper v. Simmons. 2005. 543 U.S. 551.

Scott, Elizabeth S. 2000. "Criminal Responsibility in Adolescence: Lessons from Developmental Psychology." In *Youth on Trial: A Developmental Perspective on Juvenile Justice*. Edited by Thomas Grisso and Robert G. Schwartz, 291–324. Chicago: University of Chicago Press.

Scott, Elizabeth S., and Laurence Steinberg. 2008. *Rethinking Juvenile Justice*. Cambridge, MA: Harvard University Press.

Sherrod, M. Lynn, Brian Huff, and Steven Teske. 2008. "Childish Behavior; Criminal Behavior." *Huntsville Times*, June 1, 2008, at A23.

Silva, Karol, Elizabeth P. Shulman, Jason M. Chein, and Laurence Steinberg. 2016. "Peers Increase Late Adolescents' Exploratory Behavior and Sensitivity to Positive and Negative Feedback." *Journal of Research on Adolescence* 26(4): 696–705.

Smith, Robert J., and Justin D. Levinson. 2012. "The Impact of Implicit Racial Bias on the Exercise of Prosecutorial Discretion." *Seattle University Law Review* 35(3): 795–826.

Soung, Patricia. 2011. "Social and Biological Constructions of Youth: Implications for Juvenile Justice and Racial Equity." *Northwestern Journal of Law and Policy* 6(10): 428–444.

St. George, Donna. 2011. "Judge Steve Teske Seeks to Keep Kids with Minor Problems Out of Court." *Washington Post*, October 17, 2011.

Status Offense Reform Center. 2014. *Notes from the Field, Clayton County, Georgia.*

Steinberg, Laurence. 2009. "Adolescent Development and Juvenile Justice". *Annual Review of Clinic Psychology* 5: 459–485.

Steinberg, Laurence. 2014. *Age of Opportunity: Lessons from the New Science of Adolescence.* New York: Houghton Mifflin Harcourt Publishing Company.

Steinberg, Laurence, and Elizabeth Cauffman. 1999. "The Elephant in the Courtroom: A Developmental Perspective on the Adjudication of Youthful Offenders." *Virginia Journal of Social Policy and the Law* 6(3): 389–417.

Steinberg, Laurence, He Len Chung, and Michelle Little. 2004. "Reentry of Young Offenders from the Justice System: A Developmental Perspective." *Youth Violence and Juvenile Justice* 2(1): 21–38.

Steinberg, Laurence, and Kathryn C. Monahan. 2007. "Age Differences in Resistance to Peer Influence." *Developmental Psychology* 43(6): 1531–1543.

Steinberg, Laurence, Dustin Albert, Elizabeth Cauffman, Marie Banich, Sandra Graham, and Jennifer Woolard. 2008. "Age Differences in Sensation Seeking and Impulsivity as Indexed by Behavior and Self-report: Evidence for a Dual Systems Model." *Developmental Psychology* 44(6): 1764–1778.

Steinberg, Laurence, Elizabeth Cauffman, Jennifer L. Woolard, Sandra A. Graham, and Marie T. Banich. 2009a. "Are Adolescents Less Mature than Adults? Minors' Access to Abortion, the Juvenile Death Penalty, and the Alleged APA 'Flip-Flop.'" *American Psychologist* 64(7): 583–594.

Steinberg, Laurence, Sandra Graham, Lia O'Brien, Elizabeth, Cauffman, and Marie T. Banich. 2009b. "Age Differences in Future Orientation and Delay Discounting." *Child Development* 80(1): 29–44.

Steinberg, Laurence, Elizabeth Cauffman, and Kathryn C. Monahan. 2015. "Psychosocial Maturity and Desistance from Crime in a Sample of Serious Juvenile Offenders." *OJJDP Juvenile Justice Bulletin* 1–12.

Tanenhaus, David S. 2005. "Degrees of Discretion: The First Juvenile Court and the Problem of Difference in the Early Twentieth Century." In *Our Children, Their Children.* Edited by Darnell F. Hawkins and Kimberly Kempf-Leonard, 105–121. Chicago: University of Chicago Press.

Todd, Andrew R., Kelsey C. Thiem, and Rebecca Neal. 2016. "Does Seeing Faces of Young Black Boys Facilitate the Identification of Threatening Stimuli?" *Psychological Science* 27(3): 384–393.

Tonry, Michael. 2010. "The Social, Psychological, and Political Causes of Racial Disparities in the American Criminal Justice System." *Crime and Justice* 39: 273–312.

Trinkner, Rick, and Ellen S. Cohn. 2014. "Putting the 'Social' Back in Legal Socialization: Procedural Justice, Legitimacy, and Cynicism in Legal and Nonlegal Authorities." *Law and Human Behavior* 38(6): 602–617.

U.S. Department of Education: Office for Civil Rights. 2018. *2015–16 Civil Rights Data Collection: School Climate and Safety.*

Weigard, Alexander, Jason Chein, Dustin Albert, Ashley Smith, and Laurence Steinberg. 2014. "Effects of Anonymous Peer Observation on Adolescents' Preference for Immediate Rewards." *Developmental Science* 17(1): 71–78.

Wis. Stat. Ann. § 938.01(2)(e).

CHAPTER 23

CORPORATE CRIMINAL LAW UNBOUNDED

MIRIAM H. BAER

23.1 Introduction

It is an uncontroversial proposition that criminal law differs significantly from other fields of law. It harnesses the state's power to deprive its citizens of liberty; it communicates society's condemnation of misconduct; and it imposes upon its targets a stigma substantially different in kind and magnitude from other legal sanctions (Ristroph 2019).

Criminal law is also the creation of the state; our fellow citizens cannot easily imprison us, but police officers and prosecutors can and often do (Ristroph 2017). Accordingly, to justify and restrain the state's awesome powers, theorists have promoted a series of limitations on criminal lawmaking and prosecution. These limitations organize themselves into three principles: legality, culpability, and limited punishment (Kadish et al. 2017). Collectively, they provide a normative roadmap for prosecutors, the primary actors tasked with initiating, proving, and resolving violations of criminal law.

Facially, these precepts apply universally across state and federal penal systems. As Alice Ristroph has recently observed, criminal law's limiting principles purport to protect all offenders, rich or poor, and to constrain criminal lawmaking pertaining to all offenses, from the most minor to the most serious (Ristroph 2020). To be sure, these limiting principles are largely aspirational, and some might conclude they barely function at all, or provide a convenient pretext for more malevolent aims (Ristroph 2020). Nevertheless, at their best, they promote the rule of law by preventing arbitrary abuses of power. When legal actors actually adhere to them, they contribute to a fair and legitimate criminal justice system (Natapoff 2017, describing top of "penal pyramid"). When our legal actors and institutions lose sight of them, criminal law becomes tarnished in the eyes of many and rightfully finds itself the target of sustained and profound reform efforts.

One category of crime has all but ignored these limiting principles: the criminal punishment of corporations and other business entities.[1] In matters of lawmaking, ascription of fault, and imposition of punishment, corporate prosecution repeatedly diverges from traditional understandings of what criminal law is, how it should be made, and how it should be implemented. This is not merely a case of falling short of one's aspirations; rather, it is a case of ignoring internal limitations altogether. And interestingly enough, whereas the academy derides the rest of criminal law for its perceived lawlessness, corporate crime is either overlooked or compartmentalized as a topic deserving of disparate treatment. Accordingly, whereas much of today's criminal law scholarship seeks to restrain the government's enforcement and criminal lawmaking powers, contemporary corporate crime scholarship adopts a decidedly different tone. If "do less" has become the slogan for the rest of criminal law, "do more" is the rallying cry where corporate prosecutions are concerned.

What is to account for this distinction in treatment? Perhaps it is attributable to the physical and practical impossibility of placing an organization in jail (Thomas 2019), or to the fact that corporations are not vested with the dignity and liberty interests of individual persons. "The supposition that corporations are entitled to some of the legal protections extended to natural persons is riddled with controversy, to say the least" (Husak 2014). Perhaps, too, it arises out of the power differential between corporations and criminal defendants. Across numerous sectors, corporations are increasingly seen as the engines of the rich and powerful, violating laws and imposing substantial costs on others, all with apparent impunity (Stewart 2013, 261–72). Individual defendants, by contrast, have long endured a system of socio-legal control that dehumanizes and over-punishes them (Levin 2019). No wonder, then, that individual defendants attract the bulk of reformers' sympathies. They need the help a lot more than corporations.

This attitude is understandable but ignores corporate crime's many failings. A corporate crime regime that is unmoored from the rest of criminal law vests tremendous power in the executive branch, and there is no reason to believe federal prosecutors will be any more adept in using their vast powers to regulate corporate entities than they have been in other fields of social engineering. If the specter of unrestrained prosecutorial discretion concerns us, it ought to concern us as applied to corporate offenders too, however unsympathetic those offenders may be (Levin 2019).

To their credit, a number of scholars have attempted to make corporate criminal law look and function more like the rest of criminal law. William Laufer has urged the adoption of an open-textured liability rule that he refers to as "constructive fault" (Laufer 1994, 715).[2] Others have floated their own theories of liability (Abril and Olazabal 2006; Lederman 2000), as have numerous jurists (Gruner 2004, 3.03[4][a], cataloguing judicial approaches). Thus far, however, Congress has shown no interest in codifying these theories of corporate criminal liability. Moreover, as prosecutors become more adept in fashioning sophisticated "deferred prosecution agreements" with corporate defendants, the content and procedure underlying these extrajudicial dispositions increasingly threaten to overshadow more basic questions, such as why we punish corporate actors at all.

Thus, it comes as no surprise that corporate crime stubbornly fails to track "the general part of the criminal law" (Laufer 1994; Laufer and Strudler 2000, 1286). Instead, it operates largely unbound by criminal law's foundational principles. Some might argue that prosecutors benefit from this lack of constraint; others might just assuredly claim that the corporate defendants themselves are the primary beneficiaries of this vacuum. A few might go so far as to say that corporate crime's untethering underscores its illegitimacy (Alschuler 2009; Fischel and Sykes 1996; Hasnas 2009). Most, however, justify corporate crime's unique characteristics by citing a well-worn necessity thesis: corporate criminal law and its evolving enforcement regime enable prosecutors to identify and punish wrongdoers *and* impose a degree of regulation that would be impossible to achieve directly given our current political climate. Corporate crime is thus a means towards securing two valuable ends: the possibility for prosecutions of individual offenders, and the increased regulation of business entities. It may be inconsistent with criminal law's most revered principles, but the corporate prosecution project preserves at least some degree of accountability.

It is difficult to rebut this necessity thesis because its premises are largely correct. Over the past three decades, a confluence of political, economic, and legal factors has rendered it extremely difficult for regulatory institutions to devise, enforce, and oversee corporate behavior through traditional forms of ex ante regulation (Brown 2011; Farber 2013). By comparison, "punishment" has received far more institutional support than regulation (Baer 2012; Levin 2019). Nevertheless, "governing through crime" (Simon 2007) can become counterproductive when the punishment in question reflects negative sentiment more than sober statistical findings. More importantly, regulation that is the product of bad process is hardly cause for celebration. If much of what occurs under the corporate crime moniker is a watered-down version of regulatory oversight, then we should at least admit that is what we are doing. Moreover, we should keep firmly in mind the fact that the forces that have so effectively hamstrung ex ante regulation might eventually do just the same thing to ex post punishment-as-regulation. Indeed, some would say that is already the case; as of this writing, the prosecution and quasi-punishment of corporations under DPAs dropped noticeably under the first twenty months of the Trump administration (Garrett 2020) and may fall even more.

Instrumental justifications are also problematic insofar as they dissuade scholars from developing a sustainable theory of collective fault. There may well be situations in which most of us would agree that an entity is *deserving* of punishment for an act or series of acts or omissions that occurred within that entity's conceptual space. In *those* cases the argument for corporate punishment looks more like the traditional retributive case. But that "desert" boundary—the one that our society would theoretically agree upon if asked—would likely produce fewer offenders than the rule that currently triggers corporate criminal liability. Accordingly, corporate crime finds itself in a sort of Catch-22. So long as its defenders sense a need for quasi-regulation, they will resist efforts to narrow and codify it. At the same time, so long as it remains uncodified, corporate crime's normative foundations will remain underdeveloped, leaving much of its articulation to federal prosecutors and the corporate defense attorneys with whom they periodically spar.

The remainder of this chapter unfolds as follows. The first section summarizes the basic rules of corporate criminal liability. The next section recites criminal law's fundamental tenets and highlights ways in which corporate punishment diverges from these principles. The chapter then considers the normative implications of an "unbound" corporate criminal law, and the concluding section argues for legislative reforms that would not only "bind" corporate criminal law, but also impose needed restraints on the prosecutors who currently implement it.

23.2 A Quick Primer

Since the turn of the twentieth century, corporations and other business organizations have been criminally liable for their employees' crimes, provided those employees have acted within the scope of their employment and with at least a partial purpose to benefit the corporation (Garrett 2014, 35–36; Khanna 1996, 1488–1490). This broad rule of *respondeat superior* liability dates back to the Supreme Court's decision in *New York Central & Hudson Railroad Co. v. United States* (1909), wherein it held that a corporation could legally be treated as a "person" for purposes of the Elkins Act (Alexander and Cohen 2015, 543).

Prior to the 1800s, courts declined to hold corporations liable on the ground that corporate entities lacked moral agency (Thomas 2018). Instead, courts treated criminal acts as *ultra vires*—i.e., undertaken without shareholders' authority and therefore subject to reversal (Lipton 2010; Thomas 2018). Eventually, municipal corporations came under attack in the mid-1800s for failing to maintain public bridges and highways (Laufer 1999, 1362–1363). The industrial revolution and emergence of legislation such as the Sherman Antitrust Act directed greater attention to for-profit corporations and the specter of corporate wrongdoing (Lipton 2010).

The Supreme Court altered corporate criminal liability's trajectory in its watershed *New York Central* case.[3] In *New York Central*, the Supreme Court upheld the provision of the 1903 Elkins Act that held that corporations could be prosecuted for their employees' failure to comply with the tariffs set by the Interstate Commerce Commission. The railroad contended that its prosecution would result in the punishment of "innocent stockholders . . . without due process of law" (492). The Court disagreed. Corporations had already become responsible for their employees' behavior in tort cases, provided the employee was acting in the scope of his employment and for the benefit of the principal. If imputation of responsibility was appropriate in the tort context, the Court reasoned, then it was just as appropriate in the criminal context. To decide otherwise would all but cripple Congress's nascent regulation of interstate commerce.

From there, *respondeat superior* blossomed into a robust doctrine, eventually replacing *ultra vires* as the dominant approach toward corporate criminal behavior (Lipton 2010). Today, any entity, be it a corporation, partnership, non-profit, or some other type of organization (e.g., LLC), may be held liable for its employees' violations of federal law, provided that (1) the employee acted "within the scope of her employment," and (2) she acted with *an* intent to benefit the corporation.

Subsequent lower court opinions have explored each prong's doctrinal boundaries, and as a result, neither element is particularly difficult to prove (Gruner 2004). Assuming the government can identify an actual wrongdoer, the leap from individual to corporate liability is relatively easy. The employee's behavior renders the corporate actor responsible, regardless of the corporation's knowledge of or efforts to block such behavior. Moreover, the fact that the employee was acting primarily to further her own ends is largely irrelevant; so long as she harbored *an* intent to benefit the corporation—by boosting its overall revenues or stock price, for example—*respondeat superior* liability applies.

Based on the foregoing, scholars overwhelmingly agree that *respondeat superior* casts a rather wide net, and in some cases, too wide (Abril and Olazabal 2006, 112–113). At the same time, the rule can be maddeningly underinclusive. Liability may be difficult to establish when there exists no single wrongdoer (Moorh 2007), or it may fall short in those cases where the employee undertakes her crime solely to further her own ends (Sheley 2019). In the grand scheme of things, however, the underinclusive cases pale in comparison to the overinclusive ones. Moreover, in cases where prosecutors have been unable to identify a single wrongdoer, at least one court has devised a means of aggregating and imputing knowledge (*United States v. Bank of New England, N.A.* 1987).[4]

Notwithstanding the foregoing, *respondeat superior*'s deployment in trial cases is rare because so few corporations take their cases to trial (Laufer and Strudler 2000). The *real* law of corporate criminal liability is determined by neither courts nor legislatures, but rather by the federal prosecutors who negotiate guilty pleas and extrajudicial agreements with corporate boards. Although some might argue the pressure to forego a trial and plead out a corporate case differs little from the rest of criminal law, it is helpful first to review the reasons corporations and prosecutors alike are so eager to enter into extrajudicial agreements that skirt the criminal justice system's conventional processes.

23.3 Collateral Consequences and Alternatives to Indictment

Corporations, as a practical matter, cannot be jailed (Coffee 1981). Rather, they can be fined, denied participation in government programs, ordered to make various governance changes, or, in the most extreme cases, stripped of their charter (Garrett 2014).

The collateral consequences of corporate prosecution pose a near intractable problem for policymakers and prosecutors. For at least *some* industries, consequences such as debarment and charter removal threaten systemic costs and externalities the government would prefer to avoid (Gilchrist 2014). A few challenge this collateral costs claim as an exaggeration (Markoff 2013), but most accept the assertion that *some* consequences would likely befall a financial or health care institution were its parent company to be indicted with absolutely no agreement in place regarding its charter, its licenses, and its ability to participate in federal and state programs (Podgor 2018, 935–936). Some companies really are "too big to jail" (Garrett 2014; Werle 2019), and more importantly, indict without warning.

Recognizing this problem, prosecutors have devised a series of alternatives to an outright indictment, which also tend to avoid or mitigate the worst of conviction's collateral consequences (Alexander and Arlen 2018; Alexander and Cohen 2015). Depending on one's perspective, they have either devised an innovative approach that reduces and avoids unnecessary costs or have instead leveraged *respondeat superior*'s drawbacks to accrue powers more properly left to other branches of government.

Resolutions of corporate investigations fall along a continuum of outcomes. In the more egregious cases, the corporation or its subsidiary might be forced to plead guilty to an agreed-upon Information, often with an additional agreement that the corporation will still be permitted to continue most or all of its business lines (Alexander and Arlen 2018). At the other end of the spectrum—and increasingly more often under the Trump administration (Garrett 2020)—the corporation may avoid liability altogether if it catches and discloses misconduct early and aggressively. For cases that fall in the middle, the corporation will be compelled to enter into either a Deferred or Non-prosecution Agreement, which are described below.

A Deferred Prosecution Agreement is a bit of a misnomer, as it represents the government's agreement *not* to prosecute the corporate defendant *ever*, provided the defendant undertakes the actions set forth in the agreement (Baer 2016). Although the prosecutor files the agreement in court in order to toll the Speedy Trial Act's provisions,[5] the Second and D.C. Circuits have each held that lower courts have little to no authority to review the agreement's substantive details.[6] As a result, the substance and implementation of the agreement fall squarely within the prosecutor's discretion; since the prosecutor could decide to decline the case altogether, she retains just as much discretion to craft an agreement that avoids criminal liability and secures a mix of extrajudicial reforms.

Contemporary DPAs and NPAs have sought ambitious reforms in corporate governance and culture (Finder and McConnell 2006), although some would argue that those reform efforts are spotty at best (Garrett 2014). Many agreements include the corporation's admission of certain facts, although no statute requires these admissions (Alexander and Arlen 2018). The agreements often require the corporate offender to pay financial sanctions (i.e., "fines"—although not always explicitly labeled as such), and to engage in a number of general and specific governance reforms (Alexander and Arlen 2018). Operational reforms ("improve the compliance program") appear to be more common than board-level governance reforms ("create a Board level compliance committee") (Armour et al. 2020b).

To ensure some level of uniformity among its prosecutors, the Department of Justice has promulgated a series of memos advising of the general principles that prosecutors should consider prior to entering into alternative agreements with business organizations. These memos, known formally as the Federal Principles of Prosecution of Business Organizations (the "Federal Principles") have been memorialized in the Justice Manual, which until September 2018 was widely known as the United States Attorneys' Manual.[7]

The Federal Principles include broad and fairly subjective factors, including:

- the nature of the wrongdoing and its pervasiveness within the organization;
- the corporation's efforts to prevent misconduct through its compliance program;
- the corporation's voluntary disclosure of the wrongdoing and subsequent cooperation efforts with officials;
- the collateral consequences of indicting and criminally prosecuting the corporation;
- and the availability of alternative remedial measures.[8]

Putting aside the most obvious of cases at either ends of the spectrum, it would not take too much effort to imagine one prosecutor drawing fairly different conclusions from another regarding one or more of these factors. Accordingly, concerns regarding unfair treatment, lack of uniformity, and lack of transparency pervade much of the DPA literature (Garrett 2014; Reilly 2015).

Extrajudicial agreements and the process that underlies their negotiation have incited much controversy.[9] Some of this criticism pertains to the opaque process that produces them (Garrett 2014). Some of it is directed at agreements themselves, contending they are insufficiently punitive and deliver only the most superficial of reforms (Uhlmann 2013). And finally, some contend that the fear of criminal liability may cause corporations to generate expensive and counterproductive policing costs, which will be felt most keenly by mid- and lower-level employees (Baer 2009). Whatever their shortcomings, DPAs, NPAs, and declinations are notable for the ways in which they have evolved in a purely ad hoc manner, almost completely divorced from criminal law's troika of internal limiting principles. Whether bad or good, they function very differently from the "rest" of criminal law.

23.4 Criminal Law's Limitations

One of oldest and most popular of American criminal law casebooks, Kadish, Schulhofer, and Barkow's *Criminal Law and Cases*, introduces its students to criminal law's familiar tenets in an early chapter: legality, culpability, and proportionality (Kadish et al. 2017). As many agree, these pillars are, to varying degrees, more aspirational than real. At least one scholar has argued that these "limitations" not only are unreal, but have also played an indirect role in fueling mass incarceration (Ristroph 2020).

Notwithstanding these concerns, concepts such as legality, culpability and proportionality have become stalwarts of the criminal law canon. They have guided and shaped criminal law's implementation and scholarly discourse, even as they fail to live up to their ambitions. I offer the briefest of overviews in this section.

23.4.1 Legality

The legality principle embraces a series of constitutional and jurisprudential rules intended to ensure that individuals receive advance notice of what constitutes a criminal offense. It also prevents enforcement officials from arbitrarily declaring particular conduct prohibited after the fact and thereby abusing their powers (Jeffries 1985; Robinson 2005).

Legality elevates the legislature above the executive and judiciary (Jeffries 1985). Its requirement that laws be written in advance applies not only to the content of criminal prohibitions, but also to the punishments that flow as a result of such violations. (Even here, a wide range of punishment—such as "zero to twenty years' imprisonment" apparently suffices.) Finally, it erects a series of additional limitations on open-ended lawmaking. When penal laws themselves are so indeterminate that jurists experience difficulty in inferring their meaning, they become vulnerable either to limiting concepts such as the rule of lenity, or to being overturned on account of constitutional vagueness concerns (Solan 1998). And although some states continue to permit "common law" criminal lawmaking (Hessick 2019), federal courts have long held to the maxim that there exists no such thing as "federal criminal common law" (*United States v. Hudson & Goodwin* 1812; *Liparota v. United States* 1985, 424).[10]

23.4.2 Culpability

Culpability is the shorthand we lend to criminal law's general requirement that individuals act with a malevolent state of mind.[11] As the Supreme Court intoned in *Morissette v. United States* (1952), more than a half-century ago:

> The contention that an injury can amount to a crime only when inflicted by intention . . . . is as universal and persistent in mature systems of law as belief in freedom of the human will and a consequent ability and duty of the normal individual to choose between good and evil.[12]

Individuals who choose to harm others, to place others at risk of harm, or to willfully ignore the state's dictates are said to deserve some degree of punishment (Ferzan 2002, 188, explaining that punishment's culpability component represents "an assessment of the actor's choice"). Thus, criminal law does not punish a person on account of her status. Nor does it ordinarily permit punishment under a so-called strict liability theory, at least not in those instances where the legislature has been silent or unclear (Levin 2019, 19).[13]

Concededly, legislatures can and *do* criminalize negligent or purely non-culpable behavior, but courts require them to do so plainly (*Staples v. United States* 1994), and scholars have contended such statutes should subject their targets to little more than the slightest of punishments, even if actual practice suggests otherwise (Sayre 1933; but see Huq and Lakier 2018, documenting the emergence of regulatory crimes that threaten more serious consequences). Thus, when adhered to, the principle of culpability restrains criminal lawmaking and affirms the view that criminal liability should be "based on a conscious choice to do wrong" (Simon 2007, 188; quoted in Levin 2019).

Culpability also restrains criminal prosecutors, either by forcing them to establish the wrongdoer's mental state, or by forcing them to present lesser-included offenses to a jury, depending on the jurisdiction's procedural rules (Crespo 2018; Levin 2019, 8–9). Moreover, culpability further restrains prosecutors insofar as it shapes the public's expectations. Cases that lack jury appeal or appear to be a variant of prosecutorial overreach may well include situations in which the offender acted without choice or in ignorance of relevant facts (Offit 2019, 1089, describing federal prosecutors' reluctance to pursue highly technical financial structuring cases unaccompanied by additional evidence of wrongdoing).

None of this is to deny the prosecutor's leverage throughout an investigation and prosecution. In nearly all cases, the prosecutor enjoys the upper hand. Nevertheless, strong culpability norms (not to mention well-written rules designed to serve those norms) can at least limit how well she plays that hand. Law matters, and it matters quite a bit when it shapes the public's understanding of what a "reasonable" exercise of prosecutorial discretion ought to look like.

23.4.3 Limited Punishment

Two related principles of criminal punishment further limit prosecutors in their pursuit of offenders. The proportionality principle provides that an offender's punishment should not exceed the level of harm he or she imposes on victims or society at large (Bagaric et al. 2017, 1021). The concept known as *parsimony* holds that sentencers should impose no more punishment than is necessary to achieve consequential goals (Tonry 2017). Thus, the judge seeking general deterrence should impose a sentence no greater than necessary to persuade others not to commit the same offense. And a regime interested in securing rehabilitation should limit its interventions to those that are data-tested and no more intrusive than necessary to prevent future violations of law (Slobogin 2011).

Of the three principles, limited punishment appears to be least obeyed in practice. The Supreme Court appears to have all but abandoned the task of reviewing sentencing regimes for proportionality. The federal sentencing statute speaks of parsimony (18 U.S.C. § 3553), but defendants rarely win appeals on grounds that a judge has violated Section 3553's parsimony obligation. A few state court systems have taken the proportionality obligation more seriously (Schneider 2012), but even in these cases, the aim seems to be one of correcting aberrations and outliers, rather than ensuring a true fit between the offense and the proscribed sentence. And sentencing regimes remain stubbornly immune to expertise on rehabilitation and risks of re-offending (Bagaric et al. 2017, 786, criticizing "continued disregard of expert knowledge and empirical evidence" in sentencing).

Notwithstanding these shortfalls, parsimony and proportionality still serve important functions in our political discourse. Legislators, tired of overstretched prison budgets and of shouldering the costs of mass incarceration, recently have shown a bi-partisan interest in reducing sentences and adopting non-prison alternatives. Politicians—including elected district attorneys—have successfully emphasized policing and prison reform in their election campaigns.[14] Thus, proportionality and parsimony still possess the ability to constrain prosecutors, albeit in a more indirect manner than either legality or culpability principles. For at least *some* politicians, the imposition of unnecessary costs on an individual offender and her community is no longer a safe political bet in today's society.

23.5 Corporate Crime Unbounded

How do corporate prosecutions differ from prosecutions of natural persons? This section analyzes this question in regard to criminal law's internal limitations. The point is not that corporate prosecutions fall short of criminal law's core principles. The same could be said for prosecutions of individual offenders. Rather, the difference in the corporate context is that practitioners, jurists, and observers seem far more willing to abandon these principles where corporate offenders are concerned. Corporate criminal law does more than simply diverge from principles of legality, culpability, and limited punishment. It largely pays no attention to these restraints *at all*. Moreover, its scholars seem far more willing to accept this state of affairs than those who write on the subject of individual punishment. I discuss the possible reasons for this phenomenon in later sections. Before doing that, I first describe the degree to which corporate crime functions differently from the rest of criminal law.

23.5.1 Corporate Crime's (Lack of) Legality

The primary doctrine holding corporations criminally liable for their employees' wrongs arises not out of a specific statutory definition of corporate liability, but instead from the Supreme Court's decision in *New York Central* and its relevant progeny (Alschuler 2009). Admittedly, Congress has defined corporations and other business entities as "persons" within the federal criminal code.[15] It has also, at times, imposed specific obligations on corporate entities, as in the Bank Secrecy Act, which threatens financial institutions with criminal liability for failing to report suspicious activity in bank accounts. Nevertheless, corporate criminal liability is derived primarily from judicial opinions (Alschuler 2009).

Corporate crime's legality problem grows more noticeable the more one attempts to uncover the "real" basis of criminal liability. Whatever the law on the books may be, the law on the ground looks far different from *respondeat superior*'s strict, unbending rule. As any superficial review of the DOJ's press releases demonstrates, the government prosecutes corporations for many reasons, but it rarely pursues a corporation *solely* because its employee, acting within the scope of her authority, happened to commit a crime with an intention to benefit her employer. To the contrary, prosecutors pursue and seek DPAs from corporations because "the organization" has played some role in affirmatively encouraging the underlying criminality, or has acquiesced in the offense, or is responsible for putting in place structures or policies it knew or should have known would produce such behavior.

In other words, we "punish" corporate entities because of things they have done, things they failed to do, and things they did, knowing they were placing others at severe risk. We do not, as a general matter, punish corporate entities *solely* because they happen to be engaged in a wholly legal, pre-defined relationship with a malevolent employee. *Respondeat superior* may be the formal rule of corporate criminal liability across federal jurisdictions, but the rule on the ground is something quite different.

Thus, the shadow law of corporate criminal liability differs quite a bit from the actual one. Some academics see this as cause for celebration, or at least relief (Laufer and Strudler 2000). Still, a law on the books that diverges so sharply from the law on the ground generates a number of problems. First, since neither a legislature nor even a court has articulated the actual rule governing corporate prosecutions, corporate crime invites—in fact, demands—substantial exercises of prosecutorial discretion. Second, so long as it remains unwritten, the *real* law of corporate criminal liability remains under-theorized and in flux. Unlike *respondeat superior*, the shadow law of corporate criminal liability actually arises out of some notion of organizational-level misconduct. Although several scholars have interrogated these concepts (Sepinwall 2017; Thomas 2018, 2019), their debates remain separate from the day-to-day practice of corporate prosecution and punishment.

23.5.2 Culpability

Corporate criminal liability also diverges from criminal law's veneration of personal fault as a basis for punishment, as it holds the corporation vicariously and strictly liable for the behavior of its employees. Whatever role culpability plays in criminal law, it plays almost no role in *corporate* criminal liability.

The standard account of culpability holds an individual responsible for her own behavior and the conduct of those she purposely aids or solicits. More aggressive theories of group liability hold the individual criminally liable for the behavior she foreseeably triggers. For example, the "natural and probable consequences" doctrine imposes on aiders and abettors liability for *other crimes* that could be said to be the "natural and probable consequence" of the crime in which they were complicit. Similarly, in jurisdictions that follow the infamous *Pinkerton* conspiracy doctrine (*Pinkerton v. United States* 1946), one is not merely responsible for the crimes to which one has agreed, but also for the crimes one's co-conspirator commits, provided those crimes are foreseeable and undertaken in furtherance of the conspiracy (Beale 2009, 1514–1515).

These extension doctrines have become infamous among criminal law scholars because they elide distinctions between intentional and unintentional conduct. Sarah Sun Beale analogizes them to corporate criminal liability because they premise liability for a more serious crime on one's willing engagement in some underlying activity (Beale 2009). Thus, if you have no issue with *Pinkerton* or the natural and probable consequences doctrine, you ought to have no problem with corporate criminal liability. And even if you *do* take issue with those doctrines, you might still defend corporate criminal liability (as Beale does) because of the corporation's great capacity for harm.

Beale's analogy glosses over one problem: none of the standard doctrines Beale cites envisions the application of strict vicarious liability on account of a person's *legal* conduct (Baer 2021). Doctrines such as *Pinkerton* and the natural and probable consequences doctrine each load additional liability onto an offender's initial decision to engage in wrongdoing. Under the standard *Pinkerton* formulation, a decision to engage in Crime *x* as part of a conspiracy triggers liability for Crime *y* regardless of whether the defendant would independently meet Crime *y*'s *mens rea* requirements.

Corporate criminal liability goes one step further. It punishes the corporation on account of its *legal* relationship with its employee, *and* on account of its fictional status as a legal person. This last point is key. Corporate entities do not arise out of thin air; they are the creation of legislatures. The corpus of laws known collectively as "corporate law" does far more than *permit* corporate relationships; it actively *encourages* capital formation through corporate and alternative entities (Thomas 2019).

Now, it may be that the *shadow* law of corporate criminal liability is more grounded in familiar notions of fault. For example, if the state prosecutes and punishes a corporation because its owners and top managers willfully created an atmosphere conducive to fraud or foreign bribery, it can say that it is adhering to the culpability principle. But the state does not *have* to constrain itself to this rule, and it has no obligation to prove any elements of culpability in court. The state can pursue the faulty corporation alongside the faultless one, provided it can identify an employee who committed a crime and did so with a partial intention to benefit the corporation. Corporate crime, in other words, is not bound by a rule of culpability; it is bound, instead, by a rule of employment.

23.5.3 Proportionality and Parsimony

The final manner in which corporate crime diverges from other areas of criminal law is that its proponents often downplay proportionality and parsimony. Instead, scholars often argue for deeper governance reforms including changes in the corporation's character (Diamantis 2018), behavior in the marketplace (Garrett 2007), and internal governance systems (Cunningham 2004). These reform efforts rarely mention the limiting principles that otherwise preoccupy discussions of criminal punishment. In the corporate crime world, experimentation and intervention are unalloyed goods.

For example, for the punishment of individual offenders, criminal law scholars have persuasively argued that criminal rehabilitation may become a recipe for intrusions on an individual's dignity and liberty, and exacerbate biases already embedded in the system (Eaglin 2013). To address these worries, scholars have argued that rehabilitative regimes must be based in scientific data and establish a strong nexus between the underlying offense and the additional conduct the court seeks to reform (Slobogin 2011).

In contrast to these limiting principles, *corporate* rehabilitation efforts are decidedly more expansive. This is true partially because the corporation is a juridical fiction (Diamantis 2018, downplaying dignity and liberty concerns). But it is also the case because scholars quite transparently believe corporate rehabilitation should be deployed as a substitute for more conventional forms of regulation (Husak 2014). As a result, scholars seem far more amenable to interventions that would be anathema, or at least be met with substantial skepticism, were they imposed directly on individuals.

23.6 The Role of Prosecutors

Corporate crime enforcement provokes reactions quite different from the universal cry that the criminal justice system is broken. Instead, the reactions to corporate crime enforcement fall within one of several camps. There are those who believe prosecutors are moving in the right direction, but should firm up transparency in their decision-making processes (Alexander and Arlen 2018); those who profess that prosecutors are not punishing or reforming corporations nearly *enough* for their actual or supposed transgressions (Garrett 2014; Uhlmann 2013); and those who sincerely believe prosecutors and legislatures should aim for a narrower criminal law that seeks solely to punish and that leaves conventional regulatory aims to administrative agencies (Baer 2016). In sum, most reformers seek to change and not abolish the practice of corporate prosecutions, and many presume that federal prosecutors will continue to play an important role in the identification and redress of corporate wrongdoing (Buell 2018).

Ordinarily, the strongest argument for prosecuting corporations is not found in retributive theory. Particularly where the company itself is a publicly held company, it will be nearly impossible to establish that shareholders played any role in the company's wrongdoing. Even where the corporate "entity" is concerned, the ascription of fault and blame remains a difficult task. Accordingly, the stronger of the major arguments for corporate criminal liability is the claim that the fear of criminal punishment optimally deters crime. The corollary of this claim is that for the crimes that remain *un*deterred, corporate liability vastly improves the government's ability to identify and punish the individuals who perpetrated wrongdoing within the corporation's confines. That is, corporate crime *deters* and where it falls short of its deterrence mission, it *incapacitates* guilty entities and individuals alike. (This is, of course, the theoretical justification for the practice.)

When deterrence and incapacitation are its twin aims, corporate crime's scholarship often focuses on incentives and liability standards. Strict liability is problematic because it fails to reward corporations for investing in monitoring and detection; a negligence standard is equally problematic because it encourages inefficient activity levels and is prone to factual and interpretive error. Thus, a so-called composite regime emerges as the best of all options (Arlen 1994; Arlen and Kraakman 1997). This regime holds the corporation strictly responsible for its employees' crimes, but dramatically reduces the severity of punishment whenever the corporation voluntarily monitors and self-discloses wrongdoing to public authorities.

Because it encourages the corporation to invest in self-policing and to report wrongdoing promptly, the composite regime easily improves upon strict vicarious liability. Many would say the United States Sentencing Guidelines and DOJ's prosecutorial charging principles reflect elements of this approach, but these policies remain inconsistent with the composite regime's teachings insofar as they take into account many *other* factors that have little to do with self-reporting and deterrence (Arlen 2012, criticizing the Organizational Sentencing Guidelines). More importantly, for certain types of systemically important firms, composite liability is a non-starter. The government simply cannot indict certain types of firms; if firms know this too, they harbor far less incentive to disclose wrongdoing to authorities (Werle 2019).

Moreover, the firm's internal monitoring efforts are only as strong as the executives and managers who oversee its compliance function (Alschuler 2009; Armour et al. 2020a). The *corporation* may harbor an incentive to monitor and disclose wrongdoing, but the corporate executives guilty of such wrongdoing have every incentive to hide what they have done for as long as they can. Thus, regardless of whether a given firm is "too big to fail," the composite regime may falter when high-level executives themselves perpetrate and personally benefit from the corporation's crimes.

All is not lost. To the extent the composite system succeeds in inducing some corporate firms to monitor and report wrongdoing, it does so because it invests the corporation's board of directors with a specific, non-negotiable oversight obligation. Board members—particularly independent ones—have the most to lose in terms of reputation if they allow the company to go under. Accordingly, the threat of corporate punishment reduces the specter of managerial obstruction by animating one corporate constituent (the Board) to exercise greater oversight over a different one (corporate management), through the use of the corporation's compliance function (Miller 2014). This, in turn, slowly changes corporate norms and culture.

Corporate punishment begets other benefits. In an adversarial fight that might otherwise be more evenly matched than the average street crime case, it lends prosecutors and government investigators tremendous leverage (First 2010). It lightens the prosecutor's load, since compliance officers and corporate defense lawyers do much of initial leg-work in terms of interviewing witnesses and collecting documents (Buell 2007), and it removes potential constitutional impediments to collecting evidence (Griffin 2007; Podgor and Green 2013).

The strongest argument for corporate liability is thus largely procedural and instrumental. We employ an impossibly wide definition of corporate crime because we want corporations to help us identify morally culpable and potentially harmful individuals. Along the way, we might reform some companies and their fellow travelers. This instrumental use of *substantive* organizational liability to procure largely *procedural* benefits where individual prosecutions are concerned mirrors Stuntz's infamous observation that legislatures often expand substantive criminal law in order to elide policing hurdles set by rules of constitutional criminal procedure (Stuntz 1997).

Were prosecutors simply using corporate crime to leverage information from one party (the corporation) to prosecute another party (the guilty corporate executive), we might conclude that corporate crime operates no differently from the rest of criminal law. But corporate crime endows the prosecutor with yet another function, which is the power to indirectly regulate corporate governance through corporate compliance mandates (Griffith 2016; Arlen 2016).

When we view the corporate prosecution as merely a stand-in for regulation, much of what passes for corporate criminal practice becomes a feature and not a bug. The Department of Justice's Principles of Prosecution no longer stick out as vague, unbinding guidelines in contravention of the legality principle's command that legislatures write criminal law. Rather, they look instead like a blueprint for informal or negotiated rule-making (Krawiec 2003). DPAs and NPAs no longer register alarm in those who fear excessive prosecutorial power and insufficient judicial oversight; instead, they are upheld as healthy versions of traditional, structural regulation (Garrett 2007), or experimental new governance (Hess and Ford 2008; but see Baer 2009, questioning new governance claim).

Here again, the question remains whether the outcome—the generation of *some* regulation, albeit not nearly as strong as many would prefer—is worth the costs. When more traditional forms of regulation falter, the democratic process itself provides straightforward methods for undoing regulatory commands. And when antiregulatory impulses become too strong, democratic processes *also* provide a means for eventually altering the deregulatory trajectory and injecting new rules and oversight into different industries. These salutary feedback loops fade, however, when prosecutors attempt to mimic regulation's effect through deferred prosecution agreements (Arlen 2016). Because the DPA process is so lacking in transparency, it is often difficult to know why a given reform was included or left on the table, much less whether those reforms have actually borne fruit several years down the road. Thus, DPAs and similar agreements suffer the same democratic deficits as pretextual prosecutions, a category Professors Richman and Stuntz critiqued long ago (Richman and Stuntz 2005). In the same way a pretextual prosecution fails to inform the populace of the actual harm the prosecutor seeks to punish, the DPA and NPA similarly leave the public in the dark on harms, goals, and outcomes. Prosecutors promise to procure "better culture," "stronger compliance," and "less crime," but are rarely forced to justify in writing and on the record *specific* governance goals, *specific* means for attaining those goals, much less set forth the *specific* evidence that verifies the company's progress in achieving those goals. The federal corporate prosecutor thus remains unaccountable to the public, albeit in ways far different from the assistant district attorney tasked with overseeing thousands of cases that churn through the criminal justice system.

23.7 Moving Forward

Corporate crime represents a substantial departure from the rest of criminal law. It exists at odds with the legality principle and often rejects familiar rules of culpability and limited punishment. Corporate crime is thus *unbounded* by criminal law's familiar internal limitations. Whether this is cause for celebration or concern rests largely upon one's justification for prosecuting and punishing corporate entities. Preventing corporate obstruction, leveraging the company's internal monitoring controls, and re-invigorating government control where regulation would otherwise be impossible are all plausible explanations for the system we have. But the process still leaves a bad taste in one's mouth, precisely because it dilutes criminal law's meaning and undermines its legitimacy.

How, then, to fix corporate crime's unboundedness? The path is not impossible to imagine: Congress could, at long last, enact a series of statutes explicitly defining corporate fault in criminal cases. It could plausibly borrow from the Model Penal Code, which defines corporate liability more narrowly in many cases, imposing liability only for those crimes put into play by the firm's board or directors or "high managerial" agents (Model Penal Code § 2.07[1][c]; Ainslie 2006; Hefendehl 2000). It could also borrow from its European neighbors, some of whom have rejected the concept entirely in lieu of civil enforcement or have narrowed liability to those offenses triggered by a designated group of persons in control of the firm (Diskant 2008).

Alternatively, Congress could adopt a formal but open-textured definition of corporate crime. It might also exempt certain underlying crimes from corporate liability altogether, or pair an explicit form of omission liability ("failure to prevent fraud") with an affirmative compliance defense.[16] And finally, Congress might place restrictions on the type of federal collateral penalties that induce corporations and prosecutors to short-circuit the judicial process in the first place. In other words, Congress might narrow the consequences of corporate prosecution in order to make prosecutions, convictions, and judicial sentences more likely in the first place (Baer 2016).

Collectively, these limitations would bring corporate crime closer to what is commonly referred to as the general part of criminal law. For some, however, this effort would be perceived as a cynical attempt to please corporate interests while still pretending to care about corporate crime. For economists, reforms like these might upset the deterrence ecosystem that arises out of two-tiered system that premises leniency on corporate monitoring and self-reporting. These are difficult challenges, and ones not likely to abate any time soon. But we should address them head on.

An unbounded corporate criminal law is not without its benefits. In the right hands, it promotes deterrence, identifies wrongdoers, and potentially defends against an overly aggressive antiregulatory agenda. In the *wrong* hands, however, it can wreak havoc. Moreover, in anyone's hands, it is apt to generate skepticism and alienate the general public.

As criminal law scholars embark on a significant and long awaited effort to reform the criminal justice system, corporate crime scholars would do well to return to the question of corporate crime's relationship with the rest of criminal law. If we are serious about legality, culpability, and limited punishment, then we should think long and hard about how those principles ought to govern corporate crime's content and procedural framework. And if we are just as certain that we want to jettison these restraints, then we should ask once again why the label "criminal" has become so essential to the project of regulating corporate behavior.

Notes

1. For the sake of clarity, I refer to the punishment of for-profit business entities as "corporate criminal liability" throughout the remainder of this chapter. The federal code treats corporations, partnerships, and hybrids as equivalents (1 U.S.C. § 1; 18 U.S.C. § 18; Gruner 2004, § 3.02).
2. Constructive fault "considers a wide range of states of mind derived from organizational attributes, features, processes, and structures in relation to the actions of corporate agents" (Laufer 1994, 715).
3. Some contend this change was already in the works and that the Court merely affirmed a growing phenomenon in the lower courts (Diskant 2008).
4. Although *Bank of New England* affirms the aggregation of knowledge for certain offenses, more recent cases have rejected the aggregation of a willful or purposeful state of mind. *United States ex rel. Heathcote Holdings Corp. v. William K. Walthers, Inc.* (2011) reviews cases that declined to employ a "collective" scienter or "collective" intent approach for proving corporate fraud.
5. "Because a DPA involves the formal initiation of criminal charges, the agreement triggers the Speedy Trial [Act]" (*United States v. Fokker Servs, BV*. 2016, 737).
6. For two examples, see *United States v. HSBC Bank USA, NA* (2017)—where the appellate court held that the district court "impermissibly encroached" upon the Executive Branch's Article II power when it attempted to supervise aspects of the government's agreement with HSBC—and *United States v. Fokker Servs, BV* (2016, 738–739), where the appellate court vacated the district court's denial of a motion for exclusion under the Speedy Trial Act.
7. The change in the name of the Manual is explained in U.S. Department of Justice (2018).
8. In addition to these basic factors, the Department has increasingly signaled its willingness to decline prosecution altogether when the corporation voluntarily fully discloses its employees' wrongdoing (Garrett 2020). Declination was first floated as an option solely for foreign bribery cases in the Department's FCPA Pilot Program in April 2016. In November

2017, the Department announced its intention to make the program a permanent one and make declination a more prominent part of its policy (Jaeger 2017). In March 2018, the Department further announced its intention to have the FCPA Corporate Enforcement Policy serve as "nonbinding guidance" for corporate prosecutions outside the FCPA.
9. For a representative critique, see *United States v. Saena Tech Corp.* (2015).
10. None of this is to deny the fact that federal courts often *do* engage in a form of criminal lawmaking, such as occurs when judges "fill the interstices of open-textured statutory provisions" (Kahan 1994, 347).
11. Blackstone famously posited: "to constitute a crime against human laws, there must first be a vicious will, and secondly an unlawful act consequent upon such vicious will" (Blackstone [1769] 2016, 21).
12. *Morissette v. United States* 1952, 250–251.
13. Amy Sepinwall is notable for her rejection of this restraint, although she readily admits that fault has played a foundational role in criminal punishment (Sepinwall 2017, 2015).
14. See Russell M. Gold in Chapter 16 of this volume.
15. See n. 2 above.
16. The United Kingdom holds corporations criminally liable under a "Failure to Prevent Bribery" statute and a "Failure to Prevent Tax Evasion" provision. Firms prosecuted under these provisions may raise as an affirmative defense the fact that they maintained an adequate compliance program.

References

Abril, Patricia S., and Ann Morales Olazabal. 2006. "The Locus of Corporate Scienter." *Columbia Business Law Review* 2006(1): 81–166.

Ainslie, Elizabeth K. 2006. "Indicting Corporations Revisited: Lessons of the Arthur Andersen Prosecution." *American Criminal Law Review* 43: 107–23.

Alexander, Cindy R., and Jennifer Arlen. 2018. "Does Conviction Matter? The Reputation and Collateral Effects of Corporate Crime." In *Research Handbook on Corporate Crime and Financial Misdealing*. Edited by Jennifer Arlen, 87–149. Northampton, MA: Edward Elgar Publishing.

Alexander, Cindy R., and Mark Cohen. 2015. "The Evolution of Corporate Criminal Settlements: An Empirical Perspective on Deferred Prosecution, Non-Prosecution and Plea Agreements." *American Criminal Law Review* 52(3): 537–594.

Alschuler, Albert W. 2009. "Two Ways to Think About the Punishment of Corporations." *American Criminal Law Review* 46(4): 1359–1392.

Arlen, Jennifer. 1994. "The Potentially Perverse Effects of Corporate Criminal Liability." *Journal of Legal Studies* 23(2): 833–867.

Arlen, Jennifer. 2012. "The Failure of the Organizational Sentencing Guidelines." *University of Miami Law Review* 66(2): 321–362.

Arlen, Jennifer. 2016. "Prosecuting beyond the Rule of Law: Corporate Mandates Imposed through Deferred Prosecution Agreements." *Journal of Legal Analysis* 8(1): 191–234.

Arlen, Jennifer, and Marcel Kahan. 2017. "Corporate Governance Regulation through Non-Prosecution." *University of Chicago Law Review* 84(1): 323–387.

Arlen, Jennifer, and Reinier Kraakman. 1997. "Controlling Corporate Misconduct: An Analysis of Corporate Liability Regimes." *N.Y.U. Law Review* 72(4): 687–779.

Armour, John, Jeffrey Gordon, and Geeyoung Min. 2020a. "Taking Compliance Seriously." *Yale Journal of Regulation* 37(1): 1–66.

Armour, John, Brandon Garrett, Jeffrey Gordon, and Geeyoung Min. 2020b. "Board Compliance." *Minnesota Law Review* 104(3): 1191–1273.
Baer, Miriam H. 2009. "Governing Corporate Compliance." *Boston College Law Review* 50(4): 949–1019.
Baer, Miriam H. 2012. "Choosing Punishment." *Boston University Law Review* 92(2): 577–642.
Baer, Miriam H. 2016. "Too Vast to Succeed." *Michigan Law Review* 114(6): 1109–1136.
Baer, Miriam H. 2021. "Three Conceptions of Corporate Crime (And One Avenue For Reform)." *Law and Contemporary Problems* 84:__ (forthcoming)
Bagaric, Mirko, et al. 2017. "Bringing Sentencing into the 21st Century: Closing the Gap between Practice and Knowledge by Introducing Expertise into Sentencing Law." *Hofstra Law Review* 45(3): 785–850.
Beale, Sara Sun. 2009. "A Response to the Critics of Corporate Criminal Liability." *American Criminal Law Review* 46(4): 1481–1506.
Blackstone, William. (1769) 2016. *Commentaries on the Laws of England*. Vol. 4, at 21. Reprint, Oxford: Oxford University Press.
Buell, Samuel. 2007. "Criminal Procedure within the Firm." *Stanford Law Review* 59(6): 1613–1670.
Buell, Samuel W. 2018. "Why Do Prosecutors Say Anything? The Case of Corporate Crime." *North Carolina Law Review* 96: 823–858.
Coffee, John C., Jr. 1981. "'No Soul to Damn, No Body to Kick': An Unscandalized Inquiry into the Problem of Corporate Punishment." *Michigan Law Review* 79(3): 386–459.
Crespo, Andrew Manuel. 2018. "The Hidden Law of Plea Bargaining." *Columbia Law Review* 118(5): 1303–1424.
Cunningham, Lawrence A. 2004. "The Appeal and Limits of Internal Controls to Fight Fraud, Terrorism, Other Ills." *Journal of Corporation Law* 29(2): 267–336.
Diamantis, Mihailis. 2018. "Clockwork Corporations: A Character Theory of Corporate Punishment." *Iowa Law Review* 103(2): 507–570.
Diskant, Edward B. 2008. "Comparative Corporate Criminal Liability: Exploring the Uniquely American Doctrine through Comparative Criminal Procedure." *Yale Law Journal* 118(1): 126–176.
Eaglin, Jessica M. 2013. "Against Neorehabilitation." *SMU Law Review* 66(1): 189–226.
Ferzan, Kimberly Kessler. 2002. "Don't Abandon the Model Penal Code Yet! Thinking Through Simon's Rethinking." *Buffalo Criminal Law Review* 6: 185–217.
First, Harry. 2010. "Branch Office of the Prosecutor: The New Role of the Corporation in Business Crime Prosecutions." *North Carolina Law Review* 89(1): 23–98.
Finder, Lawrence D., and Ryan D. McConnell. 2006. "Devolution of Authority: The Department of Justice's Corporate Charging Policies." *St. Louis University Law Journal* 51(1): 1–52.
Fischel, Daniel, and Alan O. Sykes. 1996. "Corporate Crime." *Journal of Legal Studies* 25(2): 319–350.
Garrett, Brandon L. 2007. "Structural Reform Prosecutions." *Virginia Law Review* 93(4): 853–958.
Garrett, Brandon L. 2014. *Too Big to Jail: How Prosecutors Compromise with Corporations*. Cambridge, MA: Belknap Press.
Garrett, Brandon L. 2020. "Declining Corporate Prosecutions." *American Criminal Law Review* 57(1): 109–155.

Gilchrist, Gregory M. 2014. "The Special Problem of Banks and Crime." *University of Colorado Law Review* 85(1): 1–52.

Griffin, Lisa Kern. 2007. "Compelled Cooperation and the New Corporate Criminal Procedure." *N.Y.U. Law Review* 82(2): 311–382.

Griffith, Sean J. 2016. "Corporate Governance in an Era of Compliance." *William and Mary Law Review* 57: 2075-2140.

Gruner, Richard S. 2004. *Corporate Criminal Liability and Prevention*. New York: Law Journal Press.

Hasnas, John. 2009. "The Centenary of a Mistake: One Hundred Years of Corporate Criminal Liability." *American Criminal Law Review* 46(4): 1329–1358.

Hefendehl, Roland. 2000. "Corporate Criminal Liability: Model Penal Code Section 2.07 and the Development of Western Legal Systems." *Buffalo Criminal Law Review* 4: 283–300.

Hess, David, and Cristie L. Ford. 2008. "Corporate Corruption and Reform Undertakings: A New Approach to an Old Problem." *Cornell International Law Journal* 41(2): 307–346.

Hessick, Carissa Byrne. 2019. "The Myth of Common Law Crimes." *Virginia Law Review* 105(5): 965–1024.

Huq, Aziz, and Genevieve Lakier. 2018. "Apparent Fault." *Harvard Law Review* 131(6): 1525–1598.

Husak, Douglas. 2014. "Social Engineering as an Infringement of the Presumption of Innocence: The Case of Corporate Criminality." *Criminal Law & Philosophy* 8: 353–369.

Jaeger, Jaclyn. 2017. "Announcing the New FCPA Corporate Enforcement Policy." *Compliance Week*, November 29, 2017.

Jeffries, John Calvin, Jr. 1985. "Legality, Vagueness, and the Construction of Penal Statutes." *Virginia Law Review* 71(2): 189–246.

Kadish, Sanford H., Stephen J. Schulhofer, and Rachel E. Barkow. 2017. *Criminal Law and Its Processes: Cases and Materials*. 10th ed. New York: Wolters Kluwer.

Kahan, Dan M. 1994. "Lenity and Federal Common Law Crimes." *Supreme Court Review* 1994: 345–428.

Khanna, Vikramaditya S. 1996. "Corporate Criminal Liability: What Purpose Does It Serve." *Harvard Law Review* 109(7): 1477–1534.

Krawiec, Kimberly D., 2003. "Cosmetic Compliance and the Failure of Negotiated Governance." *Washington University Law Quarterly* 81(2): 487–544.

Laufer, William S. 1994. "Corporate Bodies and Guilty Minds." *Emory Law Journal* 43(2): 647–730.

Laufer, William S. 1999. "Corporate Liability, Risk Shifting and the Paradox of Compliance." *Vanderbilt Law Review* 52(5): 1341–1420.

Laufer, William S., and Alan Strudler. 2000. "Corporate Intentionality, Desert and Variants of Vicarious Liability." *American Criminal Law Review* 37(4): 1285–1312.

Lederman, Eli. 2000. "Models for Imposing Corporate Criminal Liability: From Adaptation and Imitation toward Aggregation and the Search for Self-Identity." *Buffalo Criminal Law Review* 4(1): 641–708.

Levin, Benjamin. 2019. "Mens Rea Reform and Its Discontents." *Journal of Criminal Law & Criminology* 109(3): 491–558.

Liparota v. United States. 1985. 471 U.S. 419.

Lipton, Daniel. 2010. "Corporate Capacity for Crime and Politics: Defining Corporate Personhood at the Turn of the Twentieth Century." *Virginia Law Review* 96(8): 1911–1964.

Markoff, Gabriel. 2013. "Arthur Andersen and the Myth of the Corporate Death Penalty." *University of Pennsylvania Journal of Business Law* 15(3): 797–842.
Miller, Geoffrey. 2014. *The Law of Governance, Risk Management, and Compliance*. New York: Wolters Kluwer.
Moorh, Geraldine Szott. 2007. "Of Bad Apples and Trees: Considering Fault Based Liability for the Complicit Corporation." *American Criminal Law Review* 44(4): 1343–1364.
Morissette v. United States. 1952. 342 U.S. 246.
Natapoff, Alexandra. 2017. "The Penal Pyramid." In *The New Criminal Justice Thinking*. Edited by Sharon Dolovich & Alexandra Natapoff, 3–31. New York: NYU Press.
New York Central & Hudson Railroad Company v. United States. 1909. 212 U.S. 481.
Offit, Anna. 2019. "Prosecuting in the Shadow of the Jury." *Northwestern University Law Review* 113(5): 1071–1120.
Pinkerton v. United States. 1946. 328 U.S. 670.
Podgor, Ellen S. 2018. "White Collar Shortcuts." *University of Illinois Law Review* 2018(3): 925–968.
Podgor, Ellen S., and Bruce A. Green. 2013. "Unregulated Internal Investigations: Achieving Fairness for Corporate Constituents." *Boston College Law Review* 54(1): 73–126.
Reilly, Peter. 2015. "Justice Deferred Is Justice Denied: We Must End Our Failed Experiment in Deferring Corporate Criminal Prosecutions." *BYU Law Review* 2015(2): 307–358.
Richman, Daniel C. and William J. Stuntz. 2005. "Al Capone's Revenge: An Essay on the Political Economy of Pretextual Prosecution." *Columbia Law Review* 105: 583–639.
Ristroph, Alice. 2017. "The Constitution of Police Violence." *UCLA Law Review* 64(5): 1182–1245.
Ristroph, Alice. 2019. "An Intellectual History of Mass Incarceration." *Boston College Law Review* 60: 1949–2010.
Ristroph, Alice. 2020. "The Curriculum of the Carceral State." *Columbia Law Review* 120: 1634–1709.
Robinson, Paul H. 2005. "Fair Notice and Fair Adjudication: Two Kinds of Legality." *University of Pennsylvania Law Review* 154(2): 335–398.
Rubin, Edward L. 2005. "Images of Organizations and Consequences of Regulation." *Theoretical Inquiries in Law* 6(2): 347–390.
Sayre, Francis Bowes. 1933. "Public Welfare Offenses." *Columbia Law Review* 33(1): 55–88.
Schneider, Gregory S. 2012. "Sentencing Proportionality in the States." *Arizona Law Review* 54(1): 241–276.
Sepinwall, Amy J. 2015. "Crossing the Fault Line in Corporate Criminal Liability." *Journal of Corporation Law* 40(2): 439–482.
Sepinwall, Amy J. 2017. "Faultless Guilt: Toward a Relationship-Based Account of Criminal Liability." *American Criminal Law Review* 54(2): 521–570.
Slobogin, Christopher. 2011. "Prevention as the Primary Goal for Sentencing: The Modern Case for Indeterminate Dispositions in Criminal Cases." *San Diego Law Review* 48(4): 1127–1172.
Solan, Lawrence M. 1998. "Law, Language and Lenity." *William & Mary Law Review* 40(1): 57–144.
Staples v. United States. 1994. 511 U.S. 600.
Stuntz, William J. 1997. "The Uneasy Relationship between Criminal Procedure and Criminal Justice." *Yale Law Journal* 107(1): 1–76.

Teichman, Doron. 2017. "Convicting with Reasonable Doubt: An Evidentiary Theory of Criminal Law." *Notre Dame Law Review* 93(2): 757–810.

Thomas, W. Robert. 2018. "How and Why Corporations Became (and Remain) Persons under Criminal Law." *Florida State University Law Review* 45(2): 479–538.

Thomas, W. Robert. 2019. "Incapacitating Criminal Corporations." *Vanderbilt Law Review* 72(3): 905–974.

Tonry, Michael. 2017. "Fairness, Equality, Proportionality and Parsimony: Toward a Comprehensive Juriprudence of Just Punishment." In *Penal Censure: Engagements within and beyond Desert Theory*. Edited by Antje du Bois-Pedain and Anthony E. Bottoms, 277–298. Oxford: Oxford University Press.

Uhlmann, David M. 2013. "Deferred Prosecution and Non-Prosecution Agreements and the Erosion of Corporate Criminal Liability." *Maryland Law Review* 72(4): 1295–1344.

United States ex rel. Heathcote Holdings Corp. v. William K. Walthers, Inc. 2011. 779 F. Supp. 2d 735 (N.D. Ill.).

U.S. Department of Justice. 2018. "Press Release: Department of Justice Announces Rollout of Updated United States Attorneys' Manual." September 25.

United States v. Fokker Servs. 2016. 818 F.3d 733 (D.C. Cir.).

United States v. Hudson & Goodwin. 1812. 11 U.S. (7 Cranch) 32.

United States v. HSBC Bank USA. 2017. 863 F.3d 125 (2d Cir.).

United States v. Saena Tech Corp. 2015. 140 F. Supp. 3d 11 (D.D.C.).

Werle, Nick. 2019 "Prosecuting Corporate Crime When Firms Are Too Big to Jail: Investigation, Deterrence and Judicial Review." *Yale Law Journal* 128(5): 1366–1438.

CHAPTER 24

LAW ENFORCEMENT AGENT DEFENDANTS AND PROSECUTORS

STEPHEN RUSHIN

24.1 Introduction

PROSECUTORS face unique challenges when pursuing criminal charges against a police officer or other law enforcement agents. These challenges have been on full display in two recent, prominent cases from St. Louis County, Missouri. The first case began on August 9, 2014, when police officer Darren Wilson shot and killed an unarmed black teenager named Michael Brown in Ferguson, Missouri. Many of us are familiar with the events that followed. Protests erupted throughout Ferguson. Local police engaged in days of heated confrontation with protestors who demanded justice for Brown's death. The U.S. Department of Justice opened an investigation of the Ferguson Police Department to determine whether the agency was engaged in a pattern of unconstitutional or unlawful behavior in violation of federal law (Apuzzo and Fernandez 2014). Given the underlying political and legal circumstances, St. Louis County Prosecuting Attorney Robert McCulloch faced significant public pressure to bring charges against Wilson. Under Missouri law, McCulloch had two options. He could either use his statutory authority to file charges against Wilson, provided he could prove that probable cause existed for such charges. Alternatively, McCulloch could present his case to a grand jury, which would decide whether such probable cause existed.

McCulloch opted to present his case to the grand jury. While McCulloch's office directly filed most criminal cases in St. Louis County, it was unsurprising that his office turned to a grand jury in such a highly sensitive case. But something unusual happened during this grand jury proceeding. In most grand jury proceedings, the prosecutor is only obligated to present evidence that incriminates the criminal suspect, in hopes of demonstrating probable cause. This is typically an easy standard to satisfy—hence why some colloquially suggest that a competent prosecutor could indict a "ham sandwich" (Levin 2014).

McCulloch took a different path. He decided to provide the grand jury with *all* evidence in the case, including both evidence that incriminated Wilson *and* potentially exculpatory evidence. As one media outlet explained, this approach was "virtually without precedent in the law of Missouri or anywhere else" (Toobin 2014). McCulloch turned the grand jury into a mini-trial, and he seemingly acted as an advocate both for Wilson and the State of Missouri. Faced with this exculpatory evidence, the grand jury chose not to indict Wilson for Brown's killing (Davey and Bosman 2014).

Only a few years later, St. Louis County found itself embroiled in another hotly contested criminal prosecution of a police officer. This case stemmed from the killing of Anthony Smith inside his own vehicle by St. Louis police officer Jason Stockley in 2011. Immediately after the shooting, Stockley claimed to have found an unregistered firearm inside of Smith's vehicle. Prosecutors alleged that Stockley had planted the gun in Smith's vehicle. To back up their claim, prosecutors presented dash camera footage of Stockley rummaging through his personal bag immediately before he entered Smith's vehicle. Prosecutors also presented audio of Stockley stating that, during his pursuit of Smith, he was "going to kill this motherf—er." And prosecutors presented evidence showing that investigators found only Stockley's DNA on the firearm recovered from inside of Smith's vehicle (Hart 2017).

For years after the incident, though, prosecutors at the state and federal level seemed unwilling to pursue charges against Stockley, despite the fact that the St. Louis Board of Police Commissioners settled a federal lawsuit stemming from the incident for approximately $900,000. It wasn't until 2016 that Stockley faced criminal charges for the killing (Byers 2016). As the trial neared, Stockley asked to waive his right to a jury, and instead requested a bench trial. Over the prosecutor's objection, the trial court granted Stockley's request for a bench trial. Ultimately, in an unusually detailed verdict, the trial court judge found Stockley not guilty (Chappell 2017).

These two cases, separated by only a few miles, illustrate many of the challenges that prosecutors face in approaching criminal cases involving police officers as defendants. In recent years, a growing body of research has documented the various barriers to and complexities surrounding criminal investigations and prosecutions of police officers. In the wake of the grand jury's failure to indict Darren Wilson in Ferguson, some have wondered aloud whether McCulloch treated Wilson differently because he was a police officer (Hill and Schabner 2014). In addition, the failed prosecution of Wilson raised some questions about whether the St. Louis County Prosecuting Attorney's Office was sufficiently detached from the Ferguson Police Department so as to conduct a fair investigation of Wilson's actions—a fear that was at least somewhat reduced by the independent assessment by the U.S. Department of Justice that Wilson did willfully deprive Brown of his constitutional rights (Byers 2015).

The Stockley verdict also raised important questions related to the criminal prosecution of police officers. Like the failed effort to prosecute Wilson, the multi-year delay in filing charges against Stockley despite the existence of DNA and video evidence may lead some to question whether local officials could be impartial in prosecutions of police officers. Some may worry that Stockley's use of a bench trial robbed the public of a legitimate opportunity to make factual findings about his guilt or innocence. And still others may worry that the Stockley case fundamentally demonstrated the extraordinary challenges in proving criminal conduct by police officers beyond a reasonable doubt, even in an era of widespread cell phone, body, and dash cameras (Berman, Lowery, and deGrandpre 2017).

The purpose of this chapter is to explore some of the complex problems arising from criminal investigations and prosecutions of police officers. It ultimately argues that criminal prosecutions of police present unique challenges for prosecutors, many of which are not present in prosecutions of other criminal defendants. This likely contributes to the relative rarity of prosecutions and convictions of police officers for professional misconduct, including the killing of civilians. The first part of this chapter presents the available evidence on how often police officers are subject to criminal prosecutions under both federal and state criminal statutes. In doing so, this part considers many of the existing barriers to prosecutions of police officers. The second part of this chapter then presents some ways that policymakers can reform the rules surrounding the criminal prosecution of police defendants.

24.2 When Police Become Defendants

Police officers most frequently become criminal defendants in one of two ways: an officer may become a defendant if his or her actions violate state criminal law, or if the federal government uses its narrow authority to allege that the officer deprived a person of her civil rights. In either case, existing literature suggests that police officers are sometimes treated differently than civilian suspects. At every nearly stage, from the investigation of alleged criminal conduct to the adjudication of guilt, structural, legal, and institutional barriers make it difficult to secure convictions of police defendants. The subsections that follow will explore the process of investigating, charging, and convicting police officers for criminal behavior. The first subsection explores how this process works at the state and local level. Then, the next subsection looks at how this process works at the federal level.

24.2.1 Challenges Facing State and Local Prosecutions of Police Officers

24.2.1.1 *Detecting and Investigating Police Misconduct*

Prosecutors are often positioned to both detect and investigate police officer misconduct. But the role of the prosecutor within the criminal justice system—particularly their close working relationship with police officers—creates opportunities for significant conflicts of interest that may call into question a prosecutor's impartiality. Most commonly, police officers become criminal defendants when they engage in acts that violate state criminal law. It appears that most jurisdictions give the local police department the power to investigate allegations of police misconduct that rises to the level of criminal behavior. Internal affairs divisions within a police department commonly handle these investigations, though some jurisdictions give this investigatory authority to professionals outside of the local police department (Jacobi 2000). And a relatively small number of police departments in large American cities give civilian review boards some meaningful role in investigating police wrongdoing. But these civilian review boards often have limited investigatory, subpoena power, or decision-making authority (Ofer 2016).

Thus, in at least some cases of criminal acts by police officers, prosecutors take on significant investigative responsibilities. In carrying out these responsibilities, Professor Alexa P. Freeman has argued "[l]ocal prosecutors who ordinarily work closely with the police face an impossible conflict of interest between their desire to maintain working relationships and their duty to investigate and prosecute police brutality" (Freeman 1996, 719). Professor Laurie L. Levenson has reiterated this sentiment, explaining that "prosecutors often enjoy too close of a relationship with local police and are therefore reluctant to turn against those with whom they have worked" (Levenson 1994; Levenson 2001, 22). And this problem is hardly new. Scholars have recognized this tension for decades, with scholars like Professor Louis B. Schwartz recognizing as far back as 1970 that local prosecutors could not be "an effective instrument for controlling police violence" because of the "hopeless conflict of interest" involved in such cases (Schwartz 1970, 1023–1024). These realizations have led many scholars to call for legal reforms that would ensure the impartial investigation and prosecution of police misconduct by outside agents.

Another emerging thread of scholarship has argued that District Attorney's Offices should harness their close working relationship with law enforcement agents to serve as a check on police misconduct. For example, Professor Erwin Chemerinsky has persuasively argued that prosecutors are actually uniquely positioned to identify and respond to possible officer misconduct during the investigation of criminal conduct. Using the Rampart Scandal in Los Angeles as an example, Professor Chemerinsky showed that, with adequate controls in place, the Los Angeles District Attorney's Office could have identified the pattern of misconduct ongoing in the Rampart Division before it spiraled out of control. For example, the District Attorney's Office could have adopted procedures for deputy prosecutors to report cases where a police officer was suspected of lying in a criminal proceeding, and it could track cases declined or dismissed because of officer credibility problems. Professor Chemerinsky also suggested that the District Attorney's Office could play a more substantial role in reporting to the scene of officer-involved shootings in order to interview participants and witnesses as soon as the scene is secure. And he argued that the District Attorney's Office could alter the present incentive structure so as to reward attorneys not just for securing convictions, but also for efforts to identify perjury and misconduct by officers (Chemerinsky 2001).

24.2.1.2 *Limitations on Investigations of Police Officers*

Police union contracts, law enforcement officer bills of rights (LEOBRs), and other state and local laws frequently limit the techniques that can be used during internal investigations of police officers, generally giving police officers more protections than similarly situated civilian suspects (Fisk and Richardson 2017; Joseph 2016; Keenan and Walker 2005; Levine 2016b; McKesson, Sinyangwe, Elzie, and Packnett 2016; Rushin 2017a; Walker 2015). Admittedly, many of these labor protections are designed to apply specifically to the investigation of internal disciplinary matters, and not necessarily criminal conduct. But in practice, investigators may not initially know whether the alleged officer misconduct qualifies as merely a violation of internal policy or a criminal act. And officers suspected of criminal behavior are sophisticated actors who are likely to invoke their *Miranda* protections to prevent interrogations. Thus, in practice, it seems highly likely that these labor protections provide limitations on how investigators gather evidence against police officers, particularly when supervisors require officers to answer questions for an internal disciplinary interview.

Take, for example, the events surrounding the killing of Laquan McDonald by former Chicago police officer Jason Van Dyke. After Van Dyke shot and killed McDonald, officers on the scene claimed that McDonald had advanced towards them while swinging a knife in an "aggressive, exaggerated manner," forcing Van Dyke to open fire in self-defense (Mills et al. 2015). Van Dyke had been subject to more complaints than 96.7 percent of all Chicago police officers in the years leading up to the shooting, including allegations of excessive use of force and the use of a racial slur. And Van Dyke's actions had previously resulted in the city paying out $350,000 in civil damages after he allegedly used excessive force during a traffic stop (McLaughlin 2015). Despite all of this, the Chicago Police Department had never punished or even flagged Van Dyke's behavior as potentially problematic (Rushin 2017a). How had Van Dyke slipped through the cracks of the city's disciplinary process for so long? And how did multiple officers on the scene of Laquan McDonald's killing concoct the same, demonstrably false accounting of the events?

Part of the answer may lay in the protections afforded to Van Dyke and other Chicago police officers as part of the city's police union contract and the Illinois Uniform Peace Officer Disciplinary Act. Because of these labor protections, investigators in Chicago were barred from interviewing officers immediately after officer-involved shootings, potentially giving them an opportunity to coordinate their stories so as to deflect blame. The union contract also required the city to erase portions of officer disciplinary records, limiting the ability of Chicago's then-existing Independent Police Review Authority to consider an officer's disciplinary history when examining new complaints against an officer. And under state law, investigators in Illinois were generally unable to initiate investigations of police officers based on anonymous complaints (Rushin 2017a). These protections stand in stark contrast to the way that police treat civilians during criminal investigations. As just one example, civilian suspects are routinely subject to coercive interrogation tactics that many police union contracts and LEOBRs bar investigators from using against law enforcement suspects (Levine and Rushin 2018).

Empirical studies by civil rights activists, media outlets, and scholars have found that Chicago's police union contract is hardly unique. Police union contracts and LEOBRs frequently give officers rigid waiting periods before interrogations can begin, require investigators to turn over incriminating evidence to officers before an interrogation, purge disciplinary records after set lengths of time, establish statutes of limitations on internal investigations, limit the involvement of civilians in internal investigations, ban anonymous complaints against officers, and mandate complicated disciplinary appeals procedures that often involve the use of binding arbitration. A number of critics have argued that these regulations unnecessarily impair the collection of evidence against police officers (Keenan and Walker 2005; Levine 2016b; McKesson, Sinyangwe, Elzie, and Packnett 2016; Rushin 2017a). Others have claimed that collective bargaining or the protections afforded by union contracts and LEOBRS may contribute to increases in officer misconduct or use of force against civilians (Dharmapala, McAdams, and Rappaport 2018; Rad 2018). Thus, prosecutors and police investigators must often navigate these complex labor law limitations on their investigative abilities, which may sometimes limit their ability to build a criminal case against a police officer.

24.2.1.3 *Charging Decision, Grand Juries, and Conflicts of Interest*

Once an investigation has been completed, prosecutors wield considerable discretion in deciding whether to file charges against a police officer for a violation of a criminal statute. In fact, prosecutors often have nearly complete and unreviewable authority to decide whether or not to pursue criminal charges against a police officer (or any criminal suspect for that matter) (Stuntz 2001). A prosecutor's charging decision is "among the most opaque made by any actor in the legal system" (Levine 2016c, 753). After a charging decision is made, some jurisdictions require prosecutors to seek an indictment before a grand jury, particularly for serious felony offenses, while other jurisdictions give prosecutors the option to directly file charges. But even when a prosecutor brings a case to a grand jury, she can still control what evidence is presented to the grand jury, as illustrated by the example from Ferguson, Missouri, at the start of this chapter. As Professor Kate Levine has explained, "when the police are the suspects, the usual charge and indictment process appears to unravel" (Levine 2016c, 755).

In these police suspect cases, some "prosecutors use their full arsenal of procedural discretion when a police-suspect's liberty and reputation is on the line: they conduct thorough pre-charge investigations, credit an officer's version of events, and either exercise their option to present exculpatory evidence to a grand jury, or in many cases, decline to charge altogether" (Levine 2016c, 756). Other times, prosecutors are careful to impanel "special grand juries to investigate police related deaths" so as to "insulate themselves from the final decision, while appearing to fulfill the public desire for an independent review" (McKinley and Baker 2014). This stands in stark contrast to how prosecutors often treat civilian suspects, where prosecutors often aggressively pursue all possible charges and sometimes present limited or skewed facts, as needed, to secure indictments from grand juries (Kuckes 2006). All of this has led some to argue that a "structural conflict of interest arises when local prosecutors are given the discretion and responsibility to investigate and lead cases against the police" (Levine 2016a, 1496).

24.2.1.4 *Obtaining a Conviction*

If a prosecution of a police officer proceeds to a trial, the best available evidence suggests that factfinders are less likely to convict him (or her) than other similarly situated criminal defendants (Kindy and Kelly 2015). The seemingly low rate of criminal convictions of police officers may be explained by a few factors. For one thing, critics have argued that juries are often more sympathetic to police officers than other criminal defendants. As Professor Rachel Harmon has argued, prosecutions of police officers are often difficult because "victims of police misconduct often make problematic witnesses" and because "juries frequently believe and sympathize with defendant officers" rather than alleged victims of police wrongdoing (Harmon 2010, 9). Additionally, victims of police brutality are themselves often individuals suspected of criminal behavior. Under such circumstances, juries may feel reluctant to order criminal punishment against a police officer, who claims he was "just trying to do his job." Ultimately, as Professor Barbara Armacost has explained, "[t]he fact that the victim is viewed as unsympathetic and unreliable contributes to jurors' natural reluctance to brand a police officer a criminal and to send him to prison" (Armacost 2004, 466).

Given all of these barriers, how often are police officers subject to criminal charges for professional misconduct? It is difficult to provide a definitive answer to this question. This is in part because policing in the United States is highly decentralized. We are not a nation of one police force, but rather thousands of decentralized federal, state, and local police departments that employ hundreds of thousands of individual officers (Rushin 2017b). As a general rule, we keep few consistent, national statistics on police behavior (Rushin 2016). Perhaps nothing better illustrates this than comments made by then Director of the Federal Bureau of Investigations James Comey, soon after the events in Ferguson: "It's ridiculous that I can't tell you how many people were shot by the police last week, last month, last year" (Schmidt 2015).

As explained in the next subsection, a handful of scholars and media outlets have attempted to determine how many police officers have been subject to criminal charges and convictions over the last several years. Their data generally suggests that criminal charges are rare, and convictions even rarer.

24.2.1.5 *Frequency of State and Local Prosecutions*

In recent years, important efforts by scholars, media outlets, and civil rights advocates have shed additional light on the number of criminal prosecutions of police officers at the state and local level. Perhaps most prominently Professor Philip M. Stinson has pioneered the collection of data on "criminal arrest cases" against police officers. Professor Stinson has used media reports to estimate the number of police officers arrested for various types of criminal offenses from 2005 to 2013. By coding these records, Professor Stinson identified approximately 9,088 criminal arrests of 7,518 state and local peace officers over this time period, involving everything from relatively minor to serious criminal offenses (Stinson 2018). Given that there are around 18,000 state and local law enforcement agencies in the United States, this means that the typical American police department saw an average of 0.06 officer arrests per year over this nine-year period.

Others like the *Washington Post*, the *Guardian*, and Mapping Police Violence have focused specifically on the frequency of police killings of civilians and prosecutions of police officers for these killings. Perhaps most prominently, the *Washington Post* found that, despite the estimated 10,000 to 11,000 individuals killed by law enforcement between 2005 and 2015, only fifty-four police officers faced criminal charges related to these killings. And only eleven of those cases actually resulted in a criminal conviction—meaning that only one in one thousand police killings seems to result in a criminal conviction of a police officer (Kindy and Kelly 2015).

The relatively rare rate of convictions of police officers may actually be normatively desirable. Take instances where an officer uses force against a civilian. Use of force in many situations may be fully justifiable. Police commonly encounter individuals at their most vulnerable and in moments of crisis, where another person's behavior may require the officer to use force to protect themselves or others from serious harm. Under such situations, we should expect police to utilize force. Thus, it is difficult to accurately pinpoint the normatively desirable level of police prosecutions and police convictions each year. Nevertheless, it seems likely the current rate of criminal prosecutions and convictions of police each year underrepresents the number of cases that warranted prosecution or conviction.

24.2.2 Challenges to Federal Prosecutions of Police Officers

Given all of the barriers to state and local prosecutions of police officers, some have pointed to federal prosecutions as an obvious solution. Congress has authorized the U.S. Attorney General under 18 U.S.C. § 242 to seek criminal charges against police officers who willfully deprive individuals of their civil rights. This statute, passed after the Civil War, was designed in part to provide newly freed slaves with additional assurance that the federal government would use criminal charges to punish state and local officials who deprived them of their civil rights, even if the state or local prosecutor failed to act (Johnson and Bridgmon 2009).

Federal prosecutions of law enforcement agents theoretically work around many of the barriers to criminal accountability described above. Federal prosecutors and the Federal Bureau of Investigation need not abide by the terms of police union contracts or LEOBRs in investigating a police officer's conduct. And because federal prosecutors are less likely to work with local police officers, there are fewer concerns about the potential for conflicts of interest. But this does not mean that federal prosecution under § 242 meaningfully fills the gap left by the lack of state and local prosecutions (Armacost 2004). Overall, the best evidence available suggests that prosecutions and convictions of police officers under this statute are exceedingly rare (Johnson and Bridgmon 2009). One estimate found that federal prosecutors generally attempted charges in less than 1 percent of all potentially actionable § 242 cases (Rushin 2014, 3203). Some of this may be explained by the fact that § 242 does not provide a general cause of action against all criminal conduct by police, but rather only criminal conduct in which the police officer "willfully" deprived a person of their civil rights.

In *Screws v. United States* (1945), the U.S. Supreme Court held that the term "willfully" in § 242 requires federal prosecutors to prove that a state actor acted intentionally and with the purpose of violating someone's constitutionally protected rights. This relatively high threshold for proving guilt under § 242 means that it can be difficult for prosecutors to win a case against a police officer accused of violating § 242 (Armacost 2004). The available empirical evidence also suggests that the federal government only has limited resources to pursue criminal prosecutions pursuant to § 242 (Rushin 2014). This means that, while § 242 prosecutions may somewhat fill the gap left by state and local inaction, they remain a highly imperfect and incomplete solution.

24.3 Moving Forward

So where do we go from here? Are there reforms that states can make to ensure that police officers engaged in criminal conduct are subject to the same investigations and prosecutions as civilian suspects? Researchers have recommended a number of possible reforms that states and municipalities could take to ensure rigorous and fair investigations and prosecutions of police officers who break the law. The subsections that follow will consider some of the most common reforms advocated by scholars and civil rights advocates to improve the investigation and prosecution of police officers accused of criminal conduct.

24.3.1 Outsourcing Investigations and Prosecutions of Police Officers

One way that states and localities could reform the prosecution of police misconduct is by passing statutes or establishing formal protocols that outsource the investigation and prosecution of alleged crimes by police officers. Professor Levine has made just such an argument. Using conflict-of-interest law, she has argued that local prosecutors should almost always be removed from cases involving the prosecution of police misconduct. As she persuasively argues, "[e]lected district attorneys, who are subject to intense pressure from police unions, and their line attorneys who must rely on law enforcement for the success of every case they try, have a clear conflict of interest when the tables are turned and they must decide whether to bring charges and lead cases against police-defendants" (Levine 2016a, 1483). Even if a prosecutor's office has a "special unit designated to deal with police crimes," Professor Levine believes that this will not be sufficient to insulate these prosecutors from potential conflicts of interest (1485). Given these realities, she recommends that prosecutors remove all cases involving misconduct by local police officers to a different office—be that a different district attorney's office, the state attorney general's office, or the federal prosecutor's office. This would result in all charging decisions being made by an independent office, and not the local prosecutor.

In 2014, Wisconsin passed a law that requires just such outsourcing of criminal prosecutions of police misconduct that include officer-involved deaths of civilians. The law also provided a number of other measures to ensure transparency and accountability. The law was a response to the killing of an unarmed 21-year-old man named Michael Bell, Jr., in Kenosha, Wisconsin. As was routine at that time, the internal affairs division of the Kenosha Police Department handled the investigation of the incident thereafter. According to witnesses on the scene, one of the officers shouted that Bell had taken one of the officer's guns, leading to the use of deadly force. Within forty-eight hours, the department concluded that the shooting was justified and that the officer had not engaged in any misconduct.

After lab reports indicated that Bell's DNA and fingerprints were not found on the officer's gun, Bell's father began an effort to change the Wisconsin law. He used the $1.75 million settlement the family received from their wrongful death suit against the Kenosha Police Department "to fund a grassroots campaign" involving ads in major newspapers, on radio stations, and on television. They also erected billboards in Milwaukee with the slogan, "When Police Kill, Should They Judge Themselves?" The campaign worked, as Wisconsin eventually became the first state in the country to establish a law requiring independent investigations of police killings of civilians (NPR 2014).

The law provides two major requirements when a police officer is involved in the death of a civilian. First, the law requires local law enforcement agencies in Wisconsin to create policies that transfer investigative authority in such cases to an outside agency that has sufficient training and expertise to handle such a case. And second, if the outside agency deems the death to be justified, the agency must release all relevant investigative documents to the public (Palmer 2016).

Since the passage of the Wisconsin measure, at least one other state—Connecticut—has passed a similar law (Yan and Fantz 2015). Admittedly, outsourcing investigations of police-involved deaths of civilians may not solve all of the problems discussed in this chapter. Police departments are still likely to demand protections from internal investigations via police union contracts and LEOBRs. Juries may remain unwilling to convict a police officer. And while bench trials may be available, they may also diminish the role of the public in overseeing the administration of the criminal justice system. In fact, one examination found that all of the first nine fatal police-involved shootings in Wisconsin investigated under the new law were found justified by the outside investigating agency (Halsted 2014).

But these limitations aside, The Wisconsin model provides a viable path forward to reduce some of the most problematic conflicts of interest inherent in the investigation and prosecution of police officers suspected of criminal behavior. It will likely serve as a model for other states in the future.

24.3.2 Grand Juries

Others have argued that states should consider legislation that regulates the use of grand juries in police misconduct cases. Some, like Professor Peter L. Davis, have argued that truly independent grand juries may serve as a check on a prosecutor's decision to decline prosecution in cases of police brutality. Professor Davis starts with the premise that, given the absence of consistent internal disciplinary action by local police departments, prosecutors must aggressively enforce criminal prohibitions against police officers in order to deter police violence effectively. Given that existing conflicts of interest may prevent prosecutors from bringing criminal charges against officers, Professor Davis recommends that states provide citizens with direct access to grand juries—either directly or through an impaneling judge—in cases where a prosecutor has declined to press charges. Specifically, at the time of his research, Professor Davis found that Alabama, California, Colorado, Georgia, Louisiana, Maryland, Minnesota, Nebraska, Tennessee, Texas, and West Virginia all provided citizens with a common law, constitutional, or statutory right to circumvent the discretion of the prosecutor and present evidence of violations of state law directly to grand juries. And in three states—Illinois, Maine, and North Carolina—he found that judges had discretion to allow citizens to directly access grand juries (Davis 1994).

Others have worried that grand juries do not provide enough transparency and public accountability. Civil rights advocates have criticized grand juries as ineffective vehicles for charging police officers, in part because "the grand jury process is [often] secret and court records associated with it are sealed" (Gross 2015). This sentiment grew after the grand juries failed to indict police officers responsible for the deaths of Eric Garner in New York and Michael Brown in Ferguson. In response, at least one state—California—passed legislation that prevented prosecutors from using grand juries in cases of police use of deadly force. Instead, the law forced prosecutors to decide whether or not charges were appropriate. Since prosecutors are generally elected officials, the hope was that this measure would result in more transparency in cases of alleged police brutality and provide the public with an accountability mechanism.

While an appeals court ultimately struck down this California law, the measure raises some broader questions (Thanawala 2017). Will prosecutors more effectively exercise charging authority than grand juries? And do grand juries present a real barrier to police accountability, because of their secretive nature, because grand juries are unwilling to indict police, or because prosecutors can use them as a vehicle to obtain whatever outcome they want? More research may be necessary on these points.

24.3.3 Facilitating Investigations by Loosening Internal Investigation Procedures for Police Officers

Finally, there is one immediate step that municipalities could take to ensure that prosecutors have the tools to treat police officers comparably to similarly situated civilians. Communities could scale back some labor protections for police officers to facilitate quicker and more robust investigations of officer misconduct. This might, in turn, provide prosecutors with stronger evidence on which to base charging decisions in cases of police misconduct. To be clear, as Professor Levine and I have argued in the past, police officers deserve protections from abusive investigation techniques during internal and criminal investigations (Levine and Rushin 2018). And scholars like Professor Levine have persuasively argued that policymakers should not just exclusively focus on the scaling back of protections for police officers under internal investigations; instead, we could use this as an opportunity to give civilians some of the same procedural protections currently offered to police suspects (Levine 2016b). But procedural protections during investigations must not become so cumbersome as to impede reasonable investigations.

Many of the current protections given to police officers appear to go too far. For example, in response to a national survey, police chiefs across the United States almost uniformly claim that delaying interrogations meaningfully impedes investigators' ability to elicit incriminating information from a suspect. Additionally, police chiefs almost uniformly report that providing suspects with access to incriminating information before an interrogation harms interrogations and impedes the search for the truth (Rushin and DeProspo 2019). Despite the widespread recognition that these tactics impede investigations, a large number of police departments give police officers these very protections when they must undergo interrogations about suspected misconduct (Rushin 2017b).

By partially scaling back some of the more burdensome procedural protections currently afforded by police union contracts and LEOBRs, communities could increase the probability that prosecutors have sufficient evidence to pursue criminal charges against police officers where such charges are warranted. But advocates may face an uphill battle, as police unions are likely to push back strongly against these kinds of reforms. And as illustrated by recent union contract negotiations in cities like Austin, Texas, communities should be prepared to provide officers with other benefits, like higher pay or improved benefits, in exchange for eliminating these protections during internal investigations (Hall 2017).

24.4 Conclusion

Prosecutors face distinctive challenges in prosecuting police officers for criminal conduct. No doubt, this chapter only scratches the surface of this complex topic. It is critically important for prosecutor's offices to approach this topic with care. Failure to do so may contribute to a miscarriage of justice and have significant career implications for an elected district attorney. Thus, it may be fitting to end this chapter with a cautionary anecdote, illustrating the consequences of a prosecutor's office mishandling (at least in the eyes of the public) a case involving a law enforcement officer defendant.

In the wake of his decision to present exculpatory evidence to a grand jury after the killing of Michael Brown, Robert McCulloch faced enormous backlash, both in Ferguson and nationally. Despite demands from the public that he recuse himself from the case and assign a special prosecutor, McCulloch decided to handle the case himself (Berman 2014). He assured the public that he would be "fair and impartial in every matter." But when McCulloch not only chose to present exculpatory evidence before a grand jury, but also to publicly announce that he agreed with the grand jury's decision to not indict Darren Wilson, McCulloch faced a new problem: a political challenger. Wesley Bell, a black city council member from Ferguson, decided to run against McCulloch in the primary.

Almost four years to the day after Brown's death, voters in the democratic primary ousted McCulloch, making Wesley Bell the prosecuting attorney of St. Louis County (Wootson 2018). There is little doubt that McCulloch's decisions in the Wilson case contributed to his electoral defeat. While McCulloch still stands by his decisions, the event is a sobering reminder that few prosecutorial decisions will receive more public attention than those involving law enforcement agent defendants. It is in the interest of every prosecutor's office to develop policies that minimize conflicts of interest, ensure impartiality, and promote public accountability in these sensitive cases.

REFERENCES

Apuzzo, Matt, and Manny Fernandez. 2014. "Justice Dept. Inquiry to Focus on Practices of Police in Ferguson." *New York Times*, September 3.

Armacost, Barbara E. 2004. "Organizational Culture and Police Misconduct." *George Washington Law Review* 72(3): 453–546.

Berman, Mark. 2014. "NAACP Calls for Special Prosecutor in Michael Brown Shooting Case." *Washington Post*, August 21.

Berman, Mark, Wesley Lowery, and Andrew deGrandpre. 2017. "Police and Protestors Clash in St. Louis After Former Officer Who Shot Black Driver Acquitted on Murder Charges." *Washington Post*, September 16.

Byers, Christine. 2015. "Justice Department Finds that Ferguson Officer Did Not Violate Michael Brown's Rights." *St. Louis Post-Dispatch*, March 5.

Byers, Christine. 2016. "Former St. Louis Cop Arrested, Charged with First-Degree Murder for 2011 Police Shooting." *St. Louis Post-Dispatch*, May 17.

Chappell, Bill. 2017. "Former St. Louis Police Officer is Acquitted of Murder in Anthony Lamar Smith Case." *NPR*, September 15.

Chemerinsky, Erwin. 2001. "The Role of Prosecutors in Dealing with Police Abuse: The Lessons of Los Angeles." *Virginia Journal of Social Policy & the Law* 8(2): 305–327.

Davis, Peter L. 1994. "Rodney King and the Decriminalization of Police Brutality in America: Direct and Judicial Access to the Grand Jury as Remedies for Victims of Police Brutality When the Prosecutor Declines to Prosecute." *Maryland Law Review* 53(2): 271–357.

Davey, Monica, and Julie Bosman. 2014. "Protests Flare after Ferguson Police Officer Is Not Indicted." *New York Times*, November 24.

Dharmapala, Dhammika, Richard H. McAdams, and John Rappaport. 2018. "Collective Bargaining and Police Misconduct." University of Chicago Public Law & Legal Theory Paper Series, No. 655.

Fisk, Catherine, and L. Song Richardson. 2017. "Police Unions." *George Washington Law Review* 85(3): 712–799.

Freeman, Alexa P. 1996. "Unscheduled Departures: The Circumvention of Justice Sentencing for Police Brutality." *Hastings Law Journal* 47(3): 677–777.

Gross, Allie. 2015. "California Becomes First State to Ban Grand Juries in Police Shooting Cases." *Mother Jones*, August 13.

Hall, Katie. 2017. "In New Contract, Police Agree to More Accountability for Higher Raises." *Austin American Statesman*, October 25.

Halsted, Gilman. 2014. "9 Fatal Police-Involved Shootings Were Investigated under New Law in 2014." *Wisconsin Public Radio*, December 29.

Hart, Benjamin. 2017. "St. Louis Protests End in Violence after White Officer Found Not Guilty of Murder." *New York Magazine*, September 17.

Hill, James, and Dean Schabner. 2014. "Ferguson Grand Jury 'Unfair,' Michael Brown Family Lawyer Says." *ABC News*, November 23.

Harmon, Rachel. 2010. "Promoting Civil Rights through Proactive Policing Reform." *Stanford Law Review* 62(1): 1–68.

Jacobi, John V. 2000. "Prosecuting Police Misconduct." *Wisconsin Law Review* 2000: 789–853.

Johnson, Brian R., and Phillip B. Bridgmon. 2009. "Depriving Civil Rights: An Exploration of 18 U.S.C. 242 Criminal Prosecutions 2001–2006." *Criminal Justice Review* 34(2): 196–209.

Joseph, George. 2016. "Leaker Police Files Contain Guarantees Disciplinary Files Will Be Kept Secret." *The Guardian*, February 7.

Keenan, Kevin M., and Samuel Walker. 2005. "An Impediment to Police Accountability? An Analysis of Statutory Law Enforcement Officers' Bills of Rights." *Boston University Public Interest Law Journal* 14(2): 185–244.

Kindy, Kimberly, and Kimbriell Kelly. 2015. "Thousands Dead, Few Prosecuted." *Washington Post*, April 11.

Kuckes, Niki. 2006. "The Democratic Prosecutor: Explaining the Constitutional Function of the Grand Jury." *Georgetown Law Journal* 94(5): 1265–1318.

Levenson, Laurie L. 1994. "The Future of State and Federal Civil Rights Prosecutions: The Lessons of the Rodney King Trial." *UCLA Law Review* 41(3): 509–608.

Levenson, Laurie L. 2001. "Police Corruption and New Models for Reform." *Suffolk University Law Review* 35(1): 1–46.

Levinson, Reade. 2017. "Across the U.S., Police Contracts Shield Officers from Scrutiny and Discipline." *Reuters*, January 13.

Levin, Josh. "The Judge Who Coined 'Indict a Ham Sandwich' Was Himself Indicted." *Slate*, November 25, 2014.

Levine, Kate. 2016a. "Who Shouldn't Prosecute the Police." *Iowa Law Review* 101(4): 1447–1496.

Levine, Kate. 2016b. "Police Suspects." *Columbia Law Review* 116(5): 1197–1258.

Levine, Kate. 2016c. "How We Prosecute the Police." *Georgetown Law Journal* 104(4): 745–776.

Levine, Kate, and Stephen Rushin. 2018. "Interrogation Parity." *University of Illinois Law Review* 2018(5): 1685–1704.

McKesson, DeRay, Samuel Sinyangwe, Johnetta Elzie, and Brittany Packnett. 2016. "Police Union Contracts and Police Bill of Rights Analysis." *Campaign Zero*. June 29.

McKinley, James C., and Al Baker. 2014. "Grand Jury System, with Exceptions, Favors the Police in Fatalities." *New York Times*, December 7.

McLaughlin, Elliot C. 2015. "Chicago Police Officers Had History of Complaints before Laquan McDonald Shooting." *CNN*, November 26.

Mills, Steve, Jeremy Gorner, Todd Lighty, Annie Sweeney, Stacy St. Clair, and Jason Meisner. 2015. "Laquan McDonald Police Reports Differ Dramatically from Video." *Chicago Tribune*, December 5.

NPR. 2014. "In Wisconsin, A Decade-Old Police Shooting Leads to New Law." *NPR*, December 13.

Ofer, Udi. 2016. "Getting It Right: Building Effective Civilian Review Boards to Oversee Police." *Seton Hall Law Review* 46(4): 1033–1062.

Palmer, Jim. 2016. "Wisconsin a Model with Outside Investigations of Police Shootings." *San Francisco Chronicle*, May 26.

Rad, Abdul N. 2018. "Police Institutions and Police Abuse: Evidence from the US." University of Oxford.

Rushin, Stephen. 2014. "Federal Enforcement of Police Reform." *Fordham Law Review* 82(6): 3189–3247.

Rushin, Stephen. 2016. "Using Data to Reduce Police Violence." *Boston College Law Review* 57(1): 117–166.

Rushin, Stephen. 2017a. "Police Union Contracts." *Duke Law Journal* 66(6): 1191–1266.

Rushin, Stephen. 2017b. *Federal Intervention in American Police Departments*. New York: Cambridge University Press.

Rushin, Stephen, and Atticus DeProspo. 2019. "Interrogating Police Officers." *George Washington Law Review* 87(3): 646–705.

Schmidt, Michael S. "F.B.I. Director Speaks Out on Race and Police Bias." 2015. *New York Times*, February 12.

Schwartz, Louis B. 1970. "Complaints against the Police: Experience of the Community Rights Division of the Philadelphia District Attorney's Office." *University of Pennsylvania Law Review* 118(7): 1023–1035.

Screws v. United States. 1945. 325 U.S.91.

Stinson, Philip. 2018. "The Henry A. Wallace Police Crime Database." Bowling Green State University.

Stuntz, William J. 2001. "The Pathological Politics of Criminal Law." *Michigan Law Review* 100(3): 505–600.

Thanawala, Sudhin. 2017. "California Court: Grand Juries Can Probe Police Shootings." *KQED News*, January 11.

Toobin, Jeffrey. 2014. "How Not to Use a Grand Jury." *New Yorker*, November 25.

Walker, Samuel. 2015. *The Baltimore Police Union Contract and the Law Enforcement Officers' Bill of Rights: Impediments to Accountability*.

Wootson, Cleve R., Jr. 2018. "Voters Oust Prosecutor Accused of Favoring Ferguson Officer Who Killed Michael Brown." *Washington Post*, August 8.

Yan, Holly, and Ashley Fantz. 2015. "Police Kill Teen: Why Wisconsin's Investigation Will Be Different." *CNN*, March 10.

CHAPTER 25

PROSECUTING MISDEMEANORS

JENNY ROBERTS[1]

25.1 Introduction

ALTHOUGH felonies and particularly violent crime tend to get the most media, public, and legislative attention in the United States, misdemeanors make up the bulk of the criminal legal system. Misdemeanors comprise approximately 75 percent of all criminal court cases, and prosecutors and police file more than 13 million misdemeanor cases each year (Natapoff 2018, 256–258; Stevenson and Mayson 2018, 737, 745). Misdemeanor arrest rates are even higher, with prosecutors declining to file charges on some of those arrests.

While these statistics demonstrate that most people in the criminal legal system are charged with low-level offenses, there is no uniform definition of the term "misdemeanor." It is generally understood to mean a criminal offense with a maximum punishment of one year in jail, but every state legislature can use the term "misdemeanor" however it chooses. For example, in Maryland the misdemeanor of assault—which includes threats without physical contact—carries up to ten years' imprisonment. In New York, that same threat is a "violation," a category that falls below misdemeanor in the state's Penal Law and carries a maximum of fifteen days' imprisonment. Further, many localities have their own codes and ordinances, which may include misdemeanor charges. Still, while a misdemeanor is whatever the legislature says it is, most jurisdictions divide their criminal offenses into felonies and misdemeanors, with the latter carrying a maximum one-year jail sentence.

There are also a wide variety of misdemeanor offenses, ranging from fairly serious to extremely minor, from a social harm perspective. The newly approved Model Penal Code: Sentencing ("MPC") suggests two levels of classification, "Misdemeanors" and "Petty Misdemeanors." The Commentary discusses how some jurisdictions might want more than two separate categories but cautions that a criminal code with too many levels may make "sensible classification of crimes, in the abstract and in relation to one another, . . . difficult or impossible."[2]

Prosecutors play a critical role in misdemeanor cases. They have ethical and professional duties to take a variety of factors into consideration at every stage of a criminal case, from the charging decision through any sentence or later expungement recommendation. As other chapters in this book discuss, due to prosecutors' near-unfettered discretionary power, many commenters consider them to be the most powerful actors in criminal cases.[3] Yet in many instances, prosecutors either fail to properly exercise their discretion in low-level cases or are completely absent from the charging and adjudicatory processes, effectively leaving misdemeanor decision-making to the police and judiciary.

This chapter begins by discussing the need for informed, non-biased prosecutorial decision-making, given the enormous volume of misdemeanor arrests and the structural and institutional realities that weaken the role of other criminal legal system actors involved in misdemeanors. It then examines the prosecutor's role in misdemeanor cases at several key stages in the process: charging, bail determinations, plea bargaining, sentencing, expungement and sealing, and post-conviction claims of innocence. The chapter draws on actual examples of prosecutorial practices, as well as theoretical and empirical research about the exercise of prosecutorial discretion.

25.2 Prosecutorial Discretion and Mass Misdemeanor Criminalization

In nations that follow a civil law tradition, prosecutorial discretion is not an integral part of the criminal legal system because, at least in theory, all crimes detected must be prosecuted and there is little to no plea bargaining (Luna 2014, 7). While many of these jurisdictions actually do have avenues for discretion, they have neither the high volume of misdemeanor cases nor the severe collateral consequences of a criminal record found in the United States. This section thus focuses on the role of prosecutorial discretion in the United States, where it is a central function in criminal, and particularly in misdemeanor, cases.

In the United States, there are a variety of structural, institutional, and practical reasons that prosecutors hold so much discretionary power, and this power effectively determines the outcome in most misdemeanor cases. These reasons include legislative deferral to prosecutors through enactment of broad and overlapping criminal laws; heavy enforcement of low-level offenses, particularly in those jurisdictions following a "broken windows" or "order maintenance" approach to policing; weak to non-existent judicial review of misdemeanor convictions; and the lack of any defense counsel in many misdemeanor cases in some jurisdictions, or counsel with unethically high workloads in others. After exploring how these non-prosecutorial institutions, actors, and policies enhance prosecutorial power in misdemeanor cases, this section discusses several factors unique to the centrality of prosecutorial discretion in the mass misdemeanor context. Most troubling are the well-documented racial disparities in the misdemeanor realm, particularly in certain categories of cases. Another factor is the need to mitigate the myriad and disproportionate effects of a misdemeanor case, due to the ever-growing number of so-called "collateral" consequences that flow from even a minor criminal record. Yet another is the fact that prosecutors with the least experience are generally handling misdemeanor cases.

25.2.1 Prosecutorial Power in Misdemeanor Cases

Legislatures have handed police and prosecutors enormous power in the misdemeanor realm by passing numerous and overlapping misdemeanor crime statutes. The result is a patchwork of misdemeanor prohibitions that cover such broad swaths of everyday behavior that prosecution of even a fraction of offenders would be impossible. Many of these offenses are *mala prohibita*, or unlawful simply because a statute says so, as compared to offenses that criminalize morally blameworthy conduct. The conduct criminalized in *mala prohibita* offenses raises an important threshold question for prosecutors, which is whether any adjudication in a criminal court is the proper or fair outcome. Although not directly discussing misdemeanors, William Stuntz's description of the legislative process for criminal law is certainly apt in this context:

> Legislators have good reason to criminalize more than they (or the public) would want punished in order to increase the likelihood and reduce the cost of punishing the conduct they (and the public) do want punished. There is no reason to believe criminal law, on its face, accurately captures the range of behavior the public thinks worthy of serious sanction. Indeed, there is good reason to believe the opposite.
> (Stuntz 2001, 570–571)

That "good reason to believe the opposite" has been borne out in recent ballot measures approving marijuana legalization and elections of a number of so-called progressive prosecutors who ran on platforms promising less prosecution of low-level public order and drug offenses. Even in jurisdictions where minor marijuana possession remains a misdemeanor, some prosecutors have announced that they will no longer pursue such charges (Krasner 2018a; Office of the State's Attorney for Baltimore City 2019, 14). This recent, but still limited, push-back demonstrates a growing public awareness of and discomfort with mass misdemeanor criminalization.

Scholars have captured some of this discomfort by distinguishing between factual ("I didn't do it") and normative ("I did it, but I did not thereby offend the public's moral code") innocence (Amar 1997, 90). An example of normative innocence might be jaywalking, a misdemeanor in some jurisdictions (and a traffic infraction in others). In Georgia, "improperly crossing a roadway" carries up to twelve months in jail.[4] This is not simply a law on the books. In Atlanta in 2014, police officers issued 266 tickets for this offense, and in some cases actually arrested and detained individuals. Prosecutors dismissed at least some of those arrests when the defendants later appeared in court, and one such defendant (who was detained for eight hours before being released) described the prosecutor as laughing when he saw the charges (Huddleston 2014). Perhaps the prosecutor felt that a person should not be saddled with a criminal conviction for the alleged behavior, or perhaps the dismissal was a matter of expediency in a busy urban courtroom. Or the prosecutor might have determined that the time already spent in detention, combined with the experience of the arrest, was sufficient punishment and any other outcome would be disproportionate. The prosecutor might have also been aware of serious racially disparate levels of arrest in this and other quality of life offenses (Natapoff 2018, 153). Whatever the reason for the post-charge dismissal, prosecutorial discretion to guard against serious abuse of policing and punishment powers and to protect against unintended collateral consequences plays a critical role in the ultimate outcome of these and similar cases.[5]

Jaywalking is just one example of how law enforcement officials in some jurisdictions make frequent arrests for low-level misdemeanor offenses as part of a larger approach that has been termed "broken windows," "zero tolerance," or "order maintenance" policing. This theory of policing, conceived by social scientists James Wilson and George Kelling, claims that serious crime can be prevented by addressing a neighborhood's minor physical and social disorders (Kelling and Wilson 1982). Allowing broken windows and other public space disorder to go without response, the theory goes, attracts serious crime. Although Wilson and Kelling did not call for a response in the form of mass misdemeanor arrests, that is the method that many law enforcement agencies pursued. Implementing broken windows theory in a number of urban jurisdictions in the early to mid-1990s, police made large numbers of arrests for offenses like loitering, trespassing, disorderly conduct, and jumping a subway turnstile. There is well-established empirical critique of the effectiveness of this mass-misdemeanor-arrest approach to lowering serious crime (Harcourt 2005, 84–89). This approach has also resulted in heavily racially disproportionate policing and prosecution (Howell 2014). While not all jurisdictions implement broken windows policing, misdemeanors—many of them very minor and *mala prohibita*—make up the vast majority of criminal court dockets around the nation. Whatever legislative and law enforcement decision-making led to misdemeanors comprising almost 80 percent of criminal cases, the result is that the prosecutor's discretionary function is critical in light of these realities.

The hydraulic pressure that mass misdemeanor criminalization places on both the lower criminal courts and individuals charged with misdemeanors plays out in highly troubling ways. For example, one study of Florida's misdemeanor courts revealed that almost 70 percent of defendants entered a guilty or "no contest" plea at their arraignment,[6] meaning the case started and ended at the first appearance. Eighty-two percent of arraignments lasted three minutes or less, with 91 percent finishing within five minutes (Smith and Maddan 2011, 15). These disturbing findings—in a state where almost half a million individuals face misdemeanor charges each year—illustrate how the police decision to arrest and the prosecutor's decision to file and pursue a case essentially determine the outcome of the case. Prosecutors' leverage to gain misdemeanor convictions is particularly high with defendants who are detained on bail they cannot afford. In minor misdemeanor cases, prosecutors often make "time-served" offers (sometimes with probation after release); accepting that offer is the only way the individual can get out of jail. It is difficult to characterize guilty pleas under such circumstances as the voluntary and just outcome for adjudication of a criminal case, even if they pass constitutional muster. Prosecutors also hold significant leverage in jurisdictions that require many court appearances over an extended period of time before there is a misdemeanor hearing and trial. Individuals who are not detained but have work and family obligations, or difficulty getting transportation to court, may choose an early guilty plea even when they want a trial, to avoid the punishing process of seeking full adjudication (Feeley 1979).

The same Florida study revealed that only 34 percent of defendants were represented by defense counsel at their arraignment and that half of those appearing without counsel ended up waiving their right to representation, often in highly questionable and sometimes blatantly unconstitutional proceedings (Smith and Maddan 2011, 15). This last finding illustrates yet another systemic failure that results in further lack of accountability mechanisms for prosecutors in misdemeanor cases. The Supreme Court has held that there is a right to counsel in misdemeanor cases only when the defendant is sentenced to an actual or suspended sentence of imprisonment.[7] While most state statutes set a lower threshold for the right to counsel and thus provide for defense lawyers in a great number of misdemeanor cases, too often there is chronic underfunding and overloading of public defense systems (American Bar Association 2017). In yet other jurisdictions, such as the counties in the Florida study, individuals are pressured or even misled into waiving their right to counsel in misdemeanor cases. The result is the absence of a robust defense bar check on mass misdemeanor criminalization.

The role of prosecutorial discretion becomes even more elevated in a system with little to no judicial review of most misdemeanor cases. First, high case volume means that lower criminal courts judges spend little time on each misdemeanor case. These rushed judges often do not seriously consider even those issues that defense counsel might raise, let alone raise such issues on their own. In many jurisdictions, almost no misdemeanors make it to the suppression hearing or trial stage, so that improper police conduct, or even lack of guilt, is not adjudicated and exposed. Even fewer misdemeanors are heard on appeal, for a variety of reasons that might include prosecutorial insistence on waiver of the right to appeal in a plea agreement and defendants' lack of information about, or staying-power to pursue, a lengthy appeal. This means that appellate judges have almost no opportunity to check such things as legislative vagueness in a misdemeanor statute or sufficiency of the evidence.

These are just some of the surrounding systemic circumstances that highlight the importance of the prosecutorial function in the misdemeanor arena and demonstrate how "the need for equitable discretion tends to rise as crime severity falls" (Bowers 2010, 1658).

25.2.2 Special Considerations for Misdemeanor Prosecutors

Independent of these institutional and structural challenges, prosecutors in the United States are considered "ministers of justice,"[8] a facet of their role that encompasses a variety of duties. These include promoting a fair, legitimate, and unbiased criminal legal system, advancing public safety (Howell 2014, 289; Zacharias 1991, 57), and seeking only punishment that is proportionate to the offense. Despite this minister of justice role, the United States has a misdemeanor crisis, with more than 13 million new cases filed in the lower criminal courts each year. It is worth noting three issues that cut across all levels of misdemeanor prosecution and thus merit close consideration at every stage: the disproportionate effect of even minor misdemeanor arrests and convictions on defendants' lives well in excess of any carceral sentence due to myriad and growing collateral consequences; the persistent and consistent empirical reality of a racially biased criminal legal system that is particularly pronounced in misdemeanor cases; and the fact that it is often inexperienced prosecutors who handle misdemeanor cases.

Even when a misdemeanor case leads to little or no jail time, "there is no such thing as a low-stakes misdemeanor" (Roberts 2017, 171). This is because there are a host of so-called collateral consequences that can flow from a misdemeanor conviction (or sometimes even a mere arrest), even though these consequences are not part of the sentence the judge imposes. For example, a public urination conviction in California—if the conviction is under a state statute prohibiting the exposure of private parts in public or any place where there are others present "to be offended or annoyed thereby"—will lead to mandatory lifetime sex offender registration under that state's registry law.[9] Many misdemeanor convictions, including almost all drug possession convictions, make an individual subject to mandatory deportation.[10] A less formal example is that an arrest that was later dismissed can still be listed on a state's public criminal records website, to be found by an employer or landlord who might then decline to offer the individual a job or housing.[11] These consequences, particularly in an era of broadly available electronic criminal records and background screening, can completely overshadow any penal consequence for a misdemeanor case (Jain 2018, 963–964; Roberts 2011, 227; Roberts 2017, 187). Aggravating their disproportionate effect is the fact that many individuals in the lower criminal courts are not represented by counsel, or over-burdened counsel fails to warn them about (and may not themselves even be aware of) these hidden consequences.

There are at least two major reasons prosecutors should be attentive to collateral consequences in misdemeanor cases. First, criminal punishment must be proportionate, and prosecutors should avoid outcomes in criminal cases that lead to the imposition of unintended and overly harsh consequences. They can do this by taking the major, relevant collateral consequences into account in making decisions about charging, plea bargaining, sentencing recommendations, and any post-conviction petition for sealing or expungement. Second, there is now significant evidence that the collateral consequences of convictions can undermine public safety by setting up barriers to employment, housing, education, and other opportunities tied to lower rates of recidivism (Duane et al. 2017). Particularly for low-level misdemeanor offenses, prosecutors should determine whether the public safety benefit of prosecution (if there is any) outweighs the public safety harm of a court record or conviction.

These disproportionate effects of a misdemeanor conviction fall particularly heavily on individuals in poor and minority communities. For example, public health studies over many years document similar levels of marijuana use among Black and White individuals, yet arrest rates for marijuana possession are consistently higher for Black individuals, exponentially so in many jurisdictions. In Iowa, the District of Columbia, Minnesota, and Illinois, Black individuals were seven and a half to eight times more likely to be arrested for marijuana possession than White individuals; in Wisconsin, Kentucky, and Pennsylvania, Black individuals were five to six times more likely to face such arrests. The New York City Police Department's "order-maintenance" policy concentrated resources on quality-of-life arrests based on the theory that this would lead to a drop in violent crime. However, under the policy, police stopped Black and Latino individuals at significantly higher rates than Whites, even though Whites stopped were twice as likely to be in possession of a weapon (ACLU 2013, 18, 66–67, 92–94).

A number of factors external to the prosecutor's office—such as the definition of various misdemeanors, judicial review of convictions on appeal, or ethical codes and professional standards—all guide prosecutorial discretion more in theory than in practice, particularly when it comes to misdemeanors. It is individual prosecutors' own background and sense of justice, as well as the structure and culture of the particular office, that actually determine how misdemeanor prosecutors will exercise their discretion. In many jurisdictions, misdemeanor prosecutors are the least experienced and often in their first job out of law school. These new attorneys might not be afforded, or even be comfortable with, much leeway in exercising their discretion. Junior prosecutors may be expected to stick closely to guidelines or even strict policies on plea bargaining or sentence recommendations in misdemeanor cases. However, supervisors and elected prosecution office heads also have an interest in allowing junior attorneys to develop professionally, in part by learning how to exercise discretion, even if within certain boundaries. While the degree of autonomy for misdemeanor prosecutors will vary from office to office, it can often be the case that inexperienced prosecutors lack perspective and fail to exercise much discretion at all for even the most minor of offenses (Levine and Wright 2012, 1121–1122).

All of these aspects of the prosecutor's duties call for particular attention to the need for the robust and well-informed exercise of discretion in a mass misdemeanor system.

25.3 The Exercise of Prosecutorial Discretion at Various Stages of a Misdemeanor Case

In the United States, the prosecutorial function is decentralized, with thousands of separate offices at the county and local level. Some offices handle all levels of cases, while a smaller number handle only misdemeanors (Wright 2012, 363). While this means that there are many different ways an office might approach misdemeanor prosecutions, most prosecutors are making key decisions at several core stages of a misdemeanor case.

As this section will describe, there are a number of significant stages for the exercise of prosecutorial discretion in a misdemeanor case. Filing or declining to file charges is the greatest use of prosecutorial power, but declinations rarely if ever happen in some jurisdictions. Once the case is filed in court, prosecutors' decisions and recommendations will influence the path of that case from the setting of bail through any sentencing proceeding. Even after sentencing or other disposition of the case, prosecutors can play an important role in individual or systemic instances of wrongful misdemeanor convictions as well as any sealing or expungement mechanism for relief from the myriad consequences of a criminal record.

25.3.1 Case Screening: Charging or Declination

For any level of criminal offense, the prosecutor's initial decision to file charges is a critical juncture, as it initiates the adversarial process and thus many statutory and constitutional rules and protections. Further, the filing of charges leads to creation of a court record. This alone is significant in the data era, as court records are generally free or cheap and easily viewed through electronic databases, whereas arrest records might be harder to access.[12] The decision to convert an arrest into a formal criminal proceeding is particularly significant in misdemeanor cases, which can last many months and—in some jurisdictions—through many court appearances. This requires the defendant, and sometimes the victim, to miss work and travel to court. For these and related reasons, Malcolm Feeley aptly described the lower criminal courts as a place where "the process is the punishment" (Feeley 1979). Today, an open misdemeanor case also means that employers and others can view the on-line record during the pendency of the case (and longer in many jurisdictions) even if all charges are later dismissed.

An individual arrested for a misdemeanor offense will generally either be held to appear in front of a judicial officer or issued a summons or other similar document with a future date to appear in court. It is usually at this point, before the initial court appearance, that prosecutors first interact with a misdemeanor case. And it is at this point that the prosecutor must decide whether to file charges and what charges to file. It is worth noting that in some jurisdictions, the arresting police officer chooses and files the charges and might also prosecute the case in court (Natapoff 2018, 71). However, when actual prosecutors are involved, they can decline to file formal charges in an individual case after a person has been arrested.[13] This is generally called a "declination," although there are variety of names across jurisdictions (such as "no papering" in the District of Columbia).[14] The 2017 update to the Model Penal Code's sentencing provisions uses the term "deferred prosecution," which it defines as "the practice of declining to pursue charges against an individual believed to have committed a crime in exchange for completion of specified conditions" (Model Penal Code 2017). An example of a such a conditional pre-charge declination would be an agreement to forego the filing of a charge of driving with a license suspended for failure to pay parking tickets upon proof of payment of (or perhaps a payment plan for) the tickets.

One might expect to find high misdemeanor declination rates, particularly for quality-of-life or other low-level arrests. These are generally victimless, low-profile offenses that comprise a significant percentage of many jurisdictions' misdemeanors. For example, in New York City in 2012, marijuana offenses and non-larceny theft (which includes turnstile jumping) made up almost 35 percent of all misdemeanor arrests (Kohler-Hausmann 2014, 630). In other jurisdictions, driving with a suspended license—with most suspensions based on failure to pay parking tickets or other fines or fees—crowd the misdemeanor docket (NACDL 2009, 26). While national data reflecting the full array of misdemeanor arrests is not available, FBI statistics show that, of the 10.8 million total estimated arrests in the United States in 2015, more than 1 million were in the categories of "liquor laws," "drunkenness," "disorderly conduct," and "vagrancy" (FBI 2015). Further, the fact that many prosecutors are overwhelmed with the sheer number of misdemeanors would suggest particularly robust declination rates for this level of offense (Gershowitz and Killinger 2011, 267–270).

But the opposite is true, at least in some states. For example, Iowa prosecutors' declination rate for public order misdemeanors in 2008 was substantially lower than any other offense category. The declination rate for simple misdemeanors, the most minor level in Iowa's three tiers of misdemeanor offenses, was 0.5 percent, which is significantly lower than the overall felony declination rate of 7 percent and lower than the rate for any other level of crime. New York had similar trends for 2005–2008 (Bowers 2010, 1716–1717). The declination rate for misdemeanors in Alaska in 2015 was 3.7 percent (Natapoff 2018, 70).

There are a number of explanations for these low misdemeanor declination rates. For example, prosecutors in some jurisdictions make heavy use of deferred adjudication (a post-filing mechanism for dismissal, usually upon fulfillment of certain conditions) during plea bargaining and have little time to spend on each case (Smith and Maddan 2011). With this focus on speed and efficiency over full adjudication on the merits, prosecutors have little incentive to weed out cases before they are filed. Indeed, some offices devote few to no resources to screening misdemeanor cases. Issa Kohler-Hausmann has described New York City's system of mass misdemeanor case filings with a high percentage of post-filing conditional dismissals as one of "managerial justice," designed to mark individuals over time without regard to guilt or innocence (Kohler-Hausmann 2014).

Another institutional dynamic is that junior attorneys are often making misdemeanor declination decisions. They lack experience and perspective, and likely have very little time to make the critical charging decision. Further, police officers are the only witnesses in many misdemeanors, particularly quality-of-life or public order cases, and it can be difficult for a junior prosecutor to challenge officers during screening, both in terms of asking hard questions (for example about the constitutionality of a search) and for the actual decision to decline to file charges. Indeed, one major study described a county where the supervising prosecutor "had a policy of accepting all or nearly all cases brought by the police department and dismissing problem cases later in the process; in effect, the unit was not screening cases at the start of the process" (Frederick and Stemen 2012, 79). However, the other county in the study had higher declination rates for certain categories of screened misdemeanor cases that came from the jurisdiction's primary municipal police department, demonstrating again how varied practices can be across jurisdictions (Frederick and Stemen 2012, 162–163).

Although almost all prosecutorial decision-making is effectively immune from review (Davis 2007), the screening function is particularly non-transparent. Unlike other prosecutorial decision points—bail requests, plea offers, sentencing recommendations—screening is conducted behind closed doors and without defense counsel or judicial involvement, before the procedural protections of the adversarial system are in place for a defendant.

Low misdemeanor declination levels can be seen as problematic for several reasons. Legislatures have criminalized behaviors common to a wide range of individuals, many of them quite minor. Prosecutors play a significant role in such a system, and the failure to exercise charging discretion is a central factor in misdemeanor overcriminalization (Husak 2008). The failure to screen out cases can also signal to the police that they should continue their misdemeanor arrest practices, which have led to the extraordinary rate of 13.2 million arrests per year and has been even higher in the past (Stevenson and Mayson 2018, 737). Further, weak screening can be a factor in wrongful misdemeanor convictions of innocent individuals, examples of which can be found on the National Registry of Exonerations (Roberts 2018, 780–781).

Prosecutorial failure to exercise the discretion to decline misdemeanor cases is particularly problematic in a criminal legal system with widely documented racial disparities. Babe Howell has argued that low declination rates in minor misdemeanor cases, in light of these racial disparities as well as failures of procedural justice, are an abdication of the prosecutor's ethical and professional responsibility duty to do justice (2014, 287).

Recently, a number of communities have voted for change. In several major jurisdictions, voters elected new prosecutors based on reform promises that directly or indirectly touch on a number of issues relevant to misdemeanor cases, including racial disparities and overcriminalization. These promises include declination policies for entire classes of offenses, rather than on a case-by-case basis. For example, in 2016 in Harris County (Houston), Texas—the third most populous county in the United States—Kim Ogg was the first Democrat elected District Attorney in almost forty years. Ogg's campaign promises included offering pre-charge diversion for marijuana possession of up to four ounces (Dart 2017). In Corpus Christi, Texas voters elected Mark Gonzalez, a 37-year-old defense attorney with "Not Guilty" tattooed on his chest, as their chief prosecutor. Gonzalez also promised, among other things, to divert minor marijuana cases (Bella 2018).

Another "progressive prosecutor," Larry Krasner of Philadelphia, publicly released a policy memo in 2018 that included a section directing his line prosecutors to "decline certain charges." The misdemeanors in the section included possession of marijuana "regardless of weight," paraphernalia or buying from a person when the related drug is marijuana, and prostitution charges against a sex worker unless that person has three or more prior prostitution convictions (in which case the person would be referred to a specialized court) (Krasner 2018a). At the same time, Krasner hired almost forty new attorneys, most of them recent law school graduates, who will likely be the ones to carry out the declination policy (Mitchell 2018). It may be that such personnel shifts are necessary for major policy changes, at least in some jurisdictions. The 2018 campaign promises of Rachael Rollins, Boston's first African American woman elected as chief prosecutor, included even more misdemeanor declination categories. In addition to all drug possession, her list of fifteen types of charges with a default policy of declination that could be bypassed only in exceptional circumstances and with supervisory permission, included trespassing, larceny under $250, disorderly conduct, disturbing the peace, minor driving offenses, and some resisting arrest charges (Rachael Rollins n.d.).

Although it is too early to assess how these declination policies will affect misdemeanor prosecutions in the relevant jurisdictions, there is some data that demonstrates significant change. For example, after Ogg instituted her new marijuana policy in Harris County, case filings dropped drastically. There were 11,098 misdemeanor marijuana cases filed in 2014. For the eighteen months beginning with the new policy's effective date of March 2017, there were only 1,842 misdemeanor marijuana cases in the Harris County courts, and those cases are likely explained by failures to complete the pre-charge diversion program, possession in a school zone (not covered by the policy), or charges that were dropped down from felony to misdemeanor (Reichman 2018).

It is significant that some of these declination policies are memorialized and publicly available, as this will facilitate accountability. The Model Penal Code's sentencing provision relating to deferred prosecution agreements (MPC 2017, 6.02A[14]) calls for the adoption and publication of standards:

> Each prosecutor's office shall adopt and make publicly available written standards for its use of deferred-prosecution agreements. The standards should address:
>
> (a) the criteria for selection of cases for the program;

(b) the content of agreements, including the number and kinds of conditions required for successful completion;

(c) the grounds and processes for responding to alleged breaches of agreements, and the possible consequences of non-compliance; and

(d) the benefits afforded upon successful completion of agreements.

The MPC also provides for maintaining records and data on deferred prosecutions, including demographic information on such factors as economic status, race, and gender of the participating individuals. Such data will be critical to review and study of declinations, something that has been difficult in the past due to lack of transparency.

In other countries, prosecutorial screening and declination decisions might also play a role in misdemeanor cases. For example, Dutch prosecutors follow national guidelines for charging in a wide variety of cases. They can decline to file charges when it does not serve the public interest to pursue a case, and also have the authority to offer pre-charge programs, fines, or community service. Ronald Wright has described this discretionary power as "similar to counterparts in the United States, managing the volume in the criminal courts through dismissals or declinations" (Wright 2012, 365). However, in Europe, the so-called "right to be forgotten"—which allows individuals to request internet search engines to remove links to their name in certain circumstances—means that minor criminal records may not cause as great an obstacle to housing, employment, and other facets of daily life as they do in the United States (EU General Data Protection Regulation 2016, Art. 17[2]; *Google Spain SL. v. Agencia Española de Protección de Datos* 2014).

In many countries, prosecutors are at least theoretically constrained by the principle of legality, which calls for compulsory charges any time there is probable cause to believe that a crime was committed. However, particularly in recent years and in low-level cases, prosecutors and courts are in fact exercising discretion to decline or use some type of conditional deferral mechanism in large numbers of cases (Goldstein and Marcus 1977, 280; Lewis 2006, 151–153). In Brazil, for example, prosecutors have discretion to offer what is called "consensual justice" in certain minor offenses carrying no more than two years' incarceration. Although there are several formal mechanisms available to carry out consensual justice, the end result is that the defendant who fulfills the agreed-upon conditions will end up without a criminal record (Sousa 2019). Despite these examples, there is far less written about prosecutors in other countries than U.S. prosecutors, and very little empirical work on prosecutorial discretion (Wade 2008).

The exercise of prosecutorial discretion to decline or file charges is the most important decision-making point in a misdemeanor case. In the United States, the mere creation of a court record, combined with a potentially long process of adjudication, can far outweigh any direct penal sanction the individual faces, particularly in low-level misdemeanors. Even if a misdemeanor case is filed and later dismissed, there can be significant process costs and collateral consequences. However, once a prosecutor decides to file misdemeanor charges, the next most significant event is the prosecutor's bail recommendation.

25.3.2 Bail Recommendations

Some misdemeanor arrests lead to release and a summons to appear in court on a later date. In other cases, the individual is held after arrest to appear in court for a bail determination. In many jurisdictions in the United States, a judge or magistrate determines pretrial detention or release at the defendant's first appearance, although some states allow non-lawyers to preside over this and other stages of a misdemeanor case (*Montana v. Davis* 2016). The judge or other official has a variety of options depending on the relevant statute, usually ranging from releasing the defendant on their own recognizance (with or without conditions) to setting cash bail or a bond amount (e.g., Tex. Crim. Proc. Code Ann. § 17).

The bail determination drives the outcome in many misdemeanor cases. One recent study of hundreds of thousands of misdemeanor cases found that defendants detained on a misdemeanor are 25 percent more likely to be convicted and 43 percent more likely to get a jail sentence than similarly situated defendants who were released. Studies and data in other jurisdictions with large cities demonstrate a similar effect of pretrial detention on misdemeanor case outcomes (Heaton, Mayson, and Stevenson 2017, 717, 732–733). In addition to case outcome effects, pre-trial detention can lead to lost workdays or total job loss, resulting in serious economic consequences for individuals and families (Gold 2019, 540–541).

The prosecutor often plays a key role in the bail determination process, particularly in jurisdictions where defendants have no representation unless they hire a private lawyer who appears at this early stage (Heaton, Mayson, and Stevenson 2017, 730).[15] Prosecutors likely filed the actual charges and have seen police reports and other documents that even the judge determining bail might not yet be able to view. There are a few jurisdictions that have banned cash bail for most misdemeanors, but prosecutors in these jurisdictions can sometimes still request bail upon demonstrating a threat to public safety or a flight risk in a particular case.[16]

In some jurisdictions, a significant percentage of individuals held on bail in a misdemeanor case are unable to pay the set amount, at least immediately following the bail determination (Criminal Justice Agency 2014, 23). Unfortunately, there is ample evidence that judges routinely violate statutory and constitutional prohibitions on detaining individuals based solely on their inability to pay bail (Open Society Justice Initiative 2011).[17] Prosecutors have ethical and professional duties to adhere to these prohibitions, and thus have an important role to play when they are aware of any violations and when making bail recommendations more generally. Although more likely due to public pressure from recent organized movements to end cash bail in misdemeanor cases than such an awareness, some chief prosecutors have recently announced that they will stop seeking bail in most minor misdemeanor cases.

Many of the same offices discussed above that have recently instituted declination policies have also announced new misdemeanor bail policies. In Philadelphia, one of District Attorney Larry Krasner's campaign promises was to reform the "broken cash bail system." In 2018, he published a list of twenty-five specific charges, which included many misdemeanors, for which his office would no longer seek monetary bail absent exceptional circumstances (Krasner for District Attorney n.d.; Krasner 2018b). New York City's two largest District Attorney's offices issued directives in 2017 and 2018 to their prosecutors to stop requesting bail in a number of low-level misdemeanor cases (New York County District Attorney 2018). In Orlando, Florida, newly elected State Attorney Aramis Ayala followed up on a campaign promise by announcing in mid-2018 that her office would no longer seek bail for individuals charged in nine categories of non-violent misdemeanors, unless there was a risk of flight or violence (Lotan and Chen 2018).

As with declination, the effects of these new bail policies are not yet clear. Still, there is recent evidence of prosecutors' ability to influence judges' misdemeanor bail decisions. In the Texas county that includes Houston, average bail for misdemeanor marijuana cases in 2014 was $2,500 for Black defendants and $1,500 for White defendants. After Kim Ogg took office, she announced a policy of agreeing to personal bonds, where the individual is released upon a promise to pay a set amount should he fail to return to court, rather than seeking cash bail in minor misdemeanor cases. The average bail amount under this policy dropped to $500 for both Black and White defendants in this category of cases (Reichman 2018), although it is worth noting that $500 remains unaffordable for many defendants.

Bail drives outcomes and consequences in misdemeanor cases, and prosecutors play a significant role in bail determinations. When an individual is held on misdemeanor bail that they cannot afford, the prosecutor has particular leverage in the next step in the process, plea bargaining.

25.3.3 Plea Bargaining and Sentencing Recommendations

Driven by policing decisions followed by low declination rates, misdemeanor offenses make up three-quarters of criminal court dockets nationwide. With this volume, plea bargaining becomes a significant stage in such cases. "Plea bargaining" is used here to include any agreement between the government and the defendant about a reduction or substitution in charges (charge bargaining) or a specific sentence (sentence bargaining), or both. While a plea bargain requires the participation and eventual agreement of both defendant and prosecutor, the ability to extend a plea offer represents a major area of prosecutorial discretion. Even if there is no agreed-upon bargain and a defendant instead pleads guilty to a misdemeanor charge and asks the judge to impose a sentence, the prosecutor's sentencing recommendation will likely influence the judge's decision.

Unfortunately, there are well-documented racial disparities in misdemeanor plea bargaining. For example, one study of Wisconsin cases—controlling for a large number of variables, including criminal history and type of charge—found that "white defendants are 74.72% more likely than Black defendants to see all misdemeanor charges carrying a potential imprisonment sentence dropped, dismissed or amended to lesser charges" and that "black defendants convicted of a misdemeanor are more likely to be punished by incarceration than white defendants" (Berdejó 2018, 1216).

Once misdemeanor charges are filed and a court record is created, one of the most favorable dispositions that a prosecutor can offer (short of an outright dismissal) is some type of deferred adjudication. While the term for this mechanism varies from jurisdiction to jurisdiction, "deferred adjudication" is used here to refer to any disposition of a case that does not result in a final judgment of conviction. A deferred adjudication can occur before or after a guilty plea (or admission of facts sufficient for a guilty plea) and will usually be dependent on the defendant's fulfillment of certain agreed-upon conditions. For an example of a pre-plea deferred adjudication, a prosecutor might agree to docket a misdemeanor shoplifting case for three months in the future with a promise to dismiss the charges should the defendant successfully complete a set number of community service hours or an educational program about shoplifting during that time period. Many drug courts use a post-plea deferred adjudication model, requiring prosecutorial consent and a guilty plea for participation. A defendant might plead guilty to misdemeanor possession of heroin with a promise that the guilty plea will be vacated and dismissed upon successful completion of drug treatment; the actual treatment plan, location, and length is generally determined by drug court staff working with treatment providers.[18] However, should the defendant ultimately fail to complete the program, the judge will proceed to sentencing as the defendant has already entered a guilty plea. Depending on the relevant jurisdiction's law, a deferred adjudication agreement (particularly of the post-plea variety) may be conditioned upon consent of the judge.[19]

Some prosecutors may prefer post-plea deferred adjudications because they offer the carrot of an eventual dismissal but retain the stick of an eventual conviction (and imposition of sentence) if the defendant fails to complete his part of the bargain. However, a guilty plea that is later vacated or sometimes even a mere admission of facts of the underlying offense can form the basis for the imposition of collateral consequences so severe as to easily overwhelm any direct punishment. For example, under federal immigration law, a lawful permanent resident (regardless of years in and connection to the United States or lack of connection to a country of origin) is mandatorily deportable based upon admission of "sufficient facts to warrant a finding of guilt" along with any form of "punishment, penalty, or restraint on . . . liberty" in any drug offense other than a "single offense involving possession for one's own use of 30 grams or less of marijuana" (8 U.S.C. § 1227[a][2][B][i]).

While this is an extreme (although not unusual) example, such consequences mean that prosecutors should be particularly attuned to the structure and content of plea bargains. Prosecutors' goals include enhancing public safety and seeking punishment that is proportional to the offense. Yet research shows that a criminal conviction can pose barriers to work and housing, and that stable work and housing are critical factors in avoiding recidivism. There are many other examples of the disproportionate effect of a misdemeanor conviction (Jain 2018; Roberts 2017). Other than a pre-filing declination, a pre-plea deferred adjudication mechanism offers the most robust avenue for prosecutors to avoid unintended or disproportionate collateral consequences.

Given the volume of cases that most misdemeanor prosecutors handle, and the relatively early stage at which plea bargaining might begin (and often end), prosecutors often base plea offers on any information in the file in front of them in court and on the defendant's criminal history (Frederick and Stemen 2012, 135). It will generally be up to defense counsel, or to the defendant directly if they are not represented by counsel, to raise any collateral consequences or other mitigating information with the prosecution during plea bargaining. Still, prosecutors might also themselves raise potentially relevant collateral consequences during plea bargaining for practical reasons. For example, defense counsel might be unaware of, and thus fail to bargain so as to avoid, a severe collateral consequence of a misdemeanor, such as sex offender registration. In some jurisdictions, defense counsel's failure to advise their client about such registration can form the basis for a post-conviction collateral attack on the conviction on the grounds of ineffective assistance of counsel (*People v. Fonville* 2011, 986–997). To protect the finality of any guilty plea in such circumstances, a prosecutor aware of registration consequences may decide to raise the issue with counsel, and may agree to a bargain that avoids registration where it is deemed unnecessary. Often, this means a plea offer that is similar to the original charge but does not lead to the undesired consequence. It could even mean an exchange of enhanced punishment for avoidance of the consequence (Love, Roberts, and Logan 2018, § 8.7).

While attention to collateral consequences may result in misdemeanor plea offers that avoid unintended consequences, this is not the only consideration in misdemeanor plea bargaining. For example, in many jurisdictions, probation is a common sentence for a misdemeanor conviction, even if the term of probation is intended to last only as long as it takes the defendant to pay a fine imposed as part of the sentence. Here, the prosecutor may exercise discretion to offer a charge bargain that does not allow a sentence of probation or a sentence bargain that does not include probation. Similarly, in sentence bargaining, the prosecution may agree to a non-incarceratory sentence in exchange for a plea of guilty to the original charge, where the defendant's primary goal is to avoid incarceration.

Although judges actually impose the sentence in a criminal case, a charge bargain can lower the range of incarceration available to the judge or further narrow the judge's discretion where the bargain is to a charge that does not allow a jail (or even a probationary) sentence. Even when the prosecutor is recommending a particular sentence as part of an agreed-upon bargain with the defendant, lower court judges facing heavy dockets will generally accept those sentence bargains (McConkie 2015, 69). The prosecutor's role here is particularly important in light of existing racial disparities in sentencing. For example, after controlling for age, gender, criminal history, and a number of other factors in misdemeanor cases in a Wisconsin county, one study found that "the rate of incarceration for black defendants is 17.1% higher than that of white defendants, a difference representing 40.1% of the average incarceration rate for misdemeanor convictions" (Berdejó 2018, 1213). While judges imposed these sentences (and could have rejected those that were too high or low), and thus bear some responsibility for these disparate outcomes, charge and sentencing bargaining likely led to these differences in many instances, putting the onus squarely on the prosecutor for such injustices.

As with charging decisions and bail recommendations, there is a lack of transparency for the exercise of prosecutorial discretion during plea bargaining. Prosecution offices do not generally have publicly available or even written misdemeanor plea bargaining policies. However, defense attorneys who regularly handle misdemeanor cases in a jurisdiction will learn the "going offer" on particular types of offenses, often dependent upon the defendant's criminal history. These offers are likely due to more informal prosecutorial policies that may be technically advisory but that junior prosecutors generally try to follow (Frederick and Stemen 2012, 72–73). Still, such policies are not public and not uniformly applied. For example, one study found that almost all prosecutors in a large suburban county regularly used internal "round-tabling" sessions—a process where "all members of the [prosecutorial] unit discuss the specific charges to file, the plea offer to make, or whether a particular case should be dismissed"—"with the exception of the misdemeanor unit which was comprised of the least experienced [Assistant District Attorneys]." In units using round-tabling, there was "a great deal of consistency in outcomes across cases" (Frederick and Stemen 2012, 49, 283).

25.4 Post-Conviction: Sealing and Expungement, and Innocence Claims

There are two significant ways in which prosecutors are involved in misdemeanors after a conviction and sentencing. First, prosecutors might play a role in the sealing or expungement of a misdemeanor criminal record. Second, prosecutors will be involved in any post-conviction claim of innocence in a misdemeanor case. As with other stages of a misdemeanor case, prosecutorial discretion and advocacy can be a major influence in the ultimate outcome of either of these types of proceedings, although in both areas the prosecutor's power may be circumscribed by law or practice.

25.4.1 Sealing and Expungement

At the very end of the criminal process, prosecutors are sometimes involved in the sealing or expungement process. The terms "sealing" or "expungement" often have different meanings under different state law,[20] ranging from actual destruction of some types of criminal records in a few states to limitations on public access to the record in others. While this mechanism is available for at least some types of misdemeanor criminal records in most jurisdictions, the variation in approaches means that prosecutors are involved in varying degrees, or sometimes not at all (Murray 2018). For example, in Maryland, "[u]nless the State's Attorney files an objection to the petition for expungement within 30 days after the petition is served, the court shall pass an order requiring the expungement of all police records and court records about the charge" (Md. Code

Ann., Crim. Proc. § 10-105. In other jurisdictions, non-conviction records—such as dismissals or deferred adjudications—might be automatically sealed, without the need for a petition or involvement by the prosecutor (Love, Roberts, and Logan 2018, § 7:17).

Several prosecutor's offices have announced blanket policies relating to expungement of certain classes of misdemeanors. For example, citing "numerous hurdles in the expungement statutes that would require expenditure of enormous resources to determine whether expungement might be possible," the Baltimore City State's Attorney instead filed a motion to vacate almost five thousand marijuana possession convictions, "[i]n light of the disproportionate enforcement of marijuana possession laws and the collateral consequences of such convictions on communities of color" (Office of the State's Attorney for Baltimore City 2019, 14). When California voters legalized possession and recreational use of marijuana, the initiative included a provision allowing individuals convicted of the covered offenses to petition for a charge reduction from felony to misdemeanor or dismissal of lower-level marijuana offenses. The San Francisco District Attorney, citing the war on drugs' disproportionate harm to communities of color, announced that his office would review, recall and resentence nearly 5,000 felony marijuana convictions and would dismiss and seal more than 3,000 misdemeanors that were sentenced prior to the initiative's passage (Parvini, Lin II, Chang 2018).

Prosecutors have also played a major role in some legislative debates about the passage or broadening of relevant statutory schemes. For example, Pennsylvania passed the Clean Slate Act in 2018, which made sealing of some non-violent conviction records automatic after ten years, with no hearing, fees, or prosecutorial involvement (2018 Pa. Laws 402-56). The head prosecutor from Allegheny County, which includes the city of Pittsburgh, wrote an editorial in support of the legislation (Zappala 2017). In 2013, Indiana enacted what was, at that time, one of the most comprehensive expungement laws in the United States. A former prosecutor who went on to the Indiana state legislature spearheaded passage of this law (Dugan 2015, 1337). He articulated fiscal reasons for his support as well as a focus on reformation over vindication in the state constitution but observed that many prosecutors across the state remained "ardent opponents" of the law (Collateral Consequences Resource Center 2014).

Increasingly, prosecutors have become directly involved in individual expungement cases, usually by holding expungement clinics or fairs (Trischitta 2018). At these events, line prosecutors and other prosecution office employees assist those seeking to seal or expunge a criminal record and often interact directly with these individuals. There are a number of potential ethical, professional, and practical issues that arise when prosecutors engage with individuals seeking expungement (Murray 2018). These issues include client confidentiality and the scope of the lawyer-client relationship (assuming formation of such a relationship), conflicts of interests (as the prosecutor's office would file any opposition to a petition should the individual actually be—or become—ineligible for expungement), and the appearance of impropriety (for appearing to handle both sides of a case). Thus, while prosecutorial embrace of the need for sealing and expungement mechanisms to allow individuals to move beyond a criminal record, and their increasing assistance in the process, is a positive development, this new area is one in which prosecution offices should act cautiously and with clearly articulated standards.

25.4.2 Misdemeanor Wrongful Convictions

As Brandon L. Garrett describes in Chapter 8 of this book, after a conviction prosecutors are sometimes involved—either on an adversarial or, increasingly, a non-adversarial basis—in "identify[ing], remedy[ing], and prevent[ing] wrongful convictions." However, most of these efforts, and thus most exonerations, have been in high-level felony cases.

As of early 2019, the National Registry of Exonerations included data and narratives for eighty-nine misdemeanor wrongful convictions (National Registry of Exonerations 2019). As misdemeanor cases almost never involve DNA and with few resources devoted to revealing and reopening claims of misdemeanor wrongful convictions, this number surely represents only a tiny percentage of innocent individuals convicted of misdemeanors (National Registry of Exonerations 2015). Fifty-eight of these documented misdemeanor exonerations came out of Harris County, Texas, where hundreds of people were convicted of drug offenses in cases later shown to involve no controlled substances (National Registry of Exonerations 2019). In many of these cases, a drug field test showed what later turned out to be erroneous positive results for a controlled substance. All of the individuals in these cases had pleaded guilty rather than seeking a trial, usually after being held on bail they could not afford. When a journalist discovered the "no controlled substance" scandal, he contacted the Harris County District Attorney's (D.A.) Conviction Review Section. The D.A.'s office was proactive after this point, working for several years to strike wrongful convictions in these cases and instituting procedural changes for pending cases to get full laboratory tests more rapidly and before any guilty plea that involved jail time (Roberts 2018, 795–800).

As Chapter 8 describes, there are now conviction integrity or conviction review units in some thirty jurisdictions in the United States. However, some prosecutors will only review felony wrongful conviction claims (Hollway 2016, 40–43). While is it unlikely that offices or units with such case eligibility limits would ignore a claim of mass wrongful misdemeanor convictions such as the Harris County scandal, prosecutors might consider new standards to encompass a wider variety of claims.

25.5 Conclusion

There is ample doctrinal and scholarly attention paid to the near-unfettered discretion of the prosecutor in the United States. In other nations, such discretion is increasingly accepted as part of the reality of the criminal legal system even where it is not formally recognized. Yet little attention has been paid to the prosecutor's role in misdemeanor cases, although that is starting to change. There is a small but growing body of scholarship addressing prosecutors' ethical, professional, and constitutional duties in low-level cases, particularly where there are serious racial disparities in the enforcement of these offenses. There is also a nascent but high-profile movement of so-called progressive prosecutors, many of whom focused on mass misdemeanor criminalization in their campaigns and have now started to implement promised reforms.

In an era where even the most minor of criminal records can affect an individual's ability to get work and housing and to access educational and other opportunities, the prosecutorial function in misdemeanor cases has taken on new significance. While misdemeanor arrest numbers have recently fallen in many jurisdictions, by conservative estimates there are still 13.2 million misdemeanor cases filed in the United States each year, an astonishingly high number. This is part of a larger criminal system crisis, in the form of a country where one in three adults has some sort of arrest or conviction record (Love, Roberts, and Logan 2018, § 5.1).

The power and responsibility to mitigate the unintended harms of a misdemeanor arrest are especially important where non-prosecutorial institutions have failed to provide meaningful limits on misdemeanor criminalization. The judiciary has largely abdicated its role in the lower criminal courts, often simply processing the high volume of misdemeanor cases as quickly as possible and sometimes fostering a coercive atmosphere without regard to accuracy or justice. While legislatures and police are also central to this mass misdemeanor criminalization crisis, prosecutors retain significant power to lower overall misdemeanor case filings, to negotiate just bargains in cases they do file, to seek proportionate sentences that account for the collateral consequences of a misdemeanor charge, and to consider post-conviction mechanisms for relief where appropriate.

Prosecutors in many jurisdictions exercise very little of their enormous discretion in misdemeanor cases. Time will tell whether a newly attentive electorate and a fresh prosecutorial approach to misdemeanors will begin to roll back the extreme overuse and consequent disproportionate impact of misdemeanor prosecutions in the United States.

Notes

1. I thank Emily Ford for her excellent research assistance.
2. Model Penal Code: Sentencing § 6.01(4).
3. For more detail, see Matt Barno and Mona Lynch in Chapter 2 of this volume.
4. Ga. Stat. § 40-6-92 (prohibiting "Crossing at Other than Crosswalks"); Ga. Stat. § 40-6-1 (categorizing traffic offenses as misdemeanors); Ga. Stat. § 17-10-3 (allowing maximum misdemeanor punishment of up to $1,000 fine or up to twelve months imprisonment).
5. It is worth noting that in some jurisdictions, a prosecutor might not even be involved in such a minor misdemeanor.
6. A "no contest" or *nolo contendere* plea has the same legal effect as a plea of guilty, even though the defendant does not admit guilt during such a plea (e.g., Fl. R. Crim. Pro. Rule 3.170).
7. *Alabama v. Shelton* (2002); *Scott v. Illinois* (1979); *Argersinger v. Hamlin* (1972).

8. Model Rules of Professional Conduct, Rule 3.8 comment 1 ("A prosecutor has the responsibility of a minister of justice and not simply that of an advocate").
9. See Cal. Penal Code § 290 (requiring all individuals subject to Sex Offender Registration Act to register for life); Cal. Penal Code § 314 (prohibiting indecent exposure).
10. For more detail on collateral immigration consequences, see Jennifer Chacón in Chapter 21 of this volume.
11. There are laws in some states that protect individuals from discrimination based on a criminal record, at least where there is no nexus to the employment sought (e.g., New York State Human Rights Law § 15-290; New York Attorney General's Office 2019).
12. Law enforcement agencies generally maintain arrest records. Although not as easy to access as court records, arrest records can themselves lead to various employment, housing, and other collateral consequences.
13. Law enforcement can also decline to arrest even when there is probable cause, instead issuing a formal or informal warning. In addition to ending the encounter at a very early stage, this means that there is no potentially damaging arrest record. However, even mere contact with the police can cause its own sort of harm, particularly if such interactions are persistent—such as in neighborhoods where young Black men are consistently stopped and frisked (Meares 2017, 1529–1530).
14. Prosecutorial dismissals at a later stage of a case, after charges have been filed, are discussed below in the "Plea Bargaining" section.
15. The Supreme Court has held that the right to counsel guaranteed by the Sixth Amendment attaches "at the first appearance before a judicial officer at which a defendant is told of the formal accusation against him and restrictions are imposed on his liberty" (*Rothgery v. Gillespie County* 2008, 194). However, attachment of the right to counsel is only a first step. The actual *presence* of counsel is only required at post-attachment events that constitute a "critical stage" of the criminal process, and "the need for counsel's presence" is what makes a stage critical (212). The Court has not definitively determined that a bail hearing is always a critical stage (although there is certainly strong support for that position). There are thus jurisdictions where bail is set and defendants are held without representation (Class Action Complaint 2015). Although a number of lawsuits have challenged (in some cases successfully) their use, set "bail schedules" are also in place in some jurisdictions. Even here, prosecutors might be able to seek departure from the schedule and thus have an effect on the bail determination (Heaton, Mayson, and Stevenson 2017, 730).
16. For example, N.J.S.A. § 2A:162-15 sets out New Jersey's statutory presumption of "pretrial release by non-monetary means" in most cases, with authorization for departures upon motion of a prosecutor; any such motion is subject to clear and convincing evidence that no condition will ensure a return to court, safety for a person or the community, or against obstruction of the criminal justice process. Relatedly, a N.J. Attorney General Directive establishes a "pretrial detention decision-making framework" for the three categories in which prosecutors are statutorily authorized to seek bail in otherwise presumptive release cases (N.J. Attorney General Directive 2016).
17. In *O'Donnell v. Harris Cty., Texas* (2017), the court noted that judges rarely adjust bail and, therefore, indigent defendants who cannot pay bail either plead guilty or remain detained.
18. For further discussion, see Salmon Shomade in Chapter 9 of this volume.
19. Some jurisdictions also have mechanisms for the judge to offer pre- or post-plea deferred adjudications. These range from a dismissal of a case in the interest of justice (e.g.,

N.Y. Crim. Proc. § 210.40), to a post-plea "probation before judgment" where the court will eventually vacate the guilty plea upon completion of a term of probation (e.g., Md. Code Ann., Crim. Proc. § 6-220). This section focuses on deferred adjudications that come out of a plea bargaining process and thus involve prosecutorial participation and consent.

20. With very limited exceptions, there is no federal sealing or expungement law.

References

8 U.S.C. § 1227(a)(2)(B)(i).

2018 Pa. Laws 402-56.

Alabama v. Shelton. 2002. 535 U.S. 654.

Amar, Akhil R. 1997. *The Constitution and Criminal Procedure: First Principles*. New Haven: Yale University Press.

American Bar Association. 2017. *The Rhode Island Project: A Study of the Rhode Island Public Defender System and Attorney Workload Standards*. Chicago: American Bar Association.

American Civil Liberties Union. 2013. *The War on Marijuana in Black and White*.

Argersinger v. Hamlin. 1972. 407 U.S. 25.

Bella, Timothy. 2018. "The Most Unlikely D.A. in America." *Politico Magazine*, May 6.

Berdejó, Carlos. 2018. "Criminalizing Race: Racial Disparities in Plea-Bargaining," *Boston College Law Review* 59(4): 1187–1250.

Bowers, Josh. 2010. "Legal Guilt, Normative Innocence, and the Equitable Decision Not to Prosecute." *Columbia Law Review* 110(7): 1655–1726.

Cal. Health & Safety Code § 11361.8.

Cal. Penal Code § 290.

Cal. Penal Code § 314.

Chen, Elsa Y. 2008. "Cumulative Disadvantage and Racial and Ethnic Disparities in California Felony Sentencing." In *Racial and Ethnic Politics in California: Continuity and Change*. Edited by Bruce Cain and Sandra Bass, vol. 3, 251–274. Berkeley, CA: Institute of Government Studies Press, University of California.

Class Action Complaint. 2015. *Varden v. City of Clanton*, No. 2:15-CV-34-MHT (M.D. Ala. January 15, 2015), Doc. 1.

Collateral Consequences Resource Center. 2014. *Indiana's New Expungement Law the Product of 'Many, Many Compromises.'* December 15.

Criminal Justice Agency. 2014. *CJA Annual Report 2014*.

Dart, Tom. 2017. "Houston's New District Attorney Stands by Her Bold Move to Decriminalize Marijuana." *The Guardian*, April 18.

Davis, Angela J. 2007. *Arbitrary Justice: The Power of the American Prosecutor*. Oxford: Oxford University Press.

Duane, Marina, Nancy La Vigne, Mathew Lynch, and Emily Reimal. 2017. *Criminal Background Checks: Impact on Employment and Recidivism*. Washington, D.C.: Urban Institute.

Dugan, Joseph C. 2015. "I Did My Time: The Transformation of Indiana's Expungement Law." *Indiana Law Journal* 90(3): 1321–1364.

EU General Data Protection Regulation. 2016. O.J. L 119, 04.05.2016, Art. 17(2).

Federal Bureau of Investigation (FBI). 2015. *Crime in the United States: Table 29*.

Feeley, Malcolm M. 1979. *The Process Is the Punishment: Handling Cases in a Lower Criminal Court*. New York: Russell Sage Foundation.

Fl. R. Crim. Pro. Rule 3.170.

Frederick, Bruce, and Don Stemen. 2012. *The Anatomy of Discretion: An Analysis of Prosecutorial Decision Making—Technical Report*. Vera Institute of Justice, NCJRS Document 240334.

Gershowitz, Adam M., and Laura R. Killinger. 2011. "The State Never Rests: How Excessive Prosecutor Caseloads Harm Criminal Defendants." *Northwestern University Law Review* 105(1): 261–302.

Gold, Russell M. 2019. "Jail as Injunction." *Georgetown Law Journal* 107(3): 501–560.

Goldstein, Abraham, and Martin Marcus. 1977. "The Myth of Judicial Supervision in Three 'Inquisitorial' Systems: France, Italy, and Germany." *Yale Law Journal* 87(2): 240–283.

Google Spain SL. v. Agencia Española de Protección de Datos, Case C-131/12, (2014) E.C.R. I (delivered 13 May 2014).

Harcourt, Bernard E. 2005. *Illusion of Order: The False Promise of Broken Windows Policing*. Cambridge, MA: Harvard University Press.

Heaton, Paul, Sandra Mayson, and Megan Stevenson. 2017. "The Downstream Consequences of Misdemeanor Pretrial Detention." *Stanford Law Review* 69(3): 711–794.

Hollway, John. 2016. *Conviction Review Units: A National Perspective*. University of Pennsylvania Law School, Public Law Research Paper No. 15-41.

Howell, Babe. 2014. "Prosecutorial Discretion and the Duty to Seek Justice in an Overburdened Criminal Justice System." *Georgetown Journal of Legal Ethics* 27(2): 285–334.

Huddleston, David. 2014. "Jailed for Jaywalking: Pedestrian Crime Lands Some behind Bars." *WSB-TV*, November 3.

Husak, Douglas. 2008. *Overcriminalization: The Limits of the Criminal Law*. Oxford: Oxford University Press.

Jain, Eisha. 2018. "Proportionality and Other Misdemeanor Myths." *Boston University Law Review* 98(3): 953–980.

Kelling, George L., and James Q. Wilson. 1982. "Broken Windows: The Police and Neighborhood Safety." *The Atlantic*, March.

Kohler-Hausmann, Issa. 2014. "Managerial Justice and Mass Misdemeanors." *Stanford Law Review* 66(3): 611–694.

Krasner for District Attorney. n.d. "On the Issues." Accessed February 11, 2019.

Krasner, Larry. 2018a. "New Policies Announced February 15, 2018." *Philadelphia District Attorney*, February 15.

Krasner, Larry. 2018b. "Larry Krasner Announces End to Cash Bail in Philadelphia for Low-Level Offenses." *Philadelphia District Attorney's Office*, February 21.

Levine, Kay L., and Ronald F. Wright. 2012. "Prosecution in 3-D." *Journal of Criminal Law and Criminology* 102(4): 1119–1180.

Lewis, Chris. 2006. "The Prosecution Service Function within the English Criminal Justice System." In *Coping with Overloaded Criminal Justice Systems: The Rise of Prosecutorial Power Across Europe*. Edited by Jörg-Martin Jehle and Marianne Wade, 151–184. Berlin, Germany: Springer.

Lotan, Gal Tziperman, and Adelaide Chen. 2018. "Aramis Ayala's New Bail Policy: Who Will Benefit?" *Orlando Sentinel*, May 23.

Love, Margaret Colgate, Jenny Roberts, and Wayne Logan. 2018. *Collateral Consequences of Criminal Convictions: Law, Policy, and Practice*. 3rd ed. Minneapolis: Thomson West.

Luna, Erik. 2014. "Sentencing." In *The Oxford Handbook of Criminal Law*. Edited by Markus D. Dubber and Tatjana Hörnle, 964–987. Oxford: Oxford University Press.

McConkie, Daniel S. 2015. "Judges as Framers of Plea Bargaining." *Stanford Law & Policy Review* 26(1): 61–118.

Md. Code Ann., Crim. Proc. § 6-220.

Md. Code Ann., Crim. Proc. § 10-105.

Meares, Tracey. 2017. "Policing and Procedural Justice: Shaping Citizens' Identities to Increase Democratic Participation." *Northwestern Law Review* 111(6): 1525–1536.

Mitchell, Max. 2018. "Krasner Beefs up Philadelphia Prosecutor Ranks with 38 New Hires." *The Legal Intelligence*, September 11.

Model Penal Code. 2017. *Sentencing § 6.01(4)*. Proposed Final Draft. Philadelphia: American Law Institute.

Model Rules of Professional Conduct. 2016. *Rule 3.8, comment 1*. Chicago: American Bar Association.

Montana v. Davis. 2017. 383 Mont. 281, cert. denied, 137 S. Ct. 811.

Murray, Brian. 2018. "Unstitching Scarlet Letters?: Prosecutor Discretion and Expungement." *Fordham Law Review* 86(6): 2821–2872.

Natapoff, Alexandra. 2018. *Punishment without Crime: How Our Massive Misdemeanor System Traps the Innocent and Makes America More Unequal*. New York: Basic Books.

National Association of Criminal Defense Lawyers. 2009. *Minor Crimes, Massive Waste: The Terrible Toll of America's Broken Misdemeanor Courts*.

National Registry of Exonerations. 2015. *Why So Few Misdemeanor Exonerations?* October 6.

National Registry of Exonerations. 2016. *Exonerations in 2016*.

National Registry of Exonerations. 2019. *Misdemeanor*. Accessed February 26.

N.J.S.A. § 2A:162-15.

New York Attorney General's Office. 2019. "New York State Human Rights Law." Division of Human Rights.

New Jersey Attorney General. 2016. "Law Enforcement Directive No. 2016-6." Department of Law and Public Safety, 56–60, October 11.

New York County District Attorney. 2018. "Manhattan and Brooklyn District Attorney's Offices End Requests for Bail in Most Misdemeanor Cases." January 9.

New York State Human Rights Law § 15-290.

N.Y. Crim. Proc. § 210.40.

O'Donnell v. Harris Cty., Texas. 2017. 251 F. Supp. 3d 1052, 1131 (S.D. Tex.), aff'd as modified, 882 F.3d 528 (5th Cir. 2018), and aff'd as modified sub nom.

Office of the State's Attorney for Baltimore City. 2019. *Reforming a Broken System: Rethinking the Role of Marijuana Prosecutions in Baltimore City*. January.

Open Society Institute. 2011. *The Socioeconomic Impact of Pretrial Detention: A Global Campaign for Pretrial Justice Report*. New York: Open Society Institute.

Parvini, Sarah, Rong-Gong Lin II, Cindy Chang. 2018. "San Francisco Will Wipe Out Thousands of Marijuana Convictions Dating to 1975." *Los Angeles Times*, January 31.

People v. Fonville. 2011. 804 N.W.2d 878 (Mich. Ct. App.).

Rachel Rollins for District Attorney. n.d. "Charges to Be Declined." Accessed January 17.

Reichman, Jeff. 2018. "The Decline of Low-Level Marijuana Cases in Harris County." *January Advisors*, September 30.

Roberts, Jenny M. 2011. "Why Misdemeanors Matter: Defining Effective Advocacy in the Lower Criminal Courts." *UC Davis Law Review* 45(2): 277–372.

Roberts, Jenny M. 2017. "Informed Misdemeanor Sentencing." *Hofstra Law Review* 46(1): 171–214.

Roberts, Jenny M. 2018. "The Innocence Movement and Misdemeanors." *Boston University Law Review* 98(3): 779–836.

Rothgery v. Gillespie County. 2008. 554 U.S. 191.

Scott v. Illinois. 1979. 440 U.S. 367.

Smith, Alisa, and Sean Maddan. 2011. *Three-Minute Justice: Haste and Waste in Florida's Misdemeanor Courts*. Washington, D.C.: National Association of Criminal Defense Lawyers.

Sousa, Marllon. 2019. "Plea Bargaining in Brazil: [Im]proving Criminal Trials through the Balance between the Utilitarian Justice and the Defendant's Fundamental Rights." SJD dissertation, American University Washington College of Law.

Stevenson, Megan, and Sandra Mayson. 2018. "The Scale of Misdemeanor Justice." *Boston University Law Review* 98(3): 731–778.

Stuntz, William J. 2001. "The Pathological Politics of Criminal Law." *Michigan Law Review* 100(3): 505–600.

Tex. Crim. Proc. Code Ann. § 17.

Trischitta, Linda. 2018. "Thursday in Lauderdale Lakes: The Next Broward County Criminal Record Expungement Workshop." *Sun-Sentinel*, May 15.

Wade, Marianne. 2008. "The Januses of Justice: How Prosecutors Define the Kind of Justice Done across Europe." *European Journal of Crime, Criminal Law and Criminal Justice* 16(4): 433–456.

Wright, Ronald F. 2012. "Community Prosecution, Comparative Prosecution." *Wake Forest Law Review* 47(2): 361–372.

Zacharias, Fred. 1991. "Structuring the Ethics of Prosecutorial Trial Practice: Can Prosecutors Do Justice?" *Vanderbilt Law Review* 44(1): 45–114.

Zappala, Stephen A., Jr. 2017. "Clean the Slate for Nonviolent Offender." *Pittsburgh Post-Gazette*, December 8.

CHAPTER 26

PROSECUTORS AND NATIONAL SECURITY

KENT ROACH

26.1 Introduction

Although national security prosecutions are relatively rare, their stakes are extremely high. Prosecutors play a critical role in mediating competing demands of secrecy and disclosure. As in other cases, they mediate relations with the police. In the national security context, however, they also work with intelligence agencies and foreign partners.

The prosecutorial role reveals much about the challenges of applying rule of law and criminal justice values to the realm of national security. On the one hand, the prosecutor can be a powerful agent of greater respect for legality and human rights. On the other hand, prosecutors who fail to manage effectively the divide between the often secret world of national security and the more public world of the criminal courts may hasten a process whereby the state's national security activities become an exception to the rule of law, often carried out by means that are less restrained and less transparent than criminal prosecutions.

What are national security cases? The national security context includes espionage and other forms of foreign influence, as well as offenses related to the disclosure or leakage of secret information. Although these threats may increase in the future, much of the limited information that is available about the prosecutorial role in national security cases arises in the context of terrorism prosecutions in domestic courts, which will be the focus of this chapter. Fortunately, the terrorism prosecution context raises many of the same challenges that are present in other national security cases, making it a valuable case study.

National security prosecutions may be some of the most difficult and challenging of all prosecutions, for multiple reasons. First, they often involve the use of complex or rarely used charges and investigative powers. Second, they sometimes require cooperation with intelligence agencies and foreign governments, who both may resist the disclosures required by prosecutions. Third, they may force difficult decisions about whether a possible prosecution should be declined or abandoned because of competing public interests, most notably in maintaining secrecy. Such issues provide challenges to the independence of prosecutors from political direction (Edwards 1980; Roach 2010b; Stenning 2010). Finally, the high stakes of national security prosecutions, including their potential effects on the whole of government and on other nations, place pressures on the ethical role of prosecutors. These include dangers to human rights, the impartial application of the rule of law, entrapment, and miscarriages of justice (Dyzenhaus 2006; Roach 2019b).

The first part of this chapter focuses on the operational challenges that prosecutors face in national security cases. These include demands for specialization that may be difficult to fulfill given the relative rarity of national security prosecutions; the availability of special investigative powers not normally available in other criminal cases; exceptionally broad and complex offenses; and the demands of federalism and international cooperation. In addition to these challenges, prosecutors often play a dominant role in reconciling the competing demands of secrecy and disclosure and mediating the very different incentives and organizational cultures of the police and intelligence agencies (Roach 2010c). They must manage disclosure, which can become voluminous with increasing surveillance capabilities. National security prosecutions, especially those involving terrorism, can become complex mega-trials involving multiple defendants and offenses (Canadian Commission of Inquiry 2010). Finally, prosecutors must balance competing demands for guilty pleas and defendant cooperation with public expectations that all those who commit often broadly defined national security offenses be punished severely.

The second part of the chapter will build on the largely descriptive work of the first part by isolating a few ethical and normative challenges that run throughout the many operational aspects of the prosecutorial role in national security cases. These include the challenges of ensuring that often exceptional national security laws are enforced in a manner consistent with the rule of law and human rights and of maintaining the related balance between legitimate claims of secrecy and demands for disclosure to ensure fairness to the accused and disclosure of state misconduct. Prosecutors need to recognize that the risk of human rights abuses, such as entrapment and miscarriages of justice, hangs over many national security investigations and prosecutions. Another overarching ethical challenge for prosecutors in national security cases is the need to maintain prosecutorial independence and discretion while recognizing that the whole of government and whole of society can be affected by the many difficult decisions that prosecutors must make in national security cases.

26.2 Operational Challenges

26.2.1 Investigative Powers and Assistance

National security law may allow the state to use a variety of investigative powers that may not be available in other criminal cases. For example, Australia, Canada, and the

United Kingdom all allow preventive arrests of terrorism suspects on lesser grounds than ordinary arrest powers (Roach 2011). In Canada, the use of such powers requires the consent of either the provincial or federal Attorney General. In the United Kingdom, Australia, Canada, and France prosecutors can also seek control orders or peace bonds, including various forms of house arrests, as a means of imposing controls on suspects. These controls can be imposed on lower quantum of proof standards than required for a criminal prosecution and are often subject only to a deferential form of review by the judiciary. In the United States, terrorism suspects have at times been detained by the use of material witness warrants (Barnes 2012). The use of such extraordinary powers has been controversial and can cast doubt on the legitimacy of national security prosecutions. Functionally, they may be substitutes for allowing an investigation (often with electronic surveillance and/or undercover operatives) to continue that could produce more evidence of national security crime.

In some cases, officials use pretextual or so-called Al Capone strategies to arrest or detain targets of national security investigations for other crimes or violations of immigration or other laws (Richman and Stuntz 2005). This may be an attractive option for both investigators and prosecutors who desire to prevent threats to national security and/or the disclosure of intelligence methods and sources. At the same time, however, these alternatives are often less restrained (Roach 2011) and less transparent (Richman and Stuntz 2005) than criminal prosecutions. In short, prosecutors who advise in national security investigations face dilemmas between the need to prevent grave threats to national security and the need to ensure that subsequent prosecutions are possible. A complicating factor is that a national security prosecution may risk the disclosure of important sources and methods of continuing intelligence-gathering.

Susan Hemmings, a leading U.K. prosecutor, has observed that "prosecutors work with the police and the security services much earlier than they used to and may advise long before suspects are arrested" (Hemmings 2010, 957). The ethical challenges of the "embedded prosecutor" to prosecutorial independence will be examined in the third section of this chapter, but at this juncture it should be noted that many of the investigative tools in national security cases may differ from ordinary investigative tools. In the United Kingdom, for example, warrants in national security cases are granted by the elected and responsible Minister, not by an independent judge. The quid pro quo, though, is that the fruits of such surveillance are generally not admissible in criminal proceedings (Syrett 2015, 178). This represents an explicit policy decision to favor the state's interests in maintaining secrecy over its interests in facilitating the criminal prosecution of terrorists. It may also help explain why British terrorism offenses are notoriously broadly defined. For example, they include "membership in a terrorist organization" and "possessing information that is useful to the commission of terrorism" (Roach 2011). This breadth may make it easier to prosecute such offenses without the use of electronic surveillance. Based on her interviews with national security prosecutors in England, West (2018, 85–86) reports that prosecutors select some terrorist charges such as speech offences related to terrorism, rather than broader offences such as preparation for terrorism, in order to limit the disclosure of sensitive information.

In the United States, under the *Foreign Intelligence Surveillance Act* (FISA) originally enacted in 1978, warrants for electronic surveillance can be obtained on the basis of probable cause to believe that those subject to surveillance are foreign powers or their agents. (This is distinct from probable cause to believe that one has committed a crime.) The USA Patriot Act, enacted in the immediate aftermath of the 9/11 terrorist attacks, was designed to facilitate the use of FISA warrants by declaring that foreign intelligence-gathering no longer had to be the sole purpose of a FISA warrant. In 2008, FISA was again expanded to allow a warrant where there was a reasonable belief that a foreign target was outside of the United States, even if one party to the communication was in the United States. Courts have generally been deferential to these expanded powers and to their use as evidence in criminal prosecutions, despite concerns that they avoid the probable cause standard imposed for other crimes (Said 2015, 74–78).

26.2.2 Overcriminalization by Complex and Rarely Used Offenses

William Stuntz perceptively observed that extensive use of broadly defined criminal offenses effectively transfers to police and prosecutors the power to decide whom among the many guilty will be charged and prosecuted (Stuntz 2001). Although he made these comments in the context of ordinary American criminal justice, they are especially true in the context of national security prosecutions in many democracies (Tadros and Hodgson 2009; West 2018).

As with respect to ordinary crime, overcriminalization raises legitimacy concerns. Just as there are concerns that prosecutorial power has been disproportionately wielded against African Americans, Hispanic, and Indigenous people in the ordinary criminal justice system, there are concerns that prosecutorial power in the national security area has been disproportionately focused on Muslims (Said 2015, 2018). There were also concerns that the Obama Administration aggressively used Espionage Act provisions first enacted during World War I against those who leaked or possessed leaked classified information (Ryan 2018). Prosecutions based on illegal foreign influence also raise concerns about prosecutorial partiality and may increase in prominence with increased international tensions between Western democracies and China and Russia.

The statutory breadth of offenses that might be violated long before any completed act of terrorism occurs provides prosecutors with much discretion in deciding whether and what charges should be brought. A prosecutorial decision to lay a terrorism charge may also result in publicity, pre-trial detention, exposure to high sentences and post-sentence controls. A recent international study has concluded: "prosecutorial discretion operates as a final safeguard of sorts given the life-altering implications of a terrorism conviction and the already-discussed substantive and procedural human rights concerns of especially early intervention" (Paulussen and Pitcher 2018, 24). It cites as an example the decision of Australian terrorism prosecutors to drop charges against Jamie Williams, who fought with Kurdish forces against Daesh; a spokesperson for the Commonwealth Attorney General stated that the Attorney General "has a broad discretion and is able to take into account a number of factors," but in this case "it would be inappropriate to comment further" (25). The authors warn, however, that such exercise of discretion may result in an uneven and discriminatory application of the law. The breadth of criminal law gives prosecutors much discretion and power to decide whether to charge a national security suspect with ordinary criminal offences, with multiple and overlapping national security offences, or with no charges at all.

26.2.3 Specialization

Special investigative powers and complex offenses in the national security area suggest that those who prosecute national security offenses should have special expertise and security clearances to access classified information.

For example, the United Kingdom's Crown Prosecution Service has a Special Crime and Counter-Terrorism Division (SCCTD), and most of its work concerns terrorism prosecutions (U.K. Crown Prosecution Service 2018). This division works closely with both specialized police units and intelligence agencies. It has developed experience with the frequently transnational elements of international terrorism prosecutions and the demands of disclosure and public interest immunity applications to limit disclosure in terrorism prosecutions (West 2018, 82–83).

In 2010, a royal commission in Canada recommended the creation of a specialized unit among federal prosecutors to handle terrorism prosecutions. It stressed that specialization would improve the prosecutor's ability to manage competing interests in secrecy and disclosure and better coordinate with provincial prosecutions and domestic and foreign intelligence agencies (Canadian Commission of Inquiry 2010). But no such specialization has occurred, even though Canada's federal Director of Public Prosecutions has about five hundred prosecutors. One reason is the comparative rarity of national security prosecutions. This is a recurring dilemma in national security prosecutions: their highly complex and coordinated nature demands specialized expertise, but their relative rarity makes it difficult to develop and maintain such expertise. At the end of 2019, the Canadian government announced its intention to establish a specialized Director of Terrorism Prosecutions (Trudeau 2019), but it remains to be seen whether this office will be housed within the Attorney General's department thus allowing direct supervision by the Attorney General who sits in Cabinet or whether it will be situated in the Director of Public Prosecutions office in which case the Attorney General's role would only be by means of public directives (Roach 2010b). In 2015, one such directive was issued in which the Attorney General of Canada directed the DPP to ensure that terrorism cases were identified and assigned to prosecutors at the earliest opportunity. It also instructed prosecutors to provide timely communications, advice, and (when necessary) consent for investigative measures and prosecutions to investigative agencies (Attorney General of Canada 2015)

26.2.4 Whole of Government Approaches

Prosecutors play a key coordinating function with respect to ordinary crime, often providing some of the only links with the police as investigators and with correctional officials. At the same time, there are concerns that prosecutors make many decisions "flying blind" and "flying solo" (Wright 2017). In the national security context, however, such blindness may result in disasters that could affect both national security and foreign relations.

The idea that prosecutors should consult with others in government has been long recognized. For instance, in 1951, Sir Hartley Shawcross, then Attorney General for England and Wales, articulated what has become known as the Shawcross doctrine: in order to inform himself, the Attorney General "may... consult with any of his colleagues in the government and indeed... would in some cases be a fool if he did not... the assistance of his colleagues is confined to informing him of particular considerations which might affect his own decision, and does not consist, and must not consist, in telling him what that decision ought to be" (Stenning 2010, 457).

Prosecutors in national security matters need to consult a range of national security actors, including intelligence agencies, the department of foreign affairs, the military, and foreign allies. The U.S. Attorney's manual, for example, counsels that "when national security issues arise during a criminal prosecution, they must be resolved through careful coordination... with high level officials from the intelligence, military and foreign affairs communities" (U.S. Attorney General 2018, 9–90.010). It advises that each office should have a National/International Security Coordinator with top security clearance to "be the initial point of contact for the office on matters relating to foreign relations, intelligence and national defense."

In Canada and in many other common law countries that use a Director of Public Prosecutions (DPP) as a means to ensure that prosecutorial power is exercised independently and free from partisan political interest (Edwards 1984), there are special challenges in ensuring that prosecutors are properly informed about the whole of government implications for their exercise of prosecutorial powers. Many of these acts contemplate that the only interaction between the DPP and others in government will be through public directives from the Attorney General. Such transparency may be difficult to achieve given the "whole of government" implications of many national security prosecutions, leading some to recommend that Attorneys General, who can be advised by Cabinet colleagues about the foreign policy and other implications of terrorism prosecutions, assume responsibility for them (Canadian Commission of Inquiry 2010; Roach 2010b).

26.2.5 Federalism

Federalism also presents significant challenges. Even if federal prosecutors have exclusive prosecutorial authority over some national security offenses or can take over existing prosecutions, local investigators and prosecutors may be in a better position to prosecute crimes that may be precursors to terrorism. A 2005 study of various local and state prosecutors in the United States found that many were focused on prosecuting precursor crimes to suspected terrorism, such as identity theft and money laundering. The study highlighted the challenges of coordinating national and more local prosecutorial strategies (Nugent 2005).

In Canada, both federal and provincial prosecutors have jurisdiction to prosecute terrorism crimes under the federal Criminal Code, but the Security Offences Act provides that the federal Attorney General can pre-empt provincial prosecutions if the criminal offense also constitutes a threat to the national security of Canada. So far this power has not been invoked, and many terrorism prosecutions have been conducted jointly by federal and provincial prosecutors. One complication, however, is that in 2006 all federal prosecutions were assigned to a Director of Public Prosecutions, who holds office in good behavior for a set term. This reform follows best practices in many Commonwealth countries (Edwards 1984) but was not pursued with significant attention to its impact on national security prosecutions, which constitute only a small minority of all federal prosecutions (Roach 2010b).

26.2.6 International Co-operation

A significant amount of classified information in international terrorism and foreign influence prosecutions may have been obtained by foreign allies. Under a process known as caveats, the foreign agencies that compiled the information must generally consent to any further disclosure of the information. This is an important protection for the type of international information sharing that the United Nations and others have encouraged in the post-9/11 era. It also provides some safeguards to ensure that the information remains reliable and is not used in ways that may infringe human rights.

Susan Hemmings has commented on the difficulties produced by international cooperation in terrorism investigations, such as the challenges of proving "clear lines of continuity where evidence has been gathered in a theatre of war or in a country that is unsafe or unstable" (Hemmings 2010, 956). Her comments were made in 2010 but are particularly important given the post-2014 emphasis on foreign terrorist fighters as a security threat.

Many post-9/11 terrorism offenses are defined as crimes of universal jurisdiction, meaning that they can be potentially prosecuted in countries where the relevant events are not alleged to have occurred. As Maximo Langer has observed, the prosecution of crimes of universal jurisdiction can impose significant international relations costs on those countries that prosecute crimes alleged to have been committed in other countries (Langer 2011). Wadie Said has drawn a parallel between U.S. assertions of universal jurisdiction in terrorism and drug cases, arguing that this approach has produced "a system of worldwide enforcement housed in the American justice system where law enforcement and prosecutors have almost limitless discretion to investigate and bring charges" (Said 2018). He has also warned that exceptions and deference to prosecutorial powers in the national security context will migrate and influence other criminal justice powers.

26.2.7 Informants

The use of informants creates dilemmas and imposes responsibilities on prosecutors in all criminal cases but poses special challenges in national security cases. National security informants may be especially incentivized to participate and perhaps to lie because they may face prosecution under broad and severe offenses relating to terrorism or foreign influence and/or deportation to countries with poor human rights records.

National security informants may also require special protection from possible retaliation by terrorist groups or foreign powers. Prosecutors may seek to shield the disclosure of identifying information about informers under various evidentiary privileges, but this may become impossible if the informant played an active role in the events that are the subject matter of the charges. For example, prosecutors abandoned several high-profile Canadian terrorism prosecutions, including one against the alleged mastermind of the 1985 Air India bombing that killed 331 people, when it became clear that to proceed the disclosure of a key informant would be necessary. Another complicating factor in the Air India case was that many witnesses were originally recruited by Canada's civilian intelligence agency, who promised them anonymity in part because the intelligence agency's mandate did not include prosecutions. Prosecutors eventually forced many of these witnesses to testify; they placed some in witness protection after one possible witness was assassinated (Roach 2010a). Nevertheless, the informants who were originally promised anonymity were understandably reluctant witnesses. Such reluctance contributed to the 2005 acquittal of two men charged as part of the wide-ranging Air India conspiracy. In the end, only one person was convicted of manslaughter out of a terrorist conspiracy that resulted in 331 deaths (Canadian Commission of Inquiry 2010).

Based on her interviews with English national security prosecutors, Leah West has reported that prosecutors sometimes decline to file certain terrorism charges in order to prevent the disclosure of the identity of informants and human sources. She quotes one UK national security prosecutor: "you don't charge where you have to disclose something. You find a way to charge something else. . . ." (West 2018, 85–86, 104). This use of charging decisions to minimize disclosure obligations depends both on the variety of offences available and the breadth of disclosure rules. Both the United Kingdom and the United States have less broad disclosure obligations than Canada. Unlike Canada and the United Kingdom, the United States does not have crimes directly related to terrorist speech that may require more limited disclosure of sensitive information than broader crimes such as material support of terrorism. The use of charging decisions to protect informants from disclosure may mean that unreliable national security informants and improper handling of or illegal activities by such informants may not be revealed even when a national security investigation results in a criminal prosecution.

26.2.8 Classified Information and Special Procedures Involving Disclosure

Dealing with classified information presents practical challenges for prosecutors who require security clearances and special facilities in order to obtain access to such information. Much classified information will require the permission of its original creator for additional disclosure of the information. In many cases, the originator of the material may be domestic or foreign intelligence agencies. Disclosure and use of such information in criminal proceedings may also result in additional inquiry into whether the information was obtained through torture or other violations of human rights.

One of the greatest operational and ethical challenges facing prosecutors in national security cases is discharging disclosure obligations to the accused while at the same time respecting the state's interest in maintaining the secrecy of domestic and foreign intelligence-gathering. A complicating factor in discharging ethical and legal obligations of disclosure is that the volume of disclosure in national security prosecutions is often massive. In one Australian case, disclosure literally filled one defense lawyer's computer, making it difficult for him to read and listen to all the disclosure and resulting in trial by "edited highlights" (de Lint and Kassa 2017, 187).

If prosecutors decide that too little should be disclosed, they run the risk of a miscarriage of justice by failing to disclose exculpatory information or information that reveals human rights violations. At the same time, prosecutors can disclose too much, thereby straining the limited resources of the defense and/or compromising both intelligence-gathering and the efficiency of the trial.

In many countries there are special procedures that allow prosecutors an opportunity to obtain advance judicial permission for non-disclosure of relevant material on the grounds that the harms of disclosure to the state's national security interests outweigh the harms of non-disclosure to the accused. Sometimes these procedures allow the judge to authorize the disclosure of redacted summaries of classified material or of substituted information. In England, such proceedings are called public interest immunity proceedings; in the United States, they are conducted under the Classified Information Procedure Act (Roach 2010a).

These special procedures generally place responsibilities on prosecutors to protect the secrecy of classified information and allow ex parte communications with the judge. They also provide for judicial responsibility in balancing the competing interests of the accused in disclosure and the state in secrecy. As will be discussed in the third section of this chapter, miscarriages of justice have occurred when prosecutors or even courts have erred on the side of secrecy. In many cases, prosecutors can effectively overrule judicial orders of disclosure by terminating prosecutions or by dropping certain charges.

None of the above procedures for protecting secret intelligence from disclosure allows prosecutors to use as evidence material that has not been disclosed to the accused. This is a basic element of fairness that must be observed in just criminal justice systems. At the same time, the "substitution effects" (Roach, 2011) of such practices should not be ignored. In particular, the demand that all evidence used against the accused be disclosed may lead to the use of a variety of less restrained alternatives to criminal prosecutions, including extra-judicial killing, or military and immigration detention that do not require the disclosure of the intelligence used to justify the decision.

26.2.9 The Terrorist Trial

Trials may be more frequent in the terrorism context than other criminal contexts because of the political motivations of many accused, their desire to expose and challenge state investigative conduct, and the high sentences that they face. A greater likelihood that a terrorism case will go to trial, combined with the massive disclosure obligations and related challenges of obtaining judicial approval for non-disclosure, will place many challenges on prosecutors and the criminal justice system. Indeed, the evolution from al Qaeda to Daesh and the resurgence of far-right terrorism has made it difficult, if not impossible, to prosecute all extremists who are prepared to engage in violence or who are associated with a growing number of often small and self-radicalized groups. A Canadian royal commission warned prosecutors that they must use their discretion to ensure that trials and juries are not overwhelmed by having too many accused facing too many charges in one terrorist trial (Canadian Commission of Inquiry 2010). The terrorist trial, perhaps even more than ordinary criminal trials, is a scarce resource that prosecutors must use to best advantage.

In order to preserve limited resources and protect secrecy, prosecutors may feel intense pressure to offer discounts on sentences in order to induce guilty pleas. These discounts may be justified given the broad range of conduct covered by modern terrorism offenses and the various degrees of involvement in a planned or executed terrorist plot. Yet they may result in plea and sentence agreements that attract controversy from a public that expects harsh sentences for any offense associated with terrorism. It may also result in controversy over the legitimacy of the application of the criminal sanction when it is not accompanied by a public trial. Another related problem is the growing recognition in the United States and elsewhere that significant numbers of people have made rational or irrational decisions to plead guilty despite their innocence (Roach 2019b).

When terrorism trials are held, they will often be lengthy and expensive. In Canada, a special court room had to be built for the trial of two men eventually acquitted of the 1985 Air India bombings (Canadian Commission of Inquiry 2010). Similarly, a special courtroom outside of Scotland had to be constructed for the trial of those accused of the Lockerbie bombing. Rightly or wrongly, concerns about the security of domestic courts have been cited as a rationale for U.S. laws prohibiting the transfer of those held in military detention at Guantanamo Bay to the United States for domestic trials (Roach 2011).

Not all accused and sometimes not even their lawyers may accept the legitimacy of the court system in national security cases. This presents a risk of the politicization of the trial process that will place special demands on the prosecutor and the judge not to act in such a way that will lend credence to claims that the court is simply an instrument of state power. Many national security cases attract much pre-trial publicity and have defendants who are members of religious or political minorities. This may place pressure on the fairness of the trial and the selection of the jury in those jurisdictions which give the accused a right to trial by jury. Jury selection in national security trials presents challenges, especially in cases where there has been extensive pre-trial publicity and some prospective jurors may be prejudiced towards the accused (Roach, 2021) Trials may frequently be necessary to ensure a fair and transparent application of the criminal law to those accused of national security related crimes, but they will place many practical and normative demands on the criminal justice system, most of which will be borne by the prosecutor.

26.2.10 Sentencing

The prosecutor plays a key role in sentencing in all criminal matters, but she faces special challenges in the national security context. Both the breadth of offenses and the need to encourage reluctant participants to cooperate with authorities and testify against co-conspirators may require prosecutors to agree to drop charges and reduce sentences in a way that may seem to result in a disproportionately light sentence. For example, in the United Kingdom from September 2001 to August 2012, 56 percent of those convicted of terrorism offenses received sentences of five years imprisonment or less and only 25 percent received sentences of ten years or more (Home Office 2013). Parliament has responded to such sentences by increasing the maximum sentences of some terrorism offenses and allowing members of the public to challenge sentences in terrorism cases as overly lenient. Sentences in national security cases may be particularly high profile and controversial. This will place pressure on prosecutors.

26.3 Ethical Challenges

26.3.1 Maintaining the Rule of Law in the Face of National Security Exceptionalism

One of the main ethical challenges in the national security context is the idea that the ends justify any means. Such an approach can lead to cynicism about national security as an area where state interests prevail regardless of the rule of law. For example, terrorism prosecutions can be seen as a form of "winner's justice" and espionage prosecutions can be seen as just another form of foreign relations. As Wayne McCormack has observed, the elusiveness of a definition of terrorism in international law threatens the impartial rule of law. There are related dangers when prosecutors and other governmental lawyers apply the language of war to terrorism (McCormack 2012) and embrace questionable tactics such as entrapment (Said 2015), pre-textual prosecution (Richman and Stuntz 2005), selective and discriminatory forms of prosecutions, or heavy inducements that force the accused to plead guilty (Roach 2019b). All of these techniques can violate human rights, but they also obscure the precise threat to national security (or lack thereof) that is the subject matter of the state's intervention.

One antidote to exceptionalism is prosecutorial conduct that treats those accused of terrorism in the same fashion as those accused of other crimes, to the greatest degree possible. Such an approach can help ensure compliance with human rights standards. In addition, it can help ensure that successful prosecutions are seen as legitimate. This should mean that those convicted of terrorism and other national security threats are exposed to appropriate stigma and punishment and cannot reasonably be seen as martyrs. Susan Hemmings has stressed this criminalization approach by arguing:

> Prosecutors in the UK begin from the perspective that terrorists are criminals and that they should be tried in our mainstream criminal justice system using criminal law and procedures .... [T]errorists should not be accorded "special status" and should expect to be treated fairly and in accordance with the law.... Prosecutors make decisions in accordance with the Code for Crown Prosecutors on all types of cases, including allegations of terrorism.
>
> (Hemmings 2010, 955)

Hemmings elaborates that the twin requirements of sufficient evidence and proof that a prosecution is in the public interest "do not differ because the case is more serious, controversial or of public importance or because evidence gathering has to take to place in a theatre of war or conflict" (956). At the same time, much will depend on the independence and ethics of prosecutors.

Both terrorism laws and espionage law have been applied selectively when they serve the interest of the U.S. government. For example, agents of the Cuban government were convicted in Florida of espionage and conspiracy to murder in relation to Cuba's shooting down of planes flown by anti-Castro activists, but anti-Castro activists who were reportedly planning acts of terrorism against Cuba were not charged (Said 2015, 117–119). Another threat to the rule of law is the frequent use of pretextual or "Al Capone" charges to charge those who may be involved in terrorism or its financing with a range of other crimes, including tax evasion, obstruction of justice, and making false statements to investigators (Barnes 2012, 1646–1647) as well as immigration-related offenses. Even if the accused are factually guilty of lesser crimes, there may be unfairness in exposing them to charges that would not have been investigated or prosecuted if they were not also suspects in often intensive and intrusive national security investigations. There are also concerns in many democracies that terrorism prosecutions since 9/11 have focused on terrorism associated with al Qaeda and Daesh and not with respect to far-right terrorists who have often only been prosecuted after they have committed acts of violence (Forcese and Roach 2015, 278–280). Pretextual prosecutions and the use of immigration, administrative, or military detention may allow for greater protection of secrets and informants, but they may also understate and obscure the degree of criminality related to national security (Richman and Stuntz 2005).

26.3.2 Challenges to Prosecutorial Independence

Drawing on his extensive practical experience, David Scharia has written about a "dialogue" between courts, the military, and prosecutors in Israel, which he suggests likely does not have a parallel in any other system. In one case, the courts approved military expropriation of land, but on the understanding that the Attorney General would ensure that those from whom land was taken could continue to make partial use of the land (Scharia 2014, 145–146). In another case, a prosecutor was complimented by the Court for not using a confession obtained by improper means (153). Leaving aside whether the Court has avoided its own ethical responsibilities by such tacit forms of dialogue, such an approach places special obligations on prosecutors and governmental lawyers to act within legal constraints. As Scharia notes, however, the legislature and the public may not accept the nuanced restraints that the Israeli courts ask the prosecutor to implement: "in such cases, it is doubtful whether it is possible to assume that prosecutors or legal counsels would prefer or be able to rely on non-binding advisory messages" (231) from the Court. In other words, reliance on prosecutorial discretion may not always be an effective way to impose rule of law restraints on national security activities or to be seen to be respecting such necessary restraints.

Scharia reports how an adverse Israeli High Court comment about a failure to disclose relevant information to the accused caused Israeli prosecutors to revise their guidelines for disclosing classified information to the accused; the Court complimented prosecutors for better discharging their disclosure duties in subsequent national security cases (154). In Canada, the Federal Court has questioned the conduct of both intelligence agencies and the governmental lawyers that provide them with legal advice. The Federal Court has not hesitated to make well-publicized calls in its judgments for reviews of conduct, including that of governmental lawyers. Such reviews have taken place and one is ongoing in light of the Federal Court's most recent call in *Re Sections 12 and 21 of the Canadian Security Intelligence Service Act*, for a "comprehensive external review" because previous internal and limited reviews have identified an "institutional culture" among both government lawyers and the intelligence agencies as "undermining both the commitment to and compliance with core values including the rule of law."

In *R (on the application of Corner House Research and Others) v. Director of Serious Fraud Office* (2008), the highest court in England upheld a prosecutor's decision to stop a bribery prosecution after Saudi Arabia threatened to withdraw intelligence and other cooperation from the United Kingdom. Relying in part on this decision, Philip Stenning has questioned the reality of prosecutorial independence in high profile cases, including those made in the national security area. At the same time, Professor Stenning suggests that such an approach may not require the abandonment of the general default principle of prosecutorial independence in less exceptional cases (Stenning 2010, 464–466). Such an approach would involve an abrogation of the constitutional convention, long defended by Professor John Edwards, that there should not be direct Cabinet (or Presidential) responsibility for criminal prosecutions even in the national security domain (Edwards 1980, 86–87; Edwards 1984, 61). The convention has recently been recognized by the Supreme Court of Canada in *R. v. Cawthorne* (2016) as applying even in the national security domain of military justice.

In response to Professor Stenning, I have argued that the *Corner House* decision need not be interpreted as a rejection of prosecutorial independence, but rather as judicial deference to the exercise of prosecutorial discretion, after the prosecutor had been informed about the adverse consequences of a sensitive prosecution. In other words, this and similar cases can be reconciled with the Shawcross principle defended by Professor Edwards—that we should prevent the government from directing the exercise of prosecutorial discretion even in national security cases. At the same time, I have suggested that Directors of Public Prosecutions (who in the United Kingdom, Australia, and Canada hold office for set terms during good behavior) have the potential to disrupt "the fine balance" (Roach 2010b, 488) established by the Shawcross doctrine if the DPP or the Attorney General is inhibited from consulting with others in government to obtain information (but not direction) about the possible effects of national security prosecutions. If the DPP operates without such information, the Attorney General in most DPP systems retains the right to terminate a prosecution on the basis that it will place vital national interests in jeopardy. This, however, is different and less dangerous to the rule of law than simply allowing heads of government to dictate prosecution decisions. In my view such governmental direction of prosecutions raises concerns that governments could direct prosecutors to prosecute their enemies and not prosecute their friends (Agamben 2005; Dyzenhaus 2006).

Prosecutors and governmental lawyers are the most natural defenders of the rule of law and human rights within the government (Edwards 1984; Roach 2006). The national security context will often require prosecutors to interact with strong state actors such as intelligence agencies, the military, and the foreign service. Such interaction has the potential to restrain the state. Nevertheless, there are no guarantees that prosecutors will prevail, or that their independence will be respected when they engage with stronger state actors such as the military and the security services.

26.3.3 Miscarriages of Justice

A leading U.K. terrorism prosecutor has explained how prosecutors must examine masses of material held by the police and security agencies and how prosecutors are "conscious that they are the guardians of justice" in deciding what must be disclosed

(Hemmings 2010, 966). Hemmings also notes that prosecutors have continuing legal and ethical disclosure duties, and this may be important given that the exact nature of the accused's case may only be apparent at trial. As the accused's case becomes clearer, the prosecutor's disclosure obligations may increase; in cases that reveal exculpatory evidence or evidence that undermines the prosecutor's case, disclosure duties may extend to the post-conviction stage. In this regard, it is important to note that the English courts imposed broad disclosure on prosecutors in the wake of several miscarriages of justice being revealed in IRA terrorism cases in the early 1990s. However, both Parliament and the courts have decreased disclosure obligations since those judicial decisions because of concerns that disclosure of unused material may both lengthen terrorism trials and jeopardize the state's interest in secrecy (Roach 2010a; West, 2018). A 2017 study by the Inspectorate for the Crown Prosecution Service found significant problems both in police scheduling and prosecutorial disclosure of unused material in a random selection of the more serious cases heard in Crown Court (Crown Prosecution Service Inspectorate 2017). It remains to be seen whether wrongful convictions of the magnitude of the Irish cases will emerge in the post-9/11 era (Roach 2019a).

Prosecutors must also be aware of the dangers of miscarriages of justice when offering plea deals to those charged with national security offenses. The desire to maintain secrecy and avoid long and controversial trials may provide prosecutors with a temptation to offer suspects deals that cannot refuse. This is also a more general problem across the criminal justice system, as witnessed by increasing revelations that wrongful convictions have resulted from guilty pleas (Roach 2019b).

Some of the main causes of miscarriages of justice (tunnel vision, noble cause corruption, unreliable informants, erroneous cross-racial identification, false confessions, and guilty pleas) are likely to be present in national security cases, especially terrorism prosecutions. At the same time, major miscarriages of justice—as influential as the Birmingham Six or Guildford Four—have yet to emerge in the post-9/11 era (Roach 2019a). One hypothesis is that police and prosecutors have an improved ability to eliminate false positives. There is some evidence of this in the United Kingdom, as most terrorism-related arrests do not result in prosecutions. At the same time, common law criminal justice systems continue to place more of a value on finality than many civil law systems (Creegan 2011). Moreover, many terrorism offenses have been defined so broadly that it may be difficult for a victim of a miscarriage of justice to find new evidence (information that may be shielded by secrecy claims and be available in foreign lands) that is generally necessary to overturn a miscarriage of justice (Roach 2019a).

26.3.4 Entrapment and Other Forms of Misconduct

American prosecutors have played a key role in the use of proactive stings as a chief means to investigate terrorism cases (Richman 2003). Such stings provide prosecutors with significant advantages, as they can produce evidence of broadly defined terrorism offenses under tightly controlled circumstances that can limit disclosure that may threaten intelligence-gathering. American juries have frequently rejected entrapment defenses, often after hearing inflammatory evidence that the accused was predisposed to commit acts of terrorism (Roach 2011; Said 2015). In Canada, independent judges decide whether entrapment claims have been made out; for example, the court in *R. v. Nuttall* (2018), found that police—with the assistance of prosecutors—had effectively manufactured a terrorist crime and had manipulated two marginal and addicted converts to Islam into committing a terrorist crime. This may be the only example in North America of a terrorism prosecution being terminated on entrapment grounds. In continental procedures, the use of the informers and proactive investigations are generally subject to more ongoing judicial supervision than in North America (Ross 2007).

Although prosecutors may theoretically be subject to criminal and civil liability and professional disciplinary proceedings for various forms of misconduct, these forms of accountability are very difficult to use (Roach 2019b; Wright and Miller 2010). For example, the Attorney General of the United States and prosecutors were found to enjoy qualified immunity from civil liability for their pre-textual use of material witness warrants as a means to detain terrorist suspects without charge (*Al Kidd v. Ashford* 2011). Prosecutorial misconduct in the national security context may be shielded by claims of secrecy.

26.3.5 Prosecutors in Non-Democratic Countries

National security prosecutions in countries that are not democracies provide a special challenge to human rights. The abuse of national security laws in countries such as Egypt and Syria have both resulted in serious human rights abuses and produced pressure that facilitated the growth of al Qaeda and Daesh as the two most prominent terrorist groups of the last two decades (Roach 2011). Authoritarian regimes including China have been adept at using the language of international counter-terrorism in an attempt to justify the prosecution and mass detention of minorities in Tibet and Xianjang. Alas, prosecutors in repressive states have often been at the forefront of these movements (de Lisle 2010).

Article 18 of the 2020 Law of the People's Republic of China on Safeguarding National Security in the Hong Kong Special Administrative District, imposed on Hong Kong by China, requires the creation of a "specialized prosecution division" in national security. Prosecutors must be approved by a new "whole of government" committee "for safeguarding national security" whose activities under Article 14 are not subject to disclosure or judicial review. These prosecutors will have the power to bring prosecutions for new crimes of secession, subversion, terrorism or foreign collusion. Under Article 46, the Secretary of Justice will have the power to deprive those accused of such offences of a jury trial. In addition, prosecutorial functions in serious cases or those involving foreign governments or external elements can under Article 55 be taken over by the new Office for Safeguarding National Security appointed by and accountable to the

Chinese government in Beijing, with trials being held under Chinese criminal procedure. Depending on the context, prosecutors can serve either as agents of repression and state policy or as agents for human rights and the rule of law in the national security context.

26.4 Conclusion

Examining the operational and ethical challenges faced by prosecutors in the national security context illuminates our understanding of their role in the criminal justice system.

Prosecutors increasingly play a role in the investigative stage as they provide legal advice. This may especially be true in the national security context, where advice from prosecutors may be necessary to assist investigators to use special investigative and detention powers and to work with foreign governments. Prosecutors will play a vital role in ensuring respect for the rule of law and human rights in national security operations. In turn, there is a risk that they may become complicit in human rights violations and miscarriages of justice that may be more likely given the high stakes and secrecy that surrounds many national security activities.

Prosecutors also play a critical role in mediating the demands of intelligence-gathering (where preserving the secrecy of sources and methods is a priority) with the demands of evidence and disclosure (which require often reluctant national security actors, including intelligence agencies and foreign allies in international investigations, to reveal sources and methods). If prosecutors fail to manage the competing interests between disclosure and secrecy skillfully, national security actors may opt for the use of less restrained, less transparent, and often less fair alternatives to the criminal law, such as conducting targeted and extra-judicial assassinations, declaring suspected spies personae non gratae, and using military or administrative detention. Prosecutors may also have to use special procedures to restrict the disclosure of classified information and this can place considerable operational and ethical demands on them.

Yet another challenge is to the ability of prosecutors to exercise prosecutorial discretion independent of government direction. National security, by definition and increasingly by post-9/11 practice, is a whole of government affair. This means that prosecutors will need to consult and often work with intelligence, military, customs and border, and foreign affairs agencies with respect to national security investigations and prosecutions. Some have argued that it is unrealistic not to expect the head of government to dictate the result of prosecutorial decisions that will have a significant effect on a state's foreign relations or other vital interests (Stenning 2010). The rise of populist and authoritarian rulers in recent years has strengthened the idea that national security prosecutions will be an instrument of state policy. At the same time, such realism presents threats to the independence and ethical professionalism of prosecutors as well as to human rights and the rule of law (Edwards 1980; Roach 2010b). If prosecutors do not stand up for such values in national security investigations, it is not clear that anyone in government will. It is not an exaggeration to conclude that prosecutors in national security cases hold much of the fate of the rule of law in their hands.

References

Agamben, Giorgio. 2005. *State of Exception*. Translated by Kevin Attell. Chicago: University of Chicago Press.

Al Kidd v. Ashford. 2011. 563 U.S. 731.

Attorney General of Canada. 2015 Directive 3 under subsection 10(2) of the Director of Public Prosecutions Act 18 June 2015.

Barnes, Beau. 2012. "Confronting the One-Man Wolf Pack: Adapting Law Enforcement and Prosecutorial Responses to the Threat of Lone-Wolf Terrorism." *Boston University Law Review* 92(5): 1613–1662.

Canadian Commission of Inquiry into the Investigation of the Bombing of Air India Flight 182. 2010. *Flight 182: A Canadian Tragedy*. Vol. 3, *The Relationship between Intelligence and Evidence and the Challenges of Terrorism Prosecutions*. Ottawa: Public Works.

Classified Information Procedure Act 18 U.S.C. App. III.

Creegan, Erin. 2011. "Cooperation in Foreign Terrorism Prosecutions." *Georgetown Journal of International Law* 42(2): 491–530.

Crown Prosecution Service Inspectorate. 2017. *Making It Fair*. July 2017.

De Lint, Willem, and Wondwossen D. Kassa. 2017. "Bent into Security: Barrister Contributions to a Skewed Order in Two Terrorism Prosecutions in Australia." *Journal of Law and Society* 44(2): 169–199.

de Lisle, Jacques. 2010. "Security First: Patterns and Lessons from China's Use of National Security Threats." *National Security Law and Policy Review* 4: 397–436.

Dyzenhaus, David. 2006. *The Constitution of Law*. Cambridge: Cambridge University Press.

Edwards, John Ll. J. 1980. *Ministerial Responsibility for National Security*. Ottawa: Supply and Services.

Edwards, John Ll. J. 1984. *The Attorney General, Politics and the Public Interest*. London: Sweet and Maxwell.

Forcese, Craig, and Kent Roach. 2015. *False Security: The Radicalization of Canadian Anti-Terrorism*. Toronto: Irwin Law.

Foreign Intelligence Surveillance Act (FISA), 50 USC Ch. 36.

Hemmings, Susan. 2010. "The Practical Application of Counter-Terrorism Legislation in England and Wales: A Prosecutor's Perspective" *International Affairs* 86(4): 955–969.

Home Office. 2013. *Terrorist Arrests-Analysis of Charging and Sentence by Religion*. United Kingdom, 12 September 2013 at Table 4.1.

Langer, Máximo. 2011. "The Diplomacy of Universal Jurisdiction." *American Journal of International Law* 105(1): 1–49.

McCormack, Wayne. 2012. "Prosecuting Terrorism." In *The Prosecutor in Transnational Perspective*. Edited by Erik Luna and Marianne Wade, 293–313. New York: Oxford University Press.

Nugent, Elaine. 2005. *Local Prosecutors' Response to Terrorism*. NCJRS Document 211202. Arlington, VA: American Prosecutors Research Institute.

Paulussen, Christophe, and Kate Pitcher. 2018. *Prosecuting (Potential) Foreign Terrorist Fighters: Legislative and Practical Challenges*. Hague: International Centre for Counter-Terrorism.

R. v. Cawthorne. 2016. 1 SCR 983.

R v. Director of Serious Fraud Office. 2008. UKHL 60.

R. v. Nuttall. 2018. BCCA 479.

Re Sections 12 and 21 of the Canadian Security Intelligence Service Act, RSC 1985, c C-23 (Re). 2020. FC 616 at para 310.

Richman, Daniel. 2003. "Prosecutors and Their Agents, Agents and Their Prosecutors." *Columbia Law Review* 103(4): 749–832.

Richman, Daniel, and William Stuntz. 2005. "Al Capone's Revenge: An Essay on the Political Economy of Pretextual Prosecution." *Columbia Law Review* 105(2): 583–639.

Roach, Kent. 2006. "Not Just the Government's Lawyer: The Attorney General as Defender of the Rule of Law." *Queens Law Journal* 31(2): 598–643.

Roach, Kent. 2010a. *The Unique Challenges of Terrorism Prosecutions: Towards a Workable Relation between Intelligence and Evidence*. Ottawa: Supply and Services.

Roach, Kent. 2010b. "Prosecutorial Independence and Accountability in Terrorism Prosecutions." *Criminal Law Quarterly* 55(4): 486–507.

Roach, Kent. 2010c. "The Eroding Distinction between Intelligence and Evidence in Terrorism Investigations." In *Counter-Terrorism and Beyond*. Edited by Nicola McGarrity, Andrew Lynch, and George Williams, 48–68. New York: Routledge.

Roach, Kent. 2011. *The 9/11 Effect: Comparative Counter-terrorism*. Cambridge: Cambridge University Press.

Roach, Kent. 2019a. "Defining Miscarriages of Justice in the Context of Post-9/11 Terrorism." In *Counter-terrrorism, Constitutionalism and Miscarriages of Justice*. Edited by Genevieve Lennon, Colin King, and Carole McCartney, 187–208. Oxford: Hart Publishing.

Roach, Kent. 2019b. "Regulating the Prosecutorial Role in Wrongful Convictions." In *The Evolving Role of the Public Prosecutor*. Edited by Victoria Colvin and Philip Stenning, 249–265. Abington: Routledge.

Roach, Kent. 2021. "Trial by Jury and the Toronto 18" *Manitoba Law Journal* (forthcoming special issue of the Toronto 18 Terrorism Prosecutions)

Ross, Jacqueline. 2007. "The Place of Covert Policing in Democratic Societies: A Comparative Study of Germany and the United States." *American Journal of Comparative Law* 55(3): 493–580.

Ryan, David. 2018. "National Security Leaks, The Espionage Act and Prosecutorial Discretion." *Homeland and National Security Law Review* 6(1): 59–81.

Said, Waidie. 2015. *Crimes of Terror: The Legal and Political Implications of Federal Terrorism Prosecutions*. New York: Oxford University Press.

Said, Waidie. 2018. "Limitlessness Discretion in the Wars on Drugs and Terror." *University of Colorado Law Review* 89(1): 93–132.

Scharia, David. 2014. *Judicial Review of National Security*. New York: Oxford University Press.

Security Offenses Act, S.C. 1985. c. S-7.

Stenning, Philip. 2010. "Prosecutions, Politics and the Public Interest: Some Recent Developments in the United Kingdom, Canada and Elsewhere." *Criminal Law Quarterly* 55(4): 449–478.

Stuntz, William. 2001. "The Pathological Politics of Criminal Law." *Michigan Law Review* 100(3): 505–600.

Syrett, Keith. 2015. "The United Kingdom." In *Comparative Counter-Terrorism Law*. Edited by Kent Roach, 167–202. Cambridge: Cambridge University Press.

Tadros, Victor, and Jacqueline Hodgson. 2009. "How to Make a Terrorist Out of Nothing." *Modern Law Review* 72(6): 984–997.

Trudeau, Justin. 2019. "Mandate Letter to Minister of Justice Attorney General of Canada," December 13.

United Kingdom Crown Prosecution Service. 2018. Special Crime and Counter-Terrorism Division.

USA Patriot Act, 8 U.S. Code Section 1701 et seq.

West, Leah. 2018. "The Problem of 'Relevance': Intelligence to Evidence Lessons from UK Terrorism Prosecutions" *Manitoba Law Journal* 41(4): 57-112.

Wright, Ronald. 2017. "Prosecutors' Institutions and Incentives." *Criminology, Criminal Justice, Law and Society* 18(3): 85–100.

Wright, Ronald, and Marc Miller. 2010. "The Worldwide Accountability Deficit for Prosecutors." *Washington & Lee Law Review* 67(4): 1587–1622.

CHAPTER 27

SHRINKING THE ACCOUNTABILITY DEFICIT IN CAPITAL CHARGING

SHEROD THAXTON

27.1 Introduction

Contemporary capital punishment practices continue to face sharp criticism from both legal analysts and officials in every branch of government. Nearly a decade ago, the American Law Institute (ALI) withdrew its endorsement of the death penalty framework it had developed and promoted for over forty years (ALI 2009; Steiker and Steiker 2014). The ALI disavowed contemporary capital punishment systems, many of which were directly modeled after the ALI's prototype death penalty statute, "in light of the current intractable institutional and structural obstacles to ensuring a minimally adequate system for administering capital punishment" (ALI 2009). U.S. Supreme Court Justices Stephen Breyer and Ruth Bader Ginsburg raised concerns over the fair administration of the death penalty in 2015 (*Glossip v. Gross* 2015), and former Justice John Paul Stevens, who retired from the Court in 2010, expressly condemned the practice (Stevens 2010). The governors of Illinois (Johnson 2000), Maryland (Clines 2002), and New Mexico (Associated Press 2009), just to name a few, have openly expressed concerns over the unlawful and error-prone operation of their state capital punishment systems. Numerous prosecutors and law enforcement officials, including chiefs of police, have also advocated for the abolition of the death penalty, citing an unacceptable risk of error and excessive cost (Abbott 2008; Dieter 2009; Samuels 2008).

In addition to legal, political, and academic elites, national opinion poll data reveal that public support for the death penalty is at its lowest point in several decades (Newport 2011; Stewart 2011). Public perception of the capital punishment system has been influenced, in part, by a voluminous scholarly literature that consistently reveals not only rampant arbitrariness and capriciousness (i.e., the death penalty is not reserved for the "worst-of-the-worst" as the U.S. Constitution requires), but also racial/ethnic, gender, and geographic bias in capital charging, sentencing, and reversals on appeal (Alesina and Ferrara 2014; Gelman et al. 2004; Radelet and Borg 2000; Thaxton 2018).

These problems of arbitrariness, discrimination/bias, wrongful convictions, and cost are also interrelated. Jurisdictions with the highest reversal rates for trial error, inter alia, impose death sentences at the highest rates and in cases that are not highly aggravated (i.e., where the culpability level is relatively low). These jurisdictions also have trial judges who are subject to popular (and often highly partisan) elections (Gelman et al. 2004; Liebman et al. 2000).[1] The constellation of these factors, coupled with the fact that approximately a dozen counties in the United States are responsible for the vast majority of death sentences (and even fewer are responsible for the vast majority of actual executions), reveal that a minority of "death-prone" jurisdictions are disproportionately responsible for the miscarriages of justice observed in our capital charging-and-sentencing system (Liebman and Clarke 2011; Smith 2012; Steiker and Steiker 2005). This small group of jurisdictions also imposes significant costs on the majority of jurisdictions that do not actively pursue the death penalty, including more crime, fewer arrests for murder, and heightened risks of miscarriages of justice for non-capital defendants (Liebman and Clarke 2011).

Discouraging the overly aggressive use of the death penalty by prosecutors may be the most effective (and efficient) way to reduce the overall prevalence of error in capital charging-and-sentencing systems, as well as unnecessary expense. Prosecutorial overreaching in the capital context primarily results from both electoral politics (MacFeely 2000; McCannon 2013; Wright 2009) and prosecutors' desire to incentivize defendants' waiver of their right to trial via plea-bargaining in exchange for withdrawal of the capital charge (Thaxton 2013). Analysts have suggested numerous reforms aimed at either explicitly restricting the breadth of prosecutorial discretion or better illuminating and regulating prosecutors' discretionary choices. While some of these proposals specifically focus on capital charging-and-bargaining dynamics, the vast majority apply to charging-and-bargaining more broadly.

This essay suggests a relatively modest reform that may be especially effective in shifting some of the financial and administrative costs of inadequate charge screening, while still allowing prosecutors to retain discretion in seeking the death penalty. The proposal consists of two key components: (1) an advisory (i.e., non-binding) opinion from a reviewing authority assessing the appropriateness of a prosecutor's decision to seek the death penalty in a case based on the totality of evidence and (2) financial *and* administrative cost-shifting capable of disincentivizing "hawkish" prosecutorial behavior with respect to capital charging.[2] Specifically, a prosecutor who disregards the screening authority's negative recommendation would subject his/her jurisdiction to a hefty surcharge—the jurisdiction would have to pay a percentage of the direct and (state) collateral review court costs in any case in which the capital conviction or sentence is ultimately reversed.[3] Prosecutors rejecting the screening authority's negative recommendation and ultimately disposing of the case via a plea agreement would make the jurisdiction liable for a larger percentage of the pre-trial costs and trial costs (if a plea agreement is reached after the trial commences) in states that have split-funding arrangements. Administrative cost-shifting would come in multiple forms, including the collection and dissemination of information about prosecutors' record of reversals and the requirement that local prosecutors serve as co-counsel, of-record, in all appellate proceedings at the state and federal level. The proposal requires additional manpower and expense, but the infrequency of potential capital murder cases, relative to other serious violent felonies, makes the proposal manageable. The proposed reform is modeled, to an extent, after the federal death penalty system's requirement that federal prosecutors obtain approval from the Attorney General to pursue the death penalty (U.S. DOJ 2001). However there are several important points of departure from the federal system's framework that constitute potential improvements over both the federal model and other models that have been proposed to reduce or eliminate prosecutorial over-charging.

The chapter proceeds in three parts below. Section 27.2 discusses the Court's attempted regulation of the capital punishment process to minimize the risk of legal error. The Court's efforts have been famously described as "Slow Dancing with Death" because the Court has continually struggled with reconciling its seemingly inconsistent constitutional requirements of (1) reserving the death penalty for only the worst-of-the-worst offenders and (2) requiring individualized charging-and-sentencing determinations that permit legal actors broad discretion in seeking and imposing the death penalty (Banner 2002; Foley 2003; Liebman 2007).[4] The Court's failure to clearly articulate and enforce the legal standards it has set forth leaves many state-level criminal justice actors—primarily prosecutors—with insufficient guidance as to how to adhere to the substantive dictates of the Eighth Amendment for the use of the death penalty: limiting its application to those defendants who not only commit the most heinous crimes, but who are also least deserving of mercy from both a moral and legal standpoint. Indeed, as many prosecutors struggle to hack through the doctrinal thicket, their use of the death penalty has become increasingly motivated by, or susceptible to, political, financial, and administrative pressures, despite the Court's explicit (though inconsistently enforced) signaling that such practices are unconstitutional.

Section 27.3 of this chapter provides a description of the sources of error in the administration of capital punishment and the reasons for their persistence, and then summarizes recent research focused on detecting those errors in death penalty cases. Section 27.4 presents a proposal targeted at curbing prosecutorial overreaching in capital cases. The proposal develops several cost-shifting mechanisms that should discipline prosecutors' use of the death penalty by having them internalize more of the costs associated with the hawkish use of capital punishment.

27.2 The Court, the Constitution, and the Rationalization of the Capital Charging and Sentencing Process

In *Furman v. Georgia* (1972) the Court held, five to four, that all existing capital punishment statutes (including the federal death penalty statute) were unconstitutional as applied, because they failed to articulate any principled basis for decision-makers to distinguish those limited number of defendants sentenced to death from the thousands of other similarly situated defendants who were not subject to the death penalty. All nine Justices wrote separate opinions in *Furman*, leaving the ruling without a clear holding; nevertheless, the concern over the arbitrary imposition of the death penalty was echoed by every Justice on the Court. The concurring opinions authored by Justices Stewart and White provided the narrowest ground for agreement, and therefore were deemed controlling (Baldus, Woodworth, and Pulaski 1990). Justices Brennan, Douglas, Marshall, Stewart, and White all agreed that defendants who were under the sentence of death at that time of the Court's ruling should have their death sentences vacated, in significant part, because of the risk of arbitrariness. Brennan viewed the death penalty as "little more than a lottery system"; Douglas explained that equality in the administration of the death penalty was the key consideration for the Court; Marshall noted that convicted murderers are seldom sentenced to death; Stewart famously noted that "death sentences are cruel and unusual in the same way that being struck by lightning is cruel and unusual"; and White lamented that there was no principled way to distinguish those who received the death penalty from those who did not.

Furman's holding came as a shock to many legal analysts because a year earlier, in *McGautha v. California* (1971), Justice Harlan, writing for the majority of the Court, believed that it was impossible to develop a legal formula capable of distinguishing the worst-of-the-worst cases from the vast majority of murder cases that were not capitally prosecuted, and as a result, the unstructured sentencing authority of juries did not violate defendants' due process rights. In contrast, *Furman* deemed the broad, unbridled discretion afforded to both prosecutors and capital juries as violative of the Eighth Amendment's prohibition against cruel and unusual punishment, but the Court's ruling left open the door for states to devise their own statutes that would, ostensibly, pass constitutional muster (Baldus, Woodworth, and Pulaski 1990; Haines 1996).

When the Court later approved the modified guided-discretion death penalty statutes in *Gregg v. Georgia* (1976), *Jurek v. Texas* (1976), and *Proffit v. Florida* (1976), and invalidated the mandatory death penalty statutes in *North Carolina v. Woodson* (1976) and *Roberts v. Louisiana* (1976), it underscored that not only must the death penalty be reserved for the worst-of-the-worst offenses, but even among that limited group of persons, the death penalty is only permissible for the most culpable offenders. The *Gregg* Court expressly recognized that the primary concern in *Furman* was the arbitrary and capricious manner in which defendants were being condemned to death.[5] The Court was also confident that the guided-discretion statutes enacted after *Furman* would result in greater consistency in the administration of the death penalty.

The Court's assumption, made without an evidentiary basis, that the heightened procedural regulation approach to capital punishment would satisfy the Eighth Amendment was unfortunate but unsurprising considering the fact that Georgia's statute, which was approved in *Gregg*, was closely modeled on "an untested innovation in 1962" by ALI (ALI 2009, 4). Neither the ALI, the state of Georgia, nor the Court had any reliable evidence as to whether the guided-discretion statute presented to the Court in *Gregg* was capable of eliminating or sufficiently reducing the rampant arbitrariness (and potential bias) in death penalty charging-and-sentencing practices that the Court found unconstitutional in *Furman*. Compounding the problem is the fact that, in the years since, the Court has both refused to carefully police adherence to the general dictate of *Furman* and refused to test *Gregg*'s assumption that the guided-discretion statutes would result in rational and consistently imposed death sentences (Smith 2012, 249). Instead, the Court has continually focused its attention on whether state statutes sufficiently narrowed the class of death-eligible defendants (*Godfrey v. Georgia* 1980, 420; *Walton v. Arizona* 1990, 639), what types of evidence the trier-of-fact was allowed to consider and how it could be considered (*Lockett v. Ohio* 1978, 586; *Eddings v. Oklahoma* 1982, 104; *Walton v. Arizona* 1990, 639; *Smith v. Texas* 2004, 37; *Kansas v. Marsh* 2006, 163), and which crimes and defendants were beyond the reach of the death penalty (*Coker v. Georgia* 1977, 584; *Eberheart v. Georgia* 1977, 917; *Tison v. Arizona* 1987, 137; *Atkins v. Virginia* 2002, 304; *Roper v. Simmons* 2005, 551; *Kennedy v. Louisiana* 2008, 407).

27.3 Prevalence and Sources of Capital Error

One of the strongest criticisms of the death penalty is that innocent people may have been wrongly executed. Not a single criminal justice official has gone on record admitting a wrongful execution (Radelet and Bedau 1998), but the lack of a formal admission is unsurprising, considering the professional, legal, and financial repercussions of such a revelation for the states and localities in which the wrongfully convicted are executed (Kirchmeier 2006). Prosecutors also have very little incentive to refrain from wrongdoing in murder cases because such misconduct has been treated with significant leniency (Rosen 1987; Scheck et al. 2000; Weinburg 2003).[6] These obstacles notwithstanding, scholars have produced compelling evidence that at least twenty-two innocent persons came within seventy-two hours of being executed and twenty-three persons believed to be innocent were executed (Bedau and Radelet 1987; Radelet, Bedau, and Putnam 1992). Relatedly, the risk of mistaken executions has not appeared to dissipate over time. From 1973–2014, there were 150 death row inmate exonerations, or roughly one exoneration for every nine executions (Dieter 2015; Gross et al. 2005).

While concern over the wrongful conviction of factually innocent individuals has garnered the most media attention and public scrutiny over the last several decades, other types of legal errors are highly prevalent in the capital charging-and-sentencing process (Radelet and Borg 2000). Two comprehensive studies on appellate review of capital cases reveal rampant *reversible* (i.e., harmful) error. Over two-thirds of the approximately 4,500 death sentences imposed from 1973–1995 that received appellate review were overturned (Liebman et al. 2000). Moreover, three rounds of inspection were necessary to detect a significant portion of the mistakes (Liebman et al. 2000).[7] These errors placed many defendants at risk for wrongful conviction because 82 percent of death sentences overturned resulted in a sentence less than death upon retrial (Liebman et al. 2000), and 7 percent were found to be innocent of a capital crime (Gelman et al. 2004; Liebman 2000).[8] A recent study of 368 capital habeas petitions filed in federal court from 2000–2002—constituting 60 percent of all capital habeas filings during that period—discovered that capital habeas petitions had seven times as many claims of trial error as non-capital petitions and were *thirty-five* times more likely to be granted relief (King and Hoffmann 2011, 147). The most common reasons for reversal in both capital and non-capital murder cases are eyewitness error, prosecutorial and police misconduct, false or coerced confessions, ineffective assistance of counsel, and perjury (Gross 1996). Error rates were greatest in jurisdictions that impose death sentences at higher rates, have trial judges subject to highly partisan popular elections, and impose death sentences in cases that are not highly aggravated (Gelman et al. 2004).

But judicial politics cannot account for these high reversal rates. Ninety percent of death penalty reversals were granted by judges who were elected in jurisdictions with strong support for the death penalty, and therefore potentially subject to retaliation by the electorate, and more than half of the remaining reversals were granted by federal judges appointed by Republican presidents with strong law-and-order agendas (Gelman et al. 2004, 222). Furthermore, judges hearing cases at the state post-conviction stage often reverse death sentences that were imposed in *their own* court at the trial stage, despite strong incentives to approve capital verdicts absent clear flaws with a demonstrable capacity to skew the outcome (Liebman 2002). As William Stuntz (2011) has explained, the limitations on police and prosecutors established by the Bill of Rights are easy to evade, and the promise of the Equal Protection Clause was never delivered. In fact, 60 percent of defendants sentenced to death had their errors deemed "harmless/non-prejudicial" at one of the three stages of review (Liebman 2002, 80). The U.S. Supreme Court has only identified a small class of errors, called structural errors, that it has deemed to be harmful per se because such errors are related to fundamental rights involving the actual framework in which the trial operated, and not simply the process itself (*Arizona v. Fulminante* 1991, 279). In contrast, the prejudicial impact of all non-structural errors is assessed on a case-by-case basis against the totality of the evidence (*Chapman v. California* 1967, 18). Moreover, collateral review of constitutional non-structural error is currently governed by a different (and more government-friendly) standard than direct appellate review, permitting the government to demonstrate, more easily, that the alleged error was harmless (*Brecht v. Abrahamson* 1993, 619).

This distinction between automatic reversal for structural errors and harmless error review for non-structural errors was recently muddied by the Court in *Weaver v. Massachusetts* (2017). According to *Weaver*, a structural error analysis is contingent upon how and when the claim of error is raised. When a defendant fails to preserve a claim of structural error by making a timely objection during trial, and later attributes this failure to ineffective assistance of counsel, the non-structural constitutional error standard governs. In other words, to prevail, the defendant must show, but for counsel's unprofessional errors, there is a reasonable probability that the outcome of the trial would have been different *because of the presence of structural error*. In contrast, had defendant's counsel raised a timely objection to the structural error at trial, the defendant would not have been required to show the actual effect of the structural error; the defendant would have been entitled to automatic reversal once he proved the error occurred.[9]

27.4 Surveying the Reform Landscape

Analysts have suggested numerous reforms aimed at either explicitly restricting the breadth of prosecutorial discretion or better illuminating and policing prosecutors' discretionary choices. While some of these proposals specifically focus on capital charging-and-bargaining dynamics (Hoffman, Kahn, and Fisher 2000–2001; Liebman 2002; Schornhorst 1987), the vast majority apply to charging-and-bargaining more broadly (Bar-Gill and Ben-Shahar 2009; Barkow 2009; Bibas 2009, 2011; Bowers 2008; Dervan 2011; Fairfax 2009; Gazal-Ayal 2005–2006; Gold 2011; Misner 1996; Stuntz 2004). The proposals can generally be categorized as *external* or *internal*.

27.4.1 External Reforms

External reforms highlight the intervention of legislatures, judges, community organizations, voters, victims, and their families (Bibas 2009). These proposals often take the form of narrower crime definitions (Bowers 2008; Sharon 2011), limits on plea bargaining discounts (Dervan 2011; Gazal-Ayal 2005–2006), elimination of statutory minimums (Bowers 2008; Schulhofer 1992; Stuntz 2001), compulsory broad pre-trial discovery requirements (Liebman 2000, 2002), external review of pleas and sentences (Hoffman, Kahn, and Fisher 2000–2001; Horowitz 1997; Stuntz 2004), stricter reporting requirements of discretionary choices (Misner 1996; Liebman 2002), stronger and consistent disciplinary actions for prosecutorial misconduct (Gershowitz 2009; Gross 1996; Scheck, Neufeld, and Dwyer 2000; Weinburg 2003), improved funding and training for defense counsel (Bibas 2009, 2012; Liebman 2002), the creation of a *statewide* elite capital punishment team to litigate all capital cases across the state (Smith 2011), the creation of a *national* elite capital punishment team to litigate capital trials across the nation (Gershowitz 2014), imposing a ceiling on the number of capital prosecutions that can be sought in each jurisdiction (Gershowitz 2007a), and requiring prosecutors to post a "bond" when pursuing a capital case that would be returned to the jurisdiction if the case is not overturned on appeal (Gershowitz 2007b; Misner 1996). These proposals have been characterized as naive for being too "blunt," ignoring history, and neglecting how institutional cooperation and competition typically create strong incentives for legislatures and judges to maximize prosecutorial discretion in order to minimize costs and workloads (through plea bargaining) while still appearing tough on crime (Misner 1996, 765; Rosen 1987, 773–742; Stuntz 2001, 523).

Perhaps the most consistently advocated legal reform addressing the breadth of prosecutorial discretion in capital charging is the narrowing of capital statutes. Narrowly defining death eligibility, proponents of this approach argue, will render capital charging more consistent with the spirit of *Furman*. For example, some have argued that (1) capital statutes should be restricted to only encompass between 5 to 10 percent of murders, (2) statutory aggravating factors that are only responsible for a very small percent of death sentences should be excised, (3) the motivation behind statutory aggravators that focus on defendant and victim characteristics independent of the circumstances of the crime should be subject to closer scrutiny, and (4) capital statutes that result in the death sentencing of less than 20 percent of death-eligible murderers should be invalidated (Sharon 2011; Shatz and Rivkind 1997).[10]

Proposals focused on narrowing the pool of eligible offenders for the death penalty suffer from several important shortcomings. First, they ignore the Supreme Court's repeated refusal over the past four decades to establish firm culpability thresholds for capital cases. In *Zant v. Stephens* (1983), for example, the Court explicitly held that the purpose of aggravating factors in capital statutes is to narrow the class of death-eligible cases, not to channel discretion at the penalty phase. Scholars have agreed with the Court's reasoning: such efforts would simply replicate line-drawing problems (Kennedy 1988, 1431–1433). In fact, both the U.S. Supreme Court and state supreme courts have approved of juries at the penalty phase considering additional aggravating circumstances not enumerated in the applicable capital statute when at least one statutorily defined element has been proven beyond a reasonable doubt (*Wainwright v. Goode* 1983, 78). Second, precisely crafted capital statutes may reduce the ability of prosecutors to pursue the death penalty in marginally aggravated cases—which should have some impact on error rates—but they largely fail to address other common types of error (e.g., racial bias, availability of defenses, suppression of exculpatory/impeachment evidence, etc.) (Forst 2004; Gross 1996; Lanier and Acker 2004; Natapoff 2006; Radelet, Bedau, and Putnam 1992; Scheck, Neufeld, and Dwyer 2000; Shatz and Rivkind 1997). Third, these narrowing proposals fail to link the exercise of prosecutorial discretion to fiscal accountability, which is much more likely to resonate with legislators, judges, and voters (Thaxton 2013). Finally, these proposals assume that criminal law actual drives criminal punishment, when in fact there is good reason to believe the opposite. In our current system, "law on the streets" may remain unchanged even as substantive law changes dramatically (Stuntz 2001). And this may be particularly true in the capital charging-and-sentencing context. Empirical studies consistently reveal that "legal rules" only explain a modest proportion of variation in actual charging and sentencing outcomes in death penalty cases (Berk, Weiss, and Boger 1993; Nakell and Hardy 1987; Thaxton 2017).[11] According to Black (1984, 20), legal rules are important under two conditions: when cases are socially similar or when the potential punishment is trivial. Legal doctrines and facts are often ambiguous with uncertain applications, and legal officials frequently disregard the written law, so the predictive power of rules is questionable. In discussing prosecutorial discretion, Ramsey (2002, 1318) explains that "discretion can never be completely formulaic. Holes will exist even in the tightest net of legal and ethical rules—holes that must be filled by the attorney's own judgment."

Criticisms notwithstanding, certain of these proposals—with slight modifications—may gain traction in the capital context due to the current political climate, as legislators and judges revaluate criminal justice priorities in the face of serious budget and manpower constraints. Such reforms may also be consistent with much of the Court's death penalty jurisprudence for the past four decades, which has underscored that death is qualitatively different from all other forms of punishment and requires extraordinary procedural protection against error (*Furman v. Georgia* 1972, 238; *Kennedy v. Louisiana* 2008, 407).

27.4.2 Internal Reforms

Internal proposals concentrating attention on policies and practices within prosecutor offices—such as intra-office guidelines pertaining to non-compulsory pre-trial discovery rules, limits on bargain "discounts," cooling off periods for more serious crimes, default rules that benefit defendants when plea agreement terms are ambiguous, and heightened training/supervision of "front-line prosecutors"—have become increasingly popular (Barkow 2009; Bibas 2009, 2011; Liebman 2002; Meares 1995; Misner 1996). Yet it remains unclear just how effective many of these proposed reforms would be for non-routine cases with high political and financial stakes, such as murder cases. High profile cases are typically subject to greater internal scrutiny/review by supervisorial staff, and prosecutors have less incentive (and less leeway) to offer substantial bargaining discounts. The reduced desire or ability of prosecutors to grant defendants large sentence discounts for crimes that are subject to high penalties, especially high mandatory minimums, is likely to lead these defendants to test their chances at trial, irrespective of departmental policies aimed at curbing gross prosecutorial overreaching (White 2006). This may be especially true in the capital context because the central contested issue is not the probability of conviction; rather it is the likelihood of a death sentence or sentence greater than the statutory minimum at the penalty phase, and perhaps even the expected likelihood of execution (Alschuler 2009; Ehrhard-Dietzel 2012).

Useful reforms therefore must raise the costs of making foreseeable errors in capital charging (Misner 1996; Stuntz 2001). Current capital charging-and-sentencing systems make trial error virtually costless to prosecutors—and to a lesser extent the capital defense bar[12]—because proper feedback mechanisms from appellate and post-conviction stages to trial actors are nearly non-existent. Professor James Liebman (2002, 324–325) has explained that "[t]rial-level actors benefit from the mistakes, but do not internalize the costs of those mistakes. The psychological benefit of each death sentence is high, but the cost of each mistake is low." Defeats at trial are vivid in the minds of the public, so prosecutors and police have strong incentives to search for ethically suspect ways to win marginal cases,[13] while knowing that low-status "front-line" attorneys in the Attorney General's office will be blamed for reversals and neither themselves nor other local officials will be required to answer to the full electorate for the cost of error correction (which is currently subsidized by state and federal governments) (Alarcón and Mitchell 2010; Liebman 2002). "Capital cases get off track from the start," according to Liebman (2002, 324), "where a capital conviction or sentence is a stretch given the evidence and the mitigating circumstances." By adequately discouraging poor screening decisions with respect to guilt *and* punishment, we could substantially reduce not only high error correction costs (Bowers 2008, 1179; Gazal-Ayal 2005–2006, 2306), but also the greater expense associated with pre-trial and trial stages of capital cases (Thaxton 2013).

27.5 A "Frugal" Proposition

In an effort to avoid several of the aforementioned shortcomings of existing proposals aimed at curbing prosecutorial overreaching in capital cases, I propose a modest reform that may be especially effective in shifting some of the costs of inadequate charge screening, while still allowing prosecutors to retain discretion in seeking the death penalty. As noted earlier, my proposal requires an additional layer of (non-binding) review of death charging decisions, and pairs this review with *financial* and *administrative* cost-shifting mechanisms. Also recall that my suggested disincentives for prosecutorial overreaching in capital cases take the form of holding jurisdictions financially liable for appellate costs (direct and collateral review) and holding prosecutors administratively responsible for litigating these cases, as counsel of record, on appeal.

These cost-shifting mechanisms are triggered when the prosecutor rejects the non-binding negative recommendation of an external capital charging screening committee. Some additional manpower and expense are required, but the proposal should be feasible due to the infrequency of potential capital murder cases, relative to other serious violent felonies.

The proposed reform is modeled after the federal death penalty system's requirement that federal prosecutors submit information on *all* death-eligible cases, irrespective of the prosecutor's intent seek the death penalty in those cases, and obtain prior approval from the Attorney General to pursue the death penalty (the "federal protocol").[14] The federal protocol was adopted in 1995 following the enactment of the Federal Death Penalty Act of 1994. According to the Justice Department, it was "designed to promote consistency and fairness," but the focus was on the detection and elimination of racial/ethnic bias in the imposition of the death penalty, and not on arbitrariness (U.S. DOJ 2001). While the effectiveness of the federal protocol in eliminating racial/ethnic disparities in the imposition of the death penalty at the federal level has been subject to debate,[15] this system provides a promising model to help reduce prosecutorial overreaching in state capital cases, especially when coupled with appropriate financial (dis)incentives.

27.5.1 Data Collection

Under my proposed reform, district attorney offices would be required to keep records on all cases that either result in an indictment for a death-eligible offense or could have been indicted for a death-eligible offense based on the facts of the case. They would also have to regularly report this information to a separate agency (e.g., the state attorney general or the state administrative office of the court).[16] This reporting requirement is not implausible—local police departments are required to regularly submit information on reported crimes and arrests, especially violent crime, to the state bureaus of investigation, who in turn submit this information to the Federal Bureau of Investigation (FBI) for its annual compilation of crime data (FBI 2011). The proposal would require more expansive pre-trial discovery for cases in which the prosecutor intends to seek the death penalty (Cook 2009; Liebman 2002; Schulhofer 1992), including, inter alia, candid assessments of evidentiary problems (especially problems with police investigations and eyewitnesses/confidential informants) and plausible defenses (e.g., insanity, self-defense, etc.) (Gazal-Ayal 2005–2006).[17] This would be akin to the federal protocol, where U.S. Attorneys' capital case submissions must be sent to the Criminal Division and include a death penalty evaluation form for each defendant charged with a capital offense, a detailed prosecution memorandum, copies of indictments, written materials submitted by defense counsel in opposition to the death penalty, and other significant documents and evidence as appropriate. While some scholars have cautioned that extensive discovery rights prior to trial create unnecessary risks to confidential informants, undercover officers, and witnesses (Bibas 2011), these risks can be minimized by preventing defense counsel from having access to these materials but still allowing the review committee to consider the totality of evidence. Defendants also might be asked to waive *Brady* claims and other discovery related claims in exchange for defense counsel having access to *Brady/Giglio*-relevant information at pre-screening conferences (Liebman 2002, 341).

27.5.2 Review Committee Composition

An important consideration is the actual composition of the review committee. Federal attorneys (and judges) are not subject to popular election, whereas the states' Attorneys General, district attorneys, and judges in the most active death penalty states are directly accountable to the electorate. Consequently, the federal review model may not be as robust when implemented at the state level. The lack of prosecutorial and judicial independence may pose significant problems for the fair administration of justice in the capital context (Bright and Keenan 1995); nonetheless, bills have been introduced in a small number of states that require review of prosecutorial discretion in pursuing the death penalty by the attorney general of the state (Murphy 2011). The non-binding nature of the recommendation—whether ultimately at the discretion of the attorney general or the review committee as a whole—may help guard against some of these concerns. Because constructing a committee of individuals who would be properly incentivized to reasonably identify marginal cases might be a difficult task, coordination at the federal level may be particularly meaningful in ensuring an unbiased reviewing body.

States could be made responsible for a percentage of federal post-conviction costs for all capital cases that are overturned at the federal level when the committee initially recommends pursuing the death penalty in a marginal case, perhaps with the exception of ineffective assistance of counsel claims (unless the ineffectiveness claim is tied to forfeiture doctrine/procedural default for important substantive issues). Expenses from federal post-conviction proceedings would most likely be in the form of a proportional reduction in federal assistance to states, but restrictions on sub-recipients to specifically target the relevant counties may be possible as well. The Court has held that the withholding of federal funds to states is generally permissible in the pursuit of general welfare (*South Dakota v. Dole* 1987, 203). This proposal should have the ancillary benefit of encouraging trial judges to approve reasonable defense requests for funding of mental health and investigative experts for both guilt and penalty phases in order to minimize the risk of reversal on appeal.[18]

27.5.3 Substantive Case Review

My proposed system requires the capital review committee to meet with the district attorney in the relevant jurisdiction, front-line prosecutors who are responsible for the case, and defense counsel. Similar to the federal protocol, the committee must consider, inter alia, the prosecution's theory of liability, the strength of the evidence, statutory and non-statutory aggravation, and mitigation,[19] the defendant's role in the capital offense, the defendant's willingness to plead guilty to a life or near-life term of imprisonment, and additional evidence that is probative of guilt and punishment (Federal Judicial Center 2010; Holder 2011). Defense counsel is also afforded the opportunity to present any arguments against pursuing the death penalty against her client. Defense counsel would also have access to the systemic data collected about death-eligible cases, as well as cases that could have been eligible for the death penalty based upon their specific facts, but the prosecutor declined to pursue an indictment for a capital offense.

27.5.4 Recommendations and Ramifications

After full consideration of the evidence, the reviewing committee would make a non-binding recommendation to the prosecutor with respect to pursuing the death penalty.[20] If the committee recommends that the prosecutor not pursue the death penalty and the prosecutor still decides to go forward with the capital prosecution, the legislature would require the prosecutor's jurisdiction to pay a percentage of the state appellate court costs—at both direct appeal and state post-conviction—in any case in which the capital conviction or sentence is ultimately reversed (Liebman 2002, 341). If a prosecutor rejects the committee's recommendation and pursues a capital case that is ultimately disposed of by plea agreement, she would subject her jurisdiction to liability for a larger percentage of pre-trial and trial costs (incurred prior to the plea agreement) in states that have "split-funding" arrangements (e.g., statewide systems that subsidize county prosecution and public defender offices).[21] Prosecutors would be prohibited from engaging in plea negotiations and threatening to seek the death penalty prior to seeking a recommendation from the review committee. This proposal could also easily incorporate the suggestion from other analysts that prosecutors be required to observe a "cooling off" period before seeking a recommendation for the death penalty (Bibas 2011; Liebman 2002).

The proposed review of potential capital cases by screening committees seems plausible from a resource perspective. In fact, there is striking consistency in the proportion of death-eligible cases that were noticed for the death penalty between the federal government and several states. For example, in the five years between 1995 and 2000, federal prosecutors pursued the death penalty in 183 cases and, as required under the federal protocol, submitted information on 683 death-eligible federal offenses (27 percent of death-eligible cases) (U.S. DOJ 2001). During the same time period, Georgia prosecutors sought the death penalty in 256 of 957 death-eligible cases (27 percent) (Paternoster 2007; Thaxton 2009). In Maryland, from 1978–1999, 353 of 1,311 death-eligible cases (27 percent) were noticed for the death penalty (Paternoster and Brame 2003). In the state of Washington, prosecutors sought the death penalty in 87 of

298 death-eligible cases (29 percent) (Beckett and Evans 2016). Prosecutors in Harris County, Texas sought the death penalty in 129 of 504 death-eligible cases (25.5 percent) from 1992–1999 (Phillips 2008).

The effectiveness of my proposed reform will largely turn on the ability of the financial and administrative cost-shifting to adequately disincentivize prosecutorial overreaching in potentially capital cases. The high costs of pursuing the death penalty, even in cases that are eventually resolved by plea agreement, has forced many state and local officials to reconsider the feasibility of maintaining the death penalty either in its current form or at all. Although precise assessments of the cost of capital punishment are lacking because of the diffusion costs, it is undeniable that capital cases are more expensive than comparable non-capital cases at every stage of the process (Thaxton 2013). Moreover, in the past decade, numerous state legislatures have introduced bills to abolish the death penalty or to significantly curtail its scope, in large part because of cost considerations. For example, the high cost of maintaining the death penalty figured prominently in the legislative debates resulting in the repeal of capital punishment in Delaware (2016), Illinois (2011), Maryland (2013), New Hampshire (2019), and New Mexico (2009). Evidence from Maryland suggests that each capital case costs, at minimum, $1 million more than a non-capital case, even after taking into account differential imprisonment costs (Roman et al. 2009). Capital case trial costs were five times greater and appellate costs were four times more expensive than non-capital cases. In California, the difference between the *least expensive* capital murder trial and the *most expensive* non-capital murder trial was $1.1 million, but this figure did not include costs associated with federal review of state capital convictions (California Commission on the Fair Administration of Justice 2008). A comprehensive analysis of federal post-conviction review of death sentences in California suggests that these appeals add between $635,000 and $1.58 million to each capital case beyond state expenditures (Alcarcón and Mitchell 2012). Since Californians reinstated its death penalty in 1978, nearly $4 billion has been spent on the death penalty and thirteen condemned inmates have been executed (more than $300 million per execution). Imprisoning condemned inmates on death row costs Californians an additional $100,663 per inmate per year in 2010 (Alarcón and Mitchell 2011, S107). And while reliable data are not available at the state-level, an analysis of the federal system revealed that capital cases disposed by plea were over four times more expensive than the median non-capital cases, irrespective of methods of disposition (Gould and Greeman 2010). These figures suggest that, at a minimum, cost shifting from states to counties, and from the federal government to the state government (or other sub-state units), could potentially have a significant impact on capital litigation.

Both instituting and gauging the efficacy of administrative cost-shifting is more difficult. Trial courts are much better suited to the task of avoiding erroneous death sentences, yet the costs of legally invalid death sentences are borne by others (Liebman 2002). It is politically profitable for prosecutors to (over)produce death sentences because they benefit from death sentences and do not have to internalize the costs of these legal errors, irrespective of whether those convictions are obtained while violating the statutory and constitutional rights of defendants. For example, nearly 70 percent of death sentences imposed in the United States from 1973–1995 were overturned on appeal (Liebman 2000), with the cost of error correction falling on taxpayers, low-status front-line deputy state attorneys general handling direct and state collateral appeals, appellate court judges, the families and friends of victims who endure repeated delays and retrials, and wrongly condemned inmates (Liebman 2000; Vandiver 2014).

Consequently, more effective feedback to trial officials responsible for errors is a key component of curbing the undisciplined use of the death penalty. Identifying prosecutors, by name, whose mistakes cause reversals and requiring them to appear in the brief and in court as counsel of record in all appellate proceedings is an important first step (Liebman 2002). Relatedly, data must be collected across jurisdictions throughout the state on prosecutors' reversal rates of capital cases, and this information must be disclosed to the public and media via websites and court briefs. This is especially important for prosecutors who repeatedly breach their legal and ethical duties. The reputational ripple effects of administrative cost-shifting may be significant, particularly when coupled with the financial cost-shifting described earlier. Many prosecutors in the most active capital jurisdictions have professional and political aspirations that are undergirded by a "law and order" and "win at all costs" orientation, and career upward mobility is often closely tied to maximizing convictions, irrespective of foreseeable (and sometimes intentional) deficiencies that plague their cases.

Developing an infrastructure that not only requires the collection and dissemination of information about prosecutorial overreaching (and associated misconduct), but also requires prosecutors to participate in vertical representation at the appellate level—much in the same way that public defender offices that adopt a *vertical representation* model operate—holds the promise of internalizing the costs of foreseeable mistakes.[22] My proposal also offers the potential ancillary benefit of an educative effect: by meaningfully participating in direct and collateral review proceedings, prosecutors may gain a deeper understanding of, and appreciation for, the myriad problems that result in harmful legal error and miscarriages of justice in capital cases. I do not believe my proposal risks over-penalizing prosecutors and their jurisdictions for unforeseeable mistakes because of the screening function of the review committee (aided by the participation of defense counsel) that is aimed at minimizing foreseeable arbitrariness, caprice, and bias. It is also worth noting that the substantive and procedural appellate rules require a showing of actual prejudice (i.e., harmful error) for most trial errors occurring in capital cases. As Justice Minon famously noted, "A defendant is entitled to a fair trial, but not a perfect one" (*United States v. Lutwak* 1953, 604). This principle had been codified, previously, in Federal Rule of Criminal Procedure 52(a): "Any error, defect, irregularity, or variance that does not affect substantial rights must be disregarded."

27.6 Conclusion

The legitimacy of the criminal justice system rests, largely, on the ability of its policies and procedures to reduce systematic criminal justice errors.[23] These errors may represent the sum of the costs borne by innocent or disproportionately punished individuals and are typically generated by extreme pressure to solve cases and reduce crime, as well as by the absence of professionalism among criminal justice officials (Forst 2004). The empirical literature on the operation of the death penalty consistently reveals that prosecutors' charging and plea bargaining decisions are plagued by inaccuracy, unreliability, and legally unjustified racial, gender, and regional disparities. The reasons for the persistence of these problems are undoubtedly complex, but largely unconstrained and potentially improperly motivated prosecutorial decision-making has both garnered the attention, and provoked the ire, of death penalty reformers since the Court's initial foray into rationalizing and regulating the death penalty in *Furman*. This essay outlined a proposal aimed at bringing greater accountability to prosecutors' exercise of discretion. It is important to underscore that I deem my proposal to be modest for two reasons. First, while it differs in varying degrees from existing proposals in several respects, it does not present a radical departure from the corpus of proposals articulated by other scholars also concerned with reducing/eliminating both arbitrariness, bias, and other legal errors in the capital charging-and-sentencing process.[24] This conventionality is understandable, in many respects, given the nature of the doctrinal, political, and structural constraints impacting death penalty reform. Any feasible proposal must be developed with full awareness of the (im)practicalities accompanying the administration of the government's ultimate sanction (Bright 1995; Liebman 2002; Steiker and Steiker 2015).

Second, and perhaps more importantly, I deem my proposal as modest because there are important, yet often underappreciated, limitations to technocractic thought—that is, the widely held view among lawyers and legal scholars that problems of law can be reduced to problems of technique (Black 1972). It remains an open question whether the capital punishment process is amenable to the types of "fixes" that have been successfully implemented by the federal government to substantially reduce (to varying degrees) arbitrariness, caprice, and racial/ethnic bias in previously problematic areas such as voting, housing, employment, and public education (Howe 2004). Although broad consensus exists among death penalty analysts concerning the sources of these problems—e.g., overly broad capital statutes, inadequate legal representation, decentralized decision-makers, broad charging and sentencing discretion, and overly restrictive merits review in state and federal habeas proceedings—there is considerable disagreement over whether any set of proposed remedies will produce the desired result.[25] Carol Steiker and Jordan Steiker (1995, 359) explained that "the body of doctrine produced by the Court is enormously complex and its applicability to specific cases [is] difficult to discern; yet it remains unresponsive to the central animating concerns that inspired the Court to embark on its regulatory regime in the first place. Indeed, most surprisingly, the overall effect of twenty-odd years of doctrinal head banging has been to substantially reproduce the pre-*Furman* world of capital sentencing."

All proposals aimed at repairing the "broken system" of capital punishment must fully acknowledge that inherent limitations may exist with respect to altering doctrines, policies, and practices in order to achieve even-handed administration of the death penalty. While establishing "super due process" for criminal defendants on the one hand, and encouraging "tighter" self-monitoring and self-regulation of charging and plea-bargaining practices on the other hand, may provide minor fixes to longstanding problems, it is highly unlikely that more "tinkering" is all that is needed to satisfy the still unfulfilled promise of *Furman* (*Callins v. Collins* 1994, 1141).

NOTES

1. Elected judges may be less likely to require capital trials to strictly follow reliable procedures out of fear that prosecutors will publicly blames judges for losses based on "legal technicalities" (Bright and Keenan 1995). The independence of the judiciary is further diminished by political attacks from both political parties and from candidates for judicial office (Bright 1997).
2. See Misner (1996, 719), arguing the current flaw in the evolving power of the prosecutor is the failure to force her to face the full costs of prosecutorial decisions.
3. Cost-shifting from federal post-conviction proceedings would come in the form of reductions in federal assistance to states, perhaps with restrictions on sub-recipients to specifically target offending jurisdictions.
4. In a dissenting opinion in *Walton v. Arizona* (1990), Justice Scalia highlighted the tension in the Court's capital punishment jurisprudence ruling following *Furman* and opined that the conflict was irreconcilable.
5. The risk of the discriminatory imposition of the death penalty was also emphasized by multiple Justices (Baldus, Woodworth, and Pulaski 1990).
6. Scheck, Neufeld, and Dwyer (2000) reported that not a single prosecutor had been disbarred in the 381 murder convictions that were reversed because of prosecutorial misconduct.
7. Liebman et al. (2000) discovered that state courts overturned 47 percent of death sentences (mostly on direct appeal), while 40 percent of convictions upheld by state courts were subsequently overturned by federal courts.
8. Gelman et al. (2004) report that legal innocence of the death penalty (i.e., ineligibility for the death penalty), as opposed to factual innocence, accounted for 20 percent of reversals on direct appeal.
9. The Court's ruling is somewhat perplexing because the rationale for requiring automatic reversal for structural errors is that the impact of structural errors is unamenable to harmless error analysis. The Court explained that errors are deemed "structural" for different reasons. Some structural errors will always result in fundamental unfairness, whereas others are simply too hard to measure, or they are designed to protect an interest other than preventing erroneous convictions.
10. Dissenting in *McCleskey v. Kemp* (1987), Justices Stevens and Blackmun proposed that Georgia's capital statute be limited to only the most heinous murders to reduce the arbitrary and discriminatory application of the death penalty.

11. "Whether legal rules predict [legal] behavior is an empirical rather than a conceptual question" and "rules are to be taken as an object to be explained and not, themselves, what explains law" (Horwitz 1983, 372).
12. Due to the fact that the pool of capitally charged cases is so large, the capital defense bar tends to neglect capital pre-trial, trial, and direct appellate proceedings, and focuses on procedural issues that are winnable in habeas proceedings rather than the substantive issues that are in play at the earlier stages. This is particularly true because condemned inmates' access to state-compensated attorneys shrinks, so it becomes easier for outside attorneys to intervene at the post-conviction stages (Liebman 2000, 2076).
13. Prosecutors' suppression of possibly exculpatory evidence accounted for 20 percent of reversals in capital cases from 1973–1995 (Gelman et al. 2004; Liebman et al. 2002).
14. The eventual authorization rate for these cases was 87 percent. This protocol was subsequently expanded to require the regular submission of information on all cases in which an indictment was obtained for conduct that *could* have been charged as a capital offense, irrespective of whether the prosecutor sought such an indictment (U.S. DOJ 2001).
15. Compare Baldus (2001) (unwarranted regional and race-of-victim disparities persist in the administration of the federal death penalty) with Klein et al. (2006) (failing to find race-of-defendant or race-of-victim disparities in the administration of the federal death penalty).
16. Misner (1996) suggests that states designate an existing agency or create a separate agency for the purposes of inventorying prosecutorial resources on a county-by-county and statewide basis. Several attempts were made by members of the U.S. Congress to pass a "Racial Justice Act" that would require states to maintain sufficient data on all potential cases in order to allow capital defendants and prosecutors to allege racial bias in capital charging (or the absence thereof) (Baldus, Pulaski, and Woodworth 1994).
17. Gazal-Ayal (2005–2006) posits that prosecutors may overcharge in order to coerce a defendant into accepting a plea to prevent the defendant from arguing legitimate defenses in court.
18. Compare *Britt v. North Carolina* (1971, 227) (explaining that indigent prisoners are constitutionally entitled to "the basic tools of an adequate defense or appeal, when those tools are available for a price to other prisoners") with *Ake v. Oklahoma* (1985, 77) (there is no absolute right to state-funded expert services, but many jurisdictions recognize a limited or conditional right to such experts).
19. Scholars disagree as to whether the presentation of robust mitigation during the penalty phase has a demonstrable impact on death sentences. Whereas Stetler (2018) has argued that the emphasis on mitigation litigation in the penalty phase of capital cases has led to a sharp reduction in death sentences, Smith, Cull, and Robinson (2014) identify recent research discovering that powerful mitigation evidence is ubiquitous among capital defendants who were ultimately executed.
20. From 1995–2000, the Attorney General authorized 87 percent of capital case submissions from U.S. Attorneys (U.S. DOJ 2000). The federal protocol requires approval from the Attorney General for a U.S. Attorney to withdraw the death penalty by ultimately reaching a plea agreement. Given the non-binding nature of the committee's recommendation under my proposal, no such authorization is needed from the reviewing committee; however, my proposal incorporates cost-shifting when a prosecutor rejects the committee's negative recommendation, seeks the death penalty, and ultimately reaches a plea agreement.

21. Carlson et al. (2008) provide descriptions and assessments of states' mixes of state and local funding for trial courts. California provides reimbursements to counties, minus normal salaries and expenses, when criminal trial costs seriously impair the finances of the county. One study discovered that, during a ten-year period, 1996–2005, the state reimbursed counties $45.8 million for twenty-one identifiable homicide trials—eight of which were capital trials. The three most expensive trials ranged from $3.2 million to $10.9 million (California Commission on the Fair Administration of Justice 2008, 129).
22. "Under vertical representation, one attorney represents a single defendant at every stage of the proceedings, rather than assigning specialized procedural stages to different attorneys in the office" (Wright 2011, 1527). Different versions of the vertical representation are operative throughout the country—some models terminate vertical representation after the sentencing phase, while others require the attorney to represent the client through the direct appeal. According to Wright (2011, 1527), "The continued dominance of vertical representation is an indicator that the individualistic ethic is still vibrant in public defense management. It is telling, then, that the use of vertical organizational schemes remains stronger on the public defense side than on the prosecution side."
23. In contrast, a *random error* results from the individual action of criminal justice practitioners or from circumstances beyond the control of the offender. An example of a random error would be the unintentional destruction of inculpatory evidence that permits a clearly guilty offender to evade conviction (Forst 2004).
24. While I have not provided a lengthy review of any single proposal articulated by other scholars, this chapter summarizes the various components of those proposals and reveals overlap with my proposal.
25. For example, Baldus, Pulaski, and Woodworth (1994) refute the claim that discrimination in the imposition of the death penalty is inevitable and impossible to prevent, while Howe (2004) suggests that even an increase in the due process protections—"super due process"—for capital defendants is unlikely to significantly reduce or eliminate racial bias in the capital punishment process. Similarly, Ogletree (2002, 34) cautions that the incremental procedural fixes to the capital punishment system have done little to correct or change the legacy of racial bias in criminal justice administration in America while simultaneously further entrenching the practice of capital punishment by providing the appearance of legality and impartiality.

References

Abbott, James. 2008. "Less Money, More Pain and Injustice." *Fort Worth Star-Telegram*, January 20.

Administrative Office of the United States Courts, Federal Judicial Center. 2010. *Resource Guide for Managing Capital Cases*, Vol. 2: *Habeas Corpus Review of State Capital Convictions*. Washington, D.C.: Government Printing Office.

Ake v. Oklahoma. 1985. 470 U.S. 68.

Alarcón, Arthur L., and Paula M. Mitchell. 2011. "Executing the Will of the Voters: A Roadmap to Mend or End the California Legislature's Multi-Billion-Dollar Death Penalty Debacle." *Loyola of Los Angeles Law Review* 44 (special issue): S41–S224.

Alesina, Alberto, and Eliana La Ferrara. 2014. "A Test of Racial Bias in Capital Sentencing." *American Economic Review* 104(11): 3397–3433.

Alschuler, Albert W. 2009. "Plea Bargaining and the Death Penalty." *DePaul Law Review* 58(3): 671–680.

American Law Institute. 2009. *Report of the Council to the Membership of the American Law Institute on the Matter of the Death Penalty*. Philadelphia: American Law Institute.

Arizona v. Fulminante. 1991. 499 U.S. 279.

Associated Press. 2009. "N.M. Repeals Death Penalty." *Los Angeles Times*, March 19, A15.

Atkins v. Virginia. 2002. 536 U.S. 304.

Baldus, David C. 2001. *Memorandum to the Honorable Russell D. Feingold: Re DOJ Report on the Federal Death Penalty System*. June 11.

Baldus, David C., Charles A. Pulaski, Jr., and George Woodworth. 1994a. "Reflections on the 'Inevitability' of Racial Discrimination in Capital Sentencing and the 'Impossibility' of Its Prevention." *Washington and Lee Law Review* 51(2): 359–430.

Baldus, David C., Charles A. Pulaski, Jr., and George Woodworth. 1994b. "False Attacks on the Racial Justice Acts." *Des Moines Register*, June 7, A9.

Baldus, David C., George Woodworth, and Charles A. Pulaski, Jr. 1990. *Equal Justice and the Death Penalty: A Legal and Empirical Analysis*. Boston: Northeastern University Press.

Banner, Stuart. 2002. *The Death Penalty: An American History*. Cambridge, MA: Harvard University Press.

Bar-Gill, Oren, and Omri Ben-Shahar. 2009. "The Prisoners' (Plea Bargain) Dilemma." *Journal of Legal Analysis* 1(2): 737–773.

Barkow, Rachel. 2009. "Institutional Design and the Policing of Prosecutors: Lessons from Administrative Law." *Stanford Law Review* 61(4): 869–922.

Bedau, Hugo A., and Michael L. Radelet. 1987. "Miscarriages of Justice in Potentially Capital Cases." *Stanford Law Review* 40(1): 21–179.

Berk, Richard A., Robert E. Weiss, and John C. Boger. 1993. "Chance and the Death Penalty." *Law and Society Review* 27(1): 89–110.

Bibas, Stephanos. 2009. "Prosecutorial Regulation versus Prosecutorial Accountability." *University of Pennsylvania Law Review* 157(4): 959–1016.

Bibas, Stephanos. 2011. "Regulating the Plea-Bargaining Market: From Caveat Emptor to Consumer Protection." *California Law Review* 99(4): 1117–1161.

Bibas, Stephanos. 2012. *The Machinery of Criminal Justice*. Oxford: Oxford University Press.

Black, Donald. 1972. "The Boundaries of Legal Sociology." *Yale Law Journal* 81(6): 1086–1100.

Black, Donald. 1984. "Social Control as a Dependent Variable." In *Toward a General Theory of Social Control: Fundamentals*. Vol. 1: *Studies on Law and Social Control*. Edited by D. J. Black, 1–29. New York: Academic Press.

Bowers, Josh. 2008. "Punishing the Innocent." *University of Pennsylvania Law Review* 156(5): 1117–1179.

Brecht v. Abrahamson. 1993. 507 U.S. 619.

Bright, Stephen B. 1995. "The Politics of Crime and the Death Penalty: Not 'Soft on Crime,' but 'Hard on the Bill of Rights.'" *Saint Louis University Law Journal* 39(2): 479–503.

Bright, Stephen B. 1997. "Political Attacks on the Judiciary: Can Justice Be Done amid Efforts to Intimidate and Remove Judges from Office for Unpopular Decisions?" *New York University Law Review* 72(2): 308–330.

Bright, Stephen B., and Patrick J. Keenan. 1995. "Judges and the Politics of Death: Deciding between the Bill of Rights and the Next Election in Capital Cases." *Boston University Law Review* 75(3): 759–835.

Britt v. North Carolina. 1971. 404 U.S. 226.

Callins v. Collins. 1994. 510 U.S. 1141.

Carlson, Alan, Kate Harrison, and John K. Hudzik, 2008. *Adequate, Stable, Equitable, and Responsible Trial Court Funding: Reframing the State v. Local Debate*, Rep. No. 223973. Arlington: Justice Management Institute.

Chapman v. California. 1967. 386 U.S. 18.

Clines, Francis X. 2002. "Death Penalty Is Suspended in Maryland." *New York Times*, May 10.

Coker v. Georgia. 1977. 433 U.S. 584.

Commission on the Fair Administration of Justice. 2008. *Report and Recommendations on the Administration of the Death Penalty in California*. Sacramento.

Cook, Philip J. 2009. "Potential Savings from Abolition of the Death Penalty in North Carolina." *American Law and Economics Review* 11(2): 498–529.

Dervan, Lucian E. 2011. "The Surprising Lessons from Plea Bargaining in the Shadow of Terror." *Georgia State University Law Review* 27(2): 239–298.

Dieter, Richard C. 2009. *Smart on Crime Reconsidering the Death Penalty in a Time of Economic Crisis*. Washington, D.C.: Death Penalty Information Center.

Dieter, Richard C. 2015. *Facts about the Death Penalty*. Washington, D.C.: Death Penalty Information Center.

Eberheart v. Georgia. 1977. 433 U.S. 917.

Eddings v. Oklahoma. 1982. 455 U.S. 104.

Ehrhard-Dietzel, Susan. 2012. "The Use of Life and Death as Tools in Plea Bargaining." *Criminal Justice Review* 37(1): 89–109.

Fairfax, Roger A., Jr. 2009. "Delegation of the Criminal Prosecution Function to Private Actors." *UC Davis Law Review* 43(2): 411–456.

Federal Bureau of Investigation (FBI), United States Department of Justice. 2011. *Crime in the United States, 2010: Uniform Crime Reports*. Washington, D.C.: Government Printing Office.

Federal Death Penalty Act. 1994. 18 U.S.C § 3591.

Foley, Michael A. 2003. *Arbitrary and Capricious: The Supreme Court, the Constitution, and the Death Penalty*. Westport: Praeger.

Forst, Brian. 2004. *Errors of Justice: Nature, Sources, and Remedies*. Cambridge: Cambridge University Press.

Furman v. Georgia. 1972. 408 U.S. 238.

Gazal-Ayal, Oren. 2005–2006. "Partial Ban on Plea Bargains." *Cardozo Law Review* 27(5): 2295–2350.

Gelman, Andrew, James S. Liebman, Valerie West, and Alexander Kiss. 2004. "A Broken System: The Persistent Patterns of Reversals of Death Sentences in the United States." *Journal of Empirical Legal Studies* 1(2): 209–261.

Gershowitz, Adam M. 2007a. "Imposing a Cap on Capital Punishment." *Missouri Law Review* 72(1): 73–124.

Gershowitz, Adam M. 2007b. "Pay Now, Execute Later: Why Counties Should Be Required to Post a Bond to Seek the Death Penalty." *University of Richmond Law Review* 41(4): 861–896.

Gershowitz, Adam M. 2009. "Prosecutorial Shaming: Naming Attorneys to Reduce Prosecutorial Misconduct." *UC Davis Law Review* 42(4): 1059–1106.

Gershowitz, Adam M. 2014. "An NTSB for Capital Punishment." *Texas Tech Law Review* 47(1): 151–177.

Glossip v. Gross. 2015. 136 S. Ct. 2726.

Godfrey v. Georgia. 1980. 446 U.S. 420.

Gold, Russell M. 2011. "Promoting Democracy in Prosecution." *Washington Law Review* 86(1): 69–124.

Gould, Jon B., and Lisa Greenman. 2010. *Report to the Committee on Defender Services Judicial Conference of the United States: Update on the Cost and Quality of Defense Representation in Federal Death Penalty Cases*. Washington, D.C.: Government Printing Office.

Gregg v. Georgia. 1976. 428 U.S. 153.

Gross, Samuel R. 1996. "The Risks of Death: Why Erroneous Convictions Are Common in Capital Cases." *Buffalo Law Review* 44(2): 469–500.

Gross, Samuel R., Kristen Jacoby, Daniel J. Matheson, Nicholas Montgomery, and Sujata Patil. 2005. "Exonerations in the United States, 1989 through 2003." *Journal of Criminal Law and Criminology* 95(2): 523–560.

Haines, Herbert H. 1996. *Against Capital Punishment: The Anti-Death Penalty Movement in America, 1972–1994*. Oxford: Oxford University Press.

Hoffman, Joseph L., Marcy L. Kahn, and Steven W. Fisher. 2000–2001. "Plea Bargaining in the Shadow of Death." *Fordham Law Review* 69(6): 2313–2392.

Holder, Eric H., Jr. 2011. *Memorandum to All Federal Prosecutors: Changes to Death Penalty Protocol*. Washington, D.C.: Department of Justice.

Horowitz, John A. 1997. "Prosecutorial Discretion and the Death Penalty: Creating a Committee to Decide Whether to Seek the Death Penalty." *Fordham Law Review* 65(6): 2571–2610.

Horwitz, Allan V. 1983. "Resistance to Innovation in the Sociology of Law: A Response to Greenberg." *Law and Society Review* 17(2): 369–384.

Howe, Scott. 2004. "The Futile Quest for Racial Neutrality in Capital Selection and the Eighth Amendment Argument for Abolition Based on Unconscious Racial Discrimination." *William and Mary Law Review* 45(5): 2083–2166.

Johnson, Dirk. 2000. "Illinois, Citing Faulty Errors, Bars Executions." *New York Times*, February 1, A1.

Jurek v. Texas. 1976. 428 U.S. 262.

Kansas v. Marsh. 2006. 548 U.S. 163.

Kennedy, Randall. 1988. "*McCleskey v. Kemp*: Race, Capital Punishment, and the Supreme Court." *Harvard Law Review* 101(7): 1388–1411.

Kennedy v. Louisiana. 2008. 554 U.S. 407.

King, Nancy J., and Joseph L. Hoffmann. 2011. *Habeas for the Twenty-First Century: Uses, Abuses, and the Future of the Great Writ*. Chicago: University of Chicago Press.

Kirchmeier, Jeffrey L. 2006. "Dead Innocent: The Death Penalty Abolitionist Search for a Wrongful Execution." *Tulsa Law Review* 42(2): 403–435.

Klein, Stephen P., Richard A. Berk, and Laura Hickman. 2006. *Race and the Decision to Seek the Death Penalty in Federal Cases*. Santa Monica: Rand Corporation.

Lanier, Charles S., and James R. Acker. 2004. "Capital Punishment, the Moratorium Movement, and Empirical Questions: Looking beyond Innocence, Race, and Bad Lawyering in Death Penalty Cases." *Psychology, Public Policy, and Law* 10(4): 577–616.

Liebman, James S. 2000. "The Overproduction of Death." *Columbia Law Review* 100(8): 2030–2156.

Liebman, James S. 2002. "Opting for Real Death Penalty Reform." *Ohio State Law Journal* 63(1): 315–342.

Liebman, James S. 2007. "Slow Dancing with Death: The Supreme Court and Capital Punishment, 1963-2006." *Columbia Law Review* 107(1): 1–130.

Liebman, James S., and Peter Clarke. 2011. "Minority Practice, Majority's Burden: The Death Penalty Today." *Ohio State Journal of Criminal Law* 9(1): 255–352.

Liebman, James S., Jeffrey Fagan, Valerie West, and Jonathan Floyd. 2000. "Capital Attrition: Error Rates in Capital Cases, 1973–1995." *Texas Law Review* 78(7): 1839–1865.

Lockett v. Ohio. 1978. 438 U.S. 586.

MacFeely, William S. 2000. *Proximity to Death*. Boston: Norton.

McCannon, Bryan C. 2013. "Prosecutor Elections, Mistakes, and Appeals." *Journal of Empirical Legal Studies* 10(4): 696–714.

McGautha v. California. 1971. 402 U.S. 183.

McCleskey v. Kemp. 1987. 481 U.S. 279.

Meares, Tracey L. 1995. "Rewards for Good Behavior: Influencing Prosecutorial Discretion and Conduct with Financial Incentives." *Fordham Law Review* 64(3): 851–920.

Misner, Robert L. 1996. "Recasting Prosecutorial Discretion." *Journal of Criminal Law and Criminology* 86(3): 717–777.

Murphy, Russell G. 2011. "Execution Watch: Mitt Romney's 'Foolproof' Death Penalty Act and the Politics of Capital Punishment." *Suffolk University Law Review* 45(1): 1–28.

Nakell, Barry, and Kenneth A. Hardy. 1987. *The Arbitrariness of the Death Penalty*. Philadelphia: Temple University Press.

Natapoff, Alexandra. 2006. "Beyond Unreliable: How Snitches Contribute to Wrongful Convictions." *Golden Gate University Law Review* 37(1): 107–129.

Newport, Frank. 2011. "In U.S., Support for Death Penalty Falls to 39-Year Low." *Gallup Poll News Service*, October 13.

North Carolina v. Woodson. 1976. 428 U.S. 280.

Ogletree, Charles J., Jr. 2002. "Black Man's Burden: Race and the Death Penalty in America." *Oregon Law Review* 81(1): 15–38.

Paternoster, Raymond, and Robert Brame. 2003. *An Empirical Analysis of Maryland's Death Sentencing System with Respect to the Influence of Race and Legal Jurisdiction*. College Park: University of Maryland.

Paternoster, Raymond. 2007. *The Death Penalty in Georgia, 1995–2004*. College Park: University of Maryland.

Phillips, Scott. 2008. "Racial Disparities in the Capital of Capital Punishment." *Houston Law Review* 45(3): 807–840.

Proffit v. Florida. 1976. 428 U.S. 242.

Radelet, Michael L., and Hugo A. Bedau. 1998. "The Execution of the Innocent." *Law and Contemporary Problems* 61(4): 105–124.

Radelet, Michael L., and Marian J. Borg. 2000. "The Changing Nature of Death Penalty Debates." *Annual Review of Sociology* 26(1): 43–61.

Radelet, Michael L., Hugo A. Bedau, and Constance E. Putnam. 1992. *In Spite of Innocence: Erroneous Convictions in Capital Cases*. Boston: Northeastern University Press.

Ramsey, Carolyn B. 2002. "The Discretionary Power of Public Prosecutors in Historical Perspective." *American Criminal Law Review* 39(4): 1309–1394.

Roberts v. Louisiana. 1976. 428 U.S. 325.

Roman, John K., Aaron Chalfin, and Carly R. Knight. 2009. "Reassessing the Cost of the Death Penalty Using Quasi-Experimental Methods: Evidence from Maryland." *American Law and Economics Review* 11(2):530–74.

Roper v. Simmons. 2005. 543 U.S. 551.

Rosen, Richard A. 1987. "Disciplinary Sanctions against Prosecutors for Brady Violations: A Paper Tiger." *North Carolina Law Review* 65(2): 693–744.

Samuels, Ray. 2008. "Readers Forum: Capital Punishment Is a Costly Mistake." *Contra Costa Times*, December 19.

Scheck, Barry, Peter Neufeld, and Jim Dwyer. 2000. *Actual Innocence: Five Days to Execution and Other Dispatches from the Wrongfully Convicted*. New York: Doubleday.

Schornhorst, F. Thomas. 1987. "Preliminary Screening of Prosecutorial Access to Death Qualified Juries: A Missing Constitutional Link." *Indiana Law Journal* 62(2): 295–332.

Schulhofer, Stephen J. 1992. "Plea Bargaining as Disaster." *Yale Law Journal* 101(8): 1979–2010.

Sharon, Chelsea Creo. 2011. "The Most Deserving of Death: The Narrowing Requirement and the Proliferation of Aggravating Factors in Capital Sentencing Statutes." *Harvard Civil Rights Civil Liberties Law Review* 46(1): 223–252.

Shatz, Steven F., and Nina Rivkind. 1997. "The California Death Penalty: Requiem for *Furman*?" *New York University Law Review* 72(6): 1283–1343.

Smith, Robert J. 2012. "The Geography of the Death Penalty and Its Ramifications." *Boston University Law Review* 92(1): 227–290.

Smith, Robert J., Sophie Cull, and Zoe Robinson. 2014. "The Failure of Mitigation?" *Hastings Law Journal* 65(5): 1221–1256.

Smith, Stephen F. 2011. "Localism and Capital Punishment." *Vanderbilt Law Review En Banc* 64: 105–121.

Smith v. Texas. 2004. 543 U.S. 37.

South Dakota v. Dole. 1987. 483 U.S. 203.

Steiker, Carol S., and Jordan M. Steiker. 1995. "Sober Second Thoughts: Reflections on Two Decades of Constitutional Regulation of Capital Punishment." *Harvard Law Review* 109(2): 355–438.

Steiker, Carol S., and Jordan M. Steiker. 2005. "A Tale of Two Nations: Implementation of the Death Penalty in Executing versus Symbolic States in the United States." *Texas Law Review* 84(7): 1869–1928.

Steiker, Carol S., and Jordan Steiker. 2014. "Lessons for Law Reform from the American Experiment with Capital Punishment." *Southern California Law Review* 87(3): 733–784.

Steiker, Carol S., and Jordan M. Steiker. 2015. "The American Death Penalty and the (In) Visibility of Race." *University of Chicago Law Review* 82(1): 243–517.

Stetler, Russell. 2018. "The Past, Present, and Future of the Mitigation Profession: Fulfilling the Constitutional Requirement of Individualized Sentencing in Capital Cases." *Hofstra Law Review* 46(4): 1161–1256.

Stevens, John Paul. 2010. "On the Death Sentence." *New York Review of Books*, December 10.

Stewart, Rebecca. 2011. "Number Who Prefer Death Penalty on Decline." *CNN News Polls*, October 12.

Stuntz, William J. 2001. "The Pathological Politics of Criminal Law." *Michigan Law Review* 100(3): 505–600.

Stuntz, William J. 2004. "Plea Bargaining and Criminal Law's Disappearing Shadow." *Harvard Law Review* 117(8): 2548–2569.

Stuntz, William J. 2011. *The Collapse of American Criminal Justice*. Cambridge, MA: Harvard University Press.

Thaxton, Sherod. 2009. *The Social Geometry of Death: Social Structure and Capital Punishment in Georgia, 1993–2000*. Ph.D. dissertation, Emory University, Atlanta.

Thaxton, Sherod. 2013. "Leveraging Death." *Journal of Criminal Law and Criminology* 103(2): 475–552.

Thaxton, Sherod. 2017. "Disciplining Death: Assessing and Ameliorating Arbitrariness in Capital Charging." *Arizona State Law Journal* 49(1): 137–221.

Thaxton, Sherod. 2018. "Disentangling Disparity: Exploring Racially Disparate Effect and Treatment in Capital Charging." *American Journal of Criminal Law* 45(1): 95–166.

Tison v. Arizona. 1987. 481 U.S. 137.

United States Department of Justice. 2000. *The Federal Death Penalty System: A Statistical Survey, 1988–2000*. Washington, D.C.: Government Printing Office.

United States Department of Justice. 2001. "The Federal Death Penalty System: Supplementary Data, Analysis and Revised Protocols for Capital Case Review." *Federal Sentencing Reporter* 14(1): 40–48.

United States v. Lutwak. 1953. 344 U.S. 604.

Vandiver, Margaret. 2014. "The Impact of the Death Penalty on the Families of Homicide Victims and of Condemned Prisoners." In *America's Experiment with Capital Punishment: Reflections on the Past, Present, and Future of the Ultimate Penal Sanction*. Edited by James R. Acker, Robert M. Bohm, and Charles S. Lanier, 3rd ed., 627–660. Durham: Carolina Academic Press.

Wainwright v. Goode. 1983. 464 U.S. 78.

Walton v. Arizona. 1990. 497 U.S. 639.

Weaver v. Massachusetts. 2017. 137 S. Ct. 1899.

Weinburg, Steve. 2003. *Harmful Error: Investigating America's Local Prosecutors*. Washington, D.C.: Center for Public Integrity.

White, Welsh S. 2006. *Litigating in the Shadow of Death: Defense Attorneys in Capital Cases*. Ann Arbor: University of Michigan Press.

Wright, Ronald F. 2009. "How Prosecutor Elections Fail Us." *Ohio State Journal of Criminal Law* 6(2): 581–610.

Wright, Ronald F. 2011. "*Padilla* and the Delivery of Integrated Criminal Defense." *UCLA Law Review* 58(6): 1515–1542.

Zant v. Stephens. 1983. 462 U.S. 862.

Index

Note: Page references followed by a "*t*" indicate table; "*f*" indicate figure.

For the benefit of digital users, indexed terms that span two pages (e.g., 52–53) may, on occasion, appear on only one of those pages.

ABA. *See* American Bar Association
ACCA. *See* Armed Career Criminal Act
accessory prosecution, victim-directed 390–1
accountability courts xxvii, xxxii. *See also* drug courts; veterans courts
  in Australia 197–8
  in Canada 197–8
  charging decisions and 195–6
  due process and 196–7
  focus of 184–5
  future of 199–200
  guiding principles of 183
  justifications for creation of 185–6
  misdemeanor cases and 184–5, 191
  overview of 183–4
  prosecutors' participation in 192–7
  in UK 197–9
ACE (Alternative to Court Experience) 199–200
adolescent offending. *See also* juvenile court
  acceptance of responsibility in 454
  admission of guilt in 454
  adult court transfers in 464
  alleged role in offense and 453
  brain development and 448–50
  charging discretion and 449–52, 460
  dangerousness of threat in 453
  detention and incarceration harms in 463
  developmentally appropriate responses to 452–5
  diversion programs and 450
  drug use, race and 459, 468n.3
  implicit racial bias and perceptions of culpability in 456
  independent recommendations for 454
  NDAA's National Prosecution Standards for 452
  overcriminalization of 449–52
  overview of 447–8, 467
  peer influence in 453
  positive youth development promotion and 465–7
  prosecutorial bias, race and 458
  prosecutors as gatekeepers with 448–62
  racial disparities in treatment of 447–8, 455–62
  racial stereotyping and 460
  residential treatment programs for 463–4
  school-to-prison pipeline, systemic reform opportunities and 460
  sentencing, race and 464
  seriousness of current offense in 453
  societal tolerance for normative 451
  victims' views on 466–7
  violence, race and 459
adult court, juvenile court transfer to 464
advanced metrics of prosecution activity 229
adversarial legal traditions 207–8, 351–2, 365–6
AEDPA (Anti-terrorism and Effective Death Penalty Act) 436

Aggression Replacement Therapy (ART) 466
Air India bombing, 1985 546, 548
Ake v. Oklahoma 576n.18
Alexander, Michelle 252n.9, 336
ALI (American Law Institute) 559
"alienage indifferent" model 440
"alienage neutral" model 437–8
Alliance for Safety and Justice 466
Alschuler, Albert 88–90
altering charges, at trial 129
alternative courts, diversion programs and 157
Alternative to Court Experience (ACE) 199–200
Altman, Heidi 438, 440
ambiguity, prosecutorial role 144–5
American Bar Association (ABA)
  Canons of Professional Ethics of 310
  Criminal Justice Standards of 61, 311
  on duty of candor 322
  Model Rules of Professional Conduct of 136, 139–40, 310–11
  post-conviction standards of 171–4
  professional regulation of prosecutors by 309–12
  Rule 3.6 of 315
  Rule 3.8 of 312, 317–19, 322, 323n.4
  Rule 4.2 of 316–17
  Standards for Guilty Pleas of 80
  Standing Committee on Professional Ethics of 311, 316, 319
  unfulfilled promise of 320–2
American Law Institute (ALI) 559
Andrade, Leandro 334
Anti-terrorism and Effective Death Penalty Act (AEDPA) 436
"appealable error," 163
appeals
  CVRA and 374–5
  misdemeanor cases and 517
  plea bargaining and waivers for 164
  specialized units for 172–3
  testing charges and 70
  for writ of mandamus 374–5, 377
appointments, of chief prosecutors 209, 330
Armacost, Barbara 503
Armed Career Criminal Act (ACCA) 158–9
arrest warrants 62–3
ART (Aggression Replacement Therapy) 466
audits, post-conviction 176–8
Australia
  accountability/drug courts in 197–8
  sentencing in 163
  VIS in 379
autonomy
  discretion and xxviii
  misdemeanor cases and 519
  police-prosecutorial relationships and 11–15
Ayala, Aramis 525–6

Bach, Amy 280
bail determination 525–6
bail funds, community prosecution and 422
bail reform 240, 340–1, 525–6
Bain, James 171
Baldus, David 43
Balko, Radley 38
Bank Secrecy Act 484–5
Bar authorities xxix–xxx, xxxiii. *See also* American Bar Association
  disciplinary enforcement and 314, 323n.3
  disclosure and 319
  media restrictions and 315
  overview of 309, 322–3
  persuasion efforts of 311–12
  plea bargaining and 320
  policy reforms and 311
  professional conduct codes and, adoption and interpretation of 315–20
  professional conduct codes and, limited impact of 312–15
  professional regulation of prosecutors and 309–12
  prosecutorial misconduct and 318

Rule 4.2 and 316–17
unfulfilled promise of 320–2
writings published by 311
Barbaro v. The Queen 167n.12
Barkow, Rachel 328, 481–2
Batson v. Kentucky 141
Beale, Sara Sun 486
Beckett, Katherine 439
Becton, Diana 248
Begin Again program 246
Bell, Michael, Jr. 506
Bell, Wesley 509
Bellin, Jeffrey xxiv, 343n.5
bench trials
opening statements in 122
police officer criminal conduct and 506
testing charges and 68–70
Bennett, Bill 199
Bentley, Paul 197
bias
cognitive 366, 368
diversity of staff limiting 243
implicit, adolescent culpability perceptions, race and 456
implicit, plea bargaining and 80, 88
jury selection and 120
prosecutorial, race, adolescent offending and 458
racial 37, 41, 46–7, 331, 361–2, 448, 452, 462
of witnesses 107–8, 142
Bibas, Stephanos 234
biological materials sampling, coercion and 19–20
Black Lives Matter 67, 341–2
Blackstone, William 492n.11
Blizzard, Robert 233
Blodgett, Jonathan 200–1
body-worn cameras 111–12
Bordenkircher v. Hayes 37–8
Bowman, Frank 336
Brady material 104, 178, 302, 356–7
Brady v. Maryland 356
Brady v. United States 78–9
brain development, adolescence and 448–50
Brazil
consensual justice in 524
judicial authority in 14
pre-trial inquiries in 13
prosecution in 5–6
Brazzi v. Italy 20
Breyer, Stephen 559
Britt v. North Carolina 576n.18
"broken windows" policing 514–16
Bronx Defenders 358
Brown, Darryl 331–2
Brown, Lee 231
Brown, Michael 67, 497–8, 507, 509
Buffalo Drug Treatment Court 191
Buffalo Mental Health Court 191
Buffalo Veterans Treatment Court 190–1
Bulgaria 213, 215, 219
burden of proof
as burdens of production/ persuasion 137–8
equality of arms principle and 137
presumption of innocence and 138
Bush, George H. W. 331
Bush, George W. 434–5

Calamandrei, Piero 4
Campbell's Law 251n.6
Canada
accountability/drug courts in 197–8
appointment of chief prosecutors in 209
course-based training in 220–1
curtailing political influence on chief prosecutor in 210
defense attorneys in 364–5
DPP in 543–4, 552
entrapment and national security cases in 553–4
hiring frontline prosecutors in 211
informants for terrorism cases in 546
integrating training in 221
prosecutor training in 216, 218
Securities Offences Act in 545
Security Intelligence Service Act in 551
terrorism cases and specialized units in 543
video-testimony in 386

Canons of Professional Ethics, ABA 310
capital charging xxxv
  cost-shifting mechanisms and 568–9, 572–3
  data collection and 569–70
  democratic control and 560, 575n.1
  error in, prevalence and sources of 563–5
  external reforms and 565–7
  internal reforms and 567–8
  miscarriages of justice and 560
  overview of 559–62, 574–5
  policy reforms for 560–1, 565–74
  public opinion on 560
  race and 43
  rationalization of 562–3
  review committee for, composition of 570
  review committee for, recommendations and ramification of 571–4
  review committee for, substantive quality of 570–1
  statutes for 566–7
  "super due process" and 575, 577n.25
  trial mistakes and 568, 573
Capone, Al 541, 550–1
career ambitions, courtroom workgroups and 278
Carnelutti, Francesco 29n.8
case assignment, in courtroom workgroups 276
case file. *See* dossier
case-in-chief 125
case screening process
  charging discretion and 40–1, 51–2, 59–60, 520–5
  misdemeanor cases and 522
  plea bargaining and 90
CCTV (closed circuit television) testimony 385–6
charge bargaining 160–1
charging decisions. *See also* testing charges
  accountability courts and 195–6
  checks on 62
  in civil law 129–30
  court records and 520
  criminal law hypothesis and 8
  diversion programs and 195–6
  ECHR on 8, 30n.13
  importance of 35
  judicial supervision of 11
  law enforcement and organizational conflicts over 296–9
  misdemeanor cases and 36, 42, 520–5
  performance metrics for proportionate and fair 238–9
  police officer criminal conduct and 502
  positive law on 7
  "preliminary charge," 6–7, 29n.8
  pre-trial inquiries and 6, 29n.7
  prosecution and 5–9
  sentencing and 39–40, 47–50, 90, 154–8, 560
  specialized units and 262
charging discretion xxvii–xxviii, xxxi, 413, 432
  adolescent offending and 449–52, 460
  case factors in studies on 42
  case screening process and 40–1, 51–2, 59–60, 520–5
  community prosecution and 417
  demographic factors in studies on 42–4
  empirical research on 40–9
  Equal Protection Clause and 36–7
  evidence and 42
  expansion of 38
  freedom in 38, 60–1
  grand juries and 66
  guidelines for 61
  hydraulic displacement of discretion and 39–40
  importance of 35
  institutional racism and 46–7
  legality principle and 524
  legal standards on 36–9
  local factors in studies on 47–9, 51
  mass incarceration and 49–51
  overview of 35–6, 51–3
  performance metrics for 52
  plea bargaining and 37–8, 90, 158

race and 36–7, 49–51
senior prosecutor supervision of 61
social-structural factors in studies on 44–7
state courts and 52
victim cooperation and 42
victim credibility and 44–5
Chemerinsky, Erwin 500
chief prosecutors, hiring 208–11
appointments and 209, 330
curtailing political influence and 209–11
direct public elections and 208–9, 401
children, victim testimony from 383–4
Child Victims' and Child Witnesses' Rights Act (CVCWRA) 385–6
China 554–5
CIUs. *See* conviction integrity units
civil law
charging decisions in 129–30
common law compared to 364
criminal law action compared to 7
dossier in 129
evidence presentation in 127
presumption of innocence in 138
statutory law and 9–10
witnesses in 119–20, 125
civil service, prosecutors in democracy compared to xv–xvi, 404–5
classified information, in national security cases 547–8
Classified Information Procedure Act 547
Clean Slate Act, 2018 530
Clean Slate programs 247–8
clemency xxxii, 154
discretion and 165
post-conviction criminal procedure and 174
Clinton, Bill 187
closed circuit television (CCTV) testimony 385–6
closing statements 130, 142
Code for America 247
coercion
biological materials sampling and 19–20
European Public Prosecutor's Office and 24–6
fair trial rights and 16–18
Coker v. Georgia 167n.10
collaborative models, defense attorneys and 363–4
collateral consequences
of corporate crime prosecution 479–81
court records and 520
legislatures and 328–30
misdemeanor cases and 514–15, 518–19, 527–8
performance metrics for 246–9
plea bargaining and 527–8
collateral review, testing charges and 70
collateral sanctions, plea bargaining and 159–60
Collins, Erin 184–5
Colom, Scott 235–6
colonial era, victims as prosecutors in x
Colorado Justice Review Project 177
Comey, James 503
Commission on the Future of DNA Evidence 176–7
common law 482
altering charges at trial in 129–30
civil law compared to 364
disclosure in 104–6, 113
evidence presentation in 127
reasonable doubt standard in 138
sentencing in 163
communication
interception of 17–19
prosecutor's duties with xxvi
community engagement, performance metrics for 245
community partnerships, performance metrics for 246
community policing 230–1
community prosecution xxxiv
bail funds and 422
charging discretion and 417
court watching groups and 422
democracy deficits and 416
democratic control and 415

community prosecution (*Continued*)
diversion programs and 418–20
downstream 420
goals of 414
healing circles and 419
historical development of 417–18
importance of 415–17
international tribunals and 418
LEAD (Law Enforcement Assisted Diversion) programs and 419
NGOs and 421
office values and structure implications of 423–4
over-enforcement of crimes and 418
overview of 413–15
partnership choices for 420–3
race and 414
reentry and 420
transparency and 416
trust and 414, 416
under-enforcement of crimes and 418
victim relationships in 417–18
community supervision, performance metrics for 239
composite regime, corporate crime and 488
CompStat system, NYPD 230
"concept hagiography," courtroom workgroups and 283, 285
concessions model of plea bargaining 81
conduct of prosecutors. *See* professional conduct codes; prosecutorial misconduct
conflicts of interest 313, 499–500, 504–5, 507, 509, 530–1
police officer criminal conduct and 502
Connors, Timothy 238
consensual justice, Brazil 524
consensus model of plea bargaining 81
consequentialism 137, 139
Conservative Political Action Conference 199
conservatives, mass incarceration and 199
"constructive fault," 476
conviction integrity units (CIUs) xxxii, 172, 174–6
performance metrics and 241–2
convictions. *See also* plea bargaining; post-conviction criminal procedure
capital charging and wrongful 563–5
culture of 355–6
maximizing xv
misdemeanor cases and wrongful 531
for police officer criminal conduct 503
coordinate powers, law enforcement and 292–3
Core Competencies Guide (NDCI) 193–4
corporate crime xxxv
basic rules of liability in 478–9
collateral consequences of prosecuting 479–81
composite regime and 488
"constructive fault" and 476
criminal law limiting principles and 476, 484–7
culpability principle and 485–6
deterrence and 487–8
DPAs and 476–7, 480–1, 489–90
Federal Principles of Prosecution of Business Organizations and 481
incapacitation and 487–8
indictment alternatives in 479–81
legality principle and 484–5
necessity thesis and 477
negligence standard and 488
NPAs (Non-Prosecution Agreements) and 480–1, 489–90
open-textured definitions of 490
overcriminalization and 481–2, 484
overview of 475–8
parsimony and proportionality principles and 486–7
policy reform for 490–1
power and 476
prosecutors' role in enforcement of 487–90
publicly held companies and 487–8
punishment and 477–8, 488–9
rehabilitation and 487

respondeat superior liability and 478–80, 485
Sherman Antitrust Act and 478
strict liability and 488
cost-shifting mechanisms, capital charging and 568–9, 572–3
courtroom workgroups xi, xxix, xxxiii
career ambitions and 278
case assignment in 276
"concept hagiography" and 283, 285
concerns of 279–83
defendants' perceptions of 281–2
defense attorneys in 276, 278–9, 281, 284
definition of 273, 275–6
efficiency issues with 282–3
familiarity issues within 279–80, 284
future research on 285–7
goals of 278–9
hiring and 277–8
judge assignment and 276
methodology of 274–5
models of 276–7
overview of 273–4
person-to-person defense models in 276
public opinion and 279
relationships in 274, 277–8
sponsoring organizations and 278
trial teams and 276, 279–80
variables in 283
court watching groups 422
Coy v. Iowa 385
CPIA (Criminal Procedure and Investigations Act) 126–7
CPS (Crown Prosecution Service) 7, 12–13
Creuzot, John 237
crime, as label xxiii
Crime and Punishment (Dostoevsky) 118
crime rate, violent 227
crime victims' advocates (CVAs) 376–7
Crime Victims' Rights Act (CVRA), 2004 374–5, 383
criminal conduct by police officers. *See* police officer criminal conduct
Criminal Justice Act, 2003, UK 7, 12–13
Criminal Justice Standards, ABA 61, 311
Criminal Law and Cases (Kadish, Schulhofer, Barkow) 481–2
criminal procedure. *See also* post-conviction criminal procedure
legislatures and 338–41
localism and 340–1
state and federal efforts in 339–40
Criminal Procedure and Investigations Act (CPIA) 126–7
cross-examination, of witnesses 126, 128
Crown Court, UK
closing statements in 130–1
CPIA in 126–7
evidence presentation in 126–7
jury trial classification and 121
opening statements in 122
Plea and Trial Preparation Hearing in 125–6
Special Crime and Counter-Terrorism Division and 543
trial seating arrangements in 123, 124*f*
witnesses in 127
Crown Prosecution Service (CPS) 7, 12–13
Cuccinelli, Ken 199
culpability
adolescent offending, implicit racial bias and perceptions of 456
corporate crime and 485–6
legislatures and 483
natural probable causes doctrine and 485–6
Pinkerton doctrine and 485–6
principle of 482–3, 485–6
cumulative disadvantages, plea bargaining and 87–8
CVAs (crime victims' advocates) 376–7
CVCWRA (Child Victims' and Child Witnesses' Rights Act) 385–6
CVRA (Crime Victims' Rights Act), 2004 374–5, 383
cyber investigations, fair trial rights and 17

Damaška, Mirjan 292
data collection, capital charging and 569–70

data storage 112
Davis, Angela J. 37, 406
Davis, Peter 507
death penalty xxxv. *See also* capital charging
  abolition attempts against 559
  capital statutes for 566–7
  costs of 572
  Eighth Amendment and 561–2
  empirical research on 574
  error in, prevalence and sources of 563–5
  external reforms and 565–7
  internal reforms and 567–8
  public opinion on 560
  rationalization of 562–3
Deberry, Satana 340
decarceration specialized court model 185–6
decision-making, prosecutorial 19–22. *See also* charging decisions
declination decisions 520–5
defendant rehabilitation policy 268n.2
defense attorneys xxxiv, 15–16, 19, 22–8, 196–7
  in Canada 364–5
  collaborative models and 363–4
  competence of 359
  in courtroom workgroups 276, 278–9, 281, 284
  data access and 112
  disclosure and trustworthiness of 110
  ethics of offices of 358–9
  fairness and 353–4
  gender of 361–2
  geographical factors and 360
  holistic defender model and 358
  individual factors and 360–1
  in international systems 364–8
  in military justice system 363
  misdemeanor cases, plea bargaining and 529
  no-contact rule and 316–17
  "open file" disclosure and 356
  overview of 351–2, 368–9
  plea bargaining and 77, 354–5, 367–8
  politics of 361
  prosecutorial misconduct and attacks on 142–3
  prosecutors compared to 351
  prosecutors' tensions with 361–3
  race of 361–2
  reform prosecutors and 364
  rewards of 361
  roles of 352–5
  social architecture of offices of 357–60
  in South Africa 365–6
  in specialized units 363
  in Sweden 367
  in UK 365
  in US system 352–63
  victim impact statement and 379
  victim testimony and 383–4
  zealous 358
deferred adjudication 527
deferred prosecution agreements (DPAs)
  corporate crime and 476–7, 480–1, 489–90
  misdemeanor cases and 520–1, 523–4
democracy, prosecutors in civil service compared to xv–xvi, 404–5
democracy deficits 416
democratic control
  capital charging and 560, 575n.1
  community prosecution and 415
  direct public elections of chief prosecutors and 208–9, 401
  election effect and 403–5
  through elections, measuring 401–3
  electoral accountability and xv–xvi, xxxiv, 208–9, 405–6
  in France 406–7
  in Germany 406
  independence and 405–9
  in Italy 406
  overview of 399–400
  police officer criminal conduct and 509
  through prosecutorial decisions, measuring 403–5

prosecutor selection/appointment and 59–60, 145, 153–4, 400–1
transparency and 408, 409nn.8,10
in UK 406–7
U.S. Attorneys' appointment and removal and 402–3
Denmark
course-based training in 220–1
hiring entry-level prosecutors in 213
hiring frontline prosecutors in 211
integrating training in 221
prosecutor training in 216
deontology 137–8
Department of Education, Office for Civil Rights of 460–1
Department of Homeland Security (DHS) 434, 436–7
desistance factors, performance metrics and 239–40
determinate sentencing 39
deterrence, corporate crime and 487–8
DHS (Department of Homeland Security) 434, 436–7
Dietrich v. The Queen 118–19
digital evidence 103–4, 111–14
Director of Public Prosecutions (DPP), Canada 543–4, 552
direct public elections, of chief prosecutors 208–9, 401
disclosure (discovery)
approaches to 104–7
Bar authorities and 319
Brady material and 356–7
broad 108–9
in common law 104–6, 113
competing interests in 107–11
defense attorney trustworthiness and 110
digital evidence and 111–14
ethics and obligations of 319
of exculpatory evidence 66–7, 78–9, 104–7, 547
of incriminating evidence 104–5
judicial authority and 108–10
justification for pre-trial 101–2
of material evidence 319
models of 102
narrow 108–9
in national security cases 547–8
obligations xxxii
"open file," 356
overview of 101–4
plea bargaining and 79, 102
police-prosecutorial relationships and 301–2
policy reform for 111–14
prosecutor trustworthiness and 110
security and 103–4, 111–14
in state courts 102–3, 106, 110–11
technology and 103, 111–14
terminology of 104
time and cost of 102
timing of 105
UK practices of 105–6, 110
of unused evidence 104–5
of witnesses 104–5, 107–8
discretion. *See also* charging discretion
autonomy and xxviii
clemency and 165
in criminal justice xii–xiii
hydraulic displacement of xxvii, 39–40
importance of 59
misdemeanor cases and 514–29
parole and 164–5
recidivism likelihood and 60
sentencing xxvii, 336
shape of xxvii–xxviii
terrorism cases and 542–3
triage and xxvii
discretionary adjudication, prosecution decision-making and 19–22
"discretionary mandatories," race and 335–7
discretionary sanctions, plea bargaining and 159
distributive fairness 134–6
diversion programs xxvii, xxxii. *See also* drug courts; veterans courts
adolescent offending and 450
alternative courts and 157

diversion programs (*Continued*)
charging decisions and 195–6
community prosecution and 418–20
due process and 196–7
focus of 185
future of 199–200
guiding principles of 183
justifications for creation of 185–6
non-US 197–9
overview of 183–4
performance metrics for 236–7
post-adjudication programs and 186
prosecutors' participation in 192–7
sentencing and 154–8
diversity of staff, performance metrics for 243
DNA testing, post-conviction 171, 173–4
domestic violence cases
police-prosecutorial relationships and 294–5
specialized units for, effectiveness of 264–5
Domestic Violence Project, Cleveland 265
Donovan, T. J. 247–8
dossier, in trials 129
Double Jeopardy Clause, Fifth Amendment 332–3
Dougherty, Michael 237
downstream community prosecution 420
DPAs. *See* deferred prosecution agreements
DPP (Director of Public Prosecutions), Canada 543–4, 552
Dripps, Donald 339
Drug Court Office, of Department of Justice 188
drug courts
in Australia 197–8
in Canada 197–8
justification for creation of 186–8
NDCI's *Core Competencies Guide* for 193–4
non-adversarial approach in 189–90
organizational structure of 191–2
origins of 187
prosecutors' participation in 192–7
staffing sessions and 189
team in 189
"Ten Key Components" of 188–9, 192–3
in UK 197–9
veterans courts compared to 191–2
drug sentencing, mandatory minimum sentences and 156, 158–9, 336–7
drug use, adolescent offending, race and 459, 468n.3
duality, prosecutorial role 144–5
due process 37–8, 75–6, 80, 562
accountability courts and 196–7
diversion programs and 196–7
model 119, 287n.5
plea bargaining and 80
super 575, 577n.25
testing charges for 70
violation of 142, 189, 196–7
Due Process Clause 36, 62, 68–9, 292–3
Dupree, Mark 241
duty of candor, ABA on 322

Eagly, Ingrid 437–9, 441
ECHR (European Court of Human Rights) 8, 18, 30n.13
education
performance metrics promoting 245–6
school-to-prison pipeline and 460
Egypt 554
851 enhancements 159, 335
Eighth Amendment, death penalty and 561–2
EIO. *See* European Investigation Order
Eisenstein, James 273, 275–6, 278–9, 283
election effect 403–5
elections, measuring democratic control through 401–3
electoral accountability xv–xvi, xxxiv, 208–9, 405–6. *See also* democratic control
electronically stored information (ESI) 103–4, 111–14
Elkins Act 478
embedded prosecutors, national security cases and 541

empirical research 218
case factors in 42
on charging discretion 40–9
on death penalty 574
demographic factors in 42–4
"gap studies" and 40–1
on judicial discretion 81
local factors in 47–9, 51
on plea bargaining, new directions for 86–8
on plea bargaining, Wave I 81
on plea bargaining, Wave II 81–3
on plea bargaining, Wave III 83–6
social-structural factors in 44–7
entrapment, national security cases and 553–4
entry-level prosecutors, hiring 213–14
EPPO. *See* European Public Prosecutor's Office
equality of arms principle 137
Equal Protection Clause
charging discretion and 36–7
prosecutorial misconduct at jury selection and 141
race and 43
error, capital 563–5
ESI (electronically stored information) 103–4, 111–14
Espionage Act 542
espionage law 550–1
ethics
Canons of Professional Ethics, ABA 310
of defense attorneys' offices 358–9
disclosure obligations and 319
national security/terrorism cases and 549–55
professional conduct codes' limited impact and 312–15
prosecutorial, at trials 136–9
of prosecutors' offices 355–7
regulation of 320–1
Standing Committee on Professional Ethics, ABA 311, 316, 319
Eurodefensor, European Public Prosecutor's Office and need of 27–8
European Court of Human Rights (ECHR) 8, 18, 30n.13
European Investigation Order (EIO)
law enforcement and 22–3
national implementation of 23–4
private parties requesting 22
prosecutorial powers in 22–4
European Public Prosecutor's Office (EPPO)
coercion and 24–6
Eurodefensor and 27–8
human rights and 24–5
independent oversight issues with 26–7
Permanent Chamber of 26–7
procedural rules issues with 27–8
transnational investigative powers of 24–8
Evans, Heather 439
evidence
charging discretion and 42
civil law presentation of 127
common law presentation of 127
digital 103–4, 111–14
exclusionary rule doctrine of Fourth Amendment and 300
exculpatory, disclosure of 66–7, 78–9, 104–7, 547
France and presentation of 127–8
Germany and presentation of 127–8
grand juries and 67
hearsay, in preliminary hearings 64
incriminating, disclosure of 104–5
of innocence, post-conviction 173–4
material, disclosure of 319
plea bargaining and 84
presentation of, in trial 125, 141
protecting 107–8
rebuttal 126
technology and 103
UK and presentation of 126–7
unused, disclosure of 104–5
exceptionalism, national security 549–51
exclusionary rule doctrine, of Fourth Amendment 300

exculpatory evidence, disclosure of 66–7, 78–9, 104–7, 547
executive branch, prosecution and 144, 215–17
exoneration 165–6, 174–5, 531
expediency principle 207–8
expertise xv–xvi. *See also* hiring; training
expert witnesses 125
exploding plea offers 79, 89
expungement 153–4, 165, 247–8, 529–31
external reforms, capital charging and 565–7
extrajudicial sanctions, plea bargaining and 159

facility dogs, for emotional support of victims 386–7
fact bargaining 161
factual innocence 138, 165–6, 515–16
Fair Sentencing Act, 2010 338
fair trial rights
  coercion and 16–18
  cyber investigations and 17
  defense attorneys and 353–4
  international human rights law and 15
  objectives for 134–6
  prosecution interference with, safeguards and 16–19
false guilty pleas 79, 84–5
familiarity, within courtroom workgroups 279–80, 284
family separations, immigration enforcement and 434–5
Fast Track program 435
FCPA Corporate Enforcement Policy 491n.8
federalism, national security cases and 544–5
Federal Principles of Prosecution of Business Organizations 481
Feeley, Malcolm 76, 295, 520
Feeney Amendment 334
Felony Justice (Eisenstein and Jacob) 283
felony reentry prosecutions, immigration enforcement and 435
FFT (Functional Family Therapy) 466
FIA (Formerly Incarcerated Advisory) Board 247
Fifth Amendment
  Double Jeopardy Clause of 332–3
  grand jury indictment and 65
  self-incrimination and 142, 302
firearms cases sentencing, mandatory minimum sentences and 158–9
FIRST STEP Act (Formerly Incarcerated Reenter Society Transformed Safely Transitioning Every Person Act) 200–1
FISA (Foreign Intelligence Surveillance Act) 542
Fisher, George xi
Floyd, George 341–2
Foreign Intelligence Surveillance Act (FISA) 542
Formerly Incarcerated Advisory (FIA) Board 247
Formerly Incarcerated Reenter Society Transformed Safely Transitioning Every Person Act (FIRST STEP Act) 200–1
Fortune v. South Carolina 142–3
Fourteenth Amendment, US 136
  Due Process Clause 36, 62, 68–9, 292–3
Fourth Amendment 62
  exclusionary rule doctrine of 300
Foxx, Kim 235–6, 340
France
  democratic control in 406–7
  discretionary adjudication, prosecution decision-making in 21–2
  evidence presentation in 127–8
  hiring frontline prosecutors in 211
  hiring tests in 213
  penal orders in 133–4
  training with judiciary in 214–15
Freeman, Alexa 500
frontline prosecutors, hiring 211–14
  entry-level 213–14
  selection criteria in 212–13
Functional Family Therapy (FFT) 466
Furman v. Georgia 562–3, 575

gang-related crimes, specialized units for 265–6
"gap studies," 40–1
Garner, Eric 67, 341–2, 507
Garrett, Brandon 531
Gascón, George 247
gender
in charging discretion studies 42–4
of defense attorneys 361–2
disparities by xxx
jury selection and 140
plea bargaining and 43–4, 82, 85
violence based on 263, 376–7, 380
Germany
appointment of chief prosecutors in 209
closing statements in 131
curtailing political influence on chief prosecutor in 210
democratic control in 406
discretionary adjudication, prosecution decision-making in 21–2
evidence presentation in 127–8
German Code of Criminal Procedure 123
penal orders in 133–4
prosecutor's role in trials in 144–5
training with judiciary in 214–15
trial seating arrangements in 123, 124*f*
trial stages in 135*t*
Victims' Rights Amendment in 390
video-testimony in 386
Gershowitz, Adam 235, 251n.7, 293–4, 300
Gilchrist, Peter 242
Ginsburg, Ruth Bader 559
"girl courts," 185
Gold, Russell 300, 406
Goldstein, Stanley 197
Gonzales, Alberto 402–3
Gonzalez, Eric 236, 247–8, 440
Gonzalez, Mark 522–3
Graham v. Florida 167n.10, 447
grand juries xxxi
abolition efforts against 65
authority of 64
charging discretion and 66
criticisms of 66–7
evidence and 67
Fifth Amendment and indictment by 65
historical evolution of 64–5
lay participation in 66
police officer criminal conduct and 502, 507–8
police officer criminal conduct and lack of indictments from 67
policy reforms for 67–8
probable cause hearings compared to 66
probable-cause standard of 67
testing charges and 64–8
transparency and 507
Green, Bruce xxiv–xxv
Gregg v. Georgia 562–3
Groebner, Robert, Jr. 241
Guantanamo Bay detention 548

Haney López, Ian 46
Harlan, John Marshall 66
Harmon, Rachel 303, 503
Haynesworth, Thomas 173–4
healing circles, community prosecution and 419
hearsay evidence, in preliminary hearings 64
Heise, Michael 336
Hemmings, Susan 541, 545, 550, 552–3
hiring xxxii–xxxiii
appointments and 209, 330
chief prosecutors 208–11, 401
courtroom workgroups and 277–8
curtailing political influence and 209–11
direct public elections and 208–9
entry-level prosecutors 213–14
frontline prosecutors 211–14
national consistency in 212
overview of 207–8, 221–3
selection criteria in 212–13
tests in 213
Holder, Eric 179
holistic defender model 358
Hora, Peggy 188

horizontal alignment of law enforcement 292–3
horizontal prosecution models 259–61, 268, 286, 292
Horton, Willie 331
Howell, Babe 522
human rights. *See* international human rights law
human smuggling, immigration enforcement and 435–6
human trafficking, immigration enforcement and 435–6
Hungary 210
Hurtado v. California 66
Hutchinson, Asa 199
hydraulic displacement of discretion xxvii, 39–40
Hynes, Charles 175

ICC (International Criminal Court) 139, 142
ICC (Interstate Commerce Commission) 478
ICE (Immigration and Customs Enforcement) 437
IIRIRA (Illegal Immigration Reform and Immigrant Responsibility Act) 436
"illegal alien punishment" model 439
Illegal Immigration Reform and Immigrant Responsibility Act (IIRIRA) 436
Illinois Uniform Peace Officer Disciplinary Act 501
Immigrant Defense Project 440
Immigrant Legal Resource Center 440
Immigration and Customs Enforcement (ICE) 437
Immigration and Nationalist Act, 1996 437
immigration enforcement xxxiv, 402–3, 547–8, 550–1
  "alienage indifferent" model and 440
  "alienage neutral" model and 437–8
  consultants on 440
  criminal prosecution consequences for 436–41
  family separations and 434–5
  Fast Track program and 435
  federal migration offenses and 431
  felony reentry prosecutions and 435
  human smuggling, human trafficking and 435–6
  "illegal alien punishment" model and 439
  legislatures and 431–2
  mass removals and 436–7, 443n.1
  misdemeanor cases and 433–4, 527
  Operation Streamline and 433–4
  overview of 431–3, 443
  performance metrics and 248–9
  plea bargaining and 86–7, 160
  policy reforms and 432
  prosecution and 433–6
  sentencing and 161
  state laws and 441–2
  Trafficking Victims Protection Act of 2000 and 432, 442
  victims and 442–3
  War on Drugs and 431–2
  witnesses and 442–3
"immigration enforcement" model 438–9
impartiality, judicial authority and 29n.1
implicit bias 331, 361–2, 448. *See also* bias
  adolescent culpability perceptions, race and 456
  checking 458
  plea bargaining and 80, 88
  research on development of 462
  training 243
incapacitation, corporate crime and 487–8
incarceration reduction, performance metrics for 235
incentives, performance metrics and 249–50
incriminating evidence, disclosure of 104–5
independence
  adolescent offending recommendations and 454
  democratic control and 405–9

European Public Prosecutor's Office oversight issues and 26–7
judges' tradeoff with accountability and 407–8
national security cases and prosecutorial 551–2
prosecutors' professional relationships and xxviii–xxx
Independent Police Review Authority 501
indeterminate sentencing 39
informants, in national security cases 546–7
information, victims' rights legislation and 376
innocence, new evidence of, post-conviction 173–4
Innocence Project xvii, 165–6, 177
post-conviction DNA testing and 171
inquisitorial legal traditions 207–8, 351–2, 366–8
In re Dean 379–80
In re Winship 68–9
institutional racism, charging discretion and 46–7
interest group pressure, legislatures and 330–1
internal reforms, capital charging and 567–8
International Criminal Court (ICC) 139, 142
International Criminal Tribunals 132
international human rights law
European Public Prosecutor's Office and 24–5
fair trial rights and 15
terrorism cases and 549–50
international tribunals 132, 418
Interstate Commerce Commission (ICC) 478
intrusive investigations
coercion and 16–18
judicial authority and 18–19
investigative authorities, private parties interacting with 15–16
investigative tactics, safeguarding 107–8
Italy
coercive sampling of biological materials in 19–20
curtailing political influence on chief prosecutor in 209–10
democratic control in 406
discretionary adjudication, prosecution decision-making in 21–2
European Investigation Order national implementation in 23
judicial authority in pre-trial inquiries in 11–12
notitia criminis registration in 6–7, 11–12, 30n.10, 30n.12, 31n.17
penal orders in 133
pre-trial inquiries in 6–7, 29n.7
private parties interacting with investigative authorities in 15–16
prosecutors in 4, 29n.1
Rocco code in 9

Jacob, Herbert 273, 275–6, 278–9, 283
Japan
hiring frontline prosecutors in 211
training with judiciary in 215
J.E.B. v. Alabama ex rel. T.B. 141
John D. and Catherine T. MacArthur Foundation 229–30.
See also MacArthur Foundation
Jones-Wright, Genevieve 245
judges
accountability-independence tradeoff for 407–8
assignment of, courtroom workgroups and 276
prosecutors as 132–4
judicial authority
in Brazil 14
disclosure and 108–10
impartiality and 29n.1
intrusive investigations and 18–19
in Italy 11–12
in pre-trial inquiries 10–15
in Spain 10–11, 13–14

judicial discretion 336
empirical research on 81
restraints on 39–40
sentencing and 51–2, 153, 160
judicial management 132
judicial monitoring specialized court model 185–6
judicial supervision
of charging decisions 11
for plea bargaining 89
judiciary, training with 214–15
Jurek v. Texas 562–3
jury selection 120, 140
jury trials
evidence presentation in 126–7
facility dogs in 387
history of 76
in national security cases 548–9
opening statements in 122
plea bargaining sacrificing rights to 37–8
sentencing "penalty" of 75–6, 158
Sixth Amendment and 69
testing charges and 68–70
in UK 121
voir dire in 120
justice objectives, at trial 134–6
juvenile court xxxiv, 155, 447–8. *See also* adolescent offending
adult court transfer from 464

Kadish, Sanford 481–2
Kansas v. Garcia 441–2
Kelling, George 516
Kenna v. District Court 378
Kennedy, Anthony 75
Kennedy, James 186, 193
Kenya 263
Klein, Herbert 187
Koch Foundation 341–2
Kohler-Hausmann, Issa 521–2
Krasner, Larry
bail reform and 240, 525–6
charging discretion of 235–6
conviction integrity units and 241
election of 285
immigration enforcement consultants and 440
misdemeanor declination decisions of 523
Krumholz, Sam 402

Lane, Eric 196
Langbein, John xii–xiii
Laufer, William 476
Laura and John Arnold Foundation xvii
law enforcement 291–2. *See also* police officer criminal conduct
adolescent culpability perceptions and implicit racial bias of 456
body-worn cameras and 111–12
charging decision conflicts with 296–9
community policing and 230–1
coordinate powers and 292–3
dashboard cameras and 111–12
detachment and xxix
disclosure and prosecutorial interaction with 301–2
European Investigation Order and 22–3
horizontal alignment of 292–3
performance metrics in, evolution of 230–1
police shootings and 302–3, 341–2
prosecutors as gatekeeper and 293–6
"stop and frisk" and 298–9
training and monitoring, prosecutorial role in 299–301
as witnesses 126
law enforcement officer bills of rights (LEOBRs) 501–2
LEAD (Law Enforcement Assisted Diversion) program 235–6, 419
legality principle xii, 207–8, 482
charging discretion and 524
corporate crime and 484–5
legislatures and 482
legal sufficiency policy 268n.2
legislatures xxix, xxxiii. *See also* policy reforms

collateral consequences and 328–30
cost considerations and 337–8
criminal procedure and 338–41
culpability and 483
"discretionary mandatories," race and 335–7
Feeney Amendment and 334
immigration enforcement and 431–2
interest group pressure and 330–1
lack of judicial intervention and 332–3
legality principle and 482
localism and 340–1
overview of 327–9, 341–2
pathological politics and 327–32
police shootings and 341–2
public choice theory and 330–1
sentencing law and 328, 333–8
"soft on crime" problems for 331–2
state and federal criminal procedure efforts and 339–40
substantive criminal law and 329–33
LEOBRs (law enforcement officer bills of rights) 501–2
Levenson, Laurie L. 500
Levine, Kate 302–3, 502, 505–6, 508
Lewis, Michael 229
Liebman, James 568
limited punishment principle 483–4, 486–7, 518–19
limiting principles, of criminal law 475–6, 481–4
localism, criminal procedure and 340–1
Lynch, Gerald xi
Lynch, Mona 434

MacArthur Foundation 84. *See also* John D. and Catherine T. MacArthur Foundation
Magistrates' Court, UK
closing statements in 130–1
evidence presentation in 126
jury trial classification and 121
opening statements in 122–3
mala in se ix–x
mala prohibita offenses ix–x, 515–16
Malik, Mina 199–200
mandatory minimum sentences xxxi, 154
"discretionary," race and 335–7
drug sentencing and 156, 158–9, 336–7
851 enhancements and 159, 335
firearms cases sentencing and 158–9
leverage of 334–5
plea bargaining and 158–9
race and 48, 51–2
rise of 335
sentencing below 162
mandatory prosecution 144, 156
Mapping Police Violence 504
marijuana
legalization 153–5, 515
possession charges, declination of 522–3
possession charges, expungement of 530
Marin County Restorative Justice Program (MCRJ) 238
Maryland v. Craig 385–6
mass incarceration xv, 354
charging discretion and 49–51
conservatives and 199
cost of 163, 484
limiting principles of criminal law and 481–2
misdemeanor cases and 514–20
plea bargaining and 75–6
policy reform for 341–2
public opinion on 233
race and 227, 242
in US compared to world 227
War on Drugs and 49, 336
mass removals, immigration enforcement and 436–7, 443n.1
material evidence, disclosure of 319
McCaffery, Barry 192–3
McCleskey v. Kemp 43, 575n.10
McConkie, Dan 113
McCormack, Wayne 549–50
McCulloch, Robert 497–8, 509
McDonald, Laquan 501
McGautha v. California 562

McLeod, Allegra 185–6
MCRJ (Marin County Restorative Justice Program) 238
Measures for Justice 52, 84, 87
media
  law violation portrayals in xxiii
  restrictions, Bar authorities and 315
  trials and attention from 403–4
Meese, Edwin 199
mental health courts (MHCs) 192
mentoring of prosecutors, training and 219
Metcalfe, Christi 280, 284
MHCs (mental health courts) 192
Miami Drug Court 183–4, 187
migration offenses, federal 431
military justice system 363
Miller, Marc 48
Miller v. Alabama 167n.10, 447
miscarriages of justice
  capital charging and 560
  national security cases and 552–3
misconduct. *See* prosecutorial misconduct
misdemeanor cases xxxv, 297
  accountability courts and 184–5, 191
  appeals and 517
  autonomy and 519
  bail determination and 525–6
  "broken windows" policing and 516
  charging decisions and 36, 42, 520–5
  classification of 513–14
  collateral consequences and 514–15, 518–19, 527–8
  court records and 520
  declination decisions and 520–5
  deferred adjudication and 527
  definition of 513
  discretion and 514–29
  DPAs and 520–1, 523–4
  expungement of 529–31
  factual innocence and 515–16
  immigration enforcement and 433–4, 527
  mala prohibita offenses and 515
  marijuana legalization and 515
  mass incarceration and 514–20
  normative innocence and 515–16
  overview of 513–14, 531–2
  petty 513–14
  plea bargaining and 86, 158, 354, 526–9
  post-conviction criminal procedure and 529–31
  prevalence of 513
  proportionality principle and 518–19
  prosecutorial power in 515–18
  race and 85, 457–8, 519, 522–3, 526–7
  recidivism and 518–19, 527
  right to counsel and 517, 533n.15
  screening 522
  sealing and 529–31
  sentencing recommendations and 526–9
  special considerations for 518–20
  wrongful convictions and 531
Model Penal Code 490, 513–14, 523–4
Model Rules of Professional Conduct, ABA 136, 139–40, 310–11
money bail reform 340–1, 525–6
Moneyball (Lewis) 229
Morales, Stephanie 247
Morgenthau, Robert 339
Morisette v. United States 482
Mosby, Marilyn 248, 298
MST (Multisystemic Therapy) 466
MTFC (Multidimensional Treatment Foster Care) 466
Multidimensional Treatment Foster Care (MTFC) 466
Multisystemic Therapy (MST) 466
Murphy, Sigurd 190

NAAG (National Association of Attorneys General) 217–18
NAAUSA (National Association of Assistant United States Attorneys) 328, 334
NACDL (National Association of Criminal Defense Lawyers) 177, 311
NAPC (National Association of Prosecutor Coordinators) 217–18

National Association of Assistant United States Attorneys (NAAUSA) 328, 334
National Association of Attorneys General (NAAG) 217–18
National Association of Criminal Defense Lawyers (NACDL) 177, 311
National Association of Prosecutor Coordinators (NAPC) 217–18
National District Attorneys Association (NDAA) 217–18, 311, 328, 452
National Drug Court Institute (NDCI) 193–4
National Drug Court Professional Association 188
National Exoneration Registry 174–5
National Forensic Science Commission 177–9
National Institute of Standards and Technology (NIST) 177–8
National Legal Aid and Defender Association (NLADA) 196–7
National Prosecution Standards, NDAA 452
National Registry of Exonerations 84–5, 531
national security cases xxxv
  challenges of 539–49
  classified information in 547–8
  disclosure in 547–8
  embedded prosecutors and 541
  entrapment and 553–4
  Espionage Act and 542
  ethical challenges with 549–55
  exceptionalism and 549–51
  federalism and 544–5
  FISA and 542
  informants in 546–7
  international co-operation for 545–6
  international human rights and 549–50
  investigative powers and assistance in 540–2
  miscarriages of justice and 552–3
  in non-democratic countries 554–5
  overcriminalization and 542–3
  overview of 539–40, 555–6
  Patriot Act and 542
  pretextual prosecutions and 550–1
  prosecutorial independence and 551–2
  rule of law maintenance and 549–51
  sentencing in 549
  specialization for 543–4
  trials in 548–9
  types of 539
  warrants and 541
  whole of government approaches to 544
natural and probable consequences doctrine 485–6
NDAA (National District Attorneys Association) 217–18, 311, 328, 452
NDCI (National Drug Court Institute) 193–4
necessity thesis, corporate crime and 477
negligence standard, corporate crime and 488
Nelson, Melissa 229–30
ne procedat judex ex officio 3, 29n.1
the Netherlands
  appointment of chief prosecutors in 209
  entry-level hiring process in 213
  mentoring in 219
  training with judiciary in 215
net-widening 330, 436–7
new evidence of innocence, post-conviction 173–4
New York Central & Hudson Railroad Co. v. United States 478, 484–5
New York Police Department (NYPD) 230
New Zealand 163
NGOs (non-governmental organizations) 421
NIST (National Institute of Standards and Technology) 177–8
NLADA (National Legal Aid and Defender Association) 196–7
no-contact rule 316–17
"no drop" policies 264
Nolan, James 188, 195, 197–8
non-criminal specialized courts 186

non-governmental organizations (NGOs) 421
non-prosecution agreements (NPAs) 480–1, 489–90
normative innocence, misdemeanor cases and 515–16
North Carolina v. Alford 78–9
North Carolina v. Woodson 562–3
notification, victims' rights legislation and 376
notitia criminis registration, Italy 6–7, 11–12, 30n.10, 30n.12, 31n.17
NPAs (non-prosecution agreements) 480–1, 489–90
NYPD (New York Police Department) 230

Obama, Barack 433–5, 437, 542
OCR (Office for Civil Rights) 460–1
office cultures, training and 219
Office for Civil Rights (OCR) 460–1
office management
  community prosecution implications for 423–4
  fragmentation and xiv
  prosecutors and xi–xii
  social architecture and 355–7
Office of Inspector General (OIG) 178
Ogg, Kim 340, 522–3, 526
OIG (Office of Inspector General) 178
"open file" disclosure 356
opening statements 122, 141
Operation Hardcore, Los Angeles 266
Operation Streamline, immigration enforcement and 433–4
Operation Wetback 443n.1
opportunity principle 144
order maintenance policing 514–16
order maintenance specialized court model 185–6
ordinal proportionality in sentencing 80
Organization for Scientific Area Committees (OSAC) 177–8
outsourcing investigations and prosecution, for police officer criminal conduct 505–7
Ouziel, Lauren 233, 299
overcriminalization
  corporate crime and 481–2, 484
  national security cases and 542–3
  of normal adolescent behavior 449–52
over-enforcement of crimes, community prosecution and 418
Oyler v. Boles 36

Packer, Herbert 287n.5
Padilla v. Kentucky 438
parole xxxii
  community supervision and 239
  discretion and 164–5
  prosecutorial recommendations for 154
parsimony principle 483–4, 486–7
partnership choices, for community prosecution 420–3
pathological politics 341–2
  legislatures and 327–32
Patriot Act 542
Payne v. Tennessee 378
peer influence, in adolescent offending 453
penal orders
  defendant absence and 124–5
  in France 133–4
  in Germany 133–4
  in Italy 133
  overview of 132
  reviewing and opposing 133–4
performance metrics, for prosecutors xv, xxx, xxxiii
  advanced metrics and 229
  charging discretion and 52
  for collateral consequences and reentry 246–9
  for community engagement, trust and well-being 245
  for community partnerships 246
  for community supervision reform 239
  conviction integrity units and 241–2
  criminal justice system's history of 230–3
  current landscape of 227–8
  desistance factors and 239–40
  for diversion programs 236–7

for diversity of staff 243
for education promotion 245–6
for fairness and justice improvements 240
immigration enforcement and 248–9
implementation of 250
for incarceration reduction 235
incentives, promotion practices and 249–50
law enforcement and evolution of 230–1
for needless arrest reduction 235–6
overview of 227–30, 250–1
policy reforms and 233–4
poverty penalty addressed with 240–1
for pre-trial detention reduction 240–1
for prevention 245–6
for procedural fairness improvements 243–5
for proportionate and fair sentencing and charging 238–9
for racial disparities in criminal justice system 242–3, 252n.9
reorientation of 231–3
for restorative justice programs 237–8
review processes and 241–2
tracking 250
transparency and 232
twenty-first-century goals for 234–49
for victim satisfaction 244–5
persecutio criminalis 6
person-to-person defense models, in courtroom workgroups 276
persuasion, burden of proof and 137–8
petty misdemeanors 513–14. *See also* misdemeanor cases
Pinkerton doctrine 485–6
Plea and Trial Preparation Hearing (PTPH) 125–6
plea bargaining xxxii. *See also* sentencing
abolition efforts against 88–9
appeal waivers in 164
Bar authorities and 320
case screening process and 90
charge bargaining and 160–1
charging discretion and 37–8, 90, 158
collateral consequences and 527–8
collateral sanctions and 159–60
concessions model of 81
consensus model of 81
controversies with 75–6
cumulative disadvantages and 87–8
defense attorneys and 77, 354–5, 367–8
deferred adjudication and 527
disclosure and 79, 102
discretionary sanctions and 159
due process and 80
election effect and 403–4
empirical research on, new directions for 86–8
empirical research on, Wave I 81
empirical research on, Wave II 81–3
empirical research on, Wave III 83–6
evidence and 84
exploding 79, 89
extrajudicial sanctions and 159
fact bargaining and 161
false guilty pleas and 79, 84–5
gender and 43–4, 82, 85
historical rise of 76–7
immigrants and 86–7, 160
implicit bias and 80, 88
in international systems 367–8
judicial supervision for 89
jury trial rights sacrificed in 37–8
mandatory minimum sentences and 158–9
mass incarceration and 75–6
misdemeanor cases and 86, 158, 354, 526–9
normative perspectives on 78–81
origins of xi
overview of 75–6
policy reforms in 88–91
in popular culture 158
prosecutorial power in 77–8
punishment ceilings and 89–90
race and 82–3, 85–7
regulation of 75, 77
sentence bargaining and 161
sentencing reductions and 47, 49–50, 80, 82–4, 154, 158–64

plea bargaining (*Continued*)
socio-economic status and 85–6
stages of 87
standards for 80
transparency and 79–80, 88, 529
ubiquity of 75
victims and guidelines for 382–3
written 89
police officer criminal conduct xxxv
bench trials and 506
charging decisions and 502
conflicts of interest and 502
convictions for 503
democratic control and 509
detecting and investigating 499
federal prosecution of, challenges to 504–5
frequency of state and local prosecutions of 503
grand juries and 502, 507–8
grand juries and lack of indictments for 67
internal investigation procedures for, loosening 508
LEOBRs and 501–2
limitations on investigations into 501
outsourcing investigations and prosecution for 505–7
overview of 497–9, 508–9
police shootings and 302–3, 341–2
policy reforms for 505–8
prosecution challenges with 499–504
Rampart Scandal and 500
union contracts and 501–2
police-prosecutorial relationships xxix, xxxiii, 10–15, 30n.10. *See also* law enforcement
autonomy and 11–15
benefits of 294–5
charging decision conflicts in 296–9
disclosure and 301–2
domestic violence cases and 294–5
downsides of 295
goals of 295
horizontal alignment and coordinate powers in 292–3
overview of 291–2, 303–4
police shootings and 302–3, 341–2
prosecutors as gatekeeper and 293–6
training and monitoring in 299–301
police shootings 302–3, 341–2
policy reforms
bail and 240, 340–1, 525–6
Bar authorities and 311
for capital charging 560–1, 565–74
for collateral consequences and reentry 246–9
for community engagement, trust and well-being 245
for community partnerships 246
for community supervision 239
conviction integrity units and 241–2
for corporate crime 490–1
desistance factors and 239–40
for disclosure 111–14
for diversity of staff 243
for education promotion 245–6
for fairness and justice improvements 240
for grand juries 67–8
immigration enforcement and 432
for incarceration reduction 235
incentives, promotion practices and 249–50
for mass incarceration 341–2
for needless arrest reduction 235–6
performance metrics for prosecutors and 233–4
in plea bargaining 88–91
for police officer criminal conduct 505–8
poverty penalty addressed with 240–1
for pre-trial detention reduction 240–1
for prevention 245–6
for procedural fairness improvements 243–5
for proportionate and fair sentencing and charging 238–9
for prosecution xvi–xvii

for racial disparities in criminal justice system 89–90, 242–3, 252n.9, 455–6, 459–60, 466–7, 522–3
recidivism and 239
for restorative justice programs 237–8
review processes and 241–2
school-to-prison pipeline and opportunities for 460
for victim satisfaction 244–5
politics
curtailing influence of, hiring and 209–11
of defense attorneys 361
pathological 327–32
prosecutor lobbying organizations and 311, 328, 333–5
prosecutor professional associations and 309–12, 317–18, 320
"soft on crime" problems for 331–2
populism xv–xvi
positive law
on charging decisions 7
prosecution and 5–6
positive youth development, adolescent offending and 465–7
post-adjudication programs 186
post-arraignment, testing charges and 68
post-conviction criminal procedure xxxii
ABA standards for 171–4
audits and 176–8
clemency and 174
conviction integrity units and 172, 174–6
DNA testing in 171, 173–4
expungement and 529–31
misdemeanor cases and 529–31
new evidence of innocence and 173–4
OIG and 178
overview of 171–2, 178–9
sealing and 529–31
sentencing review units and 176
special investigation units and 178
specialized appeals units and 172–3
wrongful convictions and 531
post-traumatic stress disorder (PTSD) 190, 195
post-trial, testing charges and 70
poverty penalty, performance metrics addressing 240–1
power
coordinate, law enforcement and 292–3
corporate crime and 476
European Investigation Order and prosecutorial 22–4
European Public Prosecutor's Office's transnational investigative 24–8
misdemeanor cases and prosecutorial power in 515–18
national security cases and investigative 540–2
plea bargaining and prosecutorial 77–8
PPP (Prosecutors and Politics Project) 402
practical experience, training and 218–19
"preliminary charge," 6–7, 29n.8
preliminary hearings 36, 63–5, 70
presumption of innocence, burden of proof and 138
pretextual prosecutions 550–1
pre-trial detention 14, 63, 240–1, 328–9, 525. *See also* bail reform
pre-trial inquiries
in Brazil 13
charging decisions and 6, 29n.7
criminal law action and complex dynamics of 9–10
in Italy 6–7, 29n.7
judicial authority in 10–15
prosecution and 5–9
"pseudo-offenses" and 11–12
relational networks in 9–16
against unknown persons 7
prevention, performance metrics for 245–6
principle of legality. *See* legality principle
Principles of Federal Prosecution 61, 489
prison overcrowding 342
privacy, victims' rights legislation and 376

private parties
European Investigation Order requests by 22
investigative authorities interacting with, in prosecution 15–16
private prosecution, victim-directed
accessory 390–1
international 390
public prosecution compared to 4–5
US 389–90
proactive prosecution x–xi
probable cause hearings
following warrantless arrest, testing charges and 63
grand juries compared to 66
probable-cause standard, of grand juries 67
probation violations, sentencing and 164
procedural economy 132
procedural fairness 134–9
performance metrics for improving 243–5
procedural identity 132
procedural justice 144, 373–4, 391, 522
procedural rules, European Public Prosecutor's Office issues with 27–8
production, burden of proof and 137–8
professional conduct codes
adoption and interpretation of 315–20
limited impact of 312–15
professional regulation of prosecutors 309–12
Proffit v. Florida 562–3
progressive prosecutors 236, 338–41, 416–17, 515, 522–3, 531–2
promotion practices, performance metrics and 249–50
proportionality principle 483–4, 486–7, 518–19
Prosecution and Racial Justice Project, Vera Institute of Justice 459–60
prosecution/prosecutors. See *specific topics*
"prosecution stand by," in UK 121–2
prosecution studies xxiv. *See also* empirical research
deductive and inductive approaches to xxiv–vi
prosecutorial discretion. *See* discretion
prosecutorial misconduct xxxii, 139–44
Bar authorities and 318
Brady disclosures and 302, 356–7
at closing statements 142
defense attorney attacks and 142–3
impact of 143
at jury selection 140
at opening stage 141
at presentation of evidence 141
Prosecutors and Politics Project (PPP) 402
"pseudo-offenses," pre-trial inquiries and 11–12
PTPH (Plea and Trial Preparation Hearing) 125–6
PTSD (post-traumatic stress disorder) 190, 195
public choice theory 330–1, 339
public interest immunity proceedings, UK 547
publicly held companies, corporate crime and 487–8
public opinion
courtroom workgroups and 279
on death penalty 560
on mass incarceration 233
sentencing and 153–4
public prosecution, private prosecution compared to 4–5
public trust, prosecutors as fiduciary of xxiv–xxv
punishment ceilings 89–90

Quatman, John 140

race
adolescent culpability perceptions, implicit bias and 456
adolescent offending and disparities by 447–8, 455–62
bias and 37, 41, 46–7, 331, 361–2, 448, 452, 462

capital charging and 43
charging discretion and 36–7, 49–51
in charging discretion studies 42–4
community prosecution and 414
of defense attorneys 361–2
democracy deficits and 416
"discretionary mandatories" and 335–7
disparities by xxx, 44–5, 48–50, 89–90, 162, 242–3, 252n.9, 447–8, 455–62
drug use, adolescent offending and 459, 468n.3
Equal Protection Clause and 43
institutional racism and 46–7
jury selection and 140
mandatory minimum sentences and 48, 51–2
mass incarceration and 227, 242
misdemeanor cases and 85, 457–8, 519, 522–3, 526–7
performance metrics for criminal justice system disparities by 242–3, 252n.9
plea bargaining and 82–3, 85–7
prosecutorial bias, adolescent offending and 458
school-to-prison pipeline, systemic reform opportunities and 460
sentencing, adolescent offending and 464
sentencing disparity by 48–52, 83–4, 160, 162, 336, 528
stereotyping and 331, 460
violence, adolescent offending and 459
War on Drugs and 530
Racine, Karl 238
Rampart Scandal, Los Angeles 500
reactive prosecution x–xi
reasonable doubt standard
in common law 138
testing charges and 68–9
recidivism 457
discretion and likelihood of 60
misdemeanor cases and 518–19, 527
policy reforms and 239
pre-trial detention and 240
veterans courts and 191
reentry
community prosecution and 420
performance metrics for 246–9
reform. *See* policy reforms
reform prosecutors 364
rehabilitation
corporate 487
defendant 268n.2
Reinventing Justice (Nolan) 195
relational networks
in pre-trial inquiries 9–16
public bodies and 10–15
remand detention, prosecution and 14–15, 31n.19
Reno, Janet 176–7, 183–4, 187, 192–3
residential drug treatment programs 419
residential treatment programs, for adolescent offending 463–4
respondeat superior liability 478–80, 485
restorative justice programs 237–8
review committee, for capital charging
composition of 570
recommendations and ramification of 571–4
substantive quality of 570–1
review processes, performance metrics and 241–2
Rice, Tamir 67
Richman, Daniel 298, 489–90
right to be heard, victims' rights legislation for 377–80
right to be present, victims' rights legislation for 377
right to counsel 89–90, 136, 196–7, 339, 355, 364–5, 517, 533n.15
Ristroph, Alice 475
Roberts v. Louisiana 562–3
Rocco code, Italy 9
Roiphe, Rebecca xxiv–xxv
role ambiguity, of prosecutor 144–5
role duality, of prosecutor 144–5
Rollins, Rachael 235–6, 244, 248–9, 523
Roper v. Simmons 167n.10, 447
Rosen, Jeffrey 248

royal absolutism, prosecutors and 3
Rule 3.6, ABA 315
Rule 3.8, ABA 312, 317–19, 322, 323n.4
Rule 4.2, ABA 316–17
rule of law, national security cases maintaining 549–51
Rules Enabling Act 113
Russell, George 190–1
Russell, Robert 185
R (on the application of Corner House Research and Others) v. Director of Serious Fraud Office 551–2
R. v. Nuttall 553–4
R. v. Stinchcombe 110–11

Safety and Justice Challenge 84
Satterberg, Dan 237, 245
SCCTD (Special Crime and Counter-Terrorism Division), UK 543
Scharia, David 551
school-to-prison pipeline, systemic reform opportunities and 460
Schulhofer, Stephen 47, 481–2
Schwartz, Louis 500
screening. *See* case screening process
Screws v. United States 505
sealing, of misdemeanor cases 529–31
Securities Offences Act, Canada 545
security. *See also* national security cases
  data 112
  disclosure and 103–4, 111–14
Security Intelligence Service Act, Canada 551
selecting charges. *See* charging discretion
self-incrimination
  Fifth Amendment and 142, 302
  witnesses and 125–6
sentence bargaining 161. *See also* plea bargaining
sentencing xxxii. *See also* mandatory minimum sentences; plea bargaining
  adolescent offending, race and 464
  alternative courts and 157
  in Australia 163
  below guideline 162
  charging decisions and 39–40, 47–50, 90, 154–8, 560
  in common law 163
  determinate 39
  discretion xxvii, 336
  diversion programs and 154–8
  drug 156, 336–7
  851 enhancements and 159, 335
  federal and state collaboration for 156
  in firearms cases 158–9
  immigration enforcement and 161
  indeterminate 39
  judicial discretion and 51–2, 153, 160
  jury trials and "penalty" of 75–6, 158
  limited punishment principle and 483–4, 518–19
  maximizing xv
  misdemeanor cases and recommendations for 526–9
  in national security cases 549
  in New Zealand 163
  ordinal proportionality in 80
  overview of 153–5, 166
  parsimony principle and 483–4
  performance metrics for proportionate and fair 238–9
  plea bargaining and reductions in 47, 49–50, 80, 82–4, 154, 158–64
  probation violations and 164
  process of 161–4
  proportionality principle and 483–4, 486–7, 518–19
  public opinion and 153–4
  punishment ceilings and 89–90
  race and disparity in 48–52, 83–4, 160, 162, 336, 528
  review units for 176
  in terrorism cases 549
  three strikes laws and 159, 333–4
  timing of 131
  "trial penalty" and 158
  "trial tax" and 82–3
  in UK 163
  venue manipulation for 156
  witnesses in 162

Sentencing Commission, US 39, 51–2
sentencing law
  cost considerations and 337–8
  "credit-card-sentencing policy" and 338
  "discretionary mandatories," race and 335–7
  Feeney Amendment and 334
  legislatures and 328, 333–8
Sentencing Reform Act, 1984 39, 160
September 11th attacks 542
Sexual and Gender-Based Violence Crimes Unit 263
sexual assault cases
  charging discretion and demographics in 43–4
  specialized units for, effectiveness of 261–4, 269n.4
  state-funded attorneys for 388–9
  victim credibility in 44–5
Shawcross, Hartley 544
Shawcross doctrine, UK 544, 552
Sherman Antitrust Act 478
Sixth Amendment 533n.15
  jury trials and 69
Sklansky, David xxv, 89, 145, 231–2, 299
Smith, Anthony 498–9
Smith, Jack 190
social architecture
  of defense attorneys' offices 357–60
  of prosecutors' offices 355–7
societies, criminal justice and ix–x
socio-economic status
  disparities by xxx
  plea bargaining and 85–6
  poverty penalty, performance metrics addressing 240–1
"soft on crime" problems, for politicians 331–2
Soros, George xvii
South Africa 210–11
  defense attorneys in 365–6
South Korea
  course-based training in 220–1
  curtailing political influence on chief prosecutor in 210
  hiring frontline prosecutors in 211
  hiring tests in 213
  prosecutor training in 217
Spain
  European Investigation Order national implementation in 23–4
  judicial authority in 13–14
  judicial authority in pre-trial inquiries in 10–11
Special Crime and Counter-Terrorism Division (SCCTD), UK 543
specialized criminal courts. *See* accountability courts; diversion programs; drug courts
specialized units xxxiii
  advantages of 259–60
  advocates for 260
  for appeals 172–3
  charging decisions and 262
  defense attorneys in 363
  for domestic violence, effectiveness of 264–5
  for gang-related crimes, effectiveness of 265–6
  overview of 259–61, 266–8
  post-conviction 178
  research regarding 267–8
  for sexual assault, effectiveness of 261–4
Special Victims Counsel (SVC) 388–9
Speedy Trial Act 480
staffing sessions, drug courts and 189
Standards for Guilty Pleas, ABA 80
Standing Committee on Professional Ethics, ABA 311, 316, 319
state, criminal law and creation of 475
status courts 185
statutory law, civil law action and 9–10
Steiker, Carol 574–5
Steiker, Jordan 574–5
Steinberg, Laurence 448
Stenning, Philip 551–2
stereotyping, racial 331, 460
Stevens, John Paul 559

Stinson, Philip 503–4
Stockley, Jason 498–9
"stop and frisk," 298–9
Streamline cases 433–4
strict liability, corporate crime and 488
Stuntz, William xii, 38, 329–31, 489–90, 515, 542, 564–5
substantive criminal law
  lack of judicial intervention and 332–3
  legislatures and 329–33
  pathological politics and 329–32
  public choice theory and 330–1
substantive fairness 134–6
substantive justice 117, 144, 171
summary trials xxvii
  closing statements in 130–1
  evidence presentation in 126–7
  opening statements in 122–3
super due process 575, 577n.25
"super due process," capital charging and 575, 577n.25
supplementing charges, at trial 129
SVC (Special Victims Counsel) 388–9
Swain v. Alabama 140–1
Sweden
  appointment of chief prosecutors in 209, 330
  defense attorneys in 367
  mentoring in 219
  prosecutor training in 215–16
Switzerland 210
system efficiency policy 262, 268n.2

TASC (Treatment Alternatives to Street Crimes) 188
Taylor, Breonna 67
technology, disclosure and 103, 111–14
"Ten Key Components," of drug courts 188–9, 192–3
Ten Tenets of Fair and Effective Problem-Solving Courts (NLADA) 196–7
termination of proceedings, by prosecutors 20–2
terrorism cases xxxv, 540–1
  Canadian specialized units for 543
  challenges of 539–49
  classified information in 547–8
  definitions of 541
  disclosure in 547–8
  discretion and 542–3
  entrapment and 553–4
  ethical challenges with 549–55
  federalism and 544–5
  informants in 546–7
  international co-operation for 545–6
  international human rights and 549–50
  investigative powers and assistance in 540–2
  miscarriages of justice and 552–3
  in non-democratic countries 554–5
  overcriminalization and 542–3
  overview of 539–40, 555–6
  Patriot Act and 542
  pretextual prosecutions and 550–1
  prosecutorial independence and 551–2
  rule of law maintenance and 549–51
  sentencing in 549
  specialization for 543–4
  trials in 548–9
  as universal jurisdiction crimes 545–6
  whole of government approaches to 544
testing charges xxxi
  arrests pursuant to warrant and 62–3
  for due process 70
  formal charges and 64–70
  grand juries and 64–8
  initial charges and 62–4
  overview of 59, 70–1
  post-arraignment and 68
  post-trial, appeal, collateral review and 70
  preliminary hearings and 63–4
  probable cause hearing following warrantless arrest and 63
  purpose of 61–2
  reasonable doubt standard and 68–9
  trial and 68–70
TF-CBT (Trauma Focused Cognitive Behavioral Therapy) 466

therapeutic jurisprudence specialized court model 185–6
Thompson, Kenneth 175
three strikes laws 159, 333–4
Trafficking Victims Protection Act, 2000 432, 442
training xxx, xxxii–xxxiii
  course-based 219–21
  implicit bias 243
  integrating 221
  with judiciary 214–15
  of law enforcement, prosecutorial role in 299–301
  mentoring and 219
  office cultures and 219
  overview of 207–8, 221–3
  practical experience and 218–19
  prosecutors in executive branch and 215–17
  in regional and local jurisdictions 217–18
  strategies for 214–18
transnational criminal justice
  European Investigation Order prosecutorial powers and 22–4
  European Public Prosecutor's Office investigative powers of 24–8
  prosecutors in 22–8
transparency
  community prosecution and 416
  democratic control and 408, 409nn.8,10
  grand juries and 507
  performance metrics for prosecutors and 232
  plea bargaining and 79–80, 88, 529
  victims' issues with 382
Trauma Focused Cognitive Behavioral Therapy (TF-CBT) 466
Treatment Alternatives to Street Crimes (TASC) 188
triage
  discretion and xxvii
  purposes of xii–xiii
"trial penalty," 76, 158. *See also* "trial tax," sentencing and
trials. *See also* bench trials; jury trials; summary trials
  altering/supplementing charges at 129
  capital charging and mistakes at 568, 573
  case-in-chief in 125
  closing statements in 130, 142
  conduct of prosecutors in xxxii, 119, 139–44
  definition of 118–19
  dossier in 129
  election effect and 403–4
  evidence presentation in 125, 141
  identity of defendants in 123
  judgment and 130
  jury selection in 120, 140
  justice and fairness objectives at 134–6
  media attention from 403–4
  in national security cases 548–9
  normative framework of 119
  opening stage of 122, 141
  penal order and defendant absence in 124–5
  prosecutorial ethics at 136–9
  prosecutorial misconduct at 139–44
  prosecutor's role in 117–18, 134–45
  seating arrangements in 123, 124*f*
  sentencing timing in 131
  stages of 119–32, 135*t*
  in terrorism cases 548–9
  testing charges and 68–70
trial sufficiency policy 262, 267, 268n.2
"trial tax," sentencing and 82–3
trial teams, courtroom workgroups and 276, 279–80
Trump, Donald 433–4, 437
  First Step Act and 200–1
trust
  community prosecution and 414, 416
  disclosure and 110
  performance metrics for community engagement and 245
  public, prosecutors as fiduciary of xxiv–xxv

Turner, Jenia 79, 112–13
21 Principles for the 21st Century Prosecutor 452–3

Uganda 263
UK. *See* United Kingdom
under-enforcement of crimes, community prosecution and 418
union contracts, police 501–2
unitary structure, of prosecution 8–9
United Kingdom (UK). *See also* Crown Court, UK; Magistrates' Court, UK
accountability/drug courts in 197–9
Criminal Justice Act of 2003 and 7, 12–13
Crown Prosecution Service in 7, 12–13
defense attorneys in 365
democratic control in 406–7
disclosure practices in 105–6, 110
evidence presentation in 126–7
hiring frontline prosecutors in 211
jury trials in 121
mentoring in 219
Plea and Trial Preparation Hearing in 125–6
"prosecution stand by" in 121–2
prosecutorial independence in national security cases in 551–2
public interest immunity proceedings in 547
sentencing in 163
Shawcross doctrine in 544, 552
Special Crime and Counter-Terrorism Division of 543
trial seating arrangements in 123, 124*f*
trial stages in 135*t*
video-testimony in 386
United States ex rel. Heathcote Holdings Corp. v. William K. Walthers, Inc. 491n.4
United States v. Armstrong 36–7
United States v. Bank of New England 491n.4
United States v. Booker 39, 48, 167n.9
United States v. Fokker Services BV 491n.6
United States v. HSBC Bank USA, NA 491n.6
universal jurisdiction crimes, terrorism as 545–6
unknown persons, pre-trial inquiries against 7
upstream community prosecution 418–20
Urban Institute 250
U.S. attorneys, appointment and removal of 402–3

values, community prosecution implications for 423–4
Vance, Cyrus 243
Van Dyke, Jason 501
venue manipulation, for sentencing 156
Vera Institute of Justice xvii, 87, 459–60
vertical prosecution models xxxiii
advantages of 259–60
advocates for 260
for domestic violence cases, effectiveness of 264–5
for gang-related crimes, effectiveness of 265–6
horizontal prosecution compared to 259
overview of 259–61, 266–8
research for 267–8
for sexual assault cases, effectiveness of 261–4
veterans courts 185
drug courts compared to 191–2
justification for creating 190
origins of 190–1
PTSD and 190, 195
recidivism and 191
Victim and Witness Protection Act, 1982 374–5
Victim Impact Program (VIP) 263–4
victim impact statement (VIS) 378–9
victims xxxiv
accessory prosecution directed by 390–1
adolescent offending and views of 466–7
burnout and 381–2
charging discretion and cooperation with 42
charging discretion and credibility of 44–5

clinic attorneys for 387–8
community prosecution relationships with 417–18
courtroom protections for 384–7
emotions of 380–2
facility dogs for emotional support of 386–7
immigration enforcement and 442–3
legal representation for, enforcement of 387–9
overview of 373–4, 391–2
plea bargaining guidelines for 382–3
private prosecution directed by, international 390
private prosecution directed by, US 389–90
prosecution and meaningful participation of 380–4
as prosecutors, in colonial era x
satisfaction of, performance metrics for 244–5
shielding and 385–6
state-funded attorneys for sexual assault 388–9
testimony of 383–4
transparency issues for 382
Victims of Crime Act, 1984 374–7
Victims' Rights Amendment, Germany 390
Victim's Rights and Restitution Act, 1990 374–5
victims' rights legislation (VRL)
clinic attorneys and 387–8
courtroom protections and 384–7
coverage of 375
for information and notification 376
legal representation and, enforcement of 387–9
overview of 374–5
potential of 391
for privacy 376
rights encompassed by 375–80
for right to be heard 377–80
for right to be present 377
state-by-state 374
video surveillance 103, 111–12
video testimony 385–6
Violence Against Women Act 376–7
Violent Crime Control and Law Enforcement Act, 1994 374–5, 442
VIP (Victim Impact Program) 263–4
VIS (victim impact statement) 378–9
voir dire 120
voters. *See* democratic control
voting rights, felons and 330–1, 343n.8
VRL. *See* victims' rights legislation

War on Drugs
immigration enforcement and 431–2
mass incarceration and 49, 336
race and 530
warrantless arrests 63
warrants
arrests pursuant to, testing charges and 62–3
national security cases and 541
Washtenaw County Peacemaking Court (WCPC) 238
Watkins, Craig 175
WCPC (Washtenaw County Peacemaking Court) 238
Weaver v. Massachusetts 565
West, Leah 546
Wethering, Gerald 187
Williams, Jamie 542–3
Wilson, Darren 67, 497–8, 509
Wilson, James 516
Wilson, Jennifer Kelly 195
wiretaps 103
witnesses
bias of 107–8, 142
children as 383–4
in civil law 119–20, 125
cross-examination of 126, 128
in Crown Court 127
disclosure of 104–5, 107–8
expert 125
immigration enforcement and 442–3
law enforcement as 126
preparing/guiding of 128–9

witnesses (*Continued*)
- protecting 107–8
- redirect examination and 126
- self-incrimination and 125–6
- in sentencing 162
- victim testimony and 383–4

Wollard, Orville 334
workgroups. *See* courtroom workgroups
Wright, Ronald 48, 401–2, 524
writ of mandamus 374–5, 377
written dossier. *See* dossier
written plea bargaining 89
wrongful convictions
- capital charging and 563–5
- of misdemeanor cases 531

Young v. United States ex rel. Vuitton et Fils 389–90
youth. *See* adolescent offending

Zant v. Stephens 566–7
"zero tolerance" policing 516
Zirilli v. The Queen 167n.12
Zozula, Christine 194–5